PRAISE FOR *SECONDARY LENSES ON LEARNING*

There are few materials to choose from when it comes to outreach efforts with high schools. What is so exciting about the *Secondary Lenses on Learning* materials is the ways in which the process brings together a team to collect and analyze data and form an action plan.

—Dan Chazan
Associate Professor of Curriculum and Instruction
University of Maryland

The readings in each session bring current research and knowledge into the seminar. They are relevant, accessible, and thought provoking. The video clips provide glimpses into real classrooms with diverse students, inviting participants to reflect on the possibilities for all students. The focus questions push the participants to think deeply and to examine their own beliefs and attitudes. From a professional development provider's perspective, these materials lend themselves to working with schools across a region or within a single school division. These materials can easily be used as the core of a graduate course for school-based mathematics leadership teams.

—Vickie Inge
Director of Mathematics Outreach
University of Virginia

Repeatedly, we find the success of professional development in schools and school systems correlates directly to two key factors: (1) the establishment of sustained, high-functioning professional communities of teachers and school leaders who share a vision and goals for reform and whose professional learning is contextualized in the everyday, authentic work of mathematics learning, teaching, and leadership; (2) the participation of school leaders in ongoing content-based leadership development. The *Secondary Lenses on Learning* materials address these two factors in particularly powerful ways and will be a mainstay of our work with leadership teams. To quote the principal from one school team that participated in our pilot program: "Unlike most schools in the state, my school saw growth in our mathematics student achievement this year. The *Secondary Lenses on Learning* seminar was extremely valuable in improving skills for staff and learning for students."

—Linda Foreman, Director
Teachers Development Group

These materials definitely make a distinct contribution to the field. They bring together current mathematics education research, case studies, and classroom examples in a very sound professional development model that is targeted to secondary leaders. This project fills a major gap for math education leaders and professional developers. We now have an excellent tool for helping us to work with school and district leaders.

—Lisa Matthews
Math Field Specialist
New Mexico State University

As the principal of a middle school, I was able to participate in the *Lenses on Learning* training. The research articles and other materials have been invaluable as our district has adopted a standards-based math curriculum in Grades 6–8. *Lenses on Learning* provided the necessary background to be able to firmly support the need for this kind of math instruction in order to defend the district's adoption to a few disgruntled parents. The training also provided me with hands-on experiences so that I better understand the student and teacher behaviors associated with developing a deep understanding of math and the process standards associated with it.

—Dawn Tinsley, Principal
Moriarty Middle School
Moriarty, NM

SECONDARY LENSES ON LEARNING

Team Leadership for Mathematics in Middle and High Schools

Participant Book

Catherine Miles Grant
Valerie L. Mills
Mary Bouck
Ellen Davidson
with Barbara Scott Nelson
and Steve Benson

A Joint Publication

CORWIN
A SAGE Company

EDC
Education Development Center, Inc.

This work was supported by the National Science Foundation under Grant No. ESIE Grant #-0353277, awarded to Education Development Center. Any opinions, findings, conclusions, or recommendations expressed here are those of the authors and do not necessarily reflect the views of the National Science Foundation.

For information:

Corwin
A SAGE Company
2455 Teller Road
Thousand Oaks, California 91320
(800) 233-9936
Fax: (800) 417-2466
www.corwinpress.com

SAGE India Pvt. Ltd.
B 1/I 1 Mohan Cooperative Industrial Area
Mathura Road, New Delhi 110 044
India

SAGE Ltd.
1 Oliver's Yard
55 City Road
London EC1Y 1SP
United Kingdom

SAGE Asia-Pacific Pte. Ltd.
33 Pekin Street #02-01
Far East Square
Singapore 048763

Printed in the United States of America

Library of Congress Cataloging-in-Publication Data

Secondary lenses on learning participant book: Team leadership for mathematics in middle and high schools/Catherine Miles Grant . . . [et al.].
    p. cm.
"A joint publication with the Education Development Center."
ISBN 978-1-4129-7279-6 (cloth)
ISBN 978-1-4129-7280-2 (pbk.)
    1. Mathematics—Study and teaching (Middle shool) 2. Mathematics—Study and teaching (Secondary) I. Grant, Catherine Miles.

QA11.2.S45 2009
510.71′2—dc22   2009015982

This book is printed on acid-free paper.

09   10   11   12   13   10   9   8   7   6   5   4   3   2

Acquisitions Editor:	Dan Alpert
Associate Editor:	Megan Bedell
Production Editor:	Melanie Birdsall
Copy Editor:	Tina Hardy
Typesetter:	C&M Digitals (P) Ltd.
Proofreader:	Wendy Jo Dymond
Cover Designer:	Karine Hovsepian

Sessions Chart

SESSION NUMBER	SESSION TITLE	DATE
Session 1	What Does It Mean to *Know* Algebra? (Content)	
Session 2	What Does High-Quality Instruction Look Like? (Instruction)	
Session 3	How Can Assessment Support Learning and Instruction? (Formative Assessment)	
Session 4	How Can We Hold High Expectations and Provide Strong Support for *All* Students? (Equitable Practices)	
Session 5	How Can Professional Development Enable Teachers to Improve Student Achievement? (Practice-Based Professional Development)	
Session 6	How Can School Leaders Advance Their Mathematics Program Toward Success for All? (Mathematics Improvement Process)	

Contents

Foreword

You have in your hands a powerful tool for improving the teaching and learning of mathematics in your secondary schools. *Secondary Lenses on Learning* provides an opportunity for school-based mathematics improvement teams, composed of individuals in a range of roles (principal, math teacher, department head, guidance counselor, district curriculum director, and others), to step away from a narrow focus on test data in order to learn about larger systemic issues that impact students' opportunity to learn mathematics. Resources and explorations provided during daylong sessions will pique your interest in engaging in classroom observations and collecting targeted data between sessions. As your team gathers details about the strengths and weaknesses of your mathematics program, you will also learn strategic moves that others have used to address many of your emerging problems. Your team will leave the six-session seminar with both short-term and long-term plans designed to improve student learning in mathematics in significant ways.

During the 2006–2007 school year, I was fortunate to have served as the Field Test Director for *Secondary Lenses on Learning*. My appreciation for the potential impact of these resources grew as I organized the field test of early drafts of these materials, facilitated several local seminars, and analyzed participant data to learn about the impact of *Secondary Lenses on Learning*. Findings from an analysis of surveys administered to field test participants prior to their enrollment in *Secondary Lenses on Learning* show that there was a high degree of variability among the school leaders in our sample, in terms of their knowledge of mathematics for teaching and their beliefs about how students learn mathematics and how it should be taught. Some team members in our sample came into the seminar with knowledge and beliefs about mathematics learning and teaching that positioned them well for the tasks they were responsible for leading; others did not.

Through participation in *Secondary Lenses on Learning*, the majority of participants, whether working in administrative or primarily instructional roles, made progress in their ability to identify and articulate a rationale for practices that attend to students' thinking and challenge and extend students' mathematical understanding. In other words, survey data reveal shifts in pedagogy scores preseminar to postseminar, indicating a move from more traditional to reform views of teaching. There was movement from (a) thinking of mathematics teaching as demonstrating procedures and immediately correcting mistakes, to (b) valuing particular features of practice such as using concrete or semiconcrete contexts, working in groups, or using multiple representations, to (c) recognizing effective practice as offering students and teachers extended opportunities to identify what students understand and have yet to learn and then offering open-ended tasks that have the potential to challenge all learners. Participants in all roles made progress along this continuum.

Not only did the seminar provide experiences that impacted beliefs and knowledge about effective mathematics teaching and learning, the six sessions also provided an opportunity for teams to bond together in ways not often afforded by meetings within the typical school setting. Beginning with the first session, participants identified ways that they individually and collectively contribute to the mathematics program. Most were surprised to learn of numerous overlaps in their efforts and how little they knew about each other's work. Data collected between sessions added detail to these overlaps and highlighted a current lack of coordination in efforts to improve students' success in mathematics classes. Candor built as teams identified strengths and weaknesses within their setting related to curriculum, instruction, assessment, and opportunities and supports for learning. The work in the final session of developing a short-term and long-term improvement plan highlighted the team's common commitment to significant change. Most groups shifted from being collections of competent, committed, and hard-working individuals to informed, focused, and collaborative teams poised for action.

Developing a shared understanding of effective practice, a strategic plan for improving the mathematical understanding of all students, and an appreciation of and support for the work of the full range of people responsible for the teaching and learning of mathematics, will not happen by simply enrolling in this seminar. In order to gain maximum benefit from participation, be strategic as you select members of your team and gain their pledge to full participation in seminar sessions and the work between sessions. Your common commitment to exploring aspects of your work that may be hampering students' learning of mathematics has the potential to make a significant impact on student learning and achievement.

May your work as a mathematics site improvement team become strengthened and focused because you commit to making time to learn, assess, and plan together, through *Secondary Lenses on Learning: Team Leadership for Mathematics in Middle and High Schools.*

—Virginia C. Stimpson
Field Test Director, Secondary Lenses on Learning
Mathematics Education, College of Education
University of Washington

Acknowledgments

Project Staff

Catherine Miles Grant, Education Development Center

Valerie L. Mills, Oakland Schools

Mary Bouck, Michigan State University

Ellen Davidson, Simmons College

Barbara Scott Nelson, Education Development Center

Steve Benson, Lesley University

Helen Lebowitz, Education Development Center

Project Evaluator

Virginia C. Stimpson, University of Washington

External Reviewers

Ben Ford, Sonoma State University

Vickie Inge, University of Virginia

Advisory Board

Nancy Alexander, Charleston, WV, Public Schools

Diane Briars, Mathematics Education Consultant

Daniel Chazan, University of Maryland

Mark Driscoll, Education Development Center

Will J. Jordan, Temple University

Joshua Paris, Brookline, MA, Public Schools

Mark Smylie, University of Illinois at Chicago

Pilot-Test Facilitators and Sites

Kathy Bodie, K–12 Mathematics Coordinator, Arlington, MA, Public Schools

Mary Eich, K–8 Mathematics Coordinator, Newton, MA, Public Schools

Dennis McCowan, Mathematics Chair, Weston, MA, Public Schools

Richard Houde, Retired Assistant Superintendent, Weston, MA, Public Schools

Valerie L. Mills, Supervisor and Mathematics Education Consultant for Oakland Schools, MI

Mary Bouck, PROM/SE Director of Capacity Building, Michigan State University

Teresa Ballard, Mathematics Coordinator, Battle Creek Public Schools, MI

These pilot tests took place under the auspices of the Education Collaborative of Greater Boston (EDCO); the Massachusetts Secondary School Administrators Association (MSSAA); Oakland Schools, Oakland County, Michigan; and Promoting Rigorous Outcomes in Mathematics and Science (PROM/SE), Michigan State University.

Field-Test Sites and Facilitators

Albuquerque, NM (Franny Dever, Lisa Matthews, Bill Schrandt, Becca Campos)

Colorado Springs, CO (Russ Peters, Barb Wilson)

Greater Philadelphia Mathematics Science Partnership, PA (Adina Laver, Debbie McKinney)

Teachers Development Group, OR (Linda Foreman, Kathy Pfaendler)

Charleston, WV (Deborah Seldomridge, Judy Pomeroy)

Video Development

Peter Shwartz, Dellaruth Video

Special Thanks to

Sandie Gilliam and her students at the San Lorenzo Valley High School

Students at the Prospect Hill Academy Charter School

Elizabeth Jones, Mathematics Consultant; Clare Earley, Teachers Development Group; Mari Halladay, Education Development Center

And all those upon whose work *Secondary Lenses on Learning* builds.

■ PUBLISHER'S ACKNOWLEDGMENTS

Corwin gratefully acknowledges the contributions of the following reviewers:

Lori Gibson, Math Staff Developer (6–12)
Bismarck Public Schools, Bismarck, ND

Vickie L. Inge, Director of Mathematics Outreach
University of Virginia, Charlottesville, VA

Lisa Matthews, Math Field Specialist
New Mexico State University, Mora, NM

Judy Mumme, Senior Project Director
WestEd, Sheridan, MT

Virginia C. Stimpson, College of Education
University of Washington, Seattle, WA

About the Authors

Catherine Miles Grant is a Senior Research and Development Associate at Education Development Center (EDC). Her research and development work centers on supporting principals and other school and district leaders to provide informed, strategic, and coherent leadership for their mathematics programs. Grant directs the National Science Foundation–funded *Secondary Lenses on Learning* project and associated facilitator institutes, coordinates EDC's *Lenses on Learning* outreach initiatives, and also works with the Wallace-funded *School Leadership Project* to better align principal preparation programs with the needs of schools. She is the major author of three sets of *Lenses on Learning* professional development materials: *Team Leadership for Mathematics in Middle and High Schools, Instructional Leadership in Mathematics,* and *Supervision: Focusing on Mathematical Thinking.* She was a senior researcher with *Putting Something on the Line,* a Spencer-funded study of links between ideas about mathematics, learning, and teaching and elementary school principals' practice. She was also an evaluator on the Boston Public Schools' National Science Foundation–funded *Lead Learners in Mathematics* project. Prior to joining EDC, Grant was a senior research associate at TERC in Cambridge, Massachusetts. Grant has also worked as a classroom teacher, resource teacher, district mathematics coordinator, and curriculum developer.

Valerie L. Mills is Supervisor and Mathematics Education Consultant for Oakland Schools, a Michigan intermediate agency serving 28 districts and 240,000 students. Beginning as a high school mathematics teacher more than 30 years ago, she has also served as Mathematics Department Chair, Mathematics Coordinator, and Director of Curriculum in the Ypsilanti and Ann Arbor school districts in Michigan. Other recent projects include a middle school mathematics professional development project, Beyond Implementation: Focus On Challenge And Learning (BI:FOCAL), and a five-year Mathematics/Science Partnership project with 15 high needs schools. Mills was a teacher-author on the Core Plus Mathematics Project, past president of the Michigan Council of Teachers of Mathematics, and past chair of the National Council of Teachers of Mathematics' Academy Services Committee. Mills has been awarded the Michigan Mathematics Education Service Award, the Presidential Award for Excellence in Mathematics Teaching, and the Milken National Educator Award. She is a frequent speaker at state and national meetings and has advised mathematics education projects throughout the country.

Mary Bouck is the PROM/SE Director of Capacity Building where she oversees all professional development for the project. (PROM/SE stands for Promoting Rigorous Outcomes in Mathematics and Science and is a National Science Foundation-supported research and development project at Michigan State University.) She also serves as a Visiting Academic Specialist in the Division of Science and Mathematics Education and Department of Teacher Education at Michigan State University. Bouck is a former mathematics teacher and school administrator, finishing her 30-year public school career as a superintendent. During this time, she worked in rural as well as urban schools. As an experienced educator, she has developed curriculum materials for elementary and middle grades and was a member of the writing group for the National Council of Teachers of Mathematics' Principles and Standards for School Mathematics. Bouck is an experienced professional development leader and a leader in promoting change in mathematics education. Her research interests include the development of teachers, teacher-leaders, and administrators.

Ellen Davidson is an Assistant Professor in the Department of Education at Simmons College with a focus on mathematics education. She taught for many years in SummerMath for Teachers, a National Science Foundation–funded in-service program at Mount Holyoke College. She was on the original *Lenses on Learning* development team and was one of the designers for *Lenses on Learning* professional development materials: *Instructional Leadership in Mathematics* and *Supervision: Focusing on Mathematical Thinking.* Davidson directed the *Lenses on Learning Facilitator Institutes* and has facilitated *Lenses on Learning* courses for administrators in the Boston and Chicago public schools. Davidson has extensive experience as a classroom teacher, mathematics coach, and mathematics specialist. Integrating her commitment to equity in education, Davidson is also an author of *Open Minds to Equality: A Sourcebook of Learning Activities to Affirm Diversity and Promote Equity*, published by Rethinking Schools.

■ ABOUT THE CONTRIBUTORS

Barbara Scott Nelson is Senior Scientist and Director of the Center for the Development of Teaching at Education Development Center, Inc., Newton, Massachusetts. Her research focuses on school and district administrators' practical judgment—in particular, how administrators' ideas about the nature of mathematics, learning, and teaching, affect their administrative practice. She has published numerous articles on administrator and teacher learning and edited two volumes on teacher learning: *Mathematics Teachers in Transition*, with Elizabeth Fennema, and *Beyond Classical Pedagogy*, with Terry Wood and Janet Warfield. Her recent book, *The Effective Principal: Instructional Leadership for High-Quality Learning*, was written with Annette Sassi and published by Teachers College Press. This book reports on research on the impact that elementary principals' knowledge of mathematics and how it is learned and taught has on their practice of instructional leadership. She is currently directing a large, multimethods study of elementary and middle school principals' leadership content knowledge for mathematics and how it affects their work.

Steve Benson is Associate Professor of Mathematics at Lesley University and Codirector of the Master of Science for Teachers program at the University of New Hampshire. He was formerly a research scientist in the Center for Mathematics Education at Education Development Center and has held faculty positions at St. Olaf College, Santa Clara University, University of New Hampshire, and University of Wisconsin–Oshkosh. Throughout his career, Benson has been deeply involved in the design and facilitation of preservice and inservice professional development programs for mathematics teachers at all grade levels. He is the lead author of the Corwin publication *Ways to Think About Mathematics: Activities and Investigations for Grade 6–12 Teachers.*

Part I
Useful Tools

SECONDARY LENSES ON LEARNING OBSERVATION AND REFLECTION GUIDE FOR A MATHEMATICS LESSON

■ MATHEMATICAL CONTENT

STUDENTS	TEACHERS
What mathematical *concepts* and *procedures* are students working on in this lesson? What specific mathematical *concepts* are perplexing for particular students? What are specific examples of students working on the following mathematical process skills (National Council of Teachers of Mathematics, 2000)? • *Problem solving* (applying and adapting a variety of appropriate strategies to solve problems, e.g., identifying patterns and relationships among quantitative variables) • *Reasoning and proving* (e.g., making and investigating mathematical conjectures, developing and evaluating solution strategies) • Engaging in *mathematical communication* (e.g., organizing and consolidating mathematical thinking through communication; using mathematical language, models, and symbols to express mathematical ideas; analyzing and evaluating the mathematical thinking and strategies of others) • *Making connections* (among mathematical ideas and to contexts outside of mathematics) • *Working with multiple representations* to make sense of problematic situations and to organize, record, and communicate mathematical ideas (e.g., using numerical and verbal expressions, graphic and tabular models, and symbolic expressions of the models)	What are the mathematical goals (*concepts* and/or *procedures*) of this lesson? What evidence is there that this lesson is part of a set of lessons that balances work with concept development and procedures? In what ways does this lesson afford opportunities for students to develop mathematical process skills (National Council of Teachers of Mathematics, 2000)? • Problem solving • Reasoning and proving • Engaging in mathematical communication • Making connections • Working with multiple representations What is the fit between the mathematical goals of the lesson, the content of the tasks, and their levels of cognitive demand?

Source: National Council of Teachers of Mathematics. (2000). *Principles and Standards for School Mathematics.* Reston, VA: Author.

INSTRUCTION ■

STUDENTS	TEACHERS
What are specific examples of students doing the following? • Making sense of specific mathematical concepts • Making connections between mathematical concepts, representations, solution strategies, and procedures • Persisting when solving challenging tasks • Learning through substantive discourse or "math talk" • Making and testing out mathematical conjectures • Judging for themselves the reasonableness of solutions	In what ways does the teacher's instruction reflect strengths in the following? • Knowledge of the mathematics • Mathematical knowledge needed for teaching • Knowledge of the curriculum—within and across grade levels What evidence is there that the teacher works with student ideas in the following ways? • Takes students through a clear learning path of new concepts that begins by accessing students' existing knowledge and builds on it • Utilizes multiple solution strategies intentionally • Works to "debug" wrong answers What evidence is there that the teacher supports students to develop mathematical proficiency with both factual knowledge and conceptual frameworks in the following? • Focuses instruction on helping students make sense of mathematical concepts and procedures • Helps students make connections between and among mathematical concepts, representations, multiple solution strategies, and procedures • Provides opportunities for students to consolidate understandings and procedures and begin to see ideas as instances of larger categories • Facilitates learning for struggling students without undermining their learning opportunities or the cognitive demand of tasks What evidence is there that the teacher works with the class to develop a community-centered learning environment in the following ways? • Supports students in expressing their thinking, seeking and giving help, and monitoring learning • Models mathematical thinking and appropriate use of vocabulary

■ FORMATIVE ASSESSMENT

STUDENTS	TEACHERS
What evidence is there that students are monitoring their own learning? What evidence is there that students are using feedback from the teacher and other students to extend and/or correct their understanding of a mathematical concept or procedure? What evidence is there that students expect that learning mathematics requires listening or otherwise working to understand their peers' thinking, as well as the teacher's? What evidence is there that students expect that complete correct solutions frequently include an explanation of their thinking as well as the solution?	What evidence is there that the teacher listens, analyzes, and adjusts instruction based on student comments and work? What opportunities does the teacher create during this lesson to support *formative* assessment by doing the following? • Expecting students to make their current mathematical thinking visible to themselves, other students, and the teacher (e.g., questions asked probe for understanding; existence of effective student-to-student mathematical discourse in pairs, small groups, and the whole group) • Encouraging students to evaluate their own and others' thinking (e.g., questions asked in class, on assignments) What evidence is there that *summative* assessments used in the class do the following? • Include tasks that assess both conceptual understanding and procedural knowledge • Offer feedback to students that provides direction for their next learning steps • Offer opportunities to learn from and revise work in response to input from the teacher and or peers

CONNECTIONS BETWEEN THE CLASSROOM ■ AND SCHOOLWIDE SYSTEMS

Class _____

Level of Class _____ Number of Students _____

Population of Students in the Classroom (race, gender, free or reduced-price lunch qualification and/or participation) _____

_____

Length of Class Period and Percentage of Time Spent on Instruction _____

_____

Evidence of Match Between the Needs of the Particular Class Population and the Knowledge and Experience of the Assigned Teacher _____

_____

_____

Evidence of Alignment of Lesson Content With Course Curriculum _____

_____

_____

Evidence of Use of Instructional Approaches Targeted in Mathematics Program Improvement Plan _____

_____

_____

Evidence That the Environment Is Conducive to, and Focused on, Effort, Learning, and Achievement _____

_____

_____

Sufficiency of Instructional Materials Needed in the Lesson (textbooks, calculators, rulers, and other math tools) _____

_____

_____

_____

LEVELS OF THE MATH-TALK LEARNING COMMUNITY

Action Trajectories for Teacher and Student

Overview of Shift Over Levels 0–3

The classroom community grows to support students acting in central or leading roles and shifts from a focus on answers to a focus on mathematical thinking.

A. Questioning	B. Explaining Mathematical Thinking	C. Source of Mathematical Ideas	D. Responsibility for Learning
Shift from teacher as questioner to students and teacher as questioners.	Students increasingly explain and articulate their math ideas.	Shift from teacher as the source of all math ideas to students' ideas also influencing direction of lesson.	Students increasingly take responsibility for learning and evaluation of others and self. Math sense becomes the criterion for evaluation.

Level 0

Traditional teacher-directed classroom with brief answer responses from students.

A. Questioning	B. Explaining Mathematical Thinking	C. Source of Mathematical Ideas	D. Responsibility for Learning
Teacher is the only questioner. Short frequent questions function to keep students listening and paying attention to the teacher. *Students give short answers and respond to the teacher only. No student-to-student math talk.*	*No or minimal teacher elicitation of student thinking, strategies, or explanations; teacher expects answer-focused responses. Teacher may tell answers.* *No student thinking or strategy-focused explanation of work. Only answers are given.*	*Teacher is physically at the board, usually chalk in hand, telling and showing students how to do math.* *Students respond to math presented by the teacher. They do not offer their own math ideas.*	*Teacher repeats student responses (originally directed to her) for the class. Teacher responds to students' answers by verifying the correct answer or showing the correct method.* *Students are passive listeners; they attempt to imitate the teacher and do not take responsibility for the learning of their peers or themselves.*

Level 1

Teacher beginning to pursue student mathematical thinking. Teacher plays central role in the math-talk community.

A. Questioning	B. Explaining Mathematical Thinking	C. Source of Mathematical Ideas	D. Responsibility for Learning
Teacher questions begin to focus on student thinking and focus less on answers. Teacher begins to ask follow-up questions about student methods. As a student answers a question, other students listen passively or wait for their turn.	Teacher probes student thinking somewhat. One or two strategies may be elicited. Teacher may fill in explanations herself. Students give information about their math thinking usually as it is probed by the teacher (minimal volunteering of thoughts). They provide brief descriptions of their thinking.	Teacher is still the main source of ideas, though she elicits some student ideas. Teacher does some probing to access student ideas. Some student ideas are raised in discussions, but are not explored.	Teacher begins to set up structures to facilitate students listening to and helping other students. The teacher alone gives feedback. Students become more engaged by repeating what other students say or by helping another student at the teacher's request. This helping mostly involves students showing how they solved a problem.

Level 2

Teacher modeling and helping students build new roles. Some co-teaching and co-learning begins as student-to-student talk increases. Teacher physically begins to move to side or back of the room.

A. Questioning	B. Explaining Mathematical Thinking	C. Source of Mathematical Ideas	D. Responsibility for Learning
Teacher continues to ask probing questions and also asks more open questions. She also facilitates student-to-student talk, e.g., by asking students to be prepared to ask questions about other students' work. Students ask questions of one another's work on the board, often at the prompting of the teacher. Students listen to one another so they do not repeat questions.	*Teacher probes more deeply to learn about student thinking and supports detailed descriptions from students. Teacher open to and elicits multiple strategies.* Students usually give information as it is probed by the teacher with some volunteering of thoughts. They begin to stake a position and articulate more information in response to probes. They explain steps in their thinking by providing fuller descriptions and begin to defend their answers and methods. Other students listen supportively.	*Teacher follows up on explanations and builds on them by asking students to compare and contrast them. Teacher is comfortable using student errors as opportunities for learning.* Students exhibit confidence about their ideas and share their own thinking and strategies even if they are different from others. Student ideas sometimes guide the direction of the math lesson.	*Teacher encourages student responsibility for understanding the mathematical ideas of others. Teacher asks other students questions about student work and whether they agree or disagree and why.* Students begin to listen to understand one another. When the teacher requests, they explain other students' ideas in their own words. Helping involves clarifying other students' ideas for themselves and others. Students imitate and model teacher's probing in pair work and in whole-class discussions.

Level 3

Teacher as co-teacher and co-learner. Teacher monitors all that occurs, still fully engaged. Teacher is ready to assist, but now in more peripheral and monitoring role (coach and assister).

A. Questioning	B. Explaining Mathematical Thinking	C. Source of Mathematical Ideas	D. Responsibility for Learning
Teacher expects students to ask one another questions about their work. The teacher's questions still may guide the discourse. Student-to-student talk is student-initiated, not dependent on the teacher. Students ask questions and listen to responses. Many questions are "Why?" questions that require justification from the person answering. Students repeat their own or other's questions until satisfied with answers.	*Teacher follows along closely to student descriptions of their thinking, encouraging students to make their explanations more compete; may ask probing questions to make explanations more complete. Teacher stimulates students to think more deeply about strategies.* Students describe more complete strategies; they defend and justify their answers with little prompting from the teacher. Students realize that they will be asked questions from other students when they finish, so they are motivated and careful to be thorough. Other students support with active listening.	*Teacher allows for interruptions from students during her explanations; she lets students explain and "own" new strategies. (Teacher is still engaged and deciding what is important to continue exploring.) Teacher uses student ideas and methods as the basis for lessons or miniextensions.* Students interject their ideas as the teacher or other students are teaching, confident that their ideas are valued. Students spontaneously compare and contrast and build on ideas. Student ideas form part of the content of many math lessons.	*The teacher expects students to be responsible for co-evaluation of everyone's work and thinking. She supports students as they help one another sort out misconceptions. She helps and/or follows up when needed.* Students listen to understand, then initiate clarifying other students' work and ideas for themselves and for others during whole-class discussions as well as in small group and pair work. Students assist each other in understanding and correcting errors.

TASK ANALYSIS GUIDE

LOWER-LEVEL DEMANDS	HIGHER-LEVEL DEMANDS
Memorization Tasks • Involve either reproducing previously learned facts, rules, formulae, or definitions OR committing facts, rules, formulae, or definitions to memory. • Cannot be solved using procedures because a procedure does not exist or because the time frame in which the task is being completed is too short to use a procedure. • Are not ambiguous—such tasks involve exact reproduction of previously seen material and what is to be reproduced is clearly and directly stated. • Have no connection to the concepts or meaning that underlie the facts, rules, formulae, or definitions being learned or reproduced.	**Procedures With Connections Tasks** • Focus students' attention on the use of procedures for the purpose of developing deeper levels of understanding of mathematical concepts and ideas. • Suggest pathways to follow (explicitly or implicitly) that are broad general procedures that have close connections to underlying conceptual ideas as opposed to narrow algorithms that are opaque with respect to underlying concepts. • Usually are presented in multiple ways (e.g., visual diagrams, manipulatives, symbols, problem situations). Making connections among multiple representations helps to develop meaning. • Require some degree of cognitive effort. Although general procedures may be followed, they cannot be followed mindlessly. Students need to engage with the conceptual ideas that underlie the procedures in order to successfully complete the task and develop misunderstanding.
Procedures Without Connections Tasks • Are algorithmic. Use of the procedure is either specifically called for or its use is evident based on prior instruction, experience, or placement of the task. • Require limited cognitive demand for successful completion. There is little ambiguity about what needs to be done and how to do it. • Have no connection to the concepts or meaning that underlie the procedure being used. • Are focused on producing correct answers rather than developing mathematical understanding. • Require no explanations or explanations that focus solely on describing the procedures that were used.	**Doing Mathematics Tasks** • Requires complex and nonalgorithmic thinking (i.e., there is not a predictable, well-rehearsed approach or pathway explicitly suggested by the task, task instructions, or a worked-out example). • Requires students to explore and understand the nature of mathematical concepts, processes, or relationships. • Demands self-monitoring or self-regulation of one's own cognitive processes. • Requires students to access relevant knowledge and experiences and make appropriate use of them in working through the task. • Requires students to analyze the task and actively examine task constraints that may limit possible solution strategies and solutions. • Requires considerable cognitive effort and may involve some level of anxiety for the students due to the unpredictable nature of the solution process required.

Part II

Session Introductions and Readings

Session

What Does It Mean to Know *Algebra?*

(Content)

As suggested by the NCTM Principles and Standards 2000, an overarching focus for algebra is on developing student ability to represent and analyze relationships among quantitative variables. From this perspective, variables are not letters that stand for unknown numbers— they are quantitative attributes of objects (like measurements of size), patterns, or situations that change in response to change in other quantities or with the passage of time. Understanding and predicting patterns of change in variables emerges as the most important goal of algebra . . .

—Fey and Phillips (2005)

It is no secret that schools are challenged to meet demands for increased breadth and depth in the mathematical knowledge that students need to acquire in order to graduate from high school and prepare for transitions to college or the work force. Algebra, in particular, is of great concern given its emphasis in high-stakes assessments and ongoing conversations about its "gatekeeper" role.

What is equally true is that, as a field, we know a great deal about what needs to be in place if students—all students—are to grow in their knowledge and achievement in mathematics. Decades of research and practice point to a number of key elements that need to be in place in middle and high school mathematics programs if students—all students— are to experience improved achievement in mathematics. Three cornerstones of a complete and coherent educational system are content, instruction, and assessment. The first three sessions of *Secondary Lenses on Learning* examine each of these topics, in turn, in the context of algebra.

Research also prompts us to address other dimensions of our mathematics programs, building on what is known about promising classroom practice and continuing to carry the focus to the entire school as a system. How do our schools go about analyzing what may be contributing to the success or failure of subgroups of students? What do we communicate to students about what we believe about their capacity to learn powerful and useful mathematics? How closely aligned are schoolwide policies and practices to those beliefs? What systems and programs are in place to provide support for students when they struggle? What kinds of opportunities are provided for our teachers to learn and plan together, and how closely tied are these to the authentic work of mathematics learning and teaching? What opportunities are there for us, as leaders (in both administrative and instructional roles), to *come together* for sustained shared learning and reflecting about effective research-based practices for advancing student learning in mathematics? What processes are in place for critical players to work together to analyze and plan based on the strengths and needs of our own buildings' mathematics programs? *Secondary Lenses on Learning* is designed to provide you and your team with such opportunities.

This seminar begins with a session focused on content, built around the question, "What does it mean to *know* algebra—beyond simply knowing how to apply a series of procedures?" It offers the opportunity to do the following:

- Examine characteristics of a challenging algebra curriculum that is accessible to all middle and high school students
- Explore what it means to develop a stance of inquiry and ongoing learning about mathematics education within a community of learners
- Consider the potential of a mathematics leadership team to facilitate continuous improvement in mathematics education
- Examine the connections among educators in different positions and consider that each has a practice that may need to grow in order to ensure that all students are successful in mathematics

Readings and Focus Questions to Prepare for Session 1

(Two Homework Readings)

In preparation for the first session, please read the following two articles and prepare the focus questions that follow.

Reading 1.1   Usiskin, Z. (2005). Should all students learn a significant amount of algebra? In C. Greenes & C. Findell (Eds.), *Developing students' algebraic reasoning abilities* (pp. 4–16). Lakewood, CO: National Council of Supervisors of Mathematics.

Reading 1.2   Fey, J. T., & Phillips, E. D. (2005). A course called algebra 1. In C. Greenes & C. Findell (Eds.), *Developing students' algebraic reasoning abilities* (pp. 33–45). Lakewood, CO: National Council of Supervisors of Mathematics.

These two articles describe foundational experiences to prepare students for more formal work with algebra in middle and high schools. These ideas are discussed in Session 1. Prepare for the discussion in the following way:

1. Please select *one significant* quote or section that struck you about the question posed by Usiskin: *Should all students learn a significant amount of algebra?*

   Be prepared to explain the significance of the quote you selected to a small group, including how it resonated with you. Also be prepared to contribute to a small-group discussion of other participants' selected quotes or sections.

2. Take notes about the following question: *What are the characteristics of school algebra described in the two readings, and what is the rationale?*

APPROACH	RATIONALE

READING 1.1

Should All Students Learn a Significant Amount of Algebra?

Zalman Usiskin

The algebra we teach to students can be traced back through the Greek mathematician Diophantus to the Babylonians over 3500 years ago. However, the language we use in today's algebra is relatively new as mathematics goes, dating back only to the French mathematician Viète in 1591 and the systematization of the content by Euler in 1770. In the United States as recently as 1910, less than 15% of the age cohort entered high school and only they studied any algebra (Goldin, 2003). I estimate that 1 in 20 people studied a second year of algebra.

Through the 20th century the situation changed dramatically. By 1972, virtually all students entered high school and about 72% of them were taking one year of algebra. About half of those students took a second year of algebra. Algebra was still viewed as a high school subject and introduced before grade 9 only to perhaps 10% of students. Yet by 1998, algebra was being introduced to virtually all students before grade 10: 25% of students studied algebra before grade 9, and more than 90% of students were taking one year of algebra by the end of the grade 9. Approximately two-thirds of students were studying a second year of algebra in grade 10 or 11 (National Center for Educational Statistics, 2002).

In the first year of algebra, students are typically taught linear equations and inequalities, graphing of lines, operations with polynomial expressions (including factoring), laws of positive integer powers, linear systems, square roots, simple quadratics, and maybe, rational expressions. In the second year, they are most likely to begin with a review of first-year algebra and then be taught rational powers and n^{th} roots, operations with matrices, general notions of functions, linear and quadratic functions, logarithms and exponential functions, sequences, and perhaps some combinatorics and probability (Dossey and Usiskin, 2000). When I speak of *a significant amount of algebra*, I mean this amount.

I noted that students are *taught* these subjects. I did not write that they *learn* them. Many colleges require these subjects but many students have to take remedial algebra courses in college. In some areas of the United States, all students, including those not planning to go to college, and even those who might not finish high school, are obliged to take two years of algebra. Is this wise? I will try to examine this question in as unbiased a manner as I can, recognizing that as a person who has gone to college and who works with mathematics, I am likely to be biased in favor of increased amounts of schooling and the place of my subject in that schooling.

ARITHMETIC IS EVERYWHERE, ALGEBRA IS HIDDEN ■

Most people realize that they need to know arithmetic. Whole numbers, fractions, decimals, and percents are everywhere. Just pick up a newspaper or magazine, open to any page at random, and count the numbers on it. I have examined the uses of numbers in newspapers around the world and in almost every country, a daily newspaper has a median of about 125 numbers on its pages.

Algebra is different. Scan a daily newspaper and you are not likely to see any algebraic formulas. Adults may be handicapped by a lack of knowledge of arithmetic, but lack of knowledge of algebra does not seem too debilitating. Items for sale in stores have lots of numbers on them and no algebra. Even scientific publications meant for the educated public and with many in them tend to have little if any algebra.

> Adults may be handicapped by a lack of knowledge of arithmetic, but lack of knowledge of algebra does not seem too debilitating.

Yet algebra *must* be important, for if algebra were not important, why would we require all students to study it? To say "You need algebra for college," or "You won't do well on some exams without it" is true. But these reasons do not tell us why algebra is so important that it has become a required element in the mathematics curriculum of almost every secondary school student in the world.

When people are required to learn a subject that they feel they do not need, will not use, and that requires work to learn, there are predictable results. Many of them will dislike the subject and they will be proud of their dislike. No one makes fun of reading. No one makes fun of arithmetic. But people make fun of algebra. My favorite cartoon of this type was drawn by a high school student, Brad Haak, whose mother was a mathematics teacher.

This attitude towards algebra is passed on from generation to generation.

Brad Haak's View of Algebra

■ THE REASONS FOR ALGEBRA

There is a practical reason for learning algebra. *Algebra is a gatekeeper.* A knowledge of algebra is required for any college in the United States or Canada that has any selectivity. Without algebra, a person is kept from doing many jobs or entering many job-training programs. Algebra is such a significant gatekeeper that at least one educator has called the study of algebra a *civil right.*

> Algebra is a gatekeeper.

Again, however, knowing that algebra is a gatekeeper begs the question. Why is algebra considered so important that its study is required? I offer some reasons intrinsic to algebra.

Algebra Is the Language of Generalization

Here is the rule for multiplication of fractions:

To multiply two fractions, multiply their numerators to get the numerator of the product, and then multiply their denominators to get the denominator of the product.

For example,

$$\left(\frac{2}{3}\right)\left(\frac{4}{5}\right) = \frac{(2)(4)}{(3)(5)} = \frac{8}{15}$$

What is the rule in the language of algebra?

$$\left(\frac{a}{b}\right)\left(\frac{c}{d}\right) = \frac{(a)(c)}{(b)(d)} = \frac{ac}{bd}$$

Not only is the language of algebra shorter than the English, but it also looks like the arithmetic. For this reason, the language of algebra is *easier* than everyday language.

As we all know, there are formulas for area as simple as $A = LW$ (in a rectangle, area equals length times width) that come in handy if any person is looking for a place to live and wants to know how much floor space or wall space there is, or if a person is sewing clothes and wants to determine the amount of material that is needed. There are formulas for perimeter that tell how long a fence a person might need for a field or how much ribbon is needed to tie a package. There are all sorts of formulas in sports, from the calculation of winning percentages to the probability that a team will win any number of games in a row. Income tax, sales taxes, discounts, and virtually every money matter involves applying some formula. People can get along without the formulas (most people do) but they are less likely to be fooled by someone misinterpreting them if they themselves can work with the algebra.

Algebra Enables a Person to Answer All the Questions of a Particular Type at One Time

Suppose you have a date of some event in history (in the Gregorian calendar) and you want to know the day of the week that it occurred. You can figure the day out by working from today's day and date back, accounting for leap years (trying to remember which leap years are the exceptions) and you will get your answer. But if you have many questions of this type, then you want a formula.

One such formula is

$$W = d + 2m + \left\lfloor \frac{3(m+1)}{5} \right\rfloor + y + \left\lfloor \frac{y}{4} \right\rfloor - \left\lfloor \frac{y}{100} \right\rfloor + \left\lfloor \frac{y}{400} \right\rfloor + 2$$

where

d = the day of the month of the given date

m = the number of the month of the year, with January and February regarded as the 13th and 14th months of the previous year. The other months are numbered 3 to 12 as usual.

y = the year.

This formula tells you on which day of the week a particular date in the Gregorian calendar will occur, even years into the future. Here the symbol means to round the number inside it down to the nearest integer. For instance, for February 7, 2004, $d = 7$, $m = 14$, and $y = 2003$, and so

$$\begin{aligned} W &= 7 + 2(14) + \left\lfloor \frac{3(14+1)}{5} \right\rfloor + 2003 + \left\lfloor \frac{2003}{4} \right\rfloor - \frac{2003}{100} + \frac{2003}{400} + 2 \\ &= 7 + 28 + 9 + 2003 + 500 - 20 + 5 + 2 \\ &= 2534 \end{aligned}$$

Once W is computed, divide W by 7 and the remainder is the day of the week with Saturday = 0, Sunday = 1, and so on, until Friday = 6. That is, determine the least nonnegative residue of W modulo 7. We find that $2534 = 7 \cdot 362$, so the remainder is 0 and February 7, 2004 fell on a Saturday.

Algebra Is the Language of Relationships Among Quantities

Everyone should know the meanings of certain mathematical relationships that are more and more present in everyday language:

- growing exponentially
- growing logarithmically
- varying directly
- varying inversely
- inverse square law
- line of best fit (statistics, but also algebra)
- rate at which a rate is changing (calculus, but also algebra)
- approaching asymptotically
- extrapolation, interpolation

Algebra Is a Language for Solving Certain Types of Problems

It used to be that the only problems that involved translation from words into mathematics in algebra texts—the so-called *word problems* or *story problems*—involved age, motion, coins, work, and mixtures. Now textbooks are just as likely to have problems that involve everyday situations. How much of a particular food can you eat and stay within a particular diet? If the population of a town is *x* and growing at some rate, what will the population be some years from now? When there is a formula relating two quantities, if you know one quantity, you can find the other, and today's technology has made it possible to work with far more complicated formulas than one could deal with even 25 years ago. The use of a graphing calculator makes it possible to find solutions to practical problems through graphing even when we do not have an algorithm to solve the equation algebraically. Graphs of functions and other relationships among variables are the geometry of algebra, and this geometry would not exist without the algebra that drives it.

Algebra Is the Study of Structures with Certain Properties

An algebraic formula such as $A = LW$ would not have much advantage over its translation into words (area = length times width) were it not for the fact that operations on numbers have properties that enable formulas and other equations to be manipulated. As we all know, when $A = LW$, then (by dividing both sides by L), $\frac{A}{L} = W$.

What this means is that from one formula we can deduce others. So, because we know algebra, we do not have to memorize a separate formula to determine a side of a rectangle from its area. The power of deduction is not appreciated much by the uneducated public, but it is an extraordinarily powerful tool. The power of deduction is related to the next reason for algebra.

Algebra Shows That Our Universe Possesses Order

We are all familiar with the use of algebra to explain *number tricks,* such as telling whether an integer is divisible by 9 by adding its digits. But algebra does more than just explain why number tricks work; its language explains many aspects of our universe. It is no coincidence that within 100 years after Viète's work in algebra, Newton and Leibniz independently developed the calculus, Newton could use this calculus to explain Kepler's laws, and so we learned why the orbits of the planets are essentially elliptical. Algebra helps to explain what to expect from the random flipping of coins, the odds of winning a lottery, whether a building can withstand the weights and other forces that will act on it, how to ship oil around the world with the least cost, how long it will take for the Earth's population to double at various rates of growth, and myriads of other activities.

All of these examples involve everyday real events. If we are asking about algebra for *all* students, our case is not strengthened by appealing to physics or other subjects that students who do not take algebra would also probably not take. Even so, the following reason for studying algebra is of fundamental importance.

Algebra Is a Prerequisite for Virtually All Other Mathematics

In the book simply titled *Why Math?*, Rodney Driver (1986) covers a wide range of areas of mathematics, including arithmetic, algebra, geometry, vectors, combinatorics, and probability. But common to all these areas is algebra. The soul of mathematics may lie in geometry, but algebra is its heart.

Thus, without a knowledge of algebra, people

- lose control over parts of their lives,
- must rely on other people to do these things for them,
- are more likely to make unwise decisions,
- will not be able to understand many everyday ideas, and
- will not be able to comprehend ideas discussed in chemistry, physics, the earth sciences, economics, business, psychology, and many other areas.

Thus, if two of the purposes of schooling are to create informed citizens and to optimize the work opportunities for our students, then the study of algebra is a must.

IF ALGEBRA IS SO IMPORTANT, WHY HAVE ■ SO MANY ADULTS—EVEN EDUCATED ADULTS— BEEN ABLE TO LIVE NICELY WITHOUT IT?

It is common for adults today to speak of algebra and other mathematics beyond arithmetic as if they are important only to a few people. For instance, here is a quote from a Chicago daily newspaper a few years ago:

> When the regular season begins in three weeks, Friday night's Bulls preseason opener will become about as significant as algebra formulas learned in high school. (Jackson, 1994)

What was John Jackson, the sportswriter who wrote the article, thinking when he wrote this? To himself he must have thought, "The preseason opener is meaningless. What is the most meaningless thing I can think of? Aha! It's algebra formulas!"

Clearly Mr. Jackson knows that many of the sports statistics that are printed in his newspaper are calculated using algebraic formulas, for he is undoubtedly a college graduate. However, these writers and other adults avoid the formulas whenever they can. They are like people who go to a foreign country but do not know enough of the language to converse with native speakers in that country. Even though I do not know Dutch, I can get along, but I will never appreciate the richness of the culture, and I will not be able to learn as much as I could if I knew Dutch. In my travel there, I am forced to depend on signs that have been translated into English.

So it is with most adults and algebra. People can live without algebra, but as a result they cannot appreciate as much of what is going on around them. They cannot participate fully. They are more likely to make unwise decisions and will find themselves with less control over their lives. They live in the same world, but they do not see or understand as much of its beauty, structure, and mystery.

> People can live without algebra, but.... They are more likely to make unwise decisions and will find themselves with less control over their lives.

THE DISJUNCTURE BETWEEN ■ ALGEBRA AND SCHOOL ALGEBRA

Algebra in many classrooms does not at all present the picture of the vibrant, widely applicable subject that I have described. Instead of being taught as a living language with a

> Algebra needs to turn on students rather than turn them off.

logical structure and many connections between its topics and other subjects, algebra is taught as a dead language with a myriad of rules that seem to come from nowhere, and with applications that are viewed as puzzles, like chess problems. That so many well-educated adults wonder why they studied algebra is testimony to the disjuncture between such an important subject and the way it is presented in schools.

In the past, when only a very small percent of the population needed to learn algebra, we could be content with the algebra course as a gatekeeper. But today we cannot afford to weed out so many students. Algebra needs to *turn on* students rather than turn them off.

To remove this disjuncture, there has been in some places a paradigm shift in the teaching and learning of algebra. This paradigm shift in attitude towards school algebra is the reason that one sees such a different approach to the subject in some contemporary materials for secondary schools. Using graphs, technology, applications, and mathematical structure, the best contemporary materials more accurately picture *the what* and *the why* of algebra than many traditional materials did. Applications are used to motivate the subject. Transitions are carefully made from arithmetic to algebra, and connections are given to geometry, statistics, and other mathematics. Algebra is changed from a skill-dominated experience, in which problems exist to practice skills, to a problem-centered experience in which skills are developed in order to solve interesting problems.

> Algebra is changed from a skill-dominated experience, in which problems exist to practice skills, to a problem-centered experience in which skills are developed in order to solve interesting problems.

■ ACHIEVING ALGEBRA FOR ALL— IS IT THEORETICALLY POSSIBLE?

It is commonly thought that mathematics has levels of abstraction. Algebra is more abstract than arithmetic. Calculus is more abstract than algebra. Higher algebra is more abstract than calculus. In a theoretical sense, in the sense of generalization, this is true. Each subject generalizes some of what has come before it. But how abstract is algebra, really? All of my work with the *University of Chicago School Mathematics Program* (UCSMP) has convinced me that algebra is inherently no more abstract than everyday written language, but it is made more abstract by us. Learning algebra should be no more difficult than learning a new language. Any student who can learn to read possesses the ability to learn algebra.

Why do I feel this way? Because we have learned many things about algebra. First, algebra starts earlier than its formal study, whether we want it to or not. The equation $3 + \_\_ = 7$ can be considered as algebra; the use of an underline is no different than the use of a letter. So first- or second-grade students do algebra problems; we just don't tell them, perhaps because we don't want to scare the teachers.

We have found no age cutoff with respect to the learning of variable. Even very young students can evaluate formulas and can graph. We should not have been surprised. Variable is supposed to be an abstract concept, but variables are introduced quite early in some countries' curricula and seem to be easier to learn early. Is the use of a letter such as A for area or x for an unknown any more abstract than the use of the letter symbol p for the sound /p/? Surely there is an age cutoff; babies will not learn variables. But at the secondary level, from grade 6 or 7 up, it seems that the earlier the better.

> Any student who can learn to read possesses the ability to learn algebra.

Second, the use of applications concretizes algebra, motivates it, makes it easier. We know that algebra can be approached theoretically, such as through field properties, but this approach does not work with many students. On the other hand, we also know that we can approach algebra through formulas and through generalizations of patterns, and that this approach does work. It isn't automatic; competence does not come in one day or even one week or one month. But situating algebra in contexts that give reasons for studying the subject at the same time that teachers illustrate the concepts changes a person's view of algebra forever. I know that many of you reading this would not return to the way you used to teach algebra.

But let me raise a caution. I do not wish to be interpreted as suggesting that a teacher can just go into a classroom of students and teach them algebra in some correct way and they will learn. There *are* prerequisites to learning algebra. If a symbol is to stand for a number, as variables usually do, you have to know something about numbers. You have to know that a number can be represented in many ways, that 6 can be written as $\sqrt{36}$ and as $\frac{12}{2}$ and as 6.000, and that if $x = 6$, then x can be written in any of those ways, too. You need to know what it means for one number to be close to another in value. If you have the expression $x + y$, you need to know what the + sign means independently of what the numbers x and y are. These and other arithmetic ideas are necessary for success in algebra. But they can be learned by virtually all students.

For these reasons, I believe that virtually all students can learn algebra. But is it realistically possible?

ACHIEVING ALGEBRA FOR ALL ■

To achieve algebra for all students, I think that we have to change the attitudes toward algebra that most of the public have. To do this, it helps to look at how arithmetic became a subject that everyone felt they needed to learn.

Remember that arithmetic, too, is a relatively new subject. The algorithms that we use for multiplication and division were invented mostly in Italy in the 1400s. Expecting everyone to be competent in the four fundamental operations is a phenomenon of the past 300 years. It took great numbers of people participating in trade and using numbers every day, the invention of numeration systems and algorithms—e.g., the use of decimals by Simon Stevin—that made it relatively easy for people to compute, and the widespread availability of paper and pencil (or pen and ink) that made it possible to record the work. Do we have that for algebra? *Can* we have that for algebra?

The answer is that we are closer than most people think. A large percentage of the people who use a computer today work with spreadsheets. They do not think they are doing algebra when they use Excel and other spreadsheets because this does not look like school algebra. To most people, algebra is supposed to be hard. Algebra is supposed to be something you do not understand.

But working with a spreadsheet *is* algebra. The names of the variables are A1, A2, A3, B1, B2, and so forth. Each time we ask the spreadsheet to calculate something and put it in another cell we are writing an algebraic formula. For example, if in cell C1 we type = A1 + B1, then we are naming the variable C1. The spreadsheet does the calculation for us, of course. Each time that we copy a formula to other cells, we are creating a function. The function may be explicitly defined or it may be an iterative sequence, but it is a function either way. Most spreadsheet programs allow us to graph the explicitly defined functions. With either the graph or by successive approximation, we can solve many equations. Also, almost all spreadsheet programs have a form of summation notation that makes for a very easy transition to traditional Σ-notation:

$$\text{SUM (A1:A5) is so similar to } \sum_{i=1}^{5} A_i$$

Thus algebra capability is in almost every computer, on virtually every business desk. People who think they do not know algebra are using this capability.

Spreadsheets do not do all that we view as algebra. But most that is left can be done by computer algebra systems, CAS. Want to factor a trinomial? Then put the trinomial into a TI-92 or Casio-cfx 9700g and give the instruction to factor. Want to solve a cubic exactly? Put the cubic into the CAS system and give the instruction to solve. Want to differentiate a function? Want to find a definite or indefinite integral? Want to solve a differential equation? For more complex mathematics, you may need *Mathematica* or *Maple*, but if there is an algorithm for the process, then there is a CAS system that performs that algorithm.

Paper-and-pen and, more recently, paper-and-pencil has been the technology that we have used for the past 400 years to do arithmetic. Paper-and-pen became dominant not because people understood why the algorithms work. They still don't! Paper-and-pencil won because its algorithms were more widely applicable. I believe we are now in the same situation with computers and algebra. In time, the computer algorithms embodied in spreadsheets and automatic graphers and CAS systems will become the algebra that everyone uses and recognizes. Spreadsheets will be employed to help introduce the language of algebra to students, and CAS systems will be used to perform the complex manipulations.

This does not mean that paper-and-pencil algebra will become obsolete. They will not become obsolete any more than mental arithmetic has become obsolete. People will still need to know how to solve simple equations and do simple manipulations by hand. And, perhaps more importantly, they will need to be able to translate from real and fanciful situations to mathematics and vice-versa. Algebra is more important than ever. School algebra is not obsolete, but it needs to change to touch the everyday lives of students and their families in order to be relevant to all students, and it needs to recognize its relationships with technology in order for the public to be comfortable with the notion of algebra for all.

> Algebra is more important than ever.

■ REFERENCES

Dossey, J., and Usiskin, Z. (2000). *Mathematics education in the United States—2000, A capsule summary.* Reston, VA: National Council of Teachers of Mathematics.

Driver, R. (1986). *Why math?* New York, NY: Springer Verlag.

Goldin, C. The Human Capital Century, www.educationnext.org/20031/73.html.

Jackson, J. (October 15, 1994). "Bulls Bow in OT," Chicago, IL: *Chicago Sun-Times.*

National Center for Education Statistics. (2002). *The condition of education 2002* (pp. 157, 215–6). Washington, DC: U.S. Government Printing Office.

READING 1.2

A Course Called Algebra I

James T. Fey

Elizabeth Difanis Phillips

It is essential for students to learn algebra both as a style of mathematical thinking, involving the formalization of patterns, functions, and generalizations, and as a set of competencies involving the representations of quantitative relationships.

—Silver, 1997

In recent efforts to plan and develop standards-based school mathematics curricula, no topic has occupied more time and energy of teachers, curriculum developers, and educational policy-makers than algebra. Since the original conception of the NCTM *Curriculum and Evaluation Standards for School Mathematics* in 1989, many conditions have changed in school mathematics. None of those changes has greater implications for the middle school than the broadly endorsed expectation that *all students* should study the equivalent of a year-long college preparatory course in elementary algebra, preferably in eighth grade (or even earlier for talented students). The original conception of the *Standards* algebra strand was to prepare students to be successful in high school algebra—allowing time in the eighth grade curriculum to address important topics in geometry, probability, and statistics as well as some algebra. The new educational policy conditions, including the NCTM *Principles and Standards for School Mathematics* 2000, have forced us to struggle with hard questions about the algebra we teach.

WHAT ARE THE MOST IMPORTANT ■ ALGEBRAIC IDEAS AND SKILLS FOR STUDENTS TO LEARN IN ALGEBRA?

Is the algebra that was *right* for 20th-century mathematical preparation still the right mathematical preparation for the high-tech 21st century? Is the algebra that prepares the most able and interested students for mathematics-intensive careers an appropriate course for *all students?* Should algebra be taught in a year-long course called Algebra I?

The algebra that most adults remember from their own high school mathematics is what the late Robert Davis (1986) once described as a *dance of symbols*—a maze of procedures for manipulating symbolic expressions, equations, and inequalities in search of the value for that elusive *x*. Those same adults will probably remember that when symbol manipulation

Source: Reprinted with permission from *Developing Students' Algebraic Reasoning Abilities* © 2005 National Council of Supervisors of Mathematics, courtesy of the National Council of Supervisors of Mathematics and J.T Fey and E. Phillips.

rules were put to use, it was typically to solve an array of almost notorious story problems about moving trains, relative ages of parents and their children, or combinations of coins. For most students in earlier generations, the net result of algebra instruction was generally a fragile mastery of quite limited technical skills, training in routine procedures for solving non-authentic problems, and a strong distaste for the subject.

What are the big ideas for beginning algebra that students should acquire on their way to the kind of competence in quantitative reasoning that will be required in their work and personal lives as adults? Some of the most thoughtful analyses of this question have come from the head of the University of Chicago School Mathematics Project secondary program, Zalman Usiskin. In 1988, Usiskin wrote a chapter in the NCTM yearbook with the title *Conceptions of School Algebra and Uses of Variable*. He asked readers to think about the ways that variables (or letters) are used in various expressions and what those uses of letters suggest about the role of algebra in mathematics. Each of the following items involves one or more *mathematical letters*, but collectively they call to mind a diverse array of algebraic ideas and operations.

$$A = bh \hspace{4cm} [1.2a]$$

This *formula* gives a recipe for calculating the area of any parallelogram from its base and height measurements.

$$40 = 5x \hspace{4cm} [1.2b]$$

This *equation* calls for discovering value(s) of the variable that will make the algebraic sentence a true statement.

$$x^2 - a^2 = (x + a)(x - a) \hspace{3cm} [1.2c]$$

This *identity* is a true statement for any values of the variable x and the parameter a. Such identities are used to write given expressions in equivalent forms that might prove insightful or computationally efficient.

$$x = x + 1 \hspace{4cm} [1.2d]$$

This sentence can be viewed as an equation with an empty solution set, but it is also the kind of algebraic expression that occurs in loops of computer programs or in cell formulas of spreadsheets to indicate that one value of a variable is to be replaced by another value.

$$y = 0.15x + 75 \hspace{3.5cm} [1.2e]$$

This equation defines a linear function that might give the daily earnings of a restaurant server who is paid $75 plus tips of 15% on value of food and drink served.

$$S = [n(n + 1)] \div 2 \hspace{3.5cm} [1.2f]$$

This equation is a familiar formula for a number pattern $S = 1 + 2 + \ldots + n$. (The sum of consecutive counting numbers starting with one.)

What do these examples say about the nature of algebra and what algebra instruction ought to be about at the middle school level? What do students need to understand and be able to do in order to cope with the families of problems illustrated by the six examples? How can an algebra curriculum be organized so that it includes the ideas embedded in these examples but is also coherent and encompasses *meaningful* learning experiences?

WHAT IDEAS AND WHAT ORGANIZATION OF THESE IDEAS WILL GIVE A COHERENCE TO ALGEBRA I? ■

One way to outline a comprehensive and coherent framework for middle school algebra is to focus on the overriding objective of developing student ability to represent and analyze relationships among quantitative variables. From this perspective, variables are not letters that stand for unknown numbers. Rather, they are quantitative attributes of objects (like measurements of size), patterns, or situations that change in response to change in other quantities or with the passage of time. The most important goals of mathematical analysis in such situations are understanding and predicting patterns of change in variables. The letters, symbolic expressions, equations or inequalities of algebra are tools for representing what we know or what we want to figure out about a relationship between variables. Algebraic procedures for manipulating symbolic expressions into alternative equivalent forms are also means to the goal of insight into relationships between variables. To help students acquire quantitative reasoning skills we have discovered that almost all of the important tasks to which algebra is usually applied can develop naturally as aspects of this endeavor. Our framework for thinking about algebra can be expressed with a kind of diagram that has become common in discussions of mathematics curriculum.

> A comprehensive and coherent framework for middle school algebra might focus on the overriding objective of developing student ability to represent and analyze relationships among quantitative variables.

Our framework for thinking about goals of school algebra is illustrated well by the following diagram that suggests important connections between algebraic thinking and the problems within and outside of mathematics to which it is productively applied (Figure 1.2a). Algebraic thinking is prompted by recognition of relationships between quantitative variables or numerical patterns in problematic situations. When quantitative relationships, patterns, and questions have been represented by the efficient symbolic expressions of algebra, problem solvers can apply a variety of algorithmic symbolic manipulations and graphic or numeric strategies to find mathematical answers or to gain insight into the situation of interest. Then those answers and insights must be checked for validity and meaning in the problem settings from which they arose. Of course, the interplay of representation, algebraic reasoning, and interpretation is dynamic and interactive in both directions at each interface between problem settings and formal mathematics.

To operate in this mathematical arena, students need a variety of key dispositions, understandings, and specific technical skills from algebra:

- Disposition to look for key quantitative variables in problem situations and relationships among variables that reflect *cause-and-effect*, predictable *change over time*, or pure *number patterns.*
- A repertoire of significant and common patterns to recognize and apply to problems.
- Ability to represent relationships between variables in words, graphs, organized data tables, and with symbolic expressions.
- Ability to draw inferences from represented relationships by estimation from tables and graphs and by exact reasoning using symbolic manipulations.
- Judgment to translate deductions back to the original problem situations with reasoned sensitivity to limitations of the original modeling process.

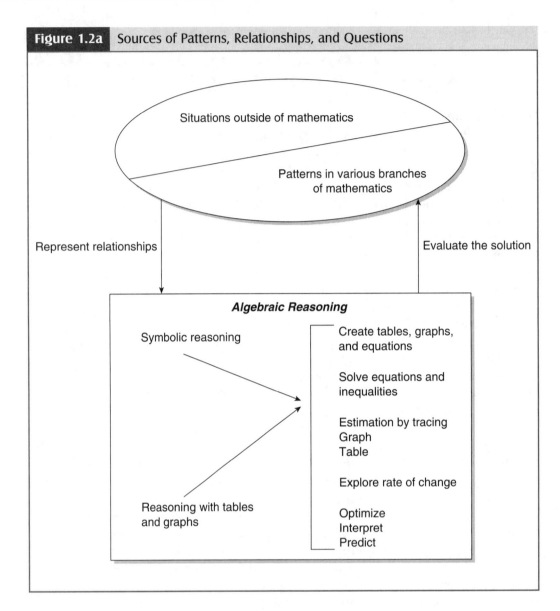

| **Figure 1.2a** | Sources of Patterns, Relationships, and Questions |

■ HOW TO TEACH THE CONTENT: LEARNING WITHIN INTERESTING CONTEXTS

The circumstances in which students learn also affect what is learned. The *what to teach* and the *how to teach it* are inextricably linked. Our content framework and a growing body of research on teaching and learning suggest that students should begin their algebraic experiences by exploring algebraic ideas that have been embedded in interesting contexts that involve important mathematical ideas. These contexts help the students develop understanding and proficiency with the embedded ideas, and they also serve as means for students to recall these ideas when needed.

> Contexts help the students develop understanding and proficiency with the embedded ideas, and they also serve as means for students to recall these ideas when needed.

The view of algebra as a course in which tools for reasoning about quantitative variables are learned and learning is motivated through problem-based investigations is illustrated well by a lesson that engages students in exploring the question: How will length and thickness of a bridge affect its carrying capacity? (The problem situations in this paper are adapted from the Connected Mathematics curriculum written by Lappan, Fey, Fitzgerald, Friel, and Phillips, 1998.)

After proposing some conjectures based on their prior knowledge and intuition, students collect data about the relationship between the variables during an experiment using paper bridges. They produce graphic and tabular models of the relationships between the variables, and ultimately they search for symbolic expressions of those models. For example, the data and models might look like those shown in Figure 1.2b.

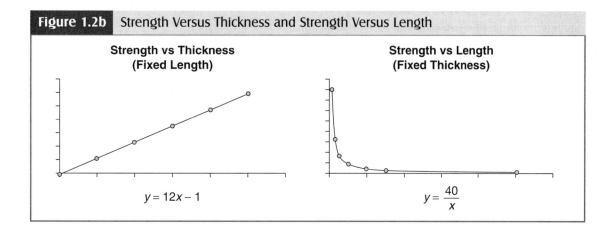

Figure 1.2b Strength Versus Thickness and Strength Versus Length

Strength vs Thickness
(Fixed Length)

$y = 12x - 1$

Strength vs Length
(Fixed Thickness)

$y = \dfrac{40}{x}$

Then, with the key relationships modeled algebraically, students may answer more specific questions that involve solving equations and inequalities.

- What bridge thickness is needed to have carrying capacity of 12? Solve $2x - 1 = 12$.
- What bridge length will have carrying capacity of 12? Solve $\dfrac{40}{x} = 12$.
- How does bridge strength change as length and/or thickness increase?

In each instance, the mathematically derived predictions should be taken back to the *real world* with caution that the model is an idealization of a pattern that involves some unpredictable variation.

To bring students to the point where they can carry out all facets of this modeling work, we need to develop their understanding of variables and relationships, ways of expressing data to reveal relationships, ways of expressing relationships in symbolic forms, and a variety of ways of drawing inferences from relationships—tabular and graphic estimation and symbolic manipulation. Therefore early in their algebra experiences students should engage in a sequence of explorations that develop a general understanding of variables and relationships and representations of these relationships. They also need to develop facility in recognizing and operating with the elementary mathematical functions that are most useful for modeling patterns and relationships. There is now a growing consensus that for beginning algebra this list of basic function families should include linear, exponential, and quadratic functions as well as some direct and inverse variation relationships.

The cornerstone of elementary algebra is the study of linear functions (NCTM, 2000). The following example illustrates the kind of reasoning one might expect from a student who understands linear functions and a strategy for developing that understanding through work on a contextual problem.

Walking Race Problem

Henri challenges his older brother Emile to a walking race. Because Emile's walking rate is faster, Emile gives Henri a 45-meter head start. Emile knows his brother would enjoy winning the race, but he does not want to make the race so short that it is obvious his brother will win. Henri walks at the rate of 1 meter per second and Emile walks at 2.5 meters per second. How long should the race be so that Henri will win in a close race?

As a beginning problem in the development of linear functions, students might approach this problem in various ways by using tables, graphs, symbolic statements, or numerical reasoning as follows.

Further questions about the situation can help students recognize important features about linear patterns of change.

- How is the walking rate of each brother represented in the table? Graph? Equation?
- Suppose Henri walks at 1.5 meters per second. How does this affect the data pattern in the table? Graph? Equation?
- How far will each brother walk in 20 seconds? Who will be ahead and by how much?
- When will Emile overtake Henri?
- How much time will have elapsed when Henri is 60 meters from the starting line?
- What information is represented by the graph points where each line crosses the *y*-axis?
- How can you represent each walking rate with symbols?

Reflection on answers to these questions will highlight the constant rate of change pattern that is fundamental to linearity and the way that rate appears as slope in the linear function graphs. The questions also lead to reasoning required to solve linear equations, inequalities, and a system of two linear equations using tables, graphs, or symbols.

Figure 1.2c Walk Race

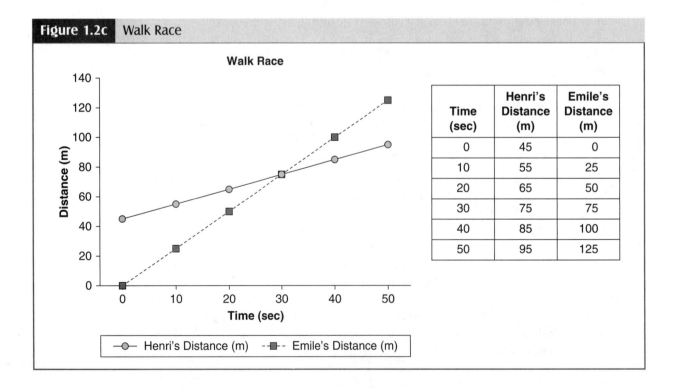

Time (sec)	Henri's Distance (m)	Emile's Distance (m)
0	45	0
10	55	25
20	65	50
30	75	75
40	85	100
50	95	125

To fully understand linear functions it is important to contrast them with nonlinear functions. The next problem contrasts exponential patterns of change with linear patterns.

Chessboard Reward Problem

A king and queen want to reward a faithful peasant. The king suggested that he would place one ruba on the first square of a chessboard, 2 rubas on the second square, 4 rubas on the third, 8 on the fourth, and so on until all 64 squares are covered. The queen suggested that she would place 10 rubas on the first square, 25 on the second square, 40 on the third square, 55 on the fifth square, and so on. The servant receives the amount of money on the last square. How many rubas will be placed on the last square of the chessboard under each plan? (See graph and table that follow in Figure 1.2d.)

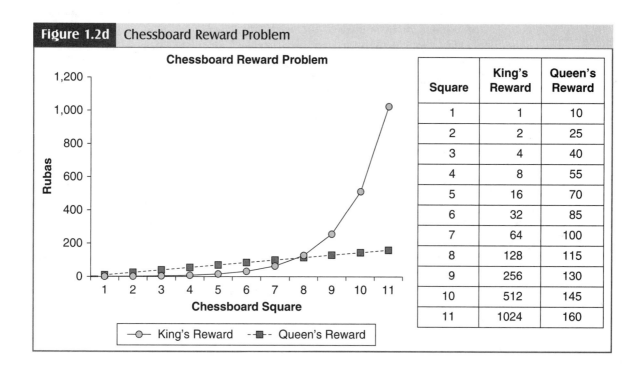

Figure 1.2d	Chessboard Reward Problem

Square	King's Reward	Queen's Reward
1	1	10
2	2	25
3	4	40
4	8	55
5	16	70
6	32	85
7	64	100
8	128	115
9	256	130
10	512	145
11	1024	160

After students have solved this particular problem by informal reasoning, they are ready to examine the situation to articulate the important mathematical ideas that are embedded in the problem.

- What are the variables? How are the patterns in the two reward plans similar and how are they different from each other?
- What symbolic forms express each of the reward patterns?
- How could you recognize patterns that are similar to the king's reward plan when the story is different?
- How can one use tables, graphs, or symbols to make predictions or answer questions about exponential functions?

Over time as students encounter new situations and new patterns of change, questions like those asked in the last two problems become *habits of mind*. What are the variables? How are they related? What is the pattern of change between the variables? How can this pattern be represented in a table, graph, or symbolic statement? What predictions can be made?

Exponential functions are accessible to beginning algebra students, and there are many applications that can be readily modeled with tables, graphs, and symbols. Most importantly, exponential functions provide an intuitive counterexample to linear functions. Patterns of change that characterize quadratic functions are more complex and can be introduced toward the end of algebra.

As students become more adept in using symbols to represent relationships and to solve problems, they can be introduced to more complex situations in which the dependent variables can often be represented with several equivalent expressions.

* * *

With this foundation of understanding based on what makes sense, students are ready to move ahead to more formal symbolic manipulation that relies heavily on structural properties of numbers and operations like the distributive property.

As students move on to quadratic functions, the distributive property is used to write quadratic expressions in expanded or factored form. Again, what is important is that students are able to go from one form to the other, and that they know what information each expression represents. Sensitivity to the value of equivalent alternative algebraic expressions includes ability to answer questions like this:

> In the case of $y = x^2 + 5x + 6$, which expression, $x^2 + 5x + 6$ or $(x + 2)(x + 3)$, would you use to locate the line of symmetry? The x-and y-intercepts? The maximum/minimum point of the graph?

Technology is a tool that permeates our lives. To use technology effectively as a tool to develop quantitative reasoning skills, students need to have control over what the technology can do for them. Using technology to gain information about a situation, generalize, and make decisions and predictions requires understanding of basic patterns of change that characterize functions, appropriate representations of these functions, and the role of equivalent expressions in functions, as well as the associated number properties that are used to create equivalent expressions and equations.

■ CONCLUSION

As the preceding problems indicate, an approach to algebra that develops skill in reasoning about quantitative variables and relationships through investigations of mathematically and contextually rich problems offers important benefits for students. First, it uses one of the most important of mathematical ideas—functions—as the conceptual core of the curriculum. Second, it helps students use multiple representations of mathematical ideas to make sense of problematic situations with numeric, graphic, verbal, and symbolic patterns and images. Finally, it encourages a cognitively natural progression from familiar concrete experiences and knowledge to the more abstract but powerful symbolic representations and operations. This is the sort of beginning algebra experience that seems right for all students—it provides a useful foundation for the kind of reasoning that all students will need to do and for further studies by those who will require more highly developed algebraic understandings and skills.

In some ways the algebra topics and concepts that we have highlighted are not so different from what students have studied in the past. What is different is that these ideas are developed within a

> A beginning algebra experience provides a foundation for the kind of reasoning that all students will need to do and for further studies by those who will require more highly developed algebraic understandings and skills.

coherent curriculum; one in which time is spent developing understanding of the important concepts, where understandings are used to build new ideas, and students are expected to make sense of new situations they encounter.

REFERENCES ■

Chazan, D. and Yerushalmy, M. (2003). On appreciating the cognitive complexity of school algebra: Research on algebra learning and directions of curricular change. In J. Kilpatrick, W. G. Martin, and D. Schifter (Eds.), *A research companion to principles and standards for school mathematics.* Reston, VA: National Council of Teachers of Mathematics, pp. 123–135.

Davis, R. (1986). What "Algebra" Should Students Learn. *Journal of Mathematical Behavior,* Volume 5, pp. 21–24.

Lappan, G., Fey, J., Fitzgerald, W., Friel, S., and Phillips, E. (1998). *Connected Mathematics.* Upper Saddle River, NJ: Prentice Hall Publishers.

NCTM. *Curriculum and evaluation standards.* (1989). Reston, VA: The Council.

NCTM. *Principles and standards for school mathematics.* (2000). Reston, VA: The Council.

Silver, E. (1997). "Algebra for All": Increasing Students' Access to Algebraic Ideas, Not Just Algebra Courses. *Mathematics Teaching in the Middle School,* 2, 4, 204–7. Reston, VA: National Council of Teachers of Mathematics.

Usiskin, Z. (1988). Conceptions of school algebra and uses of variables. In A. F. Coxford and A. P. Shulte (Eds.), *The ideas of algebra K–12* (pp. 8–19). 1988 Yearbook of the National Council of Teachers of Mathematics. Reston, VA: National Council of Teachers of Mathematics.

Usiskin, Z. (1995). Why is algebra important to learn? *American Educator,* Spring, pp. 30–37.

2 Session

What Does High-Quality Instruction Look Like?

(Instruction)

Instruction plays a critical role in students' learning of mathematics. In order to deliver high-quality instruction in mathematics, teachers need to have a deep knowledge and understanding of the subject matter at two levels: (1) one that enables them to do mathematics themselves and (2) one that enables them to teach it. In addition, effective teachers of mathematics need both general pedagogical knowledge and specific pedagogy for the teaching of mathematics (including both a deep understanding of how students learn mathematics and the capacity to elicit and build on students' mathematical thinking). They also need to know the mathematics curriculum (within the grade level[s] they teach as well as across the K–12 grades).

This session focuses on what high-quality instruction in mathematics looks like. It also provides an opportunity to discuss research findings about how people learn mathematics, as the basis for recommendations about promising instructional practices. In addition, participants explore the connection between the "cognitive demand" of tasks and opportunities to learn mathematical ideas.

This session offers the opportunity to do the following:

- Examine what is known about how people learn mathematics
- Develop an understanding of instructional strategies that promote student learning in mathematics
- Examine the types of knowledge teachers need to effectively lead mathematics instruction: (a) strong mathematics content for themselves, (b) the content needed to teach it to others, (c) pedagogy of mathematics, (d) students and how they learn, and (e) and curriculum, at and across grade levels
- Consider how various types of mathematical tasks directly affect what mathematics students have the opportunity to learn.

Readings and Focus Questions to Prepare for Session 2

(Two Homework Readings)

In preparation for the second session, please read the following two articles and prepare the focus questions that follow.

Reading 2.1 Fuson, K. C., Kalchman, M., & Bransford, J. D. (2004). Mathematical understanding: An introduction. In M. S. Donovan & J. D. Bransford (Eds.), *How students learn: mathematics in the classroom* (pp. 217–247). Washington, DC: National Research Council of the National Academies.

Reading 2.2 Stein, M. K, Smith, M. S., Henningsen, M.A., & Silver, E. A. (2000). *Implementing standards-based mathematics instruction: A casebook for professional development.* (This is a joint publication of the National Council of Teachers of Mathematics [Reston, VA] and Teachers College Press [New York]. The reading is the following chapter: "Analyzing Mathematical Instructional Tasks.")

READING 2.1 FOCUS QUESTIONS

1. Take notes on key features of the three principles of learning outlined in the reading:

Principle 1: Teachers must engage students' preconceptions and build on existing knowledge.
Principle 2: Understanding requires factual knowledge and conceptual frameworks.
Principle 3: A metacognitive approach enables students' self-monitoring.

2. How might these principles be reflected in the role of the student and the role of the teacher in a mathematics classroom that is addressing the three principles of learning?

3. How do these compare to your experiences as a mathematics student?

4. What from the reading surprised you? What resonated with you? What concerns or questions did the reading raise for you as an educator?

Mark those paragraphs or short sections that relate to your notes. Be prepared to discuss them with other participants.

READING 2.1

Mathematical Understanding

An Introduction

Karen C. Fuson

Mindy Kalchman

John D. Bransford

For many people, free association with the word "mathematics" would produce strong, negative images. Gary Larson published a cartoon titled "Hell's Library" that consisted of nothing but book after book of math word problems. Many students—and teachers—resonate strongly with this cartoon's message. It is not just funny to them; it is true.

Why are associations with mathematics so negative for so many people? If we look through the lens of *How People Learn*, we see a subject that is rarely taught in a way that makes use of the three principles that are the focus of this volume. Instead of connecting with, building on, and refining the mathematical understandings, intuitions, and resourcefulness that students bring to the classroom (Principle 1), mathematics instruction often overrides students' reasoning processes, replacing them with a set of rules and procedures that disconnects problem solving from meaning making. Instead of organizing the skills and competences required to do mathematics fluently around a set of core mathematical concepts (Principle 2), those skills and competencies are often themselves the center, and sometimes the whole, of instruction. And precisely because the acquisition of procedural knowledge is often divorced from meaning making, students do not use metacognitive strategies (Principle 3) when they engage in solving mathematics problems. Box 2.1a provides a vignette involving a student who gives an answer to a problem that is quite obviously impossible. When quizzed, he can see that his answer does not make sense, but he does not consider it wrong because he believes he followed the rule. Not only did he neglect to use metacognitive strategies to monitor whether his answer made sense, but he believes that sense making is irrelevant.

Box 2.1a   Computation Without Comprehension: An Observation by John Holt

One boy, quite a good student, was working on the problem, "If you have 6 jugs, and you want to put $\frac{2}{3}$ of a pint of lemonade into each jug, how much lemonade will you need?" His answer was 18 pints. I said, "How much in each jug?" "Two-thirds of a pint." I said, "Is that more or less than a pint?" "Less." I said, "How many jugs are there?" "Six." I said, "But that [the answer of 18 pints] doesn't make any sense." He shrugged his shoulders and said, "Well, that's the way the system worked out." Holt argues: "He has long since quit expecting school to make sense. They tell you these facts and rules, and your job is to put them down on paper the way they tell you. Never mind whether they mean anything or not."[1]

Source: Reprinted with permission from *How Students Learn: Mathematics in the Classroom* © 2005 by the National Academy of Sciences, Courtesy of the National Academies Press, Washington, DC.

A recent report of the National Research Council,[2] *Adding It Up*, reviews a broad research base on the teaching and learning of elementary school mathematics. The report argues for an instructional goal of "mathematical proficiency," a much broader outcome than mastery of procedures. The report argues that five intertwining strands constitute mathematical proficiency:

1. *Conceptual Understanding.* Comprehension of mathematical concepts, operations, and relations

2. *Procedural Fluency.* Skill in carrying out procedures flexibly, accurately, efficiently, and appropriately

3. *Strategic Competence.* Ability to formulate, represent, and solve mathematical problems

4. *Adaptive Reasoning.* Capacity for logical thought, reflection, explanation, and justification

5. *Productive Disposition.* Habitual inclination to see mathematics as sensible, useful, and worthwhile, coupled with a belief in diligence and one's own efficacy

These strands map directly to the principles of *How People Learn*. Principle 2 argues for a foundation of factual knowledge (procedural fluency), tied to a conceptual framework (conceptual understanding), and organized in a way to facilitate retrieval and problem solving (strategic competence). Metacognition and adaptive reasoning both describe the phenomenon of ongoing sense making, reflection, and explanation to oneself and others. And, as we argue below, the preconceptions students bring to the study of mathematics affect more than their understanding and problem solving; those preconceptions also play a major role in whether students have a productive disposition toward mathematics, as do, of course, their experiences in learning mathematics.

The chapters that follow on whole number, rational number, and functions look at the principles of *How People Learn* as they apply to those specific domains. In this introduction, we explore how those principles apply to the subject of mathematics more generally. We draw on examples from the Children's Math World project, a decade-long research project in urban and suburban English-speaking and Spanish-speaking classrooms.[3]

■ PRINCIPLE 1: TEACHERS MUST ENGAGE STUDENTS' PRECONCEPTIONS

At a very early age, children begin to demonstrate an awareness of number.[4] As with language, that awareness appears to be universal in normally developing children, though the rate of development varies at least in part because of environmental influences.[5]

But it is not only the awareness of quantity that develops without formal training. Both children and adults engage in mathematical problem solving, developing untrained strategies to do so successfully when formal experiences are not provided. For example, it was found that Brazilian street children could perform mathematics when making sales in the street, but were unable to answer similar problems presented in a school context.[6] Likewise, a study of housewives in California uncovered an ability to solve mathematical problems when comparison shopping, even though the women could not solve problems presented abstractly in a classroom that required the same mathematics.[7] A similar result was found in a study of a group of Weight Watchers, who used strategies for solving mathematical measurement problems related to dieting that they could not solve when the problems were presented more abstractly.[8] And men who successfully handicapped horse races could not apply the same skill to securities in the stock market.[9]

These examples suggest that people possess resources in the form of informal strategy development and mathematical reasoning that can serve as a foundation for learning more abstract mathematics. But they also suggest that the link is not automatic. If there is no bridge between informal and formal mathematics, the two often remain disconnected.

The first principle of *How People Learn* emphasizes both the need to build on existing knowledge and the need to engage students' preconceptions—particularly when they interfere with learning. In mathematics, certain preconceptions that are often fostered early on in school settings are in fact counterproductive. Students who believe them can easily conclude that the study of mathematics is "not for them" and should be avoided if at all possible. We discuss these preconceptions below.

Some Common Preconceptions About Mathematics

Preconception 1: Mathematics is about learning to compute.

Many of us who attended school in the United States had mathematics instruction that focused primarily on computation, with little attention to learning with understanding. To illustrate, try to answer the following question:

What, approximately, is the sum of $\frac{8}{9}$ plus $\frac{12}{13}$?

Many people immediately try to find the lowest common denominator for the two sets of fractions and then add them because that is the procedure they learned in school. Finding the lowest common denominator is not easy in this instance, and the problem seems difficult. A few people take a conceptual rather than a procedural (computational) approach and realize that $\frac{8}{9}$ is almost 1, and so is $\frac{12}{13}$, so the approximate answer is a little less than 2.

The point of this example is not that computation should not be taught or is unimportant; indeed, it is very often critical to efficient problem solving. But if one believes that mathematics is about problem solving and that computation is a tool for use to that end when it is helpful, then the above problem is viewed not as a "request for a computation," but as a problem to be solved that may or may not require computation—and in this case, it does not.

If one needs to find the exact answer to the above problem, computation is the way to go. But even in this case, conceptual understanding of the nature of the problem remains central, providing a way to estimate the correctness of a computation. If an answer is computed that is more than 2 or less than 1, it is obvious that some aspect of problem solving has gone awry. If one believes that mathematics is about computation, however, then sense making may never take place.

Preconception 2: Mathematics is about "following rules" to guarantee correct answers.

Related to the conception of mathematics as computation is that of mathematics as a cut-and-dried discipline that specifies rules for finding the right answers. Rule following is more general than performing specific computations. When students learn procedures for keeping track of and canceling units, for example, or learn algebraic procedures for solving equations, many view use of these procedures only as following the rules. But the "rules" should not be confused with the game itself.

The authors of the chapters in this part of the book provide important suggestions about the much broader nature of mathematical proficiency and about ways to make the involving nature of mathematical inquiry visible to students. Groups such as the National Council of Teachers of Mathematics[10] and the National Research Council[11] have provided important guidelines for the kinds of mathematics instruction that accord with what is currently known about the principles of *How People Learn.* The authors of the following chapters have paid careful attention to this work and illustrate some of its important aspects.

In reality, mathematics is a constantly evolving field that is far from cut and dried. It involves systematic pattern finding and continuing invention. As a simple example, consider the selection of units that are relevant to quantify an idea such as the fuel efficiency of a vehicle. If we choose miles per gallon, a two-seater sports car will be more efficient than a large bus. If we choose passenger miles per gallon, the bus will be more fuel efficient (assuming it carries large numbers of passengers). Many disciplines make progress by inventing new units and metrics that provide insights into previously invisible relationships.

Attention to the history of mathematics illustrates that what is taught at one point in time as a set of procedures really was a set of clever inventions designed to solve pervasive problems of everyday life. In Europe in the Middle Ages, for example, people used calculating cloths marked with vertical columns and carried out procedures with counters to perform calculations. Other cultures fastened their counters on a rod to make an abacus. Both of these physical means were at least partially replaced by written methods of calculating with numerals and more recently by methods that involve pushing buttons on a calculator. If mathematics procedures are understood as inventions designed to make common problems more easily solvable, and to facilitate communications involving quantity, those procedures take on a new meaning. Different procedures can be compared for their advantages and disadvantages. Such discussions in the classroom can deepen students' understanding and skill.

Preconception 3: Some people have the ability to "do math" and some don't.

This is a serious preconception that is widespread in the United States, but not necessarily in other countries. It can easily become a self-fulfilling prophesy. In many countries, the ability to "do math" is assumed to be attributable to the amount of effort people put into learning it.[12] Of course, some people in these countries do progress further than others, and some appear to have an easier time learning mathematics than others. But effort is still considered to be the key variable in success. In contrast, in the United States we are more likely to assume that ability is much more important than effort, and it is socially acceptable, and often even desirable, not to put forth effort in learning mathematics. This difference is also related to cultural differences in the value attributed to struggle. Teachers in some countries believe it is desirable for students to struggle for a while with problems, whereas teachers in the United States simplify things so that students need not struggle at all.[13]

This preconception likely shares a common root with the others. If mathematics learning is not grounded in an understanding of the nature of the problem to be solved and does not build on a student's own reasoning and strategy development, then solving problems successfully will depend on the ability to recall memorized rules. If a student has not reviewed those rules recently (as is the case when a summer has passed), they can easily be forgotten. Without a conceptual understanding of the nature of problems and strategies for solving them, failure to retrieve learned procedures can leave a student completely at a loss.

Yet students can feel lost not only when they have forgotten, but also when they fail to "get it" from the start. Many of the conventions of mathematics have been adopted for the convenience of communicating efficiently in a shared language. If students learn to memorize procedures but do not understand that the procedures are full of such conventions adopted for efficiency, they can be baffled by things that are left unexplained. If students never understand that x and y have no intrinsic meaning, but are conventional notations for labeling unknowns, they will be baffled when a z appears. When an m precedes an x in the equation of a line, students may wonder, Why m? Why not s for slope?

If there is no *m*, then is there no slope? To someone with a secure mathematics understanding, the missing m is simply an unstated $m = 1$. But to a student who does not understand that the point is to write the equation efficiently, the missing m can be baffling. Unlike language learning, in which new expressions can often be figured out because they are couched in meaningful contexts, there are few clues to help a student who is lost in mathematics. Providing a secure conceptual understanding of the mathematics enterprise that is linked to students' sense-making capacities is critical so that students can puzzle productively over new material, identify the source of their confusion, and ask questions when they do not understand.

Engaging Students' Preconceptions and Building on Existing Knowledge

Engaging and building on student preconceptions, then, poses two instructional challenges. First, how can we teach mathematics so students come to appreciate that it is not about computation and following rules, but about solving important and relevant quantitative problems? This perspective includes an understanding that the rules for computation and solution are a set of clever human inventions that in many cases allow us to solve complex problems more easily, and to communicate about those problems with each other effectively and efficiently. Second, how can we link formal mathematics training with students' informal knowledge and problem-solving capacities?

Many recent research and curriculum development efforts, including those of the authors of the chapters that follow, have addressed these questions. While there is surely no single best instructional approach, it is possible to identify certain features of instruction that support the above goals:

- Allowing students to use their own informal problem-solving strategies, at least initially, and then guiding their mathematical thinking toward more effective strategies and advanced understandings.
- Encouraging math talk so that students can clarify their strategies to themselves and others, and compare the benefits and limitations of alternate approaches.
- Designing instructional activities that can effectively bridge commonly held conceptions and targeted mathematical understandings.

Allowing Multiple Strategies

To illustrate how instruction can be connected to students' existing knowledge, consider three subtraction methods encountered frequently in urban second-grade classrooms involved in the Children's Math Worlds Project (see Box 2.1b). Maria, Peter, and Manuel's teacher has invited them to share their methods for solving a problem, and each of them has displayed a different method. Two of the methods are correct, and one is mostly correct but has one error. What the teacher does depends on her conception of what mathematics is.

One approach is to show the students the "right" way to subtract and have them and everyone else practice that procedure. A very different approach is to help students explore their methods and see what is easy and difficult about each. If students are taught that for each kind of math situation or problem, there is one correct method that needs to be taught and learned, the seeds of the disconnection between their reasoning and strategy development and "doing math" are sown. An answer is either wrong or right, and one does not need to look at wrong answers more deeply—one needs to look at how to get the right answer. The problem is not that students will fail to solve the problem accurately with this instructional approach; indeed, they may solve it more accurately. But when the nature of the problem changes slightly, or students have not used the taught approach for a while, they may feel completely lost when confronting a novel problem because the approach of developing strategies to grapple with a problem situation has been short-circuited.

Box 2.1b   Three Subtraction Methods

Maria's Add-Equal-Quantities Method	Peter's Ungrouping Method	Manuel's Mixed Method
$1\ \ 2\ \ ^13$ $-\ ^15\ \ 6$ $\overline{\ \ \ 6\ \ 8}$	$\overset{11}{\not{1}}\ \ \overset{14}{\not{2}}\ ^14$ $-\ \ 5\ \ 6$ $\overline{\ \ \ 6\ \ 8}$	$\overset{11}{\not{1}}\ \ \overset{14}{\not{2}}\ ^14$ $-\ \ ^15\ \ 6$ $\overline{\ \ \ 5\ \ 8}$

If, on the other hand, students believe that for each kind of math situation or problem there can be several correct methods, their engagement in strategy development is kept alive. This does not mean that all strategies are equally good. But students can learn to evaluate different strategies for their advantages and disadvantages. What is more, a wrong answer is usually partially correct and reflects some understanding; finding the part that is wrong and understanding why it is wrong can be a powerful aid to understanding and promotes metacognitive competencies. A vignette of students engaged in the kind of mathematical reasoning that supports active strategy development and evaluation appears in Box 2.1c.

It can be initially unsettling for a teacher to open up the classroom to calculation methods that are new to the teacher. But a teacher does not have to understand a new method immediately or alone, as indicated in the description in the vignette of how the class together figured out over time how Maria's method worked (this method is commonly taught in Latin America and Europe). Understanding a new method can be a worthwhile mathematical project for the class, and others can be involved in trying to figure out why a method works. This illustrates one way in which a classroom community can function. If one relates a calculation method to the quantities involved, one can usually puzzle out what the method is and why it works. This also demonstrates that not all mathematical issues are solved or understood immediately; sometimes sustained work is necessary.

Box 2.1c   Engaging Students' Problem-Solving Strategies

The following example of a classroom discussion shows how second-grade students can explain their methods rather than simply performing steps in a memorized procedure. It also shows how to make student thinking visible. After several months of teaching and learning, the students reached the point illustrated below. The students' methods are shown in Box 2.1b.

Teacher   Maria, can you please explain to your friends in the class how you solved the problem?

Maria   Six is bigger than 4, so I can't subtract here *[pointing]* in the ones.

So I have to get more ones. But I have to be fair when I get more ones, so I add ten to both my numbers. I add a ten here in the top of the ones place [pointing] to change the 4 to a 14, and I add a ten here in the bottom in the tens place, so I write another ten by my 5.

So now I count up from 6 to 14, and I get 8 ones [demonstrating by counting "6, 7, 8, 9, 10, 11, 12, 13, 14" while raising a finger for each word from 7 to 14]. And I know my doubles, so 6 plus 6 is 12, so I have 6 tens left. [She thought, "1 + 5 = 6 tens and 6 + ? = 12 tens. Oh, I know 6 + 6 = 12, so my answer is 6 tens."]

Jorge	I don't see the other 6 in your tens. I only see one 6 in your answer.
Maria	The other 6 is from adding my 1 ten to the 5 tens to get 6 tens. I didn't write it down.
Andy	But you're changing the problem. How do you get the right answer?
Maria	If I make both numbers bigger by the same amount, the difference will stay the same. Remember we looked at that on drawings last week and on the meter stick.
Michelle	Why did you count up?
Maria	Counting down is too hard, and my mother taught me to count up to subtract in first grade.
Teacher	How many of you remember how confused we were when we first saw Maria's method last week? Some of us could not figure out what she was doing even though Elena and Juan and Elba did it the same way. What did we do?
Rafael	We made drawings with our ten-sticks and dots to see what those numbers meant. And we figured out they were both tens. Even though the 5 looked like a 15, it was really just 6. And we went home to see if any of our parents could explain it to us, but we had to figure it out ourselves and it took us 2 days.
Teacher	Yes, I was asking other teachers, too. We worked on other methods too, but we kept trying to understand what this method was and why it worked. And Elena and Juan decided it was clearer if they crossed out the 5 and wrote a 6, but Elba and Maria liked to do it the way they learned at home. Any other questions or comments for Maria? No? Ok, Peter, can you explain your method?
Peter	Yes, I like to ungroup my top number when I don't have enough to subtract everywhere. So here I ungrouped 1 ten and gave it to the 4 ones to make 14 ones, so I had 1 ten left here. So 6 up to 10 is 4 and 4 more up to 14 is 8, so 14 minus 6 is 8 ones. And 5 tens up to 11 tens is 6 tens. So my answer is 68.
Carmen	How did you know it was 11 tens?
Peter	Because it is 1 hundred and 1 ten and that is 11 tens.
Carmen	I don't get it.
Peter	Because 1 hundred is 10 tens.
Carmen	Oh, so why didn't you cross out the 1 hundred and put it with the tens to make 11 tens like Manuel?
Peter	I don't need to. I just know it is 11 tens by looking at it.

(Continued)

(Continued)

Teacher	Manuel, don't erase your problem. I know you think it is probably wrong because you got a different answer, but remember how making a mistake helps everyone learn—because other students make that same mistake and you helped us talk about it. Do you want to draw a picture and think about your method while we do the next problem, or do you want someone to help you?
Manuel	Can Rafael help me?
Teacher	Yes, but what kind of helping should Rafael do?
Manuel	He should just help me with what I need help on and not do it for me.
Teacher	Ok, Rafael, go up and help Manuel that way while we go on to the next problem. I think it would help you to draw quick-tens and ones to see what your numbers mean. *[These drawings are explained later.]* But leave your first solution so we can all see where the problem is. That helps us all get good at debugging—finding our mistakes. Do we all make mistakes?
Class	Yes.
Teacher	Can we all get help from each other?
Class	Yes.
Teacher	So mistakes are just a part of learning. We learn from our mistakes. Manuel is going to be brave and share his mistake with us so we can all learn from it.

Manuel's method combined Maria's add-equal-quantities method, which he had learned at home, and Peter's ungrouping method, which he had learned at school. It increases the ones once and decreases the tens twice by subtracting a ten from the top number and adding a ten to the bottom subtracted number. In the Children's Math Worlds Project, we rarely found children forming such a meaningless combination of methods if they understood tens and ones and had a method of drawing them so they could think about the quantities in a problem (a point discussed more later). Students who transferred into our classes did sometimes initially use Manuel's mixed approach. But students were eventually helped to understand both the strengths and weaknesses of their existing methods and to find ways of improving their approaches.

Source: Karen Fuson, Children's Math Worlds Project.

Encouraging Math Talk

One important way to make students' thinking visible is through math talk—talking about mathematical thinking. This technique may appear obvious, but it is quite different from simply giving lectures or assigning textbook readings and then having students work in isolation on problem sets or homework problems. Instead, students and teachers actively discuss how they approached various problems and why. Such communication about mathematical thinking can help everyone in the classroom understand a given concept or method because it elucidates contrasting approaches, some of which are wrong—but often for interesting reasons. Furthermore, communicating about one's thinking is an important goal in itself that also facilitates other sorts of learning. In the lower grades, for example, such math talk can provide initial experiences with mathematical justification that culminate in later grades with more formal kinds of mathematical proof.

An emphasis on math talk is also important for helping teachers become more learner focused and make stronger connections with each of their students. When teachers adopt the role of learners who try to understand their students' methods (rather than just marking the students' procedures and answers as correct or incorrect), they frequently discover thinking that can provide a springboard for further instruction, enabling them to extend thinking more deeply or understand and correct errors. Note that, when beginning to make student thinking visible, teachers must focus on the community-centered aspects of their instruction. Students need to feel comfortable expressing their ideas and revising their thinking when feedback suggests the need to do so.

Math talk allows teachers to draw out and work with the preconceptions students bring with them to the classroom and then helps students learn how to do this sort of work for themselves and for others. We have found that it is also helpful for students to make math drawings of their thinking to help themselves in problem solving and to make their thinking more visible (see Figure 2.1a). Such drawings also support the classroom math talk because they are a common visual referent for all participants. Students need an effective bridge between their developing understandings and formal mathematics. Teachers need to use carefully designed visual, linguistic, and situational conceptual supports to help students connect their experiences to formal mathematical words, notations, and methods.

The idea of conceptual support for math talk can be further clarified by considering the language students used in the vignette in Box 2.1c when they explained their different multidigit methods. For these explanations to become meaningful in the classroom, it was crucially important that the students explain their multidigit adding or subtracting methods using the meaningful words in the middle pedagogical triangle of Figure 2.1b

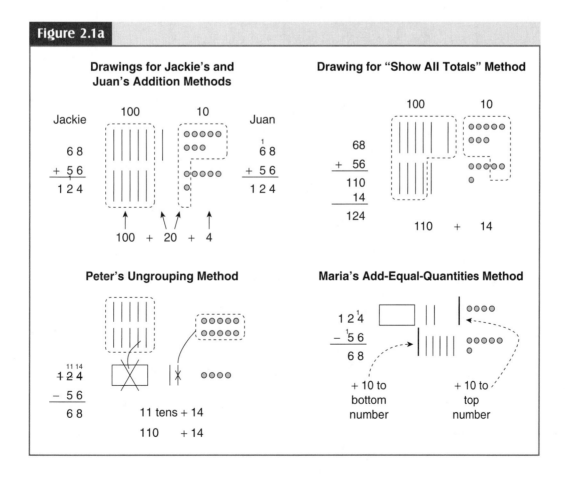

Figure 2.1a

Drawings for Jackie's and Juan's Addition Methods

Drawing for "Show All Totals" Method

Peter's Ungrouping Method

Maria's Add-Equal-Quantities Method

(e.g., "three tens six ones"), as well as the usual math words (e.g., "thirty-six"). It is through such extended connected explanations and use of the quantity words "tens" and "ones" that the students in the Children's Math Worlds Project came to explain their methods. Their explanations did not begin that way, and the students did not spontaneously use the meaningful language when describing their methods. The teacher needed to model the language and help students use it in their descriptions. More-advanced students also helped less-advanced students learn by modeling, asking questions, and helping others form more complete descriptions.

Initially in the Children's Math Worlds Project, all students made conceptual support drawings such as those in Figure 2.1a. They explicitly linked these drawings to their written methods during explanations. Such drawings linked to the numerical methods facilitated understanding, accuracy, communication, and helping. Students stopped making drawings when they were no longer needed (this varied across students by months). Eventually, most students applied numerical methods without drawings, but these numerical methods then carried for the members of the classroom the meanings from the conceptual support drawings. If errors crept in, students were asked to think about (or make) a drawing and most errors were then self-corrected.

Figure 2.1b

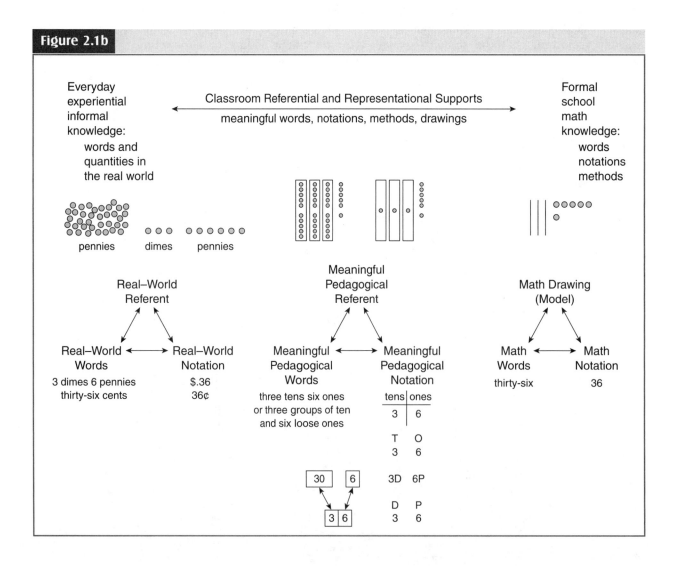

Designing Bridging Instructional Activities

The first two features of instruction discussed above provide opportunities for students to use their own strategies and to make their thinking visible so it can be built on, revised, and made more formal. This third strategy is more proactive. Research has uncovered common student preconceptions and points of difficulty with learning new mathematical concepts that can be addressed preemptively with carefully designed instructional activities.

This kind of bridging activity is used in the Children's Math Worlds curriculum to help students relate their everyday, experiential, informal understanding of money to the formal school concepts of multidigit numbers. Real-world money is confusing for many students (e.g., dimes are smaller than pennies but are worth 10 times as much). Also, the formal school math number words and notations are abstract and potentially misleading (e.g., 36 looks like a 3 and a 6, not like 30 and 6) and need to be linked to visual quantities of tens and ones to become meaningful. Fuson designed conceptual "supports" into the curriculum to bridge the two. The middle portion of Figure 2.1b shows an example of the supports that were used to help students build meaning. A teacher or curriculum designer can make a framework like that of Figure 2.1b for any math domain by selecting those conceptual supports that will help students make links among the math words, written notations, and quantities in that domain.

Identifying real-world contexts whose features help direct students' attention and thinking in mathematically productive ways is particularly helpful in building conceptual bridges between students' informal experiences and the new formal mathematics they are learning. Examples of such bridging contexts are a key feature of each of the three chapters that follow.

PRINCIPLE 2: UNDERSTANDING ■ REQUIRES FACTUAL KNOWLEDGE AND CONCEPTUAL FRAMEWORKS

The second principle of *How People Learn* suggests the importance of both conceptual understanding and procedural fluency, as well as an effective organization of knowledge—in this case one that facilitates strategy development and adaptive reasoning. It would be difficult to name a discipline in which the approach to achieving this goal is more hotly debated than mathematics. Recognition of the weakness in the conceptual understanding of students in the United States has resulted in increasing attention to the problems involved in teaching mathematics as a set of procedural competences.[14] At the same time, students with too little knowledge of procedures do not become competent and efficient problem solvers. When instruction places too little emphasis on factual and procedural knowledge, the problem is not solved; it is only changed. Both are clearly critical.

Equally important, procedural knowledge and conceptual understandings must be closely linked. As the mathematics confronted by students becomes more complex through the school years, new knowledge and competencies require that those already mastered be brought to bear. Box 1.6 in Chapter 1, for example, describes a set of links in procedural and conceptual knowledge required to support the ability to do multidigit subtraction with regrouping—a topic encountered relatively early in elementary school. By the time a student begins algebra years later, the network of knowledge must include many new concepts and procedures (including those for rational number) that must be effectively linked and available to support new algebraic understandings. The teacher's challenge, then, is to help students build and consolidate prerequisite competencies, understand new concepts in depth, and organize both concepts and competencies in a network of knowledge. Furthermore, teachers must provide sustained and then increasingly spaced opportunities to consolidate new understandings and procedures.

In mathematics, such networks of knowledge often are organized as learning paths from informal concrete methods to abbreviated, more general, and more abstract methods. Discussing multiple methods in the classroom—drawing attention to why different methods work and to the relative efficiency and reliability of each—can help provide a conceptual ladder that helps students move in a connected way from where they are to a more efficient and abstract approach. Students also can adopt or adapt an intermediate method with which they might feel more comfortable. Teachers can help students move at least to intermediate "good-enough" methods that can be understood and explained. Box 2.1d describes such a learning path for single-digit addition and subtraction that is seen worldwide. Teachers in some countries support students in moving through this learning path.

Developing Mathematical Proficiency

Developing mathematical proficiency requires that students master both the concepts and procedural skills needed to reason and solve problems effectively in a particular domain. Deciding which advanced methods all students should learn to attain proficiency is a policy matter involving judgments about how to use scarce instructional time. For example, the level 2 counting-on methods in Box 2.1d may be considered "good-enough" methods; they are general, rapid, and sufficiently accurate that valuable school time might better be spent on topics other than mastery of the whole network of knowledge required for carrying out the level 3 methods. Decisions about which methods to teach must also take into account that some methods are clearer conceptually and procedurally than the multidigit methods usually taught in the United States (see Box 2.1e). The National Research Council's *Adding It Up* reviews these and other accessible algorithms in other domains.

This view of mathematics as involving different methods does not imply that a teacher or curriculum must teach multiple methods for every domain. However, alternative methods will frequently arise in a classroom, either because students bring them from home (e.g., Maria's add-equal-quantities subtraction method, widely taught in other countries) or because students think differently about many mathematical problems. Frequently there are viable alternative methods for solving a problem, and discussing the advantages and disadvantages of each can facilitate flexibility and deep understanding of the mathematics involved. In some countries, teachers emphasize multiple solution methods and purposely give students problems that are conducive to such solutions, and students solve a problem in more than one way.

However, the less-advanced students in a classroom also need to be considered. It can be helpful for either a curriculum or teacher or such less-advanced students to select an accessible method that can be understood and is efficient enough for the future, and for these students to concentrate on learning that method and being able to explain it. Teachers in some countries do this while also facilitating problem solving with alternative methods.

Overall, knowing about student learning paths and knowledge networks helps teachers direct math talk along productive lines toward valued knowledge networks. Research in mathematics learning has uncovered important information on a number of typical learning paths and knowledge networks involved in acquiring knowledge about a variety of concepts in mathematics.

Instruction to Support Mathematical Proficiency

To teach in a way that supports both conceptual understanding and procedural fluency requires that the primary concepts underlying an area of mathematics be clear to the teacher or become clear during the process of teaching for mathematical proficiency. Because mathematics has traditionally been taught with an emphasis on procedure, adults who were taught this way may initially have difficulty identifying or using the core conceptual understandings in a mathematics domain.

Box 2.1d   A Learning Path From Children's Math Worlds for Single-Digit Addition and Subtraction

Children around the world pass through three levels of increasing sophistication in methods of single-digit addition and subtraction. The first level is direct modeling by counting all of the objects at each step (counting all or taking away). Students can be helped to move rapidly from this first level to counting on, in which counting begins with one addend. For example, 8 + 6 is not solved by counting from 1 to 14 (counting all), but by counting on 6 from 8: counting 8, 9, 10, 11, 12, 13, 14 while keeping track of the 6 counted on.

For subtraction, Children's Math Worlds does what is common in many countries: it helps students see subtraction as involving a mystery addend. Students then solve a subtraction problem by counting on from the known addend to the known total. Earlier we saw how Maria solved 14 − 6 by counting up from 6 to 14, raising 8 fingers while doing so to find that 6 plus 8 more is 14. Many students in the United States instead follow a learning path that moves from drawing little sticks or circles for all of the objects and crossing some out (e.g., drawing 14 sticks, crossing out 6, and counting the rest) to counting down (14, 13, 12, 11, 10, 9, 8, 7, 6). But counting down is difficult and error prone. When first or second graders are helped to move to a different learning path that solves subtraction problems by forward methods, such as counting on or adding on over 10 (see below), subtraction becomes as easy as addition. For many students, this is very empowering.

The third level of single-digit addition and subtraction is exemplified by Peter in the vignette in Box 2.1b. At this level, students can chunk numbers and relate these chunks. The chunking enables them to carry out make-a-ten methods: they give part of one number to the other number to make a ten. These methods are taught in many countries. They are very helpful in multidigit addition and subtraction because a number found in this way is already thought of as 1 ten and some ones. For example, for 8 + 6, 6 gives 2 to 8 to make 10, leaving 4 in the 6, so 10 + 4 = 14. Solving 14 − 8 is done similarly: with 8, how many make 10 (2), plus the 4 in 14, so the answer is 6. These make-a-ten methods demonstrate the learning paths and network of knowledge required for advanced solution methods. Children may also use a "doubles" strategy for some problems (e.g., 7 + 6 = 6 + 6 + 1 = 12 + 1 = 13) because the doubles (for example, 6 + 6 or 8 + 8) are easy to learn.

The make-a-ten methods illustrate the importance of a network of knowledge. Students must master three kinds of knowledge to be able to carry out a make-a-ten method fluently: they must (1) for each number below 10, know how much more makes 10; (2) break up any number below 10 into all possible pairs of parts (because 9 + 6 requires knowing 6 = 1 + 5, but 8 + 6 requires knowing 6 = 2 + 4, etc.); and (3) know 10 + 1 = 11, 10 + 2 = 12, 10 + 3 = 13, etc., rapidly without counting.

Note that particular methods may be more or less easy for learners from different backgrounds. For example, the make-a-ten methods are easier for East Asian students, whose language says, "Ten plus one is ten one, ten plus two is ten two," than for English-speaking students, whose language says, "Ten plus one is eleven, ten plus two is twelve, etc."

The approaches in the three chapters that follow identify the central conceptual structures in several areas of mathematics. The areas of focus—whole number, rational number, and functions—were identified by Case and his colleagues as requiring major conceptual shifts. In the first, students are required to master the concept of *quantity;* in the second, the concept of *proportion* and relative number; and in the third, the concept of *dependence* in quantitative relationships. Each of these understandings requires that a supporting set of concepts and procedural abilities be put in place. The extensive research done by Griffin and Case on whole number, by Case and Moss on rational number, and by Case and Kalchman on functions provides a strong foundation for identifying the major conceptual challenges students face in mastering these areas. This research program traced developmental/experiential changes in children's thinking as they engaged with innovative curriculum. In each area of focus, instructional approaches were developed that enable teachers to help children move through learning paths in productive ways. In doing so, teachers often find that they also build a more extensive knowledge network.

As teachers guide a class through learning paths, a balance must be maintained between learner-centered and knowledge-centered needs. The learning path of the class must also continually relate to individual learner knowledge. Box 2.1e outlines two frameworks that can facilitate such balance.

Box 2.1e   Accessible Algorithms

In over a decade of working with a range of urban and suburban classrooms in the Children's Math Worlds Project, we found that one multidigit addition method and one multidigit subtraction method were accessible to all students. The students easily learned, understood, and remembered these methods and learned to draw quantities for and explain them. Both methods are modifications of the usual U.S. methods. The addition method is the write-new-groups-below method, in which the new 1 ten or 1 hundred, etc., is written below the column on the line rather than above the column (see Jackie's method in Figure 2.1a). In the subtraction fix-everything-first method, every column in the top number that needs ungrouping is ungrouped (in any order), and then the subtracting in every column is done (in any order). Because this method can be done from either direction and is only a minor modification of the common U.S. methods, learning-disabled and special-needs students find it especially accessible. Both of these methods stimulate productive discussions in class because they are easily related to the usual U.S. methods that are likely to be brought to class by other students.

■ PRINCIPLE 3: A METACOGNITIVE APPROACH ENABLES STUDENT SELF-MONITORING

Learning about oneself as a learner, thinker, and problem solver is an important aspect of metacognition. In the area of mathematics, as noted earlier, many people who take mathematics courses "learn" that "they are not mathematical." This is an unintended, highly unfortunate, consequence of some approaches to teaching mathematics. It is a consequence that can influence people for a lifetime because they continue to avoid anything mathematical, which in turn ensures that their belief about being "nonmathematical" is true.[15]

An article written in 1940 by Charles Gragg, titled "Because Wisdom Can't Be Told," is relevant to issues of metacognition and mathematics learning. Gragg begins with the following quotation from Balzac:

> So he had grown rich at last, and thought to transmit to his only son all the cut-and-dried experience which he himself had purchased at the price of his lost illusions; a noble last illusion of age.

Except for the part about growing rich, Balzac's ideas fit many peoples' experiences quite well. In our roles as parents, friends, supervisors, and professional educators, we frequently attempt to prepare people for the future by imparting the wisdom gleaned from our own experiences. Sometimes our efforts are rewarded, but we are often less successful than we would like to be, and we need to understand why.

Box 2.1f   Supporting Student and Teacher Learning Through a Classroom Discourse Community

Eliciting and then building on and using students' mathematical thinking can be challenging. Yet recent research indicates that teachers can move their students through increasingly productive levels of classroom discourse. Hufferd-Ackles and colleagues[16] describe four levels of a "math-talk learning community," beginning with a traditional, teacher-directed format in which the teacher asks short-answer questions, and student responses are directed to the teacher. At the next level, "getting started," the teacher begins to pursue and assess students' mathematical thinking, focusing less on answers alone. In response, students provide brief descriptions of their thinking. The third level is called "building." At this point the teacher elicits and students respond with fuller descriptions of their thinking, and multiple methods are volunteered. The teacher also facilitates student-to-student talk about mathematics. The final level is "math-talk." Here students share responsibility for discourse with the teacher, justifying their own ideas and asking questions of and helping other students.

Key shifts in teacher practice that support a class moving through these levels include asking questions that focus on mathematical thinking rather than just on answers, probing extensively for student thinking, modeling and expanding on explanations when necessary, fading physically from the center of the classroom discourse (e.g., moving to the back of the classroom), and coaching students in their participatory roles in the discourse ("Everyone have a thinker question ready.").

Related research indicates that when building a successful classroom discourse community, it is important to balance the *process* of discourse, that is, the ways in which student ideas are elicited, with the *content* of discourse, the substance of the ideas that are discussed. In other words, how does a teacher ensure both that class discussions provide sufficient space for students to share their ideas and that discussions are mathematically productive? Sherin[17] describes one model for doing so whereby class discussions begin with a focus on "idea generation," in which many student ideas are solicited. Next, discussion moves into a "comparison and evaluation" phase, in which the class looks more closely at the ideas that have been raised, but no new ideas are raised.

The teacher then "filters" ideas for the class, highlighting a subset of ideas for further pursuit. In this way, student ideas are valued throughout discussion, but the teacher also plays a role in determining the extent to which specific mathematical ideas are considered in detail. A class may proceed through several cycles of these three phases in a single discussion.

The idea that "wisdom can't be told" helps educators rethink the strategy of simply telling students that some topic (e.g., mathematics) is important, and they can master it if they try. There are important differences between simply being told something and being able to experience it for oneself. Students' experiences have strong effects on their beliefs about themselves, as well as their abilities to remember information and use it spontaneously to solve new problems.[18] If their experiences in mathematics classes involve primarily frustration and failure, simply telling them, "trust me, this will be relevant someday" or "believe me, you have the ability to understand this" is a weak intervention. On the other hand, helping students experience their own abilities to find patterns and problems, invent solutions (even if they are not quite as good as expert solutions), and contribute to and learn from discussions with others provides the kinds of experiences that can help them learn with understanding, as well as change their views about the subject matter and themselves.[19]

However, research on metacognition suggests that an additional instructional step is needed for optimal learning—one that involves helping students reflect on their experiences and begin to see their ideas as instances of larger categories of ideas. For example, students might begin to see their way of showing more ones when subtracting as one of several ways to demonstrate this same important mathematical idea.

One other aspect of metacognition that is nicely illustrated in the context of mathematics involves the claim made in Chapter 1 that metacognition is not simply a knowledge-free ability, but requires relevant knowledge of the topics at hand. At the beginning of this chapter, we noted that many students approach problems such as adding fractions as purely computational (e.g., "What is the approximate sum of of $\frac{8}{9}$ plus $\frac{11}{13}$?"). Ideally, we also want students to monitor the accuracy of their problem solving, just as we want them to monitor their understanding when reading about science, history, or literature.

One way to monitor the accuracy of one's computation is to go back and recheck each of the steps. Another way is to estimate the answer and see whether there is a discrepancy between one's computations and the estimate. However, the ability to estimate requires the kind of knowledge that might be called "number sense." For the above fraction problem, for example, a person with number sense who computes an answer and sees that it is greater than 2 knows that the computation is obviously wrong. But it is "obvious" only if the person has learned ways to think about number that go beyond the ability merely to count and compute.

Instruction That Supports Metacognition

Much of what we have discussed with regard to making student thinking visible can be thought of as ongoing assessment of students. Such assessment can include students so they become involved in thinking about their own mathematical progress and that of their classmates. Such ongoing assessment can then become internalized as metacognitive self-monitoring. Classroom communication about students' mathematical thinking greatly facilitates both teacher and student assessment of learning. Teachers and students can see difficulties particular students are having and can help those students by providing explanations. Teachers can discern primitive solution methods that need to be advanced to more effective methods. They also can see how students are advancing in their helping and explaining abilities and plan how to foster continued learning in those areas.

Students can also learn some general problem-solving strategies, such as "make a drawing of the situation" or "ask yourself questions" that apply to many different kinds of problems. Drawings and questions are a means of self-monitoring. They also can offer teachers windows into students' thinking and thus provide information about how better to help students along a learning path to efficient problem-solving methods.

An Emphasis on Debugging

Metacognitive functioning is also facilitated by shifting from a focus on answers as just right or wrong to a more detailed focus on "debugging" a wrong answer, that is, finding where the error is, why it is an error, and correcting it. Of course, good teachers have always done this, but there are now two special reasons for doing so. One is the usefulness of this approach in complex problem solving, such as debugging computer programs. Technological advances mean that more adults will need to do more complex problem solving and error identification throughout their lives, so debugging—locating the source of an error—is a good general skill that can be learned in the math classroom.

The second reason is based on considerable amount of research in the past 30 years concerning student errors. Figure 2.1c illustrates two such typical kinds of errors in early and late school topics. The partial student knowledge reflected in each error is described in the figure. One can also see how a focus on understanding can help students debug their own errors. For example, asking how much the little "1's" really represent can help students start to see their error in the top example and thus modify the parts of the method that are wrong.

Early Partial Knowledge

$$
\begin{array}{r}
{}^{1}_{1} \\
2\ 6\ 8 \\
+\ 1\ 5\ 6 \\
\hline
5\ 1\ 4
\end{array}
$$

This error reflects a wrong generalization from 2-digit problems: where the little 1 is put above the left-most column. Left-most and next-left are confused in this solution. Trying to understand the meanings of the 1s as 1 ten and as 1 hundred can debug this error. The student does know to add ones, to add tens, and to add hundreds and does this correctly.

Later Partial Knowledge

1. What shape would the graph of the function $y = x^2 + 1$ have? Draw it below.

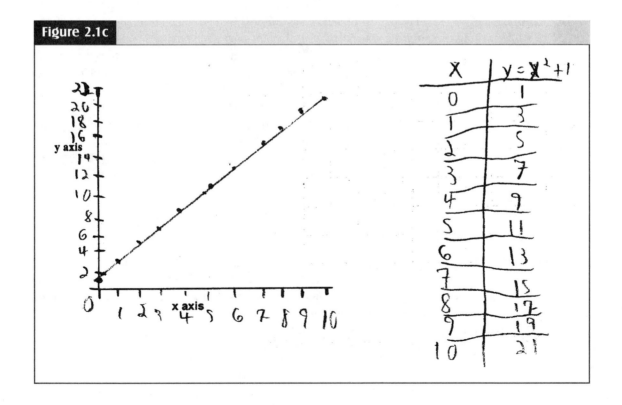

Figure 2.1c

A common error among middle school students is to treat an exponent as a coefficient or multiplier. Here, Graham has generated a table of values for the function $y = 2x + 1$ rather than $y = x^2 + 1$. This type of error has broad implications. For example, it will be difficult for students to develop a good conceptual understanding for functions and the ways in which their representations are interconnected because the graph of $y = 2x + 1$ is a straight line rather than the parabolic curve of $y = x^2 + 1$. He does know, however, how to make a table of values and to graph resulting pairs of values. He also knows how to solve for y in an equation given x.

Internal and External Dialogue as Support for Metacognition

The research summarized in *How People Learn* and *Adding It Up* and the professional experience summarized in the standards of the National Council of Teachers of Mathematics all emphasize how important it is for students to communicate about mathematics and for teachers to help them learn to do so. Students can learn to reflect on and describe their mathematical thinking. They can learn to compare methods of solving a problem and identify the advantages and disadvantages of each. Peers can learn to ask thoughtful questions about other students' thinking or help edit such statements to clarify them. Students can learn to help each other, sometimes in informal, spontaneous ways and sometimes in more organized, coaching-partner situations. The vignette in Box 2.1c illustrates such communication about mathematical thinking after it has been developed in a classroom. Experience in the Children's Math Worlds Project indicates that students from all backgrounds can learn to think critically and ask thoughtful questions, reflect on and evaluate their own achievement, justify their points of view, and understand the perspectives of others. Even first-grade students can learn to interact in these ways.

Of course, teachers must help students learn to interact fruitfully. To this end, teachers can model clear descriptions and supportive questioning or helping techniques. In a classroom situation, some students may solve problems at the board while others solve them at their seats. Students can make drawings or use notations to indicate how they thought about or solved a problem. Selected students can then describe their solution methods, and peers can ask questions to clarify and to give listeners a role. Sometimes, pairs of students may explain their solutions, with the less-advanced partner explaining first and the other partner then expanding and clarifying. Students usually attend better if only two or three of their fellow students explain their solution method for a given problem. More students can solve at the board, but the teacher can select the methods or the students for the class to hear at that time. It is useful to vary the verbal level of such explainers. Doing so assists all students in becoming better explainers by hearing and helping classmates expand upon a range of explanations. The goal in all of this discussion is to advance everyone's thinking and monitoring of their own understanding and that of other students rather than to conduct simple turn taking, though of course over time, all students can have opportunities to explain.

Seeking and Giving Help

Students must have enough confidence not only to engage with problems and try to solve them, but also to seek help when they are stuck. The dialogue that occurs in pair or class situations can help generate self-regulating speech that a student can produce while problem solving. Such helping can also increase the metacognitive awareness of the helper as he or she takes into consideration the thinking of the student being helped.

The Framework of *How People Learn:* Seeking a Balanced Classroom Environment

The framework of *How People Learn* suggests that classroom environments should at the same time be learner-centered, knowledge-centered, assessment-centered, and community-centered. These features map easily to the preceding discussion of the three principles, as well as to the chapters that follow. The instruction described is learner-centered in that it draws out and builds on student thinking. It is also knowledge-centered in that it focuses simultaneously on the conceptual understanding and the procedural knowledge of a topic, which students must master to be proficient, and the learning paths that can lead from existing to more advanced understanding. It is assessment-centered in that there are frequent opportunities for students to reveal their thinking on a topic so the teacher can shape instruction in response to their learning, and students can be made aware of their own progress. And it is community-centered in that the norms of the classroom community value student ideas, encourage productive interchange, and promote collaborative thinking.

Effective teaching and learning depend, however, on balance among these features of the classroom environment. There must be continual connections between the learner-centered focus on student knowledge and the more formal knowledge networks that are the goals of teaching in a domain. Traditional teaching has tended to emphasize the knowledge networks and pay insufficient attention to conceptual supports and the need to build on learner knowledge. Many students learn rote knowledge that cannot be used adequately in solving problems. On the other hand, an overemphasis on learner-centered teaching results in insufficient attention to connections with valued knowledge networks, the crucially important guiding roles of teachers and of learning accessible student methods, and the need to consolidate knowledge. Four such excesses are briefly discussed here.

First, some suggest that students must invent all their mathematical ideas and that we should wait until they do so rather than teach ideas. This view, of course, ignores the fact that all inventions are made within a supportive culture and that providing appropriate supports can speed such inventions. Too much focus on student-invented methods per se can hold students back; those who use time-consuming methods that are not easily generalized need to be helped to move on to more rapid and generalizable "good-enough" methods. A focus on sense making and understanding of the methods that are used is the balanced focus, rather than an emphasis on whether the method was invented by the student using it.

Second, classroom discussions may not be sufficiently guided by the teacher through the learning path. Students may talk on and on, meandering without much focus. Descriptions of student thinking may have a turn-taking, "every method is equally wonderful" flavor so that other students do not listen carefully or ask questions, but passively await their turn to talk. Different student methods may be described, but their advantages and disadvantages, or at least their similar and different features, are not discussed. There may be no building toward student-to-student talk, but everything said may be directed toward the teacher.

Third, the use of real-world situations and conceptual supports may consist more of a series of activities in which the mathematical ideas are not sufficiently salient and not connected enough to the standard math notations and vocabulary. The result may be a scattershot approach involving many different activities rather than careful choices of core representations or bridging contexts that might guide students through a coherent learning path.

Fourth, learning may not be consolidated enough because of an excessive focus on the initial learning activities. Time for consolidation of learning, with feedback loops should errors arise, is vital for mathematical fluency.

The recent Third International Mathematics and Science Study showed that teaching in the United States is still overwhelmingly traditional. However, the above caveats need to be kept in mind as teachers move forward in implementing the principles of *How People Learn*.

■ NEXT STEPS

There are some curricula that implement, at least partially, the principles of *How People Learn*. Even without extensive curricular support, however, teachers can substantially improve their practice by understanding and using these principles. This is particularly true if they can examine their own teaching practices, supported by a teaching–learning community of like-minded colleagues. Such a community can help teachers create learning paths for themselves that can move them from their present teaching practices to practices that conform more fully to the principles of *How People Learn* and thereby create more effective classrooms. Two such teacher communities, involving video clubs and lesson study, respectively, are summarized in Boxes 2.1g and 2.1h. A third approach to a teacher learning community is to organize teacher discussions around issues that arise from teaching a curriculum that supports conceptual approaches. Box 2.1i describes research summarizing one productive focus for such discussions—the use of openings in the curriculum where teachers can focus on student questions or misunderstandings.

Box 2.1g   Learning to Use Student Thinking in Teacher Video Clubs

Research indicates that teachers can develop their ability to attend to and interpret student thinking not only in the midst of class discussions, but also outside of class as they reflect on students' ideas. One model for doing so is the use of video clubs in which teachers meet together to watch and discuss video excerpts from their classrooms.[20] By providing teachers opportunities to examine student thinking without the pressure of having to respond immediately, video clubs can help prompt the development of new techniques for analyzing student thinking among teachers—techniques that teachers can then bring back to their classrooms.

Box 2.1h   Lesson Study: Learning Together How to Build on Student Knowledge

Lesson study is "a cycle in which teachers work together to consider their longterm goals for students, bring those goals to life in actual 'research lessons,' and collaboratively observe, discuss, and refine the lessons."[21] Lesson study has been a major form of teacher professional development in Japan for many decades, and in recent years has attracted the attention of U.S. teachers, school administrators, and educational researchers.[22] It is a simple idea. Teachers collaboratively plan a lesson that is taught by one group member while others observe and carefully collect data on student learning and behavior. The student data are then used to reflect on the lesson and revise it as needed. Lesson study is a teacher-led process in which teachers collaboratively identify a concept that is persistently difficult for students, study the best available curriculum materials in order to rethink their teaching of this topic, and plan and teach one or more "research lessons" that enable them to see student reactions to their redesigned unit. Ideally, a lesson study group allows teachers to share their expertise and knowledge, as well as questions related to both teaching and subject matter. Lesson study groups may also draw on knowledgeable outsiders as resources for content knowledge, group facilitation, and so on.

Note: Resources, including a handbook, videotapes, listserve, and protocols for teachers who wish to engage in lesson study, can be found at the websites of the Lesson Study Research Group at Teachers College, Columbia University: (http://www.tc.columbia.edu/lessonstudy/) and the Mills College Lesson Study Group (www.lessonresearch.net). See also Lewis (2002).

Box 2.1i   Teachers as Curriculum Designers: Using Openings in the Curriculum to Determine Learning Paths

Even when using a prepared curriculum, teachers have an important role as curriculum designers. In a study of two elementary teachers using a new textbook, Remillard[23] found that teachers made regular decisions about what parts of the teacher's guide to read, which suggestions to follow and to what ends, how to structure students' mathematical activities, and how to respond to students' questions and ideas. The decisions teachers made had a substantial impact on the curriculum experienced by students. In other words, written curriculum alone does not determine students' experiences in the classroom; this is the role of the teacher.

Remillard and Geist[24] use the term "openings in the curriculum" to denote those instances during instruction in which things do not go as described in the preset curriculum. These openings are often prompted by students' questions or teachers' observations about student understanding or misunderstanding. The authors argue that teachers must navigate these openings by (1) carefully analyzing student work and thinking, (2) weighing possible options for proceeding against one's goals for student learning, and (3) taking responsive action that is open to ongoing examination and adjustment. They suggest that teaching with curriculum guides can be improved as teachers recognize and embrace their role while navigating openings in the curriculum to determine learning paths for students.

Similarly, Remillard[25] found that teachers came to reflect on their beliefs and understandings related to their teaching and its content while involved in the very work of deciding what to do next by interpreting students' understanding with respect to their goals for the students and particular instructional tasks. Thus, some of the most fruitful opportunities for teacher learning when using a new curriculum occurred when teachers were engaged in the work of navigating openings in the curriculum.

It will take work by teachers, administrators, researchers, parents, and politicians to bring these new principles and goals to life in classrooms and to create the circumstances in which this can happen. Nonetheless, there are enough examples of the principles in action to offer a vision of the new kinds of learning that can be accessible to all students and to all teachers. Some materials to support teachers in these efforts do exist, and more are being developed. Helpful examples of the three principles in action are given in the chapters that follow. It is important to note, once again, that other projects have generated examples that implement the principles of *How People Learn.* Some of these examples can be found in the authors' references to that research and in the suggested teacher reading list. All of this work indicates that we have begun the crucial journey into mathematical proficiency for all and that the principles of *How People Learn* can guide us on this journey.

■ NOTES

1. Holt, 1964, pp. 143–144.
2. National Research Council, 2001.
3. See Fuson, 1986a, 1986b, 1990; Fuson and Briars, 1990; Fuson and Burghardt, 1993, 1997; Fuson et al., 1994, 2000; Fuson and Smith, 1997; Fuson, Smith, and Lott, 1977; Fuson, Wearne et al., 1997; Fuson, Lo Cicero et al., 1997; Lo Cicero et al., 1999; Fuson et al., 2000; Ron, 1998.
4. Carey, 2001; Gelman, 1990; Starkey et al., 1990; Wynn, 1996; Canfield and Smith, 1996.
5. Case et al., 1999; Ginsburg, 1984; Saxe, 1982.
6. Carraher, 1986; Carraher et al., 1985.
7. Lave, 1988; Sternberg, 1999.
8. De la Rocha, 1986.
9. Ceci and Liker, 1986; Ceci, 1996.
10. National Council of Teachers of Mathematics, 2000.
11. National Research Council, 2001.
12. See, e.g., Hatano and Inagaki, 1996; Resnick, 1987; Stigler and Heibert, 1997.
13. Stigler and Heibert, 1999.
14. National Research Council, 2004.
15. See, e.g., Tobias, 1978.
16. Hufferd-Ackles et al., 2004.
17. Sherin, 2000a, 2002.
18. See, e.g., Bransford et al., 1989.
19. See, e.g., Schwartz and Moore, 1998.
20. Sherin, 2000b, 2001.
21. Lewis, 2002, p. 1.
22. Fernandez, 2002; Lewis, 2002; Stigler and Heibert, 1999.
23. Remillard, 1999, 2000.
24. Remillard and Geist, 2002.
25. Remillard, 2000.

■ REFERENCES

Anghileri, J. (1989). An investigation of young children's understanding of multiplication. *Educational Studies in Mathematics, 20*, 367–385.

Ashlock, R. -B. (1998). *Error patterns in computation.* Upper Saddle River, NJ: Prentice-Hall.

Baek, J. M. (1998). Children's invented algorithms for multidigit multiplication problems. In L. J. Morrow and M. J. Kenney (Eds.), *The teaching and learning of algorithms in school mathematics.* Reston, VA: National Council of Teachers of Mathematics.

Baroody, A. J., and Coslick, R. T. (1998). *Fostering children's mathematical power: An investigative approach to k-8 mathematics instruction.* Mahwah, NJ: Lawrence Erlbaum Associates.

Baroody, A. J., and Ginsburg, H. P. (1986). The relationship between initial meaningful and mechanical knowledge of arithmetic. In J. Hiebert (Ed.), *Conceptual and procedural knowledge: The case of mathematics* (pp. 75–112). Mahwah, NJ: Lawrence Erlbaum Associates.

Beishuizen, M. (1993). Mental strategies and materials or models for addition and subtraction up to 100 in Dutch second grades. *Journal for Research in Mathematics Education, 24,* 294–323.

Beishuizen, M., Gravemeijer, K. P. E., and van Lieshout, E. C. D. M. (Eds.). (1997). *The role of contexts and models in the development of mathematical strategies and procedures.* Utretch, The Netherlands: CD-B Press/The Freudenthal Institute.

Bergeron, J. C., and Herscovics, N. (1990). Psychological aspects of learning early arithmetic. In P. Nesher and J. Kilpatrick (Eds.), *Mathematics and cognition: A research synthesis by the International Group for the Psychology of Mathematics Education.* Cambridge, England: Cambridge University Press.

Bransford, J. D., Franks, J. J., Vye, N. J., and Sherwood, R. D. (1989). New approaches to instruction: Because wisdom can't be told. In S. Vasniadou and A. Ortony (Eds.), *Similarity and analogical reasoning* (pp. 470–497). New York: Cambridge University Press.

Brophy, J. (1997). Effective instruction. In H. J. Walberg and G. D. Haertel (Eds.), *Psychology and educational practice* (pp. 212–232). Berkeley, CA: McCutchan.

Brownell, W. A. (1987). AT Classic: Meaning and skill—maintaining the balance. *Arithmetic Teacher, 34*(8), 18–25.

Canfield, R. L., and Smith, E. G. (1996). Number-based expectations and sequential enumeration by 5-month-old infants. *Developmental Psychology, 32,* 269–279.

Carey, S. (2001). Evolutionary and ontogenetic foundations of arithmetic. *Mind and Language, 16*(1), 37–55.

Carpenter, T. P., and Moser, J. M. (1984). The acquisition of addition and subtraction concepts in grades one through three. *Journal for Research in Mathematics Education, 15*(3), 179–202.

Carpenter, T. P., Fennema, E., Peterson, P. L., Chiang, C. P., and Loef, M. (1989). Using knowledge of children's mathematics thinking in classroom teaching: An experimental study. *American Educational Research Journal, 26*(4), 499–531.

Carpenter, T. P., Franke, M. L., Jacobs, V., and Fennema, E. (1998). A longitudinal study of invention and understanding in children's multidigit addition and subtraction. *Journal for Research in Mathematics Education, 29,* 3–20.

Carraher, T. N. (1986). From drawings to buildings: Mathematical scales at work. *International Journal of Behavioural Development, 9,* 527–544.

Carraher, T. N., Carraher, D. W., and Schliemann, A. D. (1985). Mathematics in the streets and in schools. *British Journal of Developmental Psychology, 3,* 21–29.

Carroll, W. M. (2001). *A longitudinal study of children using the reform curriculum everyday mathematics.* Available: http://everydaymath.uchicago.edu/educators/references.shtml [accessed September 2004].

Carroll, W. M., and Fuson, K. C. (1999). *Achievement results for fourth graders using the standards-based curriculum everyday mathematics.* Unpublished document, University of Chicago, Illinois.

Carroll, W. M., and Porter, D. (1998). Alternative algorithms for whole-number operations. In L. J. Morrow and M. J. Kenney (Eds.), *The teaching and learning of algorithms in school mathematics* (pp. 106–114). Reston, VA: National Council of Teachers of Mathematics.

Case, R. (1985). *Intellectual development: Birth to adulthood.* New York: Academic Press.

Case, R. (1992). *The mind's staircase: Exploring the conceptual underpinnings of children's thought and knowledge.* Mahwah, NJ: Lawrence Erlbaum Associates.

Case, R. (1998). *A psychological model of number sense and its development.* Paper presented at the annual meeting of the American Educational Research Association, April, San Diego, CA.

Case, R., and Sandieson, R. (1988). A developmental approach to the identification and teaching of central conceptual structures in mathematics and science in the middle grades. In M. Behr and J. Hiebert (Eds.), *Research agenda in mathematics education: Number concepts and in the middle grades* (pp. 136–270). Mahwah, NJ: Lawrence Erlbaum Associates.

Case, R., Griffin, S., and Kelly, W. M. (1999). Socioeconomic gradients in mathematical ability and their responsiveness to intervention during early childhood. In D.P. Keating and C. Hertzman

(Eds.), *Developmental health and the wealth of nations: Social, biological, and educational dynamics* (pp. 125–149). New York: Guilford Press.

Ceci, S.J. (1996). *On intelligence: A bioecological treatise on intellectual development.* Cambridge, MA: Harvard University Press.

Ceci, S. J., and Liker, J. K. (1986). A day at the races: A study of IQ, expertise, and cognitive complexity. *Journal of Experimental Psychology, 115*(3), 255–266.

Cotton, K. (1995). *Effective schooling practices: A research synthesis.* Portland, OR: Northwest Regional Lab.

Davis, R. B. (1984). *Learning mathematics: The cognitive science approach to mathematics education.* Norwood, NJ: Ablex.

De la Rocha, O. L. (1986). The reorganization of arithmetic practice in the kitchen. *Anthropology and Education Quarterly, 16*(3), 193–198.

Dixon, R. C., Carnine, S.W., Kameenui, E.J., Simmons, D.C., Lee, D.S., Wallin, J., and Chard, D. (1998). *Executive summary. Report to the California State Board of Education, review of high-quality experimental research.* Eugene, OR: National Center to Improve the Tools of Educators.

Dossey, J. A., Swafford, J. O., Parmantie, M., and Dossey, A. E. (Eds.). (2003). Multidigit addition and subtraction methods invented in small groups and teacher support of problem solving and reflection. In A. Baroody and A. Dowker (Eds.), *The development of arithmetic concepts and skills: Constructing adaptive expertise.* Mahwah, NJ: Lawrence Erlbaum Associates.

Fernandez, C. (2002). Learning from Japanese approaches to professional development. The case of lesson study. *Journal of Teacher Education, 53*(5), 393–405.

Fraivillig, J. L., Murphy, L. A., and Fuson, K. C. (1999). Advancing children's mathematical thinking in everyday mathematics reform classrooms. *Journal for Research in Mathematics Education, 30,* 148–170.

Fuson, K. C. (1986a). Roles of representation and verbalization in the teaching of multidigit addition and subtraction. *European Journal of Psychology of Education, 1,* 35–56.

Fuson, K. C. (1986b). Teaching children to subtract by counting up. *Journal for Research in Mathematics Education, 17,* 172–189.

Fuson, K. C. (1990). Conceptual structures for multiunit numbers: Implications for learning and teaching multidigit addition, subtraction, and place value. *Cognition and Instruction, 7,* 343–403.

Fuson, K. C. (1992a). Research on learning and teaching addition and subtraction of whole numbers. In G. Leinhardt, R.T. Putnam, and R. A. Hattrup (Eds.), *The analysis of arithmetic for mathematics teaching* (pp. 53–187). Mahwah, NJ: Lawrence Erlbaum Associates.

Fuson, K. C. (1992b). Research on whole number addition and subtraction. In D. Grouws (Ed.), *Handbook of research on mathematics teaching and learning* (pp. 243–275). New York: Macmillan.

Fuson, K. C. (2003). Developing mathematical power in whole number operations. In J. Kilpatrick, W. G. Martin, and D. Schifter (Eds.), *A research companion to principles and standards for school mathematics* (pp. 68–94). Reston, VA: National Council of Teachers of Mathematics.

Fuson, K. C., and Briars, D. J. (1990). Base-ten blocks as a first- and second-grade learning/teaching approach for multidigit addition and subtraction and place-value concepts. *Journal for Research in Mathematics Education, 21,* 180–206.

Fuson, K. C., and Burghardt, B. H. (1993). Group case studies of second graders inventing multidigit addition procedures for base-ten blocks and written marks. In J. R. Becker and B. J. Pence (Eds.), *Proceedings of the fifteenth annual meeting of the North American chapter of the international group for the psychology of mathematics education* (pp. 240–246). San Jose, CA: The Center for Mathematics and Computer Science Education, San Jose State University.

Fuson, K. C., and Burghardt, B. H. (1997). Group case studies of second graders inventing multidigit subtraction methods. In *Proceedings of the 19th annual meeting of the North American chapter of the international group for the psychology of mathematics education* (pp. 291–298). San Jose, CA: The Center for Mathematics and Computer Science Education, San Jose State University.

Fuson, K. C., and Fuson, A. M. (1992). Instruction to support children's counting on for addition and counting up for subtraction. *Journal for Research in Mathematics Education, 23,* 72–78.

Fuson, K. C., and Kwon, Y. (1992). Korean children's understanding of multidigit addition and subtraction. *Child Development, 63(2),* 491–506.

Fuson, K. C., and Secada, W. G. (1986). Teaching children to add by counting with finger patterns. *Cognition and Instruction, 3,* 229–260.

Fuson, K. C., and Smith, T. (1997). Supporting multiple 2-digit conceptual structures and calculation methods in the classroom: Issues of conceptual supports, instructional design, and language. In M. Beishuizen, K. P. E. Gravemeijer, and E. C. D. M. van Lieshout (Eds.), *The role of contexts and models in the development of mathematical strategies and procedures* (pp. 163–198). Utrecht, The Netherlands: CD-B Press/The Freudenthal Institute.

Fuson, K. C., Stigler, J., and Bartsch, K. (1988). Grade placement of addition and subtraction topics in Japan, mainland China, the Soviet Union, Taiwan, and the United States. *Journal for Research in Mathematics Education, 19(5),* 449–456.

Fuson, K. C., Perry, T., and Kwon, Y. (1994). Latino, Anglo, and Korean children's finger addition methods. In J. E. H. van Luit (Ed.), *Research on learning and instruction of mathematics in kindergarten and primary school,* (pp. 220–228). Doetinchem/Rapallo, The Netherlands: Graviant.

Fuson, K. C., Perry, T., and Ron, P. (1996). Developmental levels in culturally different finger methods: Anglo and Latino children's finger methods of addition. In E. Jakubowski, D. Watkins, and H. Biske (Eds.), *Proceedings of the 18th annual meeting of the North American chapter for the psychology of mathematics education* (2nd edition, pp. 347–352). Columbus, OH: ERIC Clearinghouse for Science, Mathematics, and Environmental Education.

Fuson, K. C., Lo Cicero, A., Hudson, K., and Smith, S. T. (1997). Snapshots across two years in the life of an urban Latino classroom. In J. Hiebert, T. Carpenter, E. Fennema, K. C. Fuson, D. Wearne, H. Murray, A. Olivier, and P. Human (Eds.), *Making sense: Teaching and learning mathematics with understanding* (pp. 129–159). Portsmouth, NH: Heinemann.

Fuson, K. C., Smith, T., and Lo Cicero, A. (1997). Supporting Latino first graders' ten-structured thinking in urban classrooms. *Journal for Research in Mathematics Education, 28,* 738–760.

Fuson, K. C., Wearne, D., Hiebert, J., Murray, H., Human, P., Olivier, A., Carpenter, T., and Fennema, E. (1997). Children's conceptual structures for multidigit numbers and methods of multidigit addition and subtraction. *Journal for Research in Mathematics Education, 28,* 130–162.

Fuson, K. C., De La Cruz, Y., Smith, S., Lo Cicero, A., Hudson, K., Ron, P., and Steeby, R. (2000). Blending the best of the 20th century to achieve a mathematics equity pedagogy in the 21st century. In M.J. Burke and F.R. Curcio (Eds.), *Learning mathematics for a new century* (pp. 197–212). Reston, VA: National Council of Teachers of Mathematics.

Geary, D.C. (1994). *Children's mathematical development: Research and practical applications.* Washington, DC: American Psychological Association.

Gelman, R. (1990). First principles organize attention to and learning about relevant data: Number and the animate-inanimate distinction as examples. *Cognitive Science, 14,* 79–106.

Ginsburg, H. P. (1984). *Children's arithmetic: The learning process.* New York: Van Nostrand.

Ginsburg, H. P., and Allardice, B. S. (1984). Children's difficulties with school mathematics. In B. Rogoff and J. Lave (Eds.), *Everyday cognition: Its development in social contexts* (pp. 194–219). Cambridge, MA: Harvard University Press.

Ginsburg, H. P., and Russell, R. L. (1981). Social class and racial influences on early mathematical thinking. *Monographs of the Society for Research in Child Development* 44(6, serial #193). Malden, MA: Blackwell.

Goldman, S. R., Pellegrino, J. W., and Mertz, D. L. (1988). Extended practice of basic addition facts: Strategy changes in learning-disabled students. *Cognition and Instruction, 5(3),* 223–265.

Goldman, S. R., Hasselbring, T. S., and the Cognition and Technology Group at Vanderbilt (1997). Achieving meaningful mathematics literacy for students with learning disabilities. *Journal of Learning Disabilities, March 1(2),* 198–208.

Greer, B. (1992). Multiplication and division as models of situation. In D. Grouws (Ed.), *Handbook of research on mathematics teaching and learning* (pp. 276–295). New York: Macmillan.

Griffin, S., and Case, R. (1997). Re-thinking the primary school math curriculum: An approach based on cognitive science. *Issues in Education, 3*(1), 1–49.

Griffin, S., Case, R., and Siegler, R.S. (1994). Rightstart: Providing the central conceptual structures for children at risk of school failure. In K. McGilly (Ed.), *Classroom lessons: Integrating cognitive theory and classroom practice* (pp. 13–48). Mahwah, NJ: Lawrence Erlbaum Associates.

Grouws, D. (1992). *Handbook of research on mathematics teaching and learning.* New York: Teachers College Press.

Hamann, M. S., and Ashcraft, M. H. (1986). Textbook presentations of the basic addition facts. *Cognition and Instruction, 3,* 173–192.

Hart, K. M. (1987). Practical work and formalisation, too great a gap. In J. C. Bergeron, N. Hersovics, and C. Kieren (Eds.), *Proceedings from the eleventh international conference for the psychology of mathematics education* (vol. 2, pp. 408–415). Montreal, Canada: University of Montreal.

Hatano, G., and Inagaki, K. (1996). *Cultural contexts of schooling revisited. A review of the learning gap from a cultural psychology perspective.* Paper presented at the Conference on Global Prospects for Education: Development, Culture, and Schooling, University of Michigan.

Hiebert, J. (1986). *Conceptual and procedural knowledge: The case of mathematics.* Mahwah, NJ: Lawrence Erlbaum Associates.

Hiebert, J. (1992). Mathematical, cognitive, and instructional analyses of decimal fractions. In G. Leinhardt, R. Putnam, and R. A. Hattrup (Eds.), *The analysis of arithmetic for mathematics teaching* (pp. 283–322). Mahwah, NJ: Lawrence Erlbaum Associates.

Hiebert, J., and Carpenter, T. P. (1992). Learning and teaching with understanding. In D. Grouws (Ed.), *Handbook of research on mathematics teaching and learning* (pp. 65–97). New York: Macmillan.

Hiebert, J., and Wearne, D. (1986). Procedures over concepts: The acquisition of decimal number knowledge. In J. Hiebert (Ed.), *Conceptual and procedural knowledge: The case of mathematics* (pp. 199–223). Mahwah, NJ: Lawrence Erlbaum Associates.

Hiebert, J., Carpenter, T., Fennema, E., Fuson, K. C., Murray, H., Olivier, A., Human, P., and Wearne, D. (1996). Problem solving as a basis for reform in curriculum and instruction: The case of mathematics. *Educational Researcher, 25*(4), 12–21.

Hiebert, J., Carpenter, T., Fennema, E., Fuson, K. C., Wearne, D., Murray, H., Olivier, A., and Human, P. (1997). *Making sense: Teaching and learning mathematics with understanding.* Portsmouth, NH: Heinemann.

Holt, J. (1964). *How children fail.* New York: Dell.

Hufford-Ackles, K., Fuson, K., and Sherin, M. G. (2004). Describing levels and components of a math-talk community. *Journal for Research in Mathematics Education, 35*(2), 81–116.

Isaacs, A. C., and Carroll, W. M. (1999). Strategies for basic-facts instruction. *Teaching Children Mathematics, 5*(9), 508–515.

Kalchman, M., and Case, R. (1999). Diversifying the curriculum in a mathematics classroom streamed for high-ability learners: A necessity unassumed. *School Science and Mathematics, 99*(6), 320–329.

Kameenui, E. J., and Carnine, D. W. (Eds.). (1998). *Effective teaching strategies that accommodate diverse learners.* Upper Saddle River, NJ: Prentice-Hall.

Kerkman, D. D., and Siegler, R. S. (1993). Individual differences and adaptive flexibility in lower-income children's strategy choices. *Learning and Individual Differences, 5*(2), 113–136.

Kilpatrick, J., Martin, W. G., and Schifter, D. (Eds.). (2003). *A research companion to principles and standards for school mathematics.* Reston, VA: National Council of Teachers of Mathematics.

Knapp, M. S. (1995). *Teaching for meaning in high-poverty classrooms.* New York: Teachers College Press.

Lampert, M. (1986). Knowing, doing, and teaching multiplication. *Cognition and Instruction, 3,* 305–342.

Lampert, M. (1992). Teaching and learning long division for understanding in school. In G. Leinhardt, R.T. Putnam, and R. A. Hattrup (Eds.), *The analysis of arithmetic for mathematics teaching* (pp. 221–282). Mahwah, NJ: Lawrence Erlbaum Associates.

Lave, J. (1988). *Cognition in practice: Mind, mathematics and culture in everyday life.* London, England: Cambridge University Press.

LeFevre, J., and Liu, J. (1997). The role of experience in numerical skill: Multiplication performance in adults from Canada and China. *Mathematical Cognition, 3*(1), 31–62.

LeFevre, J., Kulak, A. G., and Bisantz, J. (1991). Individual differences and developmental change in the associative relations among numbers. *Journal of Experimental Child Psychology, 52,* 256–274.

Leinhardt, G., Putnam, R. T., and Hattrup, R. A. (Eds.). (1992). The *analysis of arithmetic for mathematics teaching.* Mahwah, NJ: Lawrence Erlbaum Associates.

Lemaire, P., and Siegler, R. S. (1995). Four aspects of strategic change: Contributions to children's learning of multiplication. *Journal of Experimental Psychology: General, 124*(1), 83–97.

Lemaire, P., Barrett, S. E., Fayol, M., and Abdi, H. (1994). Automatic activation of addition and multiplication facts in elementary school children. *Journal of Experimental Child Psychology, 57,* 224–258.

Lewis, C. (2002). *Lesson study: A handbook of teacher-led instructional change.* Philadelphia, PA: Research for Better Schools.

Lo Cicero, A., Fuson, K. C., and Allexaht-Snider, M. (1999). Making a difference in Latino children's math learning: Listening to children, mathematizing their stories, and supporting parents to help children. In L. Ortiz-Franco, N.G. Hernendez, and Y. De La Cruz (Eds.), *Changing the faces of mathematics: Perspectives on Latinos* (pp. 59–70). Reston, VA: National Council of Teachers of Mathematics.

McClain, K., Cobb, P., and Bowers, J. (1998). A contextual investigation of three-digit addition and subtraction. In L. Morrow (Ed.), *Teaching and learning of algorithms in school mathematics* (pp. 141–150). Reston, VA: National Council of Teachers of Mathematics.

McKnight, C. C., and Schmidt, W. H. (1998). Facing facts in U.S. science and mathematics education: Where we stand, where we want to go. *Journal of Science Education and Technology, 7*(1), 57–76.

McKnight, C. C., Crosswhite, F. J., Dossey, J. A., Kifer, E., Swafford, J. O., Travers, K. T., and Cooney, T. J. (1989). *The underachieving curriculum: Assessing U.S. school mathematics from an international perspective.* Champaign, IL: Stipes.

Miller, K. F., and Paredes, D. R. (1990). Starting to add worse: Effects of learning to multiply on children's addition. *Cognition, 37,* 213–242.

Moss, J., and Case, R. (1999). Developing children's understanding of rational numbers: A new model and experimental curriculum. *Journal for Research in Mathematics Education, 30*(2), 122–147.

Mulligan, J., and Mitchelmore, M. (1997). Young children's intuitive models of multiplication and division. *Journal for Research in Mathematics Education, 28*(3), 309–330.

National Council of Teachers of Mathematics. (1989). *Curriculum and evaluation standards for school mathematics.* Reston, VA: National Council of Teachers of Mathematics.

National Council of Teachers of Mathematics. (1991). *Professional standards for teaching mathematics.* Reston, VA: National Council of Teachers of Mathematics.

National Council of Teachers of Mathematics. (2000). *Principles and standards for school mathematics.* Reston, VA: National Council of Teachers of Mathematics.

National Research Council. (2001). *Adding it up: Helping children learn mathematics.* Mathematics Learning Study Committee, J. Kilpatrick, J. Swafford, and B. Findell (Eds.). Center for Education, Division of Behavioral and Social Sciences and Education. Washington, DC: National Academy Press.

National Research Council. (2002). *Helping children learn mathematics.* Mathematics Learning Study Committee, J. Kilpatrick, J. Swafford, and B. Findell (Eds.). Center for Education, Division of Behavioral and Social Sciences and Education. Washington, DC: The National Academies Press.

National Research Council. (2004). *Learning and instruction: A SERP research agenda.* Panel on Learning and Instruction. M. S. Donovan and J. W. Pellegrino (Eds.). Division of Behavioral and Social Sciences and Education. Washington, DC: The National Academies Press.

Nesh, P., and Kilpatrick, J. (Eds.). (1990). Mathematics *and cognition: A research synthesis by the International Group for the Psychology of Mathematics Education.* Cambridge, MA: Cambridge University Press.

Nesher, P. (1992). Solving multiplication word problems. In G. Leinhardt, R. T. Putnam, and R. A. Hattrup (Eds.), *The analysis of arithmetic for mathematics teaching* (pp. 189–220). Mahwah, NJ: Lawrence Erlbaum Associates.

Peak, L. (1996). *Pursuing excellence: A study of the U.S. eighth-grade mathematics and science teaching, learning, curriculum, and achievement in an international context.* Washington, DC: National Center for Education Statistics.

Remillard, J. T. (1999). Curriculum materials in mathematics education reform: A framework for examining teachers' curriculum development. *Curriculum Inquiry, 29*(3), 315–342.

Remillard, J. T. (2000). Can curriculum materials support teachers' learning? *Elementary School Journal, 100*(4), 331–350.

Remillard, J. T., and Geist, P. (2002). Supporting teachers' professional learning though navigating openings in the curriculum. *Journal of Mathematics Teacher Education, 5*(1), 7–34.

Resnick, L. B. (1987). *Education and learning to think.* Committee on Mathematics, Science, and Technology Education, Commission on Behavioral and Social Sciences and Education. Washington, DC: National Academy Press.

Resnick, L. B. (1992). From protoquantities to operators: Building mathematical competence on a foundation of everyday knowledge. In G. Leinhardt, R. T. Putnam, and R. A. Hattrup (Eds.), *The analysis of arithmetic for mathematics teaching* (pp. 373–429). Mahwah, NJ: Lawrence Erlbaum Associates.

Resnick, L. B., and Omanson, S.F. (1987). Learning to understand arithmetic. In R. Glaser (Ed.), *Advances in instructional psychology* (vol. 3, pp. 41–95). Mahwah, NJ: Lawrence Erlbaum Associates.

Resnick, L. B., Nesher, P., Leonard, F., Magone, M., Omanson, S., and Peled, I. (1989). Conceptual bases of arithmetic errors: The case of decimal fractions. *Journal for Research in Mathematics Education, 20*(1), 8–27.

Ron, P. (1998). My family taught me this way. In L. J. Morrow and M. J. Kenney (Eds.), *The teaching and learning of algorithms in school mathematics* (pp. 115–119). Reston, VA: National Council of Teachers of Mathematics.

Saxe, G. B. (1982). Culture and the development of numerical cognition: Studies among the Oksapmin of Papua New Guinea. In C. J. Brainerd (Ed.), *Progress in cognitive development research: Children's logical and mathematical cognition* (vol. 1, pp. 157–176). New York: Springer-Verlag.

Schmidt, W., McKnight, C. C., and Raizen, S. A. (1997). *A splintered vision: An investigation of U.S. science and mathematics education.* Dordrecht, The Netherlands: Kluwer.

Schwartz, D. L., and Moore, J. L. (1998). The role of mathematics in explaining the material world: Mental models for proportional reasoning. *Cognitive Science, 22,* 471–516.

Secada, W. G. (1992). Race, ethnicity, social class, language, and achievement in mathematics. In D. Grouws (Ed.), *Handbook of research on mathematics teaching and learning* (pp. 623–660). New York: Macmillan.

Sherin M. G. (2000a). Facilitating meaningful discussions about mathematics. *Mathematics Teaching in the Middle School, 6*(2), 186–190.

Sherin, M. G. (2000b). Taking a fresh look at teaching through video clubs. *Educational Leadership, 57*(8), 36–38.

Sherin, M. G. (2001). Developing a professional vision of classroom events. In T. Wood, B. S. Nelson, and J. Warfield (Eds.), *Beyond classical pedagogy: Teaching elementary school mathematics* (pp. 75.93). Mahwah, NJ: Lawrence Erlbaum Associates.

Sherin, M. G. (2002). A balancing act: Developing a discourse community in a mathematics classroom. *Journal of Mathematics Teacher Education, 5,* 205–233.

Shuell, T. J. (2001). Teaching and learning in a classroom context. In N. J. Smelser and P. B. Baltes (Eds.), *International encyclopedia of the social and behavioral sciences* (pp. 15468–15472). Amsterdam: Elsevier.

Siegler, R. S. (1988). Individual differences in strategy choices: Good students, not-so-good students, and perfectionists. *Child Development, 59*(4), 833–851.

Siegler, R. S. (2003). Implications of cognitive science research for mathematics education. In J. Kilpatrick, W. G. Martin, and D. E. Schifter (Eds.), *A research companion to principles and standards for school mathematics* (pp. 1289–1303). Reston, VA: National Council of Teachers of Mathematics.

Simon, M. A. (1995). Reconstructing mathematics pedagogy from a constructivist perspective. *Journal for Research in Mathematics Education, 26,* 114–145.

Starkey, P., Spelke, E. S., and Gelman, R. (1990). Numerical abstraction by human infants. *Cognition, 36,* 97–127.

Steffe, L. P. (1994). Children's multiplying schemes. In G. Harel and J. Confrey (Eds.), *The development of multiplicative reasoning in the learning of mathematics* (pp. 3–39). New York: State University of New York Press.

Steffe, L. P., Cobb, P., and Von Glasersfeld, E. (1988). *Construction of arithmetical meanings and strategies.* New York: Springer-Verlag.

Sternberg, R. J. (1999). The theory of successful intelligence. *Review of General Psychology, 3*(4), 292–316.

Stigler, J. W., and Hiebert, J. (1999). *Teaching gap.* New York: Free Press.

Stigler, J. W., Fuson, K. C., Ham, M., and Kim, M. S. (1986). An analysis of addition and subtraction word problems in American and Soviet elementary mathematics textbooks. *Cognition and Instruction, 3*(3), 153–171.

Stipek, D., Salmon, J. M., Givvin, K. B., Kazemi, E., Saxe, G., and MacGyvers, V. L. (1998). The value (and convergence) of practices suggested by motivation research and promoted by mathematics education reformers. *Journal for Research in Mathematics Education, 29,* 465–488.

Thornton, C. A. (1978). Emphasizing thinking in basic fact instruction. *Journal for Research in Mathematics Education, 9,* 214–227.

Thornton, C. A., Jones, G. A., and Toohey, M. A. (1983). A multisensory approach to thinking strategies for remedial instruction in basic addition facts. *Journal for Research in Mathematics Education, 14*(3), 198–203.

Tobias, S. (1978). *Overcoming math anxiety.* New York: W. W. Norton.

Van de Walle, J. A. (1998). *Elementary and middle school mathematics: Teaching developmentally, third edition.* New York: Longman.

Van de Walle, J. A. (2000). *Elementary school mathematics: Teaching developmentally, fourth edition.* New York: Longman.

Wynn, K. (1996). Infants' individuation and enumeration of actions. *Psychological Science, 7,* 164–169.

Zucker, A. A. (1995). Emphasizing conceptual understanding and breadth of study in mathematics instruction. In M. S. Knapp (Ed.), *Teaching for meaning in high-poverty classrooms.* New York: Teachers College Press.

Suggested Reading List for Teachers

Carpenter, T. P. Fennema, E., Franke, M. L., Empson, S. B., and Levi, L. W. (1999). *Children's mathematics: Cognitively guided instruction.* Portsmouth, NH: Heinemann.

Fuson, K. C. (1988). Subtracting by counting up with finger patterns. (Invited paper for the Research into Practice Series.) *Arithmetic Teacher, 35*(5), 29–31.

Hiebert, J., Carpenter, T., Fennema, E., Fuson, K. C., Wearne, D., Murray, H., Olivier, A., and Human, P. (1997). *Making sense: Teaching and learning mathematics with understanding.* Portsmouth, NH: Heinemann.

Jensen, R. J. (Ed.). (1993). *Research ideas for the classroom: Early childhood mathematics.* New York: Macmillan.

Knapp, M. S. (1995). *Teaching for meaning in high-poverty classrooms.* New York: Teachers College Press.

Leinhardt, G., Putnam, R. T., and Hattrup, R. A. (Eds.). (1992). *The analysis of arithmetic for mathematics teaching.* Mahwah, NJ: Lawrence Erlbaum Associates.

Lo Cicero, A., De La Cruz, Y., and Fuson, K. C. (1999). Teaching and learning creatively with the Children's Math Worlds Curriculum: Using children's narratives and explanations to co-create understandings. *Teaching Children Mathematics, 5*(9), 544–547.

Owens, D. T. (Ed.). (1993). *Research ideas for the classroom: Middle grades mathematics.* New York: Macmillan.

Schifter, D. (Ed.). (1996). *What's happening in math class? Envisioning new practices through teacher narratives.* New York: Teachers College Press.

Wagner, S. (Ed.). (1993). *Research ideas for the classroom: High school mathematics.* New York: Macmillan.

READING 2.2 FOCUS QUESTIONS

1. According to Stein et al., what is cognitive demand with respect to mathematical tasks?

2. Why is the cognitive demand of tasks an important factor in student learning?

3. According to Stein et al., how should a curriculum and a teacher decide what kind or level of task to use for a lesson?

4. Describe what a "low-level" cognitive demand task is. Describe what a "high-level" cognitive demand task is.

5. When and why might a teacher use a low-level cognitive demand mathematics task with his or her students? When might a teacher use a high-level one?

Mark those paragraphs or short sections that seem most interesting to you. Be prepared to discuss with other participants why you think these passages are significant.

READING 2.2

Analyzing Mathematical Instructional Tasks

Mary Kay Stein

Margaret Schwan Smith

Marjorie A. Henningsen

Edward A. Silver

Mathematical tasks can be examined from a variety of perspectives including the number and kinds of representations evoked, the variety of ways in which they can be solved, and their requirements for student communication. In this book, we examine mathematical instructional tasks in terms of their cognitive demands. By cognitive demands we mean the kind and level of thinking required of students in order to successfully engage with and solve the task.

In this chapter, we describe a method for analyzing the cognitive demands of tasks as they appear in curricular or instructional materials (the first phase of the Mathematical Tasks Framework shown in Figure 1.3 in the Introduction). Unlike the remainder of the framework, which describes task evolution *during* a classroom lesson, the initial phase of the framework focuses on tasks *before* the lesson begins, that is, the task as it appears in print form or as it is created by the teacher.

Why are the cognitive demands of tasks so important? As stated in the *Professional Standards for Teaching Mathematics* (NCTM, 1991), opportunities for student learning are not created simply by putting students into groups, by placing manipulatives in front of them, or by handing them a calculator. Rather, it is the level and kind of thinking in which students engage that determines what they will learn. Tasks that require students to perform a memorized procedure in a routine manner lead to one type of opportunity for student thinking; tasks that demand engagement with concepts and that stimulate students to make purposeful connections to meaning or relevant mathematical ideas lead to a different set of opportunities for student thinking. Day-in and day-out, the cumulative effect of students' experiences with instructional tasks is students' implicit development of ideas about the nature of mathematics—about whether mathematics is something they personally can make sense of, and how long and how hard they should have to work to do so.

Since the tasks with which students become engaged in the classroom form the basis of their opportunities for learning mathematics, it is important to be clear about one's goals for student learning. Once learning goals for students have been clearly articulated, tasks can be selected or created to match these goals. Being aware of the cognitive demands of tasks is a central consideration in this matching. For example, if a teacher wants students to learn how to justify or explain their solution processes, she should select a task that is deep and rich enough to afford such opportunities. If, on the other hand, speed and fluency are the primary learning objectives, other types of tasks will be needed. In this chapter, readers will learn how to differentiate among the various levels of cognitive demand of tasks, thereby laying a foundation for more careful matching between the tasks teachers select for the classroom and their goals for student learning.

DEFINING LEVELS OF COGNITIVE ■ DEMAND OF MATHEMATICAL TASKS

The example shown in Figure 2.2a illustrates four ways in which students can be asked to think about the relationships among different representations of fractional quantities. Each of these ways places a different level of cognitive demand on students. As shown on the left side of the figure, tasks with lower-level demands would consist of memorizing the equivalent forms of specific fractional quantities (e.g., $\frac{1}{2} = .5 = 50\%$) or performing conversions of fractions to percents or decimals using standard conversion algorithms in the absence of additional context or meaning (e.g., convert the fraction 3/8 to a decimal by dividing the numerator by the denominator to get .375; change .375 to a percent by moving the decimal point two places to the right to get 37.5%). These lower-level tasks are classified as *memorization* and *procedures without connections to understanding, meaning, or concepts* (hereafter referred to simply as *procedures without connections*), respectively. When tasks such as these are used, students typically work 10–30 similar problems within one sitting.

Another way in which students can be asked to think about the relationships among fractions, decimals, and percents—one that presents higher-level cognitive demands— might also use procedures, but do so in a way that builds connections to underlying concepts and meaning. For example, as shown in Figure 2.2a, students might be asked to use a 10 × 10 grid to illustrate how the fraction $\frac{3}{5}$ represents the same quantity as the decimal .6 or 60%. Students would also be asked to record their results on a chart containing the decimal, fraction, percent, and pictorial representations, thereby allowing them to make connections among the various representations and to attach meaning to their work by referring to the pictorial representation of the quantity every step of the way. This task is classified as *procedures with connections to understanding, meaning, or concepts* (hereafter referred to simply as *procedures with connections*).

Another high-level task (classified as *doing mathematics*[1]) would entail asking students to explore the relationships among the various ways of representing fractional quantities. Students would not—at least initially—be provided with the conventional conversion procedures. They might once again use grids, but this time grids of varying sizes (not just 10 × 10) would be used. As shown in Figure 2.2a, students could be asked to shade six squares of a 4 × 10 rectangle and to represent the shaded area as a percent, a decimal, and a fraction. When students use the visual diagram to solve this problem, they are challenged to apply their understandings of the fraction, decimal, and percent concepts in novel ways. For example, once a student has shaded the six squares, he or she must determine how the six squares relate to the total number of squares in the rectangle. In Figure 2.2a, we see an example of a student's response to this task that illustrates the kind of mathematical reasoning used to come up with an answer that makes sense and that can be justified. In contrast to the tasks with lower-level demands discussed earlier, in *procedures-with-connections* or *doing-mathematics* tasks, students typically perform far fewer problems (sometimes as few as two or three) in one sitting.

Figure 2.2a	Lower-Level Versus Higher-Level Approaches to the Task of Determining the Relationships Among Different Representations of Fractional Quantities (Stein & Smith, 1998)

LOWER-LEVEL DEMANDS	HIGHER-LEVEL DEMANDS

LOWER-LEVEL DEMANDS

Memorization

What are the decimal and percent equivalents for the fractions $\frac{1}{2}$ and $\frac{1}{4}$?

Expected Student Response

$$\frac{1}{2} = .5 = 50\%$$

$$\frac{1}{4} = .25 = 25\%$$

Procedures Without Connections

Convert the fraction to $\frac{3}{8}$ a decimal and a percent.

Expected Student Response

Fraction	Decimal	Percent
$\frac{3}{8}$	.375 $8\overline{)3.000}$ $\underline{24}$ 60 $\underline{56}$ 40 $\underline{40}$	.375 = 37.5%

HIGHER-LEVEL DEMANDS

Procedures With Connections

Using a 10 × 10 grid, identify the decimal and percent equivalents of $\frac{3}{5}$.

Expected Student Response

Pictorial

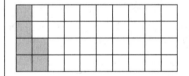

Fraction	Decimal	Percent
$\frac{60}{100} = \frac{3}{5}$	$\frac{60}{100} = .60$	.60 = 60%

Doing Mathematics

Shade 6 small squares in a 4 × 10 rectangle. Using the rectangle, explain how to determine each of the following: (a) the percent of area that is shaded, (b) the decimal part of area that is shaded, and (c) the fractional part of area that is shaded.

One Possible Student Response

(a) One column will be 10% since there are 10 columns. So four squares is 10%. Then 2 squares is half a column and half of 10% which is 5%. So the 6 shaded blocks equal 10% plus 5% or 15%.

(b) One column will be .10 since there are 10 columns. The second column has only 2 squares shaded so that would be one half of .10 which is .05. So the 6 shaded blocks equal .1 plus .05 which equals .15.

(c) Six shaded squares out of 40 squares is $\frac{6}{40}$ which reduces to $\frac{3}{20}$.

MATCHING TASKS WITH GOALS ■
FOR STUDENT LEARNING

As illustrated by the above discussion, not all mathematical tasks provide the same opportunities for student learning. Some tasks have the potential to engage students in complex forms of thinking and reasoning while others focus on memorization or the use of rules or procedures. In our work with teachers in the QUASAR Project, we discovered the importance of matching tasks with goals for student learning. Take for example the case of Mr. Johnson (Silver & Smith, 1996). Mr. Johnson wanted his students to learn to work collaboratively, to discuss alternative approaches to solving tasks, and to justify their solutions. However, the tasks he tended to use (e.g., expressing ratios such as 15/25 in lowest terms) provided little, if any, opportunity for collaboration, exploration of multiple solution strategies, or meaningful justification. Not surprisingly, class discussions were not very rich or enlightening. The discourse focused on correct answers and describing procedures, doing little to further students' ability to think or reason about important ideas associated with ratio and proportion.

Mr. Johnson's experience (and that of many teachers with whom we have worked) makes clear the need to start with a cognitively challenging task that has the potential to engage students in complex forms of thinking if the goal is to increase students' ability to think, reason, and solve problems. Although starting with such a task does not guarantee student engagement at a high level, it appears to be a necessary condition since low-level tasks virtually never result in high-level engagement (Stein, Grover, & Henningsen, 1996).

This is not to suggest that all tasks used by a teacher should engage students in cognitively demanding activity, since there may be some occasions on which a teacher might have other goals for a particular lesson, goals that would be better served by a different kind of task. For example, if the goal is to increase students' fluency in retrieving basic facts, definitions, and rules, then tasks that focus on memorization may be appropriate. If the goal is to increase students' speed and accuracy in solving routine problems, then tasks that focus on *procedures without connections* may be appropriate. Use of these types of tasks may improve student performance on tests that consist of low-level items and may lead to greater efficiency of time and effort in solving routine aspects of problems that are embedded in more complex tasks. However, focusing exclusively on tasks of these types can lead to a limited understanding of what mathematics is and how one does it. In addition, an overreliance on these types of tasks could lead to the inability to apply rules and procedures more generally, that is, to similar but not identical situations, or to recognize whether a particular rule or procedure is appropriate across a variety of situations (NCTM, 1989). Hence, students also need opportunities on a regular basis to engage with tasks that lead to deeper, more generative understandings regarding the nature of mathematical processes, concepts, and relationships.

DIFFERENTIATING LEVELS ■
OF COGNITIVE DEMAND

The Task Analysis Guide (shown in Figure 2.2b) consists of a listing of the characteristics[2] of tasks at each of the levels of cognitive demand described earlier in the chapter: memorization, *procedures without connection, procedures with connections,* and *doing mathematics.* When applied to a mathematical task (in print form), this guide can serve as a judgment template (a kind of scoring rubric) that permits a "rating" of the task based on the kind of thinking it demands of students.

For example, the guide would be helpful in deciding that the Fencing Task was an example of *doing mathematics* since the characteristics of this level most clearly describe the kind of thinking required to successfully complete the task. Specifically, no pathway is suggested by the task (i.e., there is no overarching procedure or rule that can simply be applied for solving the entire problem and the sequence of necessary steps is unspecified) and it requires students to explore pens of different dimensions and ultimately to make a generalization regarding the pen that will have maximum area for a fixed amount of fencing.

When determining the level of cognitive demand provided by a mathematical task, it is important not to become distracted by superficial features of the task and to keep in mind the students for whom the task is intended. Both of these considerations are discussed below.

Going Beyond Superficial Features

Determining the level of cognitive demand of a task can be tricky at times, since superficial features of tasks can be misleading. Low-level tasks, for example, can appear to be high-level when they have characteristics of reform-oriented instructional tasks (NCTM, 1991; Stein et al., 1996) such as requiring the use of manipulatives; using "real-world" contexts; involving multiple steps, actions, or judgments; and/or making use of diagrams. For example, some individuals have considered Martha's Carpeting Task a high-level task because it is a word problem and it is set in a real-world context. Similarly, some have considered commonly used fraction tasks—which ask students to find the sum of two proper fractions with unlike denominators and then to show the answer using fraction strips—high-level because they use manipulatives. But we would classify these tasks as low-level because typically well-rehearsed procedures (for Martha's Carpeting, the formula for determining area and for the fraction task, the rule for adding fractions with unlike denominators) are strongly implied by the problems. In both cases, the tasks would be considered to be *procedures-without-connections* tasks since there is little ambiguity about what has to be done or how to do it, there is no connection to concepts or meaning required, and the focus is on producing the correct answer.

It is also possible for tasks to be designated low-level when in fact they should be considered high-level. For example, the Lemonade Task—in which students have to determine which of two recipes for lemonade is more "lemony": Recipe A, which has 2 cups of lemon concentrate and 3 cups of water, or Recipe B, which has 3 cups of lemon concentrate and 5 cups of water—has been considered by some an example of a *procedures-without-connections* task because it "looks like" a standard textbook problem that could be solved by applying a rule or because it lacks "reform features" (such as requiring an explanation or justification). However, we have described this task as *doing mathematics* since no pathway for solving the problem is suggested (either explicitly or implicitly). Specifically, the task requires students to compare two situations and to determine which recipe has the higher proportion of concentrate. To do so, students must make sense of the problem situation and maintain a close connection to the meaning of ratio and to the question being asked. So even though tasks might "look" high- or low-level, it is important to move beyond their surface features to consider the kind of thinking they require.

Considering the Students

Another consideration when deciding the level of challenge provided by a task is the students (their age, grade level, prior knowledge and experiences) and the norms and expectations for work in their classroom. Consider, for example, a task in which students are

Figure 2.2b	The Characteristics of Mathematical Tasks at Each of the Four Levels of Cognitive Demand (Stein & Smith, 1998)

LOWER-LEVEL DEMANDS	HIGHER-LEVEL DEMANDS
Memorization Tasks • Involve either reproducing previously learned facts, rules, formulae, or definitions OR committing facts, rules, formulae, or definitions to memory. • Cannot be solved using procedures because a procedure does not exist or because the time frame in which the task is being completed is too short to use a procedure. • Are not ambiguous—such tasks involve exact reproduction of previously seen material and what is to be reproduced is clearly and directly stated. • Have no connection to the concepts or meaning that underlie the facts, rules, formulae, or definitions being learned or reproduced. **Procedures Without Connections Tasks** • Are algorithmic. Use of the procedure is either specifically called for or its use is evident based on prior instruction, experience, or placement of the task. • Require limited cognitive demand for successful completion. There is little ambiguity about what needs to be done and how to do it. • Have no connection to the concepts or meaning that underlie the procedure being used. • Are focused on producing correct answers rather than developing mathematical understanding. • Require no explanations or explanations that focus solely on describing the procedures that were used.	**Procedures With Connections Tasks** • Focus students' attention on the use of procedures for the purpose of developing deeper levels of understanding of mathematical concepts and ideas. • Suggest pathways to follow (explicitly or implicitly) that are broad general procedures that have close connections to underlying conceptual ideas as opposed to narrow algorithms that are opaque with respect to underlying concepts. • Usually are presented in multiple ways (e.g., visual diagrams, manipulatives, symbols, problem situations). Making connections among multiple representations helps to develop meaning. • Require some degree of cognitive effort. Although general procedures may be followed, they cannot be followed mindlessly. Students need to engage with the conceptual ideas that underlie the procedures in order to successfully complete the task and develop misunderstanding. **Doing Mathematics Tasks** • Requires complex and nonalgorithmic thinking (i.e., there is not a predictable, well-rehearsed approach or pathway explicitly suggested by the task, task instructions, or a worked-out example). • Requires students to explore and understand the nature of mathematical concepts, processes, or relationships. • Demands self-monitoring or self-regulation of one's own cognitive processes. • Requires students to access relevant knowledge and experiences and make appropriate use of them in working through the task. • Requires students to analyze the task and actively examine task constraints that may limit possible solution strategies and solutions. • Requires considerable cognitive effort and may involve some level of anxiety for the students due to the unpredictable nature of the solution process required.

asked to add five two-digit numbers and explain the process they used. For a fifth- or sixth-grade student who has access to a calculator and/or the addition algorithm, and for whom "explain the process" means "tell how you did it," the task could be considered routine. If, on the other hand, the task is given to a second grader who has just started work with two-digit numbers, who has base-10 blocks available, and/or for whom "explain the process" means you have to explain your thinking, the task may indeed be high-level. Therefore, when teachers select or design instructional tasks, all of these factors must be considered in order to determine the extent to which the task is likely to provide an appropriate level of challenge for their students.

■ NOTES

1. The category *doing mathematics* includes many different types of tasks that have the shared characteristic of having no pathway for solving the task explicitly or implicitly suggested and therefore requiring nonalgorithmic thinking. This category includes tasks that are nonroutine in nature, are intended to explore a mathematical concept in depth, embody the complexities of real-life situations, or represent mathematical abstractions.

2. These characteristics are derived from the work of Doyle on academic tasks (1988) and Resnick on high-level thinking skills (1987), and from the examination and categorization of hundreds of tasks in QUASAR classrooms (Stein et al., 1996; Stein, Lane, & Silver, 1997).

■ REFERENCES

Doyle, W. (1988). Work in mathematics classes: The context of students' thinking during instruction. *Educational Psychologist, 23,* 167–180.

National Council of Teachers of Mathematics (1991). *Professional standards for teaching mathematics.* Reston, VA: Author.

Resnick, L. B. (1987). *Education and learning to think.* Washington, DC: National Academy Press.

Stein, M. K., Grover, B. W., & Henningsen, M. A. (1996). Classroom instructional practices. In E. A. Silver (Ed.), *Teaching mathematics for a change: Evidence form the QUASAR project regarding the challenges and possibilities of instructional reform in urban middle schools.* Manuscript in preparation.

Stein, M. K., Lane, S., & Silver, E. A. (1997). *Classrooms in which students successfully acquire mathematical proficiency: What are the critical feature of teachers' instructional practice?* Paper presented at the annual meeting of the American Educational Research Association, New York.

In-Session Readings for Session 2

During the second session, read and discuss the following two articles:

Reading 2.3 Hiebert, J., & Stigler, J. (2004). A world of difference: Classrooms abroad provide lessons in teaching math and science. *Journal of Staff Development, 25*(4), 1–7.

Reading 2.4 Boaler, J. (1999, March). Mathematics for the moment, or the millennium? *Education Week, 18*(29), 52.

READING 2.3

A World of Difference

Classrooms Abroad Provide Lessons in Teaching Math and Science

James Hiebert

James W. Stigler

Improving classroom teaching is hard work. The literature is filled with stories of good intentions to change teaching followed by a disappointing return to traditional methods of practice. While learning how difficult it is for teachers to change the way they teach, educators also have learned that change is enabled when teachers have a clear target for change.

■ INTERNATIONAL COMPARISONS

One target for change is suggested by findings from the Third International Mathematics and Science Study (TIMSS) 1999 Video Study: Students need regular opportunities to explore mathematical relationships to develop high levels of understanding, in addition to developing skills. The reason this change is needed begins with the fact that both domestic and international assessments of achievement show that U.S. students are learning less mathematics than they could, and learning it less deeply (Silver & Kenney, 2000; Gonzales, et al., 2000). But why students are underachieving is a matter of heated debate. One hypothesis is that classroom instruction underemphasizes basic skills. Another hypothesis, from an opposite point of view, is that instruction underemphasizes conceptual understanding. The debate between skills and understanding has a long history in U.S. education and, recently, has become a central issue in the math wars (for example, see Loveless, 2001; National Council of Teachers of Mathematics, 2000; Kilpatrick, Swafford, & Findell, 2001).

It was in the context of this debate that we launched the TIMSS 1999 Video Study, the largest and most ambitious international comparison of teaching conducted to date. Random, nationally representative samples of 8th-grade lessons in mathematics and science were videotaped in a number of countries in Asia and Europe that achieve well on international comparisons. Results from the mathematics sample in the video study were released in 2003 (Hiebert, et al., 2003a) and results from the science sample are planned for release in 2004 (Roth, et al., in press). We studied a number of dimensions of teaching, including the ways classrooms are organized in the different countries, the kinds of mathematics problems presented to students, and the ways problems are worked on during classroom lessons. Can these analyses of high-achieving countries yield clues that might be relevant to the U.S. debate between skills and understanding?

Results from the study showed that high-achieving countries (Czech Republic, Hong Kong, Japan, Netherlands, Switzerland) teach 8th-grade mathematics in different ways (Hiebert, et al., 2003a). No single method of teaching appears to be necessary for high mathematics achievement. As one example, we saw a great deal of variation in the relative emphasis given in each country to problems designed to teach skills vs. problems designed to teach conceptual understanding—that is, problems that gave students opportunities to connect mathematical facts, ideas, and strategies. All countries spent some time on each type of problem, but the relative emphasis on conceptual problems varied from a high of 54% of the problems in Japan to a low of 13% in Hong Kong. (The U.S. fell in between these two, with 17%.) Japan and Hong Kong were the highest achievers in our sample, yet they were at opposite ends of the spectrum on this dimension.

A closer look revealed, however, that beneath the variability, there was a fascinating similarity among the high-achieving countries, one that distinguished them from the United States (Hiebert, et al., 2003b; Stigler & Hiebert, 2004). Although teachers in the United States presented problems of both types (practicing skills vs. "making connections"), they did something different than their international colleagues when working on the conceptual problems with students. For these problems, they almost always stepped in and did the work for the students or ignored the conceptual aspect of the problem when discussing it. Teachers in high-achieving countries differed considerably from each other in how many problems of this kind they presented, but when such problems were presented, they implemented a similar percentage of problems (about 50%) in such a way that students studied the connections or relationships embedded in the problems. Compared with their international peers, 8th graders in the United States almost never got the chance (less than 1% of the time) to explore and discuss mathematical relationships while solving these problems.

Teachers in high-achieving countries implemented at least some of these problems in the first way rather than the second way; teachers in the United States almost never did.

The significance of this finding cannot be overestimated. It says, first, that U.S. students (at least in 8th grade) are spending almost all of their time practicing skills. This is consistent with many reports from the past about the nature of mathematics teaching in this country (Fey, 1979). Teaching in the typical classroom has not changed much. The debate about how much emphasis to place on skills vs. understanding has not created opportunities for students in typical U.S. classrooms to develop both skills and understanding. We share the view with others (Kilpatrick, Swafford, & Findell, 2001) that both skills and understanding are critical. If educators agree that a balance is important, and if they take seriously the results from the TIMSS Video Study, then efforts to improve should focus on ensuring that students have some opportunities to solve challenging problems that require them to construct mathematical relationships—to develop conceptual understanding. Currently, students in typical 8th-grade mathematics classrooms are working only on skills.

Two Teaching Approaches to One Concept

Imagine the following problem:

> Find a pattern for the sum of the interior angles of a polygon.

This is a common problem in many 8th-grade curricula, and the intent is for students to explore the relationships among the measures of angles in figures with different numbers of sides and detect a pattern in the ways that the sums can be calculated.

Method 1

Teachers could implement the problem by asking students to measure the angles in various triangles, quadrilaterals, and pentagons, finding the results of 180 degrees, 360 degrees, and 540 degrees, respectively. Then they might ask students what patterns they see, whether they could predict the sum of the interior angles of six-sided figures, and, eventually, whether they could develop a rule for the sum of angles if one knew the number of sides.

Method 2

Alternatively, teachers could simply say, "There is an easy way to calculate the sum of the interior angles of a polygon—just count the number of sides, subtract two, and multiply by 180: Sum = $180(n - 2)$."

A second consequence of this finding is that curriculum reform is not enough. The percentage of mathematics problems presented in U.S. classrooms that aimed to engage students in more ambitious and creative conceptual activity was similar to several other high-achieving countries. The difference lay in how teachers implemented the problems with students. This is an issue of teaching. This is not changed by rewriting the curriculum.

In summary, the findings of the TIMSS 1999 Video Study show that different high-achieving countries have chosen different levels of emphasis with regard to skills vs. understanding. These results suggest that the exact amount of time spent on these learning goals is not the critical factor. Rather, the results suggest that some time should be devoted to practicing skills and some time devoted to developing understanding. U.S. teachers already provide practice on skills. This now needs to be balanced with solving challenging problems and discussing the relationships that can be constructed among the mathematical facts, procedures, and ideas. When working on these problems, teachers must learn how to avoid stepping in and giving the answers, and instead provide students with opportunities to think more deeply about mathematical concepts and then discuss these concepts or relationships with the students. How can teachers be supported to make this change?

■ LESSONS FROM RESEARCH

Just as educators are learning more about the features of teaching that should be targeted for improvement, and just as they are learning more about why teaching is so difficult to change, they also are learning more about professional development strategies that can support change. For starters, it is helpful to think about teaching as a cultural activity rather than as something one learns to do by studying it in school (Gallimore, 1996). That is, most teachers learn to teach by growing up in a culture, watching their own teachers teach, and then adapting these methods for their own practice. Changing teaching means changing the culture of teaching, not distributing more recommendations or holding more workshops.

How to Change Teaching

Three tips to change teaching to improve student achievement:

1. Shift priorities to spend some time daily or weekly studying teaching practices; focus on planning lessons and then reflecting on their effectiveness.

2. Provide teachers vivid examples of alternative teaching methods.

3. Have teachers learn to analyze students' work and understand their thinking to see how to adjust and improve their teaching methods.

Teaching can only change the way cultures change: gradually, steadily, over time as small changes are made in the daily and weekly routines of teaching. Consider the daily routines of most teachers. Lessons are planned (sometimes quickly, by identifying a sequence of activities), then implemented, then assessed (sometimes by watching students' reactions during the lesson, listening to students and questioning them informally, and collecting student work), and then reflected on (sometimes quickly, by making mental notes of what worked well and what didn't, who acted up, and so on). By studying how many teachers changed their teaching, we have learned that to begin the process of change, these phases of teaching must be slowed down and examined more carefully. Teachers must find ways to spend a little more time each week planning how to implement a few mathematics problems to engage students in thinking about key mathematical relationships suggested by the problem. And they must reflect, in more detail, on how students responded to these opportunities so they can improve the effectiveness with which such problems can be implemented the following day or week. Over time, these kinds of small, targeted changes in teachers' weekly routines change the culture of teaching—for the individual teacher, for the group of teachers who engage in this kind of work together, and, eventually, for the school.

Of course, changing a culture is not simple or easy. How do teachers go about the business of changing their weekly or daily routines, and what, exactly, do they do when they study teaching? We offer three suggestions.

First, finding time in the daily or weekly schedule is a key enabler. Educators often underestimate how much learning is required to teach in a different way (Cohen & Barnes, 1993) and how much time this takes. But for teachers, extra time is hard to find. A solution often is reallocating existing time rather than trying to find new time. Time spent in department meetings, grade-level meetings, and one-time workshops can be reallocated to time for studying and improving teaching in a systematic and continuing way. This shift will require changing priorities and creative scheduling, but it is the kind of commitment essential for instituting the regular, weekly collaborative study needed to improve teaching in a lasting way.

Second, teachers must be provided with vivid examples that illustrate alternative ways of teaching. If the goal is to learn how to work on mathematics problems so students can make connections to understand concepts and procedures, then teachers need images of what this kind of teaching looks like. Analyzing videos of teaching in detail and focusing intensely on the ways different teachers implement these kinds of problems can be rich learning opportunities. Studying the ways teachers present problems to students, asking students to develop problem-solving methods, comparing solution methods, looking for patterns, and comparing one problem to others provides a range of techniques that teachers can consider as they plan their own lessons. Finding useful videos is a challenge. The set of public-use videos collected as part of the TIMSS Video Study is one source. Samples of teaching do not need to show exemplary practice to be useful (Stigler & Hiebert, 1999). Examining everyday teaching, with its missed opportunities, also can be an important learning activity. Eventually, teachers can analyze videos of their own teaching, an essential experience for improving their practice.

Third, teachers must have opportunities to study students' responses to the changes teachers make in the classroom. If the goal is to learn how to implement mathematics problems so students can make connections to understand the concepts and procedures, then the critical information is whether, and to what degree, students achieve this goal. This requires information from students—how they solved the problem, how they explained their thinking, what errors they made, and so on. Learning to analyze student work and to make inferences about students' thinking can lead to significant changes in teachers' practices (Kazemi & Franke, in press).

Notice that the suggestions we offer for changing the culture of teaching to enable targeted changes in teaching practice assume many of the features recommended numerous times in the professional development literature (Darling-Hammond & Sykes, 1999; Sparks & Loucks-Horsley, 1990): situated in teachers' practice, connected to the curriculum, focused on clear student learning goals and student thinking, and continuing over time. There is growing evidence that these features are critical. But, to change cultures, educators need to appreciate the importance of examining the routines of teaching, slowing them down, and changing them, even a little. Developing a routine of planning for teaching and reflecting on teaching, with a particular learning goal in mind, can gradually but steadily change the culture of teaching.

■ CONCLUDING THOUGHTS

Everyone, including teachers, learns from everyday experiences, but usually this learning is haphazard and fleeting. Professional developers and teachers can do better than this. They can learn from carefully planned experiences. By planning to learn, teachers maximize the benefits they reap from studying their practice. This is exactly the kind of cultural change we envision. Begin with professional daily and weekly routines that are familiar—planning to teach, implementing lessons, assessing students' learning, and reflecting on how things went. Now slow down these routines and change them, even a little, by devoting more thought to how mathematics problems can be worked on with students and by studying more carefully the effects of these changes on students' thinking and understanding. Plan to learn about teaching by studying targeted instructional activities and their effects.

These ideas can be tied together by saying that teaching should have an "experiment" built in (Hiebert, Morris, & Glass, 2003). Planning to learn from teaching means setting clear learning goals (for the students and for the teacher), planning instructional activities hypothesized to achieve the learning goals for students, collecting data from students about how well the goals were achieved, and interpreting the data to revise the hypotheses and improve the lesson next time. These processes simulate experiments conducted in other settings and represent systematic, continuing, and increasingly rich professional development activities for teachers.

The payoff for teachers is the knowledge they acquire to guide improvements in their own practice. When teachers recognize that knowledge for improvement is something they can generate, rather than something that must be handed to them by so-called experts, they are on a new professional trajectory (Franke, Carpenter, Fennema, Ansell, & Behrend, 1998). They are on the way to building a true profession of teaching, a profession in which members take responsibility for steady and lasting improvement. They are building a new culture of teaching.

REFERENCES ∎

Cohen, D. K. & Barnes, C. A. (1993). Pedagogy and policy. In D. K. Cohen, M. W. McLaughlin, & J. E. Talbert (Eds.), *Teaching for understanding: Challenges for policy and practice* (pp. 207–239). San Francisco: Jossey-Bass.

Darling-Hammond, L. & Sykes, G. (Eds.). (1999). *Teaching as the learning profession: Handbook of policy and practice.* San Francisco: Jossey-Bass.

Fey, J. T. (1979). Mathematics teaching today: Perspective from three national surveys. *Arithmetic Teacher, 27*(2), 10–14.

Franke, M. L., Carpenter, T. P., Fennema, E., Ansell, E., & Behrend, J. (1998). Understanding teachers' self-sustaining, generative change in the context of professional development. *Teaching and Teacher Education, 14,* 67–80.

Gallimore, R. G. (1996). Classrooms are just another cultural activity. In D. L. Speece & B. K. Keough (Eds.), *Research on classroom ecologies: Implications for inclusion of children with learning disabilities* (pp. 229–250). Mahwah, NJ: Lawrence Erlbaum Associates.

Gonzales, P., Calsyn, C., Jocelyn, L., Mak, K., Kastberg, D., Arafeh, S., et al. (2000). *Pursuing excellence: Comparisons of international eighth-grade mathematics and science achievement from a U.S. perspective, 1995 and 1999.* (NCES 2001–028). Washington, DC: U.S. Department of Education, National Center for Education Statistics.

Hiebert, J., Gallimore, R., Garnier, H., Givvin, K. B., Hollingsworth, H., Jacobs, J., et al. (2003a). *Teaching mathematics in seven countries: Results from the TIMSS 1999 video study.* (NCES 2003–013). Washington, DC: U.S. Department of Education, National Center for Education Statistics.

Hiebert, J., Gallimore, R., Garnier, H., Givvin, K. B., Hollingsworth, H., Jacobs, J., et al. (2003b, June). Understanding and improving mathematics teaching: Highlights from the TIMSS 1999 Video Study. *Phi Delta Kappan, 84*(10), 768–775.

Hiebert, J., Morris, A. K., & Glass, B. (2003, September). Learning to learn to teach: An "experiment" model for teaching and teacher preparation in mathematics. *Journal of Mathematics Teacher Education, 6*(3), 201–222.

Kazemi, E. & Franke, M. L. (in press). Teacher learning in mathematics: Using student work to promote collective inquiry. *Journal of Mathematics Teacher Education.*

Kilpatrick, J., Swafford, J., & Findell, B. (Eds.). (2001). *Adding it up: Helping children learn mathematics.* Washington, DC: National Academy Press.

Loveless, T. (Ed.). (2001). *The great curriculum debate: How should we teach reading and math?* Washington, DC: Brookings Institution.

National Council of Teachers of Mathematics. (2000). *Principles and standards for school mathematics.* Reston, VA: Author.

Roth, K. J., Druker, S. L., Garnier, H., Lemmens, M., Kawanaka, T., Rasmussen, D., et al. (in press). *Teaching science in five countries: Results from the TIMSS 1999 video study.* Washington, DC: U.S. Department of Education, National Center for Education Statistics.

Silver, E. A. & Kenney, P. A. (Eds.). (2000). *Results from the seventh mathematics assessment of the National Assessment of Educational Progress.* Reston, VA: National Council of Teachers of Mathematics.

Sparks, D. & Loucks-Horsley, S. (1990). Models of staff development. In W. R. Houston (Ed.), *Handbook of research on teacher education.* New York: Macmillan.

Stigler, J. W. & Hiebert, J. (1999). *The teaching gap: Best ideas from the world's teachers for improving education in the classroom.* New York: Free Press.

Stigler, J. W. & Hiebert, J. (2004, February). Improving mathematics teaching. *Educational Leadership, 61*(5), 12–17.

READING 2.4

Mathematics for the Moment, or the Millennium?

Jo Boaler

People in California are worried about the mathematical performance of their children. So worried that debates about the "right" way to teach mathematics have become so metaphorically bloody they have been termed the "math wars." Much of this concern has stemmed from students' performance on state and national tests, but nobody seems to have stopped at any point to question the value of the type of knowledge assessed on these tests. I would like to halt the debate for a moment in order to pose this question: Is success on a short, procedural test the measure we want to adopt to assess the effectiveness of our students' learning? In other words, do these tests assess the sort of knowledge use, critical thought, and reasoning that is needed by learners moving into the 21st century?

One of my concerns in this area is that the current debate about standards assumes there to be one form of knowledge that is unproblematically assessed within tests. This is despite the fact that a large body of research from psychological and educational fields shows the existence of different forms of knowledge. There is also increasing evidence that students can be very successful on standard, closed tests with a knowledge that is highly inert and that they are unable to use in more unusual and demanding situations (such as those encountered in the workplace).

Test knowledge, in other words, is often the sort of knowledge that is nontransferable and is useful for little more than taking tests. To demonstrate what I mean, I would like to describe the results of a research project that monitored the learning of students who experienced completely different mathematics teaching approaches over a three-year period. In response to these different approaches, the students developed different forms of knowledge and understanding that had enormous implications for their effectiveness in real-world situations.

Two schools in England were the focus for this research. In one, the teachers taught mathematics using whole-class teaching and textbooks, and the students were tested frequently. The students were taught in tracked groups, standards of discipline were high, and the students worked hard. The second school was chosen because its approach to mathematics teaching was completely different. Students there worked on open-ended projects in heterogeneous groups, teachers used a variety of methods, and discipline was extremely relaxed. Over a three-year period, I monitored groups of students at both schools, from the age of 13 to age 16. I watched more than 100 lessons at each school, interviewed the students, gave out questionnaires, conducted various assessments of the students' mathematical knowledge, and analyzed their responses to Britain's national school-leaving examination in mathematics.

Source: As first appeared in *Education Week*, March 31, 1999. Reprinted with permission from the author, Dr. Jo Boaler.

At the beginning of the research period, the students at the two schools had experienced the same mathematical approaches and, at that time, they demonstrated the same levels of mathematical attainment on a range of tests. There also were no differences in sex, ethnicity, or social class between the two groups. At the end of the three-year period, the students had developed in very different ways. One of the results of these differences was that students at the second school—what I will call the project school, as opposed to the textbook school—attained significantly higher grades on the national exam. This was not because these students knew more mathematics, but because they had developed a different form of knowledge.

At the textbook school, the students were motivated and worked hard, they learned all the mathematical procedures and rules they were given, and they performed well on short, closed tests. But various forms of evidence showed that these students had developed an inert, procedural knowledge that they were rarely able to use in anything other than textbook and test situations. In applied assessments, many were unable to perceive the relevance of the mathematics they had learned and so could not make use of it. Even when they could see the links between their textbook work and more-applied tasks, they were unable to adapt the procedures they had learned to fit the situations in which they were working.

> Is success on a short, procedural test the measure we want to adopt to assess the effectiveness of our students' learning?

The students themselves were aware of this problem, as the following description by one student of her experience of the national exam shows: "Some bits I did recognize, but I didn't understand how to do them, I didn't know how to apply the methods properly."

In real-world situations, these students were disabled in two ways. Not only were they unable to use the math they had learned because they could not adapt it to fit unfamiliar situations, but they also could not see the relevance of this acquired math knowledge from school for situations outside the classroom. "When I'm out of here," said another student, "the math from school is nothing to do with it, to tell you the truth. Most of the things we've learned in school we would never use anywhere."

Students from this school reported that they could see mathematics all around them, in the workplace and in everyday life, but they could not see any connection between their school math and the math they encountered in real situations. Their traditional, class-taught mathematics instruction had focused on formalized rules and procedures, and this approach had not given them access to depth of mathematical understanding. As a result, they believed that school mathematical procedures were a specialized type of school code—useful only in classrooms. The students thought that success in math involved learning, rehearsing, and memorizing standard rules and procedures. They did not regard mathematics to be a thinking subject. As one girl put it, "In math you have to remember; in other subjects you can think about it."

The math teaching at this textbook school was not unusual. Teachers there were committed and hard-working, and they taught the students different mathematical procedures in a clear and straightforward way. Their students were relatively capable on narrow mathematical tests, but this capability did not transfer to open, applied, or real-world situations. The form of knowledge they had developed was remarkably ineffective. At the project school, the situation was very different. And the students' significantly higher grades on the national exit exam were only a small indication of their mathematical competence and confidence.

The project school's students and teachers were relaxed about work. Students were not introduced to any standard rules or procedures (until a few weeks before the examinations), and they did not work through textbooks of any kind. Despite the fact that these students were not particularly work-oriented, however, they attained higher grades than the hard-working students at the textbook school on a range of different problems and applied assessments. At both schools, students had similar grades on short written tests taken immediately after finishing work. But students at the textbook school soon forgot what they had learned. The project students did not. The important difference between the environments of the two schools that caused this difference in retention was not related to standards of teaching but to different approaches, in particular the requirement that the students at the project-based school work on a variety of mathematical tasks and think for themselves.

When I asked students at the two schools whether mathematics was more about thinking or memorizing, 64 percent of the textbook students chose memorizing, compared with only 35 percent of the project-based students. The students at the project school were less concerned about memorizing rules and procedures, because they knew they could think about different situations and adapt what they had learned to fit new and demanding problems. On the national examination, three times as many students from the heterogeneous groups in the project school as those in the tracked groups in the textbook school attained the highest possible grade. The project approach was also more equitable, with girls and boys attaining the different grades in equal proportions.

It would be easy to dismiss the results of this study because it was focused on only two schools, but the textbook school was not unusual in the way its teachers taught mathematics. And the in-depth nature of the study meant that it was possible to consider and isolate the reasons why students responded to this approach in the way that they did. The differences in the performance of the students at the two schools did not spring from "bad" teaching at the textbook school, but from the limitations of drawing upon only one teaching method. To me, it does not make any sense to set any one particular teaching method against another and argue about which one is best. Different teaching methods do different things. We may as well argue that a hammer is better than a drill. Part of the success of the project school came from the range of different methods its teachers employed and the different activities students worked on.

Some proponents of traditional teaching want students to follow the same textbook method all of the time. A few students are successful in such an approach, but the vast majority develop a limited, procedural form of knowledge. This kind of knowledge may result in enhanced performances on some tests, but the aim of schools must surely be to equip students with a capability and intellectual power that will transcend the boundaries of the classroom.

Session 3

How Can Assessment Support Learning and Instruction?

(Formative Assessment)

The primary use of assessment today is to measure the success of students, teachers, and schools in order to inform decisions about accountability. Tests are seen simply as an index of our success (or failure), and it is assumed that setting high standards will prompt greater effort on the part of students, teachers, and schools.

There is a great need to balance the enormous attention currently paid to *summative* assessments, particularly large-scale standardized tests, with an in-depth look at formative assessments based in the classroom. Research suggests that schools could "realize unprecedented gains in achievement if we turn the current day-to-day classroom assessment process into a more powerful tool for learning" (Stiggins, 2002, p. 761). In addition, classroom assessment is within the direct purview of teachers and administrators—whereas there is relatively little teachers and principals can do to modify or adjust the current demand for external large-scale assessments.

This session is designed to offer the opportunity to rethink current uses of assessment and to explore assessment as a tool for learning. Following the first two sessions of *Secondary Lenses on Learning*, whose foci were on content and instruction, the third session is built around assessment, the third axis of a complete three-dimensional teaching and learning system. Like the previous topics of content and instruction, there are many points along this axis on which a session might be built. Rather than try to touch on each of these points, in the interest of offering an experience with greater depth, the authors have chosen to make *formative* assessment the primary focus of this session.

This session offers the opportunity to do the following:

- Explore the scope, audience, and purposes of student assessment
- Review research findings on the role of assessment in supporting student learning
- Consider formative assessment practices that benefit student learning

Readings and Focus Questions to Prepare for Session 3

(Two Homework Readings)

In preparation for the third session, please read the following two articles and prepare the focus questions that follow.

Reading 3.1   Stiggins, R. J. (2002). Assessment crisis: The absence of assessment for learning. *Phi Delta Kappan, 83*(10), 758–776.

Reading 3.2   Black, P., Harrison, C., Lee, C., Marshall, B., & Wiliam, D. (2004). Working inside the black box: Assessment for learning in the classroom. *Phi Delta Kappan, 83*(1), 8–21.

READING 3.1 FOCUS QUESTIONS

1. According to Stiggins (2002), where are schools now with respect to their use of assessment and what is the impact of these choices on learning?

2. What opportunities does Stiggins suggest exist for improving our current uses of assessment?

Mark those paragraphs or short sections that relate to your notes. Be prepared to discuss them with other participants.

READING 3.1

Assessment Crisis

The Absence of Assessment FOR Learning

Richard J. Stiggins

If we wish to maximize student achievement in the U.S., we must pay far greater attention to the improvement of classroom assessment, Mr. Stiggins warns. Both assessment of learning and assessment for learning are essential. But one is currently in place, and the other is not.

A real voyage of discovery consists not of seeking new landscapes but of seeing through new eyes.

—Marcel Proust

If we are finally to connect assessment to school improvement in meaningful ways, we must come to see assessment through new eyes. Our failure to find a potent connection has resulted in a deep and intensifying crisis in assessment in American education. Few elected officials are aware of this crisis, and almost no school officials know how to address it. Our current assessment systems are harming huge numbers of students for reasons that few understand. And that harm arises directly from our failure to balance our use of standardized tests and classroom assessments in the service of school improvement. When it comes to assessment, we have been trying to find answers to the wrong questions.

Politicians routinely ask, How can we use assessment as the basis for doling out rewards and punishments to increase teacher and student effort? They want to know how we can intensify the intimidation associated with annual testing so as to force greater achievement. How we answer these questions will certainly affect schools. But that impact will not always be positive. Moreover, politicians who ask such questions typically look past a far more important pair of prior questions: How can we use assessment to help all our students *want* to learn? How can we help them feel *able* to learn? Without answers to these questions, there will be no school improvement. I explain why below.

School administrators in federal, state, and local education agencies contribute to our increasingly damaging assessment crisis when they merely bow to politicians' beliefs and focus unwaveringly on the question of how to make our test scores go up. To be sure, accountability for student learning is important. I am not opposed to high-stakes testing to verify school quality—as long as the tests are of sound quality.[1] However, our concern for test scores must be preceded by a consideration of more fundamental questions: Are our current approaches to assessment improving student learning? Might other approaches to assessment have a greater impact? Can we design state and district assessment systems that

Source: Stiggins, R. J. (2002). Assessment crisis: The absence of assessment for learning. *Phi Delta Kappan, 83*(10), 758–776. Reprinted by permission of the author.

have the effect of helping our students want to learn and feel able to learn?

Furthermore, the measurement community, of which I am a member, also has missed an essential point. For decades, our priorities have manifested the belief that our job is to discover ever more sophisticated and efficient ways of generating valid and reliable test scores. Again, to be sure, accurate scores are essential. But there remains an unasked prior question: How can we maximize the positive impact of our scores on learners? Put another way, How can we be sure that our assessment instruments, procedures, and scores serve to help learners want to learn and feel able to learn?

We are a nation obsessed with the belief that the path to school improvement is paved with better, more frequent, and more intense standardized testing. The problem is that such tests, ostensibly developed to "leave no student behind," are in fact causing major segments of our student population to be left behind because the tests cause many to give up in hopelessness—just the opposite effect from that which politicians intended.

Student achievement suffers because these once-a-year tests are incapable of providing teachers with the moment-to-moment and day-to-day information about student achievement that they need to make crucial instructional decisions. Teachers must rely on classroom assessment to do this. The problem is that teachers are unable to gather or effectively use dependable information on student achievement each day because of the drain of resources for excessive standardized testing. There are no resources left to train teachers to create and conduct appropriate classroom assessments. For the same reasons, district and building administrators have not been trained to build assessment systems that balance standardized tests and classroom assessments. As a direct result of these chronic, long-standing problems, our classroom, building, district, state, and national assessment systems remain in constant crisis, and students suffer the consequences. All school practitioners know this, yet almost no politicians do.

We know how to build healthy assessment environments that can meet the information needs of all instructional decision makers, help students want to learn and feel able to learn, and thus support unprecedented increases in student achievement. But to achieve this goal, we must put in place the mechanisms that will make healthy assessment possible. Creating those mechanisms will require that we begin to see assessment through new eyes. The well-being of our students depends on our willingness to do so.

THE EVOLUTION OF OUR VISION OF ■
EXCELLENCE IN ASSESSMENT

The evolution of assessment in the United States over the past five decades has led to the strongly held view that school improvement requires:

- the articulation of higher achievement *standards,*
- the transformation of those expectations into rigorous *assessments,* and
- the expectation of *accountability* on the part of educators for student achievement, as reflected in test scores.

Standards frame accepted or valued definitions of academic success. Accountability compels attention to these standards as educators plan and deliver instruction in the classroom. Assessment provides the evidence of success on the part of students, teachers, and the system.

To maximize the energy devoted to school improvement, we have "raised the bar" by setting world-class standards for student achievement, as opposed to minimum competencies. To further intensify the impact of our standards and assessments, policy makers often attach the promise of rewards for schools that produce high scores and sanctions for schools that do not.

In this context, we rely on high-stakes assessments *of learning* to inform our decisions about accountability. These tests tell us how much students have learned, whether standards are being met, and whether educators have done the job they were hired to do.

Such assessments of learning have been the norm throughout the U.S. for decades. We began with standardized college admissions tests in the early decades of the last century, and this use of testing continues essentially unchanged today. But these tests are not used merely for college admission. For decades, we have ranked states according to average SAT scores.

Meanwhile, in response to demands for accountability in public schools in the 1960s, we launched districtwide standardized testing programs that also remain in place today. In the 1970s, we began the broad implementation of statewide testing programs, and these programs have spread throughout the land. Also in the 1970s and extending into the 1980s, we added a national assessment program that continues to this day. During the 1990s, we became deeply involved and invested in international assessment programs. Across the nation, across the various levels of schooling, and over the decades, we have invested billions of dollars to ensure the accuracy of the scores on these assessments of learning. Now in 2002, President Bush has signed a school reform measure that requires standardized testing of every pupil in the U.S. in mathematics and reading every year in grades 3 through 8, once again revealing our faith in assessment as a tool for school improvement.

In the context of school improvement, we have seen assessment merely as an index of the success of our efforts. It is testimony to our societal belief in the power of standardized tests that we would permit so many levels of testing to remain in place, all at the same time and at very high cost. Clearly, over the decades, we have believed that by checking achievement status and reporting the results to the public we can apply the pressure needed to intensify—and thus speed—school improvement. At the same time, we have believed that providing policy makers and practicing educators with test results can inform the critically important school improvement decisions that are made at district, state, and federal levels.

■ THE FLAW IN THE VISION

The assessment environment described above is a direct manifestation of a set of societal beliefs about what role assessment ought to play in American schools. Over the decades, we have succeeded in carrying these beliefs to unfortunate extremes.

For example, we have believed that assessment should serve two purposes: inform decisions and motivate learning. With respect to the former, we have built our assessment systems around the belief that the most important decisions are made by those program planners and policy makers whose actions affect the broadest range of classrooms and students. The broader the reach of the decision makers (across an entire school district or state), the more weight we have given to meeting their information needs first. This is the foundation of our strong belief in the power of standardized tests. These are the tests that provide comparable data that can be aggregated across schools, districts, and states to inform far-reaching programmatic decisions.

With respect to the use of assessment to motivate, we all grew up in classrooms in which our teachers believed that the way to maximize learning was to maximize anxiety, and assessment has always been the great intimidator. Because of their own very successful experiences in ascending to positions of leadership and authority, most policy makers and school leaders share the world view that, "when the going gets tough, the tough get going." They learned that the way to succeed when confronted with a tougher challenge is to redouble your efforts—work harder and work smarter. If you do so, you win. And so, they contend, the way to cause students to learn more—and thus the way to improve schools— is to confront them with a tougher challenge. This will cause them to redouble their efforts, they will learn more, their test scores will go up, and the schools will become more effective. We can motivate students to greater effort, they believe, by "setting higher academic standards," "raising the bar," and implementing more high-stakes testing. This is the foundation of our belief in the power of accountability-oriented standardized tests to drive school improvement.

In point of fact, when some students are confronted with the tougher challenge of high-stakes testing, they do redouble their efforts, and they do learn more than they would have without the added incentive. Please note, however, that I said this is true for "some students."

Another huge segment of our student population, when confronted with an even tougher challenge than the one that it has already been failing at, will not redouble its efforts—a point that most people are missing. These students will see both the new high standards and the demand for higher test scores as unattainable for them, and they will *give up in hopelessness.*

Many political and school leaders have never experienced the painful, embarrassing, and discouraging trauma of chronic and public academic failure. As a result, they have no way of anticipating or understanding how their high-stakes testing program, whether local or statewide, could lead to even greater failure for large numbers of students. But tapping the intimidation power of standardized tests for public accountability has an effect on the success of this segment of the student population that is exactly the opposite of what we intend.

Thus it is folly to build our assessment environments on the assumption that standardized testing will have the same effect on all students. It will not. Some students approach the tests with a strong personal academic history and an expectation of success. Others approach them with a personal history and expectation of very painful failure. Some come to slay the dragon, while others expect to be devoured by it. As a result, high-stakes assessment will enhance the learning of some while discouraging others and causing them to give up. Yet, as they attempt to weave assessment into the school improvement equation, federal, state, and local policy makers seem unable to understand or to accommodate this difference.

A MORE POWERFUL VISION ■

There is another way in which assessment can contribute to the development of effective schools that has been largely ignored in the evolution of the standards, assessment, and accountability movement described above. We can also use assessments *for learning.*[2] If assessments *of learning* provide evidence of achievement for public reporting, then assessments *for learning* serve to help students learn more. The crucial distinction is between assessment to determine the status of learning and assessment to promote greater learning.

Assessments *of* and *for* learning are both important. Since we in the U.S. already have many assessments *of* learning in place, if we are to balance the two, we must make a much stronger investment in assessment *for* learning. We can realize unprecedented gains in achievement if we turn the current day-to-day classroom assessment process into a more powerful tool for learning. We know that schools will be held accountable for raising test scores. Now we must provide teachers with the assessment tools needed to do the job.

It is tempting to equate the idea of assessment *for learning* with our more common term, "formative assessment." But they are not the same. Assessment *for learning* is about far more than testing more frequently or providing teachers with evidence so that they can revise instruction, although these steps are part of it. In addition, we now understand that assessment *for learning* must involve students in the process.

When they assess *for learning,* teachers use the classroom assessment process and the continuous flow of information about student achievement that it provides in order to advance, not merely check on, student learning. They do this by

- understanding and articulating *in advance of teaching* the achievement targets that their students are to hit;
- informing their students about those learning goals, *in terms that students understand,* from the very beginning of the teaching and learning process;
- becoming assessment literate and thus able to transform their expectations into assessment exercises and scoring procedures that *accurately reflect student achievement;*
- using classroom assessments to *build students' confidence* in themselves as learners and help them take responsibility for their own learning, so as to lay a foundation for lifelong learning;
- translating classroom assessment results into frequent *descriptive feedback* (versus judgmental feedback) for students, providing them with specific insights as to how to improve;
- continuously *adjusting instruction* based on the results of classroom assessments;
- engaging students in *regular self-assessment,* with standards held constant so that students can watch themselves grow over time and thus feel in charge of their own success; and
- actively involving students in *communicating* with their teacher and their families about their achievement status and improvement.

In short, the effect of assessment *for learning,* as it plays out in the classroom, is that students keep learning and remain confident that they can continue to learn at productive levels if they keep trying to learn. In other words, students don't give up in frustration or hopelessness.

■ ARE TEACHERS READY?

Few teachers are prepared to face the challenges of classroom assessment because they have not been given the opportunity to learn to do so. It is currently the case that only about a dozen states explicitly require competence in assessment as a condition to be licensed to teach. Moreover, there is no licensing examination in place at the state or federal level in the U.S. that verifies competence in assessment. Thus teacher preparation programs have taken little note of competence in assessment, and the vast majority of programs fail to provide the assessment literacy required to enable teachers to engage in assessment *for learning.* It has been so for decades.

Furthermore, lest we believe that teachers can turn to their principals for help, it is currently the case that almost no states require competence in assessment as a condition to be licensed as a principal or school administrator at any level. Consequently, assessment training is almost nonexistent in administrator training programs. It has been so for decades.

Thus we remain a national faculty that is unschooled in the principles of sound assessment—whether assessment *of* or *for* learning. This fact has been a matter of record for decades. To date, as a nation, we have invested almost nothing in assessment *for learning*. Teachers rarely have the opportunity to learn how to use assessment as a teaching and learning tool. And our vigorous efforts to assess learning through our various layers of standardized tests cannot overcome the effects of this reality.

As a result of this state of affairs, we face the danger that student progress may be mismeasured, day to day, in classrooms across the nation. That means that all the critically important day-to-day instructional decisions made by students, teachers, and parents may be based on misinformation about student success. The result is the misdiagnosis of student needs, students' misunderstanding of their own ability to learn, miscommunication to parents and others about student progress, and virtually no effective assessment *for learning* in classrooms. The extremely harmful consequences for student learning are obvious.

RELEVANT POSITION STATEMENTS ■

The dire consequences of this assessment crisis and the urgent need for action have not gone unnoticed. For example, during the 1990s, virtually every professional association that had anything to do with teaching adopted standards of professional competence for teachers that include an assessment component.[3] This group included the American Federation of Teachers (AFT), the National Education Association (NEA), the Council of Chief State School Officers, the National Board for Professional Teaching Standards, and the National Council on Measurement in Education (NCME).

The documents that were issued included a collaborative statement of assessment competencies for teachers developed by a joint committee representing AFT, NEA, and NCME.[4] In addition to other standards, this joint statement expects teachers to be trained to choose and develop proper assessment methods; to administer, score, and interpret assessment results; to connect those results to specific decisions; to assign grades appropriately; and to communicate effectively about student achievement. It is troubling to realize that these standards are more than a decade old and still have had little impact on the preparation of teachers and administrators.

In its 2001 report, the Committee on the Foundations of Assessment of the National Research Council advanced recommendations for the development of assessment in American schools that included the following:

> *Recommendation 9: Instruction in how students learn and how learning can be assessed should be a major component of teacher preservice and professional development programs.* This training should be linked to actual experience in classrooms in assessing and interpreting the development of student competence. To ensure that this occurs, state and national standards for teacher licensure and program accreditation should include specific requirements focused on the proper integration of learning and assessment in teachers' educational experience.[5]

> *Recommendation 11: The balance of mandates and resources should be shifted from an emphasis on external forms of assessment to an increased emphasis on classroom formative assessment designed to assist learning.*[6]

Similarly, the Commission on Instructionally Supportive Assessment convened by the American Association of School Administrators, the National Association of Elementary School Principals, the National Association of Secondary School Principals, the NEA, and the National Middle School Association included the following in its list of nine requirements for state-mandated accountability tests:

> *Requirement 8: A state must ensure that educators receive professional development focused on how to optimize children's learning based on the results of instructionally supportive assessment.*[7]

We understand what teachers need to know and the proficiencies that they need to develop in order to be able to establish and maintain productive assessment environments. The challenge we face is to provide the opportunity for teachers to master those essential classroom assessment competencies. The depth of this challenge becomes clear when we realize that we must provide opportunities both for new teachers to gain these competencies before they enter the classroom and for experienced teachers who had no chance to master them during their training to gain them as well.

■ BALANCING ASSESSMENTS *OF* AND *FOR* LEARNING

Therefore, our national assessment priority should be to make certain that assessments both *of* and *for* learning are accurate in their depiction of student achievement and are used to benefit students. Since our standardized assessments *of learning* have been developed by professionals and are currently in place, they are poised to detect any improvements in the level or rate of student achievement.

But these tests provide information only once a year, and we must not delude ourselves into believing that they can serve all assessment purposes. They can reflect large-group increases or decreases in learning on an annual basis, and they can serve as gatekeepers for high-stakes decisions. They cannot inform the moment-to-moment, day-to-day, and week-to-week instructional decisions faced by students and teachers seeking to manage the learning process as it unfolds. They cannot diagnose student needs during learning, tell students what study tactics are or are not working, or keep parents informed about how to support the work of their children. These kinds of uses require assessments *for learning.* The critical question for school improvement is, What would happen to standardized test scores if we brought assessments *for learning* online as a full partner in support of student learning? Several published reviews of research reveal the startling and very encouraging answer.

In 1984 Benjamin Bloom provided a summary of research comparing standard whole-class instruction (the control condition) with two experimental interventions, a mastery learning environment and one-on-one tutoring of individual students. One hallmark of both experimental conditions was the extensive use of classroom assessment *for learning* as a key part of the instructional process. The analyses revealed differences ranging from one to two standard deviations in student achievement attributable to differences between experimental and control conditions.[8]

In their 1998 research review, Paul Black and Dylan Wiliam examined the research literature on assessment worldwide, asking if improved formative (i.e., classroom) assessments yield higher student achievement as reflected in summative assessments. If so, they asked, what kinds of improvements in classroom assessment practice are likely to yield the greatest gains in achievement?

Black and Wiliam uncovered and then synthesized more than 250 articles that addressed these issues. Of these, several dozen directly addressed the question of the impact on student learning with sufficient scientific rigor and experimental control to permit firm conclusions. Upon pooling the information on the estimated effects of improved formative assessment on summative test scores, they reported unprecedented positive effects on student achievement. They reported effect sizes of one-half to a full standard deviation. Furthermore, Black and Wiliam reported that "improved formative assessment helps low achievers more than other students and so reduces the range of achievement while raising achievement overall."[9] This result has direct implications for districts seeking to reduce achievement gaps between minorities and other students. Hypothetically, if assessment *for learning,* as described above, became standard practice only in classrooms of low-achieving, low-socioeconomic-status students, the achievement gaps that trouble us so deeply today would be erased. I know of no other school improvement innovation that can claim effects of this nature or size.

To fully appreciate the magnitude of the effect sizes cited above, readers need to understand that a gain of one standard deviation, applied to the middle of the test score distribution on commonly used standardized achievement tests, can yield average gains of more than 30 percentile points, two grade-equivalents, or 100 points on the SAT scale. Black and Wiliam report that gains of this magnitude, if applied to the most recent results of the Third International Mathematics and Science Study, would have raised a nation in the middle of the pack among the 42 participating countries (where the U.S. is ranked) to the top five.

This research reveals that these achievement gains are maximized in contexts where educators increase the accuracy of classroom assessments, provide students with frequent informative feedback (versus infrequent judgmental feedback), and involve students deeply in the classroom assessment, record keeping, and communication processes. In short, these gains are maximized where teachers apply the principles of assessment *for learning.*

Black and Wiliam conclude their summary of self-assessment by students as follows:

> Thus self-assessment by pupils, far from being a luxury, is in fact *an essential component of formative assessment.* When anyone is trying to learn, feedback about the effort has three elements: redefinition of the *desired goal,* evidence about *present position,* and some understanding of a *way to close the gap between the two.* All three must be understood to some degree by anyone before he or she can take action to improve learning.[10] (Emphasis in original.)

ANTICIPATING THE BENEFITS OF BALANCE ■

Students benefit from assessment *for learning* in several critical ways. First, they become more confident learners because they get to watch themselves succeeding. This success permits them to take the risk of continuing to try to learn. The result is greater achievement for all students—especially low achievers, which helps reduce the achievement gap between middle-class and low-socioeconomic-status students. Furthermore, students come to understand what it means to be in charge of their own learning—to monitor their own success and make decisions that bring greater success. This is the foundation of lifelong learning.

Teachers benefit because their students become more motivated to learn. Furthermore, their instructional decisions are informed by more accurate information about student achievement. Teachers also benefit from the savings in time that result from their ability to develop and use classroom assessments more efficiently.

Parents benefit as well in seeing higher achievement and greater enthusiasm for learning in their children. They also come to understand that their children are learning to manage their own lifelong learning.

School administrators and instructional leaders benefit from the reality of meeting accountability standards and from the public recognition of doing so. Political officials benefit in the same way. When schools work more effectively, both political leaders and school leaders are recognized as contributing to that outcome.

In short, everyone wins. There are no losers. But the price that we must pay to achieve such benefits is an investment in teachers and their classroom assessment practices. We must initiate a program of professional development specifically designed to give teachers the expertise they need to assess *for learning.*

■ AN ACTION PLAN

If we wish to maximize student achievement in the U.S., we must pay far greater attention to the improvement of classroom assessment. Both assessment *of learning* and assessment *for learning* are essential. One is in place; the other is not. Therefore, we must

- match every dollar invested in instruments and procedures intended for assessment *of learning* at national, state, and local levels with another dollar devoted to the development of assessment *for learning.*
- launch a comprehensive, long-term professional development program at the national, state, and local levels to foster literacy in classroom assessment for teachers, allocating sufficient resources to provide them with the opportunity to learn and grow professionally;
- launch a similar professional development program in effective large-scale and classroom assessment for state, district, and building administrators, teaching them how to provide leadership in this area of professional practice;
- change teacher and administrator licensing standards in every state and in all national certification contexts to reflect an expectation of competence in assessment both *of* and *for* learning; and
- require all teacher and administrator preparation programs to ensure that graduates are assessment literate—in terms both of promoting and of documenting student learning.

Federal education officials, state policy makers, and local school leaders must allocate resources in equal proportions to ensure the accuracy and effective use of assessments both *of* and *for* learning. Only then can we reassure families that their children are free from the harm that results from the mismeasurement of their achievement in schools. Only then can we maximize students' confidence in themselves as learners. Only then can we raise achievement levels for all students and "leave no child behind."

■ NOTES

1. For specific standards of quality, refer to Commission on Instructionally Supportive Assessment, *Building Tests to Support Instruction and Accountability* (Washington, D.C.: AASA, NAESP, NASSP, NEA, and NMSA, 2001).

2. This term was coined by Assessment Reform Group, *Assessment for Learning: Beyond the Black Box* (Cambridge: School of Education, Cambridge University, 1999).

3. See the special section on Quality Teaching for the 21st Century in the November 1996 *Phi Delta Kappan*, pp. 190–227.

4. American Federation of Teachers, National Council on Measurement in Education, and National Education Association, "Standards for Teacher Competence in Educational Assessment of Students," *Educational Measurement Issues and Practice*, vol. 9, no. 4, 1990, pp. 30–32.

5. James W. Pellegrina, Naomi Chudowsky, and Robert Glaser, eds., *Knowing What Students Know: The Science and Design of Educational Assessment* (Washington, D.C.: National Academy Press, 2001), p. 14.

6. Ibid.

7. Commission on Instructionally Supportive Assessment, p. 25.

8. Benjamin Bloom, "The Search for Methods of Group Instruction as Effective as One-on-One Tutoring," *Educational Leadership*, May 1984, pp. 4–17.

9. Paul Black and Dylan Wiliam, "Inside the Black Box: Raising Standards Through Classroom Assessment," *Phi Delta Kappan*, October 1998, p. 141. Their work is reported in more detail in idem, "Assessment and Classroom Learning," *Assessment in Education*, March 1998, pp. 7–74.

10. Black and Wiliam, "Inside the Black Box," p. 143.

READING 3.2 FOCUS QUESTIONS

1. How do Black et al. define "formative assessment"?

2. How does each of the four formative assessment tools help to support student learning? Why might adjusting classroom practices to include these tools contribute to significant changes in student achievement?

3. In what ways are these formative assessment activities related to typical instructional activities?

Mark those paragraphs or short sections that relate to your notes. Be prepared to discuss them with other participants.

READING 3.2

Working Inside the Black Box

Assessment for Learning in the Classroom

Paul Black

Christine Harrison

Clare Lee

Bethan Marshall

Dylan Wiliam

In their widely read article "Inside the Black Box," Mr. Black and Mr. Wiliam demonstrated that improving formative assessment raises student achievement. Now they and their colleagues report on a follow-up project that has helped teachers change their practice and students change their behavior so that everyone shares responsibility for the students' learning.

In 1998 "Inside the Black Box," the predecessor of this article, appeared in this journal.[1] Since then we have learned a great deal about the practical steps needed to meet the purpose expressed in the article's subtitle: "raising standards through classroom assessment."

In the first part of "Inside the Black Box," we set out to answer three questions. The first was, Is there evidence that improving formative assessment raises standards? The answer was an unequivocal yes, a conclusion based on a review of evidence published in over 250 articles by researchers from several countries.[2] Few initiatives in education have had such a strong body of evidence to support a claim to raise standards.

This positive answer led naturally to the second question: Is there evidence that there is room for improvement? Here again, the available evidence gave a clear and positive answer, presenting a detailed picture that identified three main problems: (1) the assessment methods that teachers use are not effective in promoting good learning, (2) grading practices tend to emphasize competition rather than personal improvement, and (3) assessment feedback often has a negative impact, particularly on low-achieving students, who are led to believe that they lack "ability" and so are not able to learn.

However, for the third question—Is there evidence about how to improve formative assessment?—the answer was less clear. While the evidence provided many ideas for improvement, it lacked the detail that would enable teachers to implement those ideas in their classrooms. We argued that teachers needed "a variety of living examples of implementation."

■ THE JOURNEY: LEARNING WITH TEACHERS

Since 1998, we have planned and implemented several programs in which groups of teachers in England have been supported in developing innovative practices in their classrooms, drawing on the ideas in the original article. While this effort has amply confirmed the original proposals, it has also added a wealth of new findings that are both practical and authentic. Thus we are now confident that we can set out sound advice for the improvement of classroom assessment.

The KMOFAP Project

To carry out the exploratory work that was called for, we needed to collaborate with a group of teachers willing to take on the risks and extra work involved, and we needed to secure support from their schools and districts. Funding for the project was provided through the generosity of the Nuffield Foundation, and we were fortunate to find two school districts—Oxfordshire and Medway, both in southern England—whose supervisory staff members understood the issues and were willing to work with us. Each district selected three secondary schools: Oxfordshire chose three coeducational schools, and Medway chose one coeducational school, one boys' school, and one girls' school. Each school selected two science teachers and two mathematics teachers. We discussed the plans with the principal of each school, and then we called the first meeting of the 24 teachers. So in January 1999, the King's-Medway-Oxfordshire Formative Assessment Project (KMOFAP) was born.

Full details of the project can be found in our book, *Assessment for Learning: Putting It into Practice.*[3] For the present purpose, it is the outcomes that are important. The findings presented here are based on the observations and records of visits to classrooms by the King's College team, records of meetings of the whole group of teachers, interviews with and writing by the teachers themselves, and a few discussions with student groups. Initially, we worked with science and mathematics teachers, but the work has been extended more recently to involve teachers of English in the same schools and teachers of other subjects in other schools.

Spreading the Word

Throughout the development of the project, we have responded to numerous invitations to talk to other groups of teachers and advisers. Indeed, over five years we have made more than 400 such contributions. These have ranged across all subjects and across both primary and secondary phases. In addition, there has been sustained work with some primary schools. All of this gives us confidence that our general findings will be of value to all, although some important details may differ for different age groups and subjects. Furthermore, a group at Stanford University obtained funding from the National Science Foundation to set up a similar development project, in collaboration with King's, in schools in California. Extension of our own work has been made possible by this funding. And we also acknowledge support from individuals in several government agencies who sat on the project's steering group, offered advice and guidance, and helped ensure that assessment for learning (see "Assessment for Learning," below) is a central theme in education policy in England and Scotland.

> **Assessment for Learning**
>
> Assessment for learning is any assessment for which the first priority in its design and practice is to serve the purpose of promoting students' learning. It thus differs from assessment designed primarily to serve the purposes of accountability, or of ranking, or of certifying competence. An assessment activity can help learning if it provides information that teachers and their students can use as feedback in assessing themselves and one another and in modifying the teaching and learning activities in which they are engaged. Such assessment becomes "formative assessment" when the evidence is actually used to adapt the teaching work to meet learning needs.

The Learning Gains

From our review of the international research literature, we were convinced that enhanced formative assessment would produce gains in student achievement, even when measured in such narrow terms as scores on state-mandated tests. At the outset we were clear that it was important to have some indication of the kinds of gains that could be achieved in real classrooms and over an extended period of time. Since each teacher in the project was free to choose the class that would work on these ideas, we discussed with each teacher what data were available within the school, and we set up a "mini-experiment" for each teacher.

> Many teachers do not plan and conduct classroom dialogue in ways that might help students to learn.

Each teacher decided what was to be the "output" measure for his or her class. For Grade 10 classes, this was generally the grade achieved on the national school-leaving examination taken when students are 16 (the General Certificate of Secondary Education or GCSE). For Grade 8 classes, it was generally the score or level achieved on the national tests administered to all 14-year-olds. For other classes, a variety of measures were used, including end-of-module-test scores and marks on the school's end-of-year examinations.

For each project class, the teacher identified a comparison class. In some cases this was a parallel class taught by the same teacher in previous years (and in one case in the same year). In other cases, we used a parallel class taught by a different teacher or, failing that, a nonparallel class taught by the same or a different teacher. When the project and the control classes were not strictly parallel, we controlled for possible differences in prior achievement by the use of "input" measures, such as school test scores from the previous year or other measures of aptitude.

This approach meant that the size of the improvement was measured differently for each teacher. For example, a grade-10 project class might outperform the comparison class by half a GCSE grade, but another teacher's grade-8 project class might outscore its control class by 7% on an end-of-year exam. To enable us to aggregate the results, we adopted the common measuring stick of the "standardized effect size," calculated by taking the difference between the scores of the experimental and control groups and then dividing this number by the standard deviation (a measure of the spread in the scores of the groups).

For the 19 teachers on whom we had complete data, the average effect size was around 0.3 standard deviations. Such improvements, produced across a school, would raise a school in the lower quartile of the national performance tables to well above average. Thus it is clear that, far from having to choose between teaching well and getting good test scores, teachers can actually improve their students' results by working with the ideas we present here.

■ HOW CHANGE CAN HAPPEN

We set out our main findings about classroom work under four headings: questioning, feedback through grading, peer- and self-assessment, and the formative use of summative tests. Most of the quotations in the following pages are taken directly from pieces written by the teachers. The names of the teachers and of the schools are pseudonyms, in keeping with our policy of guaranteeing anonymity.

Questioning

Many teachers do not plan and conduct classroom dialogue in ways that might help students to learn. Research has shown that, after asking a question, many teachers wait less than one second and then, if no answer is forthcoming, ask another question or answer the question themselves.[4] A consequence of such short "wait time" is that the only questions that "work" are those that can be answered quickly, without thought—that is, questions calling for memorized facts. Consequently, the dialogue is at a superficial level. As one teacher put it:

> I'd become dissatisfied with the closed Q & A style that my unthinking teaching had fallen into, and I would frequently be lazy in my acceptance of right answers and sometimes even tacit complicity with a class to make sure none of us had to work too hard. . . . They and I knew that if the Q & A wasn't going smoothly, I'd change the question, answer it myself, or only seek answers from the "brighter students." There must have been times (still are?) where an outside observer would see my lessons as a small discussion group surrounded by many sleepy onlookers. (James, Two Bishops School)

The key to changing such a situation is to allow longer wait time. But many teachers find it hard to do this, for it requires them to break their established habits. Once they change, the expectations of their students are challenged:

> Increasing waiting time after asking questions proved difficult to start with due to my habitual desire to "add" something almost immediately after asking the original question. The pause after asking the question was sometimes "painful." It felt unnatural to have such a seemingly "dead" period, but I persevered. Given more thinking time, students seemed to realize that a more thoughtful answer was required. Now, after many months of changing my style of questioning, I have noticed that most students will give an answer and an explanation (where necessary) without additional prompting. (Derek, Century Island School)

One teacher summarized the overall effects of her efforts to improve the use of question-and-answer dialogue in the classroom as follows:

> *Questioning.* My whole teaching style has become more interactive. Instead of showing how to find solutions, a question is asked and pupils are given time to explore answers together. My year 8 [grade 7] target class is now well-used to this way of working. I find myself using this method more and more with other groups.

> *No Hands.* Unless specifically asked, pupils know not to put their hands up if they know the answer to a question. All pupils are expected to be able to answer at any time even if it is an "I don't know."

Supportive Climate. Pupils are comfortable with giving a wrong answer. They know that these can be as useful as correct ones. They are happy for other pupils to help explore their wrong answers further. (Nancy, Riverside School)

Increasing the wait time can help more students become involved in discussions and increase the length of their replies. Another way to broaden participation is to ask students to brainstorm ideas, perhaps in pairs, for two to three minutes before the teacher asks for contributions. Overall, a consequence of such changes is that teachers learn more about the students' prior knowledge and about any gaps and misconceptions in that knowledge, so that teachers' next moves can better address the learners' real needs.

To exploit such changes means moving away from the routine of limited factual questions and refocusing attention on the quality and the different functions of classroom questions. Consider, for example, the use of a "big question": an open question or a problem-solving task that can set the scene for a lesson and evoke broad discussion or prompt focused small-group discussions. However, if this strategy is to be productive, both the responses that the task might generate and the ways of following up on these responses have to be anticipated. Collaboration between teachers to exchange ideas and experiences about good questions is very valuable. The questions themselves then become a more significant part of teaching, with attention focused on how they can be constructed and used to explore and then develop students' learning. Here's one teacher's thinking on the matter:

> I chose a year-8, middle-band group and really started to think about the type of questions I was asking—were they just instant one-word answers—what were they testing—knowledge or understanding—was I giving the class enough time to answer the question, was I quickly accepting the correct answer, was I asking the girl to explain her answer, how was I dealing with a wrong answer? When I really stopped to think, I realized that I could make a very large difference to the girls' learning by using all their answers to govern the pace and content of the lesson. (Gwen, Waterford School)

Effective questioning is also an important aspect of the impromptu interventions teachers conduct once the students are engaged in an activity. Asking simple questions, such as "Why do you think that?" or "How might you express that?" can become part of the interactive dynamic of the classroom and can provide an invaluable opportunity to extend students' thinking through immediate feedback on their work.

Overall, the main suggestions for action that have emerged from the teachers' experience are

- More effort has to be spent in framing questions that are worth asking, that is, questions that explore issues that are critical to the development of students' understanding.
- Wait time has to be increased to several seconds in order to give students time to think, and everyone should be expected to have an answer and to contribute to the discussion. Then all answers, right or wrong, can be used to develop understanding. The aim is thoughtful improvement rather than getting it right the first time.
- Follow-up activities have to be rich, in that they create opportunities to extend students' understanding.

Put simply, the only point of asking questions is to raise issues about which a teacher needs information or about which the students need to think. When such changes have been made, experience demonstrates that students become more active participants and come to realize that learning may depend less on their capacity to spot the right answer and more on their readiness to express and discuss their own understanding. The teachers also shift in their role, from presenters of content to leaders of an exploration and development of ideas in which all students are involved.

Feedback Through Grading

When giving students feedback on both oral and written work, it is the nature, rather than the amount, of commentary that is critical. Research experiments have established that, while student learning can be advanced by feedback through comments, the giving of numerical scores or grades has a negative effect, in that students ignore comments when marks are also given.[5] These results often surprise teachers, but those who have abandoned the giving of marks discover that their experience confirms the findings: students do engage more productively in improving their work.

Many teachers will be concerned about the effect of returning students' work with comments but no scores or grades. There may be conflicts with school policy:

> My marking has developed from comments with targets and grades, which is the school policy, to comments and targets only. Pupils do work on targets and corrections more productively if no grades are given. Clare [Lee] observed on several occasions how little time pupils spent reading my comments if there were grades given as well. My routine is now, in my target class, (i) to not give grades, only comments; (ii) to give comments that highlight what has been done well and what needs further work; and (iii) to give the minimum follow-up work expected to be completed next time I mark the books. (Nancy, Riverside School)

Initial fears about how students might react turned out to be unjustified, and neither parents nor school inspectors have reacted adversely. Indeed, the provision of comments to students helps parents to focus on the learning issues rather than on trying to interpret a score or grade. We now believe that the effort that many teachers devote to grading homework may be misdirected. A numerical score or a grade does not tell students how to improve their work, so an opportunity to enhance their learning is lost.

A commitment to improve comments requires more work initially, as teachers have to attend to the quality of the comments that they write on students' work. Collaboration between teachers in sharing examples of effective comments can be very helpful, and experience will lead to more fluency. There is, however, more involved because comments become useful feedback only if students use them to guide further work, so new procedures are needed.

> After the first INSET [inservice training meeting] I was keen to try out a different way of marking books to give pupils more constructive feedback. I was keen to try and have a more easy method of monitoring pupils' response to my comments without having to trawl through their books each time to find out if they'd addressed my comments. I implemented a comment sheet at the back of my year-8 class' books. It is A4 [letter] in size, and the left-hand side is for my comments, and the right-hand side is for the pupils to demonstrate by a reference to the page in their books where I can find the evidence to say whether they have done the work. . . . The comments have become more meaningful as the time has gone on, and the books still take me only one hour to mark. (Sian, Cornbury Estate School)

We have encountered a variety of ways of accommodating the new emphasis on comments. Some teachers have ceased assigning scores or grades at all, some teachers enter scores in their own record books but do not write them in the students' books, others give a score or grade only after a student has responded to the teacher's comments. Some teachers spend more time on certain pieces of work to ensure that they obtain good feedback and, to make time for this, either do not mark some pieces, or look at only a third of their students' books each week, or involve the students in checking the straightforward tasks.

A particularly valuable method is to devote some lesson time to rewriting selected pieces of work, so that emphasis can be put on feedback for improvement within a supportive environment. This practice can change students' expectations about the purposes of class work and homework.

As they tried to create useful feedback comments, many of the project teachers realized that they needed to reassess the work that they had asked students to undertake. They found that some tasks were useful in revealing students' understandings and misunderstandings, while others focused mainly on conveying information. So some activities were eliminated, others modified, and new and better tasks actively sought.

Overall the main ideas for improvement of feedback can be summarized as follows:

- Written tasks, alongside oral questioning, should encourage students to develop and show understanding of the key features of what they have learned.
- Comments should identify what has been done well and what still needs improvement and give guidance on how to make that improvement.
- Opportunities for students to respond to comments should be planned as part of the overall learning process.

The central point here is that, to be effective, feedback should cause thinking to take place. The implementation of such reforms can change both teachers' and students' attitudes toward written work: the assessment of students' work will be seen less as a competitive and summative judgment and more as a distinctive step in the process of learning.

Peer Assessment and Self-Assessment

Students can achieve a learning goal only if they understand that goal and can assess what they need to do to reach it. So self-assessment is essential to learning.[6] Many teachers who have tried to develop their students' self-assessment skills have found that the first and most difficult task is to get students to think of their work in terms of a set of goals. Insofar as they do so, they begin to develop an overview of that work that allows them to manage and control it for themselves. In other words, students are developing the capacity to work at a metacognitive level.

In practice, peer assessment turns out to be an important complement to self-assessment. Peer assessment is uniquely valuable because students may accept criticisms of their work from one another that they would not take seriously if the remarks were offered by a teacher. Peer work is also valuable because the interchange will be in language that students themselves naturally use and because students learn by taking the roles of teachers and examiners of others.[7] One teacher shared her positive views of peer assessment:

As well as assessing and marking (through discussion and clear guidance) their own work, they also assess and mark the work of others. This they do in a very mature and sensible way, and this has proved to be a very worthwhile experiment.

The students know that homework will be checked by themselves or another girl in the class at the start of the next lesson. This has led to a well-established routine and only on extremely rare occasions have students failed to complete the work set. They take pride in clear and well-presented work that one of their peers may be asked to mark. Any disagreement about the answer is thoroughly and openly discussed until agreement is reached. (Alice, Waterford School)

The last sentence of this teacher's comments brings out an important point: when students do not understand an explanation, they are likely to interrupt a fellow student when they would not interrupt a teacher. In addition to this advantage, peer assessment is also valuable in placing the work in the hands of the students. The teacher can be free to observe and reflect on what is happening and to frame helpful interventions:

We regularly do peer marking—I find this very helpful indeed. A lot of misconceptions come to the fore, and we then discuss these as we are going over the homework. I then go over the peer marking and talk to pupils individually as I go round the room. (Rose, Brownfields School)

However, self-assessment will happen only if teachers help their students, particularly the low achievers, to develop the skill. This can take time and practice:

The kids are not skilled in what I am trying to get them to do. I think the process is more effective long term. If you invest time in it, it will pay off big dividends, this process of getting the students to be more independent in the way that they learn and to take the responsibility themselves. (Tom, Riverside School)

One simple and effective idea is for students to use "traffic light" icons, labeling their work green, yellow, or red according to whether they think they have good, partial, or little understanding. These labels serve as a simple means of communicating students' self-assessments. Students may then be asked to justify their judgments in a peer group, thus linking peer assessment and self-assessment. This linkage can help them develop the skills and the detachment needed for effective self-assessment.

Another approach is to ask students first to use their "traffic light" icons on a piece of work and then to indicate by hands-up whether they put a green, yellow, or red icon on it. The teacher can then pair up the greens and the yellows to help one another deal with their problems, while the red students meet with the teacher as a group to deal with their deeper problems. For such peer-group work to succeed, many students will need guidance about how to behave in groups, including such skills as listening to one another and taking turns.

In some subjects, taking time to help students understand scoring rubrics is also very helpful. Students can be given simplified versions of the rubrics teachers use, or they can be encouraged to rewrite them or even to create their own. Again, peer assessment and self-assessment are intimately linked. Observers in several language arts classrooms saw children apply to their own work lessons they had learned in peer assessment. A frequently heard comment was "I didn't do that either" or "I need to do that too."

Students' reflection about their understanding can also be used to inform future teaching, and their feedback can indicate in which areas a teacher needs to spend more time. A useful guide is to ask students to "traffic light" an end-of-unit test at the beginning of the unit: the yellow and red items can be used to adjust priorities within the teaching plan. Our experience leads us to offer the following recommendations for improving classroom practice:

- The criteria for evaluating any learning achievements must be made transparent to students to enable them to have a clear overview both of the aims of their work and of what it means to complete it successfully. Such criteria may well be abstract, but concrete examples should be used in modeling exercises to develop understanding.
- Students should be taught the habits and skills of collaboration in peer assessment, both because these are of intrinsic value and because peer assessment can help develop the objectivity required for effective self-assessment.
- Students should be encouraged to keep in mind the aims of their work and to assess their own progress toward meeting these aims as they proceed. Then they will be able to guide their own work and so become independent learners.

The main point here is that peer assessment and self-assessment make distinct contributions to the development of students' learning. Indeed, they secure aims that cannot be achieved in any other way.

The Formative Use of Summative Tests

The practices of self-assessment and peer assessment can be applied to help students prepare for tests, as in tackling the following problem:

> [The students] did not mention any of the reviewing strategies we had discussed in class. When questioned more closely, it was clear that many spent their time using very passive revision [reviewing] techniques. They would read over their work doing very little in the way of active revision or reviewing of their work. They were not transferring the active learning strategies we were using in class to work they did at home. (Tom, Riverside School)

To remedy this situation, students can be asked to "traffic light" a list of key words or the topics on which the test will be set. The point of this exercise is to stimulate the students to reflect on where they feel their learning is secure, which they mark green, and where they need to concentrate their efforts, in yellow and red. These traffic lights then form the basis of a review plan. Students can be asked to identify questions on past tests that probe their "red" areas. Then they can work with textbooks and in peer groups to ensure that they can successfully answer those questions.

The aftermath of tests can also be an occasion for formative work. Peer marking of test papers can be helpful, as with normal written work, and it is particularly useful if students are required first to formulate a scoring rubric—an exercise that focuses attention on the criteria of quality relevant to their productions. After peer marking, teachers can reserve their time for discussion of the questions that give widespread difficulty, while peer tutoring can tackle those problems encountered by only a minority of students.

One other finding that has emerged from research studies is that students trained to prepare for examinations by generating and then answering their own questions outperformed comparable groups who prepared in conventional ways.[8] Preparing test questions helps students develop an overview of the topic:

> Pupils have had to think about what makes a good question for a test and in doing so need to have a clear understanding of the subject material. As a development of this, the best questions have been used for class tests. In this way, the pupils can see that their work is valued, and I can make an assessment of the progress made in these areas. When going over the test, good use can be made of group work and

discussions between students concentrating on specific areas of concern. (Angela, Cornbury Estate School)

Developments such as these challenge common expectations. Some have argued that formative and summative assessments are so different in their purpose that they have to be kept apart, and such arguments are strengthened when one experiences the harmful influence that narrow, high-stakes summative tests can have on teaching. However, it is unrealistic to expect teachers and students to practice such separation, so the challenge is to achieve a more positive relationship between the two. All of the ways we have described for doing so can be used for tests in which teachers have control over the setting and the marking. But their application may be more limited for tests in which the teacher has little or no control.

Overall, the main possibilities for improving classroom practice by using summative tests for formative purposes are as follows:

- Students can be engaged in a reflective review of the work they have done to enable them to plan their revision effectively.
- Students can be encouraged to set questions and mark answers so as to gain an understanding of the assessment process and further refine their efforts for improvement.
- Students should be encouraged through peer assessment and self-assessment to apply criteria to help them understand how their work might be improved. This may include providing opportunities for students to rework examination answers in class.

The overall message is that summative tests should become a positive part of the learning process. Through active involvement in the testing process, students can see that they can be the beneficiaries rather than the victims of testing, because tests can help them improve their learning.

■ REFLECTIONS: SOME UNDERLYING ISSUES

The changes that are entailed by improved assessment for learning have provoked us and the teachers involved to reflect on deeper issues about learning and teaching.

Learning Theory

One of the most surprising things that happened during the early INSET sessions was that the participating teachers asked us to run a session on the psychology of learning. In retrospect, perhaps we should not have been so surprised at this request. After all, we had stressed that feedback functioned formatively only if the information fed back to the learner was used by the learner in improving performance. But while one can work out after the fact whether or not any feedback has had the desired effect, what the teachers needed was a way to give their students feedback that they knew in advance was going to be useful. To do that they needed to build up models of how students learn.

So the teachers came to take greater care in selecting tasks, questions, and other prompts to ensure that students' responses actually helped the teaching process. Such responses can "put on the table" the ideas that students bring to a learning task. The key to effective learning is then to find ways to help students restructure their knowledge to build in new and more powerful ideas. In the KMOFAP classrooms, as the teachers came to listen more attentively to the students' responses, they began to appreciate more fully that learning was not a process of passive reception of knowledge, but one in which the learners were active in creating their own understandings. Put simply, it became clear that, no matter what the pressure to achieve good test scores, learning must be done by the student.

Students came to understand what counted as good work through exemplification. Sometimes this was done through focused whole-class discussion around a particular example; at other times it was achieved through the use of sets of criteria to assess the work of peers.

Engaging in peer assessment and self-assessment is much more than just checking for errors or weaknesses. It involves making explicit what is normally implicit, and thus it requires students to be active in their learning. As one student wrote:

> After a pupil marking my investigation, I can now acknowledge my mistakes easier. I hope that it is not just me who learned from the investigation but the pupil who marked it did also. Next time I will have to make my explanations clearer, as they said "It is hard to understand". . . . I will now explain my equation again so it is clear.

The students also became much more aware of when they were learning and when they were not. One class, which was subsequently taught by a teacher not emphasizing assessment for learning, surprised that teacher by complaining: "Look, we've told you we don't understand this. Why are you going on to the next topic?" While students who are in tune with their learning can create difficulties for teachers, we believe that these are exactly the kinds of problems we should want to have.

Subject Differences

From hearing about research and discussing ideas with other colleagues, the teachers built up a repertoire of generic skills. They planned their questions, allowed appropriate wait time, and gave feedback that was designed to cause thinking. They ensured that students were given enough time during lessons to evaluate their own work and that of others.

However, after a while it became clear that these generic strategies could go only so far. Choosing a good question requires a detailed knowledge of the subject, but not necessarily the knowledge that is gained from advanced study in a subject. A high level of qualification in a subject is less important than a thorough understanding of its fundamental principles, an understanding of the kinds of difficulties that students might have, and the creativity to be able to think up questions that stimulate productive thinking.[9] Furthermore, such pedagogical content knowledge is essential in interpreting responses. That is, what students say will contain clues to aspects of their thinking that may require attention, but picking up on these clues requires a thorough knowledge of common difficulties in learning the subject. Thus, while the general principles of formative assessment apply across all subjects, the ways in which they manifest themselves in different subjects may differ. We have encountered such differences in making comparisons between teachers of mathematics, science, and language arts.

In mathematics, students have to learn to use valid procedures and to understand the concepts that underpin them. Difficulties can arise when students learn strategies that apply only in limited contexts and do not realize that they are inadequate elsewhere. Questioning must then be designed to bring out these strategies for discussion and to explore problems in understanding the concepts so that students can grasp the need to change their thinking. In such learning, there is usually a well-defined correct outcome. In more open-ended exercises, as in investigations of the application of mathematical thinking to everyday problems, there may be a variety of good solutions. Then an understanding of the criteria of quality is harder to achieve and may require joint discussion of examples and of the abstract criteria that they exemplify.

In science, the situation is very similar. There are many features of the natural world for which science provides a "correct" model or explanation. However, outside school, many students acquire different ideas. For example, some students come to believe that animals are living because they move but that trees and flowers are not because they don't. Or students may believe that astronauts seem almost weightless on the moon because there is no air present. Many of these "alternative conceptions" can be anticipated, for they have been well documented. What has also been documented is that the mere presentation of the "correct" view has been shown to be ineffective. The task in such cases is to open up discussion of such ideas and then provide feedback that challenges them by introducing new pieces of evidence and argument that support the scientific model.

There are other aspects for which an acceptable outcome is less well defined. As in mathematics, open-ended investigations call for different approaches to formative assessment. Even more open are issues about social or ethical implications of scientific achievements, for there is no "answer." Thus such work has to be "open" in a more fundamental way. Then the priority in giving feedback is to challenge students to tease out their assumptions and to help them to be critical about the quality of any arguments.

> The priority in giving feedback is to challenge students to tease out their assumptions and to help them be critical about the quality of arguments.

Peer assessment and self-assessment have a long history in language arts. Both the nature of the subject and the open outcome of many of the tasks characteristically make such practices central to one of the overall aims of the discipline, which is to enhance the critical judgment of the students.

A second important function of peer assessment and self-assessment was introduced by Royce Sadler, who argued that criteria alone are unhelpful in judging the quality of a piece of work or in guiding progression, because there will always be too many variables.[10] The key lies in knowing how to interpret the criteria in any particular case, which involves "guild knowledge." Teachers acquire this knowledge through assessing student work, and it is this process that allows them to differentiate between grades and to gain a sense of how progress is achieved. Peer assessment and self-assessment provide similar opportunities for students to be apprenticed into the guild, provided the criteria of quality are clearly communicated.

In language arts, as in science and mathematics, attention needs to be paid to the central activities. Those that are the most successful are those rich tasks that provide students with an opportunity either to extend their understanding of a concept within the text or to "scaffold" their ideas before writing. Characteristically, these include small-group and pair work, with the results often being fed back into a whole-class discussion. Again, this type of work is not uncommon in language arts, the skill being to make the task sufficiently structured to scaffold learning but not so tightly defined as to limit thinking. Such activities not only provide students with a chance to develop their understanding through talk, but they also provide the teacher with the opportunity to give feedback during the course of a lesson through further questioning and guidance. The better the quality of the task, the better the quality of the interventions.

Differences between learning tasks can be understood in terms of a spectrum. At one end are "closed" tasks with a single well-defined outcome; at the other are "open" tasks with a wide range of acceptable outcomes. Tasks in language arts—for example, the writing of a poem—are mainly at the open end. But there are closed components even for such tasks— for example, the observance of grammatical or genre conventions. Tasks in, say, mathematics are more often closed, but applications of mathematics to everyday problems can require open-ended evaluations. Thus, in varying measure, the guidance needed for these two types of learning work will be needed in all subjects.

Despite these differences, experience has shown that the generic skills that have been developed do apply across subjects. One of the project's science teachers gave a talk to the whole staff about his experiences using some of the generic skills that we've been discussing and subsequently found how such practices distributed themselves throughout the disciplines:

> Art and drama teachers do it all the time, so do technology teachers (something to do with open-ended activities, long project times, and perhaps a less cramped curriculum?). But an English teacher came up to me today and said, "Yesterday afternoon was fantastic. I tried it today with my year 8s, and it works. No hands up, and giving them time to think. I had fantastic responses from kids who have barely spoken in class all year. They all wanted to say something, and the quality of answers was brilliant. This is the first time for ages that I've learnt something new that's going to make a real difference to my teaching." (James, Two Bishops School)

Motivation and Self-Esteem

Learning is not just a cognitive exercise: it involves the whole person. The need to motivate students is evident, but it is often assumed that offering such extrinsic rewards as grades, gold stars, and prizes is the best way to do it. However, there is ample evidence to challenge this assumption.

Students will invest effort in a task only if they believe that they can achieve something. If a learning exercise is seen as a competition, then everyone is aware that there will be losers as well as winners, and those who have a track record as losers will see little point in trying. Thus the problem is to motivate everyone, even though some are bound to achieve less than others. In tackling this problem, the type of feedback given is very important. Many research studies support this assertion. Here are a few examples:

- Students who are told that feedback "will help you to learn" learn more than those who are told that "how you do tells us how smart you are and what grades you'll get." The difference is greatest for low achievers.[11]
- Students given feedback as marks are likely to see it as a way to compare themselves with others (ego involvement); those given only comments see it as helping them to improve (task involvement). The latter group outperforms the former.[12]

> Students given marks are likely to see it as a way to compare themselves with others; those given only comments see it as helping them to improve. The latter group outperforms the former.

- In a competitive system, low achievers attribute their performance to lack of "ability"; high achievers, to their effort. In a task-oriented system, all attribute performance to effort, and learning is improved, particularly among low achievers.[13]
- A comprehensive review of research studies of feedback found that feedback improved performance in 60% of the studies. In the cases where feedback was not helpful, the feedback turned out to be merely a judgment or grade with no indication of how to improve.[14]

In general, feedback given as rewards or grades enhances ego involvement rather than task involvement. It can focus students' attention on their "ability" rather than on the importance of effort, thus damaging the self-esteem of low achievers and leading to problems of "learned helplessness."[15] Feedback that focuses on what needs to be done can encourage all to believe that they can improve. Such feedback can enhance learning, both directly through the effort that can ensue and indirectly by supporting the motivation to invest such effort.[16]

■ THE BIG IDEA: FOCUS ON LEARNING

Our experiences in the project all point to the need to rethink a teacher's core aim: enhancing student learning. To achieve this goal calls for a willingness to rethink the planning of lessons, together with a readiness to change the roles that both teacher and students play in supporting the learning process.

A Learning Environment: Principles and Plans

Improvement in classroom learning requires careful forethought.

> Actually thinking about teaching has meant that I have been able to come up with ideas and strategies to cope with whatever has arisen and has contributed greatly to my professional development. I now think more about the content of the lesson. The influence has shifted from "What am I going to teach and what are the pupils going to do?" toward "How am I going to teach this and what are the pupils going to learn?" (Susan, Waterford School)

One purpose of a teacher's forethought is to plan to improve teaching actions. So, for example, the planning of questions and activities has to be in terms of their learning function.

> I certainly did not spend sufficient time developing questions prior to commencing my formative training. . . . Not until you analyze your own questioning do you realize how poor it can be. I found myself using questions to fill time and asking questions which required little thought from the students. When talking to students, particularly those who are experiencing difficulties, it is important to ask questions which get them thinking about the topic and will allow them to make the next step in the learning process. (Derek, Century Island School)

Of equal importance is concern for the quality of the responses that teachers make, whether in dialogue or in feedback on written assignments. Effective feedback should make more explicit to students what is involved in a high-quality piece of work and what steps they need to take to improve. At the same time, feedback can enhance students' skills and strategies for effective learning.

There is also a deeper issue here. A learning environment has to be "engineered" to involve students more actively in the learning tasks. The emphasis has to be on students' thinking and making that thinking public. As one teacher put it:

> There was a definite transition at some point, from focusing on what I was putting into the process, to what the students were contributing. It became obvious that one way to make a significant sustainable change was to get the students doing more of the thinking. I then began to search for ways to make the learning process more transparent to the students. Indeed, I now spend my time looking for ways to get students to take responsibility for their learning and at the same time making the learning more collaborative. (Tom, Riverside School)

Collaboration between teachers and students and between students and their peers can produce a supportive environment in which students can explore their own ideas, hear alternative ideas in the language of their peers, and evaluate them.

One technique has been to put the students into small groups and give each student a small part of the unit to explain to [his or her] colleagues. They are given a few minutes' preparation time, a few hints, and use of their exercise books. Then each student explains [his or her] chosen subject to the rest of the group. Students are quick to point out such things as, "I thought that the examples you chose were very good as they were not ones in our books. I don't think I would have thought of those." Or "I expected you to mention particles more when you were explaining the difference between liquids and gases." These sessions have proven invaluable—not only to me, in being able to discover the level of understanding of some students, but to the students too. (Philip, Century Island School)

An additional advantage of such an environment is that a teacher can work intensively with one group, challenging the ideas and assumptions of its members, knowing that the rest of the class members are also working hard.

So the main actions to be taken to engineer an effective learning environment are

- plan classroom activities to give students the opportunity to express their thinking so that feedback can help develop it;
- formulate feedback so that it guides improvement in learning;
- use activities that demand collaboration so that everyone is included and challenged and train students to listen to and respect one another's ideas; and
- be sure that students are active participants in the lessons and emphasize that learning may depend less on their capacity to spot the right answer and more on their readiness to express and discuss their own understanding.

A Learning Environment: Roles and Expectations

It is one thing to plan new types of classroom activity and quite another to put them into practice in ways that are faithful to the aims they were developed to serve. Here there are no recipes to follow in a uniform way. *Inside the Black Box* was clear in stating that the effective development of formative assessment would come about only if "each teacher finds his or her own ways of incorporating the lessons and ideas that are set out above into her or his own patterns of classroom work."

A second principle is that the learning environment envisaged requires a classroom culture that may well be unfamiliar and disconcerting for both teachers and students. The effect of the innovations implemented by our teachers was to change the "classroom contract" between the teacher and the student—the rules that govern the behaviors that are expected and seen as legitimate by teachers and students.

The students have to change from behaving as passive recipients of the knowledge offered by the teacher to becoming active learners who can take responsibility for and manage their own learning.

For the teachers, courage is necessary. One of the striking features of the project was that, in the early stages, many participants described the new approach as "scary" because they felt they were going to lose control of their classes. Toward the end of the project, they spoke not of losing control but of sharing responsibility for the students' learning with the class—exactly the same process but viewed from two very different perspectives. In one perspective, the teachers and students are in a delivery/recipient relationship; in the other, they are partners in pursuit of a shared goal:

What formative assessment has done for me is made me focus less on myself but more on the children. I have had the confidence to empower the students to take it forward. (Robert, Two Bishops School)

What has been happening here is that everybody's expectations—that is, what teachers and students think that being a teacher or being a student requires you to do—have been altered. While it can seem daunting to undertake such changes, they do not have to happen suddenly. Changes with the KMOFAP teachers came slowly and steadily, as experience developed and confidence grew in the use of the various strategies for enriching feedback and interaction. For example, many teachers started by using questions to encourage thinking. Then they improved their oral and written feedback so that it brought thinking forward and went on to develop peer and self-assessment.

To summarize, expectations and classroom culture can be changed:

- by changing the "classroom contract" so that all expect that teacher and students work together for the same end: the improvement of everyone's learning;
- by empowering students to become active learners, thus taking responsibility for their own learning;
- by incorporating the changes in the teacher's role one step at a time, as they seem appropriate; and
- by sustained attention to and reflection on ways in which assessment can support learning.

■ WHAT YOU CAN DO

To incorporate some of the ideas about formative assessment into your own practice, the first step is to reflect on what you are now doing. Discussion with colleagues and observation of one another's lessons can help spark such reflection.

A next step must be to try out changes. Wholesale change can be too risky and demanding, so it is often best to think of one thing you feel confident to try—be it "traffic lights," peer assessment, improved questioning, whatever—and simply try it. If you are a teacher in a middle school or high school, try it with just one group. Or if you are an elementary teacher, try it in just one subject area. We found that, as teachers gained confidence in the power of allowing students to say what they know and what they need to know, the teachers decided that they should extend assessment for learning to the whole of their teaching.

Taking on further strategies will then lead to further progress. When several colleagues are collaborating, each starts with a different strategy and then shares findings. This process should lead to the explicit formulation of an "action plan," comprising a range of strategies to be used, in combination, preferably starting with a class at the beginning of the school year. The first reason to start at the beginning of the year is so that there can be time to accustom both teacher and students to a new way of working. The second is that it can be very difficult to change the established habits and routines in the middle of a year. The experience of a year's sustained work, with only a few classes, preferably alongside similar efforts by colleagues, can provide a firm basis for subsequent adoption of new practices on a wider scale.

Collaboration with a group trying out similar innovations is almost essential. Mutual observation and the sharing of ideas and experiences about the progress of action plans can provide the necessary support both with the tactics and at a strategic level. Support for colleagues is particularly important in overcoming those initial uncertainties when engaging in the risky business of changing the culture and expectations in the classroom.

As for any innovation, support from administrators is essential. One way administrators can support change of this kind is to help peer groups of teachers find time to meet on a regular basis. Opportunities should also be found for teachers to report to faculty and staff meetings.

The work of any group experimenting with innovations is an investment for the whole school, so that support should not be treated as indulgence for idiosyncratic practices. Indeed, such work should be integrated into a school improvement plan, with the expectation that the dissemination of fruitful practices will follow from the evaluation of a group's experiences.

> There may be a need to review school policies: an example would be a policy that, by demanding a grade on every piece of homework, prevents the serious use of comments.

At the same time, there may be a need to review current school policies because such policies can actually constrain the use of formative assessment. A notable example would be a policy that, by demanding that a score or grade be given on every piece of homework, prevents the serious use of comments. Five of the six schools in the KMOFAP project have, following the experience of their science and mathematics teachers, modified their policies to allow "comment only" marking; for two of these, the modification was that no scores or grades be given on homework throughout the school. In another example, a "target setting" system that required very frequent review was inhibiting any change in learning methods that might slow down immediate "progress" in order to produce medium- to long-term gains in learning skills. Those engaged in innovations may need formal exemption from such policies.

Thus support, evaluation, and subsequent dissemination of innovation in assessment for learning will be planned in a coherent way only if the responsibility for strategic oversight of the development is assigned to a member of the school leadership team. Our experience supports the view that to realize the promise of formative assessment by leaving a few keen individuals to get on with it would be unfair to them, while to do it by imposing a policy that requires all teachers to immediately change their personal roles and styles would be absurd.

What is needed is a plan, extending over at least three years, in which a few small groups are supported for a two-year exploration. These groups then form a nucleus of experience and expertise for disseminating their ideas throughout the school and for supporting colleagues in making similar explorations for themselves.

NOTES ■

1. Paul Black and Dylan Wiliam, "Inside the Black Box: Raising Standards Through Classroom Assessment," *Phi Delta Kappan,* October 1998, pp. 139–48. A version of this article has been published and widely sold in the United Kingdom. A booklet, published in 2002, has also been widely distributed in the UK. It covers the same issues as the article and bears the same title with the same authors. Both booklets, and further booklets in this series, are published by NFER-NELSON.

Only a few references to the literature are given here. Further information about publications and other resources can be obtained on the King's College website in the pages of the King's Formative Assessment Group. Some of the publications can be downloaded from this site: www.Kel.ac.uk/education/research/Kal.html.

2. Paul Black and Dylan Wiliam, "Assessment and Classroom Learning," *Assessment in Education,* March 1998, pp. 7–71.

3. Paul Black, Christine Harrison, Clare Lee, Bethan Marshall, and Dylan Wiliam, *Assessment for Learning: Putting It into Practice* (Buckingham, U.K.: Open University Press, 2003).

4. Mary Budd Rowe, "Wait Time and Rewards as Instructional Variables, Their Influence on Language, Logic, and Fate Control," *Journal of Research in Science Teaching,* vol. 11, 1974, pp. 81–94.

5. Ruth Butler, "Enhancing and Undermining Intrinsic Motivation: The Effects of Task-Involving and Ego-Involving Evaluation on Interest and Performance," *British Journal of Educational Psychology,* vol. 58, 1988, pp. 1–14.

6. Royce Sadler, "Formative Assessment and the Design of Instructional Systems," *Instructional Science,* vol. 18, 1989, pp. 119–44.

7. Royce Sadler, "Formative Assessment: Revisiting the Territory," *Assessment in Education*, vol. 5, 1998, pp. 77–84.

8. See, for example, Paul W. Foos, Joseph J. Mora, and Sharon Tkacz, "Student Study Techniques and the Generation Effect," *Journal of Educational Psychology*, vol. 86, 1994, pp. 567–76; and Alison King, "Facilitating Elaborative Learning Through Guided Student-Generated Questioning," *Educational Psychologist*, vol. 27, 1992, pp. 111–26.

9. See, for example, Mike Askew et al., *Effective Teachers of Numeracy: Final Report* (London: King's College London, School of Education, 1997). In this study, there was no correlation between the progress made by elementary school students in arithmetic and the highest level of mathematics studied by the teacher. Indeed, there was a nonsignificant negative correlation between the two. The students who made the most progress were taught by teachers without high levels of subject knowledge, but who emphasized the connections between mathematics concepts.

10. Sadler, "Formative Assessment and the Design of Instructional Systems."

11. Richard S. Newman and Mahna T. Schwager, "Students' Help Seeking During Problem Solving: Effects of Grade, Goal, and Prior Achievement," *American Educational Research Journal*, vol. 32, 1995, pp. 352–76.

12. Ruth Butler, "Task-Involving and Ego-Involving Properties of Evaluation: Effects of Different Feedback Conditions on Motivational Perceptions, Interest, and Performance," *Journal of Educational Psychology*, vol. 79, 1987, pp. 474–82.

13. Rhonda G. Craven, Herbert W. Marsh, and Raymond L. Debus, "Effects of Internally Focused Feedback on Enhancement of Academic Self-Concept," *Journal of Educational Psychology*, vol. 83, 1991, pp. 17–27.

14. Avraham N. Kluger and Angelo DeNisi, "The Effects of Feedback Interventions on Performance: A Historical Review, a Meta-Analysis, and a Preliminary Feedback Intervention Theory," *Psychological Bulletin*, vol. 119, 1996, pp. 254–84.

15. Carol S. Dweck, "Motivational Processes Affecting Learning," *American Psychologist* (Special Issue: Psychological Science and Education), vol. 41, 1986, pp. 1040–48.

16. Carol S. Dweck, *Self-Theories: Their Role in Motivation, Personality, and Development* (Philadelphia: Psychology Press, 2000).

Session 4

How Can We Hold High Expectations and Provide Strong Support for All Students?

(Equitable Practices)

Excellence in mathematics education rests on equity—high expectations, respect, understanding, and strong support for all students.

—The National Council of Teachers of
Mathematics' Position on Equity (2008)

While there is much in the lives of students and in society at large that is out of our schools' control, we are doing a disservice when we do not draw on what has been learned from decades of research and practice about what *can* be done to address the learning needs of students who have not experienced success in mathematics previously. We are unwittingly undermining potential opportunities for low-income and minority students when we buy into negative stereotypes about their academic ability, dilute critical content, and cluster them in low-ability mathematics classes staffed by teachers with relatively few years of experience. We are also missing critical opportunities when we don't bring individual students' experiences and insights into the center of our efforts to strengthen classroom practice and schoolwide systems.

In Session 4,

1. *We continue to develop a collective vision for school mathematics, with a focus on making significant mathematics accessible to all students.* What classroom-level approaches have been shown to be effective in addressing achievement imbalances? What conditions at the level of schoolwide systems are necessary to support such classroom practices so as to meet the needs of diverse learners?

2. *We seek to shake complacency with the status quo.* How might we reframe the stories we tell ourselves about our mathematics programs and students? Are we really doing OK by all students and according to what information? What counterindications should we be looking at? To what do we attribute the lack of success of subsets of our student population? What assumptions lie behind those attributions? What factors that *are* under our control might make a difference for these students?

3. *We reexamine what drives our planning for the mathematics program.* What information, in addition to quantitative data to track student progress, might we draw on in order to get

a more complete view of the various components of our own school's mathematics program? What possible leverage points does this information open up? Based on what we learn, what might be productive short- and long-term goals and actions? How can we build a process for continuous improvement into our mathematics program?

4. *We seek to move individual students, with all of their capabilities and difficulties, to the center of efforts to strengthen classroom practice and schoolwide systems.* In what ways might the learning climate of a school change (a) when the system is built around a belief that all students are capable of learning powerful and useful mathematics, (b) when appropriate support is provided to students when they struggle, (c) when student determination and effort result in high student achievement in mathematics, and (d) when students' experiences and insights are considered central to understanding what can be done to strengthen classroom practice and schoolwide systems, so as to address the needs of all learners?

This session offers participants the opportunity to do the following:

- Examine ways in which assumptions, attitudes, and expectations intersect with race, ethnicity, and social class to affect achievement, engagement, and curricular opportunities for various student groups
- Explore opportunities to address issues of equitable achievement at both the classroom level and at the schoolwide systems level
- Consider broadening sources of data used in assessing what helps and hinders mathematics learning and achievement

Readings and Focus Questions to Prepare for Session 4

(Readings 4.1 and 4.2 for All Participants and Readings 4.3, 4.4, and 4.5 to Be Divided Among Building Team Members)

*A*ll *participants* read the following and respond to focus questions on the template that accompany each reading:

Reading 4.1	Schoenfeld, A. H. (2002). Making mathematics work for all children: Issues of standards, testing, and equity. *Educational Researcher, 31*(1),13–25.
Reading 4.2	The Case of the Rafter School District

Divide the following three readings among members of your team, following the jigsaw format planned during the session. Be prepared to report to others on key elements of the reading, guided by the template that follows.

Reading 4.3	Ladson-Billings, G. (1997). It doesn't add up: African American students' mathematics achievement. *Journal for Research in Mathematics Education, 28*(6), 697–708.
Reading 4.4	Boaler, J. (2002). Learning from teaching: Exploring the relationship between reform curriculum and equity. *Journal for Research in Mathematics Education, 33*(4), 239–258.
Reading 4.5	Moschkovich, J. (2002). A situated and sociocultural perspective on bilingual mathematics learners. *Mathematical Thinking and Learning, 4*(2 & 3), 189–212.

READING 4.1 FOCUS QUESTIONS

1. What does Schoenfeld (2002) report about the performance differences between students who learn from traditional or reform curricula, on tests of basic skills and on tests of conceptual understanding and problem solving?

2. What conclusions about reform curricula and the performance gap between Whites and underrepresented minorities does Schoenfeld draw from research findings?

3. What four necessary conditions for providing high-quality mathematics instruction does Schoenfeld identify?

Conditions	Notes

Mark those paragraphs or short sections that relate to your notes. Be prepared to discuss them with other participants.

READING 4.1

Making Mathematics Work for All Children
Issues of Standards, Testing, and Equity

Alan H. Schoenfeld

"Mathematics Education is a civil rights issue," says civil rights leader Robert Moses, who argues that children who are not quantitatively literate may be doomed to second-class economic status in our increasingly technological society. The data have been clear for decades: poor children and children of color are consistently shortchanged when it comes to mathematics. More broadly, the type of mathematical sophistication championed in recent reform documents, such as the National Council of Teachers of Mathematics' (2000) Principles and Standards for School Mathematics, can be seen as a core component of intelligent decision making in everyday life, in the workplace, and in our democratic society. To fail children in mathematics, or to let mathematics fail them, is to close off an important means of access to society's resources. This article discusses the potential for providing high-quality mathematics instruction for all students. It addresses four conditions necessary for achieving this goal: high-quality curriculum; a stable, knowledgeable, and professional teaching community; high-quality assessment that is aligned with curricular goals; and stability and mechanisms for the evolution of curricula, assessment, and professional development. The goal of this article is to catalyze conversations about how to achieve sustained, beneficial changes.

Robert Moses (2001) argues,

> Today . . . the most urgent social issue affecting poor people and people of color is economic access. In today's world, economic access and full citizenship depend crucially on math and science literacy. I believe that the absence of math literacy in urban and rural communities throughout this country is an issue as urgent as the lack of Black voters in Mississippi was in 1961. (p. 5)

This is a powerful statement. In the simplest terms, Moses' argument is about economics and technology. Factory jobs, once "pure" physical labor, now have technological components; even forklifts in warehouses have computer modules, and the people who use the machines must be able to use the computer controls. Most important,

---

Source: Reprinted with permission from *Educational Researcher,* copyright 2002.

Author's Note: The author is grateful to Diane Briars for providing information about the Pittsburgh public schools. Thanks to Julia Aguirre, Claire Bove, Sally Goldstein, Ilana Horn, Cathy Kessel, Sue Magidson, Andy Porter, Ann Ryu, Natasha Speer, Elizabeth Stage, Joe Wagner, and Dan Zimmerlin for comments on earlier versions of this manuscript. Thanks also to the anonymous reviewers of this article and the editors of *Educational Researcher,* whose comments resulted in a significant reframing of the article.

the technological divide is going to widen over the coming years. Moses (2001) argues that those who are technologically literate will have access to jobs and economic enfranchisement, while those without such skills will not:

> Sixty percent of new jobs will require skills possessed by only 22 percent of the young people entering the job market now. These jobs require the use of a computer and pay about 15 percent more than jobs that do not. And those jobs that do not are dwindling. Right now, the Department of Labor says, 70 percent of all jobs require technology literacy; by the year 2010 *all* jobs will require significant technical skills. And if that seems unimaginable, consider this: the Department of Labor says that 80 percent of those future jobs *do not yet exist.* (pp. 8–9)

There are counterarguments to this position, perhaps the most common one being that technology is consistently being adapted to provide jobs for those who have minimal mathematical skills. Years ago, for example, McDonald's "solved" the problem of cashiers who had difficulty making change by introducing cash registers that had pictures of the items being sold on its buttons and that calculated change automatically. But this line of argument winds up in much the same place as Moses': those students with negligible skills wind up having access to the lowest paying jobs. In purely functional terms, mathematics has long been recognized as a *critical filter* (Sells, 1975, 1978). Course work in mathematics has traditionally been a gateway to technological literacy and to higher education. On such grounds alone, one could argue that there is a national obligation to insure that all students have access to high-quality mathematics instruction. The argument for economic enfranchisement is, however, only first among equals. As will be elaborated later in this article, making decisions in one's personal life, on the job, and in matters of public interest calls increasingly for quantitatively sophisticated reasoning. More than ever before, today's students need to learn to reason and communicate using mathematical ideas.

Mathematical literacy should be a goal for all students—so what makes it a civil rights issue? The answer becomes clear when one looks at the numbers. Disproportionate numbers of poor, African-American, Latino, and Native American students drop out of mathematics and perform below standard on tests of mathematical competency, and are thus denied both important skills and a particularly important pathway to economic and other enfranchisement (Madison & Hart, 1990; Miller, 1995; National Action Committee for Minorities in Engineering, 1997; National Commission on Mathematics and Science Teaching for the 21st Century, 2000; National Science Foundation [NSF], 2000). Hence conversations about the mathematical needs of American students must focus not only on what mathematics the students should learn, but also on how we as a nation can insure that all students have the opportunity to learn it.

This article addresses those issues. To set the stage it begins with a description of mathematics instruction over the second half of the 20th century, describing the nature of the mathematics studied and increasing perceptions through the 1980s of difficulties with the curriculum. There was unhappiness with the curriculum on a number of grounds: equity being first, a narrow content focus aimed at preparing students for college being second, and national security being third. Such discontent led to calls for reform, with the National Research Council (NRC) issuing *Everybody Counts* and the National Council of Teachers of Mathematics (NCTM) issuing *Curriculum and Evaluation Standards for School Mathematics* (the *Standards*) in 1989. On the basis of a decade's experience and research, NCTM issued a new vision statement, *Principles and Standards for School Mathematics* (*Principles and Standards*) in 2000.

In the years since 1989 there have been significant changes in the curriculum. Many of these changes have been controversial: Opponents of reform feared that an emphasis on process over content would result in weakening the curriculum and decrease American children's mathematical competencies. Until now, there has not been the opportunity to evaluate the potential effectiveness of reform efforts. Large-scale change is slow. It took some years after the 1989 *Standards* was issued before curricula aligned with its reform goals could be developed and implemented; it took more time still before data on their effectiveness would become available. Such data are now beginning to come in, allowing one to see if the new curricula provide a basis for achieving the content and equity goals of reform—enfranchising all students and having them learn more powerful and useful mathematics. This article presents some preliminary data indicating that there are grounds for optimism. In research on some of the first large-scale implementations of reform curricula, data indicate that reform students do as well on skills as students who study the traditional curricula, and that they do better on an understanding of concepts and problem solving. Moreover, traditional performance gaps between majority students and poor or underrepresented minorities are diminished, though not eliminated.

Those data indicate that the first few steps of reform seem to be going in the right directions. Given that, what kind of infrastructure is required to stabilize and build on this progress? Sustained, incremental progress calls for the availability of high-quality curricula; for a stable, knowledgeable, and professional teaching community; for high-quality assessment that is aligned with curricular goals; and for stability and mechanisms for the evolution of curricula, assessment, and professional development. This article briefly assesses the current state of each of these and the possibilities for improvement.

STATUS AND VISIONS OF MATHEMATICS INSTRUCTION IN THE LATE 20TH CENTURY

Cases can be made for the virtues and drawbacks of the traditional U.S. mathematics curriculum. On the plus side, the United States' stature as a world superpower has been attributed in part to our education system. Education has been viewed in our society as a democratic vehicle for advancement. Millions of citizens, from the children of immigrants to the soldiers who took advantage of the GI Bill after World War II, would give testimony to the power of education as a mechanism for social and economic advancement. More specifically, mathematics education has been viewed as providing some of the underpinnings of the nation's technological and scientific prowess. The K–12 mathematics pipeline produced large enough numbers of people with strong enough mathematical backgrounds to serve as the backbone of the nation's mathematical and scientific infrastructure.

There has also, however, been a significant downside. First, the adequacy of the mathematical content that American students learned has periodically come into question—typically at points of national crisis. The new math came about, for example, in the aftermath of Russia's successful launch of Sputnik in 1957. Another impetus for change—economic rather than military—came with the waxing and waning of the Japanese and American economies, respectively, in the 1980s (e.g., National Commission on Excellence in Education, 1983). A sense of economic jeopardy, combined with American children's poor showing on the Second International Mathematics and Science Study (McKnight et al., 1987), led to concerns about the adequacy of the traditional curriculum.

While a key issue leading to reform was the sense that American mathematics curricula were not internationally competitive, there were other reasons. There was a serious concern that the high school mathematics curriculum was designed for those who planned to enter college, focusing largely on the skills that would ultimately enable students to study calculus. In K–12 mathematics there was little emphasis on the kinds of mathematics that would enable students to make sense of the world around them—neither statistics nor mathematical modeling was part of the traditional curriculum. There was also little or no emphasis on communicating and using mathematical ideas. Typically all one needed to earn full credit on a mathematics problem was to perform some computations, arrive at the correct answer, and write the answer in a box.

If a large proportion of K–12 students had been successful in the traditional curriculum, the impetus for change might have been muted. But that was not the case. Large numbers of students failed or left mathematics, and a disproportionate number of those who left were students of color. A 1989 report from the NRC, *Everybody Counts*, made the case as follows:

> More than any other subject, mathematics filters students out of programs leading to scientific and professional careers. From high school through graduate school, the half-life of students in the mathematics pipeline is about one year; on average, we lose half the students from mathematics each year, although various requirements hold some students in class temporarily for an extra term or a year. Mathematics is the worst curricular villain in driving students to failure in school. When mathematics acts as a filter, it not only filters students out of careers, but frequently out of school itself. (p. 7)

These negative effects were not distributed equally. *Everybody Counts* (NRC, 1989) argued the importance of mathematics education as a civil rights issue:

> Low expectations and limited opportunity to learn have helped drive dropout rates among Blacks and Hispanics *much* higher—unacceptably high for a society committed to equality of opportunity. It is vitally important for society that *all* citizens benefit equally from high-quality mathematics education. (p. 7)

Myriad data document disproportionate dropout and low performance rates for students of color (e.g., Madison & Hart, 1990; Miller, 1995; National Action Committee for Minorities in Engineering, 1997; National Commission on Mathematics and Science Teaching for the 21st Century, 2000; NSF, 2000). As one example, consider the following breakdown by race of mathematics scores on the National Assessment of Educational Progress (NAEP).[1] The critical scores are at age 17, when students are about to graduate. In recent years more than two thirds of the White 17-year-olds sampled by NAEP performed at benchmark levels—that is, were deemed to know the appropriate level of mathematics. Only about 40% of the Latino 17-year-olds, and less than one third of the African-American 17-year-olds, met benchmark performance levels. A comparison of scores for 9-, 13- and 17-year-olds shows that the gap in scores between Whites and underrepresented minorities increases as students get older.

Data from the Third International Mathematics and Science Study (TIMSS) indicate that socioeconomic status (SES) correlates with performance: "The data . . . show a relationship between the relative wealth of districts and student achievement in the subject areas. . . . Those that 'have' get more" (Schmidt, 2001). Mathematics scores on the SAT also correlate astoundingly well with parental income (National Action Committee for Minorities in Engineering, 1997). And one hardly needs to provide evidence of the correlations between race and SES or race and opportunity to learn. Powerful arguments and data are given in Miller (1995). (For compelling descriptions of the reality behind the figures, see Kozol, 1992.)

Recognition of the content and equity issues highlighted above contributed to calls for reform. The NRC issued *Everybody Counts* in early 1989 and NCTM issued the *Standards* later that year. Rather than focusing simply on mathematical content, the *Standards* addressed "what it means to be mathematically literate in a world that relies on calculators and computers to carry out mathematical procedures and in a world where mathematics is rapidly growing and is extensively being applied in diverse fields" (NCTM, 1989, p. 1). In addition to identifying the content students should know, the *Standards* focused on *process:* there was to be a focus at all grade levels on problem solving, reasoning, connections (between mathematical topics and to real world applications), and the communication of mathematical ideas in written and oral form. Indeed, the very goals of mathematics education were reconceptualized. After characterizing the then-current structures and content of schooling as a product of the industrial age, the *Standards* went on to say the following:

> The education system of the new industrial age does not meet the economic needs of today. New societal goals for education include (1) mathematically literate workers, (2) lifelong learning, (3) opportunity for all, and (4) an informed electorate. (p. 3)

To the surprise of its authors and just about everyone else, the *Standards* and two subsequent volumes that focused on teaching and assessment (NCTM, 1991, 1995) catalyzed a national standards movement.

Like Horace Greeley's famous injunction "Go west, young man," the *Standards* was long on direction and short on detail—it was a vision statement rather than a blueprint. In hindsight, that was a good thing, for both political and intellectual reasons. Given the American context of curricular pluralism, no set of specific curricular recommendations would have been politically viable. More important, however, is that the publication of the *Standards* in 1989 set the mathematical community in motion. Over the following decade, a number of curricula that took very different approaches to achieving the goals of the *Standards* were developed and refined. The result has been a collection of diverse models of curricular change, and significantly enriched curricular discourse.

Similarly, NCTM's (2000) *Principles and Standards* is a vision statement for mathematics education designed to reflect a decade's experience since the publication of the original *Standards* volumes. In terms of context, there are new curricular possibilities. In 1989 a call for all students to use scientific calculators was revolutionary; today web access makes huge databases available, and students have easy access to statistical packages to examine such data. As discussed below, the original *Standards* documents were inspired by research but not grounded in large-scale empirical testing (materials for such testing did not exist in 1989). A decade later, there is a much more solid research base. There is thus strong continuity between *Principles and Standards* and its antecedents, but also some bold new perspectives enabled by a decade's experience and reflection.

The new document rests on a set of principles that make the social and intellectual commitments of its authors clear: equity (high expectations and strong support for all students); coherent curricula rather than disconnected sets of activities; teacher professionalism, including knowledge of curricula and learning; and the effective use of assessment and technology in the service of mathematics learning. The document refines the curricular focus of earlier documents, focusing on five content standards (number, algebra, geometry, measurement, data analysis, and probability) interwoven with five process standards (problem solving, reasoning and proof, connections, communication, and representation). In a deliberate break with the traditional assumption that only some students will enroll in mathematics courses that prepare them for attending college, *Principles and Standards* calls for the development of a core curriculum that prepares all students with the mathematical background for quantitative literacy, for the workplace, and for study at the college level.

Like its antecedent, *Principles and Standards* can (despite its nearly 400 pages of densely packed text) be accused of being long on vision and somewhat short on detail. It identifies some essential goals, but does not provide a blueprint for achieving them. Its authors (among whom is the author of this article) hope that, like its antecedent, the vision will come to life over the decade following its publication as the mathematical community labors to make it a reality.

■ CAN IT WORK? HOPEFUL SIGNS

The 1989 *Standards* were grounded in contemporary research on mathematical thinking and problem solving. At the same time, however, the recommendations found therein were speculative. In 1989 no curricula designed to meet the goals delineated in the *Standards* were widely available, so there had been no opportunity to test the large-scale implementation of its ideas. Thus, opponents of *reform* (as the *Standards*-based movement came to be known) could and did complain that an untested approach was being forced upon American school children. They raised concerns that the reform approach would cause a precipitous decline in students' knowledge of mathematical facts and procedures. For reasons of space, the curricula and the controversies surrounding them will not be reviewed here.[2]

The large-scale implementation and evaluation of curricula embodying the ideas in the *Standards* took some years—curricula needed to be constructed, published, adopted, and assessed. The National Science Foundation (NSF) supported the development of a number of reform curricula in the early 1990s. By the mid-1990s, some of these were available for adoption. Insofar as these were 3-, 4-, or 5-year curricular packages (typically covering one of the elementary, middle, or high school grade bands), it was not until the turn of the century that significant numbers of students had made their way through a full reform curriculum package. Now, more than a decade after the publication of the *Standards*, hard data on large-scale implementations of these curricula are beginning to come in. To briefly summarize the current state, a converging body of data indicates the following:

1. On tests of basic skills, there are no significant performance differences between students who learn from traditional or reform curricula.

2. On tests of conceptual understanding and problem solving, students who learn from reform curricula consistently outperform students who learn from traditional curricula by a wide margin.

3. There is some encouraging evidence that reform curricula can narrow the performance gap between Whites and under-represented minorities.

The remainder of this section reviews such data, focusing largely on data from Pittsburgh, Pennsylvania. The reason for devoting so much space to that review is that Pittsburgh offers an early and unusually well-documented set of results concerning the large-scale implementation of reform—including extensive data regarding the impact of reform curricula on the racial performance gap discussed above.

Pittsburgh serves about 40,000 students in 97 public schools (59 elementary, 19 middle, 11 high, and eight other). Roughly 56% of the student population is African American and 44% is White/Other; more than 60% of the students qualify for free or reduced-price lunches.

What makes the Pittsburgh Public Schools unusual is that Pittsburgh has, since the early 1990s, made a coherent systemic effort to implement standards-based education in mathematics and other subject areas. Efforts have included the delineation of content and performance standards in line with the *Standards* and the 1996 New Standards mathematics exam (New Standards, 1996); the use of standards-based assessments (specifically, the New Standards Reference Examinations, Harcourt Educational Measurement, 1996–1999) for purposes of aligning curriculum and assessment; the use of traditional assessments (specifically, the Iowa Test of Basic Skills) for comparison purposes; and standards-based instructional materials and professional development (Briars, 2001; Briars & Resnick, 2000).

The overall results of Pittsburgh's systemic efforts are seen in Figures 4.1a and 4.1b. Note that the 1996 and 1997 cohorts had studied the traditional curriculum; the 1998–2000 cohorts had studied one of the major reform curricula.

As Figure 4.1a indicates, scores on concepts and problem solving increased with the implementation of the new curriculum, and continued to rise as the teachers became increasingly familiar with it. In 1997 roughly 10% of the traditional students met or exceeded the standards for concepts or problem solving; in 2000 roughly 25% of Pittsburgh's (now reform) students met or exceeded those standards. Although there is still huge room for improvement, the fact that two and a half times as many students than before met or exceeded those standards is impressive. Of course, problem solving was not a focus of the traditional curriculum. It is in the area of skills that the most surprising data emerge. Traditional measures of skills such as the Iowa Test of Basic Skills (ITBS) show that the reform curricula more than hold their own against traditional curricula with regard to

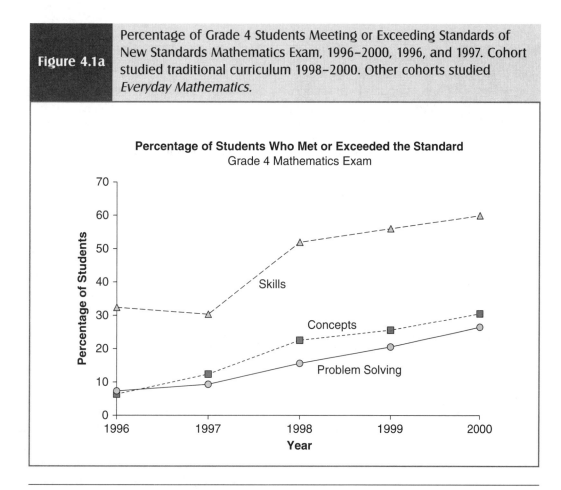

| **Figure 4.1a** | Percentage of Grade 4 Students Meeting or Exceeding Standards of New Standards Mathematics Exam, 1996–2000, 1996, and 1997. Cohort studied traditional curriculum 1998–2000. Other cohorts studied *Everyday Mathematics*. |

Source: Adapted from Briars, 2001.

skills. Even in the first year of new curriculum implementation, 1998, greater percentages of students scored above the 50th and 70th percentiles on the ITBS than in previous years, and fewer students scored below the 25th percentile. Skill scores on the New Standards examinations are more dramatic. Under the traditional curriculum, less than a third of the students met or exceeded the skill standard on the New Standards reference exam. With the new curriculum significantly more than 50% (and in 2000, 60%) do. That is, with the switch from traditional to reform curriculum the proportion of students performing well in terms of skills doubled from 1997 to 2000. In short, the fears of anti-reform groups that reform curricula would cause a decrease in student skill levels appear to be unwarranted.

Data such as these indicate that coherent approaches to teaching mathematics for conceptual understanding produce significant improvements across the board—not only in concepts and problem solving, but in skills as well. Moreover, Figure 4.1b shows that such curricula do not cream off the best students and help them do better: not only do many more students do well, as seen in Figure 4.1a, but fewer students sink to the bottom of the barrel. There seems to be some generality to such findings.

As one would expect in any district that contains nearly 100 schools, some Pittsburgh teachers embraced the proposed reforms and some did not. This raises the question of whether there were performance differences between students who experienced the curriculum as implemented (more or less) faithfully, and those that did not. Observers identified "strong implementation" teachers as those in whose classrooms students were familiar with activities and procedures specific to the *Everyday Mathematics* curriculum;

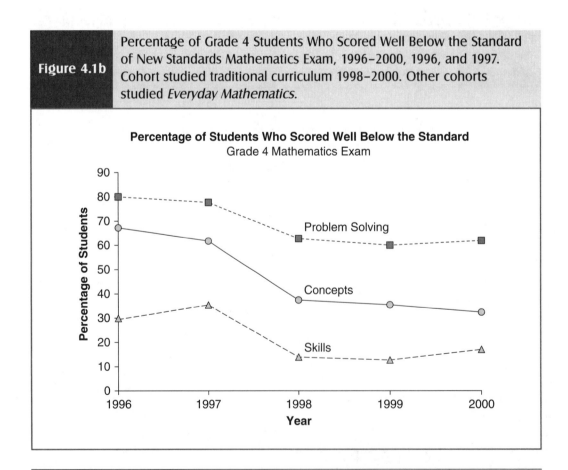

| **Figure 4.1b** | Percentage of Grade 4 Students Who Scored Well Below the Standard of New Standards Mathematics Exam, 1996–2000, 1996, and 1997. Cohort studied traditional curriculum 1998–2000. Other cohorts studied *Everyday Mathematics.* |

Source: Adapted from Briars, 2001.

curricular artifacts such as visual aids and manipulative materials were accessible and showed clear signs of use; students had frequent opportunities to work together and explain their work to each other when appropriate; displays of student work showed curriculum-specific projects and activities; and there was no evidence of the use of other programs. "Weak implementers were either not using the curriculum at all, or using it so little that the overall instruction in the classroom was hardly distinguishable from traditional mathematics instruction" (Briars & Resnick, 2000, p. 6). Strong implementation schools were identified as those in which there was strong implementation by all Grade 3 and 4 teachers in the 1996–1997 and 1997–1998 years, respectively. Weak implementation schools were identified as those in which all but one or two teachers were identified as weak implementers. Briars and Resnick (2000) created a matched sample of strong and weak implementation schools on socioeconomic grounds. They also verified that students at matched schools had "virtually identical" ITBS scores in 1995, the year before implementation of the new curriculum. Figure 4.1c represents a composite of the 1998 fourth-grade comparative student data reported in Briars and Resnick (2000). The data show that students at the strong implementation schools outperformed students at the weak implementation schools by a very wide margin. In other words, the more consistently the reform curriculum was implemented, the better students did.

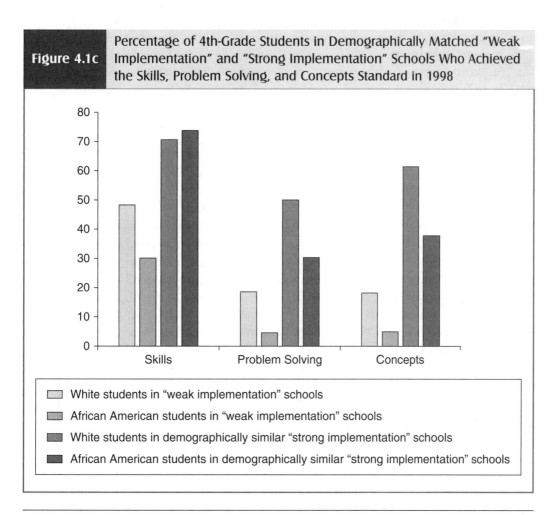

Figure 4.1c Percentage of 4th-Grade Students in Demographically Matched "Weak Implementation" and "Strong Implementation" Schools Who Achieved the Skills, Problem Solving, and Concepts Standard in 1998

☐ White students in "weak implementation" schools
▨ African American students in "weak implementation" schools
▨ White students in demographically similar "strong implementation" schools
■ African American students in demographically similar "strong implementation" schools

Source: Derived from Briars and Resnick, 2000.

Perhaps most important with regard to equity, not only did average scores on skills, concepts, and problem solving go up, but racial differences in performance diminished substantially. Figure 4.1c shows the percentage of Pittsburgh's White and African-American fourth graders in weak implementation schools and in demographically similar strong implementation schools who met the standards in skills, problem solving, and concepts on the 1998 New Standards exam. Both White and African-American students at the strong implementation schools far outperformed their counterparts at the weak implementation schools. At the strong implementation schools the performance of White and African-American students on the skills component of the test was roughly comparable.

There were still significant disparities in scores on problem solving and concepts. In the weak implementation schools, a negligible fraction (approximately 4%) of African-American students met the standards in problem solving and concepts. White students did better—approximately 18% met each standard—but the percentage is still low, and the ratio of White students to African-American students who met the standard is more than four to one. In the strong implementation schools, the percentage of African-American students meeting each of the concepts and problem solving standards is 30% or more, a more than sevenfold increase over their counterparts at the weak implementation schools. Moreover, the ratio of White students to African-American students who met those standards dropped from more than four to one to about three to two. Although this falls far short of the goal of parity, it represents very significant progress toward it.

The bottom line is that standards-based reform appears to work when it is implemented as part of a coherent systemic effort in which curriculum, assessment, and professional development are aligned. Not only do many more students do well, but the racial performance gap diminishes substantially.

The data described represent one of the first evaluations of coherent systemic efforts at mathematics reform, but they represent the tip of an emerging iceberg. Not long after the Pittsburgh data became available, the Mathematics in Michigan Convocation released data regarding Michigan students' performance on an international benchmarking study (Mullis et al., 2001). The Michigan mathematics standards are closely aligned with the *Standards,* as are the three main curricula highlighted in the Mathematics in Michigan Convocation: *Everyday Mathematics* at the elementary level, *Connected Mathematics Project* at the middle school level, and *Contemporary Mathematics in Context (Core-Plus Mathematics)* at the high school level.

The *Michigan Government News* noted on April 4, 2001, "eighth graders in the state of Michigan scored best in math and science compared to other states that participated in the Third International Mathematics and Science Study–Repeat (TIMSS-R). An 'invitational' group made up of 21 Michigan schools using criteria that stress a curriculum that aligns to the state's high standards scored even better."

It should be stressed that the invitational group contained a substantial number of schools in low-SES districts. What distinguished them, according to the article, were the curricular resources available and the alignment of curricula, standards, and assessment.

Additional data regarding large-scale implementations of reform curricula are now becoming available. For example, in the July 2001 issue of the *Journal for Research in Mathematics Education,* Riordan and Noyce describe the results of a matched comparison of traditional and reform curricula in Massachusetts, with a statewide assessment as the measure of performance:

> Fourth-grade students using *Everyday Mathematics* and eighth-grade students using *Connected Mathematics* outperformed matched comparison groups who were using a range of textbooks commonly used in Massachusetts. The gain in student performance was greater in schools farther along in their implementation of the standards-based programs. These performance gains, which were moderate in size,

remained consistent for different groups of students, across mathematical topics and different types of questions on the state test. This study supports the notion held by proponents of standards-based curriculum, that curriculum itself can make a significant contribution to improving student learning. (pp. 392–393)

Over the next few years, much more data regarding the implementation of reform curricula will become available. For example, the first volume of comprehensive evaluations of *Standards*-based instructional materials (Senk & Thompson, in press) is nearing publication. In a commentary following four chapters evaluating reform curricula at the elementary level, Ralph Putnam (in press) observes, "The first striking thing to note about the chapters is the overall similarity in their findings. Students in these new curricula generally perform as well as other students on traditional measures of mathematical achievement, including computational skill, and generally do better on formal and informal assessments of conceptual understanding and ability to use mathematics to solve problems." Commenting on the analyses of three middle school reform curricula, Chappell notes, "With respect to long-term benefits, the findings identified are convincing. They reveal that the curricula can indeed push students beyond the 'basics' to more in-depth problem-oriented mathematical thinking without jeopardizing their thinking in either area" (in press). Reviewing performance data from five high school reform curricula, Swafford (in press) writes,

> What has been presented in this section is not only extensive research on five reform curricula, but also considerable evidence that the promises of reform mathematics are real and the fears of the anti-reformers not justified. . . . [T]he preceding five chapters present ample evidence that students in reform curricula are experiencing and profiting from a broader, richer curriculum. Many would argue that it is precisely these problem solving and reasoning skills as well as a knowledge of statistics, probability and discrete mathematics that are needed, not only for future success in mathematics, but for life. (pp. 1–6)

These summaries tell a clear and consistent story: with well-designed curricula, it is possible to teach for understanding without sacrificing procedural skill. Moreover, in those cases where authors conducted studies to address the issue, the data suggest that the new curricula, though hardly eradicating performance differences between Whites and underrepresented or linguistic minorities, do tend to mitigate those differences.

There has been a significant amount of controversy, called the "math wars," regarding the implementation of reform curricula. Much of the controversy has been based on opinion and anecdote, rather than grounded in reliable data. One hopes that the nature of the dialogue can change as the evidence comes in. The fact is that reform curricula (curricula aligned with the *Standards*) can be made to work as hoped. When teachers are well supported in teaching for understanding and have good curricular materials to use, children really do learn, and racial differences in performance diminish. Given this, the policy issue that needs to be addressed is what kinds of systemic support structures will promote the successful implementation of such curricula and their progressive refinement over time? That question is the topic of the next section.

ISSUES AND OBSTACLES: ■ WHAT DOES IT TAKE TO DO IT RIGHT?

The following fundamental issues, among others, must be addressed in order to insure the sustained improvement of (mathematics) instruction in the United States: (a) high-quality curriculum; (b) a stable, knowledgeable, and professional teaching community; (c) high-quality assessment that is aligned with curricular goals; and (d) stability and mechanisms for evolution. This section evaluates the current state of each.

Issue 1: Curriculum

For perhaps the first time in American curricular history, research-based curricula grounded in an understanding of mathematical thinking, teaching, and learning are readily available. As the data in the previous section indicate, those curricula can make a substantial positive difference when properly implemented.

The current reform curricula are rudimentary in many ways and they can stand significant improvement—they represent first attempts at implementing a new set of goals for mathematics instruction. Moreover, times change and new visions emerge: *Principles and Standards* (NCTM, 2000) moves significantly beyond the 1989 *Standards*. But that vision is also evolutionary, grounded in what has been learned over the past decade. Therein lies the key. There is now a solid curricular base from which to work. Thus, two high priority goals should be to make sure that (a) the high-quality curricula currently available are actually implemented, and (b) there are mechanisms by which those curricula can be improved and updated, by means of iterative improvements in response to feedback and evolving visions of mathematical proficiency for all.

Issue 2: Teaching as a Profession

Teaching for mathematical understanding is difficult. It requires a deep understanding of the mathematics involved (see, e.g., Ma, 1999) and of how to create instructional contexts that lead students to engage with mathematics in meaningful ways. The vast majority of today's American mathematics teachers learned the traditional mathematics curriculum in the traditional way. Hence they have neither models nor experience teaching in the ways that would best facilitate their students' development of mathematical understanding.

As the data discussed in the previous section indicate, systemic alignment and sustained professional development can make a difference. When teachers are treated like professionals and they are given the opportunity to develop their skills and understandings over time, the results can be significant improvements in students' mathematical performance.

The sad fact, however, is that places where teachers are treated like professionals and are given the opportunity to develop their skills and understandings over time are few and far between. As any number of reports make clear (see, e.g., National Commission on Mathematics and Science Teaching for the 21st Century, 2000; National Commission on Teaching and America's Future, 1996), teaching is one of the most demanding and least understood or rewarded occupations in the United States. The knowledge base required for effective teaching is substantial. There are issues of subject matter knowledge, knowledge of student understanding of subject matter (pedagogical content knowledge), of understanding curricular goals, of classroom management, and more. Yet in our system, the typical expectation is that 1 year of teacher training (sometimes post-baccalaureate, sometimes not) will prepare candidate teachers to take on full responsibilities in the classroom. This is a gross underestimate of the knowledge and skills required. Worse yet, once they enter the field the vast majority of teachers have minimal opportunities for professional growth. For these reasons among others, teaching is a profession more in name than in reality.

This is a national outrage and a national pathology. This situation is not present in other nations: consider the high regard in which teachers are held in many nations around the world, and perhaps more importantly, the specifics of lesson study in nations such as Japan and China (see, e.g., Stigler & Hiebert, 1999). The expectation in those countries is that even with support, talented beginners will take a decade to evolve into fully accomplished professionals. Teachers' work is structured so that opportunities for professional growth—for example, the collaborative study, observation, and refinement of lessons and curricula that take place in lesson study—are a part of their ongoing responsibilities. There is no reason for teacher preparation and professional development to be taken any less seriously in this country. We owe it to our children.

This article begins with a discussion of mathematics education as a civil rights issue. What follows may stretch Bob Moses' ideas further than he would like, but I would argue that those of us who are interested in teacher professionalism have a great deal to learn from the civil rights movement.

Moses (2001) argued that disenfranchised voters in the American South in the 1960s were not taken seriously until *they* demanded the vote, and that by analogy, mathematics for under-represented minorities will not be taken seriously until students demand the mathematical preparation they need.

> Constructing the Mississippi Freedom Democratic Party so that sharecroppers and day workers could have a voice was radical. . . . There had been advocates for civil rights long before. . . . Nonetheless, it was when sharecroppers, day laborers, and domestic workers found their voice, stood up, and demanded change, that the Mississippi political game was really over. When these folk, people for whom others had traditionally spoken and advocated, stood up and said 'we demand the right to vote!' refuting by their voices and actions the idea that they were uninterested in doing so, they could not be refused.
>
> So to understand the Algebra Project you must begin with the idea of our targeted young people finding their voice as sharecroppers and day laborers, maids, farmers, and workers of all sorts found theirs in the 1960s. (pp. 18–20)

So it is with teaching. Real and sustained change will take place when teachers demand to be treated as professionals and welcome the concomitant responsibilities. Of course, teachers cannot go it alone. We need to help redefine the contexts of teaching, teachers' responsibilities, and accountability measures so that professionalism becomes a meaningful possibility.

Issue 3: Assessment

Depending on its nature and the relationship between assessment and the curriculum, assessment can be a positive or a negative force. Let us begin with the downside. In a research symposium devoted to examining the effects of high-stakes testing, Shepard (2001) reviewed the "effects of high-stakes accountability pressures: (a) inflated test score gains, (b) curriculum distortion, and (c) loss of intrinsic motivation to learn" (p. 1). Regarding inflated test score gains, Shepard cited numerous studies indicating that when a particular high-stakes examination is put in place, scores start out low (because students have not yet been prepared for the examination) but then rise substantially as students are prepared for the test. However, a large part of the test score gains appears to be an artifact of preparation for the particular test and not necessarily an indication that the students have learned the concepts that the tests are supposedly measuring. When other forms of tests assessing the same material in different formats are used, student performance drops substantially.

Regarding Shepard's second point, she observed that high-stakes testing affects both subject matter content and the nature of instruction. Subjects for which students are not held accountable by the assessment system tend to get decreased attention. For example, the November 21, 2001 San Francisco *Chronicle* reported that fourth- and eighth-grade Californian students' performance on the 2000 NAEP science examination was the worst in the nation. One cannot prove causality for the precipitous drop in California students' science scores compared to the rest of the nation. However, the article suggests that the drop is attributable to California's recent imposition of high-stakes testing in mathematics and English. Because there are not high-stakes exams in science, teachers' attention has been diverted away from science instruction. Perhaps more importantly, even in high priority content areas those forms of instruction that do not mesh with the assessments tend to receive decreased attention. Teachers assign fewer essay questions, for example, when understandings are to be measured by multiple-choice tests. This deprives students of important learning activities.

Shepard's (2001) third point drew from Stipek's (1996) research review of motivation and instruction. Her conclusions were,

> When teachers emphasize evaluation there is a corresponding decrease in students' intrinsic motivation and interest in the material for its own sake. When students focus on how they are doing or how they will be evaluated, they become only superficially involved in learning tasks and are much less likely to persist in trying to solve difficult problems. (p. 3)

Potential abuses and misuses of assessment were part of the American Educational Research Association's (2000) motivation for issuing its *Position Statement Concerning High-Stakes Testing in PreK–12 Education*. Indeed, numerous professional organizations, including NCTM (November 2000), have taken strong stances with regard to mathematics and the responsible use of high-stakes assessments. These include consistent recommendations that decisions affecting individual students' life chances or educational opportunities should not be made on the basis of test scores alone, and that alternative assessments should be provided where test results may not provide accurate reflections of students' abilities; that assessments should cover the broad spectrum of content and thought processes represented in the curriculum, not simply those that are easily measured; and that tests must provide appropriate accommodations for students with special needs or limited English proficiency. Unfortunately, many political jurisdictions are, in the name of "standards," violating many of these recommendations.

Having raised a cautionary flag, this discussion will turn to the positive side of assessment.

> Assessment should be a means of fostering growth toward high expectations and should support high levels of student learning. When assessments are used in thoughtful and meaningful ways, students' scores provide important information that, when combined with information from other sources, can lead to decisions that promote student learning and equality of opportunity. (NCTM, November 2000)

There are indeed positive cases. Pittsburgh, where there has been a decade-long effort to align curriculum, professional development, and assessment, provides clear and dramatic evidence of improvement. It also shows that racial differences in performance can be minimized by high-quality instruction for all. The Pittsburgh data show, and every data analysis chapter in Senk and Thompson (in press) confirms, that when students are taught for understanding their scores on skills go up. In addition to these findings, the Michigan data indicate that when standards, assessment, curriculum, and professional development are appropriately aligned, low-SES districts can perform as well on meaningful assessments as other much more wealthy districts.

Indeed, the use of well-designed assessments that are aligned with curricula can demonstrate the limitations of less comprehensive assessments. Describing recent work with the Mathematics Assessment Collaborative in California, Ridgway et al. (2000) report on a comparison of test scores using a standards-based assessment developed by the Mathematics Assessment Resource Service (MARS) and the Stanford Achievement Test (9th ed.), a traditional standardized test that is known as the SAT–9. Correlations between the two tests at various grade levels were typically around $r = 0.65$. Yet, there were consistent and important differences between the two tests.

Ridgway et al. (2000) examined the percentage of students who scored high or low on each test. Not surprisingly, students who scored high or low on one test tended to score similarly on the other: the percentage of students who scored high on both tests or low on both tests ranged between 70% and 77% in Grades 3, 5, and 7. The data regarding the remaining students tell an interesting story. At each grade, at least 3.5 times as many students scored high on the SAT–9 and low on MARS as the number of students who scored high on MARS and low on the SAT–9.

One possible explanation of these consistent differences in scores is that the MARS tests, which are explicitly designed to be aligned with *Principles and Standards* (NCTM, 2000), are much broader in conception than the SAT–9. Both assessments test for procedural mastery and for some degree of conceptual understanding. In addition, however, the MARS tests also call for having students work extended problems, communicate their results coherently, etc. These are core competencies that go untested on the SAT–9, so the SAT–9 would not identify students who are weak in these areas. In that sense, a high score on the SAT–9 runs the risk of being a *false positive*, certifying a student as competent when the student is unable to meet some very important mathematical standards. Once again, it is essential to use assessments that examine the full range of desired competencies.

Issue 4: Stability and Mechanisms for Evolution

The mathematics curriculum in the United States has seen any number of pendulum swings over the past 50 years. At mid-20th century, a very traditional curriculum focused on facts and procedures. Post-Sputnik, things got turned upside-down, and the new math introduced elementary students to sophisticated notions such as set theory. A backlash in the 1970s produced the back-to-basics movement. Standardized tests a decade later showed that students were no better at the basics than the students from the new math years; thus problem solving became the theme of the 1980s. This was superseded in the 1990s by standards-based mathematics, which, when it became highly visible, gave rise to the math wars and catalyzed the existence of what is in essence a neo-conservative back-to–back-to-basics movement. This way lies madness.

In much of the rest of the world there is evolutionary change, grounded in the assumption that if professionals keep working at something, they can make continual improvements. In China and Japan, for example, curricula change much less frequently and much more slowly than in the United States (Ma, 1999; National Institute on Student Achievement, Curriculum, and Assessment, 1998). To begin with, these curricula are carefully conceived and known to be reasonably effective. These curricula are refined on the basis of classroom observations and student performance. Teachers make the curriculum a collaborative object of study, working to find better ways to teach lessons or to improve them. In that way, gradual and sustained improvements are made.

Progress demands more than change for the sake of change, more than political rallying cries and radically new goals and tests every few years. Some stability in the system is necessary to make real progress. There is now the base for such sustained evolution. The content and process standards described in *Principles and Standards* (NCTM, 2000) represent the evolution of ideas developed in the 1989 *Standards.* A number of reform curricula, which have now been shown to produce results significantly better than the traditional curriculum, are aligned with the 1989 *Standards* and thus reasonably aligned with *Principles and Standards.* There exist at least two large-scale assessments (New Standards and MARS) aligned with the *Principles and Standards.* Thus, any educational system that desires has access to solid and well-aligned standards, curriculum, and assessments. An aligned program of professional development can contribute to the gradual strengthening of the teaching force and the iterative improvement of curricula and assessments.

■ CONCLUSION AND DISCUSSION

Curriculum

There now exist a number of well-designed, coherent mathematics curricula at various grade levels. There is substantial and mounting evidence that when teachers are adequately prepared to help students work through these curricula, the students learn not only skills and procedures, but also concepts and problem solving as well. Moreover, these curricula appear to represent a significant step toward equitable instruction. Performance gaps between Whites and underrepresented minorities, and between low- and high-SES students, though not eradicated, are far less dramatic than those typical of traditional curricula.

None of the extant curricula represent "the solution." All can stand improvement and as our vision gets clearer and more ambitious, changes will have to be made. But there is a solid base on which to build.

Teaching as a Profession

As indicated previously in this article, the nation is in big trouble here. In the current climate of accountability, teachers are increasingly being de-professionalized. Many of the current high-stakes accountability measures focus on skills. Given the stakes, many teachers feel that they deviate from skills-based instruction at their (and their students') peril. Partly because there are (real and perceived) weaknesses in the teaching force, a number of widely used skills-oriented curricula (in reading as well as in mathematics) are so prescriptive that little teacher discretion is allowed. This can lead to a downward spiral, since neither the curricula nor the work conditions under which most teachers operate provide opportunities for professional growth. It may contribute to high attrition rates, which contribute to teacher shortages, which result in the hiring of under-prepared teachers, who (in this way of thinking) would then need even more prescriptive teaching materials.

This cycle needs to be broken. In the ideal, new teachers would enter the profession with much more solid preparation for teaching than is now the case. Even then, however, it must be recognized that they are beginners who will take years to evolve into full-fledged professionals. As Garet, Porter, Desimone, Birman, and Yoon (in press) report, sustained professional development makes a difference:

> Sustained and intensive professional development is more likely to have an impact, as reported by teachers, than is shorter professional development.... Professional development that focuses on academic subject matter (content), gives teachers opportunities for "hands-on" work (active learning), and is integrated into the daily life of the school (coherence), is more likely to produce enhanced knowledge and skills.

Activities that are linked to teachers' other experiences, aligned with other reform efforts, and encouraging of professional communication among teachers appear to support change in teaching practice, even after the effects of enhanced knowledge and skills are taken into account. . . . The collective participation of groups of teachers from the same school, subject or grade is related both to coherence and active learning opportunities, which in turn are related to improvements in teacher knowledge and skill and changes in classroom practice.

The National Commission on Teaching and America's Future (1996) made its recommendation in blunt terms: "Reinvent teacher preparation and professional development" (p. 76). Specifically, it recommends "states and districts need to . . . make ongoing professional development part of teachers' daily work through joint planning, research, curriculum and assessment groups, and peer coaching" (pp. 84–86). We need to redefine teachers' work lives so that meaningful opportunities for professional growth are embedded in and seen as part of their ongoing work.

Assessment

The good news is that some high-quality standards-based assessments do exist, and that such assessments can be used productively as vehicles for positive change. The bad news is that the vast majority of high-stakes testing do not use such measures. The good tests tend to be more expensive than the others are, and they are harder for the general public to understand. We face a problem of public education and public relations.

The issue of public education is critically important. As long as the public continues to believe in the value and meaningfulness of traditional skills-based tests, reform faces a major uphill battle. There are at least three dimensions to this problem. First, there is the need to inform parents and others about the broad spectrum of mathematical understandings that is appropriate for students to learn—for example that problem solving, reasoning, and communication are essential goals of the curriculum, and that they need to be assessed.

Second, one has to counteract the very common misunderstanding that in mathematics students have to master skills before using them for applications and problem solving. People who believe this will focus first on skills, thinking that applications and problem solving can come later. The result is the traditional curriculum (and traditional skills-oriented assessments). An underlying assumption of reform is that students can develop mastery of skills through problem solving. As noted repeatedly in this article, the data bear out this hypothesis: students in reform curricula do just fine on skills, and much better than students in traditional curricula on concepts and problem solving. But the adoption of reform curricula is likely to be slow and controversial unless parents and other stakeholders come to understand the evidence and the fact that the skills first position is based on false assumptions.

Third, stakeholders in the educational system have to understand the great variability inherent in testing. People put great faith in the stability of test scores. The common metaphors of tests as thermometers or yardsticks point to the problem. When a child is sick, a difference of one or two degrees in a temperature reading is significant. Similarly, a few inches of height gain, or a few pounds' difference in weight, are taken as meaningful and important changes. Likewise, most people attribute significant meaning to particular test scores and to minor variations in them. In fact, test–retest differences on almost all standardized tests can be substantial—perhaps reflecting the fact that the student was having a good or bad day, that alternative forms of the same test did not really measure the same thing, or that the student was particularly lucky (or unlucky) in being familiar (or unfamiliar) with some aspect of the test.

Fourth, the public needs to understand the points raised in the previous section about high-stakes testing—that gains in test scores are often illusory or artifactual, and that high-stakes testing can result both in curricular deformation and in loss of intrinsic motivation for students. We stand a much better chance of having meaningful assessments if people understand these points.

Stability

Stability is essential if the nation is to move systemically toward meeting the vision of documents such as *Principles and Standards* (NCTM, 2000). There is now proof that real progress can be made: school districts such as Pittsburgh, which worked over the long term with a set of consistent goals and a systemic approach, get results. But stability is hard to come by. A decade is an eternity in the lives of those who have the most influence over what happens in schools; for most politicians, alas, the only things that count are the ones that produce results before the next election. As above, the educational research community confronts a problem of public education and public relations. In order to have a context where productive evolutionary change is possible, people have to be convinced that there is a solid base and that there are mechanisms for steady improvement. Absent either of these perceptions, there is the temptation for the quick fix—out with the old, in with the new—that typically results in change but not in progress. The issue of stability raises one last issue for discussion.

The Life Cycle of Ideas, From Research Into Practice

For those of us in educational research who hope to make a difference—and for policy makers and politicians who want to go about their business intelligently—it is essential to understand the amount of time it takes for ideas to make their way from basic research to successful large-scale implementation. Research on mathematics thinking, teaching, and learning provides an excellent case in point.

Contemporary research on mathematical thinking and problem solving, which represented a significant shift in both content and methods from previous research, began to take hold in the mid-1970s.[3] By the mid-1980s, the main dimensions of mathematical cognition—the nature and contents of the knowledge base, problem solving strategies, metacognition, and beliefs—were well established (see, e.g., Schoenfeld, 1985). Such contemporary understandings were at the foundations of the 1989 *Standards*, which, in a sharp break with tradition, gave significant emphasis to mathematical processes as well as to content; at each grade level, the first four standards concerned problem solving, reasoning, communication, and connections (across mathematical content and to real-world applications). In the early 1990s, the National Science Foundation issued a request for proposals for the development of new curricula consistent with the *Standards*. Experimental curricula were developed and published in the mid-1990s. Wide-scale implementation of those curricula took place in the late 1990s. As indicated in this article, the results of some of the first evaluations of those curricular implementations are just beginning to come in. The ideas work, and they work on a large scale. This really is an educational success story of major proportions.

It is important to note that the process just described, from basic research to large-scale implementation, took roughly 25 years. In industry that kind of research and development cycle is understood, but for the public at large and for most policy makers, that kind of time frame is beyond the imaginable. The point is not that one should expect to wait 25 years before good ideas become implemented in practice. There is a much shorter cycle for some ideas, and incremental change can be made. But, America is the land of the quick fix, at least with regard to education: whatever the problem is, we believe we can solve it, fast. This is a mistake, which leads to the kinds of pendulum swings discussed above. People need to understand that simple-minded solutions to complex problems will not work, and that progress is best made by building carefully on a well-established base. At the same time, researchers need to work consistently to bring good ideas into the world of practice. The best proof of the importance of research is documentation of its effects.

This article begins by pointing out the great importance of quantitative literacy in our society, and the history of inequities associated with mathematics education; it will end on an appropriately positive note. In recent years we have made substantial progress. Not only do the new mathematics curricula enable more students to do better, but also they decrease the traditional performance gaps between majority and traditionally under-represented minority students, and between low- and high-SES students. Such curricula, aligned with robust standards and a solid assessment system, provide a solid base on which to stand. It is time to stay the course, build on what we know, and work in evolutionary fashion toward the improvement of (mathematics) education for all students.

NOTES ■

1. NAEP trend data for 9-, 13-, and 17-year-old students covering the time period from 1978 to 1996 are available at www.nsf.ed.gov/nationsreportcard/mathematics/results/scale-ethnic.asp.

2. The Mathematics Forum at http://forum.swarthmore.edu offers numerous links to resources in mathematics education, including web sites from both pro- and anti-reform groups. A list of NSF-supported curriculum projects can be found at http://forum.swarthmore.edu/mathed/nsf.curric.html. The NSF has established four centers devoted to the support of standards-based curricula: the K–12 mathematics curriculum center available at www.edc.org/mcc, an elementary grades curriculum center at www.arccenter.comap.com, a middle grades center at http://showmecenter.missouri.edu, and a high school center at www.ithaca.edu/compass. Starting in 1998, the U.S. Department of Education commissioned panels of experts to identify "exemplary" and "promising" programs in mathematics education. Information regarding these programs and the review process by which they were selected can be found at www.ed.gov.offices/OERI/ORAD/KAD/expert_panel/math-science.html. (These awards were not uncontroversial. A large group of mathematicians and scientists opposed to reform wrote an open letter to then-Secretary of Education Richard Riley asking that the awards be rescinded.) Standards and other related information can be downloaded from NCTM at www.NCTM.org. The most prominent and anti-reform web site, with links to many others, can be found at www.mathematicallycorrect.com.

3. Any one-sentence summary is an oversimplification, of course. For a more nuanced view of the history, see Schoenfeld, 2001.

REFERENCES ■

American Educational Research Association. (2000, July). *Position statement concerning high-stakes testing in preK–12 education.* Retrieved from http://www.aera.net/about/policy/stakes.htm

Briars, D. (March, 2001). Mathematics performance in the Pittsburgh public schools. Paper presented at a conference of the Mathematics Assessment Resource Service, San Diego, CA.

Briars, D., & Resnick, L. (2000). *Standards, assessments—and what else? The essential elements of standards-based school improvement.* Unpublished manuscript.

Chappell, M. (in press). Keeping mathematics front and center: Reaction to middle grades curriculum projects' research. In S. Senk & D. Thompson (Eds.), *Standards-oriented school mathematics curricula: What does the research say about student outcomes?* Mahwah, NJ: Erlbaum.

Garet, M., Porter, A., Desimone, L., Birman, B., & Yoon, K. (in press). What makes professional development effective: Results from a national sample of teachers. *American Education Research Journal.*

Kozol, J. (1992). *Savage inequalities.* New York: Harper Perennial.

Ma, L. (1999). *Knowing and teaching elementary mathematics.* Mahwah, NJ: Erlbaum.

Madison, B. L., & Hart, T. A. (1990). *A challenge of numbers: People in the mathematical sciences.* Washington, DC: National Academy Press.

McKnight, C., et al. (1987). *The underachieving curriculum: Assessing U.S. school mathematics from an international perspective.* Champaign, IL: Stipes Publishing Company.

Michigan Government News. (2001, April 4). Retrieved from http:// www.migov.state.mi.us/gov/ PressReleases/

Miller, S. (1995). *An American imperative.* New Haven, CT: Yale University Press.

Moses, R. P. (2001). *Radical equations: Math literacy and civil rights.* Boston: Beacon Press.

Mullis, I., et al. (2001). *Mathematics benchmarking report, TIMSS 1999—Eighth grade: Achievement for U.S. states and districts in an international context.* Chestnut Hill, MA: Boston College. Retrieved from http://timss.bc.edu

National Action Committee for Minorities in Engineering. (1997). Engineering and affirmative action: Crisis in the making. New York: Author.

National Commission on Excellence in Education. (1983). *A nation at risk: The imperative for educational reform.* Washington, DC: U.S. Government Printing Office.

National Commission on Mathematics and Science Teaching for the 21st Century. (2000). *Before it's too late: A report to the nation.* Washington, DC: U.S. Department of Education.

National Commission on Teaching and America's Future. (1996). *What matters most: Teaching for America's future.* New York: Author.

National Council of Teachers of Mathematics. (1989). *Curriculum and evaluation standards for school mathematics.* Reston, VA: Author.

National Council of Teachers of Mathematics. (1991). *Professional teaching standards for school mathematics.* Reston, VA: Author.

National Council of Teachers of Mathematics. (1995). *Assessment standards for school mathematics.* Reston, VA: Author.

National Council of Teachers of Mathematics. (2000). *Principles and standards for school mathematics.* Reston, VA: Author.

National Council of Teachers of Mathematics. (2000, November). Position statement on high stakes testing. Retrieved from http://www.nctm.org/about/position_statements/highstakes.htm

National Institute on Student Achievement, Curriculum, and Assessment. (1998). *The educational system in Japan: Case study findings.* Washington, DC: U.S. Department of Education.

National Research Council. (1989). *Everybody counts: A report to the nation on the future of mathematics education.* Washington, DC: Author.

National Science Foundation. (2000). Science and engineering indicators 2000. Washington, DC: Author.

New Standards. (1996). New Standards mathematics reference examination technical summary. Pittsburgh, PA: Learning Research and Development Center, University of Pittsburgh, National Center for Education and the Economy.

Putnam, R. (in press). Commentary on four elementary mathematics curricula. In S. Senk & D. Thompson (Eds.), *Standards-oriented school mathematics curricula: What does the research say about student outcomes?* Mahwah, NJ: Erlbaum.

Ridgway, J., Crust, R., Burkhardt, H., Wilcox, S., Fisher, L., & Foster, D. (2000). *MARS report on the 2000 tests.* San Jose, CA: Mathematics Assessment Collaborative.

Riordan, J., & Noyce, P. (2001). The impact of two standards-based mathematics curricula on student achievement in Massachusetts. *Journal for Research in Mathematics Education, 32*(4), 368–398.

Schmidt, W. (2001, April 4). TIMSS press release. Retrieved from http://USTIMSS.msu.edu/ whatsnew.html

Schoenfeld, A. H. (1985). *Mathematical problem solving.* Orlando, FL: Academic Press.

Schoenfeld, A. H. (2001). Mathematics education in the 20th century. In L. Corno (Ed.), *Education across a century: The centennial volume* (pp. 239–278). Chicago: National Society for the Study of Education.

Sells, L. W. (1975). Sex, ethnic, and field differences in doctoral outcomes. Unpublished doctoral dissertation, University of California, Berkeley.

Sells, L. W. (1978). Mathematics: A critical filter. *Science Teacher, 45,* 28–29.

Senk, S., & Thompson, D. (Eds.). (in press). *Standards-oriented school mathematics curricula: What does the research say about student outcomes?* Mahwah, NJ: Erlbaum.

Shepard, L. (2001, April). Protecting learning from the harmful effects of high-stakes testing. Paper presented at the 2001 annual meeting of the American Educational Research Association, Seattle, WA.

Stigler, J., & Hiebert, J. (1999). *The teaching gap.* New York: Free Press.

Stipek, D. J. (1996). Motivation and instruction. In D. C. Berliner & R. C. Calfee (Eds.), *Handbook of educational psychology* (pp. 85–113). New York: Macmillan.

Swafford, J. (in press). Reaction to high school curriculum projects' research. In S. Senk & D. Thompson (Eds.), *Standards-oriented school mathematics curricula: What does the research say about student outcomes?* Mahwah, NJ: Erlbaum.

READING 4.2 FOCUS QUESTIONS

1. What strikes you as particularly valuable about the processes and priorities for strengthening the mathematics program at the Rafter School District?

2. What issues might Algebra Task Force members encounter as they set about enacting their plans? What might they be missing?

Mark those paragraphs or short sections that relate to your notes. Be prepared to discuss them with other participants.

READING 4.2

The Case of the Rafter School District

Four years ago, in an effort to expand educational opportunities for all students, the Rafter School District mandated that all students, in all levels, take algebra by the eighth grade. This decision was hailed by parents, who had complained bitterly about the disparities in educational opportunities for different groups of students. Some teachers agreed, and others did not. Pointing out how difficult the courses in Algebra 1 and Algebra 2 were, many felt that the change was just setting up these students for failure. But the new policy stood.

Now, four years after the mandate, it was clearly time to reconsider. Large numbers of students were, indeed, failing the eighth grade Algebra 1 class, and so had to retake it in ninth grade. Scores on the state test had not improved. Morale was low among teachers; nobody wanted to teach the lowest level class. Once again, parents were clamoring for a change.

This time the district set up an Algebra Task Force to study the situation. The committee was made up of the assistant superintendent, the middle and high school principals, a guidance counselor, the special education director, two teachers from each school, and an influential representative from the Parent Advisory Council. Over the course of several meetings they worked on several problem-based tasks from early algebra, and they discussed articles about mathematics, algebra, and equity.

In particular, they were struck by the story of Crystal, a student who might have been barred from the study of algebra because of her struggles with arithmetic. Cathy Seeley (a former mathematics teacher who later became president of the National Council of Teachers of Mathematics), tells her story in the following way:

> It would certainly be ideal to have all students be proficient in arithmetic before progressing to algebra. However, a few years ago I had an experience teaching a ninth-grade algebra class that caused me to re-examine my beliefs about necessary prerequisites for learning algebra. One particular student, whom I call Crystal, could not do fraction operations and asked if she could use a fraction calculator in the algebra . . . class. I quickly discovered that, in spite of her arithmetic deficiency, Crystal was an outstanding algebraic thinker, as long as she had her fraction calculator to help her get answers to fraction problems. To make a long story a little shorter, eventually Crystal was motivated by her success in algebra to go back and learn fractions. She continued through precalculus in high school and went on to graduate from college and graduate school.
>
> We need to be careful not to let our own beliefs about how mathematics must be organized get in the way of allowing all students the opportunity to show us what

---

Author's Note: The contents for the Rafter case are drawn from experiences in a range of schools including urban, rural, and suburban settings. [Interested participants may be interested in reading about the experience of one of these, the Railside School: Boaler, J., & Staples, M. (in press). *Creating mathematical futures through an equitable teaching approach: The case of Railside School.* Retrieved March 30, 2009, from http://www.sussex.ac.uk/education/profile205572.html]

they can do. Even though computational proficiency helps in higher-level mathematics, there is no evidence that students who are weak in some areas of computation cannot succeed in algebra or higher-level mathematics.*

Algebra Task Force members wondered how many Crystals in their school might be barred from the opportunity to move forward with their own mathematics learning if they removed the algebra requirement, because of beliefs about the way mathematics is organized and about who is ready for higher level mathematics.

The Algebra Task Force emerged from these meetings with a series of questions around which they decided to study their school in order to better understand their situation:

1. How does the content of the Algebra 1 classes offered to different levels of students compare?

2. What approaches to teaching algebra are taken in each level, and what is the cognitive demand of tasks used?

3. What opportunities for professional development are offered to support teachers in learning about how to make algebraic concepts and skills accessible to a wide range of students?

4. What teachers are assigned to the different levels of Algebra 1 classes and what criteria are used in making decisions for teachers' assignments to mathematics classes?

5. What choices about enrolling in further mathematics classes are students making, beyond what is required, and what are their reasons?

6. What is the process currently in place for advising students about placement in mathematics courses?

7. What opportunities for additional support are offered to students who are struggling in mathematics, what is the nature of these supports, and how timely is it?

The Algebra Task Force formed teams to investigate each question and agreed to share their findings at the next scheduled meeting. The team investigating Questions 1 and 2 agreed to use the *Secondary Lenses on Learning Observation and Reflection Guide* to frame their observations.

When they reconvened several weeks later and reported on their findings about the various questions, the news was indeed sobering:

*   Students in lower levels of Algebra 1 worked with significantly different content than their peers in higher levels. Although there was some variation in teaching approaches from one classroom to another, for the most part instructional practice in the lower-level mathematics classes was remarkably consistent in the paucity of opportunities provided for students to
    o work with problem-based tasks of high cognitive demand;
    o learn through substantive discourse or "math talk;"

---

*The author is Cathy Seeley. Reprinted with permission from *NCTM President's Online Chat Transcript*, September 24, 2004, copyright © 2004 by the National Council of Teachers of Mathematics. All rights reserved.

○ make connections between mathematical concepts, representations, solution strategies, and procedures; and

○ make and test out mathematical conjectures.

- Teacher professional development for mathematics was limited, and there was little time for teachers to meet together.
- Because the upper-level mathematics classes were popular among experienced teachers, the new hires were often assigned to teach the Algebra 1 classes.
- Student enrollment data showed that many students had stopped taking mathematics beyond the required Algebra 1 course, and among those that stopped a disproportionate number were low income and minority. Students to whom task force members had spoken related a general sense of disaffection and feeling that teachers didn't care.
- There was great variation in the amount of guidance offered to students with respect to selection and placement in mathematics classes and in who was involved in these consultations with students.
- While the after school program did offer some support in mathematics, there were virtually no opportunities for the afterschool instructors to meet with students' regular mathematics teachers to discuss individual students' needs. Similarly, the Special Education program operated quite separately from the regular mathematics program.

After some discussion of their findings, the Algebra Task Force came to the conclusion that the problem was too complex to be addressed merely by changing enrollment patterns as they had tried when they mandated that all students take algebra by grade 8. It was not helpful to have greater access to algebra if it only meant that significant numbers of students were likely to fail. They needed to think about adequate preparation and support for students if they were going to be successful with raising expectations for course enrollment and achievement for all students.

The Task Force established a short-term strategy and several longer-term strategies for addressing the need for better preparation and support for students.

Short-Term Strategy

Addressing the Need to Provide Additional Time and Support for Struggling Students

The Algebra Task Force decided to focus its immediate attention on coordinated responses for supporting struggling students. Its members began to consider the possibility of increasing time spent on mathematics for students who need it, through a combination of in-school and out-of-school initiatives. They wanted to ensure that the additional support offered was closely coordinated with content and approaches taken in the classroom. They decided to base their work on the framework described in Dufour's *Schools as Learning Communities*:

- *Timely.* The school quickly identifies students who need additional time and support.
- *Based on Intervention Rather Than Remediation.* The plan provides students with help as soon as they experience difficulty rather than relying on summer school, retention, and remedial courses.
- *Directive.* Instead of *inviting* students to seek additional help, the systematic plan *requires* students to devote extra time and receive additional assistance until they

have mastered the necessary concepts. (Dufour, Richard [2004, May]. Schools as Learning Communities. *Educational Leadership, 61*[8], pages 6–11)

They set up a system for collecting data about the impact on the achievement in mathematics of individual students who participated in the program of support. They also planned to follow up when students identified for support did not attend programs offered after school, in order to determine whether issues such as transportation, home responsibilities, and so on, prevented them from participating.

In addition, the task force decided to learn about initiatives to address issues of time and support taking place at other schools. Some schools they read about offered extended class periods to teach mathematics so as to allow time for all components of a lesson, augmented by individualized support for students. One particularly promising model involved pre-teaching a lesson to students who would benefit from the opportunity to preview the ideas and investigations as a foundation for fuller participation in the lesson with the entire class. Another school's block scheduling, in which courses were taken over half a school year, allowed students who failed a course at any point and were knocked out of a sequence of mathematics courses, to catch up by taking two mathematics classes in a single year. This allowed many more students to take higher-level mathematics courses over the four years of high school, even if they had difficulty with some. However, they also noted a concern about overall time lost for any given mathematics class in many models of block scheduling and so decided to learn more about other options.

Long-Term Strategy 1

The Algebra Task Force identified the need to review the mathematics curricula used in the middle school to see whether an alternative to what they were currently using might better provide all students with access to key ideas in algebra while allowing them to continue their study of important topics in other strands of mathematics. They also identified the need to engage in a thoughtful adoption and implementation process for a new high school mathematics curriculum (either integrated across mathematical strands or following the traditional course sequence) that would build on new directions planned for the middle school.

Long-Term Strategy 2

The Algebra Task Force also identified the need to significantly strengthen their professional development program so that it provided teachers with

1. a strong foundation in mathematics;

2. opportunities to rethink their pedagogy;

3. the tools to differentiate instruction in mathematics while maintaining cognitive demand; and

4. skills in conducting regular formative assessment to inform their instruction.

Long-Term Strategy 3

The Algebra Task Force identified the need to reconsider practices around tracking/achievement grouping in their school. As a first step, they made a commitment to ensuring that test scores alone would not be used as a basis for decisions that would affect students' life chances or educational opportunities. They decided to convene a meeting of teachers, guidance counselors, and the principal before the start of each year's course selection and placement process. In these meetings they would make determinations about placement that included not only results from large-scale tests, but also data from formative assessments offered in class and student portfolios that provided a view into the mathematics history of students. They also decided to reassess the ways in which they assigned teachers to classes, with an effort to place their strongest teachers (in content knowledge, in pedagogy, and in potential for connecting with students) in the math courses that were required of all students.

In addition, the Algebra Task Force decided to visit a high school that was having success with placing all incoming students into heterogeneous mathematics classes, and to visit its sending middle schools as well. They wanted to see for themselves a middle and high school curriculum that would be challenging for the full range of students. They also wanted to understand how a middle school mathematics curriculum could provide a strong foundation of proportional reasoning as a basis for students' study of Algebra 1 or the first year of an integrated high school mathematics program, while also allowing students to continue to develop their algebraic thinking and connect to important ideas in algebra, geometry, data, and elementary statistics.

READING 4.3 FOCUS QUESTIONS

(Jigsaw with other members of your team.) Please take notes about the following two questions, and be prepared to report on them to others who have not read this article.

1. What is the effect of low expectations on instructional decision making for teachers?

2. What are the features of the pedagogy of poverty that Ladson-Billings (1997) describes?

Mark those paragraphs or short sections that relate to your notes. Be prepared to discuss them with other participants.

READING 4.3

It Doesn't Add Up

African American Students' Mathematics Achievement

Gloria Ladson-Billings

Mathematics education has been heralded for its leadership role in the U.S. school reform effort (Stein, Grover, & Henningsen, 1996; Grant, Peterson, & Shojgreen-Downer, 1996). Prominent in the reform of mathematics education is the call for students not merely to memorize formulas and rules and apply procedures but rather to engage in the *processes* of mathematical thinking, that is, to do what mathematicians and other professional users of mathematics do. The revamped mathematics education program is based on engaging students in problem posing and problem solving rather than on expecting rote memorization and convergent thinking. These changes in mathematics education suggest that mathematics teaching must build on students' learning and on their ability to pose and solve problems previously considered too difficult for their age-grade levels (Carpenter & Fennema, 1988; Fennema, Franke, Carpenter, & Carey, 1993).

Despite the much talked about changes in mathematics education, African American students continue to perform poorly in school mathematics (Secada, 1992). Some have argued that African American children's poor mathematics performance is the result of a discontinuity that exists between students' home language and the perceived "precision" of mathematics and mathematical language (Orr, 1987). Others have suggested that the content of school mathematics is so divorced from students' everyday experiences that it appears irrelevant (Tate, 1994). However, few have situated the mathematics performance of African American students into the larger context of mathematics teaching and learning in U.S. schools. This discussion attempts to do just that and suggests some direction for further research on the mathematics performance of African American students.

WHY AFRICAN AMERICANS? ■

Some may ask, why focus on African American students? The telling statistics on the life chances of African Americans suggest that whenever we can improve the schooling experiences for African American students, we have an opportunity to reverse their life chances. A disturbing percentage of African American males are involved with the criminal justice system (Miller, 1997). More African American males are in jail than in college,[1] and today, for the first time in our history, more African American males than Whites are in jail (ibid.). African American students are 2 to 5 times more likely to be suspended (and at a younger age) than White students (Carnegie Corporation of America, 1984/85). The dropout rate for urban, inner-city African American youth is 36% and rising (Whitaker, 1988). And although graduation from high school is no guarantee of success in life, a life without a high school diploma is almost certain to be unsuccessful—economically and socially.

In the 1950s and 1960s civil rights leaders declared literacy to be the key to full citizenship for African Americans (Morris, 1984). If African Americans could become literate they could not be denied the franchise in those southern states that had imposed literacy tests as a condition for voting. They could begin to read and discern for themselves the political practices that could lead to liberation. Much like the work of Paulo Freire (1970), these efforts toward increased literacy for African Americans were infused with notions of developing "critical consciousness"—an ability to read both the world and the word.

Today, in the 1990s, Bob Moses, one of the stalwarts of the civil rights movement, has argued that mathematical literacy represents the "new" civil rights battleground (Jetter, 1993). Moses asserts that because of the crucial role of algebra as a curricular gatekeeper, urban students cannot continue to be tracked out of it; in the current arrangement of the curriculum, access to higher level mathematics, beginning with algebra, can mean increased educational and economic opportunity for students.

■ THE CULTURE OF THE U.S. AND THE CULTURE OF MATHEMATICS

Although this discussion is focused on African American students' mathematics achievement, it is important to situate it in the larger context of mathematics teaching and learning in the U.S. The Third International Mathematics and Science Study (TIMSS) (U.S. Office of Education, 1996) revealed that U.S. school children continue to lag behind students in other highly technological nations in mathematics and science achievement. The reasons for these lags are multiple—teachers without adequate preparation in mathematics and science, unimaginative approaches to teaching, teacher misassignment, poorly constructed textbooks. But it is more than what happens in our classrooms that contributes to the creation of a mathematically illiterate culture. Mathematics functions as a feared and revered subject in our culture. We fear it because we believe that it is too hard, and we revere it because we believe that it signals advanced thinking reserved only for the intelligentsia.

Ours is a nation where no one would readily admit to being unable to read, but many proclaim with pride their inability to balance their checkbooks or compute the amount of interest on a loan. Not knowing how to read or write carries a stigma across race, class, and gender lines. People who cannot read and write attempt to mask that fact by using a variety of strategies. They pretend that they cannot see without their eyeglasses. They rely on their memories to pretend to read what they have heard many times before, or they grasp at context clues to make meaning from the meaningless squiggles on signs and paper.

Contrast this behavior with that of people in our society who struggle with mathematics. As Stevenson reported (1992), Asian parents attributed their students' mathematics failure to lack of effort, whereas U.S. parents were more likely to suggest that their children's poor mathematics performance was attributable to a lack of innate ability. In the U.S. is found a cultural belief that either one "has it" or does not when it comes to mathematical ability, and the way to "get it" is through genetic inheritance.

As previously stated, it is acceptable in our society to be mathematically inept. Although hardly anyone will admit to being unable to read and write, Americans often matter of factly comment on their limited mathematics skills. Mathematical ability has come to be associated with "nerdiness" or "geekyness." Our cultural portrayals of the mathematically adept are White males with horn-rimmed glasses and plastic pocket protectors. These images do not prompt our children to embrace mathematics as a field of study or a necessary skill. This distortion and mystification of mathematics and its uses have contributed to our positioning it as unattainable (and undesirable).

We also have to understand that as our economy has changed, so has the role of mathematics (and science) teachers. Formerly, a high school education and a work ethic could allow one to find reasonable employment and provide for oneself and one's family. In today's more bifurcated economy, people are either highly educated (or skilled) or poorly educated (and unskilled). In the earlier era, mathematics teachers were charged with using their subject area as a curriculum sieve, sifting and winnowing to select the top students to go on to higher mathematics. In our current highly technological, global economy, few Americans can afford to be left out of high-level mathematics. Thus, today's mathematics teachers must conceive of their subject area not as a sieve but as a net that gathers in more and more students. This paradigmatic shift has been difficult for our students as a whole, but it has been particularly difficult for African American students.

But some people do well in mathematics in our society. Why? Certainly, individual differences exist that cannot be easily generalized to explain mathematical abilities. However, statistically we can see whole-group patterns that may suggest some tendencies. White middle-class male students typically do well in mathematics, as do some groups of students of Asian descent. Is there anything about the culture of mathematics that is compatible with White middle-class male students' culture and experiences? Is there anything about White middle-class male students' culture that makes it compatible with mathematics as it is taught in our schools?

Mathematics teaching in our schools emphasizes repetition; drill; convergent, right-answer thinking; and predictability.[2] Students are asked to perform similar tasks over and over. They are rarely asked to challenge the "rules" of mathematics. They are rarely asked how their prior knowledge and experience might support or conflict with school mathematics. Middle-class culture demands efficiency, consensus, abstraction, and rationality. These features of the culture are inherently neither good nor bad. However, they may reflect the experiences and understandings of one segment of our society. Boykin and Toms (1985) suggest that some features of African American cultural expression[3] include rhythm, orality, communalism, spirituality, expressive individualism, social time perspective, verve, and movement. Once again, there is nothing inherently good or bad about these cultural features. However, these kinds of cultural expression are neither reinforced nor represented in school mathematics. Further, school mathematics curriculum, assessment, and pedagogy are often closely aligned with an idealized cultural experience of the White middle class (Cohen, 1982; Joseph, 1987; Romberg, 1992). Moreover, this problem is subtle and difficult to diagnose (see e.g., Silver, Smith, & Nelson, 1995; Tate, 1995).

BEYOND SURFACE DIFFERENCES ■

But students' social context is not alone in having an impact on students' mathematics achievement. The relationship between mathematics and culture continues to be deciphered. There are those who suggest that mathematics is "culture free" and that it does not matter who is "doing" mathematics; the tasks remain the same. But these are people who do not understand the nature of culture and its profound impact on cognition (Cole, Gay, Glick, & Sharp, 1971).

Culture refers to the deep structures of knowing, understanding, acting, and being in the world. It informs all human thought and activity and cannot be suspended as human beings interact with particular subject matters or domains of learning. Its transmission is both explicit and implicit. Thus, even though African American students are a part of almost every social strata and their social context may affect what experiences they have and how they view the world, their cultural knowledge, expressions, and understandings, which may be transmitted over many generations, may share many features with African Americans across socioeconomic and geographical boundaries.

Part of the deep structure of African American culture is an affinity for rhythm and pattern.[4] African American artistic and physical expressions demonstrate these features in sophisticated ways. Jazz, gospel music, rap, poetry, basketball, sermonizing, dance, fashion—all reflect African American influences of rhythm and pattern. But these influences are rarely connected to any mathematical foundations. I am not suggesting that we should "mathematize"[5] all cultural expressions, such as art and music, but rather that it may be important to help students see the mathematical links that exist between what they know and appreciate.

School mathematics is presented in ways that are divorced from the everyday experiences of most students, not just African American students. Thus, poor mathematics performance in the U.S. cuts across cultural groups. But some disturbing patterns about the performance of African American students need to be examined. Oakes et al. (1990) found that low-income African American students are more likely to be clustered in low-ability mathematics classes. As a school's African American enrollment increases, the proportion of classes identified as high ability diminishes. Schools where African American students constitute the majority have less extensive and less demanding mathematics programs and offer fewer opportunities for students to take such gatekeeper courses as algebra and calculus that lead to increased opportunities at the college level and beyond. Oakes and her colleagues also found that schools with high concentrations of African American students tend to have fewer teachers judged to be highly qualified in mathematics.

■ TEACHING FOR HIGH PERFORMANCE IN MATHEMATICS

Although much of this discussion has dealt with the way mathematics is constructed and regarded in the U.S., I would be remiss if I did not address the notion of pedagogy. It is with changed notions of pedagogy that I believe we have the best opportunity for changing the achievement levels of African American students. My work has focused on successful teachers of African American students (e.g., Ladson-Billings, 1994, 1995). The work of such teachers is in high relief from that of what Haberman (1991) calls "the pedagogy of poverty." This pedagogy of poverty includes such routine teaching acts as "giving information, asking questions, giving directions, making assignments, monitoring seatwork, reviewing assignments, giving tests, reviewing tests, assigning homework, reviewing homework, settling disputes, punishing noncompliance, marking papers, and giving grades" (p. 290). Haberman points out that taken separately these acts might seem "normal." However, "taken together and performed to the systematic exclusion of other acts, they have become the pedagogical coin of the realm in urban schools" (p. 291).

Further, Haberman suggests that the pedagogy of poverty appeals to several constituencies (p. 291). Below I elaborate on his list of to whom this pedagogy appeals and make some connections to mathematics teaching and learning.

It Appeals to Those Who Themselves Did Not Do Well in School

Too many of the teachers assigned to urban classrooms fail to enjoy intellectual pursuits. Their own work in school was mediocre, and teaching was a choice of convenience rather than one of informed and reflective decision making. These teachers typically were not good mathematics students, and their orientation to mathematics is as a rule-governed, right-answer, "hard" discipline.

It Appeals to Those Who Rely on Common Sense Rather Than on Thoughtful Analysis

Teachers who practice this kind of pedagogy are more likely to suggest that students need to learn or do something because that is the way they learned or did it. Rather than make curricular and instructional decisions on the basis of empirical research or a systematic study of students' classroom performances, they do what "feels" right. Thus, strictly following the mathematics textbook and completing problem sets become the rule.

It Appeals to Those Who Fear People of Color and the Poor and Who Have a Need for Control

It is interesting to walk into schools or classrooms thought to be "good" urban classrooms. Often, what makes them "good" is that they are unnaturally quiet. Teachers and administrators sometimes become so consumed with the notion that African American children must be managed that they forget that they need to be taught. Maintaining order and keeping children under control become the preoccupation of the teachers Haberman describes. That order may be best maintained by, in these teachers' view, giving students mundane, routine mathematics tasks that do not invite much discussion and contestation.

It Appeals to Those Who Have Low Expectations for Children of Color and the Poor

As was previously mentioned, a notion prevails in American culture that academic excellence is a result of genetic good fortune. This concept—that some students "have it" whereas others do not—is particularly pernicious when directed toward African American students. Teachers who presume that because students are of a particular race or ethnicity they cannot be expected to perform at high levels in mathematics fail to present those students with a challenging, intellectually rigorous mathematics curriculum. Instead, their mathematics curriculum is best described as overly directive and controlling.

It Appeals to Those Who Do Not Know the Full Range of Available Pedagogical Options

It stands to reason that if teachers have not performed well in school, approach teaching unsystematically, fear their students, and hold low expectations for them, they are likely also to possess a limited teaching repertoire. Calling on past (bad) practices, these teachers tend to reproduce the kind of unimaginative, stifling pedagogy that has failed to serve students of color for many years. Their classrooms are not unlike that described by Ayers (1992, p. 259):

> Visiting a fourth-grade class, I was greeted by the teacher. "Welcome to our class," she said. "I'm on page 307 of the math text, exactly where I'm supposed to be according to board guidelines."

There was not much going on—two students were asleep, several were looking out the window, a few were reading their math books. I discovered later that virtually every student in the class was failing math. But this teacher was doing her job, moving through the set curriculum, dutifully delivering the material, passing out the grades. If the students did not learn math, that was not her responsibility.

In contrast to this pedagogy of poverty, I have had the pleasure of working with teachers who enacted a culturally relevant pedagogy. I have documented their work in a number of places (Ladson-Billings, 1994, 1995). However, in keeping with an emphasis on mathematics, I want to talk about how one teacher, whom I call Margaret Rossi, developed a pedagogy designed to ensure high mathematical achievement among African American students.

Margaret Rossi is an Italian American woman in her mid-40s. She began her teaching career in the late 1960s as a Dominican nun. She has taught students in both private and public schools, from White wealthy communities to low-income communities of color. During the study, she was teaching sixth grade in a working-class, low-income, predominantly African American school district. Although regarded as a strict teacher, she knew that students respected her for being demanding yet caring.

Mathematics in Margaret's class was a nonstop affair. She spent little or no time on classroom routines like taking roll, collecting lunch money, or dealing with classroom management. Margaret's classroom was always busy. Although her students were engaged in problem solving using algebraic functions, no worksheets were handed out, no problem sets were assigned. The students, as well as Margaret, posed problems.

From a pedagogical standpoint, I saw Margaret make a point of getting every student involved in the mathematics lesson. She continually assured students that they were capable of mastering the problems. They cheered each other on and celebrated when they were able to explain how they arrived at their solutions. Margaret's time and energy were devoted to mathematics.

Margaret moved around the classroom as students posed questions and suggested solutions. She often asked, "How do you know?" to push students' thinking. When students asked questions, Margaret was quick to say, "Who knows? Who can help him out here?" Margaret helped her students understand that they were knowledgeable and capable of answering questions posed by themselves and others. However, Margaret did not shrink from her own responsibility as teacher. From time to time she worked individually with students who seemed puzzled or confused about the discussion. By asking a series of probing questions, Margaret was able to help students organize their thinking about a problem and develop their own problem-solving strategies. The busy hum of activity in Margaret's classroom was directed toward mathematics.

All of Margaret's students participated in algebra, even though it was beyond what the district's curriculum required for sixth grade. Margaret scrounged an old set of algebra books from the district's book closet and exempted no one from the rigors of the class. One of Margaret's students was designated a special needs student. However, Margaret determined that with a few accommodations the student could remain in the classroom and benefit from her instruction. James performed well in the classroom. He participated in class discussions, posed problems as well as solved them, and accepted help from classmates when he struggled. By the end of the year, Margaret had convinced the principal that James had no need for services outside the classroom.

Although it is interesting to hear Margaret's story, it is more meaningful to understand her practice as a heuristic for solving the problem of poor mathematics achievement among African American students. Some of the tentative principles we can extrapolate from her teaching follow.

Students Treated as Competent Are Likely to Demonstrate Competence

Much of the literature on teacher expectations of student achievement helps us understand that when teachers believe in students' abilities, the students are likely to be successful. Conversely, when teachers believe that because of their race, social class, or personal economic situations students may not be intellectually able, student performance (and how it is assessed) confirms those beliefs. Margaret treated all students as if they were intellectually exceptional. She expected all of the students to perform at high levels of competence—and they did.

Providing Instructional Scaffolding for Students Allows Students to Move From What They Know to What They Do Not Know

Rather than worry over what students did not know, Margaret demonstrated the possibility of using the students' prior knowledge as a bridge to new learning. She instructed her students not to allow organization of tests or texts to distract or confuse them. She reassured them that they possessed key strategies for solving a variety of problems.

The Major Focus of the Classroom Must Be Instructional

Margaret made efficient use of her class time. From the moment the students entered the classroom until the time they were dismissed for recess, they were engaged in mathematics. Additionally, Margaret was engaged in mathematics instruction the entire time. She did not attempt to occupy the students with busy work. Instead, she was committed to the academic success of each student and accompanied each one on the instructional journey. Knowing that she was right there with them gave the students the assurance that their progress would be monitored and that they would never be allowed to stray too far off the instructional path.

Real Education Is About Extending Students' Thinking and Abilities Beyond What They Already Know

Margaret Rossi's decision to teach her sixth graders algebra even when it was not mandated by her district's curriculum was a conscious effort to demonstrate to the students that they had the capacity to learn and perform at higher and more sophisticated levels than had been demanded of them previously. Instead of attempting to maintain the students at low levels of academic performance, Margaret provided challenging content for *all* the students.

Effective Pedagogical Practice Involves In-Depth Knowledge of Students as Well as of Subject Matter

There is no disputing that effective teachers must be knowledgeable about content. Additionally, Shulman (1987) suggests that beyond a knowledge of their various content areas, teachers must know how that knowledge is best taught. Other researchers argue that teachers who are successful with diverse learners also are able to cultivate and maintain strong interpersonal relationships with their students (Foster, 1992).

Spindler and Spindler (1982) reported that teachers, perhaps unconsciously, favor those students whom they perceive to be most like them. This partiality takes the form of attending more to these students, valuing their responses more, and evaluating their performances more favorably. If teachers are to be more effective with African American students, they must develop a positive identification with them—to perceive them to be like them, that is, fully human and possessing enormous intellectual capacity.

■ FILLING THE RESEARCH VOID: "COMPLEX SITUATIONS"

One of the ways researchers might develop research agendas that respond to the need of classroom teachers and their students to improve mathematics performance is to understand the theoretical challenge of this work. A typical response to these issues is to function in a crisis-management mode—looking for ways to repair seemingly irreparable classroom situations. I suggest here that a better way to address these problems is to develop more powerful theoretical rubrics for making sense of classroom practices and student performances. Two important heuristics for creating a "way of seeing" what is happening in mathematics classrooms are found in the work of Lave and Wenger (1991) and Waldrop (1992). The former gives us an understanding of the situated nature of learning, or situated cognition. The latter helps us develop notions of complexity. Together, they might be thought of as a theory of "complex situations."

Situated cognition suggests that individuals do not learn things in a vacuum. Rather, learning occurs in social contexts. The kinds of mathematics learning that individuals do can be highly specific. Fasheh (1990) speaks of his mother's understanding of pattern because of her work as a quilter. Similarly, when teaching adults to read in the south during the 1950s and 1960s, Clark (1990) relied primarily on her students' desires to gain employment, read and study the Bible, and participate in the political process as sources of reading motivation instead of trying to teach rudiments of sound-symbol relationships. Thus, success in mathematics for African American students may need to be deeply embedded in their everyday contexts. Instead of surface connections, such as changing the names of story problem characters, teachers will need to understand the deep structures of students experiences.[6] This may mean doing some things with students that look very "unmathlike"—interviewing them, having them write autobiographies, discussing their interests. To be successful at moving from students' lives and interests to meaningful mathematics, teachers themselves will have to be very knowledgeable in mathematics. The work of Smith and Stiff (1993) illustrates this technique. Under the press of a state mandate for algebra for all students, they created a series of vignettes connected to students' interests in which they embedded the basics of algebra. Their technique called for involving students in these high-interest stories until students' interest waned. When the interest dissipated, a new story was begun. Their ability to move from story to story was linked to their knowledge of mathematics. They could (and did) embed the algebraic concepts and problems in any story. However, it was the interest in the story that kept the students engaged. This technique is important in light of the push to create high-technology programs for mathematics learning. These programs necessarily must choose some context, but they may not choose the "right" contexts.[7]

In addition to situating the teaching of mathematics in relevant student contexts, we need to recognize that human contexts or systems are necessarily complex. Casti (1994) and Waldrop (1992), constructors of "complexity theory," suggest that phenomena (or tasks) are not just "complicated," they are "complex." The classroom *is* a complicated place. But complicated phenomena and tasks typically can be reduced to the sum of their parts, whereas complex systems (e.g., human beings, communities, schools, and classrooms) are "more dynamic, more unpredictable, more alive" (Davis & Sumara, 1997, p. 117). Thus, classrooms are *both* complicated and complex.

Waldrop (1992) asserts that complex systems have three distinguishing characteristics. First they have the capacity to undergo spontaneous self-organization, in the process of somehow managing to transcend themselves. For example, in the process of solving a mathematics problem, individual students might contribute different ideas that help create a rubric or strategy for solving the problem that no one student would have developed independently. Second, complex systems are adaptive. Whether they be species, marketplaces, or individual organisms (or classrooms), they all change within changing environments (Davis & Sumara, 1997). Thus, a classroom within a dysfunctional school can be highly effective, as was true in the classrooms of the teachers I studied (Ladson-Billings, 1994). This is not to suggest that we should discourage systemic change; rather, the lack of schoolwide reform should not preclude individual teachers from developing effective practice within the system. Third, complex systems are qualitatively different from mechanical systems (e.g., cars, computers), which are "merely complicated" (Davis & Sumara, p. 118). One can understand complicated systems by analyzing each of its component parts. This analysis can make the system predictable and rule governed. Contrast that with the classroom. Merely examining each individual student (component) within the classroom tells the teacher little about the dynamic of the classroom (system). Yet, that is often precisely the approach we take. It is important to know and understand the individuals in the classroom, but it is equally important to understand how the group functions and how individuals relate to, and function with, the group.

Perhaps by melding notions of situated cognition with complexity theory we can provide teachers and researchers with a different type of lens through which to understand the classroom and a different type of tool to improve it. If we understand that the multiple contexts in which students live their lives have a variety of effects on the class system, we might begin to create the kinds of mathematics curricula and pedagogy that take full advantage of the adaptive, resilient, complex nature of learners in a classroom. Rather than presume that because of their race, culture, ethnicity, language, or other form of difference students are unable to succeed in mathematics, this lens might force us to ask how the mathematics we are teaching (and how we teach it) is changing the system. How might we construct mathematics learning situations that improve the system? When we look at other aspects of the curricula where students may be experiencing success, what can we discover about certain aspects of learning that work well in a classroom system?

Certainly enough literature documents the mathematics failure of African American students. What is lacking is the documentation of successful practice of mathematics for African American students. The challenge of improving the mathematical performance of African American students must be fought on three fronts: programmatic, personal, and political. Programmatically, we must participate in the development of meaningful and challenging curricula. Personally, we must come to develop caring and compassionate relationships with students—relationships born of informed empathy, not sympathy. Politically, we must understand that our future as a people is directly tied to our children's ability to make the most of their education—to use it not merely for their own economic gain and personal aggrandizement, but rather for a restructuring of an inequitable, unjust society. Our students have immeasurable talents and innumerable strengths. That they do not do well in school in general and in mathematics in particular just does not add up.

NOTES ■

1. The total number of African American inmates (includes all ages) exceeds the total African American male college population, which is primarily between the ages 18 and 25.

2. This description of current mathematics practice is not reflective of those school programs that have adopted the recommended NCTM curriculum Standards.

3. I do not mean to imply that there is one monolithic African American culture. However, scholars such as Nobles (1986) and Boykin and Toms (1985) have identified features extant in African American cultural expression that appear with regularity throughout African American communities.

4. It is important that this notion not be read as the stereotypical "all Black people got rhythm." Instead, what I am suggesting here is that rhythmic expressions in music, dance, art, and so on, are consistently valued and reinforced in African American cultural expression. Individuals within the culture may have no particularly rhythmic skills or interests.

5. The term *mathematize* is used to explain the practice of quantifying nonmathematical phenomena. See Putnam, Lampert, and Peterson (1990).

6. Knowing these deep structures goes beyond reading general descriptions of a culture to becoming a "student" of the specific individuals we teach.

7. For example, my daughter's middle school mathematics class participated in the highly acclaimed "Jasper Woodbury Series" created as a part of Vanderbilt University's School for Thought program. Although she completed the assignments, throughout the study she complained that she was not particularly interested in Jasper and *his* problems. The Smith and Stiff (1993) project requires that the problems emanate from students in the classroom.

■ REFERENCES

Ayers, W. (1992). The shifting ground of curriculum thought and everyday practice. *Theory Into Practice, 31,* 259–263.

Boykin, A. W., & Toms, F. (1985). Black child socialization: A conceptual framework. In H. McAdoo & J. McAdoo (Eds.), *Black children: Social, educational, and parental environments.* Beverly Hills, CA: Sage.

Carnegie Corporation of New York. (1984/85). Renegotiating society's contract with the public schools. *Carnegie Quarterly, 29/30,* 1–4, 6–11.

Carpenter, T., & Fennema, E. (1988). Research and cognitively guided instruction. In E. Fennema, T. P. Carpenter, & S. J. Lamon (Eds.), *Integrating research on teaching and learning mathematics* (pp. 2–19). Madison: National Center for Research in Mathematical Sciences Education, University of Wisconsin.

Casti, J. L. (1994). Complexification: Explaining a paradoxical world through the science of surprise. New York: HarperCollins.

Clark, S. (with Brown, C.) (Ed.). (1990). *Ready from within: A first person narrative.* Trenton, NJ: Africa World Press.

Cohen, P. C. (1982). A calculating people: The spread of numeracy in early America. Chicago: University of Chicago.

Cole, M., Gay, J., Glick, J. A., & Sharp, D. W. (1971). The cultural context of learning and thinking: An exploration in experimental anthropology. New York: Basic Books.

Davis, B., & Sumara, D. (1997). Cognition, complexity, and teacher education. *Harvard Educational Review, 67,* 105–125.

Fasheh, M. (1990). Community education: To reclaim and transform what has been made invisible. *Harvard Educational Review, 60,* 19–35.

Fennema, E., Franke, M., Carpenter, T., & Carey, D. (1993). Using children's mathematical knowledge in instruction. *American Educational Research Journal, 30,* 555–584.

Foster, M. (1992). Sociolinguistics and the African American community: Implications for literacy. *Theory into Practice, 31,* 303–311.

Freire, P. (1970). *Pedagogy of the oppressed.* New York: Continuum.

Grant, S. G., Peterson, P. L., & Shojgreen-Downer, A. (1996). Learning to teach mathematics in the context of systemic reform. *American Educational Research Journal, 33,* 509–541.

Haberman, M. (1991). The pedagogy of poverty versus good teaching. *Phi Delta Kappan, 73,* 290–294.

Jetter, A. (1993, February 21). Mississippi learning. *New York Times Magazine,* pp. 30–35, 50–51, 64, 72.

Joseph, G. C. (1987). Foundations of Eurocentrism in mathematics. *Race and Class, 28,* 13–28.

Ladson-Billings, G. (1994). The dreamkeepers: Successful teachers for African American children. San Francisco: Jossey Bass.

Ladson-Billings, G. (1995). Toward a theory of culturally relevant teaching. *American Educational Research Journal, 33,* 465–491.

Lave, J. & Wenger, E. (1991). *Situated learning: Legitimate peripheral participation.* New York: Cambridge University Press.

Miller, J. G. (1997). African American males in the criminal justice system. Kappan Special Report. *Phi Delta Kappan, 78,* K1–K12.

Morris, A. (1984). *The origins of the civil rights movement.* New York: Free Press.

National Council of Teachers of Mathematics. (1989). *Curriculum and Evaluation Standards for School Mathematics.* Reston, VA: Author.

Nobles, A. W. (1986). African psychology: Toward its reclamation, reascension, and revitalization. Oakland, CA: Black Family Press.

Oakes, J. (with Ormseth, T., Bell, R. & Camp, P.). (1990). Multiplying inequalities: The effects of race, social class, and tracking on opportunities to learn mathematics and science. Santa Monica, CA: Rand Corporation.

Orr, E. (1987). *Twice as less.* Markham, Ontario, Canada: Penguin Books.

Putnam, R., Lampert, M., & Peterson, P. (1990). *Alternative perspectives on knowing mathematics in elementary schools.* In C. Cazden (Ed.), *Review of research in education* (Vol. 16, pp. 57–150). Washington, DC: American Educational Research Association.

Romberg, T. A. (1992). Further thoughts on the standards: A reaction to Apple. *Journal for Research in Mathematics Education, 23,* 432–437.

Secada, W. G. (1992). Race, ethnicity, social class, language, and achievement in mathematics. In D. A. Grouws (Ed.), *Handbook of research on mathematics teaching and learning* (pp. 623–660). New York: Macmillan.

Shulman, L. (1987). Knowledge and teaching: Foundations of the new reform. *Harvard Educational Review, 57,* 1–22.

Silver, E. A., Smith, M. S., & Nelson, B. S. (1995). The QUASAR project: Equity concerns meet mathematics reform in the middle school. In W.G. Secada, E. Fennema, & L. Bryd (Eds.), *New directions for equity in mathematics education* (pp. 9–56). Cambridge: Cambridge University Press.

Smith, L. B. & Stiff, L. V. (1993). *Restructuring the teaching of high school general mathematics and prealgebra to the least academically prepared students.* Paper presented at the annual meeting of the American Educational Research Association, Atlanta.

Spindler, G. & Spindler, L. (1982). Roger Harker and Schönhausen: From the familiar to the strange and back again. In G. Spindler (Ed.), Doing the Ethnography of Schooling (pp. 20–46). Prospect Heights, IL: Waveland Press, Inc.

Stein, M. K., Grover, B. W., & Henningsen, M. (1996). Building student capacity for mathematical thinking and reasoning: An analysis of mathematical tasks used in reform classrooms. *American Educational Research Journal, 33,* 455–488.

Stevenson, H. (1992). *The learning gap.* New York: Summit Books.

Tate, W. F. (1994). Race, retrenchment, and the reform of school mathematics. *Phi Delta Kappan, 75,* 477–485.

Tate, W. F. (1995). School mathematics and African American students: Thinking seriously about opportunity-to-learn standards. *Educational Administration Quarterly, 31,* 424–448.

United States Office of Education. (1996). *Pursuing excellence: Initial findings from the Third International Mathematics and Science Study.* Washington, DC: Office of Educational Research and Improvement.

Waldrop, M. M. (1992). *Complexity: The emerging science at the edge of order and chaos.* New York: Simon & Schuster.

Whitaker, C. (1988, August). A generation in peril. *Ebony,* pp. 34–36.

READING 4.4 FOCUS QUESTIONS

(Jigsaw with other members of your team. Focus on the nonshaded portions of the reading.) Please take notes about the following three topics, and be prepared to report on them to others who have not prepared this reading.

Problems with the idea that traditional curricula may be more appropriate for some students	
Reasons for adding particular teaching practices to discussions about promoting equity in reform-oriented classrooms	
Particular equitable teaching practices highlighted	

Mark those paragraphs or short sections that relate to your notes. Be prepared to discuss them with other participants.

READING 4.4

Learning From Teaching
Exploring the Relationship
Between Reform Curriculum and Equity

Jo Boaler

Some researchers have expressed doubts about the potential of reform-oriented curricula to promote equity. This article considers this important issue and argues that investigations into equitable teaching must pay attention to the particular practices of teaching and learning that are enacted in classrooms. Data are presented from two studies in which middle school and high school teachers using reform-oriented mathematics curricula achieved a reduction in linguistic, ethnic, and class inequalities in their schools. The teaching and learning practices that these teachers employed were central to the attainment of equality, suggesting that it is critical that relational analyses of equity go beyond the curriculum to include the teacher and their teaching.

Please focus on the nonshaded portions of the reading.

The relationship between different teaching methods and students' understanding of mathematics is one that has fascinated teachers and researchers for decades (Benezet, 1935). When the mathematics reform movements of the 1980s were developed in different countries, they were based on the idea that open-ended problems that encourage students to choose different methods, combine them, and discuss them with their peers would provide productive learning experiences. There was considerable support for such ideas, and the last 20 years have witnessed the development of a plethora of curriculum materials that center on open-ended and contextualized mathematics problems. However, such materials and their associated teaching methods have not been well received by all parties (Battista, 1999; Becker & Jacob, 2000). Some of the objections to reform-oriented approaches have come from mathematicians and others who gained extensive understandings through more traditional routes (see, for example, Klein, 2001; Wu, 1999). Other objections have come from those who prefer to maintain the traditions of the past and who view changes to school presentations of mathematics as a challenge to the social order (Ball, 1995; Rosen, 2000). Recently, objections have come from a more unexpected source: Within the education community, some whose focus is on equity have expressed concerns that reform-oriented approaches to mathematics may not enhance the achievement of *all* students, as reformers originally hoped and claimed (Lubienski, 2000).

Lubienski (2000) monitored her own teaching of a reform-oriented classroom and noted that working-class students were less confident and successful than middle-class students. Some of the students attributed their lack of success to the open-ended nature of the work, a claim that prompted Lubienski to question the prevailing notion that reform curricular materials are advantageous for all children. Delpit (1988) has also raised questions about progressive reform movements, particularly challenging notions that they can distribute achievement more equitably. She contends that schools reproduce a "culture of power" (p. 285) and that "if you are not already a participant in the culture of power, being told explicitly the rules of that culture makes acquiring power easier" (p. 283). Delpit uses a number of examples to argue that approaches founded on principles of reform exacerbate inequalities because cultural and linguistic minority students expect and want teaching to be more direct, with explicit communication of the rules to which society attends. Delpit talks particularly about progressive approaches to reading, asserting that skills-oriented approaches may be more equitable because they teach concepts and skills directly rather than providing experiences through which students may learn them. Both Delpit and Lubienski express concerns about the limited access that some students have to new curricular approaches, raising extremely important questions for the future. In giving examples of reform-oriented approaches that, in their experience, did not reduce inequality, they also point to an urgent need for a greater understanding of the ways in which mathematics reform approaches, developed to enhance conceptual understanding, may do so more equitably.

The idea that some students may be disadvantaged by some of the reform-oriented curricula and teaching approaches that are used in schools is extremely important to consider and may reflect a certain naïveté in our assumptions that open teaching methods would be accessible to all. However, although it is very important to realize that some students may be less prepared than others to engage in the different roles that are required by open curricula, analyses that go from this idea to the claim that traditional curricula are more suitable may be very misleading. Such claims are problematic, partly because they reduce the complexity of teaching and learning to a question of curriculum, leaving the teaching of the curriculum relatively unexamined. Research has found that some reform approaches do promote equity and high achievement (e.g., Boaler, 1997a; Silver, Smith, & Nelson, 1995), and it is important to understand the conditions that supported such achievements and to examine the ways in which these reform approaches differed from others (Greeno & MMAP, 1998). This knowledge could advance our understanding of teacher practices that are productive in open environments and the teacher learning that may support them. The field of mathematics education does not currently have a nuanced or well-differentiated knowledge base about equitable teaching practices. The first wave of research into the impact of reform has tended, necessarily, to report on the relationships between students' understanding and broad teaching approaches, such as teaching through group work or whole-class discussions (Boaler, 1998; Hiebert & Wearne, 1993). In this article, I open these and other teaching practices for closer examination and contend that the differences between equitable and inequitable teaching approaches lie *within* the different methods commonly discussed by researchers. I suggest that greater insights into equity will result from an understanding of the ways in which teachers work to enact different approaches.

The idea that traditional curricula may be more appropriate for some students than for others is problematic because of its exclusive focus on curriculum. Moreover, the claim that open-ended materials and methods are less suitable for working-class or ethnic minority students is dangerous when considered within an educational system in which many already subscribe to the view that working class students cannot cope with more demanding work (Boaler, 1997a; Gutiérrez, 1996). In such a context, researchers need to be particularly careful and responsible in their reporting, making sure that they carefully examine all possible sources of equality and inequality. Haberman (1991) and Ladson-Billings (1997) have referred to the procedural teaching that is frequently offered in urban schools as a *pedagogy of poverty*, and Anyon (1980, 1981) has noted the prevalence of closed and procedural approaches in working-class schools. If observations that reform curricula do not always eradicate inequalities are not counterbalanced by investigations into the ways they may do so, reservations about reform ideas could perpetuate these deficit patterns of opportunity.

Another shortcoming of claims that traditional approaches may be better for some students is that such assertions tend to locate the problem within the students themselves. Educators must understand the needs of different groups of students not to develop negative ideas about the students' mathematical potential (Varenne & Mcdermott, 1999) but to become aware of the ways in which schools can serve all students. This will require a shift in focus away from what *students cannot do*—for example, cope well with open-ended problems—to what *schools can do* to make the educational experience more equitable. The aim of this article is to begin such an investigation, drawing on different studies that give insights into the ways that equity may be achieved. First I offer a theoretical grounding for questions of teaching and equity before moving to two examples of teaching that was organized to promote equity. I focus on the particular teaching practices that teachers used, and I argue that the field is in need of additional examples of *particular* teaching practices that reduce inequalities.

THEORIES OF CULTURAL REPRODUCTION ■

Investigations into sources of inequality have led researchers to propose that certain cultural elements mediate the relationship between people's lives and the economic structures of society (Mehan, Hubbard, & Villanueva, 1994). In this process, children learn cultural knowledge from their families—for example, ways of dressing, speaking, interacting and so on. Research suggests that children from working-class homes acquire a form of cultural capital (Bourdieu, 1986) that is different from that of children in middle- or upper-class homes and that schools recognize the cultural capital of middle-class learners. Thus, middle-class children are more likely to be perceived as effective learners merely because of their "congruency with the formal context of schooling" (Zevenbergen, 1996, p. 105).

Theories of cultural reproduction (e.g., Bourdieu & Passeron, 1977; Bowles & Gintis, 1976), which draw from both sociology and anthropology, do not deal with overt intentions or claim that teachers deliberately support students of their own gender, race, or class above others. These theories deal instead with more subtle demonstrations of power that "relate to linguistic forms, communicative strategies, and presentation of self; that is, ways of talking, ways of writing, ways of dressing, and ways of interacting" (Delpit, 1988, p. 283). Such theories are persuasive because they provide explanations for the fact that schools not only reflect but also reinforce social class disparities, despite the best intentions of educators.

Cultural reproduction theories are important to mathematics education reforms since researchers have argued that the norms of reform-oriented classrooms are consonant with the norms of White, middle-class homes. Delpit draws from Heath's data (1983) to argue that White, middle-class students are generally more accustomed to interpreting indirect statements from parents, whereas some Black and working-class students are more likely to expect facts and rules to be communicated directly. Thus, teaching approaches that expect students to discuss ideas and discover mathematical relationships through exploration may be less accessible to children who are used to receiving information more directly. There have been objections to theories of cultural reproduction on the ground that they are overly deterministic, emphasizing social and structural constraints at the expense of individual actions (Mehan, 1992; Varenne & McDermott, 1998). It is clear that students do not just assume or uncritically accept the norms of the home or school but instead play an important part in forming, accepting and, in some instances, resisting such norms

(Apple & Christian-Smith, 1991). But sociologists and anthropologists seem to agree on at least one issue: Learning to be successful in school involves understanding and following the rules of the school "game"—what Pope (1999) has defined as *doing school*—with middle-class learners frequently at an advantage. It is extremely important that movements to "reform" mathematics teaching—for example, by making it more open and contextualized—do not serve to enhance current disparities in achievement that result from subtle forms of cultural congruency. Relationships between students' expectations and predispositions and the demands of new teaching approaches are very important to consider.

Theories of cultural reproduction suggest that there are certain practices that students need to learn in school in order to be successful and that these are related to, but go beyond, an understanding of subject content (Jackson, 1989). This suggestion fits with an emerging body of research that highlights the importance of students' understanding their role in reform-oriented classrooms. Corbett and Wilson (1995) argue that those who are promoting educational reforms have generally overlooked the fact that students in reform-oriented classrooms need to develop not only new ways of working but an understanding of and a commitment to the changes in their roles: "Students must change during reform, not just as a consequence of it" (p. 12). This is a simple but important point that has been given surprisingly little attention. Thus, researchers have written extensively about the ways in which students may benefit from reforms but have paid relatively little attention to the implications of such reforms for students' roles. Cohen and Ball (2000) have termed the different practices that students need to employ and understand in school *learning practices.* One important learning practice that Corbett and Wilson (1995) draw attention to is explaining work. In traditional mathematics classrooms, students are required to produce correct answers, but in reform-oriented classrooms, they often need to go beyond correct answers and explain their methods, justifying the approaches they have used. Lubienski (2000) reported that middle-class students in her classroom were more likely than working-class students to justify their answers in keeping with the expectations of the reform curriculum that she followed. Although she used this finding as an illustration of the possible inappropriateness of open-ended curricula, it could equally be given as an example of a teaching opportunity. To be successful in the classroom, students need to master not only mathematics but also particular schooling and learning practices. Researchers need to address the important task of considering the ways in which students might learn the different practices that support successful participation in reform mathematics classrooms.

Yackel and Cobb (1996) draw attention to the norms of mathematics classrooms, distinguishing between norms that they describe as social and those that are sociomathematical. Their depiction and naming of the repeated classroom practices in which teachers and students engage and that develop gradually over time, has been extremely generative. This is partly because classroom norms, such as "what counts as an acceptable mathematical explanation and justification" (Yackel & Cobb, 1996, p. 461), pay attention to a level of detail in the enactment of teaching that has been lacking from many analyses (Lampert, 1985). Sociomathematical norms offer a lens through which to examine and describe the colors and contours of mathematics classrooms, giving names to some of the important choices to which teachers and students attend in the activity of mathematics teaching and learning. The notion of learning practices operates at a similar level of detail, drawing attention to the specific actions and practices in which students need to engage in different classrooms. Knowing when and how to take notes as a teacher talks is an example of a learning practice in which students may need to engage but that is rarely given specific attention or taught. There are many different learning practices that may give students access to the norms that are in place in their classrooms and, concurrently, to mathematical understanding and success. These range from general practices, such as asking questions or taking notes, to specific practices, such as knowing to sketch a diagram of a mathematics problem. Pólya (1971) and others have considered what successful solvers of mathematics problems do, producing lists of possible strategies. Learning practices could include such strategies as well as the other actions in which students need to engage to be successful in their mathematics classrooms. Reform classrooms require different learning practices from those called for in more traditional classrooms. If access to these practices is inequitably distributed at the present time, as Lubienski and Delpit have suggested, then it seems important to consider ways in which successful practices may be learned by all students.

The field of mathematics education does not currently have an extensive or well-developed knowledge base of the particular ways in which teachers mediate curriculum approaches to make them equitable, including, for example, the learning practices to which they may need to pay explicit attention. The development of such a knowledge base seems to have been severely hampered by the pervasive public focus on curriculum approaches. Teachers, researchers, mathematicians, and policymakers have all argued about what curricula should be used in classrooms. Although opponents and proponents of different curricula have disagreed about the importance of open-ended work or structured questions, they have rarely considered the ways in which teachers can or do manage such approaches. Yet, to be successful, the new approaches call for different kinds of teacher knowledge (Ball & Bass, 2000a, 2000b) and changes in student roles (Corbett & Wilson, 1995). The "math wars," as they have been termed in the United States, have comprised bitter battles fought in schools, districts, and the popular press as opponents and proponents of reform-oriented teaching argue their cases. Such battles are unfortunate for many reasons, not the least of which is that the broad focus on curricula necessitated by such arguments has served to reduce the learning experience to an interaction between students and curriculum. This has drawn attention away from the teaching practices that mediate student success and that require considerable understanding and support.

Cohen, Raudenbush, and Ball (2002) propose that teaching and learning be understood as a set of practices that come into play at the intersections among teachers, students, and content in environments, and they represent mathematics teaching and learning by an instructional triangle (shown in Figure 4.4a), the vertices of which are teachers, students, and content. Cohen and his colleagues suggest that learning opportunities arise at the intersections among these different variables and that few learning occasions can be understood without consideration of the contribution made by the teacher, the students, the discipline of mathematics, and the ways in which they interact within environments. They propose moreover that environments, traditionally regarded as outside influences, "become active inside instruction" (2002, p. 98).

This focus on practice is consistent with the perspective of situated theory (Greeno & MMAP, 1998; Lave, 1996; Lave & Wenger 1991), and it has profound implications for research, curriculum, and professional development. Lampert (1985) has cautioned that "efforts to build generalized theories of instruction, curriculum, or classroom management based on careful empirical research have much to contribute to the improvement of teaching, but they do not sufficiently describe the work of teaching" (p. 179). A focus on general methods of instruction, at the expense of an examination of particular teacher moves, is pervasive within and outside the education community. Broad teaching and curriculum approaches are extremely important to consider, but Ball, Cohen, Lampert and others have argued lucidly that understanding the difference between effective and ineffective teaching requires a focus on the *practices* of teaching and learning.

In the next sections of this article, I describe and examine interactions that constitute teaching and learning, as well as particular teacher moves that promote equity, by analyzing two examples of equitable teaching and learning practices—one from England and another from the United States. Both approaches were reform oriented and contributed to a reduction of linguistic, ethnic, and class inequalities. The fact that these approaches promoted equity is important, since it casts doubt on claims that reform-oriented approaches are inequitable. In the final section, I consider a more important question—what methods did the teachers use to promote equity in their mediation of the reform curriculum? I consider only a small proportion of the teachers' practices, but these will show that any reduction of the learning experience to an interaction between students and curriculum is essentially flawed, because teachers and their teaching of different curricula are central to the promotion of equity.

Figure 4.4a   Instruction as Interaction of Teachers, Students, and Content in Environments

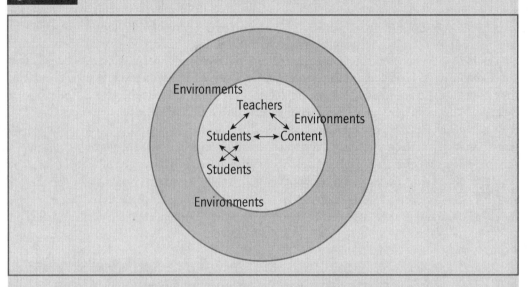

Note: From "Resources, Instruction, and Research," by D. K. Cohen, S. Raudenbush, and D. L. Ball, 2002, in *Evidence Matters: Randomized Trials in Education Research*, edited by R. Boruch and F. Mosteller (p. 88), Washington, DC: Brookings Institution Press. Copyright 2002 by the Brookings Institution Press. Reprinted with permission.

■ EVIDENCE OF EQUITABLE TEACHING

In previous issues of *JRME* (Boaler, 1998, 2000), I summarized the results of a 3-year investigation of the experiences and achievements of approximately 300 students attending secondary schools with vastly different mathematics teaching approaches in England. Both schools were situated in low-income areas and the majority of the students at both schools were White and working class. One of the schools (Phoenix Park) used an open-ended approach to mathematics; the other (Amber Hill) used a procedural, skill-based approach. I mentioned but did not expand on the fact that the students in the open-ended approach attained not only a higher level of achievement but also more equal achievement. In an earlier article (Boaler, 1997b), I investigated the relationship between mathematics achievement and social class for the 300 students from age 13, when they first encountered a different approach to mathematics, until age 16, when they reached the end of their compulsory schooling. When the 110 students in the year cohort at Phoenix Park started at the school, significant class disparities were already evident in their achievement levels. The correlation between social class[1] and mathematics attainment at that time was .43. I had not monitored the students' experiences prior to their time at Phoenix Park, but I knew that the middle schools they attended employed ability grouping and a traditional curriculum. In England, social class often correlates significantly with achievement as well as with placement in ability groups—a process presumed to contribute to social inequalities (Abraham, 1995; Ball, 1981; Tomlinson, 1987). When the students left Phoenix Park 3 years later, having worked in mixed ability groups on an open, project-based mathematics curriculum, the partial correlation between achievement and social class, after controlling for initial attainment, was only .15. At Amber Hill, where the teachers used a procedural approach to mathematics, the initial correlation between the students' attainment at age 13 and their social class was .19. It was not possible to know why the initial correlations were so different at the two schools, but the Amber Hill students had worked for the previous 2 years in mixed ability groups, whereas the Phoenix Park students had worked in groups that were tracked on the basis of ability. After 3 years of working with a procedural mathematics curriculum in ability groups, the partial correlation between achievement and social class for the 196 Amber Hill students, after controlling for initial attainment, was .30. In addition, a comparison of the Amber Hill students' initial attainment at age 13 and their ultimate attainment at age 16 revealed that 80% of those attaining above their projected potential were middle class, whereas 80% of those achieving below their projected potential were working class. At Phoenix Park, overachievers and underachievers were equally distributed among working-class and middle-class students (Boaler, 1997a, 1997b).

At the beginning of that study, the cohorts of students at the two schools were matched by gender, race, and social class, and there were no significant differences in their levels of mathematics attainment at that time. Three years later, the students at the project-based school (Phoenix Park) attained significantly higher grades on a range of assessments, including the national examination ($\chi^2 (1, N = 290) = 12.5, p < .001$). They outperformed the Amber Hill students despite the comparability of the mathematics attainment of the students in the two schools at age 13 and the extra time spent on task by students at Amber Hill, the traditional school (Boaler, 1997a). In addition, although the boys at Amber Hill earned significantly higher grades than the girls did, no gender disparities were manifest in achievement at Phoenix Park.

Thus, the school that used an open-ended approach not only achieved significant academic results for its students—whose examination results were higher than the national average, despite their school's location in one of the poorest areas of the country—but also reduced the inequalities that typically correlate with gender or social class. These results, particularly the increase in class polarization at Amber Hill, stand in direct contrast to the idea that "the algorithmic mode of instruction might provide a relatively level playing field" (Lubienski, 2000, p. 478).

The QUASAR project (Brown, Stein, & Forman, 1996; Lane & Silver, 1999; Silver, Smith, & Nelson, 1995) began with the assumption that mathematical proficiency could be attained by all students and that it would increase in poor and minority communities if teachers placed a greater emphasis on problem solving, communication, and conceptual understanding. Teachers in six urban middle schools serving socially and culturally diverse populations of students in the United States spent 5 years developing and implementing a more open and discursive mathematics curriculum. Students learned about facts and algorithms, but they also learned when, how, and why to apply procedures, which they used to solve high-level problems. There were a number of similarities between the QUASAR and Phoenix Park approaches, including mixed-ability classes, a focus on problem solving, high expectations for all students, attention to a broad array of mathematical topics, and the encouragement of discussion and justification. As measured over time, the QUASAR students' achievement revealed extremely positive results. The students made significant gains in achievement, and they performed at significantly higher levels than comparable groups of students on a range of different assessments. Furthermore, the gains were distributed equally among the different racial, ethnic, and linguistic groups of students.

The results of these and other studies (e.g., Knapp, Shields, & Turnbull, 1995) cast considerable doubt on claims that open-ended approaches are less suitable for working-class and minority children, but they also raise an important question. Why did the reform-oriented approaches of the Phoenix Park and QUASAR teachers appear to promote equality when other reform curricula have not reduced inequalities (Lubienski, 2000)? The answer to this question may be important to our field, and next I address the particular practices of teaching and learning that the Phoenix Park and QUASAR teachers employed and that appeared to have an impact on the attainment of equality.

■ A FOCUS ON TEACHING AND LEARNING PRACTICES

At Phoenix Park School the curriculum was designed by the teachers. They did not use any textbooks but instead brought together a collection of different open-ended projects that generally lasted for 2 to 3 weeks of mathematics lessons (for more information on Phoenix Park's approach, see Boaler, 1997a). The teachers designed the curriculum with teachers who came from five other schools and were part of a working group of teachers in the Association of Teachers of Mathematics (the British equivalent of NCTM). When I conducted my research study, the school had been using an open-ended approach for 2 years.

When the students arrived at Phoenix Park, many of them were immediately receptive to the open-ended mathematics approach that they encountered, despite having spent the previous 8 years working on more closed and traditional mathematics questions. However, some of the students—most of them boys—found the openness of the work extremely disconcerting. They, like some students in the Lubienski study (2000), said that they were uncomfortable with the lack of structure or direction in the problems and indicated that they would prefer a more traditional approach. These students, along with the majority of their peers at Phoenix Park, lived in severe poverty on a housing estate (similar to subsidized housing projects in the United States), where drug-related and other crimes were widespread and the police would not venture at night. When I interviewed the Phoenix Park students at the beginning of the study, they described their motivations clearly. The following comments from Shaun and Megan, two Year 9 students, are typical. (These names and the others that follow are all pseudonyms; JB is of course the author.)

Shaun   When I go into a maths lesson I usually sit down and I think—who am I going to throw a rubber [eraser] at today?

JB   Can you think of a maths lesson that you've enjoyed?

Megan   Messing about, that's what I enjoy doing.

JB   What would make maths better?

Megan   Working from books—you don't mess about if you've got a book there, you know what to do.

Although some students blamed their misbehavior on the openness of the work, the teachers did not give the students books or structure. Providing such materials and methods may have been the easiest option, but the Phoenix Park teachers believed that the open-ended approach that they used was valuable for *all* students and that it was their job to make the work equally accessible to all. They therefore developed a range of practices that served to increase the students' access to the problems and the methods they were expected to use. In the sections that follow, I describe three such practices in order to highlight these particular practices and to illustrate the importance of the detailed teacher *moves* that could become a greater part of the lexicography of mathematics education (Lampert, 1985). Where appropriate, I also include examples of similar practices from QUASAR classrooms.

Introducing Activities Through Discussion

One practice that was central to the Phoenix Park teachers' approach was introducing students to the activities through discussions in which the teachers themselves participated. This enabled the teachers to decide on the degree of support or structure students needed. In the 3 years that students attended Phoenix Park, they were never left to interpret text-based problems alone. The teachers always spent time with individuals, groups, or the whole class introducing ideas and making sure that all students knew how to start their explorations. Phoenix Park teachers would frequently ask students to gather around the board when new problems were being introduced and when homework was being assigned, in order to have some discussion of the problems posed. (More detail on the actual ways in which teachers introduced activities in Phoenix Park is given in Boaler, 2002).

Likewise, teachers in the QUASAR classrooms also spent time introducing problems. Margaret Schwan Smith (personal communication, January 18, 2001) reported that she observed one urban middle school teacher who would ask her students to read problems aloud in class and then would hold a discussion about their contexts and any unfamiliar vocabulary. Afterward, she would ask students to discuss what they thought the problems were calling for them to do, and then she would have them work in groups while she circulated to check that individual students understood what they should do. Group and class discussions of the aim of activities, the meaning of contexts, the challenging points within problems, and the access points to which students might turn were employed by Phoenix Park and QUASAR teachers to make tasks equally accessible to all students. These methods stand in contrast with those employed by teachers in many classrooms where students are left to interpret the meaning of problems from their reading of reform texts, which are often extremely wordy and linguistically demanding. The way in which work is introduced to students and the access that students are given to the mathematical ideas that they are intended to explore seems to be extremely important.

Teaching Students to Explain and Justify

A second important feature of the Phoenix Park teachers' practice was that they paid attention to the ways in which students communicated their mathematical thinking as well as the students' understanding of the need for that aspect of their work. The teachers at Phoenix Park were committed to encouraging students to explain and justify their thinking. They frequently urged individual students to explain their reasoning and communicate in more detail because the students were not used to doing so when they arrived at the school. In one of the lessons that I observed, a student gave the teacher his solution to a problem on which he had been working. His paper showed some of his methods, and a correct answer. The Year 10 teacher, whom I call Rosie Thomas, studied it for a while and then said, "Brilliant work, John, but you can't just write it down, there must be some sense to why you've done it, some logic—why did you do it that way?—explain it."

Rosie's comment "there must be some sense to why you've done it" typifies the sort of encouragement the students were given at Phoenix Park. The teachers strove to expand the way in which the students thought about mathematics, extending the students' value systems to incorporate more than the desire to attain correct answers. There was considerable evidence that they were successful in that regard, as illustrated in this excerpt from my interview with Ian, a Year 10 student:

Ian   It's an easier way to learn, because you're actually finding things out for yourself, not looking for things in the textbook.

JB   Was that the same in your last school, do you think?

Ian   No, like if we got an answer, they would say, "you got it right." Here you have to explain how you got it.

JB   What do you think about that?

Ian   I think it helps you.

In one of the lessons that I observed, the teacher asked the students to gather around the board, and then she posed the following question: "If someone new came into class and they asked you what makes a good piece of work? What does Ms. Thomas like? What would you say?" The first student offered "lots of writing"; others offered suggestions such as "have an aim," "draw a plan," and "write about patterns." Each time, the teacher came back with further questions: "Is the amount of writing important?" "What does that mean?" "Why is a plan important?" "What does a good plan look like?" "Why do we record patterns?" The students struggled over many of their explanations, but they sat around the board engrossed in this discussion for some time. The students were clearly appreciative of the opportunity to learn about valued ways of working. As they talked, the teacher kept a record of the students' suggestions on the board. After approximately 40 minutes of discussion, the teacher told the students that their task was to design a poster describing the different features of "good work." She also gave them a page that the mathematics department had prepared called "Hints for Investigations." The handout was divided into three columns—What to say, How to say it, and Making sense of it—that gave various suggestions for students. "Can you make the problem more general?" one entry asked. "Make the original problem more difficult," another suggested, and "Now explain how or why your algebraic rules work," a third prompted. The students studied the page and incorporated many of its suggestions into their posters. This lesson focused explicitly on the mathematical *learning practices* (Cohen & Ball, 2000) of explanation and justification, as well planning, labeling, drawing diagrams, and other practices that the students would need to employ in pursuing their mathematical investigations. Many of the practices were those that are valued in other reform-oriented classrooms, but teachers do not always give them such explicit attention. Teachers may assume that students will understand the need for such practices and other new methods of working. At Phoenix Park, when the teachers found that some students were not communicating their thinking or interpreting numerical answers, they devoted more time to this aspect of their teaching, assuming that the students' reluctance reflected a gap in their understanding of what was required in the work.

Making Real World Contexts Accessible

One of the reservations that Lubienski (2000) and others have expressed about reform-oriented teaching involves the use of real-world contexts. Many of the reform-oriented curricula that are used in different countries are replete with contexts that are intended to bring some realism into the mathematics classroom. I share Lubienski's concerns about the potential of these curricula for increasing the gap between low and high socioeconomic students, between boys and girls (Boaler, 1994; Murphy, 1990; Murphy, Gipps, & UNESCO, 1996), and between students of different cultural groups (Ball, 1995; Silver, Smith & Nelson, 1995; Zevenbergen, 2000) if such curricula are not carefully introduced. One of the problems presented by real-world contexts is that they often require familiarity with the situation that is described, but such familiarity cannot always be assumed. In teaching mathematics to a linguistically and culturally diverse class of elementary students, Deborah Ball (1995) found that contexts could be "unevenly familiar or interesting," a state of affairs that caused some distraction and confusion that "diminished the sense of collective purpose" in her class (p. 672). Ball led her students in explorations of theoretical, abstract, and at times esoteric mathematical concepts that fascinated the children, causing her to conclude that contexts are far from necessary for the encouragement of high-level thinking among young children.

One significant problem arises in many contexts when students are required simultaneously to engage with the contexts as though they were real and to ignore factors that would pertain to real-life versions of the tasks. As Adda (1989) puts it, we might offer students questions involving the price of sweets, but the students must remember that "it would be dangerous to answer them by referring to the price of sweets bought this morning" (p. 150). Yet, mathematics books—particularly commercially produced, reform-oriented curriculum—are full of examples of pseudo-situations that students are meant to consider. Knowing how much consideration to give to the real-world factors presented in questions has now become a form of school knowledge that students need and that appears to be inequitably distributed (Boaler, 1993, 1994; Cooper & Dunne, 1998; Zevenbergen, 2000). The QUASAR teachers addressed this issue by engaging students in conversations about the meaning of the different contexts that they encountered in questions. In one published example, the teacher introduced a question about the most economical way to buy bus tickets—as a weekly pass or as daily tickets (Silver, Smith, & Nelson, 1995). The textbook authors intended students to calculate the most cost-effective tickets, but the students, understandably, considered the variables in the question—such as how often they would use a weekly ticket and the different family members that could use it. Lubienski (2000) draws similar examples from her own classroom of students' considering given contexts and variables that would pertain in the real world—whether people would want "seconds" (another piece) of pizza, for instance, in what was intended to be a straightforward calculation of dividing a pizza into slices. When a QUASAR teacher realized that students were situating their reasoning in the context of their lives and that there was more than one correct answer to such problems, she changed her expectations and provided students with opportunities to explain their reasoning. Silver, Smith, and Nelson (1995) conclude from similar situations that "increasing the relevance of school mathematics to the lives of children involves more than merely providing 'real world' contexts for mathematics problems; real-world solutions for these problems must also be considered." (p. 41).

At Phoenix Park, the teachers rarely gave the students contextualized mathematics questions from published curricula, but they did attempt to make the different mathematical explorations relevant to the students by relating them to their lives. For example, when introducing work on statistics, the teachers asked the students to collect data that was of interest to them from newspapers and magazines. When the problems involved patterns and tessellations, they asked students to bring in patterns that they liked. In another situation, one of the teachers whom I observed suggested to a girl who was interested in babies that she investigate the admissions policy of the nursery that was attached to the school. Thus, the Phoenix Park teachers encouraged students to relate mathematics to issues and topics in their lives. They, like the QUASAR teachers, did not expect students to interpret contextualized textbook questions exactly as the textbook authors intended—that is, assuming a certain degree of reality *but not too much* (Wiliam, 1997).

Both the Phoenix Park and QUASAR teachers encouraged students to interpret mathematical and real-world variables and their relationship with one another. In doing so, these teachers were able to promote equity and help students view mathematics as a flexible means by which to interpret reality. There are important reasons for moving mathematics instruction beyond the abstract, making it extremely worthwhile to explore the ways in which teachers can accomplish this goal in a manner that treats their students equitably. The recognition that girls and boys, as well as students of different social, cultural, or linguistic groups, encounter contexts differently is relatively recent, and researchers from across the world are considering the implications of this finding (Cooper & Dunne, 1998; Zevenbergen, 2000). The recommendations that are emerging from this work center on ways in which teachers can use contexts more equitably, allowing all students to consider the constraints that real situations involve and to attend to the necessary *code switching* that may be an important and more general feature of "doing school" (Pope, 1999).

The three practices that I have highlighted were intrinsic to the Phoenix Park teachers' success in engaging students in reform-oriented mathematics investigations even though the students had not engaged in such work before they arrived at the school. After months of careful support from the Phoenix Park teachers, the students who had struggled and been extremely reluctant to accept an open approach started to become more interested in their work and more comfortable with the freedom that they were given. The change in some of the disaffected boys became most obvious when, in the 2nd year of the school (Year 10), they were taught by a student teacher who tried to teach mathematics in a more traditional way. The following extract from my observation notes records how the boys started to complain about the *closed* nature of the work that was given to them. This was very different from the approach to which they had, by then, become accustomed:

> The teacher starts the lesson by asking the class to copy what he is writing off the board. He is writing about different forms of data, qualitative and quantitative. The students are very quiet and they start to copy off the board. The teacher then stops writing for a while and tells the students about the different types of data. He then asks them to continue copying off the board. After a few minutes of silent copying Gary shouts out, "Sir, when are we going to do some work?" Leigh follows this up with "Yeah, are we going to do any work today, sir?" Barry then adds, "This is boring, it's just copying." The teacher ignores this and carries on writing and talking about data. The boys go back to copying. The teacher looks across at Lorraine, who is looking puzzled, and asks her if she "is OK"; she says, "No, not really, what does all this stuff mean?" This seems to annoy the teacher, or make him uncomfortable; he turns back to the board and continues writing. Gary persists with his questioning, this time asking, "Sir, why are we doing all this?" The teacher replies, "We are just rounding off the work you have done."
>
> After about 20 minutes of board work, the teacher asks the students to go through all of their examples of data collection that they have done over recent weeks and write down whether they are qualitative or quantitative. Peter asks, "Sir, what's the point of this? Aren't we going to do any work today?" The teacher responds with "you need to know what these words mean." Peter replies, "But we know what they mean, you've just written it on the board so we know."

This series of interactions was particularly interesting to observe because it was the group of boys who had at first been most resistant to open-ended work who now objected to the closed nature of the work the student teacher gave them. The boys repeatedly asked "whether they were going to do any work today," indicating that they did not regard copying off the board as work, probably because it did not present them with a problem to solve. When the student teacher told them to classify data as quantitative or qualitative so that they would learn what the words meant, Peter questioned the point of this because they had already been told what they meant. Yet, the mathematics teaching offered in this example is fairly characteristic of more traditional high school mathematics pedagogy in which the teacher explains what something means to students, they copy it down from the board, and then they practice some examples of their own. The degree of resistance that the students offered seems important to consider. In a different class, the regular teacher was absent one day, and when he returned, one of the boys who had been initially resistant complained about the substitute teacher they had been given. "It was terrible," the boy said. "We had this teacher who acted like he knew all the answers and we just had to find them."

My description of practices that the Phoenix Park and QUASAR teachers used to enhance students' access to the reform approaches—helping them to understand the questions posed to them, teaching them to appreciate the need for written communication and justification, and discussing with them ways of interpreting contextualized questions—includes only a small part of the teachers' repertoires of practices. Nevertheless, these examples provide some indication of the complex support that teachers using reform-oriented approaches may need to provide to students. Ball and Bass (2000a, 2000b) have offered a careful analysis of the mathematical understandings that teachers need when they engage students in collaborative explorations. Their analysis has shown that teaching approaches based on student investigations, exploration, and discussion confer on mathematics teachers additional demands that we are only now beginning to understand. Confrey (1990) observed a teacher who employed constructivist principles and recorded the particular methods that the teachers used to promote student thinking. Some of these methods, including asking students to restate problems in their own words— are similar to methods that were used by the Phoenix Park teachers to great effect. Henningsen and Stein's (1997) analysis has also been valuable in identifying the particular aspects of the QUASAR teachers' practices that supported understanding: using tasks that built on students' prior understanding, giving appropriate amounts of time, and modeling high-level performance. Such detailed investigations and descriptions of the ways teachers enact reform approaches are still rare, but they may be essential to advancing our understanding of the demands of reform-oriented teaching and the development of more appropriate learning opportunities for teachers.

DISCUSSION AND CONCLUSION ■

My brief description of the work of the Phoenix Park and QUASAR teachers is intended to serve as an illustration both of the particular teaching practices that need to be considered in mathematics classrooms and of the effectiveness of teachers who are committed to equity and the goals of open-ended work. Gutiérrez (1996, 1999, 2000, 2002) has provided more detailed and careful analyses of teachers who achieved equitable outcomes using reform curricula in low-income and culturally and linguistic diverse communities. She concluded from her work that our greatest hope for providing equitable teaching environments is to focus on teachers' *practices* (Gutiérrez, 2002), investing our time and resources in the teachers who enact reform curricula. The Phoenix Park mathematics department was relatively unusual. In England, schools rather than districts choose new teachers, and the Phoenix Park department had carefully selected new teachers who wanted to teach through open-ended projects and were dedicated to equity. In addition, the mathematics activities at the school had been chosen and designed by the teachers; these teachers shared a commitment to and knowledge of the activities they used. This is different from the scenario that often plays out in American schools in which the district chooses both the curriculum and the teachers. Reform-oriented curricula are often used by teachers who have received no training in their use and have no commitment to the materials. Although the Phoenix Park mathematics department may be unusual, the results that it achieved are nonetheless an important illustration of what can be done. The role of the teacher in securing high-level equitable teaching environments has been minimized in debates surrounding curriculum (Becker & Jacob, 2000). Yet, it seems that the teachers' mediation of different curricular approaches is central to the attainment of equity. Furthermore, advancing awareness of the particular learning practices that are required to make reform-oriented approaches accessible to all students appears to be an important stage in the process.

Sociologists propose that open approaches to learning not only give access to a depth of subject understanding but also encourage a personal and intellectual freedom that should be the right of all people in society (Ball, 1993; Willis, 1977). Moreover, they suggest that opportunities for higher-level thinking are inequitably distributed in schools, a situation that serves to maintain the structural class inequalities that exist in many societies. Willis (1977) characterizes this state of affairs as a process by which "working-class kids" are prepared for "working-class jobs." Anyon (1981) has supplied some insight into this relationship, finding that schools in poor and working-class areas "discouraged personal assertiveness and intellectual inquisitiveness in students and assigned work that most often involved substantial amounts of rote activity" (p. 203). The situation at Amber Hill school conformed to this finding in that the mathematics teachers offered a structured, procedural approach and explained to me in interviews that they needed to do so because the students were from poor backgrounds and would not have been able to cope with open-ended work. This was not a malicious belief—the teachers simply believed that students did not receive the support at home that they needed to cope with work that was linguistically and conceptually demanding, so they provided them with more structure to help them. The Phoenix Park teachers did not hold these beliefs; they thought that all students could benefit from open-ended work and that the students' home lives should not be a barrier to their pursuit of mathematical explorations.

Anyone and others suggest that teachers tend to offer working-class students more structure, presenting mathematics as a closed domain with clear rules to follow. Other researchers have noted a relationship between the level of the mathematics and the degree of structure provided. Thus, some teachers believe that students who experience more difficulty should be given more structure (Confrey, 1990; Orton & Frobisher, 1996). This view is easy to understand, particularly by those of us who have been in teaching situations when a student has expressed frustration at trying to understand a concept and the provision of a structured procedure would have encouraged immediate success. But my observations of teaching and learning within high and low attainment groups of students and my interviews with students in these groups (Boaler, Wiliam, & Brown, 2000) have demonstrated the importance of questioning the relationship between level of achievement and structure. In addition, the Phoenix Park teachers demonstrated that students of all levels and from all backgrounds could be assisted to develop a conceptual understanding of the mathematics with which they were engaged. These teachers did not succumb to the temptation to spoon-feed students who sought such help, and the rewards of their hard work were the students' achievements. This is not to suggest that teachers should never make decisions to provide students with additional structure, only that such decisions should not correlate with mathematics level or social class. As long as we set conceptual understanding as a goal for students, it is imperative that it be a goal for *all* students. Teachers who are aware that students of low SES or low achievement levels encounter difficulties in interpreting open work must accompany this knowledge by a drive to understand the students' experiences and provide action to make the teaching of open-ended approaches equitable.

The different teachers whose work I have reviewed in this article all spent time sharing understanding of the learning practices that students needed for their work on open-ended mathematics problems. The advances that they made in giving equitable access to these approaches demonstrate two important points. First, an understanding of the ways in which open-ended approaches promote equity will involve a consideration of the *detailed* practices of teaching and learning that occur in classrooms (Chazan & Ball, 1999). Researchers and others will need to delve inside the general teaching approaches that have been the subject of discussion of recent years. Second, such work may contribute to helping mathematics teachers replace the "pedagogies of poverty" (Haberman, 1991, p. 290), which often predominate in low income and minority communities, with pedagogies of power.

NOTE ■

1. Social class was determined using the information from the Office of Population Censuses and Surveys (1980).

REFERENCES ■

Abraham, J. (1995). *Divide and school: Gender and class dynamics in comprehensive education.* London: Falmer Press.

Adda, J. (1989). The mathematics classroom as a microsociety. In C. Keitel, P. Damerow, A. Bishop, & P. Gerdes (Eds.), *Mathematics, education, and society* (pp. 149–150). Paris: United Nations Educational Scientific.

Anyon, J. (1980). Social class and the hidden curriculum of work. *Journal of Education, 162*(1), 67–92.

Anyon, J. (1981). Schools as agencies of social legitimization. *International Journal of Political Education, 4,* 195–218.

Apple, M., & Christian-Smith, L. (1991). The politics of the textbook. In M. Apple & L. Christian-Smith (Eds.), *The politics of the textbook* (pp. 1–21). London: Routledge.

Ball, D. L. (1995). Transforming pedagogy: Classrooms as mathematical communities—A response to Timothy Lensmire and John Pryor. *Harvard Educational Review, 65,* 670–677.

Ball, D. L., & Bass, H. (2000a). Bridging practices: Intertwining content and pedagogy in teaching and learning to teach. In J. Boaler (Ed.), *Multiple perspectives on mathematics teaching and learning* (pp. 83–104). Westport, CT: Ablex Publishing.

Ball, D. L., & Bass, H. (2000b). Making believe: The collective construction of public mathematical knowledge in the elementary classroom. In D. Phillips (Ed.), *Yearbook of the National Society for the Study of Education: Constructivism in education* (pp. 193–224). Chicago: Chicago University Press.

Ball, S. J. (1981). *Beachside comprehensive.* Cambridge, England: Cambridge University Press.

Ball, S. J. (1993). Education, majorism, and the "curriculum of the dead." *Curriculum Studies, 1,* 195–214.

Battista, M. (1999). The mathematical miseducation of America's youth. *Phi Delta Kappan, 80,* 425–433.

Becker, J., & Jacob, B. (2000). California school mathematics politics: The anti-reform of 1997–1999. *Phi Delta Kappan, 80,* 529–537.

Benezet, L. P. (1935). The teaching of Arithmetic I: The story of an experiment. *Journal of the National Education Association, 24,* 241–244.

Boaler, J. (1993). The role of contexts in the mathematics classroom: Do they make mathematics more "real"? *For the Learning of Mathematics, 13*(2), 12–17.

Boaler, J. (1994). When do girls prefer football to fashion? An analysis of female underachievement in relation to "realistic" mathematics contexts. *British Educational Research Journal, 20,* 551–564.

Boaler, J. (1997a). *Experiencing school mathematics: Teaching styles, sex, and setting.* Buckingham, England: Open University Press.

Boaler, J. (1997b). Setting, social class, and survival of the quickest. *British Educational Research Journal, 23,* 575–595.

Boaler, J. (1998). Open and closed mathematics: Student experiences and understandings. *Journal for Research in Mathematics Education 29,* 41–62.

Boaler, J. (2000). Exploring situated insights into research and learning. *Journal for Research in Mathematics Education, 31*(1), 113–119.

Boaler, J. (2002) *Experiencing school mathematics: Traditional and reform approaches to teaching and their impact on student learning.* Mahwah, New Jersey: Lawrence Erlbaum Associates.

Boaler, J., Wiliam, D., & Brown, M. (2000). Students' experiences of ability grouping: Disaffection, polarisation, and the construction of failure. *British Educational Research Journal, 27,* 631–648.

Bourdieu, P. (1986). The forms of capital. In J. Richardson (Ed.), *Handbook of theory and research for the sociology of education* (pp. 241–258). New York: Greenwood Press.

Bourdieu, P., & Passeron, J.-C. (1977). *Reproduction in education, society, and culture.* Beverly Hills, CA: Sage.

Bowles, S., & Gintis, H. (1976). *Schooling in capitalist America: Educational reform and the contradictions of economic life.* New York: Basic Books.

Brown, C. A., Stein, M. K., & Forman, E. A. (1996). Assisting teachers and students to reform their mathematics classroom. *Educational Studies in Mathematics, 31,* 63–93.

Chazan, D., & Ball, D. L. (1999). Beyond being told not to tell. *For the Learning of Mathematics 19*(2), 2–10.

Cohen, D., & Ball, D. L. (2000, April) *Instructional innovation: Reconsidering the story.* Paper presented at the annual meeting of the American Educational Research Association, New Orleans, LA.

Cohen, D. K., Raudenbush, S., & Ball, D. L. (2002). Resources, instruction, and research. In R. Boruch & F. Mosteller (Eds.) *Evidence matters: Randomized trials in education research* (pp. 80–119). Washington, DC: Brookings Institution Press.

Confrey, J. (1990). What constructivism implies for teaching mathematics. In R. B. Davis, C. A. Maher, & N. Noddings (Eds.), *Constructivist views on the teaching and learning of mathematics* (pp. 107–124). Reston, VA: NCTM.

Cooper, B., & Dunne, M. (1998). Anyone for tennis? Social class differences in children's responses to national curriculum mathematics testing. *The Sociological Review, 46,* 115–148.

Corbett, D., & Wilson, B. (1995). Make a difference with, not for, students: A plea to researchers and reformers. *Educational Researcher, 24*(5), 12–17.

Delpit, L. (1988). The silenced dialogue: Power and pedagogy in educating other people's children. *Harvard Educational Review, 58,* 280–298.

Greeno, J. G., & Middle School Mathematics Applications Project [MMAP]. (1998). The situativity of knowing, learning, and research. *American Psychologist, 53,* 5–26.

Gutiérrez, R. (1996). Practices, beliefs, and cultures of high school mathematics departments: Understanding their influence on student advancement. *Journal of Curriculum Studies, 28*(5), 495–529.

Gutiérrez, R. (1999). Advancing urban Latina/o youth in mathematics: Lessons from an effective high school mathematics department. *The Urban Review, 31*(3), 263–281.

Gutiérrez, R. (2000). *Advancing Latina/o urban youth in mathematics: The power of teacher community.* Paper presented at the research presession of the annual meeting of the National Council of Teachers of Mathematics, Chicago.

Gutiérrez, R. (2002). Enabling the practice of mathematics teachers in context: Towards a new equity research agenda. *Mathematical Thinking and Learning, 4*(2).

Haberman, M. (1991). The pedagogy of poverty versus good teaching. *Phi Delta Kappan, 73,* 290–294.

Heath, S. B. (1983). *Ways with words.* Cambridge: Cambridge University Press.

Henningsen, M., & Stein, M. K. (1997). Mathematical tasks and student cognition: Classroom-based factors that support and inhibit high-level mathematical thinking and reasoning. *Journal for Research in Mathematics Education, 28,* 524–549.

Hiebert, J., & Wearne, D. (1993). Interactional tasks, classroom discourse, and students' learning in second-grade arithmetic. *American Educational Research Journal, 30,* 393–425.

Jackson, A. (1989, Spring). Minorities in mathematics: A focus on excellence not remediation. *American Educator, 5,* 22–27.

Klein, D. (2001). *A brief history of American K–12 mathematics education in the 20th century.* Retrieved August 1, 2001, from http://www.mathematicallycorret.com

Knapp, M., Shields, P. M., & Turnbull, B. J. (1995). Academic challenge in high poverty classrooms. *Phi Delta Kappan, 76,* 770–776.

Ladson-Billings, G. (1997). It doesn't add up: African American students' mathematics achievement. *Journal for Research in Mathematics Education, 28,* 697–708.

Lampert, M. (1985). How do teachers manage to teach? Perspectives on problems in practice. *Harvard Educational Review, 55,* 178–194.

Lane, S., & Silver, E. A. (1999). Fairness and equity in measuring student learning using a mathematics performance assessment: Results from the QUASAR project. In A. L. Nettles & M. Nettles (Eds.), *Measuring up: Challenges minorities face in educational assessment* (pp. 97–120). Boston: Kluwer Academic.

Lave, J. (1996). Teaching, as learning, in practice. *Mind, Culture, and Activity, 3*(3), 149–164.

Lave, J., & Wenger, E. (1991). *Situated learning: Legitimate peripheral participation.* New York: Cambridge University Press.

Lubienski, S. (2000). Problem solving as a means towards mathematics for all: An exploratory look through the class lens. *Journal for Research in Mathematics Education, 31,* 454–482.

Mehan, H. (1992). Understanding inequality in schools: The contribution of interpretive studies. *The Sociology of Education, 65*(1), 1–20.

Mehan, H., Hubbard, L., & Villanueva, I. (1994). Forming academic identities: Accommodation without assimilation among involuntary minorities. *Anthropology and Education Quarterly, 25,* 91–117.

Murphy, P. (1990). Assessment and gender. *Cambridge Journal of Education, 21,* 203–214.

Murphy, P., Gipps, C., & UNESCO (Eds.). (1996). *Equity in the classroom: Towards effective pedagogy for girls and boys.* London: Falmer.

The Office of Population Censuses and Surveys [OPCS] (1980). *Classification of occupations 1980* London: HMSO.

Orton, A., & Frobisher, L. (1996). *Insights into learning mathematics.* London: Cassell.

Pólya, G. (1971). *How to solve it: A new aspect of mathematical method.* Princeton, NJ: Princeton University Press.

Pope, D. (1999). *Doing school: "Successful" students' experiences of the high school curriculum.* Unpublished doctoral dissertation. Stanford University, California.

Rosen, L. (2000). *Calculating concerns: The politics of representation in California's "math wars."* Unpublished doctoral dissertation. University of California, San Diego.

Silver, E. A., Smith, M. S., & Nelson, B. S. (1995). The QUASAR project: Equity concerns meet mathematics reforms in the middle school. In W. G. Secada, E. Fennema, & L. B. Adajian (Eds.), *New directions in equity in mathematics education* (pp. 9–56). New York: Cambridge University Press.

Tomlinson, S. (1987). Curriculum option choices in multi-ethnic schools. In B. Troyna (Ed.), *Racial inequality in education* (pp. 92–108). London: Tavistock.

Varenne, H., & McDermott, R. (1999). *Successful failure: The school America builds.* Boulder, Colorado: Westview Press.

Wiliam, D. (1997). Relevance as MacGuffin in mathematics education. *Chreods, 12,* 8–19.

Willis, P. (1977). *Learning to labor: How working class kids get working class jobs.* New York: Columbia University Press.

Wu, H. (1999). Basic skills versus conceptual understanding. *American Educator/American Federation of Teachers 23*(3), 14–22.

Yackel, E., & Cobb, P. (1996). Sociomathematical norms, argumentation, and autonomy in mathematics. *Journal for Research in Mathematics Education, 27,* 458–477.

Zevenbergen, R. (1996). Constructivism as a liberal bourgeois discourse. *Educational Studies in Mathematics, 31,* 95–113.

Zevenbergen, R. (2000). "Cracking the code" of mathematics classrooms: School success as a function of linguistic, social, and cultural background. In J. Boaler (Ed.), *Multiple perspectives on mathematics teaching and learning.* (pp. 201–224). Westport, CT: Ablex Publishing.

READING 4.5 FOCUS QUESTIONS

(Jigsaw with other members of your team. Focus on the nonshaded portions of the reading.)
Please take notes about the following three topics, and be prepared to report on them to others who have not prepared this reading.

Strengths and limitations of view of language as acquiring vocabulary	
Strengths and limitations of view of language as constructing multiple meanings	
Strengths in an approach that supports particular mathematics discourse practices	

Mark those paragraphs or short sections that relate to your notes. Be prepared to discuss them with other participants.

READING 4.5

A Situated and Sociocultural Perspective on Bilingual Mathematics Learners

Judit Moschkovich

My aim in this article is to explore 3 perspectives on bilingual mathematics learners and to consider how a situated and sociocultural perspective can inform work in this area. The 1st perspective focuses on acquisition of vocabulary, the 2nd focuses on the construction of multiple meanings across registers, and the 3rd focuses on participation in mathematical practices. The 3rd perspective is based on sociocultural and situated views of both language and mathematics learning. In 2 mathematical discussions, I illustrate how a situated and sociocultural perspective can complicate our understanding of bilingual mathematics learners and expand our view of what counts as competence in mathematical communication.

Please focus on the nonshaded portions of the reading.

Language-minority students remain severely underrepresented in technical and scientific fields (Secada, 1992), there are wide gaps between the performances of White and Latino students (Educational Testing Service, 1991), and mathematics courses in middle schools and high schools continue to function as a "critical filter" for some Latino students (Oakes, 1990). Although the educational reform movement has attempted to address the needs of language-minority students, it may be leaving a substantial number of these students unaffected (Gándara, 1994; Valadez, 1989). If mathematics reforms are to include language-minority students, research needs to address the relation between language and mathematics learning from a perspective that combines current perspectives of mathematics learning with current perspectives of language, bilingualism, and classroom discourse. This research can then facilitate the design of curriculum and instruction that will address the needs of language-minority students and ultimately support the success of these students in mathematics.

Despite the steadily increasing population of U.S. students who are classified as limited in English proficiency (estimated to be 5 million with 1 million of these in California, mostly Latinos), there has been little research addressing these students' needs in mathematics classrooms. Early studies of bilingual students learning mathematics framed the challenges that bilingual Latino students faced in terms of solving word problems, understanding vocabulary, or translating from English to mathematical symbols (Cocking & Mestre, 1988;

Source: "A Situated and Sociocultural Perspective on Bilingual Mathematics Learners," Judit Moschkovich, *Mathematical Thinking and Learning*, 4 (2–3): 189–212, Copyright © 2002, Lawrence Erlbaum Associates, Inc., reprinted by permission of the publisher (Taylor & Francis, http://informaworld.com).

Author's Note: The research reported here was supported in part by National Science Foundation Grant 96065. I thank the colleagues who read earlier drafts of this article and the reviewers of this special issue, especially Juan Guerra for helping me to communicate in my second language.

Cuevas, 1983; Cuevas, Mann, & McClung, 1986; Mestre, 1981, 1988; Spanos & Crandall, 1990; Spanos, Rhodes, Dale, & Crandall, 1988). This focus was reflected in recommendations for mathematics instruction for English-language learners that emphasized vocabulary and comprehension skills (Dale & Cuevas, 1987; MacGregor & Moore, 1992; Rubenstein, 1996).

In contrast, more recent research on mathematics learning has focused on how students construct knowledge, negotiate meanings, and participate in mathematical communication. Although several studies have focused on these issues in monolingual mathematics and science classrooms (Cobb, Wood, & Yackel, 1993; Forman, 1996; Lemke, 1990; Pimm, 1987; Pirie, 1991; Richards, 1991), researchers have only recently begun to consider mathematical communication in language-minority classrooms (Adler, 1998; Brenner, 1994; Khisty, 1995; Khisty, McLeod, & Bertilson, 1990; Moschkovich, 1999; Rosebery, Warren, & Conant, 1992; Thornburg & Karp, 1992). Although these studies are a beginning step, there is a need for more research on how language-minority students learn mathematics from a perspective that includes mathematical communication as an integral aspect of learning mathematics.

Mathematics curriculum and teaching standards have come to reflect this current model of mathematics learning that emphasizes communication (National Council of Teachers of Mathematics, 1989). As mathematics classrooms shift from a focus on primarily silent and individual activities (Cazden, 1986; Stodolsky, 1988) to more verbal and social ones (Cobb et al., 1993; Flores, Sowder, Philipp, & Schapelle, 1996; Forman, 1996), bilingual Latino students face new challenges and opportunities in learning mathematics. In reform-oriented mathematics classrooms, students are no longer grappling primarily with acquiring technical vocabulary, developing comprehension skills to read and understand mathematics textbooks, or solving traditional word problems. Students are now expected to communicate mathematically, both orally and in writing, and participate in mathematical practices, such as explaining solution processes, describing conjectures, proving conclusions, and presenting arguments.

Some concerns that stem from these reforms are how bilingual Latino students will be affected by this emphasis on mathematical communication and how classroom instruction can support these students in learning to communicate mathematically. In this article, I address these concerns by proposing and exploring three perspectives for describing mathematics learning and its relation to language. The first perspective emphasizes vocabulary and describes learning mathematics as the acquisition of vocabulary. The second perspective emphasizes word meanings, uses the concept of registers (Halliday, 1978), and describes learning mathematics as the construction of multiple meanings across the everyday and mathematical registers. The third perspective emphasizes the situated[1] and sociocultural nature of language and mathematics learning, uses the concept of Discourses as defined by Gee (1996, 1999), and describes learning mathematics as participation in mathematical Discourse practices. An important practical implication of this situated– sociocultural perspective is that it allows us to more fully describe the variety of resources that students use to communicate mathematically.

In this article, I first summarize the main features of these three perspectives, detailing how a situated–sociocultural perspective can inform the study of mathematical communication in classrooms with bilingual students. Because of their critical importance to the distinctions I make between these three perspectives, I also briefly describe how concepts such as register, discourse, bilingualism, and code switching can be understood from a situated–sociocultural perspective. Next, I examine excerpts from mathematical discussions in classrooms with bilingual students using these three perspectives. Finally, I argue that a situated–sociocultural perspective complicates our view of how bilingual students learn mathematics and expands what counts as competence in communicating mathematically. A situated–sociocultural perspective is useful for avoiding deficiency models of bilingual learners, developing detailed descriptions of the resources that students use to communicate mathematically, and helping teachers build on these resources during instruction.

■ THREE PERSPECTIVES OF BILINGUAL MATHEMATICS LEARNERS

Next, I propose three perspectives for thinking about how bilingual students learn mathematics: acquiring vocabulary, constructing meanings, and participating in discourses. I find these three categories useful for organizing and understanding work on the relation between learning mathematics and language. These perspectives are not meant to represent any one researcher, theorist, or school but are instead offered as composite (and perhaps caricatured) summaries of three theoretical stances I believe are reflected in work in this area. I critique the acquiring vocabulary and constructing multiple-meanings perspectives. My purpose, however, is not to point out how previous work was right or wrong but to examine the limitations we face when using these two perspectives and to describe a progression in terms of the complexity of the phenomena each one includes. I offer the third view, a situated–sociocultural perspective, as an option for complicating how we think about language in learning mathematics and expanding what counts as competence in mathematical communication.

Acquiring Vocabulary

One way to describe bilingual mathematics learners is that students are acquiring vocabulary. This first perspective defines learning mathematics as learning to carry out computations or solve traditional word problems, and it emphasizes acquiring vocabulary as the central issue that second-language learners are grappling with when learning mathematics. This view of learning mathematics is reflected in the early research on bilingual mathematics learners, which focused primarily on how students understood individual vocabulary terms or translated traditional word problems from English to mathematical symbols (e.g., Mestre, 1981; Spanos et al., 1988). Recommendations for mathematics instruction for English-language learners have also tended to emphasize vocabulary and comprehension skills (Dale & Cuevas, 1987; MacGregor & Moore, 1992; Olivares, 1996; Rubenstein, 1996).

Although an emphasis on vocabulary may have been sufficient in the past, this perspective does not include current views of what it means to learn mathematics. Mathematics learning is now seen not only as developing competence in completing procedures, solving word problems, and using mathematical reasoning but also as developing sociomathematical norms (Cobb et al., 1993), presenting mathematical arguments (Forman, 1996), and participating in mathematical discussions (Lampert, 1990). In general, learning to communicate mathematically is now seen as a central aspect of what it means to learn mathematics.

Research from this perspective has typically been concerned with individual students solving word problems as a paradigmatic case of what it meant to learn mathematics (another paradigmatic case was computation). This perspective may have been useful for describing traditional classroom instruction that focused on solving word problems and individual computation, and it may thus be limited to such cases. Solving word problems was also the prototypical example of how mathematics and language intersect in the classroom. However, in many mathematics classrooms today, students are not grappling primarily with acquiring technical vocabulary, developing comprehension skills to read and understand mathematics textbooks, or solving traditional word problems. (This shift has occurred, in part, because traditional word problems are no longer seen as a paradigmatic case of mathematics learning.) Students are expected to participate in classroom mathematical practices that go beyond solving computation or word problems on a worksheet (Ball, 1991; Forman, 1996; Silver & Smith, 1996). In many classrooms, teachers are incorporating many forms of mathematical communication, and students are expected to participate in a variety of oral and written practices, such as explaining solution processes, describing conjectures, proving conclusions, and presenting arguments. Reading textbooks and solving traditional word problems are thus no longer the best examples of how language and learning mathematics intersect.

The vocabulary perspective also presents a simplified view of language that uses, perhaps implicitly, the notion of a *lexicon*. A lexicon is "the list of all words and morphemes of a language that is stored in a native speaker's memory; the internalized dictionary" (Finegan & Besnier, 1989, p. 528). In particular, this perspective does not address the multiple meanings of words. Ultimately, knowing vocabulary is only one part of the story of learning mathematics (or in the case of the following quote, science):

> It is not the knowing of a term in and of itself that matters one way or another; rather we found ourselves wondering how we use a particular term, with what intentions, what we are assuming about what others in the conversation might or might not know, and what that term made clear for us or what in fact we understood about the phenomena we had named. (Rosebery & Warren, 1998, p. 7)

An emphasis on vocabulary has crucial implications for instruction. In particular, this perspective can affect how teachers assess a student's competence in communicating mathematically. For example, if we focus on a student's failure to use a technical term, we might miss how a student constructs meaning for mathematical terms or uses multiple resources, such as gestures, objects, or everyday experiences. We might also miss how the student uses important aspects of competent mathematical communication that are beyond a vocabulary list.

Constructing Multiple Meanings

A second perspective for thinking about bilingual mathematics learners describes learning mathematics as constructing multiple meanings for words rather than acquiring a list of words. This perspective uses the notion of the mathematics register. Halliday (1978) defined *register* in the following way:

> A register is a set of meanings that is appropriate to a particular function of language, together with the words and structures which express these meanings. We can refer to the "mathematics register," in the sense of the meanings that belong to the language of mathematics (the mathematical use of natural language, that is: not mathematics itself), and that a language must express if it is being used for mathematical purposes. (p. 195)

A register is a language variety associated with a particular situation of use. Some examples of registers are legal talk and baby talk. An important and subtle distinction is that between lexicon and register. Unlike the notion of lexicon, the notion of register depends on the situational use of much more than lexical items and includes phonology, morphology, syntax, and semantics as well as nonlinguistic behavior. The notion of register thus involves some aspects of the situation, whereas that of lexicon does not.

Because there are multiple meanings for the same term, students who are learning mathematics can be described as learning to use these multiple meanings appropriately. Several examples of such multiple meanings have been described: the phrase "any number" means "all numbers" in a math context (Pimm, 1987); "a quarter" can refer to a coin or to a fourth of a whole (Khisty, 1995); and in Spanish, *un cuarto* can mean "a room" or "a fourth" (Khisty, 1995).

These multiple meanings can create obstacles in mathematical conversations because students often use the colloquial meanings of terms, whereas teachers (or other students) may use the mathematical meaning of terms. One example is the word *prime*, which can have different meanings, depending on whether it is used in "prime number," "prime time," or "prime rib." In Spanish, *primo* also has multiple meanings; it can mean "cousin" or "prime number," as in the phrase "número primo." Another example of multiple meanings is Walkerdine's (1998) description of the differences between the meanings of *more* in the mathematics classroom and at home. Although in a classroom situation, *more* is usually understood to be the opposite of *less*, at home the opposite of *more* is usually associated with *no more*, as in "I want more paper" and "There is no more paper."

The multiple-meanings perspective considers differences between the everyday and mathematical registers and describes how students' language use can move closer to the mathematics register by becoming more precise and reflecting more conceptual knowledge (Forman, 1996; Moschkovich, 1996, 1998; O'Connor, 1992). Learning mathematics involves, in part, a shift from everyday to more mathematical and precise meanings. For example, one important difference between the everyday and the school mathematics registers may be the meaning of relational terms such as *steeper* and *less steep* and phrases such as "moves up the y axis" and "moves down the y axis." Meanings for these terms and phrases that may be sufficiently precise for everyday purposes may prove to be ambiguous for describing lines in the context of a mathematical discussion (Moschkovich, 1996).

A refinement of students' descriptions of mathematical situations can be understood as a movement toward the mathematics register, where descriptions are more precise and reflect more conceptual knowledge. However, the mathematics register does not consist only of technical terms such as *slope* and *intercept*. Students refine their descriptions by connecting even nontechnical phrases such as "the line will be steeper" or "the line will move up on the y axis" to conceptual knowledge about lines and equations (Moschkovich, 1998).

Moving across two national languages, for example, English and Spanish, may complicate moving across two registers. For example, the distinction between the following two uses of *más* ("more") is crucial in a mathematics context:

- Hay cuatro más _____ que _____. [There are four more _____ than _____.]
- Hay cuatro veces más _____ que _____. [There are four times as many _____ as _____.]

These two sentences refer to two different mathematical situations, and yet the word *más* is used in both cases.

Emphasizing multiple meanings can shift the focus from examining how students acquire vocabulary to asking how students negotiate the meaning of mathematical terms. This second perspective shifts our view of learning mathematics from acquiring words to developing meanings for those words, from learning words with single meanings to understanding multiple meanings, and from learning vocabulary to using language in situations. The multiple-meanings perspective certainly adds complexity to our view of how language and learning mathematics intersect. Although a focus on the mathematics register has served to point out possible sources of misunderstanding in classroom conversations, using this perspective also has certain pitfalls that are important to avoid.

First, when using the multiple-meanings perspective, we need to be careful not to interpret the notion of register as a list of technical words and phrases. This interpretation reduces the concept of mathematical register to vocabulary and disregards the role of meaning in learning to communicate mathematically. Second, when using this perspective, we also need to be careful to include the situational context of utterances. Although words and phrases do have multiple meanings, these words and phrases appear in talk as utterances that occur within social contexts, and much of the meaning of an utterance is derived from the situation. For example, the phrase "give me a quarter" uttered at a vending machine clearly has a different meaning than saying "give me a quarter" while looking at a pizza. The utterance "Vuelvo en un cuarto de hora" ("I will return in a quarter of an hour") said as one leaves a scene has a clearly different meaning than "Limpia tu cuarto" ("Clean your room"), uttered while looking toward a room. When we analyze mathematical conversations, it is important to consider how resources from the situation, such as objects and gestures, point to one or another sense, such as whether *cuarto* means "room" or "quarter."

A third important limitation of the multiple-meanings perspective is that the differences between the everyday register and the mathematics register are not always a source of difficulty for students. Students use not only mathematical resources but also resources from the everyday register to communicate about a mathematical situation. Forman (1996) offered evidence of this in her description of how students and teachers interweave the everyday and academic registers in classroom discussions. Similarly, Moschkovich (1996) described how students used the metaphor that a steeper line is harder to climb than a line that is less steep to compare the steepness of lines on a graph and clarify the meaning of their descriptions of lines. One example presented in this article shows how students used another metaphor from everyday experiences, that the ground is the x axis, to elaborate the meaning of their descriptions of straight lines.

Although differences between the everyday and mathematical registers may sometimes present obstacles for communicating in mathematically precise ways and everyday meanings can sometimes be ambiguous, everyday meanings and metaphors can also be resources for understanding mathematical concepts. Rather than emphasizing the limitations of the everyday register in comparison to the mathematics register, it is important to understand how the two registers serve different purposes and how everyday meanings can provide resources for mathematical communication.

The acquiring vocabulary and constructing multiple-meanings perspectives can have an important impact on instruction. Either of these perspectives can be interpreted as emphasizing the obstacles that bilingual students face as they move from their first language to English or from the everyday register to the mathematics register. Any perspective that focuses on obstacles can easily turn into a deficiency model (Garcia & Gonzalez, 1995; González, 1995) of bilingual students as mathematics learners. The everyday register and students' first language can, in fact, be used as resources for communicating mathematically. Instruction in mathematical communication needs to consider not only the obstacles that bilingual students face but also the resources these students use to communicate mathematically.

Although mathematical communication certainly involves the use of words and constructions and the development of multiple meanings, it is also more than these. Communicating mathematically also includes using multiple resources and participating in mathematical practices, such as abstracting, generalizing, being precise, achieving certainty, explicitly specifying the set of situations for which a claim holds, and tying claims to representations.

Participating in Mathematical Discourse Practices

The two perspectives summarized previously for describing bilingual students learning mathematics, acquiring vocabulary, and understanding multiple meanings provide some analytical tools for clarifying how bilingual students learn mathematics. In this section, I explore how using the notion of Discourses (Gee, 1996, 1999) and a situated–sociocultural view of mathematics cognition, language, and bilingual learners can provide us with an even more complex and detailed view of bilingual students learning mathematics.

A situated–sociocultural perspective has important implications for instruction. The first two perspectives frame the relation between learning mathematics and language in terms of the discontinuities between first and second languages or the differences between the everyday and the mathematics register. In contrast, a situated–sociocultural perspective can be used to describe the details and complexities of how students, rather than struggling with the differences between the everyday and the mathematical registers or between two national languages, use resources from both registers and languages to communicate mathematically. A situated–sociocultural perspective thus moves away from the description of obstacles and deficiencies to a description of resources and competencies and widens what counts as competence in mathematical communication.

The situated and sociocultural discourse perspective described here uses a situated perspective of learning mathematics (Greeno, 1994) and the notion of Discourses (Gee, 1996) to build on previous work on classroom mathematical and scientific discourse (Cobb et al., 1993; Lemke, 1990; Rosebery et al., 1992). This perspective implies, first, that learning mathematics (or science) is viewed as a discursive activity (Forman, 1996; Lemke, 1990; Rosebery et al., 1992). From this perspective, learning mathematics is described as participating in a community of practice (Cobb & Hodge, 2002; Forman, 1996; Lave & Wenger, 1991; Nasir, 2002), developing classroom sociomathematical norms (Cobb et al., 1993), and using multiple material, linguistic, and social resources (Greeno, 1994). This perspective assumes that learning is inherently social and cultural, "whether or not it occurs in an overtly social context" (Forman, 1996, p. 117); that participants bring multiple views to a situation; that representations have multiple meanings for participants; and that these multiple meanings for representations and inscriptions are negotiated through conversations.

Situated perspectives of cognition (Brown, Collins, & Duguid, 1989; Greeno, 1994; Lave & Wenger, 1991) present a view of learning mathematics as participation in a community where students learn to mathematize situations, communicate about these situations, and use resources for mathematizing and communicating. From this perspective, learning to communicate mathematically involves more than learning vocabulary or understanding meanings in different registers. Instead, communicating mathematically is seen as using social, linguistic, and material resources to participate in mathematical practices.

To ground the subsequent discussion, I briefly describe how several concepts—*practices, bilingualism, code switching,* and *Discourses*—are defined from a situated–sociocultural perspective. These notions are not intended to be used as isolated concepts but are meant to be couched within a situated–sociocultural theoretical framework. I use the term *practices* in the sense described by Scribner (1984): "to highlight the culturally organized nature of significant literacy (*or mathematical* [italics added]) activities and their conceptual kinship to other culturally organized activities involving different technologies and symbol systems" (p. 13).

Rather than defining a *bilingual learner* as an individual who is proficient in more than one language, I use a situated–sociocultural definition of bilingual learners as those students who participate in multiple-language communities. As described by Valdes-Fallis (1978), "natural" bilinguals are "the product of a specific linguistic community that uses one of its languages for certain functions and the other for other functions or situations" (p. 4). Work in sociolinguistics has shown that code switching is one of many resources available to bilingual speakers. Code switching is a rule- and constraint-governed process and a dynamic verbal strategy in its own right rather than evidence that students are deficient or "semilingual." One conclusion about code switching that is relevant to the examination of mathematics learning in classrooms with bilingual students is that code switching should not be seen as primarily a reflection of language proficiency or the ability to recall (Valdes-Fallis, 1978).

I take a view of discourse as more than sequential speech or writing, using Gee's (1996) definition of *Discourse:*

> A Discourse is a socially accepted association among ways of using language, other symbolic expressions, and "artifacts," of thinking, feeling, believing, valuing and acting that can be used to identify oneself as a member of a socially meaningful group or "social network," or to signal (that one is playing) a socially meaningful role. (p. 131)

Next, I highlight some distinctions between the notions of register, discourse, and Gee's (1996) definition of *Discourses.* Gee's definition is not the usual one used in linguistics textbooks, which define *discourse* as "a sequence of sentences that 'go together' to constitute a unity, as in conversation, newspaper columns, stories, personal letters, and radio interviews" (Finegan & Besnier, 1989, p. 526). According to Gee's definition, Discourses are more than sequential speech or writing and involve more than the use of technical language; they also involve points of view, communities, and values. Mathematical Discourses (in Gee's sense) include not only ways of talking, acting, interacting, thinking, believing, reading, and writing but also mathematical values, beliefs, and points of view of a situation.

Gee (1999) also discussed the meaning of words:

> A situated view of the meaning of words means that the meanings of words are not stable and general. Rather words have multiple and ever changing meanings created for and adapted to specific contexts of use. At the same time, the meanings of words are integrally linked to social and cultural groups in ways that transcends individuals. (p. 40)

With this view of word meaning, if vocabulary or registers are seen as stable and general or are defined as individual phenomena, a situated–sociocultural perspective is not compatible with either the acquiring vocabulary or the constructing multiple meaning perspectives. Although register markers include vocabulary, phonology, morphology, syntax, and semantics, in mathematics education we may have focused mainly on the semantic aspects of register. Although the notion of register can be interpreted to include nonlinguistic behavior, such as interactional patterns and body language, the notion of Discourses as defined by Gee explicitly highlights the use of gestures and raises the use of artifacts. Although register may be an inherently social concept, Gee's definition of Discourse reminds (and perhaps forces) us to include more than words and meanings. Gee (1999) emphasized that "Discourses always involve more than language" (p. 25) and that aspects other than language, such as interactional and nonlanguage symbol systems, should be included in discourse analysis. Gee's definition of Discourses directs us to consider the importance of gestures, artifacts, practices, beliefs, values, and communities in mathematical communication.

Participating in classroom mathematical Discourse practices can be understood in general as talking and acting in the ways that mathematically competent people talk and act. These practices involve much more than the use of technical language. Gee (1996) used the example of a biker bar to illustrate the ways that any Discourse involves more than technical language. To look and act like one belongs in a biker bar, one has to learn much more than a vocabulary. Although knowing the names of motorcycle parts, makes, and models may be helpful, it is clearly not enough. In the same way, knowing a list of technical mathematical terms is not sufficient for participating in mathematical Discourse.

There is no one mathematical Discourse or practice (for a discussion of multiple mathematical Discourses, see Moschkovich, 2002). Mathematical Discourses involve different communities (mathematicians, teachers, or students) and different genres (explanations, proofs, or presentations). Practices vary across communities of research mathematicians, traditional classrooms, and reformed classrooms. However, even within each community, there are practices that count as participation in competent mathematical Discourse. As Forman (1996) pointed out, particular modes of argument, such as precision, brevity, and logical coherence, are valued. In general, being precise, explicit, brief, and logical and abstracting, generalizing, and searching for certainty are highly valued activities in mathematical communities. For example, claims are applicable only to a precisely and explicitly defined set of situations, as in the statement "Multiplication makes a number bigger, except when multiplying by a number smaller than 1." Many times, claims are also tied to mathematical representations, such as graphs, tables, or diagrams. Generalizing is also a valued practice, as in the statements "The angles of any triangle add up to 180 degrees," "Parallel lines never meet," or "$a + b$ will always equal $b + a$." Imagining (e.g., infinity or zero), visualizing, hypothesizing, and predicting are also valued Discourse practices.

A situated–sociocultural perspective focusing on participation in mathematical Discourse practices can serve to broaden the analytical lens, complicate our view of language, and generate different questions. In the next section, I use the following questions, selectively and loosely following Gee's (1999) questions for Discourse analysis, to examine two mathematical discussions:

1. *Situated Meanings.* What are the situated meanings of some of the words and phrases that seem important in the situation?

2. *Resources.* What are the multiple resources students use to communicate mathematically? What sign systems are relevant in the situation (speech, writing, images, and gestures)? In particular, how is "stuff" other than language relevant?

3. *Discourses.* What Discourses are involved? What Discourses are being produced in this situation? What Discourses are relevant (or irrelevant)? What systems of knowledge and ways of knowing are relevant (and irrelevant) in the situation? How are they made relevant (and irrelevant) and in what ways? What connections are made to Discourses outside the immediate situation? In particular, what Discourse practices are students participating in that are relevant in mathematically educated communities or that reflect mathematical competence?

■ MATHEMATICAL DISCUSSIONS IN CLASSROOMS WITH BILINGUAL STUDENTS

The two examples presented next are used to show the complexity that the use of a situated and sociocultural perspective as an analytical lens brings to the study of bilingual mathematical discussions. The first example shows how the vocabulary perspective can fail to capture students' competencies in communicating mathematically. The second example shows that the multiple-meanings perspective is not sufficient for describing all of the resources that students use.

Example 1: Describing a Pattern

The first example is from a classroom of sixth-grade through eighth-grade students in a summer mathematics course. The students constructed rectangles with the same area but different perimeters and looked for a pattern to relate the dimensions and the perimeter of their rectangles. Following is a problem similar to the one they were working on:

1. Look for all the rectangles with area 36 and write down the dimensions.

2. Calculate the perimeter for each rectangle.

3. Describe a pattern relating the perimeter and the dimensions.

In this classroom, there was one bilingual teacher and one monolingual teacher. A group of four students were videotaped as they talked in their small group and with the bilingual teacher (mostly in Spanish). As they attempted to describe the pattern in their group, they searched for the word for *rectangle* in Spanish. The students produced several suggestions, including *ángulo* ("angle"), *triángulo* ("triangle"), *rángulos*, and *rangulos*. Although these students attempted to find a term to refer to the rectangles, neither the teacher nor the other students provided the correct word, *rectángulo* ("rectangle"), in Spanish.

Later, a second teacher (monolingual English speaker) asked several questions from the front of the class. One of the students in this small group, Alicia, tried to describe a relation between the length of the sides of a rectangle and its perimeter:

Teacher B   *[Speaking from the front of the class]* Somebody describe what they saw as a comparison between what the picture looked like and what the perimeter was.

Alicia   The longer the, ah . . . the longer *[traces the shape of a long rectangle with her hands several times]* the, ah . . . the longer the rángulo *[rangle]*, you know the more the perimeter, the higher the perimeter is.

An analysis of this excerpt using the vocabulary perspective would focus on this student's failed attempt to use the right word, *rectangle*. Focusing on how missing vocabulary was an obstacle would not do justice to how this student successfully communicated a mathematical description. If we were to focus only on Alicia's inaccurate use of the term *rángulo*,[2] we might miss how she used resources from the situation and how her statement reflected practices valued in mathematical Discourse. Using the vocabulary perspective to analyze this student's attempt (or failure) to use the right word would disregard her use of situational resources to communicate mathematically. If we move from a focus on the right word, we can begin to see this student's competence. Alicia's comsspetence only becomes visible if we use a perspective of communicating mathematically that includes gestures and objects as resources.

A situated–sociocultural perspective allows us to consider the nonlanguage resources from the situation that the student used. Alicia used gestures to illustrate what she meant, and she referred to the concrete objects in front of her, the drawings of rectangles, to clarify her description. Alicia also used her native language as a resource. She interjected an invented Spanish word into her statement. In this way, a gesture, objects in the situation, and the student's first language served as resources for describing a pattern. Even though the word that she used for rectangle does not exist in either Spanish or English, it is very clear from looking at the situation that Alicia was referring to a rectangle. It is also clear from her gestures that even though she did not mention the words *length* or *width*, she was referring to the length of the side of a rectangle that was parallel to the floor.

Using a situated–sociocultural perspective, we can also ask what mathematical Discourse practices are relevant to this situation. Describing patterns is considered a paradigmatic practice in mathematics, so much so that mathematics is often defined as "the science of patterns" (Devlin, 1998, p. 3). Alicia certainly described a pattern correctly. The rectangle with area 36 that has the greatest perimeter (74) is the rectangle with the longest possible length, 36, and shortest possible width, 1. As the length gets longer, say in the comparison of a rectangle of length 12, width 3, and perimeter 30 with a rectangle of perimeter 74, the perimeter does in fact become greater. Although Alicia was missing crucial vocabulary, she did appropriately (in the right place, at the right time, and in the right way) use a construction commonly used in mathematical communities to describe patterns, make comparisons, and describe direct variation: "The longer the _____, the more (higher) the _____."

A situated–sociocultural perspective opens the way for seeing complexity and competence. Analyzed from this perspective, this example, instead of highlighting only the obstacles this student faced, points to the way the student used resources from the situation to communicate mathematically. Including not only vocabulary but also the gestures and objects provided the tools for describing the details of what this competence entailed. Making a connection to mathematical Discourse practices also widened what counts as competence.

Different implications for instruction follow from the vocabulary and situated–sociocultural perspectives. Certainly, Alicia needs to learn the word for rectangle, ideally in both English and Spanish, but instruction should not stop there. Rather than only providing the correction of her use of *rángulo* or the recommendation that she learn vocabulary, instruction should also build on Alicia's use of gestures, objects, and description of a pattern.

Example 2: Clarifying a Description

Although the first example fits the expectation that bilingual students need to acquire vocabulary, the vocabulary perspective was not sufficient to describe the student's competence. The second example highlights the limitations of the vocabulary perspective for describing mathematical communication when students are not missing vocabulary. In the following discussion, the two students were not struggling with missing vocabulary in either Spanish or English. Instead, they used both languages for a purpose not related to vocabulary, clarifying the mathematical meaning of a description. The vocabulary perspective seems particularly limited for analyzing such cases.

The second example was taken from an interview after school. These two ninth-grade students had been in mainstream English-only mathematics classrooms for several years. One student in this example, Marcela, had some previous mathematics instruction in Spanish. These two students were working on the problem shown in Figure 4.5a.

They had graphed the line $y = -0.6x$ on paper and were discussing whether this line was steeper or less steep than the line $y = x$ (see Figure 4.5b).

Giselda first proposed that the line was steeper, then less steep. Marcela had repeatedly asked Giselda if she was sure. After Marcela proposed that the line was less steep, she proceeded to explain this choice to Giselda:

Marcela   No, it's less steeper.

Giselda   Why?

Marcela   See, it's closer to the *x* axis *[looks at Giselda]*. . . . Isn't it?

Figure 4.5a Problem for Example 2

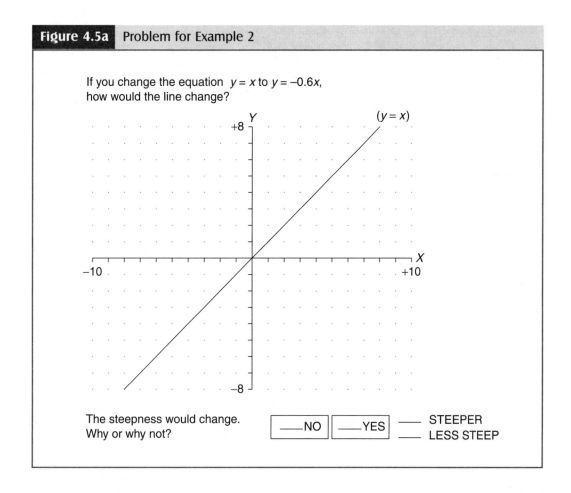

If you change the equation $y = x$ to $y = -0.6x$, how would the line change?

The steepness would change. Why or why not?

☐ ____ NO   ☐ ____ YES   ____ STEEPER   ____ LESS STEEP

Figure 4.5b Lines Drawn by Marcela and Giselda

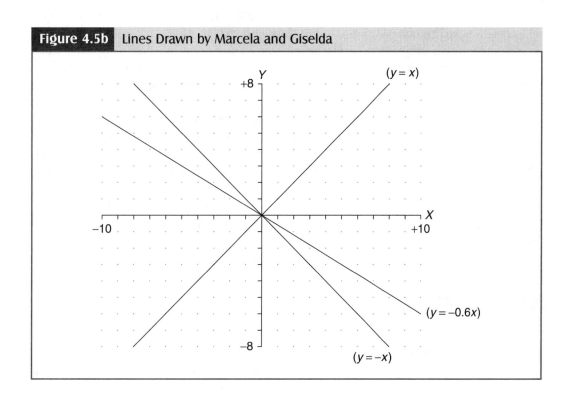

Giselda   Oh, so if it's right here . . . it's steeper, right?

Marcela   Porque fíjate, digamos que este es el suelo, entonces, si se acerca más, pues es menos steep. . . . 'Cause see this one *[referring to the line* y = x*]* . . . is . . . está entre el medio de la *x* y de la *y*. Right? *[Because look, let's say that this is the ground, then, if it gets closer, then it's less steep. . . . 'Cause see this one is between the x and the y. Right?]*

Giselda   *[Nods in agreement.]*

Marcela   This one *[referring to the line* y = –0.6x*]* is closer to the *x* than to the *y*, so this one *[referring to the line* y = –0.6x*]* is less steep.

The vocabulary perspective is not very useful for analyzing this example. Marcela, rather than struggling with vocabulary or using Spanish to fill in for a missing English word, used her first language to clarify a mathematical description. The following analysis shows how Marcela's competence involved more than knowing the meanings of *steeper* and *less steep*.

If we use a multiple-meanings perspective, we can begin to see that in this discussion, the two students were clarifying and negotiating the meanings of *steeper* and *less steep*. We could say that Marcela used the mathematics register as a resource to communicate mathematically. She used two constructions common in the school mathematics register: "Let's say this is _____" and "if _____, then _____."

However, the multiple-meanings perspective is not sufficient for describing Marcela's competence. Using a situated–sociocultural perspective, we can ask, which nonlanguage resources from the situation did she use? This student used not only mathematical artifacts—the graph, the line *y* = *x*, and the axes—but also everyday experiences as resources.

The premise that meanings from everyday experiences are obstacles for communicating mathematically does not hold for this example. In fact, Marcela used her everyday experiences and the metaphor that the *x* axis is the ground ("Porque fíjate, digamos que este es el suelo" ["Because look, let's say that this is the ground"]) as resources for explaining her description. Rather than sorting out multiple meanings between two registers, she used an everyday situation to clarify her explanation.

Using a situated–sociocultural perspective, we can also ask, what aspects of mathematical Discourse practices are relevant to this situation? Marcela's explanations echoed mathematical Discourse practices that go beyond the use of constructions from the mathematics register. First, Marcela explicitly stated an assumption, a discursive practice valued in mathematical Discourse, when she said, "Porque fíjate, digamos que este es el suelo" ("Because look, let's say that this is the ground"). Second, she supported her claim by making a connection to mathematical representations, another valued discursive practice in mathematical Discourse. She used the graph, in particular the line *y* = *x* and the axes, as references to support her claim about the steepness of the line. A situated–sociocultural perspective can help us to see that Marcela was participating in two discursive practices that reflect important values, stating assumptions explicitly and connecting claims to mathematical representations.

■ CONCLUSIONS

This area of study brings together different views of mathematics learning and of language. Work in mathematics education provides us with several ways to think about what it means to learn mathematics. Learning mathematics can be seen as learning to carry out procedures and solve traditional word problems, constructing meanings, or participating in mathematical discourse practices. Work on bilingual mathematics learners needs to be informed by current views of learning mathematics as sense making (Lampert, 1990; Schoenfeld, 1992), developing sociomathematical norms (Cobb et al., 1993), and learning to participate in mathematical Discourse practices (Brenner, 1994; Brown et al., 1989, Forman, 1996; Forman, McCormick, & Donato, 1998; Greeno, 1994; Lave & Wenger, 1991). There are also different views of language as vocabulary, registers, and Discourses. The study of mathematics learning in classrooms with bilingual students also needs to be informed by current perspectives on communication in classrooms (Ballenger, 1997; Cazden, 1986, 1993; Heath, 1983; Mehan, 1979) and bilingualism (Hakuta & Cancino, 1977; Valdes-Fallis, 1978; Zentella, 1997).

A perspective of learning mathematics as acquiring vocabulary has been used to describe how students learn to solve English word problems and understand mathematical texts. A perspective of learning mathematics as constructing multiple meanings across registers has uncovered possible misunderstandings in classroom conversations. This second perspective has been useful in pointing out ways to support English-language learners in communicating mathematically: clarifying multiple meanings, addressing the conflicts between two languages explicitly, and discussing the different meanings students may associate with mathematical terms in each language.

However, these two perspectives have limitations. Seeing learning mathematics as acquiring vocabulary is not sufficient for describing different types of mathematical discussions, situational resources, or student competence. Focusing on the obstacles between the everyday and the mathematics register can obscure how everyday meanings can be resources for mathematical discussions. Both of these perspectives can be interpreted as reducing mathematical discourse to the use of vocabulary or presenting a deficiency model of bilingual students as mathematics learners. An accurate description of mathematical communication for bilingual students needs to include not only an analysis of the difficulties but also the multiple resources students use to communicate mathematically. A situated–sociocultural perspective can broaden the analytical lens and generate different questions, such as a consideration of the situational resources students use and the ways that mathematical Discourses are relevant to a situation.

The first example of a bilingual mathematical discussion showed that even when students are missing a word, students' first language and aspects of the situation, such as gestures and objects, can be resources for communicating mathematically. The second example showed that the everyday register and a student's first language can be resources rather than obstacles for learning mathematics. Although the first example showed students who recognized a difficulty in finding the right vocabulary term, not all bilingual mathematical discussions serve this purpose. The students in the second example used both languages to explain a problem solution rather than finding or translating a word.

The previous examples illustrated several aspects of how bilingual students communicate mathematically that only become visible when a situated–sociocultural perspective is used:

- Learning to participate in mathematical Discourse is not merely or primarily a matter of learning vocabulary. During conversations in the mathematics classroom, students are also learning to participate in valued mathematical Discourse practices, such as being precise or using representations to support claims.
- Some of the resources bilingual students use to communicate mathematically are gestures, objects, everyday experiences, their first language, code switching, and mathematical representations.
- There are multiple uses of Spanish in mathematical conversations between bilingual students. Some students use Spanish to label objects. Other students use Spanish to explain a concept, justify an answer, or describe a mathematical situation.

- Bilingual students bring varied competencies to the classroom. For example, even a student who is missing vocabulary may be proficient in using mathematical constructions or presenting clear arguments.

The situated–sociocultural perspective used to examine these two mathematical discussions can expand and complicate our view of how bilingual students learn mathematics. Even when students are learning to communicate mathematically in their second language, they are doing much more than finding the right word or struggling with multiple meanings (Ballenger, 1997). As students participate in mathematical discussions, they are using resources such as their first language, gestures, and objects. They are also participating in Discourse practices that reflect the values of the discipline, such as being explicit about assumptions, connecting claims to representations, imagining, hypothesizing, and predicting. If we use a situated–sociocultural definition of Discourse, we can widen what counts as competence. To do this, we should maintain two central assumptions: Discourses are more than language; and meanings are multiple, changing, situated, and sociocultural.

Implications for Instruction

Any perspective that focuses on the obstacles bilingual students face can easily become a deficiency model (Garcia & Gonzalez, 1995; González, 1995) of bilingual students as mathematics learners. Descriptions of mathematical discussions in classrooms with bilingual students need to consider not only the obstacles that students face but also the resources students use to communicate mathematically. A situated–sociocultural perspective points to several aspects of classroom instruction that need to be considered. Classroom instruction should support bilingual students' engagement in conversations about mathematics that go beyond the translation of vocabulary and involve students in communicating about mathematical concepts.

A situated–sociocultural perspective on learning mathematics can help to shift the focus of mathematics instruction for English-language learners from language development to mathematical content. The two examples presented show that English-language learners can and do participate in discussions where they grapple with important mathematical content, even if they do not always use the right words and even if they switch from English to Spanish. One of the goals of mathematics instruction for bilingual students should be to support all students, regardless of their proficiency in English, in participating in discussions about mathematical ideas. Teachers can move toward this goal by providing opportunities for bilingual students to participate in mathematical discussions and by learning to recognize the resources that bilingual students use to express mathematical ideas.

ssClassroom conversations that include the use of gestures, concrete objects, and the student's first language as legitimate resources can support students in learning to communicate mathematically. Instruction needs to support students' use of resources from the situation or the everyday register, in whichever language students choose. Lastly, assessments of how well students communicate mathematically need to consider more than their use of vocabulary. These assessments should include how students use the situation, the everyday register, and their first language as resources as well as how they make comparisons, explain conclusions, specify claims, and use mathematical representations.

Understanding the mathematical aspects of what students say and do can be difficult when teaching, perhaps especially when working with students who are learning English. It may not be easy (or even possible) to sort out which aspects of a student's utterance are the result of the student's conceptual understanding or of a student's English-language proficiency. However, if the goal is to support student participation in mathematical discussions, determining the origin of an error is not as important as listening to the students and uncovering the mathematical competence in what they are saying and doing. It is only possible to uncover students' mathematical competence if we use a complex perspective of what it means to communicate mathematically.

NOTES ■

1. I use the term *situated* to mean "local, grounded in actual practices and experiences" (Gee, 1999, p. 40). Although situated can be understood to mean sociocultural, for the sake of clarity, I use the term *situated–sociocultural.*

2. Although the word does not exist in Spanish, it might be best translated as "rangle," perhaps a shortening of the word *rectángulo.*

REFERENCES ■

Adler, J. (1998). A language of teaching dilemmas: Unlocking the complex multilingual secondary mathematics classroom. *For the Learning of Mathematics, 18,* 24–33.

Ball, D. L. (1991). What's all this talk about "discourse"? *Arithmetic Teacher, 39,* 44–47.

Ballenger, C. (1997). Social identities, moral narratives, scientific argumentation: Science talk in a bilingual classroom. *Language and Education, 11,* 1–14.

Brenner, M. (1994). A communication framework for mathematics: Exemplary instruction for culturally and linguistically diverse students. In B. McLeod (Ed.), *Language and learning: Educating linguistically diverse students* (pp. 233–268). Albany: State University of New York Press.

Brown, J. S., Collins, A., & Duguid, P. (1989). Situated cognition and the culture of learning. *Educational Researcher, 18,* 32–42.

Cazden, C. (1986). Classroom discourse. In M. C. Wittrock (Ed.), *Handbook of research on teaching* (pp. 432–463). New York: Macmillan.

Cazden, C. (1993). Vyogtsky, Hymes, and Bakhtin: From word to utterance to voice. In E. Forman, N. Minnick, & C. A. Stone (Eds.), *Contexts for learning: Sociocultural dynamics in children's development* (pp. 197–212). New York: Oxford University Press.

Cobb, P., & Hodge, L. L. (2002/this issue). A relational perspective on issues of cultural diversity and equity as they play out in the mathematics classroom. *Mathematical Thinking and Learning, 4,* 249–284.

Cobb, P., Wood, T., & Yackel, E. (1993). Discourse, mathematical thinking, and classroom practice. In E. Forman, N. Minick, & C. A. Stone (Eds.), *Contexts for learning: Sociocultural dynamics in children's development* (pp. 91–119). New York: Oxford University Press.

Cocking, R., & Mestre, J. (Eds.). (1988). *Linguistic and cultural influences on learning* mathematics. Hillsdale, NJ: Lawrence Erlbaum Associates, Inc.

Cuevas, G. J. (1983). Language proficiency and the development of mathematics concepts in Hispanic primary school students. In T. H. Escobedo (Ed.), *Early childhood bilingual education: A Hispanic perspective* (pp. 148–163). New York: Teachers College Press.

Cuevas, G. J., Mann, P. H., & McClung, R. M. (1986, April). *The effects of a language process approach program on the mathematics achievement of first, third, and fifth graders.* Paper presented at the annual meeting of the American Educational Research Association, San Francisco.

Dale, T., & Cuevas, G. (1987). Integrating language and mathematics learning. In J. Crandall (Ed.), *ESL through content area instruction: Mathematics, science and social studies* (pp. 9–54). Englewood Cliffs, NJ: Prentice Hall.

Devlin, K. (1998). *The language of mathematics.* New York: Freeman.

Educational Testing Service. (1991). *The state of inequality.* Princeton, NJ: Author.

Finegan, E., & Besnier, N. (1989). *Language its structure and use.* New York: Harcourt Brace Jovanovich.

Flores, A., Sowder, J., Philipp, R., & Schapelle, B. (1996). Orchestrating, promoting, and enhancing mathematical discourse in the middle grades: A case study. In J. T. Sowder (Ed.), *Providing a foundation for teaching middle school mathematics* (pp. 275–299). Albany: State University of New York Press.

Forman, E. (1996). Learning mathematics as participation in classroom practice: Implications of sociocultural theory for educational reform. In L. Steffe, P. Nesher, P. Cobb, G. Goldin, & B. Greer (Eds.), *Theories of mathematical learning* (pp. 115–130). Mahwah, NJ: Lawrence Erlbaum Associates, Inc.

Forman, E., McCormick, D., & Donato, R. (1998). Learning what counts as a mathematical explanation. *Linguistics and Education, 9,* 313–339.

Gándara, P. (1994). The impact of the education reform movement on limited English proficient students. In B. McLeod (Ed.), *Language and learning: Educating linguistically diverse students* (pp. 45–70). Albany: State University of New York Press.

Garcia, E., & Gonzalez, R. (1995). Issues in systemic reform for culturally and linguistically diverse students. *Teachers College Record, 96,* 418–431.

Gee, J. (1996). *Social linguistics and literacies: Ideology in Discourses* (3rd ed.). London: Falmer.

Gee, J. (1999). *An introduction to Discourse analysis: Theory and method.* New York: Routledge.

González, N. (1995). Processual approaches to multicultural education. *Journal of Applied Behavioral Science, 31,* 234–244.

Greeno, J. (1994, August). *The situativity of learning: Prospects for syntheses in theory, practice, and research.* Paper presented at the annual meeting of the American Psychological Association, Los Angeles.

Hakuta, K., & Cancino, H. (1977). Trends in second-language-acquisition research. *Harvard Educational Review, 47,* 294–316.

Halliday, M. A. K. (1978). Sociolinguistics aspects of mathematical education. In M. Halliday (Ed.), *The social interpretation of language and meaning* (pp. 194–204). London: University Park.

Heath, S. B. (1983). *Ways with words: Language, life, and work in communities and classrooms.* New York: Cambridge University Press.

Khisty, L. L. (1995). Making inequality: Issues of language and meanings in mathematics teaching with Hispanic students. In W. G. Secada, E. Fennema, & L. B. Adajian (Eds.), *New directions for equity in mathematics education* (pp. 279–297). New York: Cambridge University Press.

Khisty, L. L., McLeod, D., & Bertilson, K. (1990). Speaking mathematically in bilingual classrooms: An exploratory study of teacher discourse. *Proceedings of the Fourteenth International Conference for the Psychology of Mathematics Educator, 3,* 105–112.

Lampert, M. (1990). When the problem is not the question and the solution is not the answer: Mathematical knowing and teaching. *American Educational Research Journal, 27,* 29–64.

Lave, J., & Wenger, E. (1991). *Situated learning: Legitimate peripheral participation.* New York: Cambridge University Press.

Lemke, J. (1990). *Talking science.* Norwood, NJ: Ablex.

MacGregor, M., & Moore, R. (1992). *Teaching mathematics in the multicultural classroom.* Melbourne, Australia: University of Melbourne, Institute of Education.

Mehan, H. (1979). *Learning lessons: Social organization in the classroom.* Cambridge, MA: Harvard University Press.

Mestre, J. (1981). Predicting academic achievement among bilingual Hispanic college technical students. *Educational and Psychological Measurement, 41,* 1255–1264.

Mestre, J. (1988). The role of language comprehension in mathematics and problem solving. In R. Cocking & J. Mestre (Eds.), *Linguistic and cultural influences on learning mathematics* (pp. 201–220). Hillsdale, NJ: Lawrence Erlbaum Associates, Inc.

Moschkovich, J. N. (1996). Moving up and getting steeper: Negotiating shared descriptions of linear graphs. *The Journal of the Learning Sciences, 5,* 239–277.

Moschkovich, J. N. (1998). Resources for refining conceptions: Case studies in the domain of linear functions. *The Journal of the Learning Sciences, 7,* 209–237.

Moschkovich, J. N. (1999). Supporting the participation of English language learners in mathematical discussions. *For the Learning of Mathematics, 19*, 11–19.

Moschkovich, J. N. (2002). An introduction to examining everyday and academic mathematical practices. In M. Brenner & J. Moschkovich (Eds.), *Everyday and academic mathematics in the classroom.* Reston, VA: National Council of Teachers of Mathematics.

Nasir, N. (2002/this issue). Identity, goals, and learning: Mathematics in cultural practice. *Mathematical Thinking and Learning, 4*, 213–247.

National Council of Teachers of Mathematics. (1989). *Curriculum and evaluation standards for school mathematics.* Reston, VA: Author.

Oakes, J. (1990). *Multiplying inequalities: The effects of race, social class and tracking on opportunities to learn mathematics and science.* Santa Monica, CA: Rand Corporation.

O'Connor, M. C. (1992). *Negotiated defining: The case of length and width.* Unpublished manuscript, Boston University, School of Education.

Olivares, R. A. (1996). Communication in mathematics for students with limited English proficiency. In P. C. Elliott & M. J. Kenney (Eds.), *Communication in mathematics: K–12 and beyond—1996 yearbook* (pp. 219–230). Reston, VA: National Council of Teachers of Mathematics.

Pimm, D. (1987). *Speaking mathematically: Communication in mathematics classrooms.* London: Routledge.

Pirie, S. (1991). Peer discussion in the context of mathematical problem solving. In K. Durkin & B. Shire (Eds.), *Language in mathematical education: Research and practice* (pp. 143–161). Philadelphia: Open University Press.

Richards, J. (1991). Mathematical discussions. In E. von Glasersfeld (Ed.), *Radical constructivism in mathematics education* (pp. 13–51). Dordrecht, The Netherlands: Kluwer Academic.

Rosebery, A., & Warren, B. (Eds.). (1998). *Boats, balloons, and classroom video: Science teaching as inquiry.* Portsmouth, NH: Heinemann.

Rosebery, A., Warren, B., & Conant, F. (1992). Appropriating scientific discourse: Findings from language minority classrooms. *The Journal of the Learning Sciences, 2*, 61–94.

Rubenstein, R. N. (1996). Strategies to support the learning of the language of mathematics. In P. C. Elliott & M. J. Kenney (Eds.), *Communication in mathematics: K–12 and beyond—1996 yearbook* (pp. 214–218). Reston, VA: National Council of Teachers of Mathematics.

Schoenfeld, A. H. (1992). Learning to think mathematically: Problem solving, metacognition, and sense-making in mathematics. In D. Grouws (Ed.), *Handbook for research on mathematics teaching and learning* (pp. 334–370). New York: Macmillan.

Scribner, S. (1984). Studying working intelligence. In B. Rogoff & J. Lave (Eds.), *Everyday cognition: Its development in social context* (pp. 9–40). Cambridge, MA: Harvard University Press.

Secada, W. (1992). Race, ethnicity, social class, language and achievement in mathematics. In D. Grouws (Ed.), *Handbook for research on mathematics teaching and learning* (pp. 623–660). New York: Macmillan.

Silver, E., & Smith, M. (1996). Building discourse communities in mathematics classrooms: A worthwhile but challenging journey. In P. C. Elliott & M. J. Kenney (Eds.), *Communication in mathematics: K–12 and beyond—1996 yearbook* (pp. 20–28). Reston, VA: National Council of Teachers of Mathematics.

Spanos, G., & Crandall, J. (1990). Language and problem solving: Some examples from math and science. In A. M. Padilla, H. H. Fairchild, & C. M. Valadez (Eds.), *Bilingual education: Issues and strategies* (pp. 157–170). Beverly Hills, CA: Sage.

Spanos, G., Rhodes, N. C., Dale, T. C., & Crandall, J. (1988). Linguistic features of mathematical problem solving: Insights and applications. In R. Cocking & J. Mestre (Eds.), *Linguistic and cultural influences on learning mathematics* (pp. 221–240). Hillsdale, NJ: Lawrence Erlbaum Associates, Inc.

Stodolsky, S. (1988). *The subject matters: Classroom activity in math and social studies.* Chicago: University of Chicago Press.

Thornburg, D., & Karp, K. (1992, April). *Resituating mathematics and science instruction for language different students.* Paper presented at the annual meeting of the American Educational Research Association, San Francisco.

Valadez, C. M. (1989). Language-minority students and educational reform: An incomplete agenda. In S. Cohen & L. Solomon (Eds.), *From the campus: Perspectives on the school reform movement* (pp. 154–169). New York: Praeger.

Valdes-Fallis, G. (1978). *Language in education: Theory and practice: Vol. 4. Code switching and the classroom teacher.* Wellington, VA: Center for Applied Linguistics.

Walkerdine, V. (1998). *The mastery of reason: Cognitive development and the production of rationality.* London: Routledge.

Zentella, A. C. (1997). *Growing up bilingual: Puerto Rican children in New York.* Malden, MA: Blackwell.

Session **5**

How Can Professional Development Enable Teachers to Improve Student Achievement?

(Practice-Based Professional Development)

Each of the sessions in *Secondary Lenses on Learning* has been designed to go deeply into one of the key areas needed for knowledgeable school leadership in mathematics education. But knowing what good mathematics curriculum, instruction, and assessment looks like and sounds like is only the first step for leadership teams determined to build successful mathematics programs. Key to reaching this goal is understanding and learning to use professional development structures that facilitate change within a mathematics department and a school community.

Session 5 is designed to broaden understandings of the nature and potential of high-quality professional development, by creating the opportunity to experience professional development approaches that are centered in the practice of teaching. While the focus for this session is practice-based professional development, participants will also have the opportunity to again look deeply at a variety of building/instructional factors that influence student achievement.

This session offers participants the opportunity to do the following:

- Broaden their understanding of the nature and potential of professional development
- Experience professional development approaches centered in the practice of teaching mathematics
- Explore instructional decisions that influence student learning and achievement

Readings and Focus Questions to Prepare for Session 5

(Three Homework Readings)

In preparation for Session 5, we have selected three readings to provide an overview of current thinking in the area of effective professional development. Please read and be prepared to discuss the following:

Reading 5.1 Smith, M. S. (2001). *Practice-based professional development for teachers of mathematics.* Reston, VA: National Council of Teachers of Mathematics.

Reading 5.2 Loucks-Horsley, S., Love, N., Stiles, K., Mundry, S., & Hewson, P. (2003). *Designing professional development for teachers of science and mathematics* (2nd ed.). Thousand Oaks, CA: Corwin.

Note: For Reading 5.2, *all participants* should read the opening section of *Designing Professional Development for Teachers of Science and Mathematics.*

Jigsaw the professional development strategies in the subsequent pages so that each member of the team has only one or two strategies to read. The professional development strategies in this section include the following:

- Curriculum Alignment and Materials Selection (pages 214–219)
- Curriculum Implementation (pages 220–224)
- Study Groups (pages 224–229)
- Case Discussions (pages 229–235)
- Examining Student Work and Thinking and Scoring Assessments (pages 235–240)
- Immersion in Problem Solving in Mathematics (pages 240–243)

Reading 5.3   Stein, M. K., Smith, M., Henningsen, M., & Silver, E. (2000). *Implementing standards-based mathematics instruction: A casebook for professional development.* Reston, VA: National Council of Teachers of Mathematics.

Take notes using the focus questions that follow, and be prepared to discuss and create a poster with answers to each of the questions during Session 5.

READINGS 5.1, 5.2, AND 5.3 FOCUS QUESTIONS

1. Describe important characteristics and related ideas about classroom-based professional development as described in the Smith (2001) and Loucks-Horsley et al. (2003) readings. How might this support the work of teachers?

2. For each of the strategies you were assigned to read in the Loucks-Horsley et al. reading, answer the following questions:

   a. What aspects of practice could this professional development strategy address for teachers and other educators?

   b. What resources are required for implementation?

   c. How might this work translate into improved student achievement?

3. What does the Mathematical Task Framework (MTF) describe (Reading 5.3)?

4. Why is the MTF important to the work of teachers?

Mark those paragraphs or short sections that relate to your notes. Be prepared to discuss them with other participants.

READING 5.1

Practice-Based Professional Development for Teachers of Mathematics

Margaret Schwan Smith

MAKING THE CASE FOR REFORMING ■ PROFESSIONAL DEVELOPMENT

The professional development of teachers is a key ingredient in improving our nation's schools (Darling-Hammond and Sykes 1999). The perceived importance of professional development is directly related to the ambitious nature of the reform goals and standards that have been put into place over the past decade by the National Council of Teachers of Mathematics (1989, 1991, 1995, 2000), state departments of education, and the National Board for Professional Teaching Standards (1997). These documents call for students who can reason about challenging and complex problems that give rise to significant mathematical understandings. It also calls for teachers who can appropriately support students' learning by creating environments that foster communication, inquiry, and investigation. Meeting these goals and standards will require a great deal of learning on the part of teachers, the vast majority of whom were taught and learned to teach under a paradigm of instruction and learning in which memorization, repetition, speed, and correct answers were of paramount importance.

The kind of learning that will be required of teachers has been described as *transformative* (involving sweeping changes in deeply held beliefs, knowledge, and habits of practice) as opposed to *additive* (involving the addition of new skills to an existing repertoire) (Thompson and Zeuli 1999). Teachers of mathematics cannot successfully develop their students' reasoning and communication skills in ways called for by the new reforms simply by using manipulatives in their classrooms, by putting four students together at a table, or by asking a few additional open-ended questions. Rather, they must thoroughly overhaul their thinking about what it means to know and understand mathematics, the kinds of tasks in which their students should be engaged, and, finally, their own role in the classroom.

Teachers cannot be expected to undergo changes as profound as this—totally refurbishing their knowledge, beliefs, and habits of practice—on the basis of professional development as we know it. For most teachers in the United States, professional development includes mandated district-sponsored staff development and elective participation in courses, workshops, and summer institutes, often given by university-based teacher educators. District-sponsored staff development typically offers a menu of training options (workshops, special courses, or in-service days) designed to transmit a specific set of ideas, techniques, or materials to teachers (Little 1993). For example, teachers may be asked to select workshops from a list that includes training on the use of computers, cooperative group instruction, or assessment by portfolio. Such approaches treat teaching as routine and technical (Little 1993), encourage tinkering around the edges of practices rather than undertaking a total overhaul of practice (Huberman 1993), and may or may not relate specifically to the teaching of mathematics. In addition, they provide teachers with limited access to intellectual resources outside the teaching community and provide limited opportunities for meaningful collegial interactions within the teaching community (Little 1993).

Courses given by members of a university faculty are often associated with degree or certification programs and generally have an academic rather than an applied focus. These courses are often taught in a manner that is inconsistent with the ways in which we are asking teachers to teach or ways that will allow even the successful student to construct adequate or appropriate knowledge (Ball 1991; Silver 1994). Although workshops and summer institutes sponsored by teacher educators can be more practice-oriented, they generally include limited follow-up support for implementation. Like district staff development, one-day sessions or even two-week institutes usually do not take into account the positive and negative factors within the school environments to which teachers return and hence may have little impact on practice. In addition, both district staff development and university-sponsored workshops and courses are usually planned without any input from those for whom the professional development is intended (Fullan 1991). Generally, both of these types of professional development activities result in a disconnected and decontextualized set of experiences from which teachers derive additive benefits (i.e., the addition of new skills to their existing repertoires). They have not been designed to produce the kind of in-depth reexamination of beliefs that is necessary to inspire the changes required for the newer, more complex forms of teaching that are being recommended.

To support instructional change in mathematics, new forms of professional development are needed for teachers at all stages of their careers—forms that can affect teachers' actions and interactions in the classroom and lead to improved learning outcomes for all students. Little (1993) has argued that these new approaches should build teachers' capacity for complex, nuanced judgments about the process of mathematics teaching and learning. Others have argued that teachers must have, at a minimum, deep and flexible understandings of the mathematics that they will teach (Simon and Blume 1994; Thompson and Thompson 1996; Sowder et al. 1998). This is particularly critical since, as Ball contends, in the "reform" view of mathematics teaching, "the conception of content is more uncertain than a traditional view of mathematics as skills and rules, the view of children as thinkers more unpredictable" (1993, p. 394).

Several approaches to teacher professional development have been successful in assisting teachers in adopting reform-oriented instructional practice. For example, some have facilitated change by assisting teachers to learn new mathematical topics in ways that reflect the style of teaching and learning that reformers advocate for classrooms (e.g., Simon and Schifter 1991; Wilcox et al. 1991). Others have focused on helping teachers understand important nuances of students' mathematical thinking (e.g., Carpenter et al. 1989) and the ways in which intellectually productive social interactions can be developed and maintained in order to facilitate students' learning of key mathematical ideas (e.g., Cobb et al. 1991). What we have learned from the efforts of these and other researchers lays the foundation for the approach proposed in this book.

■ SITUATING PROFESSIONAL DEVELOPMENT IN PRACTICE

The first chapter argued that professional development as we now know it will not transform teachers' knowledge, beliefs, and habits of practice. In this chapter, we turn our attention to describing a program of professional development that has the potential to build teachers' capacity for innovative practice and ultimately to impact student learning. As indicated in the introduction, this book takes the stand that the professional development of teachers should be situated in practice. In this view the everyday work of teaching would become the object of ongoing investigation and thoughtful inquiry (Ball and Cohen 1999). Teachers would develop an understanding of subject matter, of pedagogy, and of students as learners—critical components of a teacher's knowledge base for teaching (NCTM 1991; National Board for Professional Teaching Standards 1997; Shulman 1986)—by investigating tasks that are central to teaching. Rather than learning theories and applying them to the practice of teaching, theories or general principles emerge from closely examining practice.

Hence, "samples of authentic practice"—materials taken from real classrooms—would become the curriculum for teacher education by providing opportunities for critique, inquiry, and investigation. For instance, a mathematical task along with a carefully selected set of student responses is one such example (Stylianou and Smith 2000). Teachers could be asked to complete the task, share various approaches that could be used to solve the task, and identify the mathematical ideas that are central to the task. The examination and analysis of student responses to the task could center on determining what students' responses reveal about students' mathematical understandings and misconceptions, the type of feedback that could be provided to specific students, and the questions that teachers could ask a particular student in order to better understand his or her way of thinking. Such a discussion is likely to enhance teachers' knowledge of mathematics content and of students as learners of mathematics.

These practice-based materials, however, are not self-enacting (Ball and Cohen 1999). Rather, they provide the raw material around which "professional learning tasks" (PLTs) can be designed (Ball and Cohen 1999, p. 27). PLTs, tasks that engage teachers in the work of teaching, can be developed in order to meet a specific goal for teacher learning and to take into consideration the prior knowledge and experience that teachers bring to the activity.

The Work of Teaching

The central tenet of this approach is that it is "centered in the critical activities of the profession—that is, in and about the practices of teaching and learning" (Ball and Cohen 1999, p. 13). One way to design professional learning tasks is to consider the cycle of teachers' work and the nature of the activities in which teachers engage as they move through the cycle.

The cycle begins with planning for instruction. Here the teacher decides what mathematical knowledge and processes she wants students to learn; determines the relevant prior knowledge and experiences on which students can draw to construct new knowledge; and creates, finds, or adapts tasks or activities that build on prior knowledge and experiences and have the potential to foster the intended learning.

The cycle continues with teaching—enacting the plan that has been developed. It is during the act of teaching that the teacher must engage students' in the task or activity, make midcourse corrections as needed to fit the needs of the students, provide "scaffolding" for students' learning so as to sustain their engagement in worthwhile mathematical activity, and formally and informally assess what students are learning.

The teacher completes the cycle with reflection. During this process, teachers must consider the level and kind of thinking in which the majority of students engaged during the lesson and what students did and said that suggested understanding of important mathematical ideas. They must also consider the ways in which the teaching may have supported or inhibited students' engagement with the task as intended. Based on an appraisal of the lesson and knowledge of the overarching mathematical goals, the cycle begins again with planning the next lesson.

Although this description may oversimplify the components of the teaching cycle, it serves to highlight the types of activities that are foundational to teachers' work and suggests potential PLTs that use authentic practice. For example, a videotape of a classroom episode could serve as the basis for several tasks that embody the work of teaching. Teachers could begin by analyzing the task that was used during instruction and by asking questions such as the following:

- What opportunities to learn mathematics are afforded by the task?
- What prior knowledge and experience would students need in order to engage in the task successfully?
- How would you expect students to go about solving the task?

Teachers could then move on to watching the video and analyzing the learning environment, responding to questions such as these:

- What decisions did the teacher make during the course of the lesson?
- What decisions were made by students?
- Who validated answers?
- Who asked the questions?
- What was the nature of the questions asked by students? By the teacher?

The investigation could continue with teachers analyzing what students seemed to be learning and how they learned it. Questions such as these might frame the analysis:

- What were the mathematical ideas with which students appear to grapple?
- What do students' solutions tell about what they know and understand?
- What factors appeared to support students' engagement in mathematical activity?
- What factors seem to hinder such engagement?

The discussion could conclude with actually planning the subsequent lesson, focusing on questions that include the following:

- What should be the mathematical target of instruction in the next lesson?
- What knowledge have students demonstrated that will serve as a foundation for constructing new knowledge?
- What task would accomplish the learning goal?

A videotape of teaching, therefore, could serve as the basis for engaging teachers in an investigation and analysis of all phases of the teaching cycle.

The videotape and students' work discussed so far represent two specific samples of practice-based materials that can serve as the basis for PLTs for teachers. The remainder of this chapter will focus on three broad categories of such materials—mathematical tasks, episodes of teaching, and illuminations of students' thinking. These materials will provide the foundation for PLTs that involve exploration and analysis.

* * *

Summary

A practice-based approach to professional development provides teachers with an opportunity to develop new levels of awareness and knowledge through consideration of samples of authentic practice. The goal of such work is to help teachers develop the capacity to see specific events that occur in the practice of teaching as instances of a larger class of phenomena. That is, generalities are abstracted from examining particular situations, and these in turn become practical wisdom that will inform teachers' practice. Instead of learning theories and applying them later to practice, teachers witness the emergence of theories from the study of practice. Ultimately, the goal is for teachers to be able to apply these generalizations to their own practice.

Samples of authentic practice are not, however, a panacea for all the shortcomings of professional education. We must be aware of the potential pitfalls as well as the promise of these materials. Ball (2001) cautions us to consider carefully the way in which we design and conduct learning experiences for teachers around records of practice. In particular, she has identified four issues that should be taken seriously as we begin to construct learning experiences that build on accounts of practice:

1. *Curricula need to be developed around records of practice.* Isolated encounters with interesting professional learning tasks that do not build on each other to lead teachers to a more robust understanding will not facilitate fundamental changes in their practices. The same care that is given to developing curricula for children needs to be given to developing curricula that is for teachers and has records of practice at its core.

2. *The records of practice do not represent a teacher's own teaching situation.* Although this aspect of a practice-based curriculum can be a strength, the curriculum should be designed so that the professional learning tasks that center on records of practice are both relevant and compelling for teachers.

3. *Records of practice provide rich detail about particular situations, but it is important to see beyond details instead of becoming caught up in them.* Teachers need to be able to see specific events as examples of more generalizable ideas about mathematics teaching and learning. Moving from particulars to generalizations may not happen in one discussion. A sustained effort needs to be made to help teachers make these connections over time.

4. *The process of examining records of practice can become so analytical that it loses its connection to the work of teaching.* The analysis of records of practice is intended to help teachers develop a knowledge base for teaching that will improve their decision making in the classroom. The process is *not* designed to help teachers become more skillful at performing analysis for its own sake. Avoiding this pitfall requires keeping the work of teaching as a focus and making connections between the task at hand and the real work that teachers do.

REFERENCES ■

Ball, Deborah Loewenberg. "Research on Teaching Mathematics: Making Subject Matter Knowledge Part of the Equation." In *Advances in Research on Teaching,* vol. 2, *Teacher's Knowledge of Subject Matter as It Relates to Their Teaching Practices,* edited by Jere Brophy, pp. 1–48. Greenwich, Conn.: JAI Press, 1991.

Ball, Deborah Loewenberg. "With an Eye on the Mathematical Horizon: Dilemmas of Teaching Elementary School Mathematics." *Elementary School Journal* 93, no. 4 (March 1993), 373–97.

Ball, Deborah Loewenberg. "A Practice-Based Approach to Teacher Education: The Potential Affordance and Difficulties." Paper presented at the annual meeting of the Association of Mathematics Teacher Educators, Costa Mesa, Calif., January 2001.

Ball, Deborah Loewenberg, and David K. Cohen. "Developing Practice, Developing Practitioners: Toward a Practice-Based Theory of Professional Education." In *Teaching as the Learning Profession: Handbook of Policy and Practice*, edited by Linda Darling-Hammond and Gary Sykes, pp. 3–32. San Francisco: Jossey-Bass, 1999.

Carpenter, Thomas P., Elizabeth Fennema, Penelope L. Peterson, Chi-Pang Chiang, and Megan Loef. "Using Knowledge of Children's Mathematics Thinking in Classroom Teaching: An Experimental Study." *American Educational Research Journal* 26, no. 4 (winter 1989), 499–531.

Cobb, Paul, Terry Wood, Erna Yackel, John Nicholls, Grayson Wheatley, Beatriz Trigatti, and Marcella Perlwitz. "Assessment of a Problem-Centered Second-Grade Mathematics Project." *Journal for Research in Mathematics Education* 22 (January 1991), 3–29.

Darling-Hammond, Linda, and Gary Sykes, eds. *Teaching as the Learning Profession: Handbook of Policy and Practice.* San Francisco; Jossey-Bass, 1999.

Fullan, Michael. *The New Meaning of Educational Change.* New York: Teachers College Press, 1991.

Huberman, Michael. "The Model of an Independent Artisan in Teachers' Professional Relations." In *Teachers' Work: Individuals, Colleagues, and Contexts*, edited by Judith W. Little and Milbrey W. McLaughlin. New York: Teachers College Press, 1993.

Little, Judith Warren. "Teachers' Professional Development in a Climate of Educational Reform," *Educational Evaluation and Policy Analysis* 15, no. 2 (1993): 129–51.

National Board for Professional Teaching Standards (NBPTS). *Middle Childhood and Early Adolescence/Mathematics: Standards for National Board Certification.* Washington, D.C.: NBPTS, 1997.

National Council of Teachers of Mathematics (NCTM). *Curriculum and Evaluation Standards for School Mathematics.* Reston, Va.: NCTM, 1989.

National Council of Teachers of Mathematics (NCTM). *Professional Standards for Teaching Mathematics.* Reston, Va.: NCTM, 1991.

National Council of Teachers of Mathematics (NCTM). *Assessment Standards for School Mathematics.* Reston, Va.: NCTM, 1995.

National Council of Teachers of Mathematics (NCTM). *Principles and Standards for School Mathematics.* Reston, Va.: NCTM, 2000.

Shulman, Lee S. "Those Who Understand: Knowledge Growth in Touching," *Educational Researcher* 15 (February 1986), 4–14.

Silver, Edward A. "Mathematical Thinking and Reasoning for All Students: Moving from Rhetoric to Reality." In *Selected Lectures from the 7th International Congress on Mathematics Education*, edited by David F. Robitaille, David H. Wheeler, and Carolyn Kieran, pp. 311–25. Quebec, Canada: Les Presses de l'Université Laval, 1994.

Simon, Martin A., and Deborah Schifter. "Towards a Constructivist Perspective: An Intervention Study of Mathematics Teachers." *Educational Studies in Mathematics* 22, no. 4 (August 1991): 309–31.

Simon, Martin A., and Glendon W. Blume. "Building and Understanding Multiplicative Relationships: A Study of Prospective Elementary Teachers," *Journal for Research in Mathematics Education* 25 (November 1994): 472–94.

Sowder, Judith, Barbara Armstrong, Susan Lamon, Martin Simon, Larry Sowder, and Alba Thompson. "Educating Teachers to Teach Multiplicative Structures in the Middle Grades." *Journal of Mathematics Teacher Education* 1, no. 2 (1998): 127–55.

Stylianou, Despina, and Margaret Schwan Smith. "Examining Student Responses: A Strategy for Developing Pre-Service Elementary Teachers' Understanding of Algebra." In *Algebra across the Grades*, 2000 Yearbook of the Pennsylvania Council of Teachers of Mathematics, edited by M. Kathleen Heid, Margaret Schwan Smith, find Glendon W. Blame, pp. 23–32. N.p.: Pennsylvania Council of Teachers of Mathematics, 2000.

Thompson, Alba G., and Patrick W. Thompson, "Talking about Rates Conceptually, Part II: Mathematical Knowledge for Teaching." *Journal for Research in Mathematics Education* 27 (January 1996): 2–24.

Thompson, Charles L., and John S. Zeuli. "The Frame and the Tapestry: Standards-Based Reform and Professional Development." In *Teaching as the Learning Profession: Handbook of Policy and Practice,* edited by Linda Darling-Hammond and Gary Sykes, pp. 341–75. San Francisco: Jossey-Bass, 1999.

Wilcox, Sandra K., Pamela Schram, Glenda Lappan, and Perry Lanier. "The Role of a Learning Community in Changing Preservice Teachers' Knowledge and Beliefs about Mathematics Education." Paper presented at the annual meeting of the American Educational Research Association, Boston, April 1991.

READING 5.2

Designing Professional Development for Teachers of Science and Mathematics

Susan Loucks-Horsley

Nancy Love

Katherine E. Stiles

Susan Mundry

Peter W. Hewson

The decision about which strategies for professional learning to include in your design is informed by all other inputs into the process of designing. (See Figure 5.2a.) The goals of the professional development program—which are grounded in the vision and in data analysis—drive the selection of specific strategies. Strategy choices are also informed by the knowledge and beliefs the designers hold about the change process, teaching, learning, professional development, and the nature of science and mathematics. The context within which the strategies will be implemented shapes the selection, combination, and sequence of the learning opportunities provided. The critical issues that influence the successful implementation and outcomes of any professional development program play a role in determining the selection of strategies. For example, building capacity for sustainability may lead to a decision to combine strategies such as immersion, curriculum implementation, and technology for professional learning to meet different teachers' needs at different times. Finally, professional learning opportunities are often the specific components of the design that are evaluated and assessed.

A word of caution—strategies in isolation do not constitute effective professional development. Strategies are frequently what professional developers "grab at"; this book emphasizes why different strategies are better choices within different contexts, for different goals and purposes, and for different circumstances. As noted above, it is the intricate interplay of all components of the design framework that informs the selection of strategies for professional learning.

This chapter describes 18 specific professional development strategies. The chapter describes each strategy according to its (a) key elements, the components of the strategy that help answer the question: How will I know it when I see it? and (b) implementation requirements, the resources and support needed to use the strategy, such as time, facilities, materials, and additional staff. Following this are various examples of ways in which the strategy has been implemented and a discussion of some of the issues and challenges faced when selecting and using the strategy. In addition, for each strategy, there are several

Source: Loucks-Horsley, S., Love, N., Stiles, K., Mundry, S., & Hewson, P. (2003). *Designing professional development for teachers of science and mathematics* (2nd ed.). Thousand Oaks, CA: Corwin.

Figure 5.2a Strategies for Professional Learning

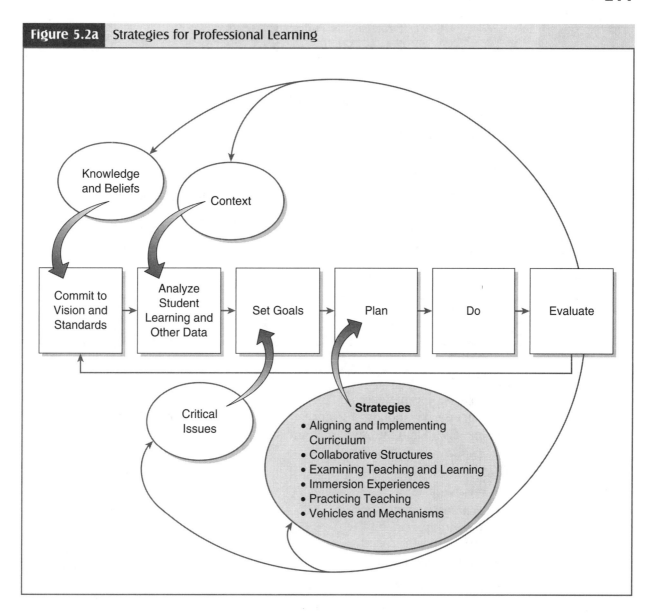

resources noted—articles, books, and Web sites—for obtaining further information and learning about specific programs or initiatives that use the strategy.

The 18 strategies are grouped into six clusters: (1) aligning and implementing curriculum, (2) collaborative structures, (3) examining teaching and learning, (4) immersion experiences, (5) practicing teaching, and (6) vehicles and mechanisms. (See Table 5.2a.) The strategies within a cluster share common underlying assumptions about teaching, learning, and professional development. Therefore, the clusters provide a framework for organizing the strategies and considering their selection and use.

As noted in previous chapters, professional development is more than offering isolated strategies. Every program, initiative, and professional development plan uses a variety of strategies in combination with one another to form a unique design. Each strategy is one piece of the puzzle, and how a designer fits strategies together depends on his or her particular circumstances. The professional development designer's challenge is to assemble a combination of learning activities that best meets the designer's specific goals and context.

Table 5.2a   Eighteen Strategies for Professional Learning

Aligning and Implementing Curriculum

- Curriculum alignment and instructional materials selection
- Curriculum implementation
- Curriculum replacement units

Collaborative Structures

- Partnerships with scientists and mathematicians in business, industry, and universities
- Professional networks
- Study groups

Examining Teaching and Learning

- Action research
- Case discussions
- Examining student work and thinking and scoring assessments

Lesson Study

- Immersion experiences
- Immersion in inquiry in science and problem solving in mathematics
- Immersion into the world of scientists and mathematicians

Practicing Teaching

- Coaching
- Demonstration lessons
- Mentoring

Vehicles and Mechanisms

- Developing professional developers
- Technology for professional development
- Workshops, institutes, courses, and seminars

From work with professional developers in science and mathematics, we identified four interconnected outcomes that often drive professional development designs in science and mathematics education:

- Increasing science and/or mathematics content knowledge
- Increasing pedagogical content knowledge
- Building a professional learning community
- Developing leadership (NISE Professional Development Strategies Working Group, 1999)

If districts are working to promote these four outcomes, as many are, it is easy to see that one strategy will not be sufficient. Instead, the designer combines different strategies to address the different outcomes, with some strategies addressing more than one outcome.

Increasing teachers' content knowledge is often best accomplished by immersing teachers in content as learners themselves. This can be accomplished through the immersion strategies, through partnerships, and in workshops/institutes. But learning content alone will not lead to changes in teaching, so designers must build in opportunities for teachers to put the content they learn into the context of teaching and provide opportunities to develop pedagogical content knowledge. This is accomplished through different strategies, such as examining student work, case discussions, curriculum work, and lesson study. Engaging in such collegial arrangements helps to address the third outcome—building a professional learning community, which can also be developed through teachers' participation in lesson study, demonstration lessons, and study groups. The final outcome is often addressed through the use of the developing professional developers strategy.

In addition to using the intended outcomes of a professional development program to guide the selection of strategies, another guide is knowing the purpose each strategy best addresses and matching it to the needs of participating teachers. Different strategies can be more appropriate for people depending on where they are in the change process. At the beginning of the process, teachers need concrete information and "how to" advice. Later they want ways to collaborate with others and assess impact.

For example, some strategies are more appropriate for building knowledge (e.g., workshops/institutes and partnerships), whereas others help teachers reflect on learning and teaching (e.g., action research, examining student work, and lesson study). The following are some different purposes for strategies:

- Strategies that focus on *developing awareness* are usually used during the beginning phases of a change, which call for introducing teachers to new approaches or content. The strategies are designed to raise awareness through the introduction of new information and to elicit thoughtful questioning on the part of the teachers concerning the new information. Examples of strategies that help to raise awareness include professional networks, demonstration lessons, and study groups.

- Strategies that focus on *building knowledge* provide opportunities for teachers to develop science and mathematics content knowledge and pedagogical content knowledge. Examples of strategies often used to build knowledge include case discussions, immersion experiences, workshops, technology for professional development, and partnerships with scientists or mathematicians.

- Strategies that help teachers *translate new knowledge into practice* engage teachers in drawing on their knowledge base to plan instruction and improve their teaching. Examples of strategies often used to help teachers translate knowledge into practice include coaching, mentoring, curriculum implementation, and demonstration lessons.

- Strategies that focus on *practicing teaching* help teachers learn through the process of using a new approach, practice, or process with their students. As they practice new moves in their classrooms, they increase their understanding and their skills. Examples of strategies often used to practice teaching are examining student work, lesson study, coaching, mentoring, and demonstration lessons.

- Strategies that provide opportunities to *reflect deeply on teaching and learning* engage teachers in examining their experiences in the classroom, assessing the impact of the changes they have made on their students, and thinking about ways to improve. These strategies also encourage teachers to reflect on others' practice, relating it to their own and generating ideas for improvement. Examples of strategies often used to help teachers reflect on their practice include action research, study groups, lesson study, case discussions, and examining student work.

The above schema is adapted from a framework devised by researchers in the Qualitative Understanding: Amplifying Student Achievement and Reasoning (QUASAR) project (Brown & Smith, 1997) to describe various ways of supporting teacher learning. The framework, in turn, reflects Shulman's (1986) model of pedagogical reasoning and action. As discussed in Chapter 2, any act of teaching is cyclical. A teacher must comprehend the material to be taught, which then must be transformed into a form that can be taught. Then, instruction takes place and is accompanied by reflection on the effectiveness in fostering student learning.

What is clear from this schema is the developmental nature of teacher learning. Other developmental models have been used by professional developers to select, combine, and sequence the strategies they use to support teacher learning. For example, the Concerns-Based Adoption Model (CBAM), discussed in Chapter 1, describes the emerging questions or concerns that educators have as they are introduced to and take on a new program, practice, or process (Hall & Hord, 2001). These concerns develop from questions that are more self-oriented (e.g., "What is it?" "How will it affect me?" and "What will I have to do?") to those that are task-oriented (e.g., "How can I get more organized?" "Why is it taking so much time?" and "How can I best manage the materials and schedules?"), and finally, when these concerns begin to be resolved, to more impact-oriented concerns (e.g., "How is this affecting students?" and "How can I improve what I'm doing so all students can learn?").

This model suggests that teacher questions can guide the selection of strategies for professional development. For example, an immersion experience in science or mathematics—that is, actually engaging in science inquiry or mathematics problem solving as learners—helps teachers see (and feel) what new teaching practices look like in action. They get a sense of new roles teachers must play, strategies for grouping and questioning, and the flow of instruction. Curriculum implementation helps teachers with their questions about the teaching task because it guides their use of materials, time management, and classroom management techniques. Teachers' more impact-oriented questions can be addressed through opportunities for them to examine student work and score student assessments or conduct action research into their own questions about student learning.

As noted previously, designers combine different strategies to meet multiple goals and to address the particular needs of the learner at a particular time. For example, over the course of a year teachers might participate in a workshop focused on teaching them to use new curriculum, have a coach who helps them implement a unit from the curriculum, and meet in a study group to review videos of their own or others' teaching and examine student work. This combination of strategies can nurture teacher learning through several stages of development and changes in teaching practice and address multiple goals—for example, improved pedagogical content knowledge and increased professional culture.

We invite professional developers to become familiar with the 18 strategies for teacher learning in this chapter and to reflect on how to best combine them to address local goals, needs, and other contextual factors.

■ CURRICULUM ALIGNMENT AND MATERIALS SELECTION

At the request of the superintendent, a group of teachers from four schools and their principals and the science curriculum specialist formed a committee to coordinate selection of curriculum materials. Their first step was to come to consensus on the criteria they would use to select from among the many science texts and kit-based materials available. They each took responsibility for some reading on trends, research, practices, and attitudes in science education and shared findings with each other. They also carefully studied and discussed the expectations for students reflected in their district, state, and national standards. From this they created a rubric for scoring the different elementary science materials they were considering. The rubric would help them measure the extent to which the curriculum materials reflected the content in the standards; engaged students in the kind of work, learning, and assessment activities recommended by research; and were developmentally appropriate. The development of the rubric resulted in substantial learning among the participants. They learned the contents of the standards as well as research on children's ideas in science and developed a shared vision of what the elementary science program for the district needed to include.

The committee obtained copies of commercially available materials to review for consideration, examining the extent to which each set of materials addressed appropriate science content, the intended learning goals for all students, and strategies for teaching, learning, and assessment. They narrowed their choice down to two different products that the committee scored the highest using their rubric. They enlisted teachers at each elementary grade level throughout the district to pilot test the two different sets of curriculum materials in their classrooms. During pilot testing, teachers engaged in short weekly sessions to reflect on what they did and examine the students' work to better understand what the students were learning and how the instructional materials supported learning. Pilot-testing teachers also met monthly with the curriculum committee to share what they, as teachers implementing the new materials, needed to enhance their ability to use the materials effectively, including science content knowledge and better understanding of inquiry-based learning. The curriculum committee responded to these needs during the pilot testing and used what they had learned to inform plans for large-scale implementation.

Based on the results, the committee and pilot-testing teachers selected one of the instructional materials for use in the coming school year and a long-term plan for implementing the new curriculum materials.

In many districts, the process of selecting curriculum materials has been simply to pick something popular with a few teachers or worse have teachers all use their own materials with little coordination. Increasingly, districts are engaging in more thoughtful analysis of the curriculum and its alignment with local and national standards. They use this curriculum analysis in combination with a deliberate materials selection process to select a coherent and focused program for all students. In addition, many districts are capitalizing on this process as an opportunity for teacher learning. The emerging strategy of curriculum alignment and selection of materials develops teachers' understanding of effective curriculum, science and mathematics education standards, content, pedagogy, and assessment.

As the above vignette illustrates, the selection committee engaged in various activities to increase teachers' knowledge including the following:

- Studying the local and national standards to identify the meaning and intent of student learning goals
- Developing a clear picture of what curriculum was needed based on the standards and student learning goals and how concepts and skills would develop in a coherent fashion through the grades
- Developing a common vision of standards-based teaching and learning
- Identifying local needs based on analysis of student learning and other data
- Using a process for selecting curriculum materials that was guided by a systematic approach to gathering evidence
- Selecting the materials, pilot testing them, and developing a plan for implementation.

Key Elements

Teachers Are Essential Participants in the Process of Aligning, Selecting, and Implementing Curriculum Materials. Many districts appoint a selection committee composed of content area coordinators and classroom teachers to conduct the initial

Key Elements of Curriculum Alignment and Materials Selection

- Teachers are essential participants in the process of aligning curriculum, selecting instructional materials, and implementing those materials.
- Teachers undertake a process of examining curriculum and instructional materials that leads to a new product and learning.
- Aligning curriculum and selecting instructional materials require a clearly articulated procedure that addresses all aspects of the process.
- Curriculum alignment and instructional materials selection is a collaborative activity.

identification of curriculum to consider for adoption. The involvement of teachers, however, often ends once the instructional materials are adopted and added to the approved district or state list. For this strategy to maximize professional learning, teachers need to stay involved throughout the whole process—from establishing learning goals to implementing instructional materials. Their involvement in studying standards and setting learning goals increases their understanding of the relationship between the curriculum and the learning goals or standards, giving them insight into the intent of the curriculum. Their active participation in pilot testing the instructional materials helps them see how the curriculum works with children, and this can inform the professional development needed to support the implementation of the materials by other teachers. Helping to shape professional development plans and monitor and support implementation is another learning opportunity for teachers.

Teachers Undertake a Process of Examining Curriculum Materials That Leads to a New Product and Learning. The outcome of alignment and selection of curriculum materials is the identification of a new or modified curriculum program aligned with standards. The selection process itself provides the opportunity for professional development. As teachers explore the standards and develop a content matrix or adopt one from commercial curriculum materials, they learn what science or mathematics content is valued in the standards, collaborate with peers and experts, examine the extent to which assessments match the content, reexamine their own classroom practices, work with others to solve problems, and interact with subject matter and pedagogy. All these activities enhance the professional growth of individual teachers and can lead to more effective teaching and learning practices.

Aligning Curriculum and Selecting Instructional Materials Require a Clearly Articulated Procedure That Addresses All Aspects of the Process. There are numerous tools and guidelines available for curriculum selection (see the Resources section). No matter which process is selected, it is critical that the following components be included:

- The formation of a team or committee with representation from teachers at the appropriate grade levels and content areas, different school sites, and administrators.
- The selection of tools and a comprehensive process to guide the examination of national and local standards, analysis of current performance levels in the appropriate grade levels and content areas, development of a content matrix that identifies student learning goals across grade levels, and the selection of the instructional materials.
- Instructional materials selection should include an analysis of the content, student learning activities, teaching activities, teacher content information, and assessment strategies. These components should be evaluated based on rubrics developed or adapted by the committee members to meet their local contexts and goals.

The selection of instructional materials should include a "prescreening" process to narrow the choices of instructional materials; a paper screen process to gather and analyze evidence from the materials to determine if they meet the established criteria and standards, using a rubric or other scoring device; pilot testing of the materials in classrooms to gather and analyze student work and other data from the classroom; selection of the final instructional materials; and full-scale implementation of the materials with accompanying professional development.

Curriculum Alignment and Instructional Materials Selection Is a Collaborative Activity.
The process of collaborating with other teachers and curriculum experts enriches the professional development opportunities. Through analysis of curriculum and discussion, teachers build their own knowledge of the content, curriculum organization and design, and content-specific pedagogy. They begin to identify content that they do not understand and plan together to address such gaps in knowledge. Often, as teachers examine the curriculum and see how and why different concepts and lessons are organized the way they are, their attitudes about what constitutes effective science or mathematics teaching and learning change. They return to their classrooms with new views. Also, by collaborating with others, teachers become less isolated in their individual classrooms and develop a broader perspective of science or mathematics education.

Implementation Requirements

District or School Administrative Support. Administrators encourage the process, provide time and incentives for teachers to participate, ensure access to resources and experts, and support ongoing, long-term improvement of the curriculum and instructional materials that are ultimately implemented.

Process for Selection Including Rubrics, Tools, and Forms for Tracking What Was Piloted and Its Results. It is essential that the process be clear to everyone involved. Using resources such as those listed later in this section will keep the team on track and document what was done and why.

Examples

The K–12 Alliance at WestEd has developed an instructional materials selection process called analyzing instructional materials (AIM). In partnership with Biological Sciences Curriculum Study (BSCS), K–12 Alliance staff are using AIM with teams of high school teachers and their school district administrators as part of the core learning experiences in the BSCS SciCenter's National Academy for Curriculum Leadership. These teams use AIM to guide their selection of and planning for implementation of inquiry-oriented, standards-based instructional materials. It is used as a professional development experience for the teams and is based on gathering evidence to analyze and select instructional materials. Leadership teams participate in professional development to help them understand the various components of AIM and to enhance their understanding of inquiry-based teaching and learning and further their common vision of best practice before they begin looking at commercially available textbooks and other materials.

The AIM process itself involves identifying criteria that are based on local, state, and national science standards for analyzing instructional materials and developing rubrics for the criteria. Several sample rubrics are provided for the teams to use to guide the development of rubrics specific to their own contexts and standards. The rubrics are designed to assess the science content, the work students do, assessment, and the work teachers do within the instructional materials. Instructional materials are assessed based on each criterion and scored according to the rubrics. Once all criteria have been assessed, the leadership team has evidence of the extent to which the instructional materials meet their criteria. This initial process, labeled the "paper screen," enables teams to narrow their selection of instructional materials to only those that are quality, inquiry-oriented, standards-based materials that meet their specific criteria. These few instructional materials are then pilot tested in classrooms. Pilot teachers participate in professional development to learn more about inquiry-based teaching and learning and the instructional materials. During pilot testing, data are gathered on the same rubric components, adding further evidence for the leadership team to consider in their selection of the final materials.

The selection process, however, does not end with the identification of one set of instructional materials. Central to the AIM process is the development of a long-term plan for professional development for all teachers who will implement the newly selected instructional materials. Leadership teams learn about the process of designing professional development for supporting curriculum implementation and about many of the strategies most successful in enhancing teachers' learning.

The ARC Center in Lexington, Massachusetts, a collaboration between the Consortium for Mathematics and Its Applications (COMAP) and three of the elementary mathematics curriculum projects supported by the National Science Foundation (NSF), works closely with schools and districts to enhance teaching and learning in mathematics. One of ARC's main strategies is to provide guidance and professional development for curriculum selection teams in districts to enhance their reform efforts in mathematics. One of these sites is the school district in Portage, Wisconsin, a small, rural school district with seven elementary schools. During the 1998–1999 school year, the district's director of instruction convened a committee to find ways that the district could improve mathematics scores on the statewide tests administered in fourth, eighth, and tenth grades. On the committee were second-through sixth-grade teachers from each of the elementary schools, who met twice a month during the academic year. The committee examined data about their own students' test scores and initiated a study to learn from other districts: "They started by looking at test data of other Wisconsin districts with demographic profiles similar to that of Portage. Of the 426 school districts in Wisconsin, they chose ten small-town, rural districts that had better mathematics scores than theirs. Committee members visited these districts, observed classes, and asked teachers questions about their mathematics programs" (COMAP, online at www.comap.com/elementary/projects/arc/stories/portage).

During their visits to other districts, the committee was encouraged to look at some of the NSF-supported mathematics instructional materials. They analyzed the materials and assessed the extent to which each set of materials addressed the state standards. After narrowing their options to two high-quality materials, they pilot tested them in fifth and sixth grade classrooms. By the end of the school year, one of those materials had been selected and adopted.

At that point, the committee took a crucial step—gaining the "buy-in" and support from classroom teachers in each of the schools. "The committee members spoke to other teachers at building meetings. They discussed the data gathering process, described the pilot tests, and shared the [instructional] materials. Their message was that the district needed to make a change, that this was an outstanding curriculum, that it would help teachers improve instruction, and that students would like mathematics and do better. The teachers supported the choice" (COMAP, online at www. comap.com/elementary/projects/arc/stories/portage). At the same time, the director of instruction was sharing identical information with each of the school principals, and parents and the community were informed of the new instructional materials through discussions. By the end of the year, each of the seven schools was supportive of the new emphasis in mathematics teaching and the school board approved the materials.

In the second year of the process, large-scale implementation was begun and classroom teachers attended numerous professional development sessions to help them learn more about the overall program and the instructional materials. By 2002, every teacher in the district was using the new curriculum and they have had positive reactions to the changes in their classrooms.

Commentary

Many of the benefits of using curriculum alignment and instructional materials selection for professional development of science and mathematics teachers have previously been identified in this section. As with any professional development strategy, however, there are challenges and issues to consider.

Time and Support. It is difficult for teachers to find the time to devote to the intensive process of examining curriculum and selecting instructional materials. Frequently, teachers are available only after school or during the summer months to devote time to this intensive effort. It is imperative that teachers who volunteer for curriculum committees are given adequate time and support for their efforts, such as reduction of class load or some other duties in exchange for their participation on the committee. It is also critical that administrators recognize that this is a long-term process and necessarily engages teachers for more than one academic year.

Selecting the Appropriate Procedure. As noted previously, numerous documents, guidelines, and procedures are available to guide the curriculum alignment and instructional materials selection processes. It is important to keep in mind that the main purpose of these processes is the professional learning and growth of the teachers involved—both those on the committee and the pilot teachers—and ultimately the selection of curriculum materials that will improve student learning. Both goals can be accomplished if care is taken in the identification of the guidelines used to facilitate the processes. In some districts, multiple-year efforts may not be feasible and shorter alignment and selection procedures may need to be identified.

Leadership Development. In addition to individual professional learning, this strategy lends itself to developing teacher leaders during the pilot testing process who can provide ongoing professional development for other teachers as they begin to implement the instructional materials. Early in the process, district-level leaders should plan for taking advantage of this knowledgeable and experienced pool of new science or mathematics leaders.

Resources

Alternatives for Rebuilding Curricula (ARC) Center. The Consortium for Mathematics and Its Applications (COMAP) (www.arccenter.comap.com).

American Association for the Advancement of Science, Project 2061, Curriculum-Analysis Procedure (www.aaas.org/project2061).

Eisenhower National Clearinghouse (ENC) (www.enc.org).

Eisenhower Regional Consortia (www.mathsciencenetwork.org).

K–12 Alliance, WestEd, California (www.k12alliance.net).

National Research Council. (1999a). *Designing mathematics or science curriculum programs: A guide for using mathematics and science education standards.* Washington, DC: National Academy Press.

National Research Council. (1999b). *Selecting instructional materials: A guide for K–12 science.* Washington, DC: National Academy Press.

National Science Foundation, Science and Mathematics Education Implementation and Dissemination Centers (www.nsf.gov).

WestEd and the WGBH Educational Foundation. (2003). *Teachers as learners: A multimedia kit for professional development in science and mathematics.* Thousand Oaks, CA: Corwin. (See Tape 3, Program 5, *Curriculum implementation: Issues and challenges,* Institute for Inquiry, Exploratorium, San Francisco.)

■ CURRICULUM IMPLEMENTATION

Sarah Johnson is a sixth-grade teacher in a district that has three middle schools, each with approximately 600 students, Grades 6 through 8. The school board has just voted to implement a new problem-centered mathematics curriculum. Sarah participated with other teachers in a preliminary meeting during the spring that provided an overview of this new curriculum, but she really has little understanding of the total program or of what it will mean for her to actually use it.

The middle school coordinator has asked Sarah to join her, one seventh- and one eighth-grade teacher, and the principal from her school, along with similar teams from each of the other two middle schools in the district to participate in a one-week residential professional development institute that will introduce them to the curriculum. At the institute, she finds 18 other middle-grades teachers and their administrators from two other districts. This will be a good opportunity to learn with teachers who are from very different districts.

At the beginning of the institute, an overview of the structure and organization of the curriculum is provided. Very quickly, the leader moves to engaging participants in doing actual activities from the first module they will teach. Sarah jumps right in, as do the rest of her team members and they work through the various activities. Sarah is particularly attentive to some of the teaching strategies that the leader is using. In particular, she likes the way the leader expects different groups to take responsibility for initiating summary discussions about problems that have been investigated. She also notes that the leader makes a point of highlighting particular learning strategies as a way of pointing out the interaction of the teaching methods used and ways to promote student engagement and problem solving.

That night, participants are given homework problems to complete for the next day. Sarah and her team meet to work together on the problems; they are challenged as they solve problems and talk about the implications for use with their students. When they arrive at the workshop the next day, the leader designates various teams to take responsibility for presenting their solutions, providing a model for a strategy that Sarah plans to use as part of her classroom structure for the next year.

As the week progresses, the participants begin to understand the structure of the curriculum and how to use it with their students. The leader makes building a community of learning seem easy; Sarah wonders how she will develop such a community with her own students but is filled with enthusiasm. As the week draws to a close, the leader focuses on planning to use the curriculum. Using the school calendar and the pacing guide provided with the curriculum, teachers from the same grade levels team up and lay out a schedule to implement the first module. Sarah feels confident about the detail provided in the teacher support materials, particularly because the curriculum has actually been field tested at a number of different sites. There are many things planned when Sarah returns to her district. She knows that the middle school coordinator is counting on her and the other teachers in her district to use the new curriculum in their classrooms this year and then to help introduce the curriculum to other teachers in their schools the following year. The principals and the middle school coordinator intend to be quite proactive in their efforts to support the teachers in developing learning communities that are oriented toward problem solving, and they will provide the teachers with opportunities for peer coaching and support group meetings. Two more one-day workshops are scheduled throughout the year with the institute leader both to provide time for discussion and to gain an understanding of other modules that will be used at each grade level. Also, the institute leader will return to the school district in the spring to conduct several one-day sessions for the other teachers in the schools.

For right now, Sarah is focused on what will happen with her students. For the first time in a long time, Sarah finds she is very excited about teaching mathematics and that the curriculum seems to reflect her beliefs about what constitutes good teaching and learning.

The implementation of new curricula in the classroom can serve as a powerful learning experience for teachers. For curriculum implementation to support professional development, plans must be designed that enable teachers to learn about, try, reflect on, and share information about teaching and learning in the context of implementing the curriculum with their colleagues. Through using curriculum in their classrooms, reporting on what happens, and reflecting with others on the strengths and weakness of different ideas and activities, teachers learn about their own teaching and their students' learning (Ball, 1996).

Curriculum implementation involves using a set of materials that includes both content and instructional guidelines. The "set" of materials may be from one publisher or developer, or it may have been selected from a variety of quality materials available and organized by the school or district for use at particular grade levels in the development of specific concepts. For curriculum implementation to serve as an effective professional development activity, it is important that the curriculum selected or organized for implementation meets quality standards for content and for appropriate teaching strategies.

Curriculum implementation that is designed for professional development focuses teachers on learning about the new curriculum and how to use it and on implementing it—not on researching, designing, testing, or revising curriculum. The teachers' time is devoted to learning the science or mathematics content necessary to teach the new curriculum, learning how to conduct the activities, learning how students learn the new material, and incorporating the new curriculum into their long-term instruction.

The goal of this professional development strategy is not only for teachers to implement a new curriculum but also for them to strengthen their knowledge of the content and pedagogy in the curriculum.

Key Elements

Quality Curriculum Materials That Are Based on Standards. Curriculum is the way content is designed and delivered. It includes the structure, organization, balance, and presentation of the content in the classroom (National Research Council [NRC], 1996a). Curriculum or instructional materials structure and organize the content and lend support for the teaching strategies and learning environments used by teachers to help their students learn. The curriculum implementation strategy relies on quality curriculum materials, carefully developed by people with expertise in content and pedagogy, and sufficiently tested for use in diverse classrooms.

Teachers Learn About the Curriculum by Teaching It and Reflecting on It. As teachers become familiar with the curriculum and go through the materials as learners, they see the various teaching strategies they will use with their students. Teachers then try the new instructional materials and teaching practices in their classrooms and regularly assess and discuss their results and progress with colleagues.

Planning and Support for the Implementation Are Critical. A plan contains the structure and timeline of the curriculum implementation (National Science Resources Center [NSRC], 1997). Teachers and professional developers work together to decide how and when the curriculum will be implemented and the milestones that will be met at different points in the implementation process. As the curriculum is introduced over a period of time, teachers are given different kinds of help and support that are tailored to their changing needs. Teachers share ideas and insights with one another as they implement the new curriculum.

> **Key Elements for Curriculum Implementation**
>
> - Quality curriculum materials that are based on standards
> - Teachers learn about the curriculum by teaching it and reflecting on it.
> - Planning and support for the implementation are critical.

They also coach one another and conduct classroom visits to support implementation. (Usually, curriculum implementation involves using an entire curriculum for all grades in the school that covers all topics of the content area instead of only one topic or one grade level. The implementation process spread over time, however, may introduce units at one grade level at a time or introduce one unit at a time at each grade level.)

Implementation Requirements

Time. Teachers must have protected and structured time to learn about the new curriculum, try it in their classrooms, and reflect with colleagues on their experiences and those of their students.

Teacher Development Opportunities. Teachers must have supported opportunities to become aware of the new curriculum, learn to manage materials in the classroom, learn any new science or mathematics content, teach the new curriculum, and assess both their own and their students' learning.

Policies. The school and district must anticipate and plan for institutionalization by ensuring that structures are in place for the continued use of the curriculum after the initial phases and ongoing professional development for all teachers and that the curriculum is part of the overall school and district goals and policy.

Ongoing Commitment and Support. Teachers and school administrators must support the curriculum implementation and accompanying professional development over time (i.e., not just for one year) and avoid becoming distracted by other innovations and competing priorities.

Mechanisms for Assessment and Evaluation. Teachers must have routine meetings and interactions with other teachers to critique and process what and how they are teaching and data must be collected to assess the extent of implementation and the interim results from the new curriculum.

Examples

Since 1995, the NSF has devoted considerable effort and funding to support curriculum implementation in districts throughout the country. The NSF has funded 87 Local Systemic Change (LSC) Through Teacher Enhancement programs in school districts. The LSC programs are designed to improve the teaching of science, mathematics, and technology by providing classroom teachers with more than 130 hours of professional development. "The LSC initiative is distinguished from previous teacher enhancement efforts by its emphasis on preparing teachers to implement designated exemplary mathematics and science instructional materials in their classrooms" (Weiss, Banilower, Overstreet, & Soar, 2002, p. 1). LSC projects have designed and implemented diverse professional development programs that emphasize increasing teachers' content knowledge and pedagogical content knowledge, deepening teachers' understanding of the ways in which students learn science and mathematics, and expanding teachers' repertoire of assessment practices. Horizon Research, Inc. (HRI) has conducted annual evaluations of all LSC projects and their findings support aligning professional development to the use of instructional materials, as noted in the following:

> Classroom observations show that teachers who participated in LSC professional development were more likely to be using the designated instructional materials,

and that the quality of the lessons taught improved with increased participation in LSC activities. Furthermore, lessons taught by teachers who had participated in at least 20 hours of LSC professional development and were using the designated instructional materials were more likely to receive high ratings for their lessons, lending support to the program's focus on professional development aimed at implementing exemplary instructional materials. (Weiss et al., 2002, p. 54)

The NSF has also supported school districts' implementation of science and mathematics curriculum through their funding of eight Implementation and Dissemination Centers in sites across the country. The centers are designed to help school districts improve student achievement in science and mathematics by helping them implement quality instructional materials. The centers work in partnership with academic institutions, corporations, educational organizations, and school districts to design and provide teacher professional development in science, mathematics, and technology.

Commentary

Although virtually all schools implement new curricula at some time, often they do not organize the implementation process around professional development that provides opportunities for teachers to reflect on and learn from their experiences over time.

There are several benefits to using curriculum implementation as a vehicle for professional development. First, such an initiative aligns professional development with three other major dimensions of the system—curriculum, instruction, and assessment. This avoids what is an all too common practice in many districts: professional development that is disconnected from and unrelated to the curriculum that teachers teach. A second and related benefit is the efficiency of teachers learning exactly what they need to teach. This contrasts with the situation in which teachers learn content and teaching strategies, but have no ready-made vehicle to put these together in their classrooms. Finally, curriculum implementation is beneficial because it provides a focus for teacher reflection. Teachers can share issues, concerns, and children's work in the context of discussing the new curriculum.

In addition to its benefits, there are also pitfalls of the curriculum implementation strategy. First, there is a tension between the "mandates" to implement a new curriculum with fidelity and teacher creativity and independence. It is important for teachers to know how much adaptation they can do and still implement the curriculum effectively. Some changes in the new curriculum (e.g., finding and developing appropriate connections to other subject areas) can enhance the materials' effectiveness. Others can be harmful (e.g., when science teachers decide that live organisms are too difficult to manage or that demonstrations work better than each student doing his or her own investigations). The nature of acceptable adaptations requires early and ongoing negotiation.

Schools can ensure continual use of the curriculum by proactively supporting all teachers and providing orientation for new teachers or teachers who change grades. The needs of teachers change over time. Initially, teachers may be focused on the "how to's" for using the new curriculum. Given the nature of problem-centered and inquiry-based curricula, this focus could span the first few years of implementation. Once teachers are comfortable with the tasks, they often become concerned with the impact of the curriculum on students' understanding. At this stage, broader considerations of the nature of the mathematics or science content being addressed and how best to understand students' thinking may surface, requiring a different orientation to professional development. Eventually, teachers may find themselves at points at which they want to "fine-tune" or make modifications in the use of the curriculum to better meet the needs of their students.

A final caveat: With this approach, there is a real danger that professional development support will stop once (or before) the curriculum is fully in place. This disregards the need for continuously increasing teacher knowledge and skills. The mechanisms for teacher reflection, sharing, assessment, and adjustment should become part of the overall school routine. As teachers become more sophisticated in curriculum use, they will want to assess the impact on student learning. Professional development can help them learn about effective ways of gathering and analyzing student learning data.

Resources

National Science Foundation's Local Systemic Change Through Teacher Enhancement Programs (www.nsf.gov).

National Science Foundation's Science and Mathematics Education Implementation and Dissemination Centers (www.nsf.gov).

WestEd. (2003). *Teachers as learners: Professional development in science and mathematics, a video library.* Thousand Oaks, CA: Corwin. (See *Standards-based curriculum implementation: Mathematics curriculum workshop.* Clark County Schools, Las Vegas, NV.)

■ STUDY GROUPS

After several years in a project focused on mathematics education reform, the teachers at McKinley Middle School were still fine-tuning their practice. Their instructional tasks were good, their curriculum sound, and their organizational and management skills honed. Somehow, however, they felt that things still were not going as well as they could. They decided that they needed to focus on the instructional tasks they were using in their classrooms. In particular, they thought that the tasks did not always seem to play out in the ways they intended. They had attended a session at a recent NCTM conference in which a framework was presented that described ways in which the cognitive demands of tasks sometimes declined as students implemented them. The teachers wanted to explore this framework further to determine if it might offer some insight into how and why their lessons sometimes did not seem to deliver their potential.

They decided to meet biweekly after school to share videotapes of their teaching and use the framework to reflect on whether or not the cognitive-demanding tasks that they usually set up in their lessons were indeed being carried out by students in a way that maintained their high-level demands. Each week, a teacher would volunteer to show a 20- to 30-minute clip of instruction that would then be discussed using the framework as a guide. A McKinley teacher commented later that year, "This sustained attention to practice was absolutely what was needed to take us over the top." Another commented that the regular group sessions were the motivating force that pushed everyone to be more critical and reflective.

Study groups are collegial, collaborative groups of problem solvers who convene to mutually examine issues of teaching and learning. They are conducted within a safe, nonjudgmental environment in which all participants engage in reflection and learning and develop a common language and vision of science and mathematics education. Study groups are not teachers gathering for informal, social, or unstructured discussions. Rather, study groups offer teachers the opportunity to come together to focus on issues of teaching and learning. The topics addressed in these groups vary from current issues in mathematics and science education to whole-school reform. Groups may be composed of small numbers of teachers interested in pursuing a topic together or subgroups of the entire school faculty addressing whole-school reform issues. Regardless of the topic or issue being addressed, study groups provide a forum in which teachers can be inquirers and ask questions that matter to them, and are based on improving student learning, over a period of time, and in a collaborative and supportive environment.

Key Elements

Study Groups Are Organized Around a Specific Topic or Issues of Importance to the Participants. One of the primary elements of this
strategy is that groups are organized around a specific topic or issue of importance to the participating teachers. These topics range from school-based concerns to curriculum and instructional issues. For example, grade-level teachers might form a study group to learn more about assessing their students' understanding of science concepts. Over a period of time, they might meet to discuss research they have read, share examples of assessments and critique the appropriateness of the assessments, or invite school or district personnel to join the group to discuss other assessment requirements and how these influence classroom practice. Other study groups might be composed of entire school faculties or departments that focus on, for example, implementing specific school improvement initiatives or increasing parental support and participation in the mathematics program.

> ### Key Elements of Study Groups
>
> - Study groups are organized around a specific topic or issues of importance to the participants.
> - Study groups have varied structures.
> - Self-direction and self-governance contribute to the success of study groups.

Study Groups Have Varied Structures. Depending on the nature of topics discussed or
issues addressed, the form study groups take varies. Makibbin and Sprague (1991) suggest four models for structuring study groups. The *implementation model* is designed to support teachers' implementation of strategies recently learned in workshops or other short-term sessions. The goal is to provide teachers with an ongoing system for discussing, reflecting on, and analyzing their implementation of strategies after the workshop has concluded. The *institutionalization model* is used once teachers have already implemented new practices in the classroom and want to continue refining and improving these practices. *Research-sharing groups* are organized around discussions of recent research and how it relates to classroom practice. *Investigation study groups* are a way for teachers to identify a topic or practice about which they would like to learn. In this model, teachers read about, discuss, and implement new strategies that are relevant in their own contexts—their teaching practices and their students' learning. These models have been successfully implemented by teachers of mathematics and science as they investigate content, instructional practices, and student learning.

Self-Direction and Self-Governance Contribute to the Success of Study Groups.
Teachers should join and form study groups voluntarily and determine their own focus for learning and the format for the sessions. Although teachers' professional learning is the goal of study groups, increasing student learning is the end result of teachers' collaboratively examining their own knowledge, skills, and abilities. Carlene Murphy and Dale Lick (2001) suggest a problem-solving cycle that can help teachers effectively structure their study groups around specific goals and needs for student achievement.

- *Data Analysis.* Analyze a wide range of data and indicators describing the status of student learning and the conditions of the learning environment.
- *Student Needs.* From the data, generate a list of student needs.
- *Categorize and Set Priorities.* Categorize student needs and prioritize categories or clusters, stating what the "problem" is.

- *Organization.* Organize study groups around the prioritized needs and specify the intended results that will indicate that the "problem" is lessened or solved.
- *Plan of Action.* Create a study group plan of action that includes specific activities or strategies to implement that will reach the intended results.
- *Implementation.* Implement the study group action plan, including data collection and tracking changes through logs or journals, and specify procedures for organizing and sustaining the group.
- *Evaluation.* Evaluate the impact of the study group effort on student performance and teacher learning, and determine plans for institutionalizing the changes.

Implementation Requirements

Time. Like most other strategies for professional development, participating in a study group requires time not only to meet and address the issues but also to do so over a long period. Some suggest a minimum of at least once a week over a period of several months (LaBonte, Leighty, Mills, & True, 1995; Murphy, 1995; Murphy & Lick, 2001). Regardless of how frequently the group meets, it is critical that groups maintain a regular schedule of consistent contact with the expectation that their work is ongoing.

Support From Administrators. The formation and success of study groups require direct support from school administrators not only for the time for the group to meet but also for support for the endeavor itself. Administrators send a clear message of the importance of professional development for teachers if time is set aside during the school day for study groups to convene. Administrators can also offer support by providing access to resources, technology, or experts when teachers request assistance in meeting their goals. In instances where whole-faculty study groups are formed, administrator support *and* participation is critical.

Membership and Substantive Topics. Teachers forming study groups must identify their members (by grade level, across grade levels, schoolwide, or department-wide) and identify a topic or issue that is "complex and substantive enough to hold the group together while individuals are developing the skills of working together as a cohesive group and developing trust and rapport" (Murphy, 1995, p. 41). For teachers just embarking on collaboration with their peers, this new format for sharing knowledge and ideas will require that they become comfortable with the process and make adjustments as they progress. In addition, if the topic selected is too narrow or can be addressed in a very few sessions, the group may find itself moving from topic to topic without really reflecting on what they are learning.

Study Group Activities. Study group participants must identify a process for how to address the issues or topics. Most study groups use a variety of activities including reading, examining school data, viewing videotapes, and discussing research; learning about new teaching and learning approaches through reading, attending workshops or other sessions, or inviting experts to work with the group; and implementing new practices in their classrooms and using the study group time to reflect on and analyze the experience both for themselves and their students. In fact, many of the other professional development strategies described in this book are often combined with study groups: examining student work and thinking, examining standards to inform curriculum alignment and selection of instructional materials, conducting action research, engaging in case discussions, partnering with scientists or mathematicians to increase content knowledge, and engaging in peer coaching and debriefing.

Group Interaction Skills. As with other strategies organized around cooperative group work, group interaction skills are critical. Successful groups have members who share a common goal and are committed to accomplishing the goal, work to create an environment of trust and openness and foster communication, believe that diversity is an asset and that each member brings something unique to the group, value risk taking and creativity, are able to plan and implement strategies, share leadership and facilitation of group processes, are comfortable with consensus decision-making procedures, and are committed to building a team that reflects deeply on their learnings.

Examples

The Maine Mathematics and Science Alliance's Governor's Academy for Science Education Leadership, modeled after WestEd's National Academy for Science and Mathematics Education Leadership, uses electronic study groups between face-to-face academy meetings, to enhance the learning of the academy's teacher leaders and to develop a learning community among the staff and participants. The Governor's Academy leaders initiated an "electronic book study group" focused on discussing and learning more about science teaching and learning by reading and discussing professional literature. One of the books for discussion was *The Teaching Gap* by James Stigler and James Hiebert (1999). The director of the Governor's Academy has extensive experience in moderating and evaluating online discussions and applied a rubric and strategies developed for the Maine LabNet to "improve the quality of thinking and discussion that goes on in online courses and electronic study groups" (P. Keeley, personal communication, June 2002).

One of the strategies was the development of reflective questioning guides, posted online, and developed by the book study facilitator prior to the start of the electronic book discussion. These reflective questions greatly enhanced the learning of the participants by focusing their thinking and online discussion on specific sections of the book and encouraged participants to connect their reading and discussion with the issues they were examining and learning about in the academy. The online discourse community took on a character of its own as participants took the responsibility for leading the discussions, keeping them lively and focused, inviting inquiry, and encouraging others to interact. When the academy participants convene in person, they debrief the entire book and reflect on the study group. Participants are then introduced to the next book and the cycle continues again between meetings. A book study has a designated timeframe and usually lasts from six to eight weeks, depending on the book, and each week a new set of reflective questions is posted. In this way, the Governor's Academy has developed an effective combination of professional development strategies for supporting and maintaining the learning of an established group of teachers that is separated geographically.

One participant's electronic contribution to the study group on the preface and Chapter 1 of *The Teaching Gap* illustrates the depth of thinking and reflection that characterizes the success of this study group in probing science teachers' thinking about issues in education and teaching.

> The authors of "The Teaching Gap" tell us that learning won't improve markedly until we help teachers increase the effectiveness of their methodology. What a simple yet profound statement! Can you IMAGINE what it would be like to have the time and support to collaborate with others on the way you teach a unit? To have it be seen as a sign of a "strong" teacher to bounce ideas for ways to teach off of your colleagues? To have the time to really evaluate the effectiveness of a lesson after you deliver it? To have the time to put the results of that evaluation to good use to

improve the lesson when it is still fresh in your mind, rather than just before you have to teach the concept again the next year?

Whenever I think about practice, I always think about how I would teach someone if I weren't in a school. When I am trying to teach my son how to change a tire, or my daughters how to tell a red fox track from a bobcat's, I do it very differently than I would if teaching it as part of a science course in my school. I wonder WHY I teach it differently; usually, it comes down to one basic thing: It is easier to teach "school" using traditional educational methods. The entire system resists anything else. I genuinely desire to improve the effectiveness of my teaching. I constantly critique my lesson plans. But without support (from somewhere) I am often blocked from using truly experiential, relevant, non-traditional methods. . . . We need to change the climate in schools to be more supportive. (P. Keeley, personal communication, June 2002).

The science study group at Averill Elementary School in East Lansing, Michigan, is a good example of a professional development program that has helped to strengthen the collaborative culture at the school. Combining the strategies of university partnerships, coaching, examining student thinking, and study groups, the program focuses on improving teaching and learning in science. A science education professor from Michigan State University observes science classrooms and scripts students' dialogue. Then she meets with teachers in a study group format to share her observations. In the study group, teachers reflect on students' thinking, the science content, and their own teaching practices. Initially, participants reported that they were intimidated by having a university professor in their classroom, but transformed their fears into excitement and powerful learning as the university partner and teachers together created a safe environment for learning. The science study group sustained itself for many years and is now being used as the mechanism for engaging teachers in a collaborative process for selecting a new science curriculum.

Commentary

Study groups require the participation of teachers who are committed to reflecting on their work and taking initiative for their own learning. It is not a strategy that lends itself to raising awareness about a topic in a short period of time but rather one that encourages teachers to "go deep" and question and reflect on their practices and their students' learning.

Because study groups necessarily involve teachers in reflection outside of the classroom, it is difficult to sustain study groups in traditional school cultures. Although they may be slow to get started in such environments, once study groups "take hold" in a school, teachers enthusiastically support their continuation. Often, administrators come to recognize their benefit and realize that study groups lend themselves well to investigations and inquiries into numerous topics and issues of concern to both teachers and the entire school community. For example, study groups concerned with finding time for professional development, using national and state standards to improve teaching and learning, or developing community support for science or mathematics reform, can benefit teachers and students while building ownership and commitment by a broader school community.

Resources

Annenberg Institute for School Reform. (n.d.). *Critical Friends Groups in Action video series: Making Teaching Public, A Community of Learners* (www.annenberginstitute.org/publications/videos.html).

Murphy, C. U. (1999). Study groups. *Journal of Staff Development, 20*(3), 49–51.

Murphy, C. U., & Lick, D. W. (2001). *Whole-faculty study groups: Creating student-based professional development.* Thousand Oaks, CA: Corwin.

CASE DISCUSSIONS ■

Sharon Friedman is a fourth-grade teacher, case writer, case discussion facilitator, and researcher involved with the Mathematics Case Methods Project. In her reflections on her involvement in case discussions, she writes the following (Barnett & Friedman, 1997):

> *When I first participated in a math case discussion, I thought that I would be examining instructional practice. I thought that I would share what I do in the classroom and hear about alternatives, which would lead to better informed decisions for my mathematics program. I was right, except for my understanding of what it means to 'examine' instructional practice. I quickly learned that the 'examination' entailed more than merely acquainting myself with various instructional methods. Through the discussions we looked deeply into the way instructional practice influenced and responded to student thinking. Any teaching practice, it seemed, had a consequence in terms of its effect on student thinking. Some curricula even led to confusion. We delved into the thoughts and misconceptions that students carry with them to our math classes, derived from past instruction, experience, and intuition. Good instructional practice, I was to discover, is an interaction between what the teacher says and the experiences he or she provides, and what the students do with it. Good practice is not, as teachers are often led to believe, a preset formula that does what it is supposed to do because the curriculum writers say so. I learned the importance of focusing the impact of my words and actions on children, on framing instruction that could anticipate student thinking as much as possible, and on responding effectively to the results. In planning, I learned to consider an interaction rather than simply a teaching method that does not take student thinking into account.*

Case discussions offer groups of teachers the opportunity to reflect on teaching and learning by examining narrative stories or videotapes that depict school, classroom, teaching, or learning situations. Cases are narratives (whether in print form or on videotape) that offer a picture of a teaching or learning event and are specifically designed to provoke discussion and reflection. They are not simply stories about teaching or learning but are, as Shulman (1992) notes, focused on events such as a teaching dilemma, students engaged in mathematics or science investigations, images of student thought processes, or teaching strategies in action.

Case discussions are used in a variety of ways with different goals and purposes. For example, educators and researchers promote the use of case discussions to examine student thinking and learning as a means of professional development. In these instances, cases are used as a window into children's thinking within a specific context. Teachers listen to students' ideas about mathematics and science and examine students' responses. By analyzing children's thinking and how their ideas are developing and by identifying what they understand and where their confusions lie, teachers become aware of how children construct their mathematical and scientific ideas. Being able to see mathematics and science through the child's eyes helps teachers know and anticipate how students may misunderstand certain concepts and enables them to choose instructional experiences that can capitalize on the child's thinking. Teachers develop a greater recognition that student misunderstandings can be a valuable teaching tool. These activities promote professional development when they cause teachers to reexamine their perceptions of students' capabilities and their own assumptions about what "understanding mathematics and science" really means (Schifter, Russell, & Bastable, 1999).

The process of reflecting on students' thinking and learning through case discussions often results in teachers "trying out" the ideas or activities contained in the cases in their own classrooms (Barnett, 1991; Davenport & Sassi, 1995; Schifter, 1994). The powerful images of students in the cases prompt teachers to wonder about the thinking of their own students, how they might pose similar problems in their classes, and what might happen as a consequence. Teachers discover that they are better able to provide their students with experiences to help them articulate their confusion and with activities that help them resolve those confusions.

In addition, when teachers confront mathematics and science issues through the lens of students' perspectives, they often increase their own mathematics and science knowledge (Heller, Kaskowitz, Daehler, & Shinohara, 2001; Schifter & Bastable, 1995). As teachers reflect on students' thinking and approaches to solving problems, and assess the reasoning of students' responses, they begin to think through the mathematics or science again for themselves, often seeing new aspects of familiar content and expanding their own understanding (Russell et al., 1995). Case discussions can also be a powerful tool for helping teachers examine their own teaching practices. In these instances, cases typically convey a contextual problem, dilemma, or issue in teaching as well as the thoughts, feelings, and internal struggles of the case teacher (Schifter, 1996b).

Cases can present "whole stories" that include an ending describing how the case teacher addressed the dilemma (Shifter, 1996b). Others stop short of describing how the case teacher handled the problem and instead end with a series of open-ended questions to be addressed by the case discussants. Some are "packed full" of information to convey the complexity of teaching (Merseth, 1991), whereas others focus on discrete instances of teaching. Finally, some cases are grouped into clusters based on cases that have one or two similar dominant themes or that illustrate different aspects of the same principle. Examining clusters of cases requires teachers to retrieve, understand, and grapple with the domain or theme in different contexts and under different conditions (Barnett & Friedman, 1997).

Whatever the focus of a case, case discussions share common goals: to increase and enrich teachers' fundamental beliefs and understanding about teaching and learning; to provide opportunities for teachers to become involved in critical discussions of actual teaching situations; and to encourage teachers to become problem solvers who pose questions, explore multiple perspectives, and examine alternative solutions (Barnett & Sather, 1992; Shulman & Kepner, 1994).

Not only is participating in case discussions a powerful professional development strategy, but also the process of writing and developing cases enhances teachers' growth and development. The act of writing cases and then discussing them with colleagues helps teachers analyze their own instructional practice.

Usually, teacher writers follow a structured case development process that progresses from identifying a topic or issue of concern to collaborative work with an editor or facilitator who helps turn the narrative into a case that has benefits for a larger audience. Most teachers who have written cases report that the writing process has a strong impact on their professional life, how they think about their teaching and students, their strategies and modes of instruction, and the ways in which they interact with colleagues regarding their experiences (Shulman & Kepner, 1994).

Key Elements

Case Materials Present a Focused View of a Specific Aspect of Teaching or Learning.
Often, observers in a classroom focus on management behaviors and miss opportunities to focus carefully on specific teaching or learning episodes. By using cases, all participants are

examining the same experience of the case teacher and students and have the immediate opportunity to reflect on those experiences during the case discussion.

Case Materials Illustrate Theory in Practice. Case discussions create a context for teachers to integrate their research-based knowledge into their view of children's learning and their own teaching and to apply this to their instructional practice. Vivid descriptions of classroom process provide grounding for theoretical principles where contexts for interpreting these abstractions are lacking (Schifter, 1994) and help teachers tie abstract learning to the complexities of real world application (Filby, 1995).

Case Materials Provide Images of Reform-Oriented Mathematics and Science Teaching and Learning. Standards-based teaching in mathematics and science requires teachers to change their beliefs about the nature of knowledge and learning and how knowledge is derived, increase their knowledge of content, and reinvent their classroom practice (Nelson, 1995). Translating the ideals of these ways of teaching and learning into actual classroom practice, however, is often the most complex and challenging task teachers face. Some cases offer an image of what reform-oriented classrooms look like and how teachers implement the principles of reform. Far from being examples of the "unattainable," teachers have found that they can identify with many of the struggles faced by teachers and students in the cases and have found them motivating and inspiring (Schifter, 1996b).

> **Key Elements for Case Discussions**
>
> - Case materials present a focused picture of a specific aspect of teaching or learning.
> - Case materials illustrate theory in practice.
> - Case materials provide images of reform-oriented mathematics and science teaching and learning.
> - Teachers interact and learn through discussions.
> - Cases are facilitated by a knowledgeable and experienced facilitator who promotes reflection by case discussants.
> - Case discussions necessarily involve effective group dynamics.
> - The cases are relevant and recognizable.

Teachers Interact and Learn Through Discussions. Through verbalization and interaction, teachers formulate ideas, learn from each other, become aware of alternative strategies and perspectives, internalize theory, critique their own and others' ideas, become aware of their own assumptions and beliefs, increase their pedagogical content knowledge, and engage in "collaborative reflection" on real problems faced by teachers (Barnett & Sather, 1992; Far West Laboratory, 1990; Filby, 1995).

When reflecting on cases that promote discussion about teacher actions, discussants may focus on what the case teacher should do next or evaluate the action that was taken. This process engages teachers in an analysis of why and how to use certain teaching strategies, challenges some of their assumptions and beliefs about the appropriate use of strategies, and broadens their repertoire of strategies for planning and implementing instruction (Shulman & Kepner, 1994). A goal of case discussions focused on teacher action is to develop in teachers an attitude of inquiry toward and strategies for inquiring about classroom practice.

Cases Are Facilitated by a Knowledgeable and Experienced Facilitator Who Promotes Reflection by Case Discussants. The facilitator helps participants tease out the facts of the case, identify and understand the problem or issues it raises, inquire into the approach taken or examine the source of students' confusion, discuss alternative actions, and reflect on the theoretical underpinnings of the action taken and discuss the consequences for learning.

Facilitation notes are often developed and published in a facilitator's guide that accompanies a casebook or video. These notes help the facilitator shape the discussions so that the richness of a case is fully explored.

Case Discussions Necessarily Involve Effective Group Dynamics. Case discussion groups establish supporting norms for interaction and commit to the long-term nature of the process. Together they establish ground rules and group norms that enhance an atmosphere of learning and trust. Participants demonstrate their commitment to improving their teaching practice and willingness to help others explore their teaching practices (Filby, 1995). (Note that groups do not always establish effective ways of working together, and this can seriously influence what participants learn.)

The Cases Are Relevant and Recognizable. Although some cases depict teaching or learning situations that reflect the "ideal image" of what teaching and learning can look like, teachers need, at least initially, to be able to identify aspects of their own teaching within a case. Ideally, teachers encounter situations similar to the cases in their own teaching and can draw on their experiences during the discussion. Once teachers feel a sense of connection with a case, they can delve deeper into how the case is either similar or dissimilar to their own teaching approaches and beliefs. For example, some cases will parallel a teacher's own approaches or philosophy and can provide opportunities to examine and evaluate the consequences of specific decisions based on those ideas. Other cases will present notions that conflict with the beliefs of the teachers and can provoke critical analysis of the perspectives presented; "wrestling with the resulting disequilibrium" is what leads to changes in teachers' thinking about teaching and learning (Barnett & Sather, 1992; Thompson & Zeuli, 1999).

Implementation Requirements

Attitudes of Participants and Facilitators. Participants must have a commitment to improving their teaching practice, a willingness to share and critically discuss aspects of practice and explore and learn the science and mathematics content addressed in cases, and be curious about important assumptions that underlie teaching and learning (Davenport & Sassi, 1995).

Skills of Facilitators. Facilitators must have an understanding of the science or mathematics being taught or learned in the case and must have the skills and experience to manage discussions that are at once intellectually stimulating, challenging, and supportive, at times confrontational, and, ultimately, useful. (See the Resources section.)

Time. Thoughtful discussions require time to unfold and become meaningful; frequently, study groups incorporate case discussions as one of the approaches to increasing their learning.

Access to Quality Cases. Cases must be clear, thorough, and well developed. (See the Resources section.)

Examples

Cases and their discussion are the focus of the Mathematics Case Methods Project at WestEd. The project aims to build the capacity of teachers to make informed strategic decisions that draw upon and anticipate student thinking through the development and analysis of mathematics cases. The cases are accounts of classroom experiences written by teachers and describe an instructional sequence in which the teacher is surprised or perplexed by students' responses or by the results of an assessment task (Barnett & Friedman, 1997). Included in the cases are descriptions or samples of student work or dialogues. The approach to examining and studying cases follows a structured format to ensure the most in-depth discussions. As Barnett (1999) outlines:

- Before beginning the discussion, group members work on a mathematics problem related to the case to help teachers, as adult learners, understand the problem.
- As they work, teachers are also asked to think about what might be confusing or difficult from the students' point of view.
- Teachers note their insights so they can be discussed.
- Teachers pair up to identify issues from the case and frame them as questions that stimulate discussion by inviting multiple points of view.
- The issues are posted on chart paper and used to focus the discussion.

Guided by the facilitator, the teachers then discuss the questions and issues raised by the case. The facilitator is a teacher with case discussion experience who has chosen to take on a leadership role and has been formally prepared to facilitate the sessions. In each case discussion, a different case is read and discussed. Barnett and Friedman identify many outcomes from teachers' participation in case discussions: The case discussions provide a powerful stimulus for changes in teachers' beliefs about how children learn and how mathematics should be taught, they lead to improvement in teachers' mathematical content knowledge, they increase the complexity of teachers' pedagogical content knowledge, and they lead to changes in teachers' classroom teaching practices.

Science Cases for Teacher Learning, a project at WestEd, develops case-based materials designed to help teachers make sense of the major ideas of kindergarten through eighth-grade physical science and examine the ways in which children think about and sometimes misunderstand those ideas. The materials combine teaching cases with facilitated hands-on explorations, structured discussion, and reflection. They are designed for flexible use: as individual cases, as multicase modules, or as a comprehensive curriculum. The professional development materials are aligned with the *National Science Education Standards*, support the implementation of standards-based curriculum, and focus on common misconceptions in science.

The cases are intentionally designed for use in conjunction with existing professional development programs and ongoing study groups. The typical unit for teacher professional learning is a discussion group of 8 to 12 teachers from the same district or project. The program takes place over one academic year and typically consists of a 24-hour curriculum (eight or more three-hour discussions, each centering on a different case). During the course of a discussion, participants examine the case from an analytic frame, thinking and reasoning aloud as they grapple with the problem at the heart of the case. Purposeful hands-on exploration and structured reflection are used to challenge ideas, causing teachers to articulate the science content they themselves do not know and reexamine their theories of science teaching. Through evidence and collaborative reasoning, teachers gain a deeper understanding of core concepts and what makes them hard to teach and hard to learn.

The facilitator has a critical role in guiding the group's inquiry process. Facilitators focus and deepen the discussion of the science, often asking teachers to draw diagrams and use hands-on materials to illustrate ideas, or use other resources to help "unpack" the core concepts. They also push the group to analyze student work and dialogue, eliciting careful consideration of what is valid *and* incorrect in students' thinking.

To optimize facilitators' use of the case-based curricula and allow for national scale up and broad impact, the project provides extensive training that builds facilitators' knowledge of science, pedagogical content, and case facilitation, thus preparing them to conduct discussions in their local areas. The typical unit for facilitator training is a cohort of 20 to 50 teacher leaders and professional development providers from multiple school districts and projects. The training takes place over one academic year and typically consists of an 80-hour curriculum. Major activities include discussion of a six- to ten-case sequence, additional science coursework, practice of case facilitation techniques, and analysis of videotaped discussions.

Commentary

Case discussions create a stimulating environment in which teachers use their expertise and professional judgment to consider underlying assumptions, analyze situations, and draw conclusions about teaching and learning. As a professional development strategy, it has many benefits. Teachers' ideas and insights are valued and challenged, leading them to reflect on and change their beliefs about how children learn and how and what they teach. Case discussions lead to increased teachers' content knowledge. They situate learning in actual practice and draw upon teachers' expertise. They provide teachers with opportunities to have in-depth conversations about teaching and learning.

Several issues surround the use of case discussions as a professional development strategy. For example, one issue is whether case discussions must be conducted face-to-face or whether they can be facilitated electronically. Bank Street College has conducted very successful electronic case discussions as part of its online courses. Outside evaluations have shown this approach to be highly valued by and beneficial to participants. There is good reason to argue, however, that because they often challenge teachers' deeply held beliefs about teaching and learning, case discussions are best conducted in person. The interpersonal, face-to-face dimension can be critical to establishing rapport and trust and to communicating disagreements in respectful and constructive ways. Preserving these benefits from the interpersonal dimension via electronic means presents a considerable challenge.

Another similar issue that has been raised is whether teachers can benefit from reading cases on their own and addressing key issues in solitary reflection. Because a serious time commitment may be required to be part of a case discussion group, it is sometimes tempting for teachers to cut the recommended corners and read about, rather than participate in, case discussions. Although teachers can certainly learn many things from reading cases, the real benefits of this strategy derive from the group process itself. It is difficult, if not impossible, to throw oneself into the kind of disequilibrium that Thompson and Zeuli (1999) have shown to be the essential step in changing beliefs and practices. In addition, the diverse contributions of the group are what determine the unique nature of each case discussion and even cause discussions of the same case to have a distinctive character.

The question of whether unfacilitated discussions are as effective as those that are facilitated is at the heart of another issue. A small group of teachers who are committed to using this approach or who are reluctant to designate a facilitator may still benefit from case discussions, but they would need very effective communication skills and would need to have at least some organized method of recording and tracking the group's progress.

The role of the facilitator in many case approaches is more than that of a guide. Particularly in those instances where the approach includes published case facilitation guides or notes, the facilitator can be responsible for encouraging the group to address certain issues raised in the guides. Without a facilitator, some of these issues might be left unexamined.

Another danger inherent in unfacilitated case discussions is that they may become more like informal discussions and lose the essence that characterizes case discussions as a professional development strategy.

Finally, people who use case discussions, and especially those who write their own cases, must be concerned about the confidentiality and ethics involved in this strategy. Case discussions must be treated like cases in other professions, such as health, law, and social services. Participants must ensure that materials such as videotape, print descriptions, and pictures are used with consent and that all materials viewed are kept confidential by the group (Kleinfeld, n.d.). This sets up the right climate as well for those interested in writing, and then sharing, their own cases.

Resources

Barnett, C., & Friedman, S. (1997). Mathematics case discussions: Nothing is sacred. In E. Fennema & B. Scott-Nelson (Eds.), *Mathematics teachers in transition.* Hillsdale, NJ: Lawrence Erlbaum.

Barnett, C., Goldstein, D., & Jackson, B. (Eds.). (1994). *Mathematics teaching cases: Fractions, decimals, ratios, and percents: Hard to teach and hard to learn? Facilitator's discussion guide.* Portsmouth, NH: Heinemann.

Barnett, C., & Ramirez, A. (1996). Fostering critical analysis and reflection through mathematics case discussions. In J. Colbert, P. Desberg, & K. Trimble (Eds.), *The case for education: Contemporary approaches for using case methods.* Needham Heights, MA: Allyn & Bacon.

Casebooks from WestEd, San Francisco: Shulman, J., & Mesa-Bains, A. (1993). *Diversity in the classroom: A casebook for teachers and teacher educators;* Barnett, C., & Tyson, P. (1994). *Enhancing mathematics teaching through case discussions;* Barnett, C., Goldstein, D., & Jackson, B. (1994). *Mathematics teaching cases: Fractions, decimals, ratios and percents—Hard to teach and hard to learn?* WestEd Eisenhower Regional Consortium for Science and Mathematics Education & Distance Learning Resource network. (1996). *Tales from the electronic frontier.*

Cases Institute. (D. Schifter, Director), Education Development Center, Newton, MA. (phone: 617–969–7100)

Center for Case Studies in Education. (R. Silverman and W. Welty, Co-Directors), Pace University, Pleasantville, NY. (phone: 914–773–3879)

Mathematics Case Methods Project, WestEd, San Francisco (www.wested.org).

Miller, B., & Kantrov, I. *A guide to facilitating cases in education.* Portsmouth, NH: Heinemann.

Miller, B., Moon, J., & Elko, S. (2000). *Teacher leadership in mathematics and science: Casebook and facilitator's guide.* Portsmouth, NH: Heinemann.

Science Case Methods Project, WestEd, San Francisco (www.wested.org).

WestEd and the WGBH Educational Foundation. (2003). *Teachers as learners: A multimedia kit for professional development in science and mathematics.* Thousand Oaks, CA: Corwin. (See Tape 3, Program 4, *Exploring science through cases,* WestEd, Oakland, CA; Tape 2, Program 1, *Exploring mathematics through Cases I,* Mt. Holyoke College, South Hadley, MA; and Tape 2, Program 2, *Exploring mathematics through cases II,* WestEd, Oakland, CA.)

EXAMINING STUDENT WORK AND THINKING AND SCORING ASSESSMENTS ■

Teachers from two middle schools were distressed because their students did not do well on the new state performance assessment. Wanting to help them do better, the teachers decided to look carefully at their students' work to uncover where the problems might lie. They selected ten students in different classrooms and then gathered and studied the students' portfolios, scoring sheets, and other records. The teachers did the assessment tasks themselves and explored several questions: What were the tasks asking? How were the responses scored? What does one need to know and be able to do to complete the task? How did the students interpret and approach the task? As a result of their discussions, the teachers were better able to "see" the students' work and understand their thinking. They listed the kinds of understandings that the assessment seemed to tap and the kinds of problems they saw in students' work. This guided subsequent discussions of how they could help students improve their performance on the state assessment and their understanding of important mathematical ideas (Ball & Cohen, 1995).

In recent years, examining student work and thinking and scoring assessments as strategies for professional learning have exponentially grown in the educational community. Numerous articles have been written describing the process as it is carried out in schools throughout the country. A quick browse on the Web reveals dozens of new sites devoted to looking at student work. Several organizations have developed protocols and guidelines for helping teachers look at student work in meaningful ways.

As Anne Lewis (1998) notes, the increase in teachers collaboratively examining student work seems to have been influenced by three education "events":

- Reform efforts that target schools as well as districts, and which encourage teachers to share responsibility for student success
- Apolitical and policy climate that wants proof that students are learning to higher standards
- The emergence of a research base that is giving teachers better clues on how to move to higher levels of learning (p. 25)

As teachers and entire faculties turn to examining student work as a means of enhancing their own and their students' learning, collaborative learning communities are developing and teachers are becoming more reflective of their practice. The benefits that are emerging from this approach to professional learning are only beginning to be studied and documented, although teachers throughout the country are submitting articles for publication in journals describing the changes in their beliefs, perceptions, approaches to teaching, and the ways in which their students are learning.

Key Elements

Teachers Confront Real Problems That They Face in Their Classrooms on a Daily Basis. The use of real student work situates teachers' learning in actual practice as they examine if their students are meeting local and national standards. Translating standards into classroom practice is a challenge and one that teachers face on a daily basis. As Graham and Fahey (1999) note, "Unless teachers and administrators can come to some fundamental understanding of how their students' work relates to a standard, they will be unable to create the conditions that will raise the work to the level of state standards."

This Strategy Engages Teachers in Examining What They Have Plenty of: Student Work. The richest discussions are stimulated by work samples that are varied in their nature and quality, require more than short answers, and include students' explanations of their thinking (e.g., why they answered the way they did and what made them do what they did). Student work can include written responses, drawings, graphs, journals, portfolios, or videotapes of interviews with students. Some facilitators of examining student work suggest various collections of student work, including "written work from several students in response to the same assignment; several pieces of work from one student in response to different assignments; one piece of work from a student who completed the assignment successfully and one piece from a student who was not able to complete the assignment successfully; work done by students working in groups; or videotape, audio tape, or photographs of students working, performing, or presenting their work" (Looking at Student Work Web site,

---

Key Elements for Examining Student Work and Thinking and Scoring Assessments

- Teachers confront real problems that they face in their classrooms on a daily basis.
- This strategy engages teachers in examining what they have plenty of: student work.
- This strategy provides a focused goal and purpose for the discussions and examination of student work.
- Teachers' learning is a result of the shared, collaborative discussions.
- Structured protocols enhance the learning experience for participating teachers.

www.lasw.org). The type of student work and the collection gathered to examine should depend on the goals and intended outcomes of the process of looking at the work.

This Strategy Provides a Focused Goal and Purpose for the Discussions and Examination of Student Work. The focus of discussion may vary. In the opening vignette to this strategy, for example, teachers had a compelling reason to examine student assessments and did so using the actual test that had been given. At other times, teachers might bring to open-ended discussion groups examples of student work that puzzle them. In some situations, teachers may begin with a rubric supplied by others to apply to a set of student work (e.g., the contents of portfolios or the results of performance tasks) or may take the opportunity to develop their own rubric through examining student work. Also, the focus for a discussion may be a videotape of children's explanations of their understanding of a problem or situation. Teachers also benefit from examining student work as they implement new curriculum. This helps to pinpoint concepts that students are finding difficult and may uncover areas of the curriculum that are not yet being fully implemented.

Teachers' Learning is a Result of the Shared, Collaborative Discussions. Although an individual teacher can certainly examine student work or reflect on student thinking in isolation, there is power in examining student work as a team. As elementary school teacher Christine Evans (1993) points out, working together greatly enhances what is possible to consider and to learn. Among her teaching group, their ideas differed about the mathematics, the tasks, and particular students. Their discussions broadened what any one person could do. Together, they began to develop shared ideas and standards that could guide their collective efforts. Creating a supportive environment in which teachers can work with each other and examine their own values about teaching and learning enhances the process, as noted by Rebecca Corwin (1997): "Doing mathematics together in a responsive group creates a safe professional community in which to explore issues and raise questions about both mathematics and pedagogy" (p. 187).

Structured Protocols Enhance the Learning Experience for Participating Teachers. As we are learning more about the most effective ways to examine student work and engage teachers in scoring assessments, it has become evident that structured protocols enhance the learning experience for participating teachers. Numerous protocols and guidelines have been developed (see the Resources section) that describe focusing questions to guide teachers as they look at student work or assessment responses and most describe processes for looking for evidence of learning in the student work, listening to colleagues' thinking and perceptions, reflecting on individual thinking, and applying what is learned and discussed to teaching practices.

Although there are numerous protocols and guidelines, they all reflect a similar structured format for engaging in the study of student work. This format includes the following:

- Identifying a focus or goal by answering the questions: What do we want to learn from the student work? What outcomes do we expect from the process? What data do we have to support our goal? How is our goal related to student performance and schoolwide goals and standards?

- Selecting student work that relates directly to the identified goal and outcomes. It is important that documentation be brought to the session that provides information on the objectives of the task the student responded to, the learning strategy or assessment strategies associated with the student work, and any other information that helps all participants better understand the context within which the student completed the work.

Who brings student work to the sessions varies according to the goals, but most groups rotate among the teachers, asking each to share responsibility for bringing student work for all to examine. Many projects refer to this teacher as the "presenting teacher" and there are specific roles in the discussions for the presenting teacher.

- Facilitated discussion of the participants' interpretations and understanding of the student work samples. This facilitation varies among projects, with some more regimented and structured than others. All of the projects, however, emphasize that it is critical to have a facilitator guide the discussions in order to ensure in-depth analysis of student learning and teacher practice. Often, this facilitation rotates among the teachers.

- Reflecting on the implications and applications of what is learned to teaching. This facilitated discussion highlights the ways in which the teachers can enhance their teaching based on what they have learned about student understanding of important concepts.

Implementation Requirements

Focused Time for Discussion and Reflection. Like many professional development opportunities, this strategy requires a focused period of time without distractions to study the material and reflect on what it suggests about students' thinking and learning needs.

The Guidance of an Experienced Content Expert. Delving deeply into understanding what students are thinking by analyzing their written work or responses on assessments requires substantial knowledge of the science or mathematics content and, in the case of examining assessments, a facilitator with expertise in assessment is helpful.

Examples

Examining student work is at the core of the Fostering Algebraic Thinking Toolkit (2000), a set of professional development materials for middle school mathematics teachers designed by staff at the Education Development Center (EDC). As lead author Mark Driscoll (2002) states, the purpose of the materials is to "focus on important mathematics; focus on mathematics as learning, as a foundation for teaching mathematics; focus on evidence-based judgment; and establish structures/norms/expectations for similar evidence-based, collegial professional development" (www.TE-MAT.org).

Teachers engaged in using the toolkit solve, discuss, and grapple with mathematical problems; introduce the problem to their students; and then bring student work to the next professional learning session. The process is designed around a conceptual framework that emphasizes the interaction between teachers reflecting on their own thinking, analyzing student thinking, and discussing with colleagues. Through this triangulation of engagement, teachers' in-depth understanding of their own mathematical knowledge is increased and they gain a more in-depth understanding of the ways in which students explore and conceptualize mathematical ideas.

The toolkit is organized around four modules that engage teachers in varied structures for deepening mathematical and pedagogical understanding: analyzing student work, listening to students, questioning in the classroom, and understanding patterns of student thinking. Teachers read interviews with small groups of students conducted by other teachers, view videotapes of students working on mathematics problems, and analyze students' responses to assessments and examine how to align instruction and assessment. Through all of these explorations, teachers have the opportunity to use data to develop evidence-based understandings of teaching and learning mathematics.

The focus on student work and thinking immerses teachers in exploring students' mathematical understandings, provides an opportunity for them to discuss what constitutes "quality work" and develop and then practice questioning strategies that extend students' thinking. This approach to practice-based professional learning incorporates many of the principles of effective professional development. As Driscoll notes, "We believe that mathematics teachers will grow professionally and become more effective to the extent that their typical experience [when using the toolkit] in professional development engages them with evidence from their practice and challenges them to refine their judgments about mathematics, learning, and teaching" (www.TE-MAT.org).

In another example, middle-school teachers worked with a mathematics educator from a nearby university to discuss the in-depth analysis of students' responses to specific performance tasks. In one task, students were asked to circle the number that has the greatest value: .08, .8, .080, or .008000. Students were to choose the number and explain their answer. Many students could select the correct answer, but they could not successfully explain how they arrived at it. For their part, teachers differed in how important they thought it was to have an explanation at all. The group examined several examples in which students had the right answer but did not understand why. One student gave an intricate, illustrated explanation; one simply noted, "it has the greatest value"; and another wrote, "the .8 is the greatest because it has no zeros before the number or after the number. The more zeros the lesser it is." With regard to this experience, Parke and Lane (1996/1997) noted the following:

> When the teachers compared the explanations, they began to see how much insight those explanations could provide into a student's level of understanding. This discussion was one of the first meaningful interactions these teachers had about their students' conceptual understandings and what they were learning in the classroom. (p. 27)

For elementary school teachers in California, examining student responses to assessment tasks has helped deepen their appreciation of the value of this activity as a professional development strategy. Assessment comes alive for them when they examine a range of student responses to the challenge to create a "Critter Museum." The teachers learn a complex scoring rubric and procedure to assist them in their scoring task. At the same time, they enhance their own understandings of important science concepts and how students exhibit what they know and are able to do (DiRanna, Osterfeld, Cerwin, Topps, & Tucker, 1995).

Commentary

There are many who see this strategy as the most powerful way to help teachers improve their practice. Clearly, it is totally "authentic" in that teachers work with products of student thinking and study closely the very thing they are responsible for improving. As professional development becomes more results oriented, there is no better way to focus on learning.

It is useful to think about how this strategy can be combined with others to optimize professional learning. For example, teachers implementing a new curriculum can bring examples of student work to follow-up sessions. Case discussions can (and often do) relate to student work, discussing in some depth what students did and what teachers can learn from that. In their action research and peer coaching, teachers can pay special attention to students who are talking to each other or working on problems or investigations and teachers can question students about what they are doing and why. Video cases of teaching, including CDs, can be accompanied by student work so that teachers viewing and discussing them can get a clearer picture of what students are learning.

When scoring assessments, teachers benefit from collaborating to develop a common rubric for scoring. They review standards and come to consensus about how they will score student work or assessment items. They practice scoring to obtain interrater reliability and discuss why they scored individual items on assessments in certain ways. This leads them to a shared view of the standards for students learning.

The most important aspect of this strategy is that teachers have access to and then develop for themselves the ability to understand the content students are struggling with and ways that they, the teachers, can help. Pedagogical content knowledge—that special province of excellent teachers—is absolutely necessary for teachers to maximize their learning as they examine and discuss what students demonstrate what they know and do not know.

Resources

Driscoll, M. (1999). *Fostering algebraic thinking: A guide for teachers in Grades 6–10.* Portsmouth, NH: Heinemann.

Driscoll, M., with Goldsmith, L., Hammerman, J., Zawojewski, J., Humez, A., & Nikula, J. (2000). *The fostering algebraic thinking toolkit.* Newton, MA: Education Development Center.

Education Development Center's Schools Around the World Web site (www.edc.org/CCT/saw2000/).

Harvard Project Zero, Collaborative Assessment Conference protocol (learnweb.harvard.edu).

Looking at Student Work Web site (www.lasw.org).

Schools Around the World (SAW) (www.edc.org/CCT/saw).

Standards in Practice (SIP), Education Trust (www.edtrust.org).

STAR Science Assessment professional development (www.maincenter.org/star.html).

Strengthening Science Inquiry Assessment and Teaching Project. WestEd (www.wested.org).

WestEd and the WGBH Educational Foundation. (2003). *Teachers as learners: A multimedia kit for professional development in science and mathematics.* Thousand Oaks, CA: Corwin. (See Tape 3, Program 3, *Assessing student work, Arizona State University East, Mesa, AZ,* and Tape 4, Program 5, *Examining content and student thinking, Urban Calculus Initiative, TERC, Cambridge, MA.*)

■ IMMERSION IN INQUIRY IN SCIENCE AND PROBLEM SOLVING IN MATHEMATICS

Elaine, Teri, Kevin, and Shelly, mathematics teacher colleagues at Riverside School, were attending a seminar at a local university. As a prelude to a discussion on open-ended investigations, the teachers were presented with and asked to explore the following problem: How many 1 ft. × 1 ft. square floor tiles would you need to make a border on the floor around the edge of a rectangular room? The group began by trying to decide what the smallest room could be that would have a tile border as described. After some discussion of the meaning of "border," they agreed that a 3 ft. × 3 ft. room would be the smallest and that it would have one tile in the interior. The group proceeded to build a model of the situation and concluded that the border would require eight tiles. At this point, Teri suggested that they look at a room that was 7 ft. × 8 ft. (She had drawn a sketch of the tile border for a 7 ft. × 8 ft. room while the other three members of the group were determining the smallest case.) Kevin suggested that they subtract the area of a 6 ft. × 5 ft. rectangle from the area of the 7 ft. × 8 ft. rectangle because this difference would result in the number of tiles on the border of the 7 ft. × 8 ft. rectangle. He used Teri's diagram to explain this solution method to the members of the group.

The teachers continued to explore different cases and to make conjectures regarding the number of square tiles in the borders of rooms with different dimensions. After much discussion and exploration, Kevin suggested an approach that seemed to "work" for rooms of any dimension. They then tested the suggested generalization and concluded that it did indeed work for any case.

Immersion in inquiry in science or problem solving in mathematics is the structured opportunity to experience, firsthand, science or mathematics content and processes. By becoming a learner of the content, teachers broaden their own understanding and knowledge of the content that they are addressing with their students. By learning through inquiry and problem solving—putting the principles of science or mathematics teaching and learning into practice and experiencing the processes for themselves—teachers are better prepared to implement the practices in their classrooms. The goal is to help teachers become competent in their content and reflective about how to best teach it. Immersion experiences are usually guided by knowledgeable and experienced facilitators with expertise in science or mathematics. The curriculum is designed specifically to highlight the processes of inquiry and mathematical problem-solving approaches to learning mathematics and science content.

Key Elements

Immersion in an Intensive Learning Experience. Teachers are immersed in an intensive experience in which they focus on learning science or mathematics and are able to pursue content in-depth. In science, they participate fully in the generation of investigable questions, plan and conduct investigations that allow them to make meaning out of the inquiry activities, collect and organize data, make predictions, and gain a broader view of the science concepts they are investigating. In mathematics, they "generate compelling questions, conduct investigations to make meaning out of mathematical activities, collect and organize data, make predictions, measure and graph, and gain a broader view of the mathematics concepts they are investigating" (Eisenhower National Clearinghouse, 1998, p. 11).

One Goal Is Learning How Students Learn Science and Mathematics. One goal of these experiences is to engage teachers in firsthand learning of what they are expected to practice in their classrooms—guiding students through inquiry-based science or mathematical problem solving.

Teachers' Conceptions About Science, Mathematics, and Teaching Change. One outcome from in-depth immersion in the processes of learning science and mathematics is a change in teachers' conceptions of the nature of science or mathematics learning and teaching. For example, as teachers begin to see science or mathematics teaching as less a matter of knowledge transfer and more an activity in which knowledge is generated through making sense of or understanding the content, they begin to see their own role as teacher changing from a direct conveyor of knowledge to a guide helping students develop their own meaning from experiences. As Schmidt (2001) proposes, "A teacher's understanding and conception of subject matter is one of the major aspects that defines teacher quality. The key is that the conceptual problem-solving aspect, together with the attendant pedagogical approaches, must be embedded in real science content" (p. 162).

> **Key Elements for Immersion in Inquiry in Science and Problem Solving in Mathematics**
>
> - Immersion in an intensive learning experience.
> - One goal is learning how students learn science and mathematics.
> - Teachers' conceptions about science, mathematics, and teaching change as a result of these experiences.

Implementation Requirement

Qualified Facilitators. Guiding teachers through the inquiry process and solving challenging mathematical problems must be a specified goal of the immersion experience and one that is carried out by someone with expertise in content and process.

Long-Term Experiences. Immersion in science inquiry and mathematical problem solving require in-depth, over-time learning that cannot be accomplished in one-shot workshops.

Examples

PROMYS is an immersion-in-mathematics experience conducted by Boston University's mathematics department and the EDC. The program is designed to enhance problem solving and open-ended exploration in high school mathematics classrooms throughout Massachusetts through immersing teachers in adult-level mathematical explorations. According to the PROMYS Web site, "The program fosters new insights into the nature of mathematical investigations and participants practice the habits of mind that are at the core of creative mathematics. Academic year workshops help teachers translate the summer experience into fundamental change in their own classrooms."

The program includes three components: the six-week summer institute focuses on immersing high school teachers in mathematical ideas, five workshops throughout the academic year translate the teacher's learning into classroom experiences for students, and a second summer institute for engagement with more advanced mathematical ideas. During the summer immersion experiences, teachers work with counselors, graduate students, research mathematicians, and previous PROMYS teachers as they solve problem sets focused on number theory. The in-depth examination of individual problem sets is enhanced through weekly "problems sessions" at which PROMYS staff help participants understand themes and ideas that connect the problem sets and focuses them on the conceptual understandings and "big ideas."

A unique aspect of PROMYS for teachers is the parallel program for students. Each participating teacher is asked to recommend a high school student to participate in the PROMYS for student program. That program engages high school students in age-appropriate experiences similar to those of the teachers—exploration of "unusually challenging problems in number theory."

At the Exploratorium's Institute for Inquiry, the professional development is deeply rooted in the belief that human beings are natural inquirers and that inquiry is at the heart of all learning. Educators personally experience the process of learning science through inquiry to stimulate thinking about how to create classrooms that are supportive environments for children's inquiry. Scientists and other educators guide teachers through the inquiry process. As teachers engage in investigations, they develop a deeper understanding of science content and the inquiry process. They also work collaboratively with other teachers to explore the application of their new knowledge and skills in the classroom.

Commentary

Even with extensive coursework in their preservice programs, many teachers come to the teaching of science or mathematics without having had opportunities to engage in science inquiry or mathematical problem solving themselves. Immersion strategies can provide an opportunity to help teachers address this gap in their learning. Immersion experiences are beneficial, but they have their drawbacks as well. Teachers with limited time and programs with limited resources may not be able to afford the time required for in-depth investigation and may opt for shorter-term experiences with, for example, the student learning materials.

Another interesting issue is where immersion in science inquiry or problem solving in mathematics best fits into a teacher's learning sequence. For example, at the City College Workshop Center in New York (see Chapter 6), Hubert Dyasi uses immersion in science inquiry to initiate teachers into a new view of science. Others may choose immersion as a more in-depth enrichment, once teachers learn to use and are comfortable with a set of materials for their students. They then gain a better understanding of how to help students explore important ideas, follow their own lines of investigation, generate alternative solutions to problems, or all three. For example, teachers implementing standards-based mathematics programs such as Investigations or Everyday Math often experience the need to increase their own content knowledge through immersion experiences.

One additional issue related to immersion experiences is the critical need to directly connect teacher learning of science and mathematics to what is taught in the classroom. For example, although an elementary school teacher might personally benefit from learning calculus, unless there is an emphasis in the immersion experience to help teachers translate the new knowledge into direct application in the classroom, the professional development aspect of the experience may be lost.

Resources

Education Development Center (EDC). Newton, MA (www.edc.org).

Exploratorium's Institute for Inquiry. San Francisco (www.exploratorium.edu/IFI).

PROMYS for Teachers, Boston University and Educational Development Center, Boston (math.bu.edu/people/promys).

WestEd and the WGBH Educational Foundation. (2003). *Teachers as learners: A multimedia kit for professional development in science and mathematics.* Thousand Oaks, CA: Corwin. (See Tape 4, Program 4, *Immersion in biotechnology, Biological Sciences Curriculum Study, Colorado Springs, CO;* Tape 3, Program 1, *Scientific inquiry, Institute for Inquiry at the Exploratorium, San Francisco;* Tape 4, Program 3, *Immersion in number theory, PROMYS, Boston University, Boston;* and Tape 2, Program 4, *Immersion in spatial reasoning, San Diego State University, San Diego, CA.*)

READING 5.3

Implementing Standards-Based Mathematics Instruction

A Casebook for Professional Development

Mary Kay Stein

Margaret Schwan Smith

Marjorie A. Henningsen

Edward A. Silver

The Mathematical Tasks Framework, shown in Figure 5.3a, was developed to guide the analysis of classroom lessons in the QUASAR Project. It provides a fluid representation of how tasks unfold during classroom instruction. In the framework, tasks are seen as passing through three phases: First, as they appear in curricular or instructional materials or as created by teachers; next, as they are set up or announced by the teacher in the classroom; and finally, as they are carried out or worked on by students. All of these, but especially the third phase (i.e., implementation), are viewed as important influences on what students actually learn (illustrated by the triangle in Figure 5.3a).

This framework was used to analyze hundreds of project lessons between 1990 and 1995. This research has yielded two major findings: (1) mathematical tasks with high-level cognitive demands were the most difficult to implement well, frequently being transformed into less-demanding tasks during instruction; and (2) student learning gains were greatest in classrooms in which instructional tasks consistently encouraged high-level student thinking and reasoning and least in classrooms in which instructional tasks were consistently procedural in nature.

As we began to share these findings with teachers and teacher educators, we found that they resonated with the way in which we had characterized mathematical instructional tasks (i.e., by their cognitive demands) and with our way of representing how tasks unfold during a lesson (i.e., task phases as depicted in the Mathematical Tasks Framework). After teachers learned about the framework, they began to use it as a lens for reflecting on their own instruction and as a shared language for discussing instruction with their colleagues. Teachers' identification with the framework led us to consider how we could take this research (both the framework and findings) and use it to create tools that would be helpful to teachers and teacher educators who are trying to improve their practice. This effort to take research into practice has culminated in this book.

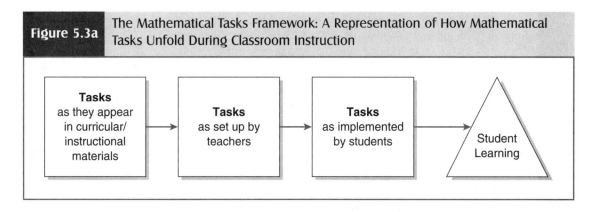

Figure 5.3a The Mathematical Tasks Framework: A Representation of How Mathematical Tasks Unfold During Classroom Instruction

USING COGNITIVELY COMPLEX ■ TASKS IN THE CLASSROOM

A major aim of the QUASAR Project was to provide students with increased opportunities for thinking, reasoning, problem solving, and mathematical communication. Student learning could not be expected to deepen or become more conceptually rich, it was argued, unless students were regularly, actively, and productively engaged with cognitively challenging mathematics.

Classroom observations conducted by project researchers suggested that most QUASAR teachers were successful in *identifying and setting up* challenging instructional tasks. Nearly three-fourths of the observed and coded instructional tasks placed high-level cognitive demands on students (Stein, Henningsen, & Grover, 1999). These same observations, however, showed that simply selecting and beginning a lesson with a high level task did not guarantee that students would actually think and reason in cognitively complex ways. In fact, only about one-third of the tasks that started out at a high-level remained that way as the students actually engaged with them (Stein et al., 1999). A variety of factors were found to conspire to reduce the level of cognitive demand of a task once it was unleashed into the classroom environment.

The Evolution of Tasks During a Lesson

The fact that tasks take on lives of their own after being introduced into classroom settings has been noted by a variety of classroom researchers (Doyle, 1988; Doyle & Carter, 1984; Stein et al., 1996). In fact, if one wishes to examine *task use in the classroom,* a reconceptualization of the term *task* is in order. As mathematical tasks are enacted in classroom settings, they become intertwined with the goals, intentions, actions, and interactions of teachers and students. Therefore, we have found the need to conceptualize mathematical instructional tasks as not only the problems written in a textbook or a teacher's lesson plan (the focus of Chapter 1), but also the *classroom activity* that surrounds the way in which those problems are set up and actually carried out by teachers and students. Defined in this way, mathematical instructional tasks become situated squarely in the interactions of teaching and learning.

When tasks are conceptualized as classroom-based activity, it is not unusual for their cognitive demands to change as they unfold during a lesson. The Mathematical Tasks Framework that was introduced earlier is a visual representation that summarizes the unfolding of tasks in response to the dynamics of teaching and learning in the classroom (see Figure 5.3a).

The first phase—tasks as they appear in curricular or instructional materials—was discussed in detail in Chapter 1. In this chapter, our focus is on the setup and implementation phases. The *setup phase* includes the teacher's communication to students regarding what they are expected to do, how they are expected to do it, and with what resources. The teacher's setup of a task can be as brief as directing students' attention to a task that appears on the blackboard and telling them to start working on it. Or it can be as long and involved as discussing how students should work on the problem in small groups, working through a sample problem, and discussing the forms of solutions that will be acceptable.

It is not unusual for a teacher to alter the cognitive demands of the task as she is setting it up for her class. In other words, she may, either purposefully or unwittingly, change the task from how it appeared in the curricular or instructional print materials from which she originally took her idea. For example, consider the Fencing Task, which appeared in the Introduction. A teacher who thinks that her students are not ready for such an open-ended problem might prepare a worksheet to guide them systematically through a set of solution steps. This worksheet might include the formulas for area and perimeter and a partially completed table that would "lead" students to the discovery that as the pen dimensions approached a square, the area approached its maximum value. The use of this worksheet would take away the challenge introduced by the unstructured nature of the task and hence change its cognitive demands.

The *implementation phase*[1] starts as soon as the students begin to work on the task and continues until the teacher and students turn their attention to a new mathematical task. During the implementation phase, both students and the teacher are viewed as important contributors to how the task is carried out. Although the students' levels of cognitive engagement ultimately determine what is learned, the ways and extent to which the teacher supports students' thinking and reasoning is a crucial ingredient in the ultimate fate of high-level tasks (Henningsen & Stein, 1997; Stein et al, 1996). For example, teachers can promote sense-making and deeper levels of understanding by consistently asking students to explain how they are thinking about the task. Or, conversely, they may cut off opportunities for sense-making by hurrying students through the tasks, thereby not allowing the time to grapple with perplexing ideas. (See Figure 5.3b for the variety of ways in which students' thinking can be supported or hindered.)

During the implementation phase, the cognitive demands of high-level tasks can easily transform, usually into less-demanding forms of student thinking. The ways in which cognitively challenging tasks typically transform during the implementation phase is discussed in depth in the next section of this chapter.

The ultimate reason for focusing on instructional tasks is to influence student learning (see final triangle in Figure 5.3a). Research has demonstrated that the cognitive demands of mathematical instructional tasks are related to the level and kind of student learning. Within the QUASAR Project, students who performed best on the QUASAR Cognitive Assessment Instrument2 were in classrooms in which tasks were more likely to be set up *and* implemented at high levels of cognitive demand (Stein & Lane, 1996; Stein et al, 1997). For these students, having the opportunity to work on challenging tasks in a supportive classroom environment translated into substantial learning gains on an instrument specially designed to measure student thinking, reasoning, problem solving, and communication. This suggests the importance of being mindful, both at the outset *and* during the various task phases, of the kinds of cognitive activity with which students *should be* and *actually are* engaged in the classroom.

Patterns of Task Setup and Implementation

In a 3-year study of classroom instruction at four QUASAR middle schools (Henningsen & Stein, 1997; Stein et al., 1996), a handful of patterns emerged that captured characteristic ways in which high-level tasks unfolded during instruction. A subsequent study including all six project sites over the full 5-year life of the project supported these findings (Stein et al., 1999). These patterns and the classroom-based factors associated with them are described below.

Maintenance of High-Level Cognitive Demands

Some tasks that were set up to place high levels of cognitive demand on student thinking were indeed implemented in such a way that students thought and reasoned in complex and meaningful ways. Take, for example, what happened in Ms. Fox's class when students were introduced to the Fencing Task. Students started out by describing an assortment of pen configurations that could be built with 24 feet of fencing. As they kept coming up with new configurations, they realized they needed to keep track of the shapes they had already tried. This led them to construct a table that identified the dimensions of each configuration along with its area. Eventually, by looking for patterns across many configurations, students arrived at a conjecture regarding the shape that produced the largest area, and then tested that conjecture with a different amount of fencing (i.e., a different perimeter). During this time, Ms. Fox circulated among the groups, asking such questions as "How do you know you have all of the possible pen configurations?" "Which has the most room?" "Do you see a pattern?" These questions led students to see the need to organize their data, make conjectures, and test them out.

Indeed, throughout our data, when tasks were enacted in this way there were usually a large number of support factors present in the classroom environment. As shown in Figure 5.3b, these included the selection of tasks that built on student's prior knowledge, appropriate teacher scaffolding of student thinking (i.e., assisting student thinking by asking thought-provoking questions that preserve task complexity), sustained pressure for explanation and meaning, and the modeling of high-level thinking and reasoning by the teacher or more capable peers.

Other tasks that were set up to place high levels of cognitive demand on students' thinking, however, exhibited declines in terms of how students actually went about working on them. When the cognitive demands of tasks declined during the implementation phase, a different set of factors tended to be operating in the classroom environment (see Figure 5.3b). These factors involved a variety of teacher-, student-, and task-related conditions, actions, and norms. Tasks that declined during the implementation phase generally transformed into one of the forms of student cognitive activity described below.

Decline Into Procedures Without Connection to Meaning

Instead of engaging deeply and meaningfully with the mathematics, students ended up utilizing a more procedural, often mechanical and shallow approach to the task. In this type of decline, one of the most prevalent factors operating in the environment was teachers' "taking over" and doing the challenging aspects of the tasks for the students.

For example, shortly after Ms. Jones gave her seventh-grade students the Fencing Task, she was dismayed to see that they were not making much progress—some students were already off-task and many others were complaining that the task was too difficult. Not knowing where to begin, the students began to urge her to give them some help. Wanting them to feel successful and stay engaged, Ms. Jones pointed out to the students that the problem involved finding the area of all the rectangles that had a perimeter of 24. She told her students that they needed to make a chart of all possibilities, starting with a 1×11, and then

Figure 5.3b Factors Associated With Maintenance and Decline of High-Level Demands

Factors Associated With the Decline of High-Level Cognitive Demands	Factors Associated With the Maintenance of High-Level Cognitive Demands
1. Problematic aspects of the task become routinized (e.g., students press the teacher to reduce the complexity of the task by specifying explicitly procedures or steps to perform; the teacher "takes over" the thinking and reasoning and tells students how to do the problem).	1. Scaffolding of student thinking and reasoning.
2. The teacher shifts the emphasis from meaning, concepts, or understanding to the correctness or completeness of the answer.	2. Students are provided with means of monitoring their own progress.
3. Not enough time is provided to wrestle with the demanding aspects of the task or too much time is allowed and students drift into off-task behavior.	3. Teacher or capable students model high-level performance.
4. Classroom management problems prevent sustained engagement in high-level cognitive activities.	4. Sustained press for justifications, explanation, and/or meaning through teacher questioning, comments, and/or feedback.
5. Inappropriateness of task for a given group of students (e.g., students do not engage in high-level cognitive activities due to lack of interest, motivation or prior knowledge needed to perform; task expectations not clear enough to put students in the right cognitive space).	5. Tasks build on students' prior knowledge.
6. Students are not held accountable for high-level products or processes (e.g., although asked to explain their thinking, unclear or incorrect student explanations are accepted; students are given the impression that their work will not "count" toward a grade).	6. Teacher draws frequent conceptual connections.
	7. Sufficient time to explore (not too little, not too much).

find the area for each using the formula area = length × width. Although Ms. Jones's actions were well intended (and understandable), when she provided students with a procedure for solving the problem, students' opportunities for mathematical dunking were diminished.

High-level tasks (such as the Fencing Task) tend to be less structured, more difficult, and longer than the kinds of tasks to which students are typically exposed. Students often perceive these types of tasks as ambiguous and/or risky because it is not apparent what they should do, how they should do it, and how their work will be evaluated (Doyle, 1988; Romagnano, 1994). In order to deal with the discomfort that surrounds this uncertainty, students often urge teachers to make these types of tasks more explicit by breaking them down into smaller steps, specifying exact procedures to be followed, or actually doing parts of the task for them. When the teacher gives in to such requests, the challenging, sense-making aspects of the task are reduced or eliminated, and the opportunity to develop thinking and reasoning skills and meaningful mathematical understandings is lost.

Decline Into Unsystematic Exploration

Unsystematic exploration differs from the other categories previously discussed since it is not used to describe tasks as they appear in curricular materials or as they are set up by the teacher and it was not represented in the QUASAR researchers' original coding scheme. Rather, this category emerged from the analysis as a way to describe some *doing-mathematics* tasks that were not proceduralized but still not adequately implemented. In this type of decline, students approached the task seriously and attempted to perform mathematical processes such as conjecturing, looking for patterns, discussing and justifying, and so forth. However, they failed to progress toward understanding the important mathematical ideas embodied in the tasks. Take, for example, Mr. Chamber's experience with the Fencing Task. Although his seventh-grade students worked conscientiously during the entire period, they focused on aspects of the problem (e.g., How big were the rabbits? How much space did the rabbits need? How much would the fencing cost?) that were not central to answering the questions posed. Although students' thinking required decision making and involved some mathematics, it did not move the students toward the generalization that the largest area for a fixed perimeter would be a square—the point of the task.

In cases such as that of Mr. Chambers, teachers appeared to desire to maintain the complexity of the task; they usually didn't take over and/or over-simplify tasks. But they also did not provide the kind and the extent of support that teachers provided when high levels of cognitive activity were maintained. For example, the sensitive, thought-provoking questions that Ms. Fox interjected at crucial points of students' explorations were absent. Another factor that seemed to be associated with this pattern was too much time for students to work on the task; without needed supports they floundered, failing to make progress toward mathematical understanding.

Decline Into Nonmathematical Activity

In these cases, students often displayed a variety of off-task behaviors such as playing absentmindedly with their manipulatives or talking with their partners about subjects far afield from mathematics. This often happened when the task was not matched appropriately to students' prior learning experiences and/ or expectations were not specific enough to guide students into an appropriate mathematical space. Another factor that played a significant role in this type of decline (to a much greater extent than in other kinds of decline) was classroom-management problems. When students were free to roam the room and talk with friends during group-work time, or to disrupt the class with requests for materials, then all students' abilities to engage with complex tasks were sacrificed.

Tasks can also decline into no mathematical activity when the teacher does not keep the focus on mathematics. In these situations, students are engaged in activity, but the activity tends to be nonmathematical in nature. For example, when Ms. Jackson used the Fencing Task in her class, she asked each student group to produce a poster on a large sheet of newsprint, showing their work in an organized way. The students' attention turned immediately to the creation of posters as works of art rather than as the result of mathematical activity, producing elaborate drawings of rabbits and pens and titling their work in calligraphy. In this situation, the teacher failed to keep an eye on the mathematics, settling instead for more affective outcomes such as students' working well together.

These four patterns—all of which began with a task classified as *doing mathematics*—represent a subset of the most prevalent patterns of task setup and implementation identified in our research. All of the prevalent patterns are identified in Figure 5.3c.[3] As shown in the figure, each pattern has been found to be associated with a set of classroom-based factors that appear to influence the path of task evolution. It is interesting to note that when the level of cognitive demand is maintained, the same five factors are generally present. When tasks decline, however, the set of factors varies depending on the nature of the decline.

Figure 5.3c	Common Patterns of Task Setup and Implementation and Most Frequently Associated Factors. For each pattern, the factors are ordered from most- to least-frequently observed

Patterns		High-Level Demands	Factors Most Often Associated With Specific Patterns of Maintenance and Decline
Task Setup	*Task Implementation*		
Doing mathematics	→ Doing mathematics	Maintained	• Task builds on students' prior knowledge • Scaffolding • Appropriate amount of time • High-level performance modeled • Sustained pressure for explanation and meaning
Doing mathematics	→ Procedures without meaningful connections	Declined	• Challenges become nonproblems • Focus shifts to correct answer • Too much or too little time
Doing mathematics	→ Unsystematic exploration	Declined	• Inappropriateness of task for students • Too much or too little time • Challenges become nonproblems
Doing mathematics	→ No mathematical activity	Declined	• Inappropriateness of task for students • Classroom management problems • Too much or too little time
Procedures with connections	→ Procedures with connections	Maintained	• Task builds on students' prior knowledge • High-level performance modeled • Appropriate amount of time • Sustained press for explanation and meaning • Scaffolding
Procedures with connections	→ Procedures with connections	Declined	• Challenges become nonproblems • Focus shifts to correct answer • Inappropriateness of the task for students

■ NOTES

1. In our framework, task implementation refers to the enactment of a task in the classroom by teachers and students. In our more current writings, including this book, we frequently use the

term *enactment* as a synonym for the term *implementation.* Enactment appears to avoid the sometimes negative connotations associated with implementation (i.e., implementation as mindless performance of mandated practices), and the misinterpretation that teachers can be thought about only as implementors rather than as constructors. By contrast, enactment connotes the view that instructional tasks are co-constructed through the thoughts and actions of the teacher and her students during the course of instruction. We have continued to label this phase "tasks as *implemented* by students" in the framework, however, in order to preserve continuity with past publications.

2. For additional information on the QUASAR Cognitive Assessment Instrument, see Lane (1993), Lane and Silver (1995), and Silver and Lane (1993).

3. The two patterns not discussed in the preceding paragraphs involve tasks which were set up as procedures with connections (see the final two patterns in the figure).

In-Session Readings for Session 5

During the fifth session, you will need the following three articles:

Reading 5.4 Smith, M. S., Silver, E. A., & Stein, M. K. (2005). *Improving instruction in algebra: Using cases to transform mathematics teaching and learning* (Vol. 2, pp. 10–27). New York: Teachers College Press. (The Cases of Catherine Evans and David Young)

Reading 5.5 Hufferd-Ackles, K., Fuson, K. C., & Sherin, M. G. (2004). Describing levels and components of a math-talk learning community. *Journal for Research in Mathematics Education, 35*(2), 81–116.

Reading 5.6 Smith, M. S. (2000). Redefining success in mathematics teaching and learning. *Mathematics Teaching in the Middle School, 5*(6), 378–386.

READING 5.4

The Cases of Catherine Evans and David Young

Margaret Schwan Smith

Edward A. Silver

Mary Kay Stein

THE CASE OF CATHERINE EVANS ■

Catherine Evans had spent most of her 20-year career teaching in self-contained classrooms (ranging from grades 1–6) where she taught all subjects. Although she taught mathematics nearly every year, she preferred to teach literature, writing, and social studies because, in her view, instruction in these areas allowed for discussions with students and opportunities for creative expression rather than focusing on memorization and procedures.

Catherine viewed teaching mathematics very differently than teaching other subjects. She described her mathematics instruction as following a regular pattern: correcting homework assigned during the previous class by reading answers and having students mark problems as correct or incorrect; presenting new material (either to the whole class or to small groups) by explaining the procedure to be learned and demonstrating a small number of sample problems; monitoring student completion of a few problems; and having students work individually on a larger set of similar problems using the preferred strategy. She saw math as the easiest period of the day, since it did not require much preparation. In addition, Catherine admitted, "probably during most of my teaching, I never thought of math as being as important as reading and writing."

Catherine Evans had been teaching at Quigley Middle School for 3 years when the opportunity arose to participate in a new math project. She was intrigued with the approach to mathematics teaching that was being proposed—one that emphasized thinking, reasoning, and communicating ideas—since these were the processes and skills that were central to her teaching in other content areas. Although she did not have any idea what this would mean in mathematics, she was ready for a new challenge and made the commitment to her colleagues to change the way mathematics was taught and learned in her classroom.

Catherine knew this would be hard, but she was confident about her abilities as a teacher. She had always been successful—her students did well on the district standardized tests, teachers in subsequent grades who had her students always remarked about how well prepared they were, and parents often requested that their children be placed in her classroom. In addition, she had a deep commitment to her students and an enthusiasm for teaching. She saw herself as someone who related well to students and was able to motivate them to learn. She felt that her humor—the ability to laugh at herself and situations—was a valuable asset in the classroom no matter what she was teaching.

Catherine Evans Talks About Her Class

5   I have been teaching the new curriculum for about 6 weeks now and I have found that my 6th-graders are not always prepared for the challenges presented. The tasks in the curriculum generally can't be solved by just using an algorithm, the solution path is not immediately evident and usually involves exploring and reasoning through alternatives, and most tasks involve providing a written explanation. If my students can't solve a problem immediately, they say, "I don't know," and give up. They have had limited experience in elementary school actually engaging actively with mathematics and expressing their thinking, and have found this to be very difficult.

6   Seeing students give up has caused me great concern. I can't buy the idea that kids don't feel bad starting off with what they perceive to be failure. When they have work they can't do or don't have the confidence to do, then I have to intervene. I decided to help kids do more verbalization in class and to get to the kids who didn't volunteer and guarantee them success by asking them to do things they couldn't fail to do right. I can't ignore the fact that success breeds success. Too many are starting out with what I'm sure they perceive to be failure.

7   In order to ensure student success, I have started to make some modifications in the curriculum, at times putting in an extra step or taking out something that seems too hard; rewriting problem instructions so that they are clearer and at an easier reading level; and creating easier problems for homework. In addition, during classroom instruction I try to break a task into small subtasks so that students can tackle one part of the task at a time.

8   We have been talking about patterns for a few weeks. The new unit that we started last week uses trains of pattern blocks arranged in a geometric sequence. The unit is supposed to help students visualize and describe geometric patterns, make conjectures about the patterns, determine the perimeters of trains they build, and, ultimately, develop a generalization for the perimeter of any train in a pattern. This unit really lays the groundwork for developing the algebraic ideas of generalization, variable, and function that students will explore in grades 6 through 8. Experiences like these lay the foundation for more formal work in algebra in 8th grade.

9   We spent some time in the beginning of this unit just making observations about the trains—the number of pattern blocks in a train, the geometric shapes that constitute a train, and the properties of a train (e.g., each train has four sides, opposite sides of the train are parallel). Students got pretty good at making observations about specific trains once we had done a few, but I had to keep reminding them that the observations needed to be mathematical. For some patterns I got some really weird responses like, "It looks like a squished pop can," or "It looks like a belt buckle." But once I reminded students that one reason for making observations was to be able to predict what larger trains were going to look like, they were able to move beyond these fanciful responses.

The Class

10   Yesterday for the first time we started determining the perimeters of the trains using the side of the square as the unit of measure. Last night's homework had been to find the perimeters of the first three trains in the pattern shown in Figure 5.4a. I also asked students to find the perimeter of the tenth, twentieth, and one-hundredth trains in this pattern. My plan for class was to begin by discussing the pattern task (Figure 5.4a) that had been assigned for homework and then have students explore another pattern.

Figure 5.4a   The Square-Pattern Train

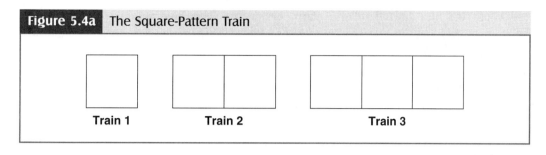

Train 1   Train 2   Train 3

Source: From *Visual Mathematics Course I, Lessons 16–30* published by The Math Learning Center. Copyright ©1995 by The Math Learning Center, Salem, Oregon. Reprinted by permission.

As students entered the classroom and got their papers out, I made a quick trip to the back of the room to check on the video camera. My colleagues and I decided to videotape some of our classes this year so that we could use the tapes to reflect on how things were going with the new curriculum and to talk about various issues that arose in using the materials. This was my first day of taping, and I was a little nervous about being on film. Students asked about the camera as they entered the classroom, but seemed unfazed by the idea of being taped. I just hoped I could forget that it was there.   11

Discussing the Square-Pattern Trains

In order to get things started, I asked students to make observations about the pattern. Shandra said that she had noticed that all of the trains were rectangles. Jake said that he noticed that the perimeter of the first train was 4. I asked him to come up and show us. When he got to the overhead he took a square tile (black) and laid an edge of the square next to each side of the train as he counted the sides. This was the procedure that we had established yesterday, illustrated in Figure 5.4b, and I was pleased to see him use it. I thanked him and he returned to his seat.   12

Figure 5.4b   Jake's Method of Finding the Perimeter of the First Train in the Square Pattern

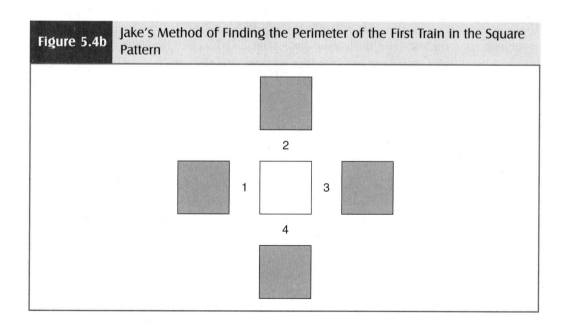

13   Since Jake had started talking about perimeters, I decided that we might as well continue in this direction. I asked Zeke what he found for the perimeter of the second train. Zeke said he thought it was 4. I asked him if he would go to the overhead and show us how he got 4. Using the diagram shown in Figure 5.4c, he explained, "The train has four sides—I just counted them 1, 2, 3, and 4."

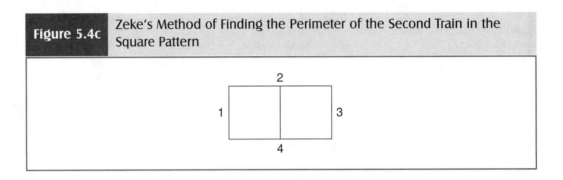

| Figure 5.4c | Zeke's Method of Finding the Perimeter of the Second Train in the Square Pattern |

14   I saw what Zeke was doing. He was counting the number of sides, not the number of units in the perimeter. The number of sides and number of units were the same in the first figure, but not in the second figure. I asked Zeke to stay at the overhead and I asked the class if someone could review what perimeter is. Danny said that it was the sides all the way around. I asked if anyone had another way to say it. Danny's definition really supported what Zeke had done, and I was looking for a definition that would cause students to question Zeke's solution. Finally Nick said that the perimeter would be 6. Nick explained, "I used Jake's way and measured all the way around the outside of the train with the square tile. It's not four because the top and bottom each have two units." Although this was not the definition I was looking for, I figured that this explanation would help students see why the perimeter was 6 and not 4.

15   At this point I decided to ask Desmond to come up and measure the perimeter of the third train for us using the procedure that Nick had just described. I have been trying all year to get him involved. Lately I have been asking him questions that I was sure he could answer. They were not meant to challenge him in any way, just help him feel successful. These experiences had an immediate positive effect on Desmond—he would actively participate in class following these episodes. So Desmond came up to the overhead and I gave him the black square and asked him to measure the third train. I really thought that this would be a simple task, but Desmond did not seem to know what to do. Since this experience was supposed to be about experiencing success, I took his hand and helped him move the square along the outside of the train, counting as we proceeded, as shown in Figure 5.4d.

16   I thanked Desmond for his help. I was sure that this would clear up the confusion. I told Zeke that a lot of people make the same mistake that he did the first time they do perimeter. Just to be sure that Zeke understood the way to find perimeter, I asked him if he could build the fourth train in the pattern. He quickly laid four squares side to side. I then asked him if he could find the perimeter by measuring. He proceeded to count the sides while moving the side of the square along the perimeter of the train—1, 2, 3, 4, 5, 6, 7, 8, 9, 10. He looked up when he finished and announced, "It will be ten!" I thanked him for hanging in there with us, and he returned to his seat.

| Figure 5.4d | Mrs. Evans Uses the Square Tile to Help Desmond Find the Perimeter of the Third Train |

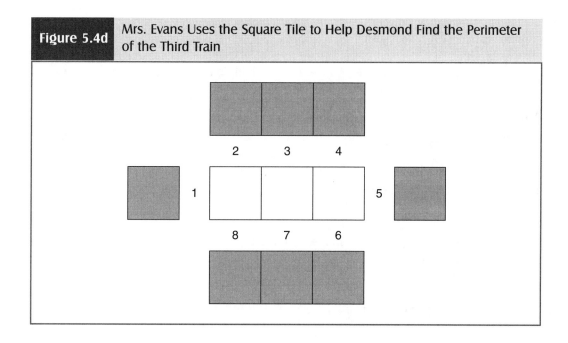

Before moving on to the next part of the assignment I asked if anybody had noticed 17
anything else about perimeter when they did just the first three. Angela had her hand up,
and I asked her what she had noticed. She explained, "On the third train there are three on
the top and three on the bottom, which makes six, and one on each end." I asked her if she
would go to the overhead and show us what she meant. Using the diagram shown in Figure
5.4e she restated, "See, there are three up here (pointing to the top of the train) and three
down here (pointing to the bottom of the train) and then one on each end.

I was surprised by this observation so early on, but knowing that it would be helpful in 18
determining the perimeters of larger trains, I asked Angela if she could use her system to
find the perimeter of the fourth train. She quickly said, "Ten." I asked her to explain. She
proceeded, "Four on the bottom and four on the top and one on each end."

Class can be pretty fast paced sometimes, with individual students, the whole class, and 19
me going back and forth in a rapid exchange. A good example of this happened at this point
as I tried to put Angela's observation to the test and see if I could get the whole class
involved in using her observation to predict future trains. Once Angela's pattern became

| Figure 5.4e | Angela's Strategy for Finding the Perimeter of the Third Train in the Square Pattern |

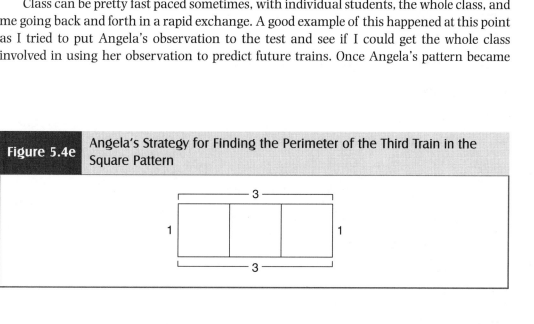

obvious to *her,* I wanted to make sure that everyone in the class saw it too. So I proceeded with the following question and answer exchange:

Me	Using your system, do you think you could do any number I say? What would you do for 10? How many on the top and the bottom?
Angela	10.
Me	How many on the ends?
Angela	2.
Me	How many all together?
Angela	22.
Me	Let's do another one. Listen to what she's saying and see if you can do it also. Angela, in train 12, how many will there be on the top and bottom?
Angela	12.
Me	And then how many will there be on the ends?
Angela	2.
Me	How many will there be all together?
Angela	26.
Me	Tamika, what's she doing?
Tamika	She's taking the train number on the top and bottom and adding two.
Me	OK, let's everybody try a few. I can pick any number. Train 50. How many will there be on the top and bottom? Everybody!
Class	50. (*With enthusiasm*)
Me	How many on the ends?
Class	2.
Me	How much all together?
Class	102.
Me	Train 100, how many on the top and bottom?
Class	100. (*Louder and with even more enthusiasm*)
Me	How many on the ends?
Class	2.
Me	How much all together?
Class	202.
Me	Train 1,000, how many on the top and bottom?
Class	1,000. (*Loudest of all*)
Me	How many on the ends?
Class	2.
Me	How much all together?
Class	2,002.

At this point I asked if they could describe anything I gave them. Another resounding "YES" answered my question. One of the things that I have found is that responding in unison really engages students and helps their confidence. When they respond in unison they feel that they are part of the group. Everyone can participate and feel good about themselves.

20

Angela's observation had really led us to finding the perimeters for any train so I decided to continue on this pathway. I asked if anyone had figured out the perimeters using a different way. I looked around the room—no hands were in the air. I wanted them to have at least one other way to think about the pattern so I shared with them a method suggested by one of the students in another class. I explained that she had noticed that the squares on the ends always have three sides—they each lose one on the inside—and that the ones in the middle always have two sides. I used train three, shown in Figure 5.4f, as an example and pointed out the three sides on each end and the two sides on the middle square.

21

I wanted to see if students understood this so I asked how many squares would be in the middle of train 50 with this system. Nick said that there would be 48. I then added that there would be 48 twos, referring to the number of sides that would be counted in the perimeter, and three on each end. I asked what 48 twos would be. Carrie said it would be 96. I then asked what the perimeter would be. Shawntay said that it would be 102. She went on to say that that was the same as what we got from train 50 when we did it Angela's way! I told the class that was right; there isn't just one way to look at it.

22

Considering a New Pattern

We had spent nearly 20 minutes on the square pattern, and it was time to move on to another pattern. I quickly got out my pattern blocks and built the hexagon-pattern train on the overhead. I told students that I wanted them to work with their partners and build the first three trains in the pattern, find the perimeters for these three trains, and then find the perimeters for the tenth, twentieth, and one-hundredth trains. I put the pattern of square trains (Figure 5.4a) that we had just finished back up on the overhead underneath the hexagon pattern and suggested that they might want to see if they could find anything that was the same for the hexagon pattern and the square pattern that would help them. Since the generalizations for the perimeters of these two trains had some similarities, I thought this would help them find the perimeters for the larger trains in the hexagon pattern.

23

After about 5 minutes students seemed to be getting restless. Since most seemed to have made progress on the task, I decided to call the class together and see what they observed about the pattern. Although this is not exactly what I asked them to do—make observations—I felt that it provided a more open opportunity for all students to have something to say. I asked Tracy what she had noticed. She said that every time you add one.

24

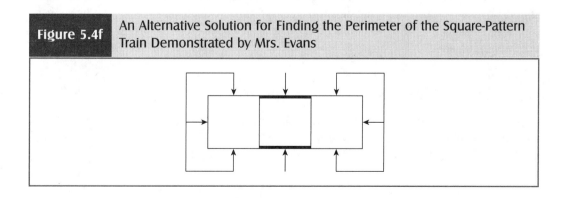

| Figure 5.4f | An Alternative Solution for Finding the Perimeter of the Square-Pattern Train Demonstrated by Mrs. Evans |

"Add one what?" I asked. "A hexagon," she responded. I then asked about the perimeter. Devon said that he discovered that it was 6. "What was six?" I asked. Devon clarified that 6 was the amount around the hexagon—around the edges on the first train. I asked Devon about the second train. He explained, "The hexagon has six around it and then you take away one for each side in the middle so it is 5 + 5 or 10. Then on the third one you still have 5 + 5 for the end ones and you add four more sides for the new hexagon you added."

25   I wanted to see if Devon realized that his observation would lead to a generalisation. I asked him if what he had discovered would tell him anything about building another train. Devon said, "Yeah. On train four there would be four hexagons. The end ones would each have five and the two middle ones would each have four." "If you were to build train 10," I asked, "could you tell me how many would have four sides and how many would have five sides?" Devon appeared to think about it for a few seconds and then responded that eight hexagons would have four sides and two hexagons would have five sides. I wanted to make sure that students understood what Devon was saying so I asked him where the two with the five sides would be. He looked at me as though I were crazy and said, "Mrs. Evans, they would have to be on the ends!"

26   Again, I wanted to see if students could use Devon's method on any train. I asked Tommy if he could describe the twentieth train. Tommy explained, "For train 20 you'd count the sides and count the ends. You subtract 2 from 20 and that would be 18 and then you multiply 18 by 4, because all the hexagons in the middle have four and then you would add 10 from the ends." I was impressed with his explanation, and he seemed to be pretty proud of himself too. I wanted to make sure that everyone had all the steps that Tommy had so nicely explained.

27   I then asked Jeremy if he could do the thirtieth train. He said that he didn't know. I felt that he probably could do this if I provided a little structure for him. I asked him how many hexagons would have five sides. He said in a questioning tone, "Two?" I nodded and said that this was correct. I then asked how many hexagons would be in the middle. He wrote something down on paper that I could not see and indicated that there would be 28. I then asked him how many sides each of the 28 hexagons would have on the perimeter. He responded more confidently this time with, "Four."

28   I then asked the class how we could write 2 fives and 28 fours. No hands shot up immediately and I glanced at the clock. Where had the time gone—the bell was going to ring any minute. I told the students that for homework I wanted them to come up with a way to calculate the perimeter of the thirtieth train and any other train we could come up with. I thought that this would push us toward more formal ways of recording calculations and, ultimately, generalizations.

Reflecting on Class Later That Day

29   The lesson was all I could have asked from the kids! They found the perimeters of the trains and were even making progress on finding generalizations. I have had this kind of a lesson about five times this year and it is very exciting. I want to see the tape as soon as possible to find other things I could have done. The kids were very proud of themselves, I think, and so was I!

Reflecting on Class Several Weeks Later

30   A few weeks after this class I had the opportunity to share a 10-minute segment of a videotaped lesson with my colleagues at one of our staff development sessions. I decided to show a segment from the pattern block lesson since I thought it had gone so well. Although

they didn't say so directly. I think they felt that I was too leading. Maybe they were right. It is easy to be too leading and feel OK about it because the kids seem happy. After all, many kids are happy with drill and practice.

I decided to go back and watch the entire tape again and see if I could look at it objectively. The lesson contained too much whole-group teacher questioning and students explaining and not enough time for students to stretch and discover independently and collaboratively. I wondered, in particular, what most students really understood about Angela's method. Sure many of them answered my questions, but were they just mindlessly applying a procedure that they had rehearsed? Did it mean anything to them? Although choral response might make kids feel good, it really masks what individual students are really thinking and what it is they understand. Just because they could come up with answers to my questions doesn't mean that they really understand or that they have any idea how to apply it. I am now left wondering what they really learned from this experience.

Reflecting at the End of the School Year

In early June, at the end-of-the-year retreat, my colleagues and I were asked to make a 10-minute presentation regarding the aspects of our teaching that we thought had changed most over the year. I began by showing a clip of one of my fall lessons—the one in which Desmond went to the overhead to measure the perimeter of the pattern train and in which I assumed control, even moving his hands. I told my colleagues, "I'd like to start with the first clip because I feel it pretty much sums up how I taught at the beginning of the year, and I'd like to show you that I really have become less directive than this tape." I showed the clip without sound. Attention was drawn to two pairs of hands on the overhead, the large pair (mine) that seemed to be moving the smaller pair (Desmond's). I explained, "You'll see Desmond comes up and I am very helpful—very directive—and move the lesson along. That was a big thing with me—to move these lessons—and if they didn't get it, I'd kinda help them do so." I added that I asked many yes or no questions very quickly and did not provide time for students to think. In contrast, I then showed video clips from the spring, in which I walked around the room, asking groups of students questions that would help them focus their efforts rather than telling or showing them what to do. For me, the differences in my actions and interactions with students on these two occasions provided evidence that I had changed.

TRANSITION ■

Catherine Evans and her colleagues continued their efforts to improve the mathematics teaching and learning at Quigley Middle School. They met frequently to talk about their work and attended professional development sessions once a month and during the summers to support their growth and development And their efforts were paying off— students were showing growth not only in basic skills but also in their ability to think, reason, and communicate mathematically.

At the beginning of the third year of the math project a new teacher joined the faculty at Quigley—David Young. Catherine and her colleagues welcomed David into their community. From their own experiences they knew how hard it was to teach math in this way. But David had something that Catherine and her colleagues did not have initially—the opportunity to work beside teachers who had experience with the curriculum.

The Case of David Young picks up at the beginning of David's second year at Quigley. He has been working with Catherine and others and has had 1 year's experience teaching this new way. Catherine is now beginning her fourth year of the math project.

■ THE CASE OF DAVID YOUNG

36   David Young has just started his second year at Quigley Middle School. The job at Quigley was at first overwhelming for David. His mathematics teacher colleagues were implementing an instructional program based on a constructivist view of learning. Although such approaches had been foundational to his teacher preparation program, his teaching up to this point had been fairly traditional. The schools he had been in for student teaching and his first year teaching did not support innovation; therefore, he had no experience putting into practice things that he had learned in his preservice training. But at Quigley the students were not passive recipients of what the teacher dished out, and drill-and-practice seemed to have a fairly limited role in instruction. Students were actually doing mathematics—exploring, making conjectures, arguing, and justifying their conclusions.

37   The enthusiasm and energy he saw in his colleagues was invigorating but also scary. His colleagues all had lots of experience, but he had almost none. He worried about his ability to be a contributing member of the community and whether he would be able to teach in a new way. David's fears were put to rest early in his first year. His colleagues were very supportive and understanding. In their monthly meetings they told him war stories about their initial experiences in teaching this new way and how they had helped one another through the tough times. They would see him at lunch, in the morning before school, or in the hallway and ask, "What are you doing today?" and How is it going?" They would give him some suggestions based on what had worked well for them, but they never told him what to do or harshly judged the decisions he made. Mostly they listened and asked a lot of questions. Over time David felt that he could ask or tell them anything. It was, he decided, the perfect place to teach.

38   During his tenure at Quigley, David had been working hard to help students develop confidence in their ability to do mathematics, which he felt in turn would influence their interest and performance in the subject. Far too many students, he thought, came to Quigley hating math in large measure because they had not been successful in it. He had talked a lot with Catherine Evans about his concerns. Catherine had been quite open about her early experiences in teaching math the new way (just 3 years ago) and her misstarts in trying to help students feel successful. David came to believe that developing confidence as a mathematics doer resulted from facing challenges and persevering in the face of them. The key, Catherine often had said, was trying to find a way to support students in solving a challenging task—not creating less challenging tasks for students to solve.

David Young Talks About His Class

39   This is the beginning of my second year teaching 6th grade with this new curriculum. The first year was rough for me and the kids as we tried to settle into our new roles in the classroom: me as the facilitator and my students as constructors of knowledge. When things did not go well my colleague Catherine was always there with a sympathetic ear and a word of encouragement. She is such a wonderful teacher—everything in her classroom seems to always go so well. (She is right next door and we have a connecting door between our rooms. Sometimes during my free period I leave the door open and listen in on what is happening over there.) Although she has repeatedly said that it was a long and painful trip from where she started to where she is today, it is hard to believe. I guess it is comforting, though, to know that if she made it, I can too.

40   Catherine and I are both teaching 6th grade this year, so we touch base nearly every day about what we are doing. We are only one month into the school year, and so far we

have been working with patterns. Up to this point we have focused primarily on numeric patterns. The new unit that we started yesterday uses trains of pattern blocks arranged in some geometric sequence. The unit is supposed to help students visualize and describe geometric patterns, make conjectures about the patterns, determine the perimeters of trains they build, and, ultimately, develop a generalization for the perimeter of any train in a pattern.

Last year this unit did not go well. There was too much teacher talk and too little time for students to think. I moved them through the entire set of exercises in one period. I felt great because I had really covered the material, but a week later it was clear that the students hadn't gained much from the experience. When I talked with Catherine about it she told me about her first time teaching this unit 3 years ago. She said that one thing she learned is that kids need time to think, to struggle, and to make sense of things for themselves. If you make it too easy for them they will never learn to figure things out for themselves. This made sense to me, but it was hard not to step in and tell them what to do. I was determined, however, to do a better job this time around.

41

The Class

Yesterday, my 6th-grade class spent some time getting familiar with the pattern blocks—identifying the shapes and determining the perimeters of the blocks. Today, they are going to make observations about trains of pattern blocks and determine the perimeters for the trains. Basically, I am just going to follow the curriculum here. It suggests giving students a pattern sequence and having them compute the perimeter for the first three or four trains and then determine the perimeter of a larger train like 10 or 20. Ultimately, the curriculum suggests asking students to imagine that they are constructing the one-hundredth train and to look for ways to find the perimeter. I will see how things go, but I hope to be able to follow this suggestion and use large numbers like 1,000 so there is no way they can build or draw the trains and count the number of sides.

42

Getting Started: The Square Tile Pattern

I started by building the pattern of squares (shown in Figure 5.4a) on the overhead and asking students to work with their partners to find the perimeters of the first 4 trains in the sequence. Emily immediately asked for pattern blocks so she could actually build the trains. This of course started a series of requests to use the blocks. I hadn't anticipated this, but I had no problem with it, either. I grabbed a few bags of blocks and dropped them off at the tables of students who had requested them.

43

Students started building the trains and quickly seemed to realize that the fourth train would have four squares. They then began to determine the perimeter and record their findings. This initial activity seemed to be pretty easy for students. After about 5 minutes I asked Derek to go to the overhead and show us how he found the perimeter for the first 3 trains. Using a technique that several students had come up with yesterday when we began exploring the perimeter of the blocks, Derek drew line segments parallel to the side of the square as he counted, as shown in Figure 5.4g, in order to show that he had counted a particular segment. Once he had completed the count he recorded the perimeter on top of the train, I asked Derek what the numbers "4," "6," and "8" represented. He responded that "these are the distance around the outside of the train in units." I asked what a unit was and he explained that he had used the side of the square as the unit. (The previous day we had discussed the fact that we were going to be measuring using the side of the square as our unit. That way we could talk about the number of units without worrying about actual measurement.)

44

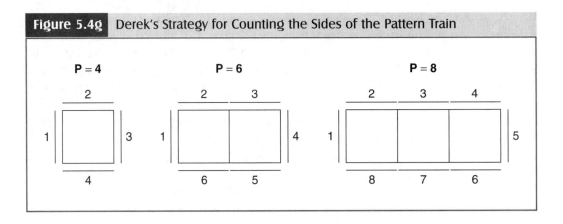

Figure 5.4g Derek's Strategy for Counting the Sides of the Pattern Train

45   I then asked the class what they thought the perimeter of the fourth train would be. Crystal said that she thought it would be 10. I asked her how she found it. She explained, "I just built the fourth one and counted the way Derek did." Jamal said that he got 10, too, but that he just added two more to the third train. I asked him to explain. He said, "When you add on one more block to the train the perimeter only gets bigger by two more units 'cause only the new piece on the top and bottom add to the perimeter." I asked the class if they had any questions for Jamal. Kirsten said that there were four sides in every square, so how could the perimeter only increase by two? Jamal went to the overhead and explained, "See, if you look at the second train there are two units on the top and bottom, and one on each side. When you go to train three and add one more square (as shown in Figure 5.4h) you still only have one unit on each end 'cause two sides of the new square are on the inside not on the perimeter."

46   I then asked students to take a few minutes and think about what the tenth train would look like, I wanted to be sure that all students had time to consider this larger train. I know that sometimes I move too quickly and don't allow enough wait time for students to think about things. This tends to work against the students who have good ideas but work at a slower pace. Since I have been waiting longer, more students have been involved.

47   I started by asking Michele what she thought the perimeter would be. She said she got 22. I asked her if she could explain to us how she got this answer. She indicated that she had built the tenth train and then counted. Although this was a perfectly good approach for the tenth figure, it was going to be less helpful when we started considering larger trains. I asked

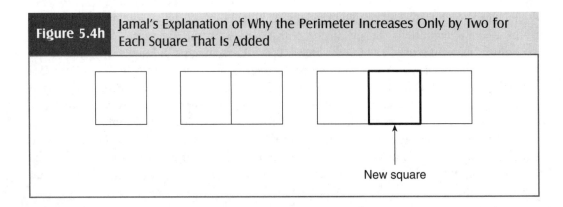

Figure 5.4h Jamal's Explanation of Why the Perimeter Increases Only by Two for Each Square That Is Added

New square

if anyone did it another way. Travis said that he got 22, too, but that he just took 10 + 10 + 2. Although his answer was correct, it was not immediately obvious why he added this set of numbers. I asked him why he did this. He explained, "See, when I looked at the first four trains I saw that the number of units on the top and bottom were the same as the number of the train. So in train one there was one unit on the top and one on the bottom. In train two there were two units on the top and on the bottom. In train three there were three units on the top and the bottom. So I figured that this would keep going, so the tenth train would have 10 units on the top and the bottom. Then for all the trains you have to add on the two sides because they never change."

I thanked Travis for sharing his strategy and asked if anyone had thought about it another way. Joseph said that he multiplied the number of squares in the train by 4, then subtracted the sides that were in the inside. I indicated that this was an interesting way to think about it and asked him if he would explain. He began, "Well, each square has four sides, so in the tenth train there would be 4 times 10 or 40 sides. But some of these are in the inside, so you have to subtract." "How did you know how many would be on the inside?" I asked. He explained, "Well, there are eight squares in the inside of the train, and each of those squares had two sides that didn't count and that gives you 16, Then there are two squares on the outside of the train and each of those had one side that didn't count, so that gave you 18. So 40 minus 18 gives you 22, and that's the answer." 48

As he finished his explanation a few hands shot up around the room. I asked the class if they had any questions for Joseph. Kendra asked how he knew that there were eight squares on the inside of the train. Joseph said that he had looked at the first four trains and noticed that the number of squares on the inside was two less than the train number—the second train had zero squares on the inside, the third train had one on the inside, and the fourth had two on the inside. I thanked Joseph for sharing his thinking about the problem with the class. I was really pleased with the two different generalizations that had been offered and decided to ask one more question before moving on to a new pattern to see if the class could apply these noncounting approaches to a larger train. 49

I asked the class if they could tell me the perimeter of the one-hundredth train. After waiting about 2 minutes for students to consider the question, I asked if anyone had a solution. Alicia said that she thought it would be 202. I asked her how she figured it out. She said she needed to draw and came up to the overhead. She drew a rectangle on the overhead (shown in Figure 5.4i) and asked us to pretend that it was 100 squares. She then continued, "Like Travis said, the number of units on the top and bottom is the train number, and then there are the two on the sides. So for the one-hundredth train, it would be 100 plus 100 plus 1 plus 1." 50

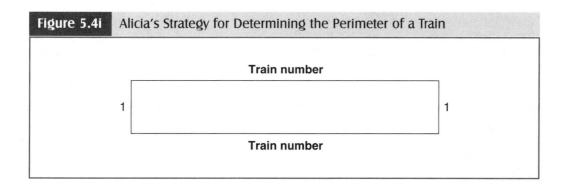

| **Figure 5.4i** | Alicia's Strategy for Determining the Perimeter of a Train |

51   I commented that this seemed like a really fast way to do the problem. At this point I decided to pass out a sheet of four additional patterns (shown in Figure 5.4j) and see if the discussion that we had about the square-pattern train would give students additional ways to think about the new patterns. Beginning with Pattern 1, I asked students to work with a partner and to sketch the fourth train in the pattern, find the perimeter of each of the four trains, and then see if they could find the perimeter of the tenth train without building the train. I knew the last condition would be a challenge for some, but I wanted them to think harder to find another way.

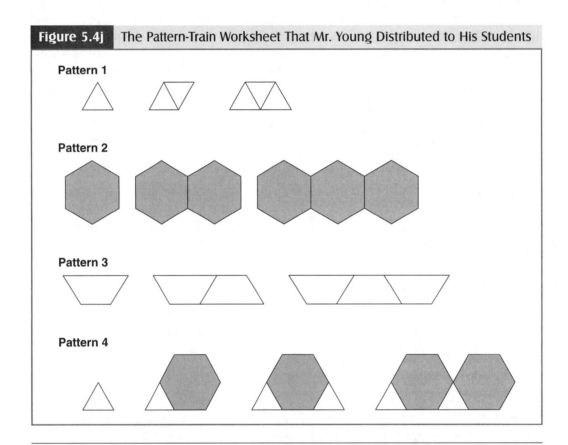

| **Figure 5.4j** | The Pattern-Train Worksheet That Mr. Young Distributed to His Students |

Source: From *Visual Mathematics Course I, Lessons 16–30* published by The Math Learning Center. Copyright ©1995 by The Math Learning Center, Salem, Oregon. Reprinted by permission.

Continuing Work: The Triangle Pattern

52   I walked around visiting the pairs as they worked on the triangle train (Pattern 1). Again students seem to quickly see the pattern—add one more triangle—and count the sides to find the perimeter. I observed several pairs starting to build the tenth train and asked them to try to find another way. I suggested that they look at the four trains they had built and see if they could find any patterns that would help them predict the tenth train. In a few cases where the students were really stuck I suggested that they try to see if they could find a connection between the train number and the perimeter as a few students had done in the last pattern.

53   Once it appeared that most pairs had made progress on this task, I asked James to come up and build the fourth train and describe the pattern. James quickly assembled the

triangles, changing the orientation each time he added one. He explained, "You just add one more triangle each time and every new one is turned the opposite way of the last one." I then asked Katie what she found for the perimeter of each train. She said that the first one was 3, the second one was 4, the third one was 5, and the fourth one was 6. I asked her what the fifth one would be. She quickly said, "Seven." I asked her how she did it so fast, and she responded, "After the first one you just add one every time. The fourth train is 6 so the fifth train would be one more."

I then asked if anyone could tell me what the perimeter of the tenth train would be. Janelle said she thought it would be 12. I asked her how she found it. She said she made a table and looked for a pattern. Since this was the first time anyone had mentioned making a table, I thought it would be worth having her explain this strategy to the class. She came up and constructed the table shown in Figure 5.4k. She explained, "I looked in the table and I saw that the perimeter kept going up by one, but that the perimeter was always two more than the train number. So that for train number 10 the perimeter would be two more, or 12." 54

Before I could even ask if anyone had done it another way, Joseph was waving his hand. He announced that he got 12 too, but that he did it another way. He said that the train number was the same as the number of triangles, just like the squares. He went on, "Since each triangle has three sides, I multiplied the number of triangles by 3. So 3 times 10 equals 30. But then, you have to subtract the sides that are in the inside. It's like the square. You take the number of triangles on the inside. For the tenth train, that would be 8. Each of those triangles has two sides that don't count and that gives you 16. Then there are two triangles on the outside of the train and each of those had one side that didn't count, so that makes 18. 30 minus 18 equals 12." 55

"Wow," I said, "there are lots of different ways to look at these trains, aren't there?" I was ready to move on, but Darrell was trying to get my attention. He said, "Aren't you gonna ask us to find the one-hundredth?" That hadn't been my plan, but if he wanted to find the one-hundredth train I was happy to oblige. I asked Darrell if he wanted to tell us what the perimeter of the one-hundredth train would be. He said, "It'll be 102. 'Cause like Janelle said it will always be two more." I asked the class if they agreed with Darrell. I saw lots of nodding heads that convinced me that we were indeed making progress. 56

Exploring Three New Patterns

I told the class that they would have 15 minutes to work with their partners on Patterns 2, 3, and 4 (see Figure 5.4j), For each pattern, they needed to sketch the fourth 57

Figure 5.4k Janelle's Table for the Triangle Train

Train Number	Perimeter
1	3
2	4
3	5
4	6

train, find the perimeter for the first four trains, and determine the perimeter for the tenth train without building the train. I wanted students to have a longer period of time for exploring the patterns without interruption. I figured that in 15 minutes everyone would at least get Pattern 2 done, and Pattern 4 would be a challenge for those who got that far since it was less straightforward than the previous patterns because the odd and even trains would be described differently.

58   As students worked on the patterns, I again walked around the room observing what they were doing, listening in on their conversations, occasionally asking a question, and reminding them that they would need to be able to justify their methods to the rest of the class. The most challenging aspect of the task for most students was finding the perimeter of the tenth train without drawing it. For Pattern 2, I encouraged them to try to find a way to talk about the perimeter of a figure in terms of the train number. "How are those two numbers related?" I asked as I moved from group to group.

Discussing the Hexagon Pattern

59   After 15 minutes all students had completed Patterns 2 and 3. Since there were only 10 minutes left in class, I thought I would have them talk about Pattern 2 before the bell rang. I started by asking Jungsen to describe the pattern and give the perimeter for the first four. She explained that each train had the same number of hexagons as the train number and that the perimeters were 6, 10, 14, and 18. "What would the perimeter of the next one be?" I asked. James said he thought it would be 24 because the hexagon had six sides and it would be six more. Michele said that she thought it would be 23, because it would be only five more because all of the sides didn't count. I asked if anyone had a different guess. Derek said that he thought it would be 22. A number of students chimed in with, "I agree!" I asked Derek to tell us how he got 22. He said that every time you added a new hexagon, you only added on four more sides. "The perimeters were 6, 10, 14, and 18. You just keep adding four."

60   I asked if anyone could explain it another way. Kirsten said that she thought she could. "Every time you add another hex," she explained, "you just add two sides on the top and two on the bottom." She pointed to the trains on the overhead (see Figure 5.4l) and continued, "If you look at train two, you have four sides on the top, four on the bottom, and the two on the ends. If you look at train three, you added one more hex, which gives you two more sides on the top and two more sides on the bottom. That gives you just four more sides."

61   I asked if anyone had found the perimeter of the tenth train. Carmen said that she thought it would be 42. I asked how she got this. She said that the tenth train would have 20 sides on the top, 20 sides on the bottom, and one on each end. I asked how she knew it would be 20. She went on to explain, "The number on top is double the train number. See, the second train has four, the third train has six, so the tenth train would have twenty."

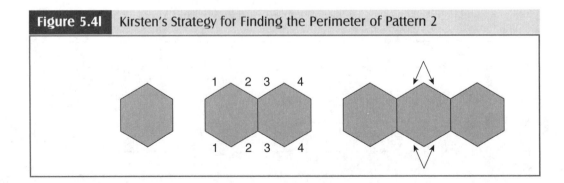

| **Figure 5.4l** | Kirsten's Strategy for Finding the Perimeter of Pattern 2 |

I thanked Carmen for sharing her solution and asked if anyone had another way. Joseph was again waving his hand. I asked Joseph if he used his method on this problem too. He said he did and explained that since each hexagon had six sides, you needed to multiply the train number by 6 to get 60. Then you needed to subtract the inside sides—that would be 18. So it would be 60 minus 18 which was 42. Kirsten asked Joseph if you always subtracted 18 for the tenth train. Joseph said that so far that seemed to work for the squares and the hexagons, but he wasn't sure if it always worked. Kirsten's question was a good one. I made a note to be sure to include a pattern for which it would not work, just to push Joseph to consider what was generalizable about his approach and what wasn't.   62

I finally asked about the perimeter of the one-hundredth train. It seemed as though everyone thought they had it this time. I took a quick look at the clock. The bell was going to ring any minute. I told students that for homework I wanted them to write down what they thought the perimeter of the one-hundredth one would be and to explain how they figured it out We would start there the next day and then jump right in and try Pattern 4.   63

READING 5.5

Describing Levels and Components of a Math-Talk Learning Community

Kimberly Hufferd-Ackles

Karen C. Fuson

Miriam Gamoran Sherin

The transformation to reform mathematics teaching is a daunting task. It is often unclear to teachers what such a classroom would really look like, let alone how to get there. This article addresses this question: How does a teacher, along with her students, go about establishing the sort of classroom community that can enact reform mathematics practices? An intensive year-long case study of one teacher was undertaken in an urban elementary classroom with Latino children. Data analysis generated developmental trajectories for teacher and student learning that describe the building of a math-talk learning community—a community in which individuals assist one another's learning of mathematics by engaging in meaningful mathematical discourse. The developmental trajectories in the Math-Talk Learning Community framework are (a) question, (b) explaining mathematical thinking, (c) sources of mathematical ideas, and (d) responsibility for learning.

Please focus on the nonshaded portions of the reading.

The successful implementation of mathematics education reform requires that teachers change traditional teaching practices significantly, and develop a discourse community in their classroom (National Council of Teachers of Mathematics [NCTM], 2000). Yet the prospect of creating such a community is daunting to many teachers; they often do not know where to begin to create the kind of discourse practices described by NCTM. The goal of this article is to introduce a framework that can help to guide teachers' work in this area and to facilitate researcher and teacher educator understanding of this process.

Source: Reprinted with permission from *Journal for Research in Mathematics Education*, copyright © 2004 by the National Council of Teachers of Mathematics. All rights reserved.

Authors' Note: The research reported in this article is based on the first author's dissertation study at Northwestern University. The research was supported by the McDonnell Foundation and by the National Science Foundation under grant no. RED-935373 and grant no. REC-90806020. The opinions expressed in these articles are those of the authors and do not necessarily reflect the views of the grantors. The authors would like to thank all of the teachers and students who have participated in this study, especially Ms. Martinez. The authors would also like to thank the reviewers for their helpful comments on earlier versions of this article.

Over the past decade, numerous studies have investigated teachers' attempts to change their mathematics instruction in light of the goals of reform (e.g., Cohen, 1990; Fennema & Nelson, 1997; Wood, Cobb, & Yackel, 1991). Some of this work highlights the need for increased subject matter knowledge and pedagogical content knowledge on the part of teachers and, in particular, the importance of providing opportunities for teachers to learn about student thinking (Fennema et al., 1996). Other research describes the many dilemmas that teachers face in trying to implement reform, and more specifically in establishing a discourse community. For example, teachers may find that students disengage somewhat as they use more challenging tasks (Romagnano, 1994; Stein, Grover, & Henningsen, 1996). In other cases, as teachers open up their classroom for students' ideas, they find it more difficult to manage the mathematical direction that instruction takes or find that students are making claims that are mathematically incorrect (Jaworski, 1994; Sherin, 2002a; Silver & Smith, 1996). A third dilemma involves teachers' sense of efficacy (J. P. Smith, 1996). Teachers find that in the context of reform, it is much more difficult to predict where a lesson will go and thus more difficult to anticipate and prepare for their role in instruction (Heaton, 2000; Sherin, 2002b; M. S. Smith, 2000). Thus, although the development of a discourse community is seen as a critical step in the implementation of reform, teachers may face difficulties and dilemmas as they make this transition.

In this article, we address this issue by introducing a theoretical framework that elaborates the development of a *math-talk learning community*. By math-talk learning community, we refer to a classroom community in which the teacher and students use discourse to support the mathematical learning of all participants. A primary goal of such a community is to understand and extend one's own thinking as well as the thinking of others in the classroom. The framework we offer extends prior research on teacher change in the context of reform by describing key components of a math-talk learning community as well as the intermediary levels along which the community develops. This description seeks to provide teachers with steps to develop their classroom into a rich math-talk learning community. Such step-by-step changes can affect classrooms on a large scale, particularly if passage through the steps can also be supported by reform-based curriculum materials (Ball & Cohen, 1996).

This article is based primarily on a case study of one teacher who began the year by teaching in a traditional manner in her urban Latino third-grade classroom. Over the course of the year, however, she had considerable success in implementing mathematics education reform, particularly in the area of whole-class discourse. Many educational reforms bypass classrooms with children from poor or non-English speaking backgrounds (Spillane, 2001) partly because such children are assumed not to be linguistically prepared to participate in reform-based practices. Thus, success in this case is particularly significant for it supports the notion that urban classrooms with students that are below grade level in mathematics *can* function and learn as a math-talk learning community.

PERSPECTIVES ON TEACHING AND LEARNING ■

Two positions anchor the perspectives on teaching and learning that frame the study reported here. First, a Vygotskian viewpoint, as articulated by Gallimore and Tharp (1990) suggests that teaching is beneficial when it "awakens and rouses to life those functions which are in a stage of maturing, which lie in the zone of proximal development" (p. 177). Thus, learning occurs when assistance is provided at opportune points in the learner's zone of proximal development. Furthermore, Vygotsky's notion of movement from the inter-psychological to the intra-psychological plane characterizes performance as moving from being assisted to being independent over time. In this study, both the teacher and the students moved through their own learning zones of proximal development. Moreover, they assisted one another in a recursive process as they moved through various levels of development. In this article, we describe the kinds of assistance provided to the students as they successfully internalized new roles in the math-talk learning community. Although the focus teacher was also provided with various means of assistance in her development (e.g., researcher interviews, implementation of a research-based curriculum, teacher meetings, and supportive administrators), describing these means of assistance is beyond the scope of this article (see Hufferd-Ackles, 1999). Instead, what is central here is the description of changes in teacher and student interactions as they moved together through learning zones of each new level of the math-talk learning community.

The other perspective that anchors this research is a constructivist and socioconstructivist view of learning (e.g., Cobb, 1994; Cobb & Bauersfeld, 1995; Cobb, Wood, & Yackel, 1990; Cobb, Yackel, & Wood, 1993). This socioconstructivist epistemology blends radical constructivism (von Glasersfeld, 1990) and sociocultural perspectives. From a radical constructivist's perspective, learning is about self-organization. Social construction of knowledge is related to a Vygotskian perspective and asserts that an individual's learning is affected by participating in a wider culture, the classroom, and the outside world (e.g., Cobb, 1994). For example, *taken-as-shared* mathematical meanings are constructed through a process of interacting in a community; these meanings become cultural representations and norms for interacting (Cobb & Bauersfeld, 1995). What is critical for our research is the notion that in a constructivist classroom, participants consider all members of the community to be constructing their own knowledge and reflecting on and discussing this knowledge.

METHOD

Participants

Four teachers from St. Peter Elementary School[1] participated in this study during the 1997–1998 school year. St. Peter is a Catholic school located in a working-class, Latino section of a large U.S. city. Ninety-eight percent of students receive scholarships toward their tuition from the parish and broader Jesuit-sponsored fundraisers. Three of the teachers were in their second year of teaching, and one teacher had no prior teaching experience. Two of the teachers were female, and two were male; two of the teachers were Latino, and two were European-American. The majority of the children in the school spoke English as their second language and Spanish as their first language. The school had one class at first, second, third, and fourth grade. The four teachers each taught one of these grades in self-contained classrooms.

As will be explained shortly in the article, the third-grade classroom became the focus of a case study. This teacher had taught for 1 year previously, and she and her students moved from second grade to third grade together. Her class of 25 students represented a wide range of achievement levels based on their performance during the previous year. Spanish was the language spoken by all of these students at home, though many students' grasp of English was also fairly strong. The teacher was bilingual and consistently monitored student comprehension of language. The students sometimes slipped into Spanish when they were excited about something or when they were working particularly hard to be understood.

Curriculum

As part of the study, the four teachers implemented the research-based mathematics curriculum, Children's Math Worlds (CMW) (Fuson et al., 1997). The CMW curriculum is based on years of research into the manner in which children learn and understand number concepts. CMW contains key conceptual supports including language and representations that help mathematics to become personally meaningful to students and that provide a context through which students can share their ideas with others. This curriculum suggests that students make mathematical drawings to solve problems and explain their thinking and label these drawings and related equations to link them to the problem situation. Because the students at St. Peter were not learning mathematics in their first language, such visual referents were particularly important. In addition, the curriculum provides support for students to use alternative methods of solving problems. It also supports teacher understanding of these alternative methods by providing information about predicted students' response to a range of activities. CMW emphasizes the building of a learning community and of meaning making for both student and teachers.

The CMW curriculum was the designated mathematics curriculum at St. Peter School for first through third grades and for part of the fourth grade. Because the teachers in this study were using instructional tasks from the curriculum, they were able to concentrate on the development of their practice rather than on the development of instructional tasks that may or may not have offered students significant opportunities to extend their mathematical thinking (e.g., Wood, Cobb, & Yackel, 1991). Prior to the teacher's departure for maternity leave, her third-grade class completed the units on two major topics: single-digit multiplication and division and multidigit addition and subtraction.

Classroom Observations

The four teachers were observed throughout the year, although each was on a slightly different observation schedule. The first-grade class was observed either once per week or every other week; the second-grade class was observed twice per week from November to February and once per week thereafter through June; the third-grade class was observed twice per week from September to mid-April (at which point the teacher left for maternity leave); and the fourth-grade class was observed twice per week in the fall and every other week in the spring. Most observations were videotaped, and those that were not were audiotaped. Following each observed class, a postobservation interview was conducted individually with each teacher with the exception of the first-grade teacher. Because the first-grade classes were conducted in Spanish, these lessons were videotaped for a Spanish-speaking researcher to analyze. That researcher conducted telephone interviews with the teacher.

Two researchers conducted most classroom visits to the second-, third-, and fourth-grade classes. One researcher videotaped the mathematics lesson, and the other took detailed notes. The priorities of the videographer in the classroom were to follow the teacher or other speaker and to record all student work on the board. For the observations that were not videotaped, there was one researcher in the room taking notes, and the lessons were audiotaped. The tapes provided permanent records for later analysis.

The first priority for note taking was to follow the teacher and document as many of his or her actions and words as possible. Notes were made of what happened during each segment of the class, important teacher and student conversations, questions, and statements, all student board work, noteworthy instructional practices, and classroom social climate (e.g., how many students raised their hands to respond to the teacher or another student). The note-taking researcher had several years of classroom teaching experience that were helpful in understanding the complexities of the teacher's role and attending to multiple simultaneous events (see Day, 1988).

During the following year, in the classroom of the third-grade teacher, seven classroom observations were conducted over the first 2 months of school. These visits focused on the formation of a math-talk learning community with the new class of students. Postobservation questions focused on the teacher's understanding of the development of this community in her classroom and on her continued math-content and math-pedagogy learning.

Teacher Meetings

All teachers met together twice monthly to discuss their mathematics teaching. These meetings were initiated by the St. Peter administrators, the principal and assistant principal, who were advocates and catalysts for reform in all subject areas. The field researcher facilitated these meetings throughout the year. Each meeting was videotaped or audiotaped.

■ DATA ANALYSIS

Phases

Data analysis consisted of three main phases. The first phase of analysis occurred during the data collection period and informed the data collection process (Miles & Huberman, 1984). Throughout this time, the field researcher, who is the first author of this article, met regularly with the other researchers to discuss the detailed observations notes that were available from the classrooms. The goal at this point was to identify significant changes that were occurring across and within the classrooms. Three researchers read the field notes independently; thus, the meetings served as a form of investigator triangulation (Denzen, 1984). Investigator triangulation also took place as data were examined in light of current literature on teacher learning and mathematics reform as well as of ongoing research on the use of CMW (see Fuson, Smith, & Lo Cicero, 1997; Fuson et al., 2000) and of the reform-based curriculum Everyday Mathematics.[2] Working hypotheses were examined as data analysis and data collection interacted (e.g., Spillane, 2000), and ensuing observations and interviews were modified to pursue issues as they were identified.

Based on this analysis, it was determined that the practice of the third-grade teacher, Ms. Martinez, had exhibited dramatic change over the course of the school year. Although there were positive changes in the direction of reform in each of the teachers' practices, Ms. Martinez's class showed the most change. It began as very traditional and moved to a fully implemented mathematical discourse community. This classroom was therefore selected as the focus of a case study.

The second phase of analysis consisted of a case study of the third-grade teacher, Ms. Martinez. This involved an analysis of classroom discourse, teacher interviews, and teacher meetings based on verbatim transcriptions of videotaped and audiotaped recordings. Transcriptions from recordings described as accurately as possible all spoken words from classroom observations. In addition to dialogue, the videotaped transcriptions contained descriptions of behavioral contexts.

There are trade-offs inherent in the use of the case-study method: in-depth understanding is gained while generalizability may be lost. To address the issue of generalizability, we added a third phase of analysis. This involved examining the results of the case study within the context of data collected in the other three classrooms. Additional observations were also conducted during the following school year to further examine the robustness of the findings. The description of the framework was modified to reflect observations in the other classrooms and in the second year to resonate with observations of other CMW classrooms and of classrooms in the Everyday Mathematics longitudinal study.

The data summarized in this article enable a detailed look at longitudinal growth across a school year. Moreover, this rich data set can help to provide the reader with an in-depth look at and understanding of the synergistic classroom life that led to the framing of a developmental trajectory that can subsequently be applied to other classroom situations (Brown, 1992; Donmoyer, 1990).

Establishing the Framework

In order to begin to classify and organize the large amounts of data collected in the case-study classroom, we established a coding system. Initially, classroom observation notes, transcripts from the classes, and teacher postobservation interviews were classified in light of a variety of themes related to mathematics reform. These were organized chronologically, with the lesson considered to be the unit of analysis. Within the lessons, examples of dialogue from classroom transcripts that had a clear beginning and end were designated as *episodes*. Each of the 60 classroom transcripts contained approximately 8 to 10 episodes. Three themes and the relationships among them soon emerged as central, and these became the focus of data analysis: *evidence of mathematics community, teacher actions,* and *student actions.* Establishing the themes as the focus illustrated that the development of the mathematics community was *linked* to specific teacher actions and/or student actions. That is, as students responded to particular kinds of actions by the teacher, the class more and more reflected ideals of mathematics reformers.

Within these actions, we identified four distinct, but related components that captured the growth of the math-talk learning community over time, and we followed their growth in the data: (a) Questioning, (b) Explaining math thinking, (c) Source of mathematical ideas, and (d) Responsibility for learning. Within each attribute, developmental trajectories in teacher actions and students' actions were derived from the data. By developmental trajectory, we refer to changes in the teacher's and students' actions that occurred over time and built successively on one another. Each trajectory consists of four levels—Level 0 through Level 3. Together, these four trajectories represent the development of the math-talk learning community in Ms. Martinez's classroom. The resulting framework titled Levels of the Math-Talk Learning Community: Action Trajectories for Teacher and Student is shown in Table 5.5a.

The articulation of the Levels of Math-Talk Learning Community framework went through cyclical revisions. The revision process continued until all episodes from all lessons in the data fit within a cell of the framework. In addition, triangulation with data from the other three St. Peter teachers (i.e., placing episodes from their transcripts in the framework) as well as with the data from the Everyday Mathematics classroom study (Mills, 1996; Mills, Fuson, & Wolfe, 1999) enabled further modifications of the Levels of Math-Talk Learning Community framework and provided confirming analysis. To check interrater reliability of the categories, another coder coded 13 classroom sessions chosen randomly from the whole course of the study (about one class every 2 weeks). Interrater agreement was 100% on all categories. Then, the members of the teacher learning research group[3] each coded 5 sessions drawn randomly from the 13 sessions. The calculated weighted agreement (Fuchs et al., 1998) was 99% for questioning, 97% for explaining, 100% for source of mathematical ideas, and 98% responsibility for learning. Together, these techniques provided support for the robustness of the framework.

Table 5.5a   Levels of the Math-Talk Learning Community: Action Trajectories for Teacher and Student

Overview of Shift Over Levels 0–3

The classroom community grows to support students acting in central or leading roles and shifts from a focus on answers to a focus on mathematical thinking.

A. Questioning	B. Explaining Mathematical Thinking	C. Source of Mathematical Ideas	D. Responsibility for Learning
Shift from teacher as questioner to students and teacher as questioners.	Students increasingly explain and articulate their math ideas.	Shift from teacher as the source of all math ideas to students' ideas also influencing direction of lesson.	Students increasingly take responsibility for learning and evaluation of others and self. Math sense becomes the criterion for evaluation.

Level 0

Traditional teacher-directed classroom with brief answer responses from students.

A. Questioning	B. Explaining Mathematical Thinking	C. Source of Mathematical Ideas	D. Responsibility for Learning
Teacher is the only questioner. Short frequent questions function to keep students listening and paying attention to the teacher. Students give short answers and respond to the teacher only. No student-to-student math talk.	*No or minimal teacher elicitation of student thinking, strategies, or explanations; teacher expects answer-focused responses. Teacher may tell answers.* No student thinking or strategy-focused explanation of work. Only answers are given.	*Teacher is physically at the board, usually chalk in hand, telling and showing students how to do math.* Students respond to math presented by the teacher. They do not offer their own math ideas.	*Teacher repeats student responses (originally directed to her) for the class. Teacher responds to students' answers by verifying the correct answer or showing the correct method.* Students are passive listeners; they attempt to imitate the teacher and do not take responsibility for the learning of their peers or themselves.

Level 1

Teacher beginning to pursue student mathematical thinking. Teacher plays central role in the math-talk community.

A. Questioning	B. Explaining Mathematical Thinking	C. Source of Mathematical Ideas	D. Responsibility for Learning
Teacher questions begin to focus on student thinking and focus less on answers. Teacher begins to ask follow-up questions about student methods and answers. Teacher is still the only questioner. As a student answers a question, other students listen passively or wait for their turn.	*Teacher probes student thinking somewhat. One or two strategies may be elicited. Teacher may fill in explanations herself.* Students give information about their math thinking usually as it is probed by the teacher (minimal volunteering of thoughts). They provide brief descriptions of their thinking.	*Teacher is still the main source of ideas, though she elicits some student ideas. Teacher does some probing to access student ideas.* Some student ideas are raised in discussions, but are not explored.	*Teacher begins to set up structures to facilitate students listening to and helping other students. The teacher alone gives feedback.* Students become more engaged by repeating what other students say or by helping another student at the teacher's request. This helping mostly involves students showing how they solved a problem.

(Continued)

Table 5.5a (Continued)

Level 2

Teacher modeling and helping students build new roles. Some co-teaching and co-learning begins as student-to-student talk increases. Teacher physically begins to move to side or back of the room.

A. Questioning	B. Explaining Mathematical Thinking	C. Source of Mathematical Ideas	D. Responsibility for Learning
Teacher continues to ask probing questions and also asks more open questions. She also facilitates student-to-student talk, e.g., by asking students to be prepared to ask questions about other students' work. Students ask questions of one another's work on the board, often at the prompting of the teacher. Students listen to one another so they do not repeat questions.	*Teacher probes more deeply to learn about student thinking and supports detailed descriptions from students. Teacher open to and elicits multiple strategies.* Students usually give information as it is probed by the teacher with some volunteering of thoughts. They begin to stake a position and articulate more information in response to probes. They explain steps in their thinking by providing fuller descriptions and begin to defend their answers and methods. Other students listen supportively.	*Teacher follows up on explanations and builds on them by asking students to compare and contrast them. Teacher is comfortable using student errors as opportunities for learning.* Students exhibit confidence about their ideas and share their own thinking and strategies even if they are different from others. Student ideas sometimes guide the direction of the math lesson.	*Teacher encourages student responsibility for understanding the mathematical ideas of others. Teacher asks other students questions about student work and whether they agree or disagree and why.* Students begin to listen to understand one another. When the teacher requests, they explain other students' ideas in their own words. Helping involves clarifying other students' ideas for themselves and others. Students imitate and model teacher's probing in pair work and in whole-class discussions.

Level 3

Teacher as co-teacher and co-learner. Teacher monitors all that occurs, still fully engaged. Teacher is ready to assist, but now in more peripheral and monitoring role (coach and assister).

A. Questioning	B. Explaining Mathematical Thinking	C. Source of Mathematical Ideas	D. Responsibility for Learning
Teacher expects students to ask one another questions about their work. The teacher's questions still may guide the discourse. Student-to-student talk is student-initiated, not dependent on the teacher. Students ask questions and listen to responses. Many questions are "Why?" questions that require justification from the person answering. Students repeat their own or other's questions until satisfied with answers.	*Teacher follows along closely to student descriptions of their thinking, encouraging students to make their explanations more compete; may ask probing questions to make explanations more complete. Teacher stimulates students to think more deeply about strategies.* Students describe more complete strategies; they defend and justify their answers with little prompting from the teacher. Students realize that they will be asked questions from other students when they finish, sothey are motivated and careful to be thorough. Other students support with active listening.	*Teacher allows for interruptions from students during her explanations; she lets students explain and "own" new strategies. (Teacher is still engaged and deciding what is important to continue exploring.) Teacher uses student ideas and methods as the basis for lessons or miniextensions.* Students interject their ideas as the teacher or other students are teaching, confident that their ideas are valued. Students spontaneously compare and contrast and build on ideas. Student ideas form part of the content of many math lessons.	*The teacher expects students to be responsible for co-evaluation of everyone's work and thinking. She supports students as they help one another sort out misconceptions. She helps and/or follows up when needed.* Students listen to understand, then initiate clarifying other students' work and ideas for themselves and for others during whole-class discussions as well as in small group and pair work. Students assist each other in understanding and correcting errors.

RESULTS ■

The central result of this research is the articulation of the framework in Table 5.5a, Levels of the Math-Talk Learning Community: Action Trajectories for Teacher and Student. This framework depicts growth in a math-talk learning community in two ways. First, it is made up of four developmental levels through which the case-study class moved. The movement through the levels is from a traditional mathematics classroom in Level 0 to a classroom embracing meaningful collaborative math-talk in Level 3. Level 0 in the framework represents a traditional, teacher-directed classroom. In the Level 1 classroom, the teacher in the study began to pursue student mathematical thinking, but still played the leading role in the math-talk learning community. In Level 2, the teacher began to stimulate students to take on important roles in the learning community and backed away from the central role in the math talk. In Level 3, the teacher coached and assisted her students as they took on leading roles in the math-talk learning community.

Second, the framework examines growth that occurred within each of four components from Level 0 to Level 3. The components that make up the framework are these: (a) questioning, (b) explaining mathematical thinking, (c) source of mathematical ideas, and (d) responsibility for learning. These components have been described in prior research as key features of an effective discourse community, although much of this work has examined each component separately. Overall, questioning and explaining have received the most attention. For example, Heaton (2000) describes her own attempt to reform her mathematics instruction and explains that learning to elicit student comments through questioning was a critical first step. Other researchers focus on teachers' ability to interpret and make sense of students' explanations during class (e.g., Schifter, 1996). Although also examined by relevant research, less work has been done to explore the role of students' contributions to the mathematical content of the lesson and of students' responsibility for the learning of their peers. For example, Sherin (2002a) discusses how control of the mathematical content of a lesson may shift between the teacher and the students, not only from lesson to lesson but also within a particular lesson. Furthermore, the notion of student responsibility for each other's learning in the context of a discourse community is most often explored from the perspective of whether or not students build on each others' ideas during class discussions (Sherin, Louis, & Mendez, 2000; M. S. Smith, 2000). Examining all four of these components—both individually and together—is an important contribution of the research reported here.

For the most part, growth occurred concurrently in each of the components of the math-talk learning community in Ms. Martinez's classroom (see Hufferd-Ackles [1999] for a more extensive analysis of this issue). The means of assistance provided by Ms. Martinez in moving through these levels is discussed later in this article.

Growth in the Components of the Math-Talk Community: Development From Level 0 to Level 3

In this section of the article, we briefly explain the growth that occurred in each component of the math-talk learning community and exemplify them with excerpts of conversations from Ms. Martinez's third-grade classroom. These excerpts illustrate the learning community's path from traditional teaching to a rich and supportive learning environment.

Component A: Questioning

The focus of this component of the math-talk learning community is on the questioner in classroom interactions. To further children's thinking about mathematics, it is important to find out what students know and how they think about mathematical concepts. Questioning of students allows their responses to enter the classroom's discourse space to be assessed and built on by others. Questioning challenges the thinking of the person being questioned by asking for further thinking about his or her work. For this reason, questioning of students is an important part of the math-talk learning community and of reform mathematics teaching. As questioning built from Level 0 to Level 3 in Ms. Martinez's classroom, there was a shift from the teacher as the exclusive questioner to students as questioners along with the teacher. Another shift took place concurrently in the questioning component of the math-talk learning community—from a focus on *questioning to find answers* to a focus on *questioning to uncover the mathematical thinking behind the answers.*

Because the Level 0 math-talk learning community resembles the traditional, teacher-centered classroom, it is the teacher who assumes the role of question-asking, and the goal of the teacher's questions is primarily to ask students to give answers to problems. Early in the year, Ms. Martinez asked Level 0 questions that required only a brief answer, and she rarely followed up the students' responses with additional, more probing questions. Because the CMW curriculum prompted her to begin asking "Why?" and "How?" of students, Ms. Martinez quickly made the transition to Level 1 questioning. The excerpt that follows shows Ms. Martinez introducing the class to arrays for the purpose of scaffolding multiplicative understanding. Level 1 questioning is apparent in the types of questions that Ms. Martinez asked and modeled. In the excerpt below and in all excerpts that follow, the actions of the teacher and students and our commentary on what was said appear in italics within parentheses.

Level 1 Questioning: Teacher pursues student thinking.

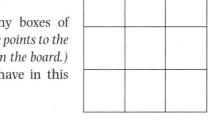

Ms. Martinez	Now, who can tell me how many boxes of cereal I have in this container? *(She points to the three-by-three array she has drawn on the board.)* How many boxes of cereal do I have in this container, Carl?
Carl	Nine.
Ms. Martinez	Nine. How did you figure that out, Carl?
Carl	Because I counted them. I counted them by 3s.
Ms. Martinez	You counted them. You counted by 3s. Can you come up and show us? *(The teacher is assisting the student to give a fuller explanation.) (Carl goes to the board to illustrate by pointing to the drawing.)*
Carl	I counted by 3s. There is 3 right here (row 1 of boxes). Right there (row 2). And there's 3 right here (row 3).
Ms. Martinez	So, it is like you are saying 3 + 3 + 3. What is another way we can count? Does anyone have another way we can count? Jimmy?
Jimmy	Um, go like this. Go like this, 3, 6, 9.

Level 2 questioning is different from Level 1 because of the shift made from the teacher as the sole questioner to the students as questioners as well. This new shift in Ms. Martinez's classroom began one day when several students were working at the board. In her efforts to engage the students who had finished the problem and were waiting in their seats, Ms. Martinez told them that they each should be thinking of one question to ask the explainers when they were finished. Liz explained her work at the board for the following problem, "Ana has 3 dolls. Maria has double the amount. How many are there all together?" To Ms. Martinez's surprise, the following dialogue took place.

Level 2 Questioning: Students begin to question.

(Liz has written this labeled equation.)

$$\begin{array}{ccc} A & d & J \\ 3 \times 2 & = & 5 \\ & d & \end{array}$$

Ms. Martinez	Okay, Santos?
Santos	I wonder why she put the 5 in there.
Ms. Martinez	Can you ask your question to Liz? *(Teacher assists student-to-student talk.)*
Santos	*(To Liz.)* Why did you put the 5 in there?
Liz	Because it says, "How many are there all together?"
Saul	How come there is a "d" under the 3?
Ms. Martinez	Can you repeat the question to Liz? *(Teacher assists student-to-student talk.)*
Saul	*(To Liz.)* How come there is a "d" under the 3?
Liz	Because it is for the dolls.
Helena	Es un . . plus? [Is it a plus?] (Liz nods in agreement.) ¿Por qué pusiste el tres y el dos junto? [Why did you put the three and the two together?]
Liz	Porque, ahi van juntos. [Because here they go together.] (Note, "J" in Liz's work stands for "all together," juntos in Spanish.)
Angel	*(To Liz.)* Why did you put the 2?
Liz	For double.

In this particular situation, Ms. Martinez could have involved herself in the discourse right away to discuss the error in Liz's solution. Instead, she waited to see if the problem in Liz's work would be clarified through the students' questioning. Students began to ask questions related to the issue of adding (3 + 2) rather than multiplying (3 × 2). Later, it took some further guidance from Ms. Martinez to resolve the issues embedded in this complex two-step problem. However, Ms. Martinez was encouraged to see the beginnings of student-to-student math talk.

At the beginning of episodes of student-to-student questioning in later classes, the teacher often prompted the questioning process with statements like "Questions for people at the board?" Initially, many of the questions that the students asked each other were modeled after questions that they had heard their teacher ask in class: for example, "What did you add?" "How did you come up with your answer?" "Can you show us on your drawing?" A positive result of this new practice was that the students in the class who were not directly involved in the discourse were actively listening to the speakers so that they did not repeat the question that another student had already asked. Sometimes students who were not outwardly participating in the questioning process gave evidence of their active listening by making comments. For example, one lower-achieving student often demonstrated active listening as he announced, "Someone already asked that."

In the following Level 3 example, students are contemplating whether one would get the same answer when adding columns of same-place-value numbers in multidigit problems from left to right or from right to left. This excerpt demonstrates the type of student-initiated questioning in order to understand one another's thinking and to understand the mathematics content that took place in the classroom when questioning reached the highest level in the framework.

Level 3 Questioning: Students initiate the questioning.

(Ms. Martinez is in the rear of the classroom, Jamie is stationed at the blackboard. He has been called on by Ms. Martinez to share his comments about whether or not it is the same to add columns of numbers left to right or right to left with the class.)

Jamie No, because if you're taking away any numbers you gotta take away from the other ones. Are you gonna start from the right?

Santos What do you mean?

Jamie Right when you're taking away, yeah, subtraction, sometimes you gotta take away from the other numbers.

Maria Sometimes you can start from the right or the left.

Jamie How? Are you going to take one from the left, I mean from the right?

Maria Sometimes it helps to write, like, when it's subtraction, from the right or sometimes from the left.

Roberto Either way, none of the numbers are going to change. Just do the same thing you're gonna do from left to right, subtract the same thing you're gonna do from right to left.

Jamie Yeah, but that's not gonna be the same answer.

Roberto If you start from right to left, you're gonna subtract something and you can subtract the same thing if you go from left to right.

Angel And when you go from left to right, it's gonna be the same answer.

Ms. Martinez Are you still not convinced, Jamie?

(At Ms. Martinez's urging, still from the rear of the classroom, the class moves on by coming up with a problem to test. A student suggests 24 + 18. Veronica solves the problem at the board by adding from left to right and then right to left. Veronica's work follows.)

Left to Right   Right to Left

$$24$$
$$+18$$
$$32$$

$$24$$
$$+18$$
$$42$$

Ms. Martinez *(To the class.)* Okay, would either method give you the right answer?

Class Yes.

Ms. Martinez Yes. But we still haven't figured out what's the right answer, have we?

Rodney *(He speaks from his seat.)* Veronica, where's the other tens? *(This is in reference to the additional ten created by the sum of 8 and 4 in the problem on the left. Veronica, in response, points to the 4 in 42 in the problem on the right.)*

Rodney *(He approaches the board while pointing at the 32 in the other problem.)* Where's the other ten?

Veronica *(She points to the 3 in 32.)* Right here?

Rodney *(He repeats.)* Where's the other ten? *(Veronica again points to the 3 in 32.)*

Rodney Yeah, but eight and four equals twelve, and you just put a two right here (pointing to the 2 in 32).

Roberto *(He speaks from his seat.)* But you can't do it! You can't do that!

Veronica Yeah, because if you put a one right here *(pointing to the chalkboard space between the numerals 3 and 2 in 32)* then it will be, uh, three hundred and twelve.

(Ms. Martinez then interjects, attempting to clarify for both Virginia and Rodney exactly what the other is saying. The discussion continues with the whole class participating. In this case, the discussion continued into the lunch period and the students asked (insisted) to continue it after recess.)

This excerpt depicts a typical instance of initiative and persistence on the part of students that was common in Level 3 situations. Several students attempted to follow, challenge, and clarify Jamie's thoughts about adding (or subtracting) from left to right. Rodney persistently pursued clarification from Veronica about her work. None of the above interactions occurred between only two people. Other students felt comfortable contributing their thoughts to the ongoing interactions. Students were no longer dependent on the teacher to initiate the process of questioning *and* to keep it going. Fewer students used the questions that the teacher had earlier modeled, but instead they focused on more specific aspects of the problem. Sometimes a student asked another student's question in different words to help the recipient understand the intent of the original question.

All students in the class asked questions, with the lower-achieving students often only mimicking what they had heard their teacher ask in a previous class or asked a simple question. However, the fact that these students were asking questions gave evidence of their comfort with being a participant in the math-talk learning community and confirmed their engagement with the discussion. By doing so, the lower-achieving students demonstrated their understanding of the general shift in the class from eliciting answers to finding out about the thinking behind the answers. At times, students seemed to ask questions because they wanted to participate, but often students earnestly wanted to pursue a specific response from the person explaining his or her work. Potential questioners were often disappointed when class ended and they did not get the opportunity to ask their question.

This excerpt also illustrates how important the teacher's role continues to be at even the highest level—Level 3. Ms. Martinez needed to intervene to clarify, to be sure that students are fully satisfied, to suggest strategies for resolving differences, and to manage time by overseeing turn taking—although much of the conversation was managed by the students.

Component B: Explaining Mathematical Thinking

We now turn to the second component of the math-talk learning community: explaining mathematical thinking. Although this component is closely connected to the process of questioning, here we attempt to focus exclusively on the process of explaining as we go through each level of the math-talk learning framework individually.

As students in Ms. Martinez's math-talk learning community became more comfortable and more able as explainers (and as Ms. Martinez began to facilitate this development), the community moved from Level 0 to Level 3 in this component. Significant support for the growth in this area was found in the social climate that the class together developed that effectively supported student explainers. Initially, standing in front of one's peers to communicate mathematical ideas was a daunting task for many students, especially shy students. Many chose to sit back down in their seats after writing work on the board rather than to accept the challenge of staying in front of the class and talking. However, as the math-talk learning community developed, students' attempts at explaining were scaffolded by supportive classroom colleagues. This support allowed the development of explaining to progress. As students learned to explain their own mathematical thinking more fully and fluidly, they made significant contributions that could then be questioned or built on by other students and assessed by the teacher.

In the Level 0 math-talk learning community, students often gave answers to Ms. Martinez's questions in one to a few words. Student explanations consisted of short interchanges between the teacher and the students. Questions asked of students by the teacher were primarily answer-focused. At times the teacher did not even wait for an answer from the students and gave it herself. The following interaction illustrates a Level 0 explanation of mathematical thinking, showing that students' explanations of their work were focused on providing the correct answers. The teacher was not looking for more explicit strategies or thinking from the students and, not surprisingly, they did not offer it. Students were solving this problem: "Joey bought 5 packs of gum at the store yesterday. Each pack has 7 sticks of gum. How many sticks of gum does he have?" In the following excerpt, Ms. Martinez provided a fuller explanation for Charlotte herself rather than have Charlotte explain.

Level 0 Explaining Mathematical Thinking: Teacher assistance focuses only on correctness of answers.

(Charlotte has drawn the following on the board.)

///// ///// ///// /////

Ms. Martinez	Okay, so how many packs has Joey bought?
Charlotte	Five.
Ms. Martinez	Five packs, so we have to draw a fifth pack, right? Draw it.

(Charlotte begins drawing a fifth pack on the board. After finishing her drawing and providing an answer, Charlotte goes back to her seat.)

///// ///// ///// ///// ///// = 25

Ms. Martinez	Okay, here's what Charlotte did. She has five times seven equals twenty-five. So she has *(pointing to each part of Charlotte's drawing at the blackboard)* one, two, three, four, five packs. Is there something that is not exactly right in here that you might have missed?
Charlotte	The answer?
Ms. Martinez	Okay what, what is wrong with the answer? First, look at the picture, okay? Is there something wrong with the picture? Are you missing something?
Charlotte	Need more sticks.
Ms. Martinez	Excuse me?
Charlotte	Need more sticks. There's only five sticks in each.
Ms. Martinez	You have *(pointing to the drawing)* one, two, three, four, five sticks. And how many is it supposed to be, Charlotte?
Charlotte	Seven.
Ms. Martinez	Seven. Because you have seven sticks of gum. Okay, that's where you went wrong, because there's seven sticks of gum. Each pack, in each pack, you need seven. *(Ms. Martinez adds the extra two sticks for each row in the drawing.)* Now she has a pack of seven sticks. Now we have five packs of seven sticks. Now, Charlotte, what is your new answer?

///// ///// ///// ///// ///// = 35
// // // // //

Charlotte	*(She pauses.)* 35?
Ms. Martinez	35, right. We have seven plus seven plus seven plus seven plus seven, which all together equals 35. Let's go on to the next problem.

In this excerpt, Ms. Martinez prompted Charlotte to correct her drawing rather than explore the reasons behind her choice of a solution. In other words, Ms. Martinez's goal was to direct Charlotte to the correct answer rather than to understand her thinking and the reason for her error. She never found out why Charlotte's original drawing started with 5 sticks per pack. In addition, Ms. Martinez described Charlotte's work to the class rather than have Charlotte explain her thinking. Had Charlotte been given the opportunity and had she possessed the capacity to explain her work, Ms. Martinez would have had more opportunity to understand her thinking process. For instance, after Charlotte commented that there were only 5 sticks (per group), Ms. Martinez did not ask her to explain herself more fully. Eventually, Ms. Martinez told the class, "Seven. Because you have seven sticks of gum." Finally, Ms. Martinez abruptly left Charlotte's problem and moved on to the next student's work without having knowledge of any of the other students' understanding of the corrected solution. In summary, this excerpt illustrates the lack of attention to student thinking in Level 0 of the developmental trajectory of explaining. This situation shows that Level 0 explaining is the counterpart to Level 0 questioning because both the questioner and explainer are focused on answers only.

Ms. Martinez made the transition to fuller student explanations of mathematical thinking in her classroom by beginning to probe students more deeply. Level 1 explanations were given as students shared information about their thinking in response to the teacher's probing. The first attempts at fuller explanations were laborious for students because they were uncomfortable responding to several consecutive questions while standing at the front of the room. Many students preferred walking over to the teacher (who was often standing nearby) and talking to her privately. The following example shows students explaining their work after solving the word problem at the board, "Carrie is playing with 6 girls. How many fingers are there in the group?"

Level 1 Explaining Mathematical Thinking: Teacher assists students in their brief initial attempts.

Ms. Martinez	Explain what you did.
Saul	6 times 7.
Ms. Martinez	Why did you write a 6?
Saul	6 girls.
Ms. Martinez	Why did you write a 7?
Ms. Martinez	*(She waits a moment.)* You can't explain? *(Saul shakes his head "no.")*
Ms. Martinez	Okay, have a seat.
Ms. Martinez	Henry, can you explain to the class why you put 6 × 5?
Henry	There are 6 girls *(pauses)* multiplied by 5. You get 30.
Ms. Martinez	Can you say it again to the class, loudly?
Henry	*(Inaudible.)*
Student in back	I can't hear. Can you say it louder?

Ms. Martinez	Henry, you have to face the audience.
Henry	6 girls multiplied by 5 *(pause)*.
Ms. Martinez	Since Henry's voice is quiet, I will repeat it for him. 6 girls counted by 5 equals 30.
Ms. Martinez	Where did you get the 5?
Henry	Because that makes 30.
Ms. Martinez	Okay, you can sit down.

This excerpt indicates that facilitating students' explaining of their thinking required patience on the part of the teacher; there were many long pauses as students considered what to say. It would have been much quicker for Ms. Martinez to show students how to arrive at an answer of 30. Furthermore, taking on the central role of explainer in the classroom discourse was uncomfortable for many students, as Saul and Henry illustrate. They were familiar with the conventional expectation that they say only a word or two and then sit down; they were not accustomed to identifying and explaining their own thinking processes.

The Level 2 explanation of mathematical thinking began after students became more comfortable with the process of communicating about such thinking. At this level, the students still required probing and some assistance in clarifying their thoughts from Ms. Martinez and, increasingly, from other students. Student explainers grew more confident that their thinking was valuable, and they became less shy about telling their mathematical ideas. They grew to expect that providing a numerical answer was not enough information. Furthermore, the classroom social norms grew to embrace and encourage student speakers. Students began to listen to one another more actively, help from other students was accepted as positive, and often students applauded after their classmates gave explanations of their work at the board. Thus, being the center of classroom discourse became less scary for students, and more students volunteered for the opportunity to tell their thoughts about the mathematics. The following excerpt demonstrates a Level 2 explanation of mathematical thinking. In this excerpt, Ms. Martinez asked Santos to explain his multidigit addition work on the board.

Level 2 Explaining Mathematical Thinking: Teacher assists students as they provide fuller, more comfortable explanations.

(Santos has written his work on the board.)

$$\begin{array}{r} {}^{1\ 1} \\ 258 \\ +\ \underline{374} \\ 632 \end{array}$$

Ms. Martinez	Santos, do you think you can explain this?
Santos	*(He stands next to his work at the board.)* Eight plus four is the two, and then the ten goes over here, over the five. That equals a hundred and thirty, the hundred goes here, over the two. You end with six hundred thirty two.
Ms. Martinez	Has he explained everything?
Class	No.
Ms. Martinez	He still hasn't explained what the ones are doing up there, has he?

Santos	Oh, well, without the ones it would be a different answer.
Ms. Martinez	What do you mean?
Santos	Without the ones, it would be five hundred and *(pause)* . . . no, yeah, five hundred and twenty-two.
Ms. Martinez	All right, but, how do you know that is the right answer and that your other answer isn't?
Santos	Because, I know how to count.
Ms. Martinez	You know how to count what?
Santos	I know how to carry. I know that you need to carry here to get the right answer.
Ms. Martinez	You know how to carry what?
Santos	I know how to carry the ones. The numbers, I know how to carry these numbers to get the answer.
Ms. Martinez	What does that mean, carry the ones?
Santos	That, you put the ones up here, on top of these, the tens and the hundreds.
Ms. Martinez	Why?
Santos	Because, it needs to be up there. The two is for twelve, and you put the one up there.
Ms. Martinez	Why?
Santos	Because if you don't put the ones, it'll be one thousand, five hundred . . . and that would be the wrong answer!

In this example, Santos demonstrated a greater comfort level at the board than Henry did in the Level 1 example. He was not surprised by or uncomfortable responding to Ms. Martinez's probing. Santos knew that he had not described all of the steps in his work. Rather than jump in herself and explain the process of making a new ten or hundred in more "correct" mathematical language, Ms. Martinez allowed Santos to explain in his own words. Santos illustrated an aspect that was recurring more frequently as the students moved to Level 2 explaining. He confidently staked a claim and continued to defend the claim using his own words. Ms. Martinez's questioning helped Santos's explaining to be more complete. Listening students could follow along more easily, and they remained more engaged. In this particular excerpt, the teacher was probing the student's thinking. In other cases at Level 2, students acted as questioners as well. The teacher's role in assisting the explaining component continued to be very important. Here, Santos needed further assistance from the teacher or from a student to explain that the ones were 1 ten and 1 hundred.

In the third level of explaining mathematical thinking, students began to defend and justify their mathematical ideas more confidently and thoroughly. Although Ms. Martinez was ready and available to probe and guide students in making their explanations more complete, their responses became more extensive and thorough and needed less assistance. During this classroom segment, students had worked together in pairs or groups to solve multidigit addition problems. The group made up of Veronica and Lou put the following work on the board and then they took their seats.

Level 3 Explaining Mathematical Thinking: Students engaged in full, confident explaining without overt assistance.

$$
\begin{array}{r}
438 \\
+\,271 \\
\hline
600 \\
100 \\
9 \\
\hline
709
\end{array}
$$

Ms. Martinez	*(She directs her question to the class.)* Questions for this group?
Maria	*(She asks Lou.)* Can you show us how you're adding? *(Veronica steps to the board next to the work she and Lou completed.)*
Veronica	*(She responds to Maria.)* You mean all of this (motioning to their work underneath the original written problem)?
Maria	Yeah. (Veronica turns to Lou, who has gotten her attention; he wants to be the one to answer).
Lou	*(He comes to the board, and begins his step-by-step explanation.)* I added the hundreds, the four and the two together, and I got six hundred. *(Veronica cuts him off and steps to the board to speak to him.)*
Veronica	No, just this. *(She points to the work just above the final answer and whispers to Lou. She then sits back down. She is directing him to explain just the final adding step, not all of the adding of the places).*
Lou	*(He points to the final hundreds place, in the answer.)* This was six hundred, and then another hundred, so that was seven hundred, and so with the ones, seven hundred and nine.
Jamie	How did he get the seven hundred? How did you get the extra hundred?
Veronica	He just said it. He just said it. He said he added, and he got the hundred.
Lou	*(He is now speaking from his seat.)* I made it with the seventy, and the thirty, which gave another hundred.

In this excerpt, Lou capably described the mathematical thinking that he used to solve the multidigit addition problem from left to right. He repeated the steps in his thinking process without the probing of Ms. Martinez and despite the interruptions by Veronica (Lou's slightly overbearing partner). Lou also took ownership of the explanation process and answered questions about it even after he finished telling about his group's approach to solving the problem and was sitting down. In Level 3 of the math-talk learning community, important information came from student discussion as well as from the teacher.

Component C: Source of Mathematical Ideas

At Level 0, the teacher presented mathematics content by standing at the board and telling students how to solve problems in a procedural manner. Students watched so that they might imitate the teacher, and then they did much of their work individually. Initially, she focused on having students copy word problems word for word from the board and solve them individually. She went from table to table and told students how to do the problems, sometimes by doing the problem for them on their papers. Students watched in order to imitate her procedures.

Ms. Martinez's class shifted to Level 1 when Ms. Martinez began to elicit student ideas as she presented content. This shift was facilitated by the conceptual focus of the curriculum. Eliciting students' ideas allowed her to uncover their previous knowledge and current misconceptions and to follow their developing understanding about the material. Student input allowed her to modify the course of lessons according to the evolving ideas of the students. The classroom excerpt below typifies Level 1 sources of contributions to teaching and learning of mathematics content. It shows Ms. Martinez standing at the board in the front of the room and beginning to modify the pace of her lesson (comparing multiplication by twos and fours) to the students' understandings. All students were sitting in their seats, and the majority appeared engaged. The class relied on the drawing below in their discussion. It showed that in the two's "count-by," there are six sets of twos between the numbers 1 and 12. In contrast, the four's "count-by" yields three sets of fours in the same number range.

Level 1 Source of Mathematical Ideas: Teacher begins to use student thinking as part of the mathematics content.

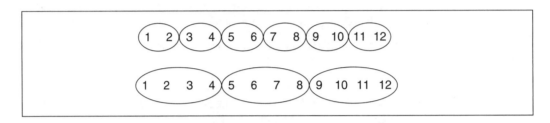

Ms. Martinez	Now, for the two's count-by you go two-four-six-eight-ten-twelve. And with the four's count-by you go four-eight-twelve. So, six fingers for the two's and three fingers for the four's. What is this three in comparison to six? If the third finger for the two's is six, what about the third finger for the four's? Charlotte?
Charlotte	Twelve?
Ms. Martinez	Twelve, good. Do we notice anything between the six and the twelve? Michael? This six right here. (*She points to the six in the number set for the two's count-by.*) And this twelve right here? (*She points to the twelve in the number set for the four's count-by.*)
Michael	Um, it'd be like times the . . . no, double the six would be twelve!
Ms. Martinez	Good. You double the six it'll be twelve. Any other number patterns that you see, Maria?
Maria	Six plus six is twelve?
Ms. Martinez	Okay, that's what Michael had said. If you double the six, it'll be twelve. Anything else about any of the numbers up here, anything that we see repeatedly? Liz?
Liz	Twenty.
Ms. Martinez	The twenty? Okay, what finger is the twenty on, Carrie? In the two's count-by, what finger?
Carrie	On the ten.
Ms. Martinez	On the ten, good. How about in the four's count-by, what finger is the twenty on?
Carrie	The fifth.

Ms. Martinez	So you used only five fingers to get to twenty in the four's count-by but you used your entire fingers to get to twenty in the two's count-by. So the twos are only taking up two numbers, which is why you use so many fingers. But the four, the four is taking up four numbers per finger, you use two numbers for one finger for the twos.

In this excerpt, students demonstrated more involvement with the lesson than they did when Ms. Martinez used the Level 0 tactics of telling students how to do mathematics. Students began to try to think about and understand the mathematics rather than merely attempt to imitate the teacher's words and actions. Thus, teaching in Ms. Martinez's room shifted from a procedural focus to one in which students were searching for meaning as the class moved from Level 0 to Level 1 in this component of the math-talk learning community.

As was evident in other Level 2 components, Ms. Martinez began to shift her physical presence to the side or to the back of the room at this point in the trajectory. It is important to note that Ms. Martinez began to allow more opportunities for students to explore content and suggest alternative and multiple methods. She did this by asking more open-ended rather than answer-driven questions. Ms. Martinez also continued to ask for other students' strategies, even after a correct one had already been presented. In doing this, Ms. Martinez demonstrated her willingness to learn the alternative strategies herself. At times, she asked students to explain their strategies more than once so that she could fully understand them. As she took on the role of co-learner in the classroom, she modeled aspects of learning from others that students later mimicked (e.g., how to ask questions to support understanding). Hearing multiple strategies allowed Ms. Martinez to assess the understanding and possible misconceptions that students held as they moved through each content domain. The following excerpt is from a class in which Ms. Martinez gave students opportunities to solve array word problems. We summarize the students' methods here rather than give the full transcript in the interest of space.

Level 2 Source of Mathematical Ideas: Student methods form much of the content.

(Santos made up the problem, "In my garden I had 4 rows and 6 columns of lettuce heads. How many lettuce heads did I have?" He drew the following picture on the board.)

In response, students offered a number of solving strategies. Angel said that you could count each lettuce head. Nick said that you could count by fours and showed how he would do that by using the vertical groupings, "4, 8, 12, 16, 20, 24." Roberto said that he would count by fives (using the horizontal groupings) and then add four (the vertical grouping left over), as shown in the diagram below.

Jimmy solved the array, "There are 6 in each row, 6 and 6 is 12, the others are 12, I added 12 and 12." After Ms. Martinez added another row to the problem, Maria counted by threes to find her solution:

Henry said he counted by tens to solve the five-by-six array problem. Ms. Martinez responded with "How can I use tens to get my answer?" Henry then showed the class how he grouped two vertical columns to make ten. There were three groups of ten. Jessie counted by twos to thirty using vertical groupings as Maria did earlier to count by threes. Ms. Martinez asked several of the students to explain

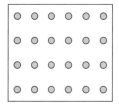

their thinking twice, which allowed her and the other students opportunities to understand the method more fully.

At Level 2, Ms. Martinez also became adept at using students' strategies that contained errors for opportunities to learn. This can be observed in the excerpt used earlier to illustrate Level 2 in the questioning trajectory. The answer for the word problem, "Ana has 3 dolls. Maria has double the amount. How many are there all together?" contained an error ($3 \times 2 = 5$). Ms. Martinez then stimulated the class to think carefully about the language of the problem to allow the students to uncover the error. The class discussion began to focus on the words *double* and *all together* and how their meanings affect the processes of problem solving in this situation.

Reaching Level 3 of the sources of mathematical ideas trajectory depended on two factors. First, students gained confidence that their ideas about mathematics were valid and important. Second, Ms. Martinez became convinced that the ideas students contributed *were* important to explore. Ms. Martinez articulated the latter in this way: "I think the kids explain it in a language that kids can understand." Therefore, she gave students discourse space when they wanted to volunteer their thoughts. At times, she would stop what she was doing and allow a student to take the chalk and explain their idea at the board. Sometimes students would expound upon a strategy that was explained in the curriculum that Ms. Martinez had not yet introduced to the class. She often recognized the importance of these student-initiated strategies after reading the curriculum and then quickly integrated them into the class discussion. For example, the following excerpt comes from a mathematics class in which Ms. Martinez was showing students a way to multiply by sixes, which builds on their knowledge of multiplying by fives. Earlier in the class, Roberto had already verbalized that this is the method he used to solve 6×7.

Level 3 Source of Mathematical Ideas: Student strategies are built on as mini-lessons.

Ms. Martinez	I am going to show you a different way to count by 6s, similar to how Roberto said.
Ms. Martinez	How many groups of 7 are there in 6×7?
Students	6. *(Ms. Martinez writes the following on the board.)*

$$6 \times 7 = 7 + 7 + 7 + 7 + 7 + 7$$
$$35 \qquad 35 + 7 = 42$$

Ms. Martinez	It is easier to multiply by 5 isn't it? *(Ms. Martinez is in the middle of explaining this strategy, and Jimmy intervenes.)*
Jimmy	I have another way.
Ms. Martinez	Okay.
Jimmy	Two of them equals 14, another two is 14, and another two is 14.
Ms. Martinez	Good, can you come up and show us? *(She hands Jimmy the chalk. Jimmy writes on the board:)*

$$7 + 7 \qquad 7 + 7 \qquad 7 + 7$$
$$14 \qquad\quad 14 \qquad\quad 14$$

(Jimmy tries to explain how he gets 14 and 14 and 14 to add up to 42. 4 and 4 and 4 and 30 . . . 14 and 14 is 28 . . . he stumbles a bit and uses his fingers to show $28 + 14 = 42$.)

Ms. Martinez	Good explaining, he didn't give up even though he was a little tongue tied.
Ms. Martinez	What Jimmy explained here is kind of like what Chris was explaining for counting by 2s.
Ms. Martinez	Okay, solve this problem in your journal. Use the way that Jimmy came up with or the way that I showed you with Roberto's help. *(She writes on the board: 6 × 9 = __)*

Both the doubling strategy used by Jimmy and the building on fives facts strategy initially introduced by Roberto were part of the curriculum lesson for this class. Instead of teaching these strategies in a traditional "telling" manner, Ms. Martinez allowed them to emerge from the students. Then she followed up to clarify and relate them. Teaching in this way, the class still explored the target mathematics content, but because of their contributions it was covered in a way that effectively engaged students.

Component D: Responsibility for Learning

As the math-talk learning community developed, responsibility for learning shifted as students became increasingly invested in their own and one another's learning of mathematics. Students began the year in Ms. Martinez's room only as passive listeners as their teacher led the class in a traditional manner. When student thinking began to be elicited, students became more engaged and involved in classroom discourse as speakers and listeners. Their responsibility for their own learning was indicated by their desire to ask questions in class, their eagerness to go to the board to demonstrate their understanding of problems, and their volunteering to engage in the work of and to assist struggling students at the board. Students grew to expect that their mathematics contributions would be positively received by the teacher and by other students. Having students' ideas in the classroom discourse space enabled students to help each other. A respect and concern for the learning of others became a by-product of Ms. Martinez's students actively engaging themselves in their own learning.

Teaching in a reform-oriented mathematics classroom is a challenging task. For students to see themselves as co-learners and co-teachers in the classroom was a substantial help to Ms. Martinez because all of the students began to see themselves as responsible, in part, for the learning of everyone in the room. One student demonstrated this aspect of the math-talk learning community after he explained his strategy for solving his 10-by-12 array at the board. He carefully explained his steps and then earnestly asked, "Teacher, do you understand?" Ms. Martinez graciously responded, "I understand completely." Chris's question illustrated that the students grew to be confident about their mathematical thinking and that they wanted the expression of their thinking to be meaningful to others, including their teacher.

From early in the school year, Ms. Martinez desired to engage all of her students in her teaching of mathematics. When the class was at Level 0 with respect to student responsibility, Ms. Martinez repeated student responses originally directed to her so that all the students in the class could hear. Students passively listened to redirected statements of their peers and did not engage in the thinking of other students. In other words, students' fundamental belief was that they needed to listen to and imitate the teacher (not other students) in order to successfully learn mathematics. In the Level 0 classroom, students did not demonstrate confidence in the ways that they solved problems. Ms. Martinez unilaterally verified the correctness or problems in student work. Students did not have the opportunity to develop a full understanding of the mathematics involved because the focus was on fixing work so the student would get the correct answer. Students were uncomfortable being in the front of the room and unaccustomed to discussing the ways in which they found their answers. Students' responses were quietly directed to the teacher and not intended for the whole class to hear. Under these conditions, Ms. Martinez assumed the role of explaining, which meant also choosing the language that would convey the initial student ideas to the class.

Ms. Martinez's class moved to Level 1 in the responsibility for learning component as she began holding her students accountable for listening to one another and as she began to focus on thinking and not just on answers in the evaluation of student work. Her explicit tactics that were intended to stimulate accountability led students to believe they should listen to what was being said by other students because they might be called upon to repeat something that was said in the course of the discussion. Ms. Martinez made an effort to ask about student thinking, but not to repeat for the students herself. She let other students start taking on this role. Although students became able to repeat what other students were saying, this did not seem to advance the class discussion. However, it did often succeed in keeping students alert in class and honed listening skills. At times, Ms. Martinez had students repeat correct and incorrect information without also making decisions or comments about the validity of the information. Although this was a move forward in terms of holding students accountable to listening to one another, the repeating process often impeded the flow of the class. As Ms. Martinez stopped to have students repeat, the continuity of the potentially meaningful discussion was often lost.

In an effort to build accountability and scaffold students into taking responsibility for their learning, Ms. Martinez abandoned this rather limiting (but perhaps a helpful transitional) practice for one that was more successful in engaging students to think about mathematics. The class shifted to Level 2 in student responsibility for learning when Ms. Martinez began having students explain the mathematical thoughts of others more fully and in *their own words*. This resulted in student listeners comparing the work of others with their own thoughts. Students were challenged to spend time trying to understand what others meant in their explanations instead of mindlessly reiterating the words used by them. At Level 2, Ms. Martinez facilitated deeper student thinking and responsibility by asking substantive questions, such as "What would you have done, Nathan? Would you have counted the same way he did?" and "What was the difference between how Michael counted and how Nathan counted?" This process required students to think more deeply about their own *and* another students' ideas. This reworking of explanations eventually helped even lower-achieving students to compare strategies. Ms. Martinez also modeled for students the questions that helped them participate in the evaluation process. By being able to decide whether or not they agreed or disagreed with the explainers, they were able to shift into the roles of critic, helper, and supporter with respect to other students' work.

The shift to Level 3 in this component of the Levels of Math-Talk Learning Community framework occurred as students took the initiative to clarify other students' work and ideas for themselves and for others during whole-class discussions and small-group interactions. The teacher alone did not give the constructive feedback for student work. Rather, it was co-evaluated by all of the participants in the math-talk learning community as part of the ongoing supportive helping process.

At Level 3, Ms. Martinez was able to have one or more students help another student while the rest of the class moved to another explanation. Thus, Ms. Martinez was able to focus on more students in the span of the classroom time while students evaluated and helped each other make corrections in their work. Ms. Martinez reported that refraining from making verbal assessments of student work when students could be making those comments was a challenging change, but she thought it had been very beneficial. Individual students also took responsibility in the Level 3 classroom by initiating group practice such as with the count-bys (e.g., count-by 6: 6, 12, 18, 24, 30, 36, 42, 48, 54, 60) during slow parts of class periods or during times when the teacher was helping individual students.

The following example of Level 3 responsibility for learning shows one student's quest for place-value understanding. Several other students became involved in assessing and assisting her understanding. Ms. Martinez acted in a supporting rather than central role in this situation.

Level 3 Responsibility for Learning: The whole class acts as teachers when students do not understand—students assist other students in understanding.

(Henry has solved this problem at the board from left to right.)

$$
\begin{array}{r}
485 \\
+\ 376 \\
\hline
700 \\
150 \\
\underline{\ 11} \\
861
\end{array}
$$

Ms. Martinez	Liz, do you have a comment?
Liz	How come he has a one over here, one in the ten and the other in the ones if there are 11 ones?
Maria	I know why, because 6 and 5 is 11 and he can't put that in one column.
Liz	*(She goes to the board.)* How come they put 1 in the tens and 1 in the ones, how come one is over here and one is over here?
Maria	6 + 5 is 11.
Ms. Martinez	Does someone else want to try to explain? *(Six students raise their hands to respond.)*
Rodney	If we put the whole thing here it would all be ones, but this is tens and ones.
Ms. Martinez	How about it Liz, understand? Satisfied? *(Pause.)* She is still a little unsatisfied. Who can try to explain?
Helena	The other time you said . . . [to add left to right] we can count first the 100s, then the 10s and then the ones, we have 11 here, we are counting ones not 10s. *(Eight students raise their hands to try to explain.)*
Chris	Because 11 has one ten.
Ms. Martinez	And?
Chris	Because 11 has one ten and you can't put 11 in the ones column.
Ms. Martinez	Why?
Chris	Because it goes in the ten column.
Ms. Martinez	But one is in the ones.
Liz	The 11s are the ones, and you put the tens and the ones.
Santos	Teacher, I think I know.

Maria	*(She has approached the board.)* 6 + 5 is 11.
Ms. Martinez	You keep saying the same thing, but what does it mean? One more person.
Saul	*(He has now joined Maria at the board.)* 11 has one ten, so it goes here *(points to the tens column).*
Santos	If you put it in the bottom, it would be 862.
Students	No, 8000 *(meaning it would be 8611, moving 8 left to the thousands place).*
Ms. Martinez	Liz still has a question.
Liz	*(strongly)* THE 11s ARE STILL THE ONES, HOW CAN YOU HAVE ONE IN THE TENS AND ANOTHER IN THE ONES?? *(She does not see eleven as 1 ten and 1 one or cannot use that knowledge here.)*
Ms. Martinez	Saul, do you get it?
Saul	It would be 8611. *(He writes this in the answer line of Henry's problem.)*
Ms. Martinez	We don't have any more time.
Students	Aaahhhhh!
Ms. Martinez	We will have to think about the best explanation for tomorrow, think about it tonight.

Liz continued to search for understanding with the students around her at the lunch table following this class. As a result of further student interactions, Liz told Ms. Martinez that she was satisfied with her understanding when the class returned from lunch.

This excerpt illustrates Ms. Martinez having chosen to involve herself as a supporter of the discussion while allowing students to take the central explaining role. Rather than resolve Liz's misconceptions herself, she gave other students opportunities to try to understand Liz's thinking and to help her by explaining in such a way that Liz would understand. Students were so engaged in the Level 3 situation that they impatiently waited to contribute to the discourse. Many clamored for the opportunity to help Liz understand the situation. Students were visibly disappointed when they had to stop interacting around this mathematical dilemma and go to lunch. Liz's press for understanding and Saul's explaining at the board illustrate the progress made by the shy students in this classroom. These particular students were initially very reluctant to share their thinking. They grew confident and comfortable enough to initiate sharing their thoughts. Liz even continued to pursue understanding in the face of many students who did not seem to share her perspective, but were instead trying to fix it.

As students learned to listen in order to understand each other's thinking in the Level 3 classroom, several positive classroom consequences resulted. For example, when a number of different solution strategies were possible for problems or situations, students listened carefully to contributions that others made to the discussion to be sure that what they would contribute would be new information. Listening to understand also launched students in the collaborative initiative to become assisters for one another, as in the excerpt above. To successfully assist one another, they needed an awareness of their own understanding of the material and they needed to understand one another's perspectives. Ms. Martinez increasingly relied on students who understood material to assist her in teaching students who did not yet fully understand. Students offered help and accepted help graciously from their fellow co-learners.

Moving Through the Levels

The case-study class moved quickly from Level 0 to Level 1 in all components of the math-talk learning framework. This movement can be attributed in part to the use of the CMW curriculum that supports a focus on student thinking and explaining of ideas. Changes similar to those in Level 1 were observed in Everyday Math classrooms (Mills, 1996; Mills, Fuson, & Wolfe, 1999).

Ms. Martinez's class then spent approximately 8 weeks at Level 1 before moving to Level 2. Because the Level 1 to Level 2 transition represents the greatest shift in the classroom—from the teacher as the central figure in the math-talk community to the students as central figures—this transition may represent a difficult change for the teacher and class to make and may take time even with students who are not also learning English.

The class operated as a Level 2 math-talk learning community for 3 months before exhibiting a majority of Level 3 characteristics. This transition to Level 3 was even more gradual than the Level 1 to Level 2 transition. Examples of Level 3 attributes occurred more frequently over time as students took on more central roles in the math-talk learning community. The class began to function fully as a Level 3 community early in March. Ms. Martinez left the school for her maternity leave early in April.

There were fluctuations from the overall upward trajectory in levels whenever new topics were introduced. Students needed to learn the new vocabulary and concepts of a new topic in order to function as a higher-level math-talk community. These drops in level were particularly apparent when the class shifted in December from their extensive work on multiplication and division to multidigit addition and subtraction.

It sometimes took the students several days to begin to resume their roles as question askers and explainers as they learned the language and representations of each new domain. During this adjustment time, Ms. Martinez functioned in a more central position and was responsible for more of the discourse. She stated, "Once I go over it and give them a sample of how I would explain, they seem to catch on better. They are more sure of what words to use and what drawings they can use, even though I tell them that whatever drawing is fine. But they are not sure if what they are going to say is right." Ms. Martinez asked many Level 1-type questions to support student familiarity with the language in the new areas of mathematics. Although Ms. Martinez resumed a more central role in these classes than she had in the preceding weeks, her goal was to familiarize students with the language of the new domain (e.g., place value) so they could resume their more significant roles in the math-talk learning community. Her growing belief in the abilities of her students motivated her to support them to participate in the math discourse quickly in each new domain. Furthermore, because the expectations of the class as a whole had changed, she noted, "When it's more of a teacher-centered class, I tend to lose kids." After brief functioning at Level 1, the class returned to higher Level 2 and Level 3 characteristics as they explored the new mathematics together.

Students' must have a grasp of the language of the domain of mathematics in order to carry on math talk both to describe one's own thinking question or extend the work of others. M. S. Smith (2000) similarly found that the teacher in her study was most directive at the beginning of a unit, and that later the class as a whole was more comfortable discussing the content. Mendez (1998) stated a similar conclusion in her study of robust mathematical discussions, "The need for significant mathematics within the students' zones of proximal development was found as another necessary condition for robustness" (p. 146). In other words, the mathematics must be accessible to students or familiar enough for them to be able to participate in meaningful discourse. As teachers move through the year, they will need to fall back to Level 1 or Level 2 to assist students in building vocabulary and concepts in new content areas. Furthermore, not every day includes extensive math talk. Some days may involve individual or student-assisting paired practice.

Teacher Actions Facilitating Transitions to New Levels

Ms. Martinez enacted particular actions to support class transitions from level to level across all of the components of the math-talk learning community, as shown in the summary in Table 5.5b. Each of these teacher actions was followed by a corresponding change in student actions. To move from Level 0 to Level 1, Ms. Martinez began to focus more on students' mathematical thinking as they arrived at answers and less on the answers themselves. To move from Level 1 to Level 2, Ms. Martinez increasingly expected students to take on substantial roles in the math-talk learning community, and she assisted them in learning these roles. Moving from Level 2 to Level 3 involved increasing expectations on Ms. Martinez's part that students would take central roles in the math-talk learning community; she gave them the space that they needed to take ownership of the roles, then she coached and assisted them as they became major participants in the math talk.

Table 5.5b   Ms. Martinez's Means of Assistance for Making the Transition to a New Level

	Means of Assistance
Level 0 to Level 1	Ms. Martinez began asking questions that focused on mathematical thinking rather than answers. She assisted students when they attempted this new task by modeling language.
Level 1 to Level 2	Ms. Martinez began to fade from the central role in the physical and discourse space and assisted students in taking on substantial roles in the discourse community. She probed for student thinking and assisted students in clarifying their thoughts when necessary. She asked questions that were open-ended rather than "fill in the blank" and sought extended descriptions of multiple student strategies.
Level 2 to Level 3	Ms. Martinez expected students to take on central roles and gave them the physical and discourse space to do so. She coached and assisted students in their participatory roles in the discourse. She expected students to assist one another voluntarily and assisted them in doing so. Ms. Martinez actively monitored interactions and remained available from the side or back of the room to assist when students needed clarification or when an interaction needed support.

Strength of the Student Community

The continuity of the community in Levels 2 and 3 was not totally dependent on the presence of Ms. Martinez. For example, continuity was apparent even when there was a substitute teacher during one observation near the end of November. In this class, individual students wrote solution strategies at the board. The substitute teacher asked students one by one to explain their work and tried to move quickly through the problems. Instead, her pace was interrupted numerous times by students saying they were not ready to move to the next problem because they had questions or comments for the student explainers. The substitute was amazed by the students' initiative. Similar events occurred after Ms. Martinez left for her maternity leave in April. Her replacement was unaccustomed to the level of involvement that the students initiated. This new teacher had to work to increase his level of expectation for the students and his own role in the mathematics classroom to fit into the existing math-talk learning community.

CONCLUSIONS AND FUTURE RESEARCH ∎

Principles and Standards for School Mathematics (NCTM, 2000) emphasizes the importance of learning in a mathematics community because it fosters students' communication of mathematical ideas and helps students to build mathematical understandings. Discussion of mathematical ideas provides opportunities for students to reason, defend, and prove their conceptions to one another. Over the course of the year, Ms. Martinez's students reached these challenging communication standards. Developing an environment where this type of math talk takes place can be a daunting task for teachers. By specifying components and levels in the creation of such an environment and by describing specific means of assistance that Ms. Martinez and her students provided to each other, this article offers assistance to others trying to build such a community. The framework can guide teachers to listen to their students, to draw out students' ideas, and to encourage students to listen to each other. Moreover, this study demonstrates that an effective math-talk learning community *can* be developed in urban classrooms, even with students still learning English. For this reason, we believe that the results described here are widely generalizable.

This research resonates with, and extends prior research on, the development of mathematical discourse. Like previous research, we have argued that opening up one's classroom to students' ideas is the critical first step in achieving a discourse community (e.g., Fennema et al., 1996). However, this article examines the steps beyond the initial Level 1 community and describes the interrelated components in a Level 2 and Level 3 discourse community.

Since its development, the math-talk framework that resulted from this study has been used with over 200 preservice and in-service teachers across multiple school settings in professional development situations. Teachers expressed the belief that the framework is accessible to them and also doable; it provided them with a vision for change. Specifically, many teachers attributed changes in their practice to conversations about the framework held in after-school mathematics meetings. The math-talk framework is one element that is possibly useful in scaffolding teacher change. Although this study focused on the change in practice of a person relatively new to the teaching profession, we have also found similar changes among more experienced teachers who discussed the framework described in this article (e.g., Drake, 2000).

Future research needs to focus more specifically on what happens during the transitions between levels in each of the components and how those transitions could be effectively supported in classrooms. It also needs to examine various ways to assist teachers in making these changes. In this research, the teacher was assisted by the research-based CMW curriculum, the reform-focused school administrators, and weekly feedback from the researcher. These together facilitated rapid change that could be studied and described over a several-month period. For widespread impact, there is a need to understand how to assist thousands of teachers in their movement through the levels of math-talk learning community with individual weekly support. Means of assistance that could be widely available are curricular supports embedded within a curriculum, materials to support teacher discussion and reflection, videos of classrooms illustrating the higher levels, and Web-based teacher assistance programs that could support answers to teacher's questions and teacher interaction and support of each other. Systems of teacher professional development that could help teacher-learning communities themselves move through math-talk levels would develop the truly expert teachers needed in the 21st century.

■ NOTES

1. Pseudonyms are used throughout this article for the school, teacher, and students.

2. The second author of this article was simultaneously conducting an empirical study of the implementation of Everyday Mathematics (see Mills, 1996; Mills, Fuson, & Wolfe, 1999).

3. Members of this group at Northwestern University included Josh Britton, Corey Drake, Kim Hufferd-Ackles, Radha Kalathil, Kim Montgomery, Miriam Sherin, and Ann Wallace.

■ REFERENCES

Ball, D. L., & Cohen, D. K. (1996). Reform by the book: What is—or might be—the role of curriculum materials in teacher learning and instructional reform? *Educational Researcher, 25*(9), 6–8, 14.

Brown, A. (1992). Design experiments: Theoretical and methodological challenges in creating complex interventions in classroom settings. *The Journal of the Learning Sciences, 2*(2), 141–178.

Cobb, P. (1994). Where is the mind? Constructivist and sociocultural perspectives on mathematical development. *Educational Researcher, 23*(7), 13–20.

Cobb, P., & Bauersfeld, H. (1995). Introduction: The coordination of psychological and sociological perspectives in mathematics education. In P. Cobb & H. Bauersfeld (Eds.), *The emergence of mathematical meaning: Interaction in classroom cultures* (pp. 1–16). Hillsdale, NJ: Lawrence Erlbaum Associates.

Cobb, P., Wood, T., & Yackel, E. (1990). Classrooms as learning environments for teachers and researchers. In R. B. Davis, C. A. Maher, & N. Noddings (Eds.), *Constructivist views on the teaching and learning of mathematics* (Journal for Research in Mathematics Education. Monograph No. 4, pp. 125–146). Reston, VA: National Council of Teachers of Mathematics.

Cobb, P., Yackel, E., & Wood, T. (1993). Learning mathematics: Multiple perspective, theoretical orientation. In T. Wood, P. Cobb, E. Yackel, & D. Dillon (Eds.), *Rethinking elementary school mathematics: Insights and issues* (Journal for Research in Mathematics Education. Monograph No. 6, pp. 21–32). Reston, VA: National Council of Teacher of Mathematics.

Cohen, D. (1990). A revolution in one classroom: The case of Mrs. Oublier. *Educational Evaluation and Policy Analysis, 12*(3), 327–345.

Day, C. (1988). The relevance and use of classroom research literature to the appraisal of teachers in classrooms: Issues of teacher learning and change. *Cambridge Journal of Education, 18*(3), 1–12.

Denzen, N. (1984). *The research act.* Englewood Cliffs, NJ: Prentice Hall.

Donmoyer, R. (1990). Generalizability and the single-case study. In E. Eisner & A. Peshkin (Eds.), *Qualitative inquiry in education: The continuing debate* (pp. 175–200). New York: Teachers College Press.

Drake, C. (2000). Stories and stages: Teacher development and mathematics education reform (Doctoral dissertation, Northwestern University, 2000). *Dissertation Abstracts International, 61,* 4273.

Fennema, E., Carpenter, T. P., Franke, M. L., Levi, L., Jacobs, V. R., & Empson, S. B. (1996). A longitudinal study of learning to use children's thinking in mathematics instruction. *Journal for Research in Mathematics Education, 27,* 403–434.

Fennema, E., & Nelson, B. S. (1997). *Mathematics teachers in transition.* Mahwah, NJ: Lawrence Erlbaum Associates.

Fuchs, L. S., Fuchs, D., Hamlett, C. L., & Karns, K. (1998). High-achieving students' interactions and performance on complex mathematical tasks as a function of homogeneous and heterogeneous pairings. *American Educational Research Journal, 35,* 227–267.

Fuson, K. C., De La Cruz, Y., Lo Cicero, A. M., Smith, S. T., Hudson, K., Ron, P., & Steeby, R. (2000). Blending the best of the 20th century to achieve a mathematics equity pedagogy in the 21st century. In M. Burke (Ed.), *Learning mathematics for a new century, 2000 yearbook* (pp. 197–212). Reston, VA: National Council of Teachers of Mathematics.

Fuson, K. C., Ron, P., Smith, S. T., Hudson, K., Lo Cicero, A., & Hufferd-Ackles, K. (1997). *Children's math worlds.* Evanston, IL: Author.

Fuson, K., Smith, S., & Lo Cicero, A. (1997). Supporting first graders' ten-structured thinking in urban classrooms. *Journal for Research in Mathematics Education, 28,* 738–766.

Gallimore, R., & Tharp, R. (1990). Teaching mind in society: Teaching schooling, and literate discourse. In L. C. Moll (Ed.), *Vygotsky and education: Instructional implication and application of socio-historical psychology* (pp. 175–205). Cambridge, UK: Press Syndicate of the University of Cambridge.

Heaton, R. M. (2000). *Teaching mathematics to the new standards: Relearning the dance.* New York: Teachers College Press.

Hufferd-Ackles, K. (1999). Learning by all in a math-talk learning community (Doctoral dissertation, Northwestern University, 1999). *Dissertation Abstracts International, 60,* 4303.

Jaworski, B. (1994). *Investigating mathematics teaching: A constructivist enquiry.* London: Falmer Press.

Mendez, E. P. (1998). Robust mathematical discussion (Doctoral dissertation, Stanford University, 1998). *Dissertation Abstracts International, 59,* 3765.

Miles, M., & Huberman, M. (1984). *Qualitative data analysis: A source book of new methods.* Beverly Hills, CA: Sage.

Mills, V. L. (1996). *Observing second-grade classrooms implementing Everyday Mathematics: What do we see of reform goals?* Paper presented at the annual meeting of the American Educational Research Association, New York, NY.

Mills, V. L., Fuson, K., & Wolfe, R. (1999). *Observing the implementation of a reform curriculum in elementary classrooms: What do we see of reform goals when teachers attempt to "do mathematics reform"?* Unpublished manuscript.

National Council of Teachers of Mathematics (2000). *Principles and standards for school mathematics.* Reston, VA: Author.

Romagnano, L. (1994). *Wrestling with change: The dilemma of teaching real mathematics.* Portsmouth, NH: Heinemann.

Sherin, M. G. (2002a). A balancing act: Developing a discourse community in a mathematics classroom. *Journal of Mathematics Teacher Education, 5,* 205–233.

Sherin, M. G. (2002b). When teaching becomes learning. *Cognition and Instruction, 20*(2), 119–150.

Sherin, M. G., Louis, D. A., & Mendez, E. P. (2000). Students' building on each other's mathematical ideas. *Mathematics Teaching in the Middle School, 6*(3), 122–125.

Shifter, D., & Fosnot, C. T. (1993). *Reconstructing mathematics education: Stories of teacher meeting the challenge of reform.* New York: Teachers College Press.

Silver, E. A., & Smith, M. S. (1996). Building discourse communities in mathematics classrooms: A worthwhile but challenging journey. In P. C. Elliott (Ed.), *Communication in mathematics, K–12 and beyond: 1996 yearbook* (pp. 20–28). Reston, VA: National Council of Teachers of Mathematics.

Smith, J. P. (1996). Efficacy and teaching mathematics by telling: A challenge for reform. *Journal for Research in Mathematics Education, 27,* 458–477.

Smith, M. S. (2000). Balancing old and new: An experienced middle school teacher's learning in the context of mathematics instructional reform. *Elementary School Journal, 100*(4), 351–375.

Spillane, J. (2000). A fifth grade teacher's reconstruction of mathematics and literacy teaching: Exploring interactions among identity, learning, and subject matter. *Elementary School Journal, 100*(4), 307–330.

Spillane, J. (2001). Challenging instruction for all students: Policy, practitioners, and practice. In S. Fuhrman (Ed.), *From the capital to the classroom: Standards based reform in the states, 100th yearbook of the National Society for the Study of Education* (pp. 217–241). Chicago: University of Chicago Press.

Stein, M., K., Grover, B. W., & Henningsen, M. (1996). Building student capacity for mathematical thinking and reasoning: An analysis of mathematical tasks used in reform classrooms. *American Educational Research Journal, 33,* 455–488.

von Glasersfeld, E. (1990). An exposition on constructivism: Why some like it radical. In R. B. Davis, C. A. Maher, & N. Noddings (Eds.), Constructivist views on the teaching and learning of mathematics (*Journal for Research in Mathematics Education.* Monograph No. 4, pp. 19–30). Reston, VA: National Council of Teachers of Mathematics.

Wood, T., Cobb, P., & Yackel, E. (1991). Change in teaching mathematics: A case study. *American Educational Research Journal, 28,* 587–616.

READING 5.6

Redefining Success in Mathematics Teaching and Learning

Margaret Schwan Smith

A major goal of current reform efforts is to help students learn mathematics with understanding. "Good" mathematical tasks are an important starting point for developing mathematical understanding, but selecting and setting up good tasks does not guarantee a high level of student engagement (Smith and Stein 1998). Using such tasks can, and often does, present challenges for teachers and students.

> **Reflection**
>
> What challenges have you faced in incorporating good mathematical tasks in the classroom?

Teachers, accustomed to establishing rules and procedures for students to follow, may have difficulty with a more nebulous set of responsibilities aimed at supporting students as they construct mathematical knowledge. Students may become frustrated with tasks that they cannot immediately solve and pressure the teacher to show them "how to do it." As a result, "good" tasks are often carried out in ways that remove the opportunities for problem solving and sense making (Doyle 1988; Stein, Grover, and Henningsen 1996) and reduce students' chances to engage in meaningful learning of mathematics (Stein and Lane 1996).

This situation occurs because teachers think that frustration and lack of immediate success are indicators that they have somehow failed their students. Teachers have no way to measure their own success when teaching is no longer defined as providing explanations and procedures or evaluating students' learning by the correctness of their solutions. According to J. P. Smith (1996), more traditional "teaching and telling" gives teachers a sense of efficacy—a perception that they have had a positive impact on students' learning—that is undermined by current efforts to reform mathematics instruction. Smith suggests that we need to establish "new moorings" for efficacy that are closely related to reform-oriented teaching to ensure that teachers will sustain their commitment to new ways of teaching.

What would constitute these "new moorings" to which Smith refers, and how will teachers come to establish these new indicators of success? Elaine Henderson (name changed), a teacher who participated in the QUASAR project, is an interesting case for exploring this question. QUASAR, which stands for Quantitative Understanding:

Source: Reprinted with permission from *Mathematics Teaching in the Middle School,* copyright © 2000 by the National Council of Teachers of Mathematics. All rights reserved.

Author's Note: This manuscript is based on the author's dissertation. An upcoming article in the *Elementary School Journal* offers a more extended discussion of Elaine Henderson and her learning during her first year of enacting an innovative curriculum (Smith, in press). The author wishes to acknowledge the helpful comments of Marjorie Henningsen on a previous draft of this article.

Amplifying Student Achievement and Reasoning, was a national project funded by the Ford Foundation to improve mathematics instruction for students attending middle schools in economically disadvantaged communities (Silver and Stein 1996; Silver, Smith, and Nelson 1995). A study of Henderson's teaching practice during her first year of implementing this innovative mathematics curriculum revealed that supporting students' engagement with "good" mathematical tasks required her to redefine what it meant for both herself and her students to be successful in mathematics class (Smith, in press). Over time, Henderson began to establish for herself new indicators that she was, in fact, having a positive impact on students' learning. I encourage you to reflect on your own experiences as you consider Henderson's practice at the beginning and end of her first year of "doing reform" in light of her changing views of success.

> **Reflection**
>
> What do you take as evidence of your success as a teacher of mathematics? What does it mean for students to be successful in your mathematics class?

BEFORE REFORM ■

Before her involvement in the QUASAR project, Henderson's goal in teaching mathematics was to ensure that her students would successfully learn the algorithms that they needed. She explained the procedures to be learned, demonstrated a small number of sample problems, monitored students' completion of a few problems, and had students work individually on a larger set of similar problems, using the strategies that she had taught.

Henderson had always considered herself to be a successful mathematics teacher—her students did well on the district standardized tests, teachers in subsequent grades who had her students always remarked that they were well prepared, and parents often requested that their children be placed in her classroom. Henderson saw herself as someone who related well to students and was able to motivate them to learn. She was always on the lookout for new ways to help her students experience success.

Henderson made the decision to participate in the QUASAR project in spring 1990 because she was intrigued by its approach to teaching mathematics, which emphasized thinking and reasoning and encouraged collaboration among students. She believed that such an approach could be beneficial to students, and she was eager to try something new. Henderson had always liked problem solving and found the tasks in the new curriculum to be more interesting than ones that she had typically used in the past. She also liked the fact that the project would give her the opportunity to work closely with her colleagues in mathematics and with teacher educators at a local university who would support the teachers' implementation efforts.

MAKING A CHANGE ■

Henderson spent several weeks working through the new curriculum with her school and university colleagues and found that she learned much about mathematics in the process. She was eager to give her students the same opportunity for learning. Early in the school year, however, Henderson began to notice that students were struggling with the tasks in the new curriculum. If they could not solve a problem immediately, which was often the case, they would just say, "I don't know" and give up. Henderson was concerned that her students were not actively participating in class. She believed that if students were not involved, they would not learn and that if they did not feel successful, they would lose their motivation to stay involved. As Henderson commented, "[I will] guarantee them success by asking them to do things they couldn't fail to do right. I can't ignore that success breeds success. Too many are starting out with what I'm sure they perceive to be failure."

Reflection

How might Henderson's alterations of tasks affect the level of challenge in the task, the kind of thinking required of students, or the mathematics that they might learn?

To ensure success, Henderson began altering problems from the curriculum. At times, she put in an extra step or took out something that she thought was too hard; she rewrote problem instructions to be clearer and created easier problems to lead up to more challenging ones. In addition, during classroom instruction, Henderson often "broke a task down" into a set of subtasks, each of which the students could complete successfully. Henderson believed that the more correct answers a student gets, the greater the learning he or she experiences. She tended to ask questions that were, as she explained, "not designed for deep thinking, just success."

A lesson on exploring patterns that took place in late October furnishes an example of how Henderson started supporting students' involvement with the new tasks. The curriculum materials suggested providing students with the first three trains in a pattern sequence, then asking students to build the fourth train. Next, the students were asked to build a larger train in the sequence, such as the tenth or fifteenth, without building all the trains in between, then discuss why they believed that the tenth or fifteenth train looked as it did. She presented the pattern shown in Figure 5.6a and gave student partners eleven minutes to write down what they noticed about each of the trains, which was a deviation from what the curriculum materials suggested. Henderson then asked students to share their observations orally and at times sent a student to the overhead projector to demonstrate an observation using overhead pattern tiles.

Figure 5.6a	Train Pattern

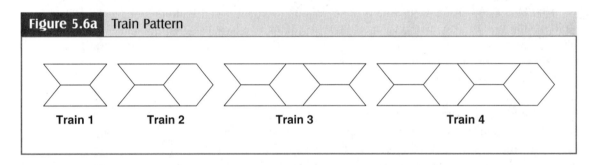

Train 1   Train 2   Train 3   Train 4

Some of the observations made by students were non-mathematical (e.g., "[the first train] looks like a squished pop can," "[the third train] looks like a belt buckle"). Others showed a basic understanding of a mathematical concept that pertained to only one train (e.g., "[the first train] has four equal sides," "[the second train has] two trapezoids and a hexagon"). A few attempted to look across trains (e.g., "they will have two [sides] that are equal and four [sides] that are equal," "trapezoids are double the number [of the train, if you replace the hexagons with trapezoids]"). Through teacher questioning, two generalizations emerged during the lesson: (1) for the even-number trains, the number of trapezoids was equal to the train number and (2) for the even-number trains, the number of hexagons was half the train number. Consider the following excerpt from the class in which Henderson tries to make sure that all her students "see" this pattern:

Ms. H.   Let's do a couple more. Listen to what he's saying, and see if you can do it also. Charles, in train 12, how many red trapezoids will there be?

Charles   Twelve.

Ms. H.   And then how many hexagons will there be?

Charles   Six.

Ms. H.   Can you do it for any even number I give you? Tony, what's he doing?

Tony	On the hexagons, he's doing the same number as the problem.
Ms. H.	On the what? Trapezoids or hexagons?
Tony	Trapezoids.
Ms. H.	The number of trapezoids is the same number as the trains.
William	And the hexagons, he's taking it in half.
Ms. H.	Take it in half for the hexagons, and it's the same for the other. OK, let's everybody try one. I can pick any even number: train 50. How many trapezoids will there be? Everybody!
SS	Fifty.
Ms. H.	How many hexagons?
SS	Twenty-five.
Ms. H.	Train 20, how many trapezoids?
SS	Twenty.
Ms. H.	How many hexagons?
SS	Ten.
Ms. H	Train 100, how many trapezoids?
SS	One hundred.
Ms. H.	How many hexagons?
SS	Fifty.
Ms. H.	All right, look up there. On train 50, will it end with two trapezoids or will it end with a hexagon?
SS	Hexagon.
Ms. H.	How do you know that? What up there tells you that? Michele, I haven't heard from you in a while.
Michele	The odds are the trapezoid, and evens are the hexagon.
Ms. H.	So you're saying to me that any number I tell you, you can tell me how it ends? Eleven.
Michele	It's odd. It would be trapezoid.

When the class was over, Henderson commented, "The lesson was all I could have asked of the kids . . . it was very exciting." She thought that the students had remained engaged throughout the period, the choral responses gave all the students an opportunity to feel good about themselves, and everyone seemed to be able to predict future trains using the generalizations.

> **Reflection**
>
> Do you agree with Henderson's assessment of how the lesson went? Why or why not? What questions might you ask of Henderson to find out more about whether the lesson was successful?

■ REFLECTING ON THE LESSON A FEW WEEKS LATER

At regular intervals over the course of the year, the classes of Henderson and her colleagues were videotaped. The videotapes and related observations were part of the ongoing efforts of the QUASAR project to document classroom practices. The videotapes were also used by teachers to reflect on their practices. At a staff-development session, Henderson volunteered to show the clip of the videotaped segment from the October lesson featuring the pattern-block sequence shown in Figure 5.6a and share their thoughts about the lesson. She commented that she had discovered that her students were not very good at observations, but she thought that they were definitely verbalizing more when she "broke it down" for them, focusing their attention on each part of a sequence rather than on the entire series.

One of the university teacher educators who was working with Henderson and her colleagues asked Henderson whether the students had progressed to the point at which they could make observations without her "breaking it down." The educator asked Henderson how long teachers need to break tasks down for students and whether Henderson thought that some of the observations would come out naturally if the students were given time and opportunity to develop them. Henderson responded that she hoped she did not always have to structure things but that her students were still at the "comfort stage" and needed this support. Once students experienced success, Henderson believed that they would try harder and would no longer need to have their learning experiences structured in this way.

The exchange with the educator appeared to have a powerful impact on Henderson. In her journal later that day, she reflected, "I need to make sure I'm not structuring too much. It is easy to be too leading and feel OK about it because the kids seem happy. After all, many kids are happy with 'shut up and add.'" Over time, Henderson continued to question her approach, wondering whether structuring the learning opportunities to ensure success would help students become competent and confident problem solvers—a central goal of the new curriculum—or whether the structuring would remove important challenging aspects from the students' mathematical experiences.

In an attempt to provide more problem-solving opportunities, during a quiz a few days later, Henderson asked students to divide a square into four congruent parts in five different ways. After students had found two solutions, they claimed that the problem could not be solved in other ways and started to give up. Henderson encouraged them to try different things to find the answer and explained to them "that they weren't really doing problem solving until they reached the point where they thought they couldn't do it." As she noted, "I'm used to the idea that their confusion means that I haven't introduced the lesson properly or have given kids something too hard. Sometimes that is true, but sometimes it is necessary to go through panic before we find solutions." Later that month, Henderson watched the entire videotape of the October pattern train lesson again and wrote the following entry in her journal:

> **Reflection**
>
> How would you say that Henderson is now defining success in mathematics teaching and learning? What appears to have changed about her definition of successful mathematics teaching and learning since the October lesson?

Students had ample opportunity to successfully predict visual pattern-block trains in this lesson, but it was set up too much for success and not enough for the frustration that goes with problem solving. Unfortunately, the lesson contained too much whole-group teacher questioning and students' explaining and not enough time for students to stretch and discover independently/ collaboratively. I made the lesson safe for the kids—no fail—which was my goal at the time. I now think I need to let them go through the frustration that goes with problem solving. The lesson probably wouldn't have looked as smooth, but I think it would have stretched the kids more. I am at a different point in my thinking than I was at the time of the lessons.

REDEFINING SUCCESS ■

Throughout the year, Henderson continued to struggle with her feelings of failure, concerns about her students' need for success, and her commitment to giving her students genuine problem-solving opportunities. For Henderson, redefining success required that she create new expectations for students of what it means to know and do mathematics and new expectations for her role in supporting students' learning. She came to believe that daily success should be measured by the extent to which students meet the expectations that she set for them and the extent to which she supported students in meeting those expectations. Henderson was effectively establishing "new moorings" for her own teaching of mathematics.

A series of lessons that Henderson conducted the next spring offers some insight into how these new moorings played out in her classroom. When the students were working in small groups or pairs on challenging problems, Henderson encouraged them to use diagrams and sketches as tools for solving problems, insisted that they be able to explain how they figured out problems, and encouraged them to consider alternative strategies. Many of Henderson's questions focused on trying to understand what students were doing as they solved the problems (e.g., "How did you get that?" "Why do you think that?" "What's happening here?") and on encouraging students to communicate (e.g., "Can you explain it to him?" "Why don't you ask your partner what she was doing first?"). When students presented their solutions at the overhead projector, the class was responsible for understanding the solutions and asking questions that would illuminate any errors in the approach. The teacher's periodic statement, "I assume that everyone understands if you have no questions," was a way of reminding students that the responsibility for understanding was theirs. Students assumed that they had given correct answers and had appropriately justified their solutions if no questions arose from their peers or the teacher, and this assumption was, in fact, true.

Although some problems were particularly difficult for students, rather than guide them step-by-step through the frustration, Henderson would ask one student to begin a problem at the overhead projector but not complete it. Henderson monitored the progress of the class but left her students to make sense of the presenter's explanation and determine how it would further their work on the problem.

Table 5.6a summarizes Henderson's new expectations for her students, her approach to supporting students in meeting the new expectations, and what she took as classroom-based evidence that students were successful. Classroom-based indicators of success, such as those found in Table 5.6a, present early evidence that changes in practice have occurred, which is a necessary first step before changes in student learning outcomes can be expected. In Henderson's situation, data collected on student performance showed that her students had grown over the year, as measured by a standardized test and an innovative performance assessment. By the end of the school year, Henderson thought that students were meeting the expectations that she had set for them and that she had done a good

> **Reflection**
>
> What can you conclude from the spring lessons about Henderson's new expectations for her students? How was she supporting students to enable them to meet her new expectations?

Table 5.6a   Key Elements in Henderson's Efforts to Redefine Success for Herself and Her Students

New Expectations for Students	Teacher Actions Consistent With Expectations	Classroom-Based Indicators of Success
Most "real" tasks take time to solve; frustration may occur; perseverance in the face of initial difficulty is important.	Use "good" tasks; explicitly encourage students to persevere; find ways to support students without removing all the challenges in a task.	Students engaged in the tasks and did not give up too easily. The teacher supported students when they "got stuck" but did so in a way that kept the task at a high level.
Correct solutions are important, but so is being able to explain how you thought about and solved the task.	Ask students to explain how they solved a task. Make sure that the quality of the explanations is valued equally as part of the final solution.	Students were able to explain how they solved a task.
Students have a responsibility and an obligation to make sense of mathematics by asking questions when they do not understand and by being able to explain and justify their solutions and solution paths when they do understand.	Give students the responsibility for asking questions when they do not understand, and have students determine the validity and appropriateness of strategies and solutions.	With encouragement, students questioned their peers and provided mathematical justifications for their reasoning.
Diagrams, sketches, and hands-on materials are important tools for students to use in making sense of tasks.	Give students access to tools that will support their thinking processes.	Students were able to use tools to solve tasks that they could not solve without them.
Communicating with others about your thinking during a task makes it possible for others to help you make progress on the task.	Ask students to explain their thinking, and ask questions that are based on students' reasoning, as opposed to how the teacher is thinking about the task.	Students explained their thinking about a task to their peers and the teacher. The teacher asked probing questions based on the student's thinking.

job in building a scaffolding for her students to support high-level thinking and reasoning.

■ SHARING YOUR REFLECTIONS

The purpose of this article is to raise questions about what it means to be successful as a teacher and as a student in reform-inspired mathematics classrooms. For Henderson, this questioning meant a year-long process of reflection on her practice and a redefinition of the factors that contribute to success. It is important to note that Henderson was not alone on her journey. She had the invaluable support of her teacher and university colleagues. I encourage you to discuss with your colleagues the issues raised in this article and to share through the "Teacher to Teacher" department in this journal your perspective on what it means to be successful.

REFERENCES ■

Doyle, Walter. "Work in Mathematics Classes: The Context of Students' Thinking during Instruction." *Educational Psychologist* 23 (February 1988): 167–80.

Silver, Edward, and Mary Kay Stein. "The QUASAR Project: The 'Revolution of the Possible' in Mathematics Instructional Reform in Urban Middle Schools." *Urban Education* 30 (January 1996): 476–521.

Silver, Edward, Margaret S. Smith, and Barbara Nelson. "The QUASAR Project: Equity Concerns Meeting Mathematics Education Reform in the Middle School." In *New Directions for Equity in Mathematics Education,* edited by Walter Secada, Elizabeth Fennema, and Lisa Adajian, pp. 9–56. New York: Cambridge University Press, 1995.

Smith, John P. "Efficacy and Teaching Mathematics by Telling: A Challenge to Reform." *Journal for Research in Mathematics Education* 27 (July 1996): 387–402.

Smith, Margaret S., and Mary Kay Stein. "Selecting and Creating Mathematical Tasks: From Research to Practice." *Mathematics Teaching in the Middle School* 3 (February 1998): 344–50.

Smith Margaret S. "Balancing Old and New: An Experienced Middle School Teacher's Learning in the Context of Mathematics Instructional Reform." *Elementary School Journal,* in press.

Stein, Mary Kay, and Suzanne Lane. "Instructional Tasks and the Development of Student Capacity to Think and Reason: An Analysis of the Relationship between Teaching and Learning in a Reform Mathematics Project." *Educational Research and Evaluation* 2 (October 1996): 50–80.

Stein, Mary Kay, Barbara W. Grover, and Marjorie Henningsen. "Building Student Capacity for Mathematical Thinking and Reasoning: An Analysis of Mathematical Tasks Used in Reform Classrooms." *American Educational Research Journal* 33 (October 1996): 455–88.

6 Session

How Can School Leaders Advance Their Mathematics Program Toward Success for All?

(Mathematics Improvement Process)

Thoughtful leadership, like thoughtful teaching, grows out of honing our vision for the work, gathering and reflecting on relevant information about the current situation in light of that vision, and building next steps from what we learn. This final session of *Secondary Lenses on Learning* is structured to launch teams on next steps for offering such thoughtful leadership for their mathematics programs.

The foundation for this work is Larry Lezotte's model of continuous improvement [Lezotte, L., & McKee, K. (2002). *Assembly required: A continuous school improvement system.* Okemos, MI: Effective Schools Products], including *Study, Reflect, Plan,* and *Implement* phases. We have "mathematized" Lezotte's model of continuous improvement for the purposes of *Secondary Lenses on Learning,* providing a process of reviewing key ideas from the five previous sessions of *Secondary Lenses on Learning,* and examining what has been learned about sites from the structured process of data collection and reflection. Based on this foundation, teams develop a draft of a mathematics program improvement plan for the building and begin planning its implementation. They also identify first steps they will take to advance mathematics in their schools and to involve other critical players in the work.

This session offers participants the opportunity to do the following:

- Examine the interconnectedness of the elements of school that contribute to mathematics achievement and the necessity of adjusting multiple aspects of the system and educators' practice in order to continuously move achievement forward
- Explore the use of data beyond state or nationally normed assessments to identify problems and plan for improvement
- Develop building mathematics program improvement plans for increasing student achievement (short and long term)
- Consider the benefits of building support for changes in mathematics education from teachers, administrators, students, parents, boards of education, and the wider community

Reading and Focus Questions to Prepare for Session 6

(One Homework Reading)

In preparation for the sixth session, please read the following article and prepare the focus questions in the page that follows.

Reading 6.1   Elmore, R. F. (2002). *Bridging the gap between standards and achievement: The imperative for professional development in education.* Washington, DC: Albert Shanker Institute.

READING 6.1 FOCUS QUESTIONS

Please read, and mark those paragraphs or short sections that seem most interesting to you. In particular, be prepared to discuss the following:

1. What does Elmore believe needs to change in schools in order for the system to survive?

2. What does Elmore state are the reasons why public schools do not improve?

3. What is the "reciprocal process" that Elmore talks about in his article?

4. What ideas and strategies does he suggest for improving schools, buildings, and student achievement?

5. How do the ideas presented by Elmore connect to the readings and discussions from the *Secondary Lenses on Learning* sessions?

Mark those paragraphs or short sections that relate to your notes. Be prepared to discuss them with other participants.

READING 6.1

Bridging the Gap Between Standards and Achievement

The Imperative for Professional Development in Education

Richard F. Elmore

THE IMPERATIVE: INVESTMENT IN ■ HUMAN SKILL AND KNOWLEDGE

The work of schools is becoming more complex and demanding while the organization of schools remains, for the most part, static and rigid. If you push hard enough on a rigid structure, eventually it will break and hurt the people in it. This is the perilous state of American public education.

The immediate cause of this situation is a simple, powerful idea dominating policy discourse about schools: That students should be held to high, common standards for academic performance and that schools and the people who work in them should be held accountable for ensuring that students—all students—are able to meet these standards. Accountability schemes come in many forms, including high-stakes student testing, district-led closure or restructuring of low-performing schools, and state takeovers of low-performing schools and districts.

The term "accountability" also can refer to many things, including rules and procedures, or to the delivery of certain types of academic content. But in this paper, I use the term only to refer to systems that hold students, schools or districts responsible for academic performance, since this is the dominant form of accountability in education today. Unfortunately, schools and school systems were not designed to respond to the pressure for performance that standards and accountability bring, and their failure to translate this pressure into useful and fulfilling work for students and adults is dangerous to the future of public education.

The standards and accountability movement is broad-based politically and persistent over time. It involves state legislators, governors, advocacy groups and professional organizations. It stems from the basic belief that schools, like other public and private organizations

---

Source: Copyright Albert Shanker Institute 2002.

Author's Note: The author wishes to thank Karen Wisniewski for her support in the preparation of this paper and Robert Floden for sharing his valuable thinking unselfishly at an important point in the research and writing. Special thanks to Deanna Burney, whose deep knowledge and wisdom about this work is an inspiration to me and to her other colleagues. And thanks to Eugenia Kemble, executive director of the Albert Shanker Institute, who is surely one of the world's most patient people.

in society, should be able to demonstrate what they contribute to the learning of students and that they should engage in steady improvement of practice and performance over time. The accountability movement expresses society's expectation that schools will face and solve the persistent problems of teaching and learning that lead to the academic failure of large numbers of students and the mediocre performance of many more. Over time, if schools improve, increased accountability will result in increased legitimacy for public education. Failure will lead to erosion of public support and a loss of legitimacy.

With increased accountability, American schools and the people who work in them are being asked to do something new—to engage in systematic, continuous improvement in the quality of the educational experience of students and to subject themselves to the discipline of measuring their success by the metric of students' academic performance. Most people who currently work in public schools weren't hired to do this work, nor have they been adequately prepared to do it either by their professional education or by their prior experience in schools. Schools, as organizations, aren't designed as places where people are expected to engage in sustained improvement of their practice, where they are supported in this improvement, or where they are expected to subject their practice to the scrutiny of peers or the discipline of evaluations based on student achievement. Educators in schools with the most severe performance problems face truly challenging conditions, for which their prior training and experience have not prepared them—extreme poverty, unprecedented cultural and language diversity and unstable family and community patterns. To work effectively under these conditions requires a level of knowledge and skill not required of teachers and administrators who work in less demanding situations, yet accountability systems expect the same level of performance of all students, regardless of social background. Hence, given the conditions of their work, some school-people regard demands for performance-based accountability as unreasonable. Throughout much of society and the economy, however, there has been a discernible shift toward performance and value-added measures of success triggered by the economic crisis of the late 1970s and early 1980s. In other high-skill, knowledge-based occupations—research and development, engineering, health care, even social services—some system of evaluation and accountability has been an important part of professional life for at least two decades. So when educators claim that they are being unfairly treated by a hostile accountability system, it's not surprising that people who work in other knowledge-intensive sectors are not particularly sympathetic.

The organization and culture of American schools is, in most important respects, the same as it was in the late nineteenth and early twentieth centuries. Teachers are still, for the most part, treated as solo practitioners operating in isolation from one another under conditions of work that severely limit their exposure to other adults doing the same work. The work day of teachers is still designed around the expectation that teachers' work is composed exclusively of delivering content to students, not, among other things, to cultivating knowledge and skill about how to improve their work.

The prevailing assumption is that teachers learn most of what they need to know about how to teach before they enter the classroom—despite massive evidence to the contrary—and that most of what they learn after they begin teaching falls into the amorphous category of "experience," which usually means lowering their expectations for what they can accomplish with students and learning to adjust to an organization that is either hostile to or unsupportive of their work. This limited view of what teachers need to know and do demands little educational leadership from administrators. And, since administrative work currently has little to do with the content of teaching, much less its improvement, it may actually act to protect teachers from various external intrusions on their isolated work.

The learning that is expected of teachers and administrators as a condition of their work also tends to be predicated on the model of solo practice. In order to advance in rank and salary, individual teachers and administrators are expected to accumulate academic credit for the university courses they take, any or all of which may be totally unconnected to their daily work. Most workplace learning also mirrors the norms of the organization—it takes the form of information about policies and practices delivered in settings disconnected from where the work of the organization is actually done.

> Despite massive evidence to the contrary, the prevailing assumption is that teachers learn most of what they need to know about how to teach before they enter the classroom.

It would be difficult to invent a more dysfunctional organization for a performance-based accountability system. In fact, the existing structure and culture of schools seems better designed to resist learning and improvement than to enable it. As expectations for increased student performance mount and the measurement and publication of evidence about performance becomes part of the public discourse about schools, there are few portals through which new knowledge about teaching and learning can enter schools; few structures or processes in which teachers and administrators can assimilate, adapt and polish new ideas and practices; and few sources of assistance for those who are struggling to understand the connection between the academic performance of their students and the practices in which they engage.

So the brutal irony of our present circumstance is that schools are hostile and inhospitable places for learning. They are hostile to the learning of adults and, because of this, they are necessarily hostile to the learning of students. They have been this way for some time. What's new about the current situation is that the advent of performance-based accountability has made the irony more visible—and may ultimately undermine the legitimacy of public education if something isn't done to change the way schools work.

Accountability must be a reciprocal process. For every increment of performance I demand from you, I have an equal responsibility to provide you with the capacity to meet that expectation. Likewise, for every investment you make in my skill and knowledge, I have a reciprocal responsibility to demonstrate some new increment in performance. This is the principle of "reciprocity of accountability for capacity." It is the glue that, in the final analysis, will hold accountability systems together (Elmore 2000). At the moment, schools and school systems are not designed to provide support or capacity in response to demands for accountability.

The imperative here is for professionals, policymakers and the public at large to recognize that performance-based accountability, if it is to do what it was intended to do—improve the quality of the educational experience for all students and increase the performance of schools—requires a strategy for investing in the knowledge and skill of educators. In order for people in schools to respond to external pressure for accountability, they have to learn to do their work differently and to rebuild the organization of schooling around a different way of doing the work. If the public and policymakers want increased attention to academic quality and performance, the *quid pro quo* is investing in the knowledge and skill necessary to produce it. If educators want legitimacy, purpose and credibility for their work, the *quid pro quo* is learning to do their work differently and accepting a new model of accountability.

THE KNOWLEDGE GAP IN PROFESSIONAL ■ DEVELOPMENT: THE IDEAL AND THE REAL

Professional development is the label we attach to activities that are designed in some way to increase the skill and knowledge of educators (Fenstermacher and Berliner 1985). In professional discourse, "professional development" is distinguished from "preservice" education by the fact that it occurs after teachers and administrators are on the job, during the routine course of their work. However, as we shall see later, this distinction is problematical in designing comprehensive approaches to the development of skill and knowledge. In practice, professional development covers a vast array of specific activities, everything from highly targeted work with teachers around specific curricula and teaching practices through short, "hit-and-run" workshops designed to familiarize teachers and administrators with new ideas or new rules and requirements, to off-site courses and workshops designed to provide content and academic credit for teachers and administrators.

So, to say that we should invest more money in "professional development" in the present context is not to say anything very meaningful. The connection between professional development, as presently practiced, and the knowledge and skill of educators is tenuous at best; its relationship to the imperative of improving instruction and student performance is, practically speaking, nonexistent (Feiman-Nemser 1983, 163). Spending more money on existing professional development activities, as most are presently designed, is unlikely to have any significant effect on either the knowledge and skill of educators or on the performance of students.

Yet, much of the literature written by researchers and practitioners about professional development seems quite sensible and useful in thinking about how to design and operate professional development activities that have some likelihood of improving teaching and learning. The research is rarely grounded in hard empirical evidence about its effects on practice or on student learning, but it certainly provides an ample basis for designing activities that could be subjected to empirical testing.

Consensus on Effective Professional Development

Educators' professional literature and academic research reflect a broad consensus on the main features of effective professional development. Exhibit 6.1a presents one summary of this consensus. This account of the consensus view draws heavily on the original standards for professional development adopted by the National Staff Development Council in 1995 (Sparks and Hirsch 1997, Sparks 1995).[1] In this view, effective professional development is focused on the improvement of student learning through the improvement of the skill and knowledge of educators. In a given school or school system, specific professional development activities would follow from a well articulated mission or purpose for the organization and that purpose would be anchored on some statement about student learning. So, for example, a school or system might say that its objective over a period of time would be to improve students' demonstrated knowledge and skill in reading, writing and mathematics as measured by portfolios of student work, curriculum-based assessments and state- or district-administered examinations. From this broad statement of purpose, the school or district might derive expectations focused more specifically on certain settings—e.g., basic reading and writing skills among students with learning problems in the primary grades, inferential and problem-solving skills in algebra in the middle grades, interpretation and analysis of expository and technical writing in the upper grades.

The point here is that professional development, if it is to be focused on student learning, at some point must be tailored to address the difficulties encountered by real students in real classrooms as well as broader systemic objectives. Similarly, effective professional development is connected to questions of content and pedagogy that educators are asking—or should be asking—about the consequences of their instructional practices on real students as well as in general questions about effective teaching practice.

Exhibit 6.1a   Professional Development: The Consensus View

- Focuses on a well-articulated mission or purpose anchored in student learning of core disciplines and skills
- Derives from analysis of student learning of specific content in a specific setting
- Focuses on specific issues of curriculum and pedagogy
  - Derived from research and exemplary practice
  - Connected with specific issues of instruction and student learning of academic disciplines and skills in the context of actual classrooms
- Embodies a clearly articulated theory or model of adult learning
- Develops, reinforces, and sustains group work
  - Collaborative practice within schools
  - Networks across schools
- Involves active participation of school leaders and staff
- Sustains focus over time—continuous improvement
- Models of effective practice
  - Delivered in schools and classrooms
  - Practice is consistent with message
- Uses assessment and evaluation
  - Active monitoring of student learning
  - Feedback on teacher learning and practice

Professional development brings the general and the externally validated in contact with the specific and the contextual. So, for example, an elementary school with persistently low reading scores and many students who have basic decoding and comprehension difficulties might focus its professional development activities on instructional strategies to improve students' skills in those domains—especially those that work well in concert with the schools' specific reading program. Or, a secondary school struggling with the introduction of a new requirement that all students demonstrate a knowledge of basic algebra might focus its professional development efforts on strategies to engage students who previously would not have been expected to master this level of mathematics.

According to the consensus view, the practice of professional development, however focused and wherever enacted, should embody a clear model of adult learning that is explained to those who participate. Those who engage in professional development should be willing to say explicitly what new knowledge and skill educators will learn as a consequence of their participation, how this new knowledge and skill will be manifested in their professional practice, and what specific activities will lead to this learning.

Professional development, in the consensus view, should be designed to develop the capacity of teachers to work collectively on problems of practice, within their own schools and with practitioners in other settings, as much as to support the knowledge and skill development of individual educators. This view derives from the assumption that learning is essentially a collaborative, rather than an individual, activity—that educators learn more powerfully in concert with others who are struggling with the same problems—and that the essential purpose of professional development should be the improvement of schools and school systems, not just the improvement of the individuals who work in them. The improvement of schools and school systems, likewise, has to engage the active support and collaboration of leaders, not just their tacit or implicit support, and this support should be manifested in decisions about the use of time and money.

Professional development in the service of improvement requires commitment to consistency and focus over the long term. The broad mission and goals that shape professional development should reflect a path of continuous improvement in specific domains of student learning. The activities should be continuous from one year to the next. As schools reach one set of objectives, they should move on to more ambitious ones and educators should demonstrate continuity and consistency in the improvement of their practice in specific domains from one year to the next. So, for example, a school district might frame broad goals for the improvement of student learning in basic academic content areas. It would then work out with each school a more specific plan of action based on the profile of that school's student population and patterns of student performance—adjusting performance expectations upward each year as the school advances.

The focus of professional development on enacted practice—the combination of academic content and pedagogy into classroom delivery that is responsive to issues of student learning in specific settings—requires that the physical location of the learning be as close as possible to where the teaching itself occurs. Hence, successful professional development is likely to occur in schools and classroom settings, rather than off-site, and it is likely to involve work with individual teachers or small groups around the observation of actual teaching. Proximity to practice also requires that the pedagogy of professional developers be as consistent as possible with the pedagogy that they expect from educators. It has to involve professional developers who, through expert practice, can model what they expect of the people with whom they are working.

Finally, successful professional development—because it is specifically designed to improve student learning—should be evaluated continuously and primarily on the basis of the effect it has on student achievement.

Potential Areas of Conflict and Disagreement

Within this broad consensus on the essentials of effective professional development there is plenty of disagreement. Associations that represent coalitions of practitioners—such as the National Staff Development Council (NSDC)—tend to present their recommendations as voluntary and consensual. They view a school system's process of creating a professional development strategy as consensus building—between the system and its community and among teachers and administrators within schools. In their words, "Everyone works together to identify strategies and develop action plans consistent with the district's overall mission" (Sparks 1995). In reality, deciding on who sets the purpose and focus of professional development is often conflict-ridden, especially in systems with high proportions of low-performing students. Student learning is a function, in part, of adult expectations; when educators work in schools where expectations for student achievement are chronically low or where expectations are highly differentiated, a consensus professional development plan may only institutionalize mediocrity and low performance. Hence, connecting professional development to the overall improvement of student achievement is likely to raise key issues about teaching and learning that may never arise through a process of simple consensus building.

Similarly, the idea of voluntarism raises the question of whether teachers should be able to choose to participate in professional development activities in their schools, whether schools should be required to participate in an overall process for determining which professional development activities should be present in their schools, and whether there should be a systemwide instructional improvement process that limits and focuses professional development activity within schools. There are two fundamental principles in tension here: the first suggests that professional development should be focused on systemwide improvement, which leads to limiting individual and school discretion; the other suggests that educators should play a major role in determining the focus of professional development, both for themselves and for their schools. These principles can be difficult to reconcile, especially in the context of an accountability system that emphasizes measurable student performance.

> Successful professional development—because it is specifically designed to improve student learning—should be evaluated continuously and primarily on the basis of the effect it has on student achievement.

Another difficult issue arises out of the relationship between professional development and personnel evaluations. If professional development occurs in close proximity to practice, then professional developers are likely to know a great deal about the strengths and weaknesses of the teachers with whom they work. Also, if principals are closely involved with the planning and implementation of the school's professional development activities, they will tend to treat the knowledge they gain from observing teacher practices as useful in their responsibility for evaluating those teachers. One possibility is that the learning objectives of professional development are corrupted by the possibility that they will be used for evaluation. Another possibility is that, in a well-functioning school, professional development is part of a seamless process of instruction and improvement for adults and children, and that it is almost impossible to pull the two apart. Whichever view you take, active pursuit of professional development is likely to create conflict around its relationship to teacher evaluation.

Finally, guidance about successful professional development fails to resolve an important issue of content versus process. In general, advocates of thoughtful, systematic approaches to school improvement (see Fullan 1991) stress that to change their schools educators need to develop skill and knowledge about the fundamentals of group problem-solving and interpersonal skills. At the same time, professional development that improves student learning must involve hard, detailed work on the fundamentals of content and pedagogy. In principle, there is no conflict between these purposes. In practice, they are likely to be in constant tension. In some senses, it is easier for educators to focus on issues of process—at the expense of issues of content and pedagogy (see below and Little 1990)—because process can be framed so as to avoid difficult questions of teacher autonomy and control. For example, we can agree, as a matter of process, to treat all issues of pedagogy as matters of personal taste. But doing so would mean that decisions about professional development would be largely personal also, disconnected from collective knowledge about best practice in the improvement of student learning. Thus, the prospects for large-scale improvement would remain dim.

THE PRACTICE OF PROFESSIONAL ■ DEVELOPMENT: THE REAL

While there is evidence that the consensus about effective professional development has influenced the way professional associations and researchers portray the field, there is little evidence that this consensus has had a large-scale effect on the practices of schools and school systems.

School systems use a more or less standard model for handling issues of professional development, and this model is largely, if not entirely, at odds with the consensus about effective practice. Few school districts treat professional development as a part of an overall strategy for school improvement. In fact, many districts do not even have an overall strategy for school improvement. Instead, districts tend to see staff development as a specialized activity within a bureaucratic structure. In some instances, there are particular people with assigned roles who work with teachers and principals around content. In other instances, professional development is a function of certain categorical programs designed to serve special student populations, such as English language learners, poor students, students with disabilities, or the gifted and talented. In many cases, individual teachers—and sometimes whole schools—are required to have a coordinated professional development plan. Yet these plans are often nothing more than a collection of teachers' individual activities over the course of a year, without a general design or specific focus that relates particular activities to an overall strategy or goal (Little 1993).

Most school systems organize formal professional development around specified days. Teachers are relieved from their regular duties to participate in activities that are usually unrelated to instructional practice, except in the broadest sense of that term. Designed to serve the widest possible audience, systemwide professional development is usually focused on specific and disconnected topics—student discipline, test preparation, district and state policy changes—and typically occurs in large-group settings away from classrooms and schools. Often these days are specified contractually through local collective bargaining agreements, so that professional development becomes associated with a specific number of discrete days disconnected from any focused strategy to equip teachers with the knowledge and skill they need to improve student learning in specific domains. More importantly, the incentive structures under which most teachers work reward them with salary increases for the courses they take on their own time and largely outside of the schools and systems in which they work, either through private vendors or colleges of education. There is usually no incentive and little guidance for aligning these courses with school and district priorities. Thus, most courses are determined by individual teacher preference.

The Gap

Whatever else one might say about the consensus view of effective professional development, it is, at the very least, a reasonable working theory for the design of large-scale professional development activities. In response to demands for accountability, it rightly aims to improve teaching practice and student learning. The main elements of the consensus view—a strong focus on systemwide and schoolwide performance goals, heavy emphasis on teachers' content knowledge and the pedagogical skills that go with effective instruction, explicit theories of adult learning, use of group settings, moving learning close to the point of practice, etc.—are all things that could be operationalized, evaluated and studied for their effectiveness in improving practice. The terms of the consensus view are sufficiently clear to be broadly communicated. The guidance of the consensus view is sufficiently broad to be applicable in a variety of settings and adaptable to a variety of contexts. And finally, the potential conflicts that arise out of the consensus view are problems that can be understood and anticipated.

The knowledge gap, then, is not so much about knowing what good professional development looks like; it's about knowing how to get it rooted in the institutional structure of schools. The problem is connecting the ideal prescriptions of the consensus model with the real problems of large-scale improvement and accountability.

Exhorting schools and school systems to engage in more enlightened professional development practices, even under the pressure of performance-based accountability, is unlikely to have much effect without more explicit guidance about how to bring these more enlightened practices into the mainstream of school life. This knowledge gap requires more explicit attention to the practice of improvement.

The Varieties and Costs of Failure

As noted above, the relationship between professional development and accountability is essentially reciprocal. It is an investment in knowledge and skill in order to achieve an end. Those who are being "developed" must consent to learning what they are being asked to do and how to do it; those who are demanding results must understand that school personnel are being asked to implement practices they currently do not know how to do. Both parties should understand that most learning occurs through experimentation and error, not through a straight linear process. It is in this domain of reciprocity that failures are most likely to occur.

Judith Warren Little suggests that the traditional "training model" of professional development—which assumes that a clearly-defined body of skills can be transferred from trainers to teachers through a well-specified process—is largely inappropriate, given the complexity of the tasks that are required for all schools to help students meet high academic standards. She recommends a variety of approaches that take explicit account of the difficult work required of teachers to meet new expectations, the level of commitment and energy they will need to learn and develop effective new practices, and the uncertainty about whether externally developed solutions will work in their specific classroom contexts (Little 1993).

More direct linkages between professional development and accountability will fail—or at the very least will be relatively ineffective—to the extent that they turn professional development into a tool for control. They will succeed to the degree that they engage teachers and administrators in acquiring knowledge and skills they need to solve problems and meet expectations for high performance. To the degree that people are being asked to do things they don't know how to do and, at the same time, are not being asked to engage their own ideas, values and energies in the learning process, professional development shifts from building capacity to demanding compliance.

The avenues for failure are many: Administrators can construct professional development as training in discrete skills that teachers feel have limited or no applicability to their real work. The level of support for teachers and administrators in learning new practices can be too weak relative to the demands that learning and implementing the new practices will make on them. Problems in connecting new practices to the specific demands that teachers face can be ignored or pushed aside by administrators or professional developers. Or, the new practices themselves may simply not work as intended.

The costs of these failures may be high: the loss of credibility for professional development as an essential activity in the organization; the loss of commitment to building the knowledge and skill that teachers and administrators need to be effective; and, an undermining of the premise of improvement—that is, the premise that investment in educators' skills and knowledge can be connected to improvement in student achievement. Later, I will speak to these issues under the heading of capacity building. For now, it is important to reinforce the idea that professional development and accountability are reciprocal processes demanding high engagement in both policy and practice, and that the long-term objective of investing in educators' skills and knowledge is to increase the capacity of schools to solve pressing problems through the application of best practice, not just to implement someone else's solutions.

■ THE PRACTICE OF IMPROVEMENT: GETTING FROM HERE TO THERE

In its simplest form, the practice of large-scale improvement is the mobilization of knowledge, skill, incentives, resources and capacities within schools and school systems to increase student learning. Strictly speaking, the practice of improvement is the sharing of a set of proven practices and their collective deployment for a common end. It is not the property of any one individual or any incumbent in any specific job. It is not the property of teachers or administrators or professional developers. It is a common set of practices shared across the profession, irrespective of roles.

Large-scale improvement intends to reach *all* students in *all* classrooms and all schools through the daily work of teachers and administrators. The idea of *improvement* means measurable increases in the quality of instructional practice and student performance over time. Quality and performance are on the vertical axis; time is on the horizontal axis; and improvement is movement in a consistently northeasterly direction.

Improvement, as we will use the term here, means engagement in learning new practices that work, based on external evidence and benchmarks of success, across multiple schools and classrooms, in a specific area of academic content and pedagogy, resulting in continuous improvement of students' academic performance over time. Improvement is not random innovation in a few classrooms or schools. It does *not* focus on changing processes or structures, disconnected from content and pedagogy. And it is *not* a single-shot episode. Improvement is a discipline, a practice that requires focus, knowledge, persistence and consistency over time.

Notice that the term "change" does not occur in any of these definitions. Change in the discourse of education is overused and under-defined. Change is generally regarded as positive, even when it achieves no discernible results. Schools are accustomed to changing—promiscuously and routinely—without producing any improvement. When I use the term change (which is rarely), I use it only to refer to specific alterations of existing structures, processes, or practices that are intended to result in improvement. In other words, change, in my vocabulary, is motivated and judged by the standard of student learning.

The practice of large-scale improvement is the process by which external demands for accountability are translated into concrete structures, processes, norms and instructional practices in schools and school systems. Professional development is the set of knowledge- and skill-building activities that raise the capacity of teachers and administrators to respond to external demands and to engage in the improvement of practice and performance.

In this context, professional development is effective only to the degree that it engages teachers and administrators in large-scale improvement. This is an intentionally narrow and instrumental view.[2] Professional development, as it is typically practiced, confuses the individual's personal growth and learning with the growth and learning of the individual that contributes to organizational performance. When teachers present individual professional development plans, for example, it is often unclear which activities are designed to enhance their individual growth and which are designed to improve their practice as teachers in a particular organization with clear goals. Likewise, courses and workshops that are offered for academic credit are often focused on the individual interests of teachers and administrators more than on the development of a shared body of skills and knowledge, necessary for schools and districts to implement a common set of successful practices.

Professional development, as I will use the term in the context of large-scale improvement, is a *collective good* rather than a private or individual good. Its value is judged by what it contributes to the individual's capacity to improve the quality of instruction in the school and school system.

HOW PROFESSIONAL DEVELOPMENT ■
CAN WORK TO IMPROVE SCHOOLS

Whether professional development improves instructional quality and academic performance depends as much on the characteristics of the organization it serves as on the characteristics of the professional development activity itself. The features of effective professional development, as described in Exhibit 6.1a, embody some very heroic assumptions about the organizational context in which the activity occurs. For example, focusing professional development on a well-articulated mission or purpose anchored in student learning assumes that leaders know what purposes the system is pursuing and can articulate them specifically enough to identify the particular professional development activities that are needed to support them. Deriving professional development from an analysis of what is needed to improve student learning assumes that the system has the capacity to capture useful, accurate information about student learning and that the people in the system have the capacity to apply that information to decisions about instructional content and professional development. Developing and sustaining group work assumes that there is time in the instructional day and that teachers and administrators have the norms and skills that are required for productive group work. And so forth down the list. At this point, one is reminded of the saying, "If we had some ham, we could have some ham and eggs—if we had some eggs." It does little good to know what quality professional development might look like if schools and school systems are incapable of supporting it.

In summary, the practice of improvement is largely about moving whole organizations—teachers, administrators and schools—toward the culture, structure, norms and processes that support quality professional development in the service of student learning. In addition, the practice of improvement at the individual and organizational levels involves mastery in several domains (see Exhibit 6.1b): knowledge and skill; incentives; and resources and capacity. The knowledge and skill domain asks what people need to know in order to improve the quality and effectiveness of their practice, and under what conditions

---

Exhibit 6.1b   Domains in the Practice of Large-Scale Improvement

Students' Knowledge and Skill

- What do students need to know and be able to do?
- Under what conditions will they learn it?

Educators' Knowledge and Skill

- What do educators need to know and be able to do to help all students succeed?
- Under what conditions will they learn it?

Incentives

- What rewards and penalties encourage large-scale improvement?
- Who will receive these incentives and who decides, using what criteria?

Resources and Capacity

- What material supports lead large-scale improvement?

they are most likely to learn it. The incentives domain asks what kinds of encouragements and rewards people should receive for acquiring this knowledge and using it to enhance performance and support improvement. The resources and capacity domain asks what level of material support and what kinds of capacities—organizational and individual—the system needs to ensure that professional development leads to large-scale improvement.

Knowledge and Skill

The practice of improvement involves the acquisition of new knowledge, connecting that knowledge with the skills necessary for effective practice and creating new settings where learning can occur. As an illustration, take what has become a central problem of performance-based accountability in secondary schools—teaching algebra to all secondary school students.

This seemingly reasonable goal raises a formidable array of practical problems. By the time students reach the ninth or tenth grade, their range of mathematics performance is usually quite wide. Historically, algebra was taught largely to college-bound students who represent the upper range of performance and, perhaps, have a higher level of motivation to master the new subject-matter. The new focus on increasing the number of students taking algebra means more algebra classes, which means more algebra teachers—all in a market where mathematics teachers are in short supply.

Most secondary schools solve this problem by drafting teachers with inadequate math skills into teaching the additional classes, typically assigning them to the classes with the lowest-achieving students. In addition, most secondary schools will continue to teach every algebra class with the methods that have always been used to teach well-prepared college-bound students, just adding sections. Using teachers whose main expertise may not be in mathematics instruction, they also layer on remedial classes—conducted after-school, by extending class periods during the regular day, or during summer sessions—to accommodate the students who fail to master the content, either because they have difficulty with math or because their algebra classes were badly-taught the first time around.

In other words, the school's response to the requirement that all students learn algebra is to make marginal adjustments in organizational structure (remedial classes, more sections), while leaving teachers' knowledge and skill essentially untouched. What this approach ignores, of course, is that the algebra requirement presents an instructional problem that few schools have faced before—how to deal with a broad range of mathematical skill and knowledge among students and teachers. Addressing this instructional problem will require that everyone involved in teaching algebra learn something new about both the content and the pedagogy required to reach students with a wide range of skill and preparation levels.

There are many other, similar examples: students in the early grades being expected to demonstrate mastery of written text in a language they don't yet comprehend; students arriving in the eighth or tenth grade who are expected to provide written interpretations of text that they don't have the literacy skills to understand; students in secondary school who perform well on tasks that involve factual recall, but who have not been taught to answer questions that require interpretation and analysis. These problems all have a common structure. In fact, at some level, they are the same problem: They all involve a fundamental issue of practice that challenges the existing structure of schools, and they all require more knowledge and skill of the people who work there. They all require people in the organization, not just to do their work differently, but to think differently about the nature and purpose of their work. And, they all require a high degree of cooperation among people with diverse roles in deploying the skills and knowledge that are necessary to help students with very different levels of interest prepare to meet common, high expectations for learning. These problems also expose the weakest aspects of schools and school systems as organizations. Their solution requires traditionally isolated teachers to act in concert with each other around common issues of content and practice and they require administrators to play a much more active role in the provision and improvement of instruction.

Interestingly, though, these problems lie in a domain about which we know a considerable amount. Here, in summary, is what the research says about the issues of knowledge and skill in the improvement of practice:

Expertise in teaching exists. It can be identified and it can be enhanced through professional development, but it doesn't necessarily support improvement in student achievement. The knowledge necessary for successful teaching lies in three domains: (1) deep knowledge of the subject-matter (i.e., history and mathematics) and skills (i.e., reading and writing) that are to be taught; (2) expertise in instructional practices that cut across specific subject areas, or "general pedagogical knowledge"; and (3) expertise in instructional practices that address the problems of teaching and learning associated with specific subjects and bodies of knowledge, referred to as "pedagogical content knowledge."

Novice teachers differ markedly from expert teachers in their command of these domains and their ability to use them. For example, they differ in the array of examples and strategies they can use to explain difficult concepts to students, in the range of strategies they can employ for engaging students who are at different performance levels, and in the degree of fluency and automaticity with which they employ the strategies they know. Professional development that results in significant changes in practice will focus explicitly on these domains of knowledge, engage teachers in analysis of their own practice, and provide opportunities for teachers to observe experts and to be observed by and to receive feedback from experts. One aspect of expertise, however, sometimes works against improvement. When the deeply embedded practices of experienced teachers run against new models of practice, when teachers are asked to challenge what they think about the range of student knowledge and skill they can accommodate in a given classroom, entrenched beliefs can work against the acquisition of new knowledge. Thus, one aspect in improving the quality of teaching is often *un*learning deeply seated beliefs and implicit practices that work against the development of new, more effective practices (Borko and Putnam 1995; Feiman-Nemser 1983; Clark and Peterson 1986).

> These problems all require people in the organization, not just to do their work differently, but to think differently about the nature and purpose of their work.

So while expertise exists, matters and can be improved, it is not true that experience equals expertise. That is, deep knowledge in the domains necessary to become a powerful and fluent practitioner does not automatically, or even reliably, come as a result of continuous practice. In fact, the evidence is substantial that the early socialization of teachers, coupled with the isolation of teaching, rather quickly socializes novices into what Feiman-Nemser calls a "utilitarian" view of teaching, characterized by narrow focus and routinization rather than active learning and the deepening of knowledge (Feiman-Nemser 1983, 156). The disjunction between experience and expertise is an issue to which we will return, but it is important to acknowledge that, in a system that values expertise and its dissemination, it may be necessary to make judgments about who has it that are at odds with the conventional view that experience inevitably leads to expertise.

Learning is both an individual and a social process. Capturing individual learning for the benefit of the group enterprise depends on structures that support interdependence in serious, substantive ways. It is now commonplace to argue, as does the consensus view of professional development, that teachers learn through social interaction around problems of practice and that the enhancement of teacher learning requires support for collegial interaction where teachers can work on new practices.

A substantial part of the research in this domain takes its conceptual guidance from the idea of "communities of practice"; that is, informal social networks of people who share concrete ideas, values and norms about their work (Lave and Wenger 1991; Wenger 1998). While it is clear that the creation of social networks can have a significant effect on the development of new practices among experienced teachers (e.g., Stein, Smith, and Silver 1999), it is also clear that certain forms of collegiality work against improvement. Mandated activities that have little or no purpose or utility, activities that stress the social aspects of collegiality over the use of collegiality to enhance instructional practice, and forms of interaction that aren't grounded in the quest to improve student achievement—all these forms of collegiality are likely to sidetrack cooperative work away from improvement (Bird and Little 1986; McLaughlin and Yee 1988; Brown, Collins and Duguid 1989; Hargreaves 1991; Huberman 1995). In general, the existing school structure, which is organized to reinforce isolated work and problem solving, makes collaboration very expensive. Thus, collaborative professional development activities that are not engaging and demonstrably useful to teachers and administrators can lead quickly to cynical compliance or outright resistance.

Practice and values change in concert. Both are important and both should be the focus of new learning for teachers and administrators. I began by stating that performance-based accountability systems are asking the people who work in schools to do things they currently don't know how to do. They are also asking many people to do things they don't think are possible and may not even believe are desirable. Experienced teachers often have very strong, fixed ideas about which students can master high academic standards and which can't. They also have very strong ideas about which kinds of practices will work for their students and which won't. These ideas are formed from experience, personal values and knowledge of pedagogy and content. By virtue of their working conditions, most teachers deal with issues of practice in a very particularistic way. Thus, more likely than not, broad guidance about instructional practice or even very specific guidance without a strong connection to the particular circumstance or specific curriculum that must be taught, will have little or no effect on practice.

Improving instructional practice requires a change in beliefs, norms and values about what it is possible to achieve as well as in the actual practices that are designed to bring achievement. In other words, improvement requires a theory of individual learning. This is a domain in which there is not likely to be a high level of disagreement about the right working theory. In the short run, it is probably more important to have an explicit working theory than it is to have any one working theory in particular. One example of a well-specified and tested theory of individual learning and improvement is Guskey's (1989) theory of attitude and perceptual change in teachers. He argues that practice changes attitudes rather than vice versa. Rather than exhorting teachers to believe that students can learn differently, or that different students can learn at higher levels, then showing teachers the practices that go with these beliefs, Guskey argues that teachers must actually try these new practices with the students for whom they believe the practices are problematical. If the new practices succeed with those students, then teachers have the opportunity to reflect on their values and attitudes, and on the changes in them that are required as a result of this experience. Guskey found that teachers who were able to use certain practices successfully "expressed more positive attitudes toward teaching and increased personal responsibility for their students' learning" (Guskey 1989, 444). He concludes that changes in attitudes and beliefs generally follow, rather than precede, changes in behavior.

> Few people willfully engage in practices that they know to be ineffective; most educators have good reasons to think that they are doing the best work they can.

An important implication of Guskey's theory is that instruction itself is probably the most potent form of professional development available to schools. This organizational reality can operate both for and against improvement. Guskey puts it this way: "The instructional practices that most veteran teachers employ are fashioned to a large extent by their experiences in the classroom. Practices that are found to 'work,' that is, those leading to desired learning outcomes, are retained; others are abandoned. Hence, a key determinant of enduring change in instructional practices is demonstrable results in terms of students' performance. Activities that are demonstrably successful tend to be repeated while those that are not successful, or for which there is no tangible evidence of success, are dropped" (Guskey, 445). It follows that, if most of what teachers learn about practice they learn from their own practice, it is imperative to make the conditions and context of that practice supportive of high and cumulative levels of achievement for all students. Which leads to the last principle under knowledge and skill, which is . . .

Context matters. Improvement requires a more or less specific understanding or theory about what matters in a given context—a classroom, a school, a school system—in line with the overall purposes and standards by which performance is being judged. Any accountability system, any system of improvement, any professional development strategy must relate the particularities of the student body, the classroom, the school and the system to the overall demands being made on the entire school system.

The level of expertise among teachers is important. It determines the starting point for work on instructional issues and, hence, the professional development capacity of schools and school systems. Teachers' level of experience, knowledge of subject matter and facility with collaborative work form the bedrock for developing group norms and forms of collaboration around specific instructional practices. The students, their prior knowledge and skill, their family and community contexts, and their previous educational experiences influence teachers' attitudes, expectations and practices. The norms, values and expectations that teachers hold about student learning and their own practice guide teachers' focus on new practices that they see as useful to their daily work. While it's possible, indeed necessary, to have broad standards of quality and performance for teaching practice and even specific priorities for which content areas and which grade levels are the priorities for professional development, this broad guidance takes complicated translation for specific schools and teachers to use it to improve the system as a whole.

In general, knowledge and skill are at the core of school improvement. If you don't know what kinds of knowledge and skill are required to improve student learning, if you can't recognize different levels of expertise in that core knowledge, and if you don't have a working theory for how to build greater expertise in teaching practice, then it's unlikely that more resources spent on professional development will make any difference to student learning.

Incentives

Any plan of improvement has to address the motives of individuals and of groups; their willingness to pursue a common purpose through collaborative activity that is likely to entail great effort, uncertainty and alteration in established norms and habits. The question of motive is especially significant for the typical school, where most people experience their work as difficult and complex without the additional burden of collaborative effort. Few people willfully engage in practices that they know to be ineffective; most educators have good reasons to think that they are doing the best work they can under the circumstances. Asking them to engage in work that is significantly different from what they are already doing requires a strong rationale and incentive. This is probably the aspect of performance-based accountability and improvement that has received the least attention.

In general, the theory of performance-based accountability is that providing communities, parents, teachers and administrators with evidence of student performance, coupled with rewards and sanctions for high and low performance, will stimulate schools and school systems to focus on doing what is necessary to improve student learning. We now know, of course, that there are serious problems with this theory: People in schools often don't know what to do to fix the problems and don't have access to the resources that are necessary to learn. Schools and school systems often do things—teaching test items rather than real content, for example—that manifestly are bad educational practice but that help them raise test scores quickly. And, under the new performance-based system, schools often compete for the students who are most likely to succeed rather than learning how to succeed in educating the students that they have.

Ideas about the use of incentives to accompany performance-based accountability are also underdeveloped. The incentives that are available to policymakers are fairly blunt instruments: publication of test scores; student promotion, retention and graduation; identification and classification of schools by performance levels; cash awards to individuals or schools; and, the takeover or reconstitution of failing schools. The characteristic that all of these incentives share is that they have virtually no relationship to the knowledge and practice of improvement. The data, the penalties, the administrative drama of designating failure or placing blame—none of these tell school people anything about how to advance student and adult learning. In other words, the important question for the design of an effective improvement process is not so much which external incentives are available to press schools for higher levels of performance, but rather what *responses* by schools and school systems are most likely to increase learning and performance.

In fact, while there are many problems with the design and implementation of performance-based accountability systems, the most serious difficulty lies with the inadequacy of the responses that schools and school systems have made to the policies. And it is mostly not their fault. Most schools are unprepared to respond effectively to any performance-based accountability system, whether well designed or poorly designed. Since school preparedness is so central, it makes sense to look at the improvement process at the classroom and school levels, then from the perspective of the broader system. What kinds of incentives are likely to engage teachers and administrators in professional development that improves practice? The research gives us some useful guidance on this question.

Internal accountability precedes external accountability and is a precondition for any process of improvement. Schools do not "succeed" in responding to external cues or pressures unless they have their own internal system for reaching agreement on good practice and for making that agreement evident in organization and pedagogy. We know this from the many studies of effective schools—that is, the schools that have the most effective professional development programs and the schools that accommodate accountability most successfully. These schools have a clear, strong internal focus on issues of instruction, student learning and expectations for teacher and student performance. In academia, we call this a strong "internal accountability system." By this we mean that there is a high degree of alignment among individual teachers about what they can do and about their responsibility for the improvement of student learning. Such schools also have shared expectations among teachers, administrators and students about what constitutes good work and a set of processes for observing whether these expectations are being met (Newmann and King, et al., 2000; Little 1993; Abelmann and Elmore, et al., 1999).

No externally administered incentive, whether it be reward or sanction, will automatically result in the creation of an effective improvement process inside schools and school systems. Nor will any incentive necessarily have a predictable effect across all schools. The effect of incentives is contingent on the capacity of the individual school or school district to receive the message the incentive carries, to translate it into a concrete and effective course of action, and to execute that action. Incentives have a differential effect, depending on the capacity of the settings in which they work, with the differential effects of accountability systems being relatively predictable. Schools with weak internal accountability systems are

> Under the new performance-based system, schools often compete for the students who are most likely to succeed rather than learning how to succeed in educating the students that they have.

likely to respond to external incentives in fragmented, incoherent and ineffective ways. Schools with relatively strong internal accountability systems are likely to respond in more effective and coherent ways.

The most direct incentives are those embedded in the work itself; the further away from the work, the less powerful and predictable is an incentive's effect. School personnel are more likely to work collaboratively to improve performance if the work itself is rewarding and if the external rewards support and reinforce work that is regarded as instrumental to increased quality and performance. Kelley, Odden, and their colleagues studied the effects of school-based performance award systems—systems that provide monetary awards to schools for gains in student achievement. They found that the actual monetary reward was often cited by teachers for its importance, but that teachers also valued their own personal satisfaction in seeing improved student achievement, opportunities to work with other teachers on instructional problems, a sense of solidarity in achieving schoolwide goals and public recognition of their success. Teachers also engaged in their own cost/benefit analysis of external performance incentives. They actively calculated the value of the rewards, tangible and intangible, against the increased pressure and stress that came with performance-based accountability, expressing doubt about the likelihood that policymakers would actually meet their commitments if schools demonstrated wide-scale improvement (Kelley and Odden, et al. 2000).

Given the atomized structure of most schools, it seems improbable that external rewards will, in and of themselves, transform these organizations into coherent, supportive environments for student and adult learning. A more likely scenario, in parallel with the Guskey argument, is that teachers and administrators will learn the value of successful collaboration from experience, then make the connection between this work and any external rewards or sanctions. It also seems probable that, within the work, visible evidence of student learning will be the most immediate motivator for continued improvement. Certainly it also makes sense to assume that teachers and school leaders will view stability in the level of resources committed to improvement as a basic condition for the investment of their own increased effort. The work itself, then, is the primary motivator for learning and improvement. If the work is not engaging and if it is not demonstrably beneficial to student learning, then any incentives are likely to produce weak and unreliable effects.

Both individual and collective incentives, skillfully designed, can support professional development and large-scale improvement. School-based incentives are collective rewards; they accrue to the school as a whole or to the individuals who work in the school on the basis of their collective performance. What about individual rewards—rewards that accrue to particular teachers and particular administrators based on their individual work? There is reason to worry that individual incentives might reinforce the existing atomization of schools. As previously stated, individual teachers accumulate points toward salary and step increases by accumulating academic credits from courses that may have no relationship to their school's performance. Many districts also offer professional development activities on a space-available basis for which teachers sign up as individuals, usually disconnected from any school-improvement plan or schoolwide priority. The large-group workshops and school-level meetings that are typical of professional development days also tend to be only loosely related to actual classroom needs. Thus, the structure of professional development reflects and reinforces the atomized, individual incentive structure of schools and school systems. This, in turn, undermines the possibility of using collective resources—the time of teachers and administrators and the money that is used to purchase outside expertise—to support a coherent and collective improvement of practice. In this instance, individual rewards and incentives work against the objective of overall improvement.

Yet it may be possible to design a system of individual rewards that reinforce large-scale improvement. Not all incentives for large-scale improvement have to be collective, and it's possible for individual incentives to play a powerful role in an overall improvement process. Odden and Kelley, for example, have proposed a knowledge- and skill-based compensation system that ties individual salary increments, step increases and bonuses to professional development activities and demonstrated competencies in domains of practice that are important to school and systemwide improvement (Kelley and Odden 1995). Thus, teachers could be rewarded for gaining and demonstrating knowledge and skill in new instructional strategies for literacy or mathematics that are tied to the school's and/or school system's performance goals. A similar, but broader, incentive would be to give increased compensation and responsibility to teachers who successfully complete the performance-based certification process of the National Board for Professional Teaching Standards (NBPTS), an independent, professional organization that focuses on the certification of teachers for advanced levels of competency. The design of the incentive structure and uses of incentives are probably more important than the types of incentives that are used.

It seems improbable, however, that a large-scale improvement process could work without strong, stable and consistent collective incentives for the improved knowledge and skill of individual educators as well as for the school's development of a more coherent internal accountability system. The addition of an external accountability system could send a strong signal that society expects school personnel to work in concert to improve student achievement. Currently, many schools are not much more than organizational fictions—places where adults interact with students in the classroom, but which have little adult interaction and a weak organizational identity in the lives of those who work there. Such organizations are not designed to engage in systematic, cumulative, collective learning about how to reach progressively higher levels of quality and performance. Thus, the fundamental problem of incentives is how to engage school personnel in work that is rewarding in some immediate, personal way, but that also encourages collaborative work around the shared purposes of the organization.

Capacity

Accountability systems and incentive structures, no matter how well designed, are only as effective as the capacity of the organization to respond. The purpose of an accountability system is to focus the resources and capacities of an organization toward a particular end. Accountability systems can't mobilize resources that schools don't have. School responses to accountability systems vary, depending on how well they manage themselves around collaborative work on instructional improvement. Accountability systems don't cause schools to improve; they create the conditions in which it is advantageous for schools to work on specific problems, to focus their work in particular ways, and to develop new knowledge and skills in their students and staff. The capacity to improve precedes and shapes schools' responses to the external demands of accountability systems.

> Accountability systems don't cause schools to improve; they create the conditions in which it is advantageous for schools to work on specific problems

Most state accountability structures are either blind or relatively ineffectual in regard to the question of capacity. Some states, notably Kentucky and Texas, provide technical assistance to failing schools, but the statewide scope of the capacity problem far exceeds states' commitment of resources to these efforts. Some states also have created networks to provide technical assistance and professional development to teachers and administrators around curriculum content, standards and performance measurements. However, most states' efforts are uninformed by any particularly powerful models of large-scale improvement. The networks are largely disconnected from the daily, detailed work of schools and so, in some ways may reinforce the isolation that exists within schools. Lack of capacity is the Achilles heel of accountability. Without substantial investment in capacity building, all that performance-based accountability systems will demonstrate is that some schools are better prepared than others to respond to accountability and performance-based incentives, namely the ones that had the highest capacity to begin with. This is not exactly what the advocates of performance-based accountability had in mind (Elmore 2001).

When experts are asked what they would do about the capacity problem in schools and school systems, they invariably recommend more spending on professional development, as if any increase in professional development activity will automatically increase capacity and student performance. The problem with this prescription is that it confuses cause and effect. If schools and school systems understood the importance of professional development to their overall performance, they would, of course, already be spending their own money on it and spending it in a targeted and coherent way. The fact that most school systems do not already have a coherent and powerful professional development system is, itself, evidence that they would not know what to do with increased professional development funding. Investing in more professional development in low-capacity, incoherent systems is simply to put more money into an infrastructure that is not prepared to use it effectively. Thus, the question of capacity precedes and coexists with the question of how much new money should be invested in professional development.

Capacity is defined by the degree of successful interaction of students and teachers around content. Defining the connection between professional development and capacity requires us to understand what capacity is, how to reach it with professional development, and what resources are available for this. If investments in it are to be directly related to improvement, the definition of capacity has to be rooted in instruction. Cohen, Raudenbush and Ball (2000) define instructional resources, or capacity, as the knowledge, skill, and material resources that are brought to bear on the interaction among students, teachers and content. They argue that none of these three elements can be treated in isolation from each other. One cannot, for example, enhance teachers' knowledge and skill without also addressing what teachers know about reaching individual students and the actual curriculum that teachers are expected to teach and students are expected to master. Likewise, you can't insist on the mastery of more rigorous content without also asking whether teachers have the requisite knowledge and skill to teach it, and where students are in their own learning relative to where the content is pitched. Nor can you "improve" student achievement without understanding what students bring to the learning, what teachers understand about student learning and in what content domain, using what curricular materials and resources, teachers and students are expected to function.

This simple, powerful model of capacity relates to the conditions under which instruction occurs. The existence of capacity in a school is evident in the interaction among teachers and students around content. Investments in capacity that do not directly affect this interaction are unlikely to improve either the quality of instruction or student learning. It also suggests that there are three entry points, or portals, for the development of capacity: teachers, students, and content. Professional development works as a capacity-building device to the extent that it enters each of these portals and acknowledges the relationship among them. The model also suggests that all schools and school systems have solutions to the problem of instructional capacity embedded in their existing teaching practices and organizational arrangements, and that enhancing capacity consists of unpacking these existing arrangements, diagnosing how they support or undermine what the school system is trying to accomplish, and changing them to be consistent with collective goals for improvement.

■ EFFECTIVE USE OF PROFESSIONAL DEVELOPMENT REQUIRES HIGH ORGANIZATIONAL CAPACITY

Returning to the relationship between professional development and organizational capacity, the Cohen, et al. model explains why investment in professional development by low-capacity schools and school systems often has no effect or a negative effect on morale and performance. Professional development affects teachers, that is, its use assumes that giving teachers new skills and knowledge enhances the capacity of teachers to teach more effectively. But, if it consists only of that, it is likely to have a modest-to-negative effect because the teacher usually returns to a classroom and a school in which the conditions of instruction and the conditions of work are exactly the same as when he or she began the professional development. The students are exactly the same. The content is exactly the same, or only slightly altered by the new materials introduced through the professional development. The teacher begins to teach and discovers that the ideas that seemed plausible during training don't seem to work in the school or classroom context.

> One cannot enhance teachers' knowledge and skill without also addressing what teachers know about reaching individual students and the actual curriculum that teachers are expected to teach.

The "real world," in the language of teachers, overwhelms the new idea, no matter how powerful or well demonstrated in theory. If this professional development cycle is run repeatedly, it produces a negative reinforcement pattern. Teachers become cynical about any new idea when no previous new idea has worked. The low capacity in this situation is the inability of the organization to support the teacher in navigating the complex interactions among the new skills and knowledge he/she has acquired, existing patterns of student engagement, and the modifications to curricula and content that may be necessary to execute the new practices in this particular setting with these particular students.

Under these circumstances, it is a gargantuan task for a teacher to actually improve his or her practice: She would have to assimilate the new knowledge and skill at a relatively high level of understanding (how one does that without actually practicing the skill repeatedly is a mystery, like learning to fly an airplane or play tennis by reading a book or watching a video tape). Immediately, she would have to transfer that knowledge into a setting in which student responses are highly unpredictable, and probably predictably disappointing on the first try. And she would somehow have to invent the curriculum materials that are necessary to align the new skill to the particular classroom: All this in real time. It seems, on its face, absurd to expect anything other than a *pro forma* response to this kind of professional development.

When you begin to describe the organizational conditions under which professional development actually contributes to instructional capacity in schools, you begin to describe an organization as it rarely exists. Such an organization would only require teachers to learn new skills and knowledge if it were prepared to support their practice of these skills in real classrooms, providing experts to work with teachers as they master these skills and adapt them to their students' responses to the new practices and materials. It would be an organization that offered consistent messages to principals, teachers and students about what goals are most important and what resources are available to support the work of meeting them. It would be an organization in which administrators, at the school and system level, think their main job is to support the interaction of teachers and students around the mastery of specific content. And, it would be a system in which no judgments about performance, of teachers or students, are made without first ensuring that the conditions for high performance have been met; a system in which no one is expected to demonstrate knowledge and skill that they haven't had the opportunity to learn.

These conditions create a formidable agenda of organizational redesign for most schools and school systems. System officials would have to have considerable expertise about the instructional practices they expect teachers to acquire. That expertise would have to entail, not just teaching teachers how to teach differently, but actually working with teachers in their classrooms to solve problems of practice in a way that supports continuous improvement. The system would have to manage its resources to support and fund the work of teachers and professional developers in sustained interaction. It would also have to set priorities, clearly stating which problems of instructional practice are central and which peripheral to overall improvement before deciding how to allocate professional development resources. Schools would have to become learning environments for teachers as well as for students. The instructional day would be designed to facilitate the learning of both groups, and the learning of educators, inside and outside of the classroom, would have to be arranged to avoid any disruption to student learning. And, it would be up to administrators to negotiate with the system at large to secure the resources necessary for implementation.

In other words, to use professional development as an instrument of instructional improvement, schools and school systems will have to reorganize themselves in order to make substantial changes in the conditions of work for teachers and students.

Effective professional development requires the development of expertise as an organizational capacity and this requires differentiated organizational roles. One of the strongest social norms among school faculty is that everyone is expected to pretend that they are equally effective at what they do. However, most people who work in schools know (or at least claim to know) who the "good" teachers are. Teachers themselves will, under the right circumstances, talk candidly about who the strong and weak teachers are reputed to be. Teachers who threaten this pretence, either by publicly distinguishing themselves as expert teachers or by being singled out as a model within their schools, may have to pay a price in social ostracism.

Yet the entire process of improvement depends on schools making public and authoritative distinctions among teachers and administrators based on quality, competence, expertise and performance. If everyone is equally good at what they do, then no one has anything to teach anyone else about how to do it better. Thus, educators' pretence of absolute equality is a major impediment to improvement and a significant factor in determining the capacity of schools to engage in effective professional development.

In a previous paper (Elmore 2000), I argued that developing the capacity to lead instruction requires a differentiated role for "leaders" and a model of distributed leadership in which those with different roles and competencies could work cooperatively around the common task of instructional improvement. This same argument applies to creating and sustaining capacity using professional development. To improve themselves, systems need to be able to identify people who know what to do, to develop the capacity of those in the organization to learn what to do, and to create settings in which people who know what to do teach those who don't. Instructional expertise is a key element of organizational capacity in regard to the use of professional development. One could argue that a school system's capacity to make productive use of professional development is directly related to its willingness to make binding and public judgments about quality and expertise.

One possible source of the presumption of equal competency is the widely held belief that teaching practice cannot be evaluated due to its highly complex, uncertain and indeterminate nature. It is easy to make mistakes in judgment about better and worse teaching, and it is particularly easy to make egregious mistakes when those who make the judgments know little about what constitutes expert practice. In most systems, the administrators who are assigned the responsibility for evaluating teachers are not selected for their expertise in instruction; indeed, most of their work has nothing to do with instruction. So it's not surprising that teachers distrust proposals for individual assessment of their quality and competence. Their misgivings are well founded.

> If everyone is equally good at what they do, then no one has anything to teach anyone else about how to do it better.

For distinctions in expertise to be credible among teachers, they have to be rooted in the core issue of instructional capacity. That is, distinctions in expertise probably won't be institutionalized unless they grow out of the work of analyzing and improving student learning. Just as individual teachers are more likely to adopt new practices after powerful improvement in student learning has been demonstrated to them, so too must the distinctions in expertise be observable in actual classroom practice before they will be generally acknowledged.

The good news: The money is probably there. The bad news: It's already being spent on something else. Just as it is probably fruitless to spend more money on professional development in schools and school systems that haven't developed the capacity to use it effectively, so too is it problematic to invest more money in professional development if schools and school systems don't know how their current monies are being spent. The purchase of time for teachers to participate in professional development on a large scale, staffing arrangements that permit some teachers to work full or part time as professional developers, the hiring of outside experts to consult on questions of design and to provide support to teachers and administrators, recruiting and training administrators with deep instructional knowledge, creating time for observation and analysis of students' responses to new types of instruction—all of these activities are very expensive, especially if they are done at scale in all schools and classrooms.

The first response of most administrators to these ideas is that they would be happy to try them if someone else would pay for them, usually meaning the next level of government above the one in which they are working. This is the theory of federalism as stated by Daniel Elazar, the renowned political scientist: The appropriate level of government to perform a given function is always the one you're working in; the appropriate level of government to pay for that function is always the one above your own.

But there is a major problem with this theory. School systems that are not spending their own professional development dollars effectively are unlikely to be more effective in spending other peoples' money. More support for professional development from any level of government is unlikely to improve practice unless schools and school districts are already using their own resources effectively.

The evidence is now substantial that there is considerable money available in most district budgets to finance large-scale improvement efforts that use professional development effectively. The money is there. The problem is that it's already spent on other things and it has to be reallocated to focus on student achievement. The sources of revenue are obvious, but using them means tackling the central problem of how schools and school systems are managed. Substantial funding can be found by reducing the staffing demands of specialized programs for teachers and students, carefully tracking differential staff patterns across schools and grade-levels, scheduling larger blocks of instructional time, refocusing categorical and special purpose funding on instructional purposes, reallocating non-instructional administrative funds to serve instructional purposes and, most importantly, reallocating and focusing existing expenditures on professional development. (See, e.g., Miles 1995; Miles and Darling-Hammond 1998.)

To say that the money is available, of course, begs the question of why it is not being spent on professional development and improved student achievement already. The answer to that question is that school systems have never had an incentive to evaluate and manage the resources they use around a coherent instructional agenda. Instead, the money that districts spend on instruction tends to be compartmentalized to meet specific external demands and specific incremental decisions at the system and school levels. As with other problems of capacity, the problem of resources can only be addressed by making the improvement of student learning the central priority and then deciding whether the available resources are adequate to the task.

A potential strength of performance-based accountability systems is that they create an incentive system in which schools and school systems are rewarded for developing a coherent focus on teaching and learning then changing their staffing arrangements and budgets to reflect this. But many schools and school systems are going to need help in understanding what must be done, as well as executing the range of actions they will have to take in order to increase their capacity to use professional development to respond to the new accountability systems. Most people in schools and school systems are not prepared for these changes. People in low-capacity schools and school systems are even less prepared. States and localities need to markedly increase the volume of information and assistance available to schools around organizational capacity issues and to engage in more open experimentation to identify more effective ways of focusing and raising capacity.

CONCLUSION: DEVELOPING ■
THE PRACTICE OF IMPROVEMENT

American public education is leaving a period in which questions of practice and its improvement were essentially pushed into the classroom, where doors were shut and teachers were left to develop their own ideas and practices, largely unsupported by the organizations in which they worked. The next stage of development in American education, propelled by the advent of performance-based accountability, requires the development of a practice of continuous school improvement—a body of knowledge about how to increase the quality of instructional practice and boost student learning on a large scale across classrooms, schools, and entire school systems. At its core is professional development, the process of professional learning for the purpose of improving student achievement.

I have tried to sketch out one view of what theoretical and practical knowledge might constitute a practice of improvement and how professional development fits into that practice. I have argued that the conventional wisdom about effective professional development provides an adequate working theory to guide practice. I have also argued that there are deep organizational and cultural reasons why schools and school systems are not likely, in their present form, to make effective use of professional development. Investing more professional development funds in systems that have not begun a serious practice of improvement is unlikely to produce any discernible increase in student learning. In order for professional development to work as a cumulative learning process, it has to be connected to the practice of improvement. In my view, that practice must entail attention to what knowledge and skill educators require to improve student learning and how people come to master that knowledge, which incentives encourage people to engage in the difficult and uncertain process of changing their teaching and administrative practice, and what resources and capacities are required to support the practice of improvement.

> Education is leaving a period in which questions of practice and its improvement were essentially pushed into the classroom, where doors were shut and teachers were left to develop their own ideas and practices.

There are several aspects of the idea of a practice of improvement that are countercultural to the current organization of American schools. We should acknowledge these conflicts explicitly, rather than pretending that they don't exist. First, the task of improvement is one that schools and school systems are not designed to do and may be one that some people who work in schools think is neither possible nor worthwhile. If you are steeped in a culture in which all practice is essentially invented in classrooms, and in which your daily worklife provides you no access to challenging ideas about how to do your work better, it is not surprising that you would think that large-scale improvement is an improbable idea.

Second, existing norms about knowledge and expertise work against improvement. The belief that experience alone increases expertise in teaching, or that those with less experience but more access to knowledge, might be qualitatively better teachers than those with more experience and less access to knowledge, works against the possibility that new knowledge can dramatically improve teaching practice. The belief, at least in public, that all teachers are equal in their skill and knowledge and that all teaching practice is the same undermines the possibility that teachers can learn from each other in powerful ways, as well as learning from experts who are not part of their immediate circle of colleagues.

Third, the existing occupational and career structure in schools and school systems is completely inadequate as a basis for improvement. Teaching is a largely undifferentiated occupation, while improvement demands that it become more differentiated—allowing teachers who have developed strong expertise in particular domains to lead the improvement of instruction in those domains by working as mentors, coaches and professional developers. Administration is a highly differentiated occupation in which the categories of specialization have little or nothing to do with the core function of the organization, which is instruction. Improvement requires a less differentiated administrative structure with more focus on the skills required for the practice of improvement. Mobility among roles is presently limited, while the practice of improvement requires flexibility and movement, so that people with expertise can move into places where their knowledge and skill can be connected to practice more immediately.

Fourth, the design of work in schools is fundamentally incompatible with the practice of improvement. Teachers spend most of their time working in isolation from each other in self-contained classrooms. In most schools and school systems, time away from the direct practice of instruction is considered time that is not spent "working." Hence, learning how to teach more effectively, if it is acknowledged at all in the structure of work, is either done on the teacher's own time through evening or summer courses, or is wedged into short periods of time released from "regular" instructional duties. The problem with this design is that it provides almost no opportunity for teachers to engage in continuous and sustained learning about their practice in the setting in which they actually work, observing and being observed by their colleagues in their own classrooms and in the classrooms of other teachers in other schools confronting similar problems of practice. This disconnect between the requirements of learning to teach well and the structure of teachers' work life is fatal to any sustained process of instructional improvement.

Fifth, the culture of passivity and helplessness that pervades many schools works directly against the possibility of improvement. Schools with weak internal accountability structures assign causality for their success or failure to forces outside their control: the students, their families, the community, the "system." Schools with strong internal accountability assign causality for their success or failure to themselves: to the knowledge and skill they bring to their work, to the power of shared values, and to the capacities of their organizations (Abelmann and Elmore, et al. 1999). The historic absence of clear guidance for schools around issues of performance and accountability has spawned an extensive and resilient culture of passivity, while the practice of improvement requires a culture of coherence and responsibility. *Teachers and administrators learn this culture of passivity and helplessness as a consequence of working in dysfunctional organizations, not as a consequence of choosing to think and behave that way. Improving the organization will change what adults learn.*

In developing a practice of improvement, it is possible to confront these contradictions more or less directly, with more or less tactical and strategic skill, but it is not possible to avoid them altogether. Grace, humility, and humor are virtues well suited to this work. The creaking and grinding sounds emerging from schools and school systems over the foreseeable future are the sounds of a nineteenth-century structure passing quickly through the twentieth century in order to confront the demands of the twenty-first. This will not always be a beautiful and edifying process. It will often look exactly like what it is, a wrenching undertaking that involves large numbers of people learning how to do something they previously did not know how to do and learning it at increasingly high levels of expertise.

So the practice of improvement is about changing three things fundamentally and simultaneously: (1) the values and beliefs of people in schools about what is worth doing and what it is possible to do; (2) the structural conditions under which the work is done; and, (3) the ways in which people learn to do the work. A powerful principle that I think derives from research and practice is that this kind of difficult, contingent, and uncertain learning is best done in close proximity to the work itself. And the work of schools is instruction.[3] Teachers acquire different values and beliefs about what students can learn by observing their own students and students like theirs in other settings, learning things that they, the teachers, might not have believed possible. Teachers and administrators learn how to connect new knowledge and skill to practice by trying to do specific things in the classroom and by asking themselves whether there is evidence that, having done these things, students are able to do things they were not able to do before. School administrators and teachers learn to change the conditions of work by trying new ideas in the context of specific curriculum content and specific instructional problems, grade-level conferences and observations around particular problems of math or literacy instruction, for example. System administrators learn to change structures and resource-allocation patterns by observing what effective practice in schools looks like and trying to figure out how to support it. Learning by these adults that is not anchored in the work is unlikely to lead to durable and supportive changes in the conditions under which the work is done. Essentially, the practice of improvement is a discipline of understanding how good work, and the learning of good work, can be supported and propagated in schools and school systems.

It is fashionable among people who work on problems of "change" and improvement in schools to argue that a deep transformation of schools will require a long time and much more money. All things in education seem to require a long time and much more money. I hope my argument in this paper brings a note of healthy skepticism on both counts. First, improvements in instruction have *immediate* effects on student learning wherever they occur, and these effects are usually demonstrable through skillful assessment and observation of students' work. The effects, in the short-term, may not be widespread; certain settings may lag behind others in seeing the effects and certain classroom and school contexts may present more difficult improvement problems than others.

> A central part of the practice of improvement should be to make the connection between teaching practice and student learning more direct and clear.

But, I think it is important to keep in mind that *students learn what they are taught,* when the teaching is done effectively and thoughtfully. So we should not peg our expectations for improvement in student performance on fancy and ambiguous theories about the uncertainty and contingency of educational "change." A central part of the discipline of improvement is the belief that if the teaching is good and powerful, and if the conditions of work enable and support that practice, then we should be able to see immediate evidence that students are learning. If we can't, then we should ask whether the teaching was really as good as we thought it was. A central part of the practice of improvement should be to make the connection between teaching practice and student learning more direct and clear. The present generation of students deserve the best practice we can give them and their learning should not be mortgaged against the probability that something good will happen for future generations. Improvements should be focused directly on the classroom experience of today's students.

I also have argued that the discipline of improvement requires major changes in the way schools and school systems manage the resources they already have: the time of teachers and administrators; the practices reflected in existing staffing patterns; administrative overhead; and, the resources already being spent, largely ineffectively, on professional development—before we can tell how much additional money is needed to engage in large-scale improvement. This is more than a low-level accounting exercise; it is fundamental to the entire process of improvement. Adding money to a system that doesn't know how to manage its own resources effectively means that the new money will be spent the same way as the old money.

Many foundations and government agencies have learned (or, more likely, haven't learned) this lesson the hard way. Yet there seems to be a kind of eternal optimism in the educational-change establishment that the next time we will get it right, that this new idea we have about *how* to give failing schools and school systems more money will make something happen that we were unable to make happen the last time. What seems clear is that the existing structure and culture of schooling is able to assimilate and deflect just about any attempt to influence it fundamentally using money as leverage. A system without a firm strategy for allocating its own money around the task of instructional improvement is like the carnivorous plant in the musical *Little Shop of Horrors*; it eats whatever it is fed and asks for more. The main work of resource allocation has to occur in schools and school systems, not in the policy and fiscal environment around them.

As this work occurs and as we get to know more about the actual resource requirements of large-scale improvement, it is quite possible that we will discover that it takes more money, maybe much more money, to do what needs to be done. But something fundamental will have changed in this process: We will actually know what the money is being spent on and what improvements in teaching practice and student learning we should expect because of it. I would love to write the paper that says why substantial infusions of new money into schools and school systems for professional development will produce higher quality instruction and higher levels of student learning. I cannot write that paper now.

Professional development is at the center of the practice of improvement. It is the process by which we organize the development and use of new knowledge in the service of improvement. I have taken a deliberately instrumental view of professional development, that it should be harnessed to the goals of the system for the improvement of student achievement, rather than driven by the preferences of individuals who work in schools. There is disagreement in the field on this point. Many people who are knowledgeable about teaching and teacher professional development argue that teachers, as professionals, should be given much more discretion and control as individuals and in collegial groups in deciding the purpose and content of professional development. Indeed, their most powerful critiques of existing professional development practices follow from the insight that mandated teacher learning is an oxymoron (Little 1993; Hargreaves 1991). Poorly organized and bad professional development can be, as many educators will testify, a deeply insulting experience.

The use of professional development for purposes of large-scale improvement raises difficult questions of authority, autonomy and control in school organization. We should not minimize these issues. It will require deep thought and skill to address them. My bias toward an instrumental view of professional development grows out my analysis of the pathologies of the existing structure and culture of schooling, as well as the knowledge that public school teachers and administrators are public professionals who are accountable for the effectiveness of their practice to public authorities and the tax paying community, as well as to their clients. Hence, it is not a threat to their professional status to argue that their publicly funded professional development should be organized around a common agenda.

This said, however, I think it wise to take a developmental view on issues of authority, autonomy, and control in decisions about professional development. The practice of improvement should create more differentiated and flexible organizations in schools and school systems. The development and distribution of competence and expertise should result in more knowledgeable and powerful people operating in "boundary roles" as mentors, teacher leaders, and professional developers, as well as more knowledgeable and powerful people in the ranks of the teaching force and administration. This distribution of expertise and leadership means that schools and school systems will have to become more consensual in the way they make decisions about issues of professional practice, including professional development. And, I have argued, issues of accountability are essentially reciprocal anyway, since I can't meet your expectations for performance unless you support my learning. So, while professional development will continue to be instrumental to improvement, I expect that it will necessarily become much more consensual in its structure of authority. Knowledge-based organizations, which is what schools will become through the practice of improvement, are organizations designed around the authority of expertise, rather than the authority of position. What you know and the effect of what you know on student learning are more important than whom you know or what your title is.

As I said at the beginning, the development of the practice and discipline of large-scale improvement is a matter of some urgency. The consequences of performance-based accountability can be disastrous (at least for some schools and deleterious for others) if schools and school systems respond to demands for increased performance by pushing harder on the existing structure of schooling and demanding more from school personnel without acknowledging that few, if any, people actually know how to do the improvement work that must by done. We are now at the stage of understanding that schools and school systems have very different responses to pressure for performance, depending on the knowledge and skill embodied in their teaching and administrative staffs, their capacity to create a strong normative environment around good teaching, and their ability to muster and manage the resources required to begin the long process of raising the level of practice. The issue is what we will do with this knowledge, whether we will use it to, once again, affirm the self-fulfilling prophecy that some schools and the students in them are "better" than others, or whether we will enable all schools to become competent and powerful agents of their own improvement.

> What you know and the effect of what you know on student learning are more important than whom you know or what your title is.

APPENDIX 6.1A: STANDARDS ■ FOR STAFF DEVELOPMENT

Context Standards

Staff development that improves the learning of all students:

- Organizes adults into learning communities whose goals are aligned with those of the school and district. (Learning Communities)
- Requires skillful school and district leaders who guide continuous instructional improvement. (Leadership)
- Requires resources to support adult learning and collaboration. (Resources)

Process Standards

Staff development that improves the learning of all students:

- Uses disaggregated student data to determine adult learning priorities, monitor progress, and help sustain continuous improvement. (Data-Driven)
- Uses multiple sources of information to guide improvement and demonstrate its impact. (Evaluation)
- Prepares educators to apply research to decision making. (Research-Based)
- Uses learning strategies appropriate to the intended goal. (Design)
- Applies knowledge about human learning and change. (Learning)
- Provides educators with the knowledge and skills to collaborate. (Collaboration)

Content Standards

Staff development that improves the learning of all students:

- Prepares educators to understand and appreciate all students, create safe, orderly and supportive learning environments, and hold high expectations for their academic achievement. (Equity)

- Deepens educators' content knowledge, provides them with research-based instructional strategies to assist students in meeting rigorous academic standards, and prepares them to use various types of classroom assessments appropriately. (Quality Teaching)
- Provides educators with knowledge and skills to involve families and other stakeholders appropriately. (Family Involvement)

Source: National Staff Development Council, 2001 (Revised)

■ APPENDIX 6.1B: GUIDING PRINCIPLES FOR TRANSFORMING PROFESSIONAL DEVELOPMENT

A number of experts and organizations have suggested that the most promising professional development programs or policies are those that[4]

- stimulate and support site-based initiatives. Professional development is likely to have greater impact on practice if it is closely linked to school initiatives to improve practice.
- support teacher initiatives as well as school or district initiatives. These initiatives could promote the professionalization of teaching and may be cost-effective ways to engage more teachers in serious professional development activities.
- are grounded in knowledge about teaching. Good professional development should encompass expectations educators hold for students, child-development theory, curriculum content and design, instructional and assessment strategies for instilling higher-order competencies, school culture and shared decision-making.
- model constructivist teaching. Teachers need opportunities to explore, question and debate in order to integrate new ideas into their repertoires and their classroom practice.
- offer intellectual, social and emotional engagement with ideas, materials and colleagues. If teachers are to teach for deep understanding, they must be intellectually engaged in their disciplines and work regularly with others in their field.
- demonstrate respect for teachers as professionals and as adult learners. Professional development should draw on the expertise of teachers and take differing degrees of teacher experience into account.
- provide for sufficient time and follow-up support for teachers to master new content and strategies and to integrate them into their practice.
- are accessible and inclusive. Professional development should be viewed as an integral part of teachers' work rather than as a privilege granted to "favorites" by administrators.

Source: Excerpted from Thomas B. Corcoran's "Helping Teachers Teach Well: Transforming Professional Development," a policy brief from the Consortium for Policy Research in Education, June 1995

■ APPENDIX 6.1C: IMPROVING PROFESSIONAL DEVELOPMENT, RESEARCH-BASED PRINCIPLES

Whatever their content and goals, professional development activities that have the characteristics below are more likely to be effective than those that do not . . .

- The content of professional development focuses on what students are to learn and how to address the different problems students may have in learning the material.
- Professional development should be based on analyses of the differences between (a) actual student performance and (b) goals and standards for student learning.
- Professional development should involve teachers in identifying what they need to learn and in developing the learning experiences in which they will be involved.
- Professional development should be primarily school-based and built into the day-to-day work of teaching.
- Most professional development should be organized around collaborative problem solving.
- Professional development should be continuous and ongoing, involving follow-up and support for further learning—including support from sources external to the school that can provide necessary resources and new perspectives.
- Professional development should incorporate evaluation of multiple sources of information on (a) outcomes for students and (b) the instruction and other processes involved in implementing lessons learned through professional development.
- Professional development should provide opportunities to understand the theory underlying the knowledge and skills being learned.
- Professional development should be connected to a comprehensive change process focused on improving student learning. (For a more detailed version of these principles, see www.npeat.org/strand2/pdprin.pdf.)

Source: From *Revisioning Professional Development: What Learner-Centered Professional Development Looks Like,* National Partnership for Excellence and Accountability in Teaching, 1999

NOTES ■

1. See Appendix 6.1a to view the NSDC's revised standards.

2. But not so very different from mainstream definitions in the literature on professional development. For example, "Staff development is defined as the provision of activities designed to advance the knowledge, skills, and understanding of teachers in ways that lead to changes in their thinking and classroom behavior. This definition limits the range of staff development to those specific activities that enhance knowledge, skills, and understanding in ways that lead to changes in thought and action." (Fenstermacher and Berliner 1985, 283). All that's missing here is the explicit connection to student learning.

3. My first tutorial on this principle was delivered by Anthony Alvarado, then-Superintendent of Community School District #2, New York City, and now Chancellor for Instruction in the San Diego Public Schools.

4. Griffin, G. 1982. "Staff Development." Paper prepared for the National Institute of Education Invitational Conference, Research on Teaching: Implications for Practice, Arlie House, VA. Washington, DC, National Institute of Education; Hodges, H. 1994. "Using Research to Inform Practice in Urban Schools: 10 Key Strategies for Success. Paper prepared for the Invitational Conference on "Improving Urban Schools: Better Strategies for Dissemination and Knowledge Utilization," sponsored by the National Center on Education for the Inner Cities, Alexandria, VA, September 8–10; Joyce, B., and B. Showers. 1982. "The Coaching of Teaching." *Educational Leadership,* 40(1): 4–10; Little, J. W. 1993. "Teachers' Professional Development in a Climate of Reform." Educational Evaluation and Policy Analysis 15(2):129–151; Loucks-Horsley, S., C. Harding, M. Arbuckle, L. Murray, C. Dubea, and M. Williams. 1987. *Continuing to Learn: A Guide Book for Teacher Development.* Andover, MA: Regional Laboratory for Educational Improvement of the Northeast and Islands and the National Staff Development Council; Price, H. 1993. "Teacher Professional Development: It's About Time." *Education Week,* 12(33), 32; National Staff Development Council. 1994. *National Staff Development Council's Standards for Staff Development: Middle level Edition.* Oxford, OH: author; Zimpher, N. L., and K. R. Howey. 1992. *Policy and Practice*

Toward the Improvement of Teacher Education. Oak Brook, IL: The North Central Regional Educational Laboratory.

■ REFERENCES

Abelmann, C. and R. F. Elmore, et. al. (1999). "When Accountability Knocks, Will Anyone Answer?" CPRE Policy Briefs. Philadelphia: University of Pennsylvania.

Alexander, P. A. and P. K. Murphy (1998). *The Research Base for APA's Learner-Centered Psychological Principles.* Washington, D.C.: American Psychological Association.

Anderson, J. R., L. M. Reder, et al. (1996). "Situated Learning and Education." *Educational Researcher,* 25(4): 5–11.

Ball, S. and C. Lacey (1984). *Subject Disciplines as the Opportunity for Group Action: A Measured Critique of Subject Sub-Cultures.* Milton Keynes, England: Open University Press.

Ball, D. L. (1993). "With an Eye on the Mathematical Horizon: Dilemmas of Teaching Elementary School Mathematics." *The Elementary School Journal,* 93(4): 373–397.

Ball, D. L. (1988). "Unlearning to Teach Mathematics." *For the Learning of Mathematics,* 8(1): 40–48.

Bird, T. and J.W. Little (1986). "How Schools Organize the Teaching Occupation." *The Elementary School Journal,* 86(4): 493–511.

Borko, H. and R. T. Putnam (1995). *Expanding a Teacher's Knowledge Base: A Cognitive Psychological Perspective on Professional Development.* New York: Teachers College Press.

Brown, J. S., A. Collins and S. Duguid (1989). "Situated Cognition and the Culture of Learning." *Educational Researcher,* 18(1): 32–42.

Bryk, A. S., S. G, Rollow, et al. (1996). "Urban School Development: Literacy as a Lever for Change." *Educational Policy,* 10(2): 172.

Carter, K. (1990). *Teachers' Knowledge and Learning to Teach.* New York: Macmillan.

Clark C. M. and P. L. Peterson (1986). *Teachers' Thought Processes.* New York: Macmillan.

Cobb, P. (1994). "Where is the Mind? Constructivist and Sociocultural Perspectives on Mathematical Development." *Educational Researcher,* 23(7): 13–20.

Cohen, D. K., S. Raudenbush and D. Ball (November 2000). "Resources, Instruction and Research." A working paper from the Center for Teaching Policy.

Cohen, D. K. (1990). "A Revolution in One Classroom: The Case of Mrs. Oublier." *Educational Evaluation and Policy Analysis,* 12(3): 311–329.

Corcoran, T. B. (June 1995). "Helping Teachers Teach Well: Transforming Professional Development." CPRE Policy Briefs. Philadelphia: University of Pennsylvania.

Darling-Hammond, L. (1990). "Instructional Policy into Practice: The Power of the Bottom Over the Top." *Educational Evaluation and Policy Analysis,* 12(3): 339–347.

Eaker, D. J., G. W. Noblit, et al. (1992). "Reconsidering Effective Staff Development: Reflective Practice and Elaborated Cultural as Desirable Outcomes." From *Effective Staff Development for School Change,* W. T. Pink and A. A. Hyde (eds.). Norwood, N.J.: Ablex.

Eisner, E. W. (1982). "An Artistic Approach to Supervision." *Supervision of Teaching.* T. J. Sergiovanni (ed.). Alexandria, Va.: Association for Supervision and Curriculum Development (ASCD).

Elmore, R. F. (2001). "Psychiatrists and Lightbulbs." Paper prepared for the American Educational Research Association by the Consortium for Policy Research in Education.

Elmore, R. F. (2000). *Building a New Structure for School Leadership.* Washington, D.C.: Albert Shanker Institute.

Feiman-Nemser, S. (1983). "Learning to Teach." In *Handbook of Teaching and Policy,* L. S. Shulman and G. Sykes (eds). New York: Longman Publishers.

Fenstermacher, G. D. (1985). "Determining the Value of Staff Development." *The Elementary School Journal,* 85(3): 281–314.

Fullan, M. (1991). *The New Meaning of Educational Change.* New York: Teachers College Press.

Grant, S. G., P. L. Peterson, et al. (1996). "Learning to Teach Mathematics in the Context of Systemic Reform." *American Educational Research Journal,* 33(2): 509–541.

Guskey, T. R. (1989). "Attitude and Perceptual Change in Teachers." *International Journal of Educational Research,* 13(4): 439–453.

Hargreaves, A. (1991). *Contrived Collegiality: The Micropolitics of Teacher Collaboration.* London, England: Sage Publications.

Hiebert, J., T. P. Carpenter, et al. (1996). "Problem Solving as a Basis for Reform in Curriculum and Instruction: The Case of Mathematics." *Educational Researcher,* 25(4): 12–21.

Huberman, M. (1995). "Networks that Alter Teaching: Conceptualizations, Exchanges and Experiments." *Teachers and Teaching: Theory and Practice,* Vol. 1, No. 2.

Kagan, D. M. (1988). "Teaching as Clinical Problem Solving: A Critical Examination of the Analogy and Its Implications." *Review of Educational Research,* 58(4): 482–505.

Kelley, C., A. Odden, A. Milanowski and H. Heneman (February 2000). "The Motivational Effects of School-Based Performance Awards." CPRE Policy Briefs. Philadelphia: University of Pennsylvania.

Kelley, C. and A. Odden (September 1995). "Reinventing Teacher Compensation Systems." CPRE Policy Briefs. Philadelphia: University of Pennsylvania.

Ladson-Billings, G. (1995). "Toward a Theory of Culturally Relevant Pedagogy." *American Educational Research Journal,* 32(3): 465–491.

Lave, J. and E. Wenger (1991). *Situated Learning: Legitimate Peripheral Participation.* New York: Cambridge University Press.

Lee, V. E. and J. S. Smith (1996). "Collective Responsibility for Learning and Its Effects on Gains in Achievement for Early Secondary School Studies." *American Journal of Education,* 104(2): 103–147.

Leinhardt, G. and J. G. Greeno (1986). "The Cognitive Skill of Teaching." *Journal of Educational Psychology,* 78(2): 75–95.

Lieberman, A. (1995). "Practices that Support Teacher Development." *Phi Delta Kappan,* 76(8): 591.

Little, J. W. (1990). "The Persistence of Privacy: Autonomy and Initiative in Teachers' Professional Relations." *Teachers College Record.*

Little, J. W. (1993). "Teachers' Professional Development in a Climate of Educational Reform." *Educational Evaluation and Policy Analysis,* 15(2): 129–151.

Loucks-Horsley, S. (1995). "Professional Development and the Learner Centered School." *Theory into Practice,* 34(4): 265–271.

McDonald, J. P. (1986). "Raising the Teacher's Voice and the Ironic Role of Theory." *Harvard Educational Review,* 56(4), 355–378.

McLaughlin, M. W. and S. M. Yee (1988). *School as a Place to Have a Career.* New York: Teachers College Press.

Miles, K. H. and L. Darling-Hammond (1998). "Rethinking the Allocation of Teaching Resources: Some Lessons from High-Performing Schools." *Developments in School Finance, 1997.* Washington, D.C.: National Center for Education Statistics.

Miles, K. H. (1995). "Freeing Resources for Improving Schools: A Case Study of Teacher Allocation in Boston Public Schools." *Educational Evaluation and Policy Analysis,* 17(4): 476–493.

Mitchell, J. and P. Marland (1989). "Research on Teacher Thinking: The Next Phase." *Teaching and Teacher Education,* 5(2): 115–128.

Munby, H. (1984). "A Qualitative Approach to the Study of a Teacher's Beliefs." *Journal of Research in Science Teaching,* 21(1): 27–38.

Munby, H. (1982). "The Place of Teachers' Beliefs in Research on Teacher Thinking and Decision Making, and an Alternative Methodology." *Instructional Science,* 11 (3): 201–225.

Nemser, S. F. (1983). *Learning to Teach.* New York: Longman.

Nespor, J. (1987). "The Role of Beliefs in the Practice of Teaching." Journal of Curriculum Studies, 19(4): 317–328.

Newmann, F. M., M. B. King, et al. (2000). "Professional Development that Addresses School Capacity: Lessons from Urban Elementary Schools." *American Journal of Education,* 108(4): 259–299.

Olson, J. (1988). "Making Sense of Teaching: Cognition vs. Culture." *Journal of Curriculum Studies,* 20(2): 167–169.

Perkins, D. N. and G. Salomon (1988). "Teaching for Transfer," *Educational Leadership,* 46(1): 22–32.

Phillips, D. C. (1995). "The Good, the Bad, and the Ugly: The Many Faces of Constructivism." *Educational Researcher,* 24(7): 5–12.

Pink, W. T. and A. A. Hyde, Eds. (1992). "Reconsidering Effective Staff Development: Reflective Practice and Elaborated Cultural as Desirable Outcomes." *Effective Staff Development for School Change.* Norwood, N.J.: Ablex.

Prawat, R. S. (1992). "Teachers' Beliefs about Teaching and Learning: A Constructivist Perspective." *American Journal of Education,* 100(3): 354–395.

Raudenbush, S. W., B. Rowan, et al. (1992). "Contextual Effects on the Self-perceived Efficacy of High School Teachers." *Sociology of Education,* 65(2): 150–167.

Shavelson, R. J. and P. Stern (1981). "Research on Teachers' Pedagogical Thoughts, Judgments, Decisions, and Behavior." *Review of Educational Research,* 51(4): 455–498.

Shulman, L. S. (1987). "Knowledge and Teaching: Foundations of the New Reform." *Harvard Educational Review,* 57(1), 1–22.

Shulman, L. S. (1986). "Those Who Understand: Knowledge Growth in Teaching." *Educational Researcher,* 15(2): 4–14.

Smylie, M. A. and J. G. Conyers (1991). "Changing Conceptions of Teaching Influence the Future of Staff Development," *Journal of Staff Development,* 12(1): 12–16.

Sparks, D. and S. Hirsh (1997). "A New Vision for Staff Development." Paper co-published by the National Staff Development Council (NSDC) and the Association for Supervision and Curriculum Development (ASCD).

Sparks, D. (1995). "A Paradigm Shift in Staff Development." *The ERIC Review,* 3(3): 5–11.

Sparks, D. and S. Loucks-Horsley (1990). *Models of Staff Development.* New York: Macmillan.

Stein, M., M. Smith and E. Silver (1999). "The Development of Professional Developers: Learning To Assist Teachers in New Settings in New Ways." *Harvard Educational Review,* 69(3), 237–269.

Stein, M. K. (1998). "Mathematics Reform and Teacher Development: A Community of Practice Perspective." From *Thinking Practices in Mathematics and Science Learning.* J. G. Greeno and S. V. Goldman (eds.). Mahwah, N.J.: Lawrence Erlbaum.

Talbert, J. E. (1995). Boundaries of Teachers' *Professional Communities in U.S. High Schools: Power and Precariousness of the Subject Department.* New York: Teachers College Press.

Wegner, E. (1998). *Communities of Practice: Learning, Meaning, and Identity.* New York: Cambridge University Press.

Part III

Team DATA Assignments

*(**D**ata **A**s a **T**ool for **A**ssessing the Mathematics Program)*

Team DATA to Collect Between Session 1 (Content) and Session 2 (Instruction)

Please work *as a team* to carry out this assignment. Each component of the data your team collects will contribute to your understanding of the current state of your site's mathematics program. It will also be critical for the work in Session 6, during which you will draft an improvement plan for your mathematics program.

Before leaving today's session, do the following:

- Make a plan for how all the data asked for will be collected and for who will be responsible for which part (Parts A and B).
- Schedule a time to meet as a team prior to the next *Secondary Lenses on Learning* session in order to compile and discuss your data (Part C).

Please be prepared to share your team's findings with other teams at the start of the next session.

Part A: Overview of DATA Assignments Between Sessions 1 and 2, page 347

Part B: Templates for Data Collection, page 348

Part C: Whole Team Reflection, page 357

PART A: OVERVIEW OF DATA ASSIGNMENTS ■ BETWEEN SESSIONS 1 AND 2

WHO	ASSIGNMENT
All Team Members	1. Using the *Secondary Lenses on Learning Observation and Reflection Guide* from this session (*Mathematical Content* section), each team member is to observe a lesson in algebra, in pairs or in a group of three. Take notes on the *Observing an Algebra Lesson* template as you observe. 2. Meet with your fellow observers to discuss what you saw, using the questions on the *Reflecting on the Lesson* template to guide and record your reflections. **Note** — You may want to explain to the teachers in the classroom being observed that you are conducting this observation as part of an assignment for a seminar in which you are enrolled.
Teachers and Mathematics Coordinators	Collect and chart information about mathematics courses, materials, and enrollment on the *Opportunities to Learn Algebraic Concepts* template.
Principals	Collect and chart information about questions you get asked about algebra and about teacher class assignments to mathematics classes on the *Questions About Algebra* template.
Guidance Counselors	Collect and chart information about questions you get asked about algebra and about further information that would be helpful on the *Questions About Algebra* template.
Central Office Administrators	Collect and chart information about student enrollment and completion of mathematics courses and about the state of the district's mathematics curriculum on the *Algebra 1 (or Integrated Mathematics) Enrollment and Completion Data and the District's Mathematics Curriculum* template.

■ PART B: TEMPLATES FOR DATA COLLECTION

Templates for Observing a Lesson in Algebra

- *Secondary Lenses on Learning Observation and Reflection Guide.* Please use the Mathematical Content portion of the guide to focus your viewing.
- *Observing an Algebra Lesson.* Please take notes on this template during the observation.
- *Reflecting on the Lesson.* Directly after observing the lesson, please meet with the others who observed the same lesson and record your reflections on this template.

Additional Templates

- *Opportunities to Learn Algebraic Concepts* (Teachers and Mathematics Coordinators)
- *Questions About Algebra; Information About Teacher Assignments* (Principals)
- *Questions About Algebra* (Guidance Counselors)
- *Algebra 1 (or Integrated Mathematics) Enrollment and Completion Data and the District's Mathematics Curriculum* (Central Office Administrators)

See Part C: Whole Team Reflection (page 357) for directions and template for a team meeting to compile and discuss data collected in Parts A and B.

Secondary Lenses on Learning Observation and Reflection Guide for a Mathematics Lesson

Mathematical Content

STUDENTS	TEACHERS
What mathematical *concepts* and *procedures* are students working on in this lesson? What specific mathematical *concepts* are perplexing for particular students? What are specific examples of students working on the following mathematical process skills (National Council of Teachers of Mathematics, 2000)? • *Problem solving* (applying and adapting a variety of appropriate strategies to solve problems—e.g., identifying patterns and relationships among quantitative variables) • *Reasoning and proving* (e.g., making and investigating mathematical conjectures; developing and evaluating solution strategies) • Engaging in *mathematical communication* (e.g., organizing and consolidating mathematical thinking through communication; using mathematical language, models, and symbols to express mathematical ideas; analyzing and evaluating the mathematical thinking and strategies of others) • *Making connections* (among mathematical ideas and to contexts outside of mathematics) • *Working with multiple representations* to make sense of problematic situations and to organize, record, and communicate mathematical ideas (e.g., using numerical and verbal expressions, graphic and tabular models, and symbolic expressions of the models)	What are the mathematical goals (*concepts* and *procedures*) of this lesson? What evidence is there that this lesson is part of a set of lessons that balances work with concept development and procedures? In what ways does this lesson afford opportunities for students to develop mathematical process skills (National Council of Teachers of Mathematics, 2000)? Reasoning and proving • Engaging in mathematical communication • Making connections • Working with multiple representations

Source: National Council of Teachers of Mathematics. (2000). *Principles and standards for school mathematics.* Reston, VA: Author.

Observing an Algebra Lesson

(All Team Members)

Please take notes on this template during the observation, using the *Mathematical Content* section of the *Secondary Lenses on Learning Observation and Reflection Guide* to focus your viewing.

STUDENTS	TEACHERS

Reflecting on the Lesson

Soon after observing the lesson, please meet with the others who observed the same lesson and record your reflections on this template.

NAME OF COURSE	NOTES
In what ways was the lesson *similar* to what Usiskin (2005) and Fey and Phillips (2005) describe or what you observed with the *How Many Toothpicks?* video?	
In what ways was the lesson *different* from what Usiskin (2005) and Fey and Phillips (2005) describe or what you observed with the *How Many Toothpicks?* video?	
What *technology* was used in the lesson, and in what ways?	

Opportunities to Learn Algebraic Concepts

(Teachers and Mathematics Coordinators)

Name of Course	Instructional Materials (Title, Publisher, Year Adopted)	Technology Availability (Calculator, Computer) and Strategic Use (Teacher Use, Student Use)	Description of Students Enrolled: Grade and Typical Performance Level (e.g., Top 20% of Grade 9 Students or Heterogeneous Mix of Students Except Lowest 10%)

Questions About Algebra

(Principals)

1. In your role, what are the three most common questions regarding learning algebra that you are asked by parents or students (or both)?

2. Which questions from parents or students regarding teaching and learning algebra have you found particularly difficult to answer? What makes these questions difficult?

3. For each of the courses offered in your building, which teachers are assigned to teach the course?

Name of Course	Level	Teacher Name and Background: (a) Years Teaching Mathematics, (b) Major and Minor

Questions About Algebra

(Guidance Counselors)

1. In your role, what are the three most common questions regarding learning algebra that you are asked by parents or students (or both)?

2. Which questions from parents or students, regarding the teaching and learning of algebra, have you found particularly difficult to answer? What makes these questions difficult?

3. What information do you have access to, as a counselor, that can be used to help students and their parents make decisions regarding what mathematics classes in which to enroll? What additional information would be useful?

4. If possible, ask other guidance counselors in your district these same questions. Record their responses here.

Most Common Questions	Questions That Are Particularly Difficult to Answer and Why

Algebra 1 (or Integrated Mathematics) Enrollment and Completion Data and the District's Mathematics Curriculum

(Central Office Administrators)

> **Note**
>
> If your team does not have a representative from the Central Office, you will need to review the following questions and decide who will secure the different parts of information requested.

1. Complete the following table to record students' enrollment and completion of Algebra 1 (or Integrated courses with equivalent rigor) in your district.

	Algebra Course	*Integrated Course (Equivalent Rigor)*
What percentage of your students take an Algebra I course or its equivalent (if using an integrated program)?	Seventh Grade _____ % Eighth Grade _____ % Ninth Grade _____ % Tenth Grade _____ % Eleventh Grade _____ % Twelfth Grade _____ %	Seventh Grade _____ % Eighth Grade _____ % Ninth Grade _____ % Tenth Grade _____ % Eleventh Grade _____ % Twelfth Grade _____ %
What percentage of your tenth-grade students have already earned a passing grade in an Algebra I course or its equivalent?	_____ %	

2. Complete the following table to describe the state of your district's mathematics curriculum.

The district has		
a. a written *K–12 mathematics curriculum* document, and	_____ Yes	_____ No
b. all mathematics teachers have a copy of it.	_____ Yes	_____ No
The district mathematics document is aligned with the current state standards and expectations (if yes, briefly explain how this was accomplished and who was involved).	_____ Yes	_____ No
The district has		
a. a document showing the alignment between grade/course-level *instructional materials* and the district and state curriculum/expectations, and	_____ Yes	_____ No
b. all mathematics teachers have a copy of this document.	_____ Yes	_____ No
The district has		
a. a written plan for how teachers are to address gaps and redundancy in their instructional materials, as compared to the district and state standards and benchmarks (if yes, briefly explain how this plan was developed and who was involved), and	_____ Yes	_____ No
b. all mathematics teachers have a copy of this plan.	_____ Yes	_____ No

PART C: WHOLE TEAM REFLECTION ■

Meet together as a whole team to compile and discuss your data. Be prepared to share your findings with teams from other schools at the next *Secondary Lenses on Learning* session.

1. Share your findings from the classroom observations.

   a. What where you struck by?

   b. What questions or issues did the observations raise?

   c. *As a Team.* On the continuum mark the approximate point on which you would place the mathematics lessons you observed. (One data point per lesson observed.)

   ←——————————————————————————————————→

| Very unlike the Usiskin (2005) and Fey and Phillips (2005) articles and the work with the *How Many Toothpicks?* task | Very similar to the Usiskin (2005) and Fey and Phillips articles and the work with the *How Many Toothpicks?* task |

2. Review and discuss the other data collected by team members.

   a. What stood out in the data you collected?

   b. What concerns or issues does this raise?

Areas to Pursue

Turn to the *Areas to Pursue* template at the end of this DATA packet (page 406).

Please review this session's Big Ideas. Then, as a team, consider and record the following:

- One or two policies or practices that you think are going well in your mathematics program with relationship to MATHEMATICAL CONTENT
- One or two issues, policies, or practices that need further investigation with relationship to MATHEMATICAL CONTENT

State what evidence you have from the data that you collected that supports your points.

Team DATA to Collect Between Session 2 (Instruction) and Session 3 (Formative Assessment)

Please work *as a team* to carry out this assignment. Each component of the data your team collects will contribute to your understanding of the current state of your site's mathematics program. It will also be critical for the work in Session 6, during which you will draft an improvement plan for your mathematics program.

Before leaving today's session, do the following:

- Make a plan for how all the data asked for will be collected and for who will be responsible for which part (Parts A and B).
- Schedule a time to meet as a team prior to the next *Secondary Lenses on Learning* session in order to compile and discuss your data (Part C).

Please be prepared to share your team's findings with other teams at the start of the next session.

PART A: OVERVIEW OF DATA ASSIGNMENTS ■ BETWEEN SESSIONS 2 AND 3

WHO	ASSIGNMENT
All Team Members	1. Using the *Secondary Lenses on Learning Observation and Reflection Guide* for this session (*Instruction* section), each team member (individually or as a group) is to observe a mathematics lesson. Look for and take notes on the ways in which the teacher addresses various components of the guide, specifically focusing on the INSTRUCTION portion. **Note** You may want to explain to the teachers in the classrooms being observed that you are conducting this observation as part of an assignment for a seminar in which you are enrolled. 2. In addition, obtain a copy of any problem(s) or task(s) that the teacher uses during your observation. You should plan to share and discuss all collected tasks with other team members when you meet. Bring a copy of these with you to the next *Secondary Lenses on Learning* session. 3. Directly after observing the lesson, please answer the questions on the *Reflecting on the Lesson* template with the others who observed the same lesson.
All Team Members	Divide responsibility for collecting data about mathematics courses and performance in your school or district, and record the information on the *Mathematics Courses* template.

■ PART B: TEMPLATES FOR DATA COLLECTION

Templates for Observing a Mathematics Lesson

- *Secondary Lenses on Learning Observation and Reflection Guide.* Please use the Instruction portion of the guide to focus your viewing.
- *Observing a Mathematics Lesson.* Please take notes on this template during the observation.
- *Reflecting on the Lesson.* Directly after observing the lesson, please answer the questions on this template with the others who observed the same lesson.

Additional Templates

- *Mathematics Courses* (divide responsibility among team members)

See Part C: Whole Team Reflection (page 365) for directions and template for a team meeting to compile and discuss data collected in Parts A and B.

Secondary Lenses on Learning
Observation and Reflection Guide

Instruction

STUDENTS	TEACHERS
What are specific examples of students doing the following?	In what ways does the teacher's instruction reflect strengths in the following?
• Making sense of specific mathematical concepts • Making connections between mathematical concepts, representations, solution strategies, and procedures • Persisting when solving challenging tasks • Learning through substantive discourse or "math talk" • Making and testing out mathematical conjectures • Judging for themselves the reasonableness of solutions	• Knowledge of the mathematics • Mathematical knowledge needed for teaching • Knowledge of the curriculum—within and across grade levels What evidence is there that the teacher works with student ideas? • Takes students through a clear learning path of new concepts that begins by accessing students' existing knowledge and builds on it • Utilizes multiple solution strategies intentionally • Works to "debug" wrong answers What evidence is there that the teacher supports students to develop mathematical proficiency with both factual knowledge and conceptual frameworks? • Focuses instruction on helping students make sense of mathematical concepts and procedures • Helps students make connections between and among mathematical concepts, representations, multiple solution strategies, and procedures • Provides opportunities for students to consolidate understandings and procedures and to begin to see ideas as instances of larger categories • Facilitates learning for struggling students without undermining their learning opportunities or the cognitive demand of tasks What evidence is there that the teacher works with the class to develop a community-centered learning environment? • Supports students in expressing their thinking, seeking and giving help, and monitoring learning • Models mathematical thinking and appropriate use of vocabulary

Observing an Algebra Lesson

(All Team Members)

1. Individually or as a group, conduct a classroom observation using the *Secondary Lenses on Learning Observation and Reflection Guide* from this session (INSTRUCTION) to focus your viewing. Look for and take notes (on the following template) on the ways in which the teacher addresses various components of the guide during instruction.

STUDENTS	TEACHERS

2. In addition, obtain a copy of any problems or tasks that the teacher uses during the lesson observed, and bring a copy to your team meeting (see Part C) as well as to the next *Secondary Lenses on Learning* session.

Reflecting on the Lesson

Soon after observing the lesson, please meet with the others who observed the same lesson.

1. Consider the ways in which this lesson was similar to, and different from, the vision of high-quality instruction described in the Session 2 readings and activities. Use the template to record your ideas.

	Similar to Vision of High-Quality Instruction	*Different From Vision of High-Quality Instruction*
Students are engaged in worthwhile mathematical tasks.		
Making sense of the mathematics is the focus of the lesson.		
The teacher works to access students' existing knowledge and builds on it.		
There is a balance between procedures and concept development.		
Students are engaged in "math talk" around concepts and reasonableness.		
There are opportunities for connecting of ideas and consolidation of learning with a feedback loop for students.		

2. Discuss: How typical would you say this lesson was of mathematics instruction in your building?

Mathematics Courses

(All Team Members)

Divide responsibility for data collection about the following topics in order to complete the following table:

Number of credits of mathematics that are required to graduate in your district			
Minimum one can do (in selection and passing of courses to meet district mathematics graduation requirement)			
Length of each required mathematics course (hours per day, days per course)	*Course*	*Minutes/Day*	*Days/Course*
Passing rates for each mathematics course for the last three years	*Course*		*Passing Rates*
Summary of your school's state assessment scores for the last three to five years: mathematics passing rates and other mathematics achievement information.	*Year*	*Passing Rate*	*(Other)*
Adequate Yearly Progress (AYP) status for mathematics			
If not making Adequate Yearly Progress (AYP), conditions that are not being met			
Further notes:			

PART C: WHOLE TEAM REFLECTION ■

1. Discuss the instruction that you saw in the mathematics lessons you observed, based on evidence collected with the framing of the INSTRUCTION section of the *Secondary Lenses on Learning Observation and Reflection Guide.* Like the stance we take while observing a classroom video, the goal is not to judge. Rather, the intent of this observation is to consider how students were making sense of the mathematics and how the teachers worked with student ideas and thinking processes in these lessons, so that you can better understand the nature of mathematics instruction in your building.

2. Share the tasks that were used during the observation and identify the cognitive demand of each task, using the Stein et al. (2000) classifications:

   a. Memorization

   b. Procedures without connections

   c. Procedures with connections

   d. Doing mathematics

Be prepared to share this information at the next *Lenses on Learning* session.

Areas to Pursue

Turn to the *Areas to Pursue* template at the end of this DATA packet (page 406).
Please review this session's Big Ideas. Then, as a team, consider and record the following:

- One or two policies or practices that you think are going well in your mathematics program with relationship to INSTRUCTION
- One or two issues, policies, or practices that need further investigation with relationship to INSTRUCTION

State what evidence you have from the data that you collected that supports your points.

Team DATA to Collect Between Session 3 (Formative Assessment) and Session 4 (Equitable Practices)

Please work *as a team* to carry out this assignment. Each component of the data your team collects will contribute to your understanding of the current state of your site's mathematics program. It will also be critical for the work in Session 6, during which you will draft an improvement plan for your mathematics program.

Before leaving today's session, do the following:

- Make a plan for how all the data asked for will be collected and for who will be responsible for which part (Parts A and B).
- Schedule a time to meet as a team prior to the next *Secondary Lenses on Learning* session in order to compile and discuss your data (Part C).

Please be prepared to share your team's findings with other teams at the start of the next session.

Part A: Overview of DATA Assignments Between Sessions 3 and 4, page 367

Part B: Templates for Data Collection, page 368

Part C: Whole Team Reflection, page 387

PART A: OVERVIEW OF DATA ASSIGNMENTS ■ BETWEEN SESSIONS 3 AND 4

Follow-Up From Session 3, to Be Processed Between Sessions and Shared at the Start of Session 4

WHO	ASSIGNMENT
Teachers, Mathematics Coordinators, and Guidance Counselors	Before the end of Session 3, each team will have worked to synthesize a master list of assessment types from among the individual assessment maps, lists or outlines of team members, and decide who will gather a sample of each widely used assessment type. Based on the decisions your team made at the end of Session 3, work together to gather a sample of each widely used assessment type on your team's master list (formative and summative, including standardized tests such as state assessment, ACT or SAT released items).
All Team Members	Meet as a whole team to review the assessment samples collected and then discuss and answer each of the questions on the Assessment DATA Summary (Part C).
All Team Members	Using the *Assessment* portion of the *Secondary Lenses on Learning Observation and Reflection Guide,* each team member (individually or as a group) is to observe a mathematics lesson. Look for examples of formative assessment strategies being used by both teachers and students based on the questions posed in the Assessment section of the guide.

To Be Analyzed During Session 4

WHO	ASSIGNMENT
Guidance Counselors	Collect and record information about the mathematics course-taking pathways of six students (two lower-achieving, two medium-achieving, and two higher-achieving) who have been in your system from seventh grade through twelfth grade. Record the information on the *Mathematics Course-Taking Pathways* template. This information will be reviewed and analyzed in Session 4 of the *Secondary Lenses on Learning* seminar.
Guidance Counselors and Teachers	Conduct interviews with a total of three to six students (one or two lower-achieving, one or two medium-achieving, and one or two higher-achieving) who are from minority or typically underrepresented groups in mathematics (such as low income, English Language Learners, or students of color). You can divide these among yourselves so that each of you interviews at least two students. Use the *Student Interviews* template to frame your interview and to record notes. This information will be reviewed and analyzed during Session 4 of the *Secondary Lenses on Learning* seminar.
Principals and Central Office Administrators	Collect and chart information about student achievement and placement in mathematics classes on the *Student Achievement and Placement* template. This information will be reviewed and analyzed during Session 4 of the *Secondary Lenses on Learning* seminar.
Principals	Collect and chart information on the *Teacher Experience, Class Level* template about grades and levels of mathematics classes taught by the most and the least experienced teachers.

■ PART B: TEMPLATES FOR DATA COLLECTION

Templates for Observing a Lesson in Algebra

- *Secondary Lenses on Learning Observation and Reflection Guide.* Please use the Assessment portion of the guide to focus your viewing.
- *Observing an Algebra Lesson.* Please take notes on this template during the observation.

Additional Templates

- *Gathering Samples of Assessment Types* (Teachers, Mathematics Coordinators, and Guidance Counselors)
- *Mathematics Course-Taking Pathways* (Guidance Counselors)
- *Student Interviews* (Guidance Counselors and Teachers)
- *Student Achievement and Placement in Mathematics Classes* (Principals and Central Office Administrators)
- *Teacher Experience, Class Level* (Principals)

See Part C: Whole Team Reflection (page 387) for directions and a template (Assessment Data Summary) for a team meeting to compile and discuss data collected in Parts and B.

Secondary Lenses on Learning
Observation and Reflection Guide

Formative Assessment

STUDENTS	TEACHERS
What evidence is there that students are monitoring their own learning? What evidence is there that students are using feedback from the teacher and other students to extend and/or correct their understanding of a mathematical concept or procedure? What evidence is there that students expect that learning mathematics requires listening or otherwise working to understand their peers' thinking, as well as the teacher's? What evidence is there that students expect that complete correct solutions frequently include an explanation of their thinking as well as the solution?	What evidence is there that the teacher listens, analyzes, and adjusts instruction based on student comments and work? What opportunities does the teacher create during this lesson to support *formative* assessment by doing the following? • Expecting students to make their current mathematical thinking visible to themselves, other students, and the teacher (e.g., questions asked probe for understanding; existence of effective student-to-student mathematical discourse in pairs, small groups, and whole group) • Encouraging students to evaluate their own and others' thinking (e.g., questions asked in class, on assignments) What evidence is there that *summative* assessments used in the class do the following? • Include tasks that assess both conceptual understanding and procedural knowledge • Offer feedback to students that provides direction for their next learning steps • Offer opportunities to learn from and revise work in response to input from the teacher and peers

Observing an Algebra Lesson

(All Team Members)

Please take notes on the following template during the observation, using the *Assessment* section of the *Secondary Lenses on Learning Observation and Reflection Guide* to focus your viewing.

STUDENTS	TEACHERS

Gathering Samples of Assessment Types

(Teachers, Mathematics Coordinators, and Guidance Counselors)

1. Work with the whole team to synthesize a master list of assessment types from among all of the individual assessment maps, lists, or outlines generated by team members.

2. Gather a sample of each widely used assessment type on the master list. Include teacher, course, and department assessments, as well as standardized tests (e.g., state assessment, ACT or SAT released items).

3. Meet as a whole team to review the assessment samples collected. Be prepared to lead a discussion with your whole team as you collectively review the assessment samples and answer each of the questions on the *Assessment Data Summary* template (Part C, page 387).

Mathematics Course-Taking Pathways

(Guidance Counselors)

Collect and record information about the mathematics trajectories of six students who have been in your system from seventh grade through twelfth grade. Choose *two lower-achieving* students, *two medium-achieving* students, and *two higher-achieving* students.

Use the template on the following pages to record data about the following, for each of the six students:

- Math classes taken (content and level)
- Grades
- Attendance
- Performance on state test and on SAT or ACT
- Placement decisions made for this student
- Interactions with a guidance counselor
- Support and enrichment provided outside of math class

Lower-Achieving Student 1

	Name/Content of Class	Level	Semester 1 Grade	Semester 2 Grade	Attendance	Notes
Grade 7						
Grade 8						
Grade 9						
Grade 10						
Grade 11						
Grade 12						

Performance on State Test	
Performance on SAT/ACT (First Time)	
Performance on SAT/ACT (Second Time)	
Performance on [Other] _____	

How Placement Decisions Were Made	
Interactions With Guidance Counselor	
Support and Enrichment Provided Outside of Math Class (e.g. tutoring, math-support lab, summer school, online course)	
Other	

Lower-Achieving Student 2

	Name/Content of Class	Level	Semester 1 Grade	Semester 2 Grade	Attendance	Notes
Grade 7						
Grade 8						
Grade 9						
Grade 10						
Grade 11						
Grade 12						

Performance on State Test	
Performance on SAT/ACT (First Time)	
Performance on SAT/ACT (Second Time)	
Performance on [Other] _____	

How Placement Decisions Were Made	
Interactions With Guidance Counselor	
Support and Enrichment Provided Outside of Math Class (e.g. tutoring, math-support lab, summer school, online course)	
Other	

Medium-Achieving Student 1

	Name/Content of Class	Level	Semester 1 Grade	Semester 2 Grade	Attendance	Notes
Grade 7						
Grade 8						
Grade 9						
Grade 10						
Grade 11						
Grade 12						

Performance on State Test	
Performance on SAT/ACT (First Time)	
Performance on SAT/ACT (Second Time)	
Performance on [Other] _____	

How Placement Decisions Were Made	
Interactions With Guidance Counselor	
Support and Enrichment Provided Outside of Math Class (e.g. tutoring, math-support lab, summer school, online course)	
Other	

Medium-Achieving Student 2

	Name/Content of Class	Level	Semester 1 Grade	Semester 2 Grade	Attendance	Notes
Grade 7						
Grade 8						
Grade 9						
Grade 10						
Grade 11						
Grade 12						

Performance on State Test	
Performance on SAT/ACT (First Time)	
Performance on SAT/ACT (Second Time)	
Performance on [Other] _____	

How Placement Decisions Were Made	
Interactions With Guidance Counselor	
Support and Enrichment Provided Outside of Math Class (e.g. tutoring, math-support lab, summer school, online course)	
Other	

Higher-Achieving Student 1

	Name/Content of Class	Level	Semester 1 Grade	Semester 2 Grade	Attendance	Notes
Grade 7						
Grade 8						
Grade 9						
Grade 10						
Grade 11						
Grade 12						

Performance on State Test	
Performance on SAT/ACT (First Time)	
Performance on SAT/ACT (Second Time)	
Performance on [Other] _____	

How Placement Decisions Were Made	
Interactions With Guidance Counselor	
Support and Enrichment Provided Outside of Math Class (e.g. tutoring, math-support lab, summer school, online course)	
Other	

Higher-Achieving Student 2

	Name/Content of Class	Level	Semester 1 Grade	Semester 2 Grade	Attendance	Notes
Grade 7						
Grade 8						
Grade 9						
Grade 10						
Grade 11						
Grade 12						

Performance on State Test	
Performance on SAT/ACT (First Time)	
Performance on SAT/ACT (Second Time)	
Performance on [Other] _____	

How Placement Decisions Were Made	
Interactions With Guidance Counselor	
Support and Enrichment Provided Outside of Math Class (e.g. tutoring, math-support lab, summer school, online course)	
Other	

Student Interviews

(Guidance Counselors and Teachers)

Conduct individual interviews with three to six students who are low income, English Language Learners, and/or students of color:

- One or two currently *achieving well* according to class placement and performance on report cards and standardized mathematics assessments
- One or two currently *achieving moderately well* according to these measures
- One or two currently *having difficulty* according to these measures

Use the questions on the templates that follow to guide your interviews.

Depending on who is on your team, you can divide these among yourselves so that each of you interviews one or two students.

Student 1

Age: _____ Grade: _____ Gender: _____ Race: _____

Free or Reduced Lunch: Yes: _____ No: _____ (Collect this information in the office, not by asking the student.)

Check:

____ Achieving well

____ Achieving moderately well

____ Having difficulty

Background notes about this student: _____

_____

_____

_____

Interview Questions

1. If you were a mathematics teacher for a day, how would you work with a student like yourself?

2. How would you rate your abilities in mathematics, and to what do you attribute this?

3. What kinds of things help you learn and understand mathematics? (Probe to get student to talk about what particulars have been helpful in specific mathematics classes.)

4. When students are struggling in mathematics generally, what help can they get (in class, outside of class)? What has been most helpful when *you* have been struggling?

5. How would you describe teachers' expectations of you as a mathematics learner?

6. Is it important for students to be successful in mathematics? Why or why not? In what ways, if any, do you see mathematics as being important for your future?

Student 2

Age: _____ Grade: _____ Gender: _____ Race: _____

Free or Reduced Lunch: Yes: _____ No: _____ (Collect this information in the office, not by asking the student.)

Check:

____ Achieving well

____ Achieving moderately well

____ Having difficulty

Background notes about this student: _____

_____

_____

_____

Interview Questions

1. If you were a mathematics teacher for a day, how would you work with a student like yourself?

2. How would you rate your abilities in mathematics, and to what do you attribute this?

3. What kinds of things help you learn and understand mathematics? (Probe to get student to talk about what particulars have been helpful in specific mathematics classes.)

4. When students are struggling in mathematics generally, what help can they get (in class, outside of class)? What has been most helpful when *you* have been struggling?

5. How would you describe teachers' expectations of you as a mathematics learner?

6. Is it important for students to be successful in mathematics? Why or why not? In what ways, if any, do you see mathematics as being important for your future?

Student 3

Age: _____ Grade: _____ Gender: _____ Race: _____

Free or Reduced Lunch: Yes: _____ No: _____ (Collect this information in the office, not by asking the student.)

Check:

____ Achieving well

____ Achieving moderately well

____ Having difficulty

Background notes about this student: _____

_____

_____

_____

Interview Questions

1. If you were a mathematics teacher for a day, how would you work with a student like yourself?

2. How would you rate your abilities in mathematics, and to what do you attribute this?

3. What kinds of things help you learn and understand mathematics? (Probe to get student to talk about what particulars have been helpful in specific mathematics classes.)

4. When students are struggling in mathematics generally, what help can they get (in class, outside of class)? What has been most helpful when *you* have been struggling?

5. How would you describe teachers' expectations of you as a mathematics learner?

6. Is it important for students to be successful in mathematics? Why or why not? In what ways, if any, do you see mathematics as being important for your future?

Student Achievement and Placement in Mathematics Classes

(Principals and Central Office Administrators)

Collect and record the following information about student achievement in mathematics on the table that follows.

Whole-School Data

1. Percentage of students from different subgroups (race or ethnicity, socioeconomics or free and reduced lunch, English Language Learner, gender) performing at *Advanced* and *Proficient* levels (level(s) designated Passing) on the state's mathematics test

2. Percentage of students from different subgroups performing at *Needs Improvement/Warning* levels (level[s] designated Not Passing) on the state mathematics test

3. Percentage of students in Grade 11 or Grade 12 with SAT or ACT scores at or above the mean, disaggregated by race and ethnicity, socioeconomics or free and reduced lunch, English Language Learner, or gender (middle schools, check with high school you need to)

4. Percentage of students in Grade 11 or Grade 12 with SAT or ACT scores at or above 700/31 (+2 standard deviations above the mean), disaggregated by race and ethnicity, socioeconomics or free or reduced-price lunch qualification, English Language Learner, or gender (middle schools, check with high schools you need to)

	Free and Reduced Lunch	Male	Female	Special Education	Black	White	Latino	Asian	English Language Learner	Other
1. Percentage Passing State Test										
2. Percentage Not Passing State Test										
3. Percentage SAT/ACT at or Above Mean										
4. Percentage SAT/ACT 2 SD Above Mean										

If your mathematics classes are tracked, collect and record information about placement of students from different subgroups in each level of mathematics courses in your building, on the following table. The following steps are intended to help you with the process of aggregating data from all the mathematics courses and grades in your building:

Step 1. List all the mathematics courses at each grade.

Step 2. If you track mathematics courses, sort the entire list of mathematics courses offered for all grades into the levels used in your building (e.g., Higher and Lower; Higher, Regular, and Lower; or Accelerated, Honors, Regular, Remedial). You may elect to sort one or more courses from any given grade into the same level (e.g., you may want to place both Honors Algebra 1 and Honors Geometry into the Higher-Level group).

Step 3. Find the approximate total student enrollment for each level (e.g., 200 students in higher level courses, 500 students in regular level courses, and 300 students in lower level courses). (Note: If you have a large number of sections for courses, consider working with a proportional sample.)

Step 4. Calculate the percentage of students in each subgroup for each level and enter the data into the following table.

If your mathematics classes are tracked . . .

	Free and Reduced Lunch	Male	Female	Special Education	Black	White	Latino	Asian	English Language Learner	Other
Percentage in Higher-Level Courses										
Percentage in Regular Level Courses										
Percentage in Lower-Level Courses										

Teacher Experience, Class Level

(Principals)

Most Experienced Teachers

If mathematics classes in your school are tracked, what grades and levels of mathematics classes are taught by the *most experienced* teachers? List the *Most Experienced Teachers'* names in the row(s) that reflects the level of courses they teach. Note that a teacher may be listed on more than one row (i.e., if Ms. Flowers [a 15-year veteran teacher] teaches the Integrated 4 courses and a lower-level Algebra course, her name would appear on the first and last lines). (You may find it helpful to refer to the list of mathematics courses, levels, and teachers from the team data collected between Sessions 1 and 2).

	Teacher	Grade	Notes *(Include years of teaching mathematics and whether this teacher has a math major or math minor. After offering the professional development survey to teachers between Sessions 4 and 5, add information about these teachers' participation in mathematics professional development.)*
Higher-Level Courses			
Regular-Level Courses			
Lower-Level Courses			

Least Experienced Teachers

If mathematics classes in your school are tracked, what levels of mathematics classes are taught by the *least experienced* teachers? List the *Least Experienced Teachers'* names in the row(s) that reflects the level of courses they teach. Note that an inexperienced teacher may be listed on more than one row (i.e., if Mr. Flowers [a third-year teacher] teaches the Integrated 4 courses and a lower-level Algebra course, then his name would appear on the first and last lines).

	Teacher	Grade	Notes (Include years of teaching mathematics and whether this teacher has a math major or math minor. After offering the professional development survey to teachers between Sessions 4 and 5, add information about these teachers' participation in mathematics professional development.)
Higher-Level Courses			
Regular-Level Courses			
Lower-Level Courses			

PART C: WHOLE TEAM REFLECTION ■

Meet together as an entire team to consider each of the following items based on the classroom observations and the assessment samples gathered. Record the team's responses on the *Assessment Types Currently Used, Strengths and Limitations* template that follows.

Assessment Data Summary

1. Are the assessment samples used primarily as assessment *of learning* or *for learning?* What opportunities do students have to learn from the assessment (samples) and what opportunities do they offer teachers to adjust instruction based on student responses?	
2. What do you notice about the types of tasks in each sample assessment and their level of cognitive demand? Do the tasks assess conceptual and/or procedural knowledge?	
3. Based on your classroom observations and the sample assessments, what are the strengths and limitations of your current assessment practices (both formative and summative)?	
4. Identify one or two changes (additions, deletions, or modifications) in your assessment practices (classroom and systemwide) that your team will consider making as part of your mathematics program improvement plan.	

Be prepared to share your thinking about Item 4 at the next session.

In addition, as a team, review the data you have collected (mathematics course-taking pathways, interviews, student achievement and placement in mathematics classes, teacher assignments) and be ready to analyze and discuss the information in detail during Session 4.

Areas to Pursue

Turn to the *Areas to Pursue* template at the end of this DATA packet (page 406).

Please review this session's Big Ideas. Then, as a team, consider and record the following:

- One or two policies or practices that you think are going well in your mathematics program with relationship to FORMATIVE ASSESSMENT
- One or two issues, policies, or practices that need further investigation with relationship to FORMATIVE ASSESSMENT

State what evidence you have from the data that you collected that supports your points.

Team DATA to Collect Between Session 4 (Equitable Practices) and Session 5 (Practice-Based Professional Development)

Please work *as a team* to carry out this assignment. Each component of the data your team collects will contribute to your understanding of the current state of your site's mathematics program. It will also be critical for the work in Session 6, during which you will draft an improvement plan for your mathematics program.

Before leaving today's session, do the following:

- Make a plan for how all the data asked for will be collected and for who will be responsible for which part (Parts A and B).
- Schedule a time to meet as a team prior to the next *Secondary Lenses on Learning* session in order to compile and discuss your data (Part C).

Please be prepared to share your team's findings with other teams at the start of the next session.

PART A: OVERVIEW OF DATA ASSIGNMENTS ■ BETWEEN SESSIONS 4 AND 5

Who	Assignment
All Team Members	1. Using all sections of the *Secondary Lenses on Learning Observation and Reflection Guide,* each team member is to observe a mathematics lesson, in a group of three (if possible). Prior to observing, decide who will be responsible for observing through the lens of the MATHEMATICAL CONTENT section, who will be responsible for observing using the lens of the INSTRUCTION section, and who will be responsible for observing using the FORMATIVE ASSESSMENT section. All observers should also use the CONNECTIONS BETWEEN THE CLASSROOM AND SCHOOLWIDE SYSTEMS section. **Note** — You may want to explain to the teachers in the classroom being observed that you are conducting this observation as part of an assignment for a seminar in which you are enrolled.) 2. Take notes on the *Observing a Mathematics Lesson* template as you observe. 3. Meet with your fellow observers to discuss what you saw, using the questions on the *Reflecting on a Mathematics Lesson With an Eye to Equity* template to guide and record your reflections.
All Team Members	Organize your team to administer a survey to each of the teachers and administrators who contribute to your mathematics program (this could include special education teachers, specifically those that teach mathematics to students or coteach in mathematics classrooms with mainstreamed students). Copy the *Survey: Mathematics Education Professional Development Activities* template. Be sure to collect all the surveys prior to meeting for your team reflection (Part C).

■ PART B: TEMPLATES FOR DATA COLLECTION

Templates for Observing a Lesson in Algebra

- *Secondary Lenses on Learning Observation and Reflection Guide.* Please use all portions of the guide to focus your viewing
- *Observing a Mathematics Lesson.* Please take notes on this template during the observation.
- *Reflecting on a Mathematics Lesson With an Eye to Equity.* Please meet soon afterward with the others who observed the lesson to reflect on your observations.

Templates for Conducting a Survey About Professional Development for Mathematics in Your Building

- *Survey: Mathematics Education Professional Development Activities.* Please make copies and distribute this survey to each of the teachers and administrators who contribute to your mathematics program. This may include special education teachers, specifically those that teach mathematics to students or coteach in mathematics classrooms with mainstreamed students. You will need to have collected the completed surveys for the scheduled team reflection meeting (Part C).

See Part C: Whole Team Reflection (page 399) for directions and template for a team meeting to compile and discuss data collected in Parts A and B.

Secondary Lenses on Learning
Observation and Reflection Guide

Mathematical Content

STUDENTS	TEACHERS
What mathematical *concepts* and *procedures* are students working on in this lesson?	What are the mathematical goals (*concepts* and *procedures*) of this lesson?
What specific mathematical *concepts* are perplexing for particular students?	What evidence is there that this lesson is part of a set of lessons that balances work with concept development and procedures?
What are specific examples of students working on the following mathematical process skills (National Council of Teachers of Mathematics, 2000)? • *Problem solving* (applying and adapting a variety of appropriate strategies to solve problems—e.g., identifying patterns and relationships among quantitative variables) • *Reasoning and proving* (e.g., making and investigating mathematical conjectures; developing and evaluating solution strategies) • Engaging in *mathematical communication* (e.g., organizing and consolidating mathematical thinking through communication; using mathematical language, models, and symbols to express mathematical ideas; analyzing and evaluating the mathematical thinking and strategies of others) • *Making connections* (among mathematical ideas and to contexts outside of mathematics) • *Working with multiple representations* to make sense of problematic situations and to organize, record, and communicate mathematical ideas (e.g., using numerical and verbal expressions, graphic and tabular models, and symbolic expressions of the models)	In what ways does this lesson afford opportunities for students to develop mathematical process skills (National Council of Teachers of Mathematics, 2000)? • Problem solving • Reasoning and proving • Engaging in mathematical communication • Making connections • Working with multiple representations What is the fit between the mathematical goals of the lesson, the content of the tasks, and their levels of cognitive demand?

Instruction

STUDENTS	TEACHERS
What are specific examples of students doing the following?	In what ways does the teacher's instruction reflect strengths in the following?
<ul><li>Making sense of specific mathematical concepts</li><li>Making connections between mathematical concepts, representations, solution strategies, and procedures</li><li>Persisting when solving challenging tasks</li><li>Learning through substantive discourse or "math talk"</li><li>Making and testing out mathematical conjectures</li><li>Judging for themselves the reasonableness of solutions</li></ul>	<ul><li>Knowledge of the mathematics</li><li>Mathematical knowledge needed for teaching</li><li>Knowledge of the curriculum—within and across grade levels</li></ul> What evidence is there that the teacher works with student ideas? <ul><li>Takes students through a clear learning path of new concepts that begins by accessing students' existing knowledge and builds on it</li><li>Utilizes multiple solution strategies intentionally</li><li>Works to "debug" wrong answers</li></ul> What evidence is there that the teacher supports students to develop mathematical proficiency with both factual knowledge and conceptual frameworks? <ul><li>Focuses instruction on helping students make sense of mathematical concepts and procedures</li><li>Helps students make connections between and among mathematical concepts, representations, multiple solution strategies, and procedures</li><li>Provides opportunities for students to consolidate understandings and procedures and begin to see ideas as instances of larger categories</li><li>Facilitates learning for struggling students without undermining their learning opportunities or the cognitive demand of tasks</li></ul> What evidence is there that the teacher works with the class to develop a community-centered learning environment? <ul><li>Supports students in expressing their thinking, seeking and giving help, and monitoring learning</li><li>Models mathematical thinking and appropriate use of vocabulary</li></ul>

Formative Assessment

STUDENTS	TEACHERS
What evidence is there that students are monitoring their own learning? What evidence is there that students are using feedback from the teacher and other students to extend and/or correct their understanding of a mathematical concept or procedure? What evidence is there that students expect that learning mathematics requires listening or otherwise working to understand their peers' thinking, as well as the teacher's? What evidence is there that students expect that complete correct solutions frequently include an explanation of their thinking as well as the solution?	What evidence is there that the teacher listens, analyzes, and adjusts instruction based on student comments and work? What opportunities does the teacher create during this lesson to support *formative* assessment by doing the following? <ul><li>Expecting students to make their current mathematical thinking visible to themselves, other students, and the teacher (e.g., questions asked probe for understanding; existence of effective student-to-student mathematical discourse in pairs, small groups, and whole group)</li><li>Encouraging students to evaluate their own and others' thinking (e.g., questions asked in class, on assignments)</li></ul>What evidence is there that *summative* assessments used in the class do the following? <ul><li>Include tasks that assess both conceptual understanding and procedural knowledge</li><li>Offer feedback to students that provides direction for their next learning steps</li><li>Offer opportunities to learn from and revise work in response to input from the teacher and peers</li></ul>

Connections Between the Classroom and Schoolwide Systems

Class _____

Level of Class _____ Number of Students _____

Population of Students in the Classroom (race, gender, free or reduced-price lunch qualification and/or participation) _____

_____

Length of Class Period and Percentage of Time Spent on Instruction _____

_____

Evidence of Match Between the Needs of the Particular Class Population and the Knowledge and Experience of the Assigned Teacher _____

_____

_____

Evidence of Alignment of Lesson Content With Course Curriculum _____

_____

_____

Evidence of Use of Instructional Approaches Targeted in Mathematics Program Improvement Plan _____

_____

_____

Evidence That the Environment Is Conducive to, and Focused on, Effort, Learning, and Achievement _____

_____

_____

Sufficiency of Instructional Materials Needed in the Lesson (textbooks, calculators, rulers, and other math tools) _____

_____

_____

Observing a Mathematics Lesson

(All Team Members)

Please take notes on the following template during the observation, using your designated section of the *Secondary Lenses on Learning Observation and Reflection Guide* to focus your viewing.

STUDENTS	TEACHERS

Reflecting on a Mathematics Lesson With an Eye to Equity

Soon after observing the lesson, please meet with the others who observed the same lesson and record your reflections on this template.

Reflections on *Mathematical Content* in the Lesson. Discuss the questions and statements from the Mathematical Content portion of the *Observation and Reflection Guide.*	
Reflections *on Instruction* in the Lesson. Discuss the questions and statements from the Instruction portion of the *Observation and Reflection Guide.*	
Reflections *on Formative Assessment* in the Lesson. Discuss the questions and statements from the Formative Assessment portion of the *Observation and Reflection Guide.*	
Reflections on *Connections Between the Classroom and Schoolwide Systems* in the Lesson. Discuss the data collected for the Connections Between the Classroom and Schoolwide Systems portion of the *Observation and Reflection Guide* for the classrooms in which you observed.	

Survey: Mathematics Education Professional Development Activities

I. What regular opportunities do you have to meet with other teachers in the mathematics department (e.g., staff meeting, common planning time, school improvement)?

Opportunities to Meet	When and How Often	Who Is Involved	What Is the Focus and What Gets Done

II. In the following tables, do the following:

A. List the mathematics professional development activities you have taken part in during the past two years (within or outside your building and district) using the content focus tables that follow. Some professional development activities may have addressed more than one category (which you should record by listing these in more than one of the tables), and some of the tables may be left blank. The table is just there to help you organize your professional development history.

B. For each of your entries, check if you found it helpful, and if so, indicate what made it helpful.

1. Mathematical Content Knowledge

Topic (e.g., Statistics, Functions-Based Algebra)	Helpful? Yes/No	What Made It Helpful for You?

2. Instructional Strategies

Topic (e.g., Differentiation, Discourse)	Helpful? Yes/No	What Made It Helpful for You?

3. Assessment

Topic (e.g., Summative, Formative)	Helpful? Yes/No	What Made It Helpful for You?

4. Instructional Materials

Topic (e.g., Textbook Adoption, Computer Software Selection, Textbook Implementation)	Helpful? Yes/No	What Made It Helpful for You?

5. Curriculum

Topic (e.g., District Curriculum Development, Alignment Study)	Helpful? Yes/No	What Made It Helpful for You?

6. Building Mathematics Leadership

Topic (e.g., Buildingwide, Districtwide, or Individually)	Helpful? Yes/No	What Made It Helpful for You?

PART C: WHOLE TEAM REFLECTION ■

Meet together as a whole team.

1. Compile and discuss your observations of all the mathematics lessons observed by team members.

   a. What where you struck by?

   b. What questions or issues did the observations raise?

2. Knowing what you know

   a. What are signs that your school reflects equitable practices and high achievement for various subgroups of students? What data support your statements?

   b. What are signs that there needs to be an improvement in equitable practices and achievement for various subgroups of students in your school?

(Use insights gained from observing mathematics lessons, as well as your analysis of the team data collected for Session 4. You may find it helpful to further organize and display your data.)

3. Read through and discuss the completed *Mathematics Education Professional Development Activities* surveys that you will have collected from all mathematics teachers, appropriate administrators, and special education teachers you included as a backdrop for Session 5 (focused on professional development). As you review the completed surveys, do the following:

   a. Notice which areas of mathematics education seem to have received little or no professional development attention and which have received the most.

   b. In the activities that were rated as helpful, look for what made them helpful.

   c. Add information about teachers' participation in professional development to the *Teacher Expertise, Class Level* template in the Team DATA Assignment between Sessions 4 and 5.

In addition to serving as a backdrop to Session 5, the data from these surveys will also contribute to planning for the Mathematics Program Improvement Plan in the final session of *Secondary Lenses on Learning.*

Areas to Pursue

Turn to the *Areas to Pursue* template at the end of this DATA packet (page 406).

Please review this session's Big Ideas. Then, as a team, consider and record the following:

- One or two policies or practices that you think are going well in your mathematics program with relationship to EQUITABLE PRACTICES AND ACHIEVEMENT
- One or two issues, policies, or practices that need further investigation with relationship to EQUITABLE PRACTICES AND ACHIEVEMENT

State what evidence you have from the data that you collected that supports your points.

Team DATA to Collect Between Session 5 (Practice-Based Professional Development) and Session 6 (Mathematics Improvement Process)

Please work *as a team* to carry out this assignment. Each component of the data your team collects will contribute to your understanding of the current state of your site's mathematics program. It will also be critical for the work in this final session, during which you will draft an improvement plan for your mathematics program.

Before leaving today's session, do the following:

- Make a plan for how all the data asked for will be collected and for who will be responsible for which part (Parts A and B).
- Schedule a time to meet as a team prior to the next *Secondary Lenses on Learning* session in order to compile and discuss your data (Part C).

Please be prepared to share your team's findings with other teams at the start of the next session.

Part A: Overview of DATA Assignments Between Sessions 5 and 6, page 402

Part B: Templates for Data Collection, page 403

Part C: Whole Team Reflection, page 404

■ PART A: OVERVIEW OF DATA ASSIGNMENTS BETWEEN SESSIONS 5 AND 6

Preparation for Session 6

WHO	ASSIGNMENT
All Team Members	Make arrangements among yourselves to ensure that the items listed on the *Further Data to Collect for Session 6* template (page 403) will be available for use during Session 6.
All Team Members	Complete the *Reflecting on Professional Development Opportunities* template (Part C, page 404).
All Team Members	Reread the *Areas to Pursue* template to which you added at the conclusion of each session (Part C, page 405).

Follow-Up to Session 5

WHO	ASSIGNMENT
All Team Members (as a Group)	1. Select an article to use as a context for a study group activity or discussion with your mathematics department faculty or other staff group from your school.
	2. Develop focus questions and a meeting agenda, and select a day and time for the study group or discussion.
	3. Run the study group or discussion.
	4. Select a day and time for the whole team to debrief the study group activity using the focus questions provided here (Whole Team Reflection Part C, page 404).

PART B: TEMPLATES FOR DATA COLLECTION ■

Templates

- *Further Data to Collect for Session 6* (All Team Members)
- *Study Group Activity* (All Team Members)

See Part C: Whole Team Reflection (page 404) for directions and template for a team meeting to compile and discuss data collected in Parts A and B.

Further Data to Collect for Session 6

(All Team Members)

Please bring the following data to Session 6:

- All prior data collected between Sessions 1 and 5 (fill in any sections you may have missed)
- A copy of the school's current school improvement plan

Study Group Activity

(All Team Members)

1. Select and use one of the following articles or one of your own choosing as the context for a study group activity or discussion with your mathematics department faculty or other staff group from your school.

   ### Selected Articles

   - Reading 5.6 (*Participant Book*, pages 302–309): Smith, M. S. (2000). Redefining success in mathematics teaching and learning. *Mathematics Teaching in the Middle School*, 5(6), 378–386.
   - Reading 2.3 (*Participant Book*, pages 76–81): Hiebert, J., & Stigler, J. (2004). A world of difference: Classrooms abroad provide lessons in teaching math and science. *Journal of Staff Development*, 25(4), 1–7.

2. Develop focus questions and a meeting agenda.

3. Select a day and time for the study group session (such as a regularly scheduled staff meeting).

4. Run the study group or discussion.

5. Select a day and time for the whole team to debrief the study group activity using the focus questions provided here (Whole Team Reflection Part C, page 404).

■ PART C: WHOLE TEAM REFLECTION

1. Ensure that all data collected for Sessions 1 through 6, as well as a copy of the school's current school improvement plan, are assembled and ready for use during Session 6.

2. With your team, please reflect on current professional development opportunities in your building and potential ones for the future. Record your ideas on the following template, *Reflecting on Professional Development Opportunities.*

3. Debrief your Study Group session by discussing the following focus questions:

   a. What did teachers seem to gain from the Study Group discussion?

   b. What professional development topics in your mathematics department might be a good match with the Study Group format for professional development?

   c. Reflecting on the Study Group experience, what seemed to be productive and what might you do differently next time?

Reflecting on Professional Development Opportunities

Using the data gathered from the Mathematics Education Professional Development Survey prior to Session 5, summarize the following:

	NOTES
1. What time is currently scheduled for professional development for improving mathematics teaching and learning and developing leadership?	Weekly Monthly Yearly
2. Do mathematics teachers have common planning times as a department? If no, do mathematics teachers have common planning times with at least one other mathematics teacher with a similar course assignment?	Mathematics teachers who have common planning time:
3. Are there times within your existing schedules that could be reallocated so as to provide *mathematics teachers and others* (e.g., administrators, special education teachers) with the opportunity to meet to focus on improving mathematics teaching and learning and on developing leadership for mathematics? If so, when?	
4. Are there times within your existing schedules that could be reallocated so as to provide the *mathematics leadership team* with the opportunity to meet to focus on mathematics program improvement and student achievement in mathematics? If so, when?	

Areas to Pursue

Turn to the *Areas to Pursue* template at the end of this DATA packet (page 406).

Please review this session's Big Ideas. Then, as a team, consider and record the following:

- One or two policies or practices that you think are going well in your mathematics program with relationship to MATHEMATICAL CONTENT
- One or two issues, policies, or practices that need further investigation with relationship to MATHEMATICAL CONTENT

State what evidence you have from the data that you collected that supports your points.

Areas to Pursue

Composite List

At the conclusion of each session you made notes regarding the issues and how they connected to the mathematics program in your buildings. Now, as a team, review the Big Ideas of the sessions and your notes. Then consider and record one or two practices or policies related to these Big Ideas that you think are going well in your mathematics program. Also identify one or two issues, practices, or policies that need further investigation with respect to the session's Big Ideas. State what evidence you have from the data that you collected that supports your view of what is working well in the mathematics program and that highlights the need to dig more deeply into particular issues, practices, or policies with relationship to the mathematics program in your building.

SESSION BIG IDEAS	GOING WELL	NEED FURTHER INVESTIGATION
Session 1: Content *What Does It Mean to* Know *Algebra?* • Examine characteristics of a challenging algebra curriculum that is accessible to all middle and high school students. • Explore what it means to develop a stance of inquiry and ongoing learning about mathematics education within a community of learners. • Consider the potential of a mathematics leadership team to facilitate continuous improvement in a mathematics program. • Examine the connections among educators in different positions and consider that each has a practice that may need to grow in order to ensure that all students are successful in mathematics.		

SESSION BIG IDEAS	GOING WELL	NEED FURTHER INVESTIGATION
Session 2: Instruction *What Does High-Quality Instruction Look Like?* • Examine what is known about how people learn mathematics. • Develop an understanding of instructional strategies that promote student learning in mathematics. • Examine the types of the knowledge teachers need to effectively lead mathematics instruction. • Consider how various types of mathematical tasks directly impact what mathematics students have the opportunity to learn.		
Session 3: Formative Assessment *How Can Assessment Support Learning and Instruction?* • Explore the scope, audience, and purposes of student assessment. • Review research findings on the role of assessment in supporting student learning. • Consider formative assessment practices that benefit student learning.		
Session 4: Equitable Practices *How Can We Hold High Expectations and Provide Strong Support for* All *Students?* • Examine ways in which assumptions, attitudes, and expectations intersect with race, ethnicity, and social class to affect achievement, engagement, and curricular opportunities for various student groups. • Explore opportunities to address issues of equitable achievement at both the classroom level and at schoolwide systems levels. • Consider broadening sources of data used in assessing what helps and hinders mathematics learning and achievement.		

SESSION BIG IDEAS	GOING WELL	NEED FURTHER INVESTIGATION
Session 5: Practice-Based Professional Development *How Can Professional Development Enable Teachers to Improve Student Achievement?* • Broaden understandings of the nature and potential of professional development. • Experience professional development approaches centered in the practice of teaching. • Explore instructional decisions that influence student achievement.		
Session 6: Mathematics Program Improvement Process *How Can School Leaders Advance Their Mathematics Program Toward Success for All?* • Examine the interconnectedness of the elements of school that contribute to mathematics achievement and the necessity of adjusting multiple aspects of the system and educators' practice to continuously move achievement forward. • Explore the use of data beyond state or nationally normed assessments to identify problems, and with research, plan for improvement. • Develop building mathematics program improvement plans for increasing student achievement (short and long term). • Consider the benefits of building support for changes in mathematics education from teachers, administrators, students, parents, boards of education, and the wider community.		

A Few Final Thoughts

It is no secret that our secondary schools are challenged by raised expectations for student enrollment in algebra and for addressing inequitable student achievement in mathematics. School and district leaders around the country are being held accountable to provide evidence of increased achievement on high-stakes tests and are pressed to *do something.* In response, they are taking action: requiring algebra for all in Grade 8, adopting new mathematics curricula, expanding afterschool and tutorial support programs, and hiring mathematics coaches.

Many such actions have merit. But experience tells us that single policies, programs, or new hires rarely, if ever, provide complete solutions to the unprecedented challenges of raised expectations for all students. Multiple innovations aren't the answer either, if they are poorly aligned or minimally understood or embraced. And without careful attention to supports needed or obstacles to be addressed, the innovations themselves are too often rejected. Such experiences reinforce the pervasive belief that the problem lies with the students themselves, and buttress complacency and acceptance of the status quo.

You, as instructional and administrative leaders, have the potential to transform schoolwide policies, programs, and practices to help *all* your students realize their mathematical potential. Together, you have been developing the necessary vision, knowledge, and shared commitments to fuel much-needed changes. And together, you can embrace processes for building, revising, and sustaining improvement efforts over time. At the heart of this work is the movement of individual students, with all of their capabilities and difficulties, to the center of efforts to strengthen classroom practice and schoolwide programs.

What might result from such collective efforts? Improved mathematics scores on high-stakes tests are a start, and a necessary one. More profoundly, these efforts will bring your schools much closer to meeting their stated goal of mathematical proficiency for all. They will add value to your students' present lives, enhance their prospects for success in college and the work force, and prepare them for broad participation in society. And such transformations can bring to you, and other adults, the satisfaction of working in schools that are making a real difference for students.

Best wishes for your continuing efforts to improve mathematics learning opportunity for students in your schools.

—The *Secondary Lenses on Learning* Team

CORWIN

A SAGE Company

The Corwin logo—a raven striding across an open book—represents the union of courage and learning. Corwin is committed to improving education for all learners by publishing books and other professional development resources for those serving the field of PreK–12 education. By providing practical, hands-on materials, Corwin continues to carry out the promise of its motto: **"Helping Educators Do Their Work Better."**

Education Development Center, Inc.

Education Development Center's mission is to enhance the quality and accessibility of education, health, and economic opportunity worldwide.